A RESIDENCE OF
TWENTY-ONE YEARS IN THE
SANDWICH ISLANDS

A. Sealey sc. N° 1 Wall st. N.Y.

Yours, truly,
H. Bingham

A RESIDENCE OF TWENTY-ONE YEARS IN THE SANDWICH ISLANDS

OR THE
CIVIL, RELIGIOUS, AND POLITICAL HISTORY OF THOSE ISLANDS

COMPRISING
A PARTICULAR VIEW OF THE MISSIONARY OPERATIONS CONNECTED
WITH THE INTRODUCTION AND PROGRESS OF CHRISTIANITY AND
CIVILIZATION AMONG THE HAWAIIAN PEOPLE

BY HIRAM BINGHAM, A.M.

MEMBER OF THE AMERICAN ORIENTAL SOCIETY, AND
LATE MISSIONARY OF THE AMERICAN BOARD

AND WITH AN INTRODUCTION TO THE NEW EDITION BY
TERENCE BARROW, PH.D.

CHARLES E. TUTTLE COMPANY
RUTLAND, VERMONT & TOKYO, JAPAN

Representatives
Continental Europe: BOXERBOOKS, INC., Zurich
British Isles: PRENTICE-HALL INTERNATIONAL, INC., London
Australasia: BOOK WISE (AUSTRALIA) PTY. LTD.
104-108 Sussex Street, Sydney 2000

Published by the Charles E. Tuttle Company, Inc.
of Rutland, Vermont & Tokyo, Japan
with editorial offices at
Suido 1-chome, 2-6, Bunkyo-ku, Tokyo, Japan

Copyright in Japan, 1981, by Charles E. Tuttle Co., Inc.

Library of Congress Catalog Card No. 77-83041

International Standard Book No. 0-8048-1252-7

First edition, 1847
Third edition, revised, published in 1849
by Hezekiah Huntington, Hartford
First Tuttle edition, 1981

PRINTED IN JAPAN

DEDICATION.

TO THE HONORABLE

𝕿𝖍𝖊 𝕬𝖒𝖊𝖗𝖎𝖈𝖆𝖓 𝕭𝖔𝖆𝖗𝖉 𝖔𝖋 𝕮𝖔𝖒𝖒𝖎𝖘𝖘𝖎𝖔𝖓𝖊𝖗𝖘 𝖋𝖔𝖗 𝕱𝖔𝖗𝖊𝖎𝖌𝖓 𝕸𝖎𝖘𝖘𝖎𝖔𝖓𝖘,

ITS OFFICERS AND MEMBERS, CORPORATE AND HONORARY,

AND ITS NUMEROUS AND GENEROUS SUPPORTERS,

THIS RECORD

OF ONE OF THEIR ACHIEVEMENTS IN RESCUING HEATHEN

NATIONS, PREPARED BY ONE, WHO, FOR A QUARTER OF

A CENTURY, HAS HAD THE HAPPINESS TO BE

EMPLOYED IN THEIR SERVICE, IS GRATEFULLY

AND RESPECTFULLY INSCRIBED,

BY THE AUTHOR.

CONTENTS

Page

CHAPTER V.

CHAPTER VI.

CHAPTER VII.

CHAPTER VIII.

CHAPTER XVI.

CHAPTER XVII.

CHAPTER XVIII.

CHAPTER XIX.

CHAPTER XXIV.

CHAPTER XXV.

CHAPTER XXVI.

EMBELLISHMENTS.

The well executed engravings on wood, by Mr. B. F. Childs, are, excepting the 6th, from sketches
taken by the writer, on the ground. The publishers have also procured an excellent steel plate
engraving, from a good Daguerreotype likeness by Mr. S. Peck.

INTRODUCTION TO THE NEW EDITION

A Residence of Twenty-One Years in the Sandwich Islands, by the Reverend Hiram Bingham, was first printed in New York in 1847. Following a second printing in 1848, a third and revised edition was published in 1849. It is this latter edition that is here reprinted.

The book provides a panoramic history of Hawaii from before its discovery in 1778 by Captain James Cook up to 1845. Hiram Bingham became Hawaii's most notable missionary, an adviser to kings and queens, and was truly one of Hawaii's most influential historical figures. His work did much to transform old Hawaii into a new Hawaii. He was a child of his time, an ardent advocate of the Calvinistic Christianity of New England, and in many ways was a bigot. He was unsympathetic to the traditional Hawaiian culture, yet his book tells us an enormous amount about Hawaiians as well as the missionary endeavors of himself and his colleagues.

Hiram Bingham was born October 30, 1789, at Bennington, Vermont. He was educated at Middlebury College and the Theological Seminary, Andover, Massachusetts. He graduated from the latter institution in 1819 and was ordained the same year at Goshen, Connecticut. After finding a wife, as was required by the American Board of Foreign Missions as an aid in resisting the temptation of native women in foreign lands, Bingham left Boston on October 23, 1819, aboard the brig *Thaddeus* bound for the Sandwich Islands. (The Hawaiian Islands were originally named the Sandwich Islands by Captain James Cook in honor of his patron, the fourth Earl of Sandwich and First lord of the British Admiralty. This was the same man who gave his name to the common sandwich by insisting that his servant bring meat between slices of bread so that he would not need to leave his beloved gambling table to eat. The name Sandwich Islands persisted throughout the nineteenth century.)

On March 30, 1820, after a journey of 160 days by way of the Atlantic, Cape Horn, and the Pacific, the *Thaddeus* hove in sight of the high peaks of the island of Hawaii. This arduous and uncomfortable journey had been endured by a party of seventeen passengers, including two ordained ministers (Hiram Bingham and Asa

Thurston), a physician, a farmer, two schoolmasters, some catechists, several wives, and a few children and Hawaiian youths, among whom was George P. Kaumuali'i, son of the king of Kaua'i.

The object of this pioneer missionary group, which was eventually followed by eleven other parties over the next twenty years, was simply to convert the Hawaiian people to Christianity and to "civilize" them. The bravery and good intentions of the early missionaries can not be questioned. Unfortunately, their teaching was of the Calvinistic, "be saved or burn" variety. Hiram Bingham, by force of his personality, soon became the unofficial leader of the group and was to dominate not only his colleagues but also many influential Hawaiians.

When the *Thaddeus* neared Kailua on the Kona Coast of Hawaii, the voyagers learned from fishermen the overwhelming news that Kamehameha the Great, unifier of the Hawaiian Islands, had died about the time they had left Boston and that his son, Liholiho (Kamehameha II), had since abolished the old *kapu* (taboo) system and had ordered the abandonment of the old Hawaiian gods and the destruction of the temples. This news was greeted with thanks to God for opening up the way to Christianity. Yet the way was not to be without obstacles. When the king met the leaders of the party at Kailua, he was uncertain about allowing them to have a free hand in evangelizing Hawaii. National rivalry was already strong, especially between France and Britain. Liholiho feared that the settlement of American missionaries in his kingdom would intensify existing antagonisms. Some foreign residents insinuated that these newcomers were the forerunners of many others who would come as agents of the American government. Eventually, however, this forlorn party was permitted to stay, on trial, for one year. Kailua did not seem suitable for mission headquarters because it appeared hot and dry, and fresh water was scarce. Most hearts were set on Honolulu, and after some delay Hiram Bingham proceeded there. One party stayed at Kailua, while others went on to Kaua'i.

Bingham successfully established himself in Honolulu as pastor and there set up a printing press as well as schools for selected Hawaiians. Eventually he directed the building of the great Kawaiahao Church. He saw that the best way to achieve his aims was to concentrate his attention on the ruling class of nobles, called *ali'i*, a method that proved effective.

Since the Hawaiians had no written script and little had been accomplished since Captain Cook and his men did their best to write down Hawaiian place names and a few words, Bingham and his fellow workers created a Hawaiian alphabet. Bingham played a major role in translating books of the Bible, composing school textbooks, and writing other literature. Difficulties with the Hawaiian language were encountered in the selection of proper consonants, since the old-time Hawaiians used a number of interchangeable sounds. The final selection of specific letters resulted in a less flexible Hawaiian language, which in due time was further defined in dictionaries. The first notable work to appear was the *Dictionary of the Hawaiian Language* published in 1838.

The importance of a written language and the value of knowledge derived from books were immediately recognized by many Hawaiians, who became rapid learners. The Hawaiians were not as benighted as Mr. Bingham and his colleagues proclaimed. If Polynesians lacked anything, it was *not* the quality of intelligence. Bingham seems to have been convinced that he had everything to offer the Hawaiians and that they had nothing to offer but their souls and their material support. His rigid theology and his harsh judgment of Hawaiian customs and manners must be accepted for what they are. We all agree that there was nothing admirable in population control by infanticide or in lacerating and mutilating the body when in sorrow or in sacrificing fellow human beings to the gods. But when Bingham arrived, Hawaii had already been subject to foreign visitors for about forty years, and most of the barbaric customs of olden times had ceased.

The value of *A Residence of Twenty-One Years in the Sandwich Islands* lies in several areas. First, it is an important documentary history of the years Bingham spent in Hawaii (1820 to 1840). The events described were in many instances witnessed by the writer, and Bingham himself was a primary maker of history in the crucial years of his sojourn. Second, the book reveals the attitudes and activities of the Calvinist missionaries who possessed both Yankee pluck and a Puritan brand of religious bigotry. As a historical work, the book ranks with half a dozen of the classic accounts of old Hawaii that begin with the journals and diaries of Captain Cook and his men. It is authoritative, and it really had no rivals from the time it was first published in 1847 until the appearance of the definitive, three-volume history, *The Hawaiian Kingdom* (1938), by Professor Ralph S. Kuykendall, and later, the less conventional view of the subject provided by Gavan Daws's *Shoal of Time: A History of the Hawaiian Islands* (1968).

At the beginning of the eighteenth century the island world of the Pacific was a romantic and pagan world. No anthropologist could imagine a more wonderful place. Cannibalism remained a part of life on many islands in the western parts of the Pacific. Human sacrifice, infanticide, cruel wars, and savagery flourished on dozens of islands. When Bingham quoted the Bible, adding his own thoughts, as he did in the opening sentences of his book, he meant exactly what he wrote: "Darkness covered the earth and gross darkness the people. This, for ages, was emphatically applicable to the isles of the great Pacific Ocean." From the point of view of Christian civilization he was right. Hawaii, however, was already a changed community. The condemnations that follow in the first chapter, and throughout the book, must be interpreted and not accepted at face value. The classic Hawaiians were a highly intelligent, well-organized people with a unique culture. Their arts of dance, chant, featherwork, carving, and the construction of temples, houses, and canoes were remarkable achievements .

With all deference to Bingham, let us say that he was not an ethnologist. He was writing according to his own lights: he wanted to save souls and civilize the Hawaiians in the way that he believed was right. That he was wrong on many points should not worry us today. We must be indulgent toward his moralizing and his sermons. When he confines himself to descriptions, we learn an enormous amount concerning Hawaiian manners and customs.

If to Bingham hula dancing was sinful, the old chants and ditties too monotonous or erotic, and the legendary lore of the Hawaiians mere foolish tales, them we must simply accept it all as an expression of the missionary mind of the time. Personally, he was a man of great courage in a world of danger. Whalers with their bottles of grog, the condemnation of those opposed to him, his worries about backsliding chiefs, wayward boy and girl converts, monarchs who liked alcohol—all these were very real problems to Bingham and his colleagues.

Actually, Hiram Bingham could have learned as much from the Hawaiians as he taught them. They were experts in the art of living. They loved song and dance, storytelling, swimming, surfing, light clothing, exposure of the body to sun, the enjoyment of sex, and eating. Today, at least in Hawaii, people have returned to many of the old Hawaiian assessments of life and have adopted what missionaries suppressed. If Hiram Bingham walked along the beaches of Waikiki or along the streets near his own church in

Honolulu, he would cry out in horror. We live in a new age, and his book must be read in the light of today.

Readers must also bear in mind that the condemnation of Captain James Cook, the Western discoverer of the Hawaiian Islands and the greatest maritime explorer in history, is quite unreasonable. Bingham's opinions are not in accord with researched accounts of Cook's visits to Hawaii and of his subsequent death at Hawaiian hands at Kealakekua Bay.

James Cook was received by the Hawaiians as the god Lono, that deity who presided over fertility and agriculture and whose return mystically occurred each year during the *makahiki* festive season. He is well known today as a humanitarian, a man of great sensitivity in dealing with the native peoples he encountered in the Pacific. He was on good terms with the Hawaiians on that fatal morning when he was killed. There is no evidence he was aware he was being identified as a particular god, or that he wanted to overthrow "idolatry" or interfere with any religious beliefs. Bingham condemns him for not acting as an evangelizing missionary.

Comments could be made in defense of other persons and new interpretations put on certain events in this book. Such comments and interpretations, however, are not among the duties of one who writes an introduction. Let it be enough to say that the Reverend Hiram Bingham was a man who could stand on his own feet. His written work is sincere, and his life was one of unrelenting labor for Hawaii and the Hawaiians. The subtitle proclaims that the book embraces "the civil, religious, and political history of those islands: comprising a particular view of the missionary operations connected with the introduction and progress of Christianity and civilization among the Hawaiian people." As we read the pages that follow, let us remember the author's intentions and salute him for his contributions to Hawaii.

Terence Barrow, Ph.D.

Honolulu

Biographical Note

The Reverend Hiram Bingham, author of *A Residence of Twenty-One Years in the Sandwich Islands*, was born in Bennington, Vermont, on October 30, 1789. With his wife, Sybil Moseley Bingham, of Hartford, Connecticut, he sailed from Boston in the brig *Thaddeus* as a member of the pioneer missionary company that arrived in Hawaii in 1820. Hiram Bingham gained prominence among his colleagues and was recognized as a leader in all matters relating to the mission. He became pastor of Kawaiahao Church, the first of the great Hawaiian churches, and an adviser to Hawaii's kings and queens. True to his calling, Bingham labored for the welfare of the Hawaiians and the advancement of civilization in Hawaii according to his lights. He played a major role in the establishment of a written Hawaiian language and as a translator of several books of the Bible. Some of Hawaii's first instructional school books were written by him. After a long and fruitful life he died on November 11, 1869, in New Haven, Connecticut.

PREFACE.

WITHIN the last half century, public attention has been attracted to the isles of the Pacific as a field of Christian missions and commercial enterprise; and the power of the Gospel has been tried on several branches of the Polynesian family.

The introduction and progress of Christianity and civilization at the Sandwich Islands, viewed in connexion with their original state, present condition, and prospects, have become a matter of interest to many who desire to see a connected account of the efforts to raise that people from their degradation and barbarism, and convert them from their idols, their cruel superstitions, and their unbridled lusts. Such a narrative I have been requested to give by those in whose judgment I confide, and with whom I have, for a quarter of a century, been specially connected.

Various parts of the History of the Sandwich Islands have been offered to the world in the publications of the American Board, and of several able writers, who have had a short acquaintance with that group—the Rev. Messrs. C. S. Stewart, Wm. Ellis, and S. Dibble; J. J. Jarves, and Charles Wilkes, Esqs., and others. But having a more perfect acquaintance with the main facts from the first attempt to rear on those shores the standard of the King of nations, " it seemed good to me also to set forth in order a declaration of those things " which came under my own observation, and those " which have been delivered to us by eye-witnesses," or have become matters of history.

" Of making many books," the reading public desires " no end," and though long accustomed to speak, write, and preach, and sometimes to think, in a foreign heathen tongue which had become familiar, I have labored to add a volume in plain English, illustrative of the character, condition, language, customs, religion, government, and pursuits of the Hawaiian people, the struggles through which they have passed, and the changes which have been wrought there by the Divine agency.

Following, in the main, the order of events which Divine Providence arranged, I have given briefly, in the first Chapter, an account of the people, for an indefinite period previous to the discovery of the Islands by Captain Cook; and in the second, their history during the subsequent forty years; and in the third, a record of preparatory measures for introducing Christianity among them, with which the reader may, if he choose, commence the narrative. Thence onward, in twenty-two successive chapters, the history of the mission and the history of the nation are interwoven, or run parallel, for ' *Twenty-One years ;*' and in the twenty-sixth chapter, for five years further, to the beginning of 1846.

I have aimed to introduce to my readers the Hawaiian people and their country, with its mountain, valley, and volcanic scenery; their rulers, teachers, friends, and opposers; their habitations, schools, churches, revivals, etc., as they appeared to myself, and to show the footprints of the nation's progress in their uphill efforts to rise amid conflicting influences. To this end, within the free outline of a ' RESIDENCE,' are incorporated such events and sketches of character from personal acquaintance, and that others may speak for themselves, such documents and extracts (sometimes without a reference) from the archives and publications of the American Board, the mission, and the native government, and other sources, as the object and unity of the work, the clearness of the narrative, and the limits of a convenient and reasonable volume would admit, and as many, too, as seemed to be required to make the volume entertaining and valuable to the rising generation, the mature Christian, the candidate for missionary toil, the teacher of religion, and the philanthropic statesman or philosopher, who would appreciate the application of the means of elevating nations, and removing barbarism, intemperance, oppression, and idolatry from the world.

To render the work the more deserving of confidence, I have availed myself of the valued criticisms and modifications suggested by the Rev. David Greene, one of the Secretaries of the American Board, to whom with others, not excepting one familiar with the prominent scenes and events described, I am greatly indebted, and through whose aid, the pleasure and advantage of the courteous reader will doubtless be promoted, the labor of preparing it more certainly rewarded, and the notes of praise to divine grace, which it is intended to multiply, be made richer and higher.

New York, June 7th, 1847.

EXPLANATIONS.

I. HAWAIIAN ORTHOGRAPHY AND PRONUNCIATION.

The pronunciation of the Hawaiian names in this volume will be made comparatively easy to the reader by observing that the vowels have the following sounds.

a, as *a* in father, art.
e, as *ey* in they, or *a* in pale.
i, as *i* in machine, or *ee* in see.

o, as *o* in no.
u, as *oo* in too.

The full accent is usually on the last vowel but one, and a secondary accent two syllables before the full. Simply to give in succession the primitive sounds of the letters of a Hawaiian name or word will accomplish a tolerably accurate pronunciation. But for further explanation of the orthography and pronunciation the reader is referred to pages 152—156.

II. THE ISLANDS.

The group of the Sandwich or Hawaiian Islands, consists of 11 which lie in the North Pacific Ocean, between 18° 50' and 22° 20' N. L., and 154° 55', and 160° 15' W. L., from Greenwich, and stretch along in a direction W.N.W. and E.S.E. about 350 miles, and contain about 6000 sq. miles.

Name.	Length.	Breadth	Height in ft.	Sq. Miles.	Pop. 1832.
HA-WAI'I,	88	68	14,500	4,000	45,792
MAU'I,	48	29	11,000	600	35,062
O-A'HU,	46	23	4,000	520	29,755
KAU-AI',	33	28	5,000	520	10,977
MO-LO-KAI',	40	9	2,800	170	6,000
LA-NAI',	17	9	1,600	100	1,600
NI-I-HAU',	7	7	800	80	1,047
KA-HO-O-LA'WE,	11	8	200	60	80
MO-LO-KI'NI, LE-HU'-A, KA-U'-LA,	Islets, scarcely more than barren rocks.				
					130,313

CLIMATE AND TEMPERATURE.—The average temperature in low southern and western locations is 75°; in northern and eastern, 72°. The lofty mountains are cool, and at their summits, cold. A summary of meteorological observations made by the missionaries at Honolulu from Aug., 1821, to July, 1822, shows the mean temperature to be 75°; N E. trade winds three-fourths of the year; rain on 40 days; highest heat observed in the shade, 88°, lowest 59°. A summary of observations made at the same place for 1838, by T. C. B. Rooke, Esq., and published in the Hawaiian Spectator, vol. i., shows the mean heat 75.8 (which nearly corresponds to that of Lahaina and Kailua), 41 rainy days, 275 fine; amount of rain, 46.8 inches. The following summary of meteorological observations made by Mr. E. Johnson, a missionary, at Waioli, Kauai, and published in the American Journal of Science and Arts, 1847, shows the mean temperature of that place to be 72°; the highest degree of heat observed in the shade, 90°, the lowest 54°; the highest in the sun, 113°; amount of rain, 85 inches.

Months and date.	FAH. THER.						WINDS.				WEATHER.									
	Average at 5½ A.M.	Average at 1 P.M.	Average at 6½ P.M	Maximum.	Minimum.	Mean.	N. E. Trades, A.M.	N. E. Trades, P.M.	Variable, A. M.	Variable, P. M.	Fair, morning.	Fair, P. M.	Cloudy, A. M.	Cloudy, P. M.	Showers, A. M.	Showers, P. M.	Rain, A. M.	Rain, P. M.	Rain at night.	Rain in inches and tenths.
April, 1845,	66.0	75.0	70.0	82.0	62.0	70.2	21	20	10	11½	9	4	4	11	10	9	7	6	17	14.0
May, "	69.6	80.3	74.0	85.0	66.0	74.6	27	4	4	11	10	5	4	14	15	1	2	10		6.0
June, "	71.6	82.6	75.0	90.0	66.0	76.4	25	27	5	3	16	17	2	1	10	10	3	3	12	4.0
July, "	72.0	82.0	75.8	86.0	69.0	76.3	30	30	1	11	9	7	7	6	9	16	6	2	21	8.0
August, "	71.6	83.2	76.9	89.0	67.0	77.2	29	29	2	2	19	15	2	5	7	8	3	3	12	5.5
Sept., "	71.4	82.6	76.6	87.0	68.0	76.8	28	27	2	3	16	12	3	4	11	13	0	1	14	5.4
Oct., "	69.6	78.5	73.8	84.0	64.0	74.0	18	16	13	15	11	10	5	3	9	10	6	8	22	18.4
Nov., "	66.7	78.3	72.0	82.0	57.0	72.3	4	4	26	26	22	19	2	4	4	4	2	3	10	5.2
Dec., "	65.2	75.0	69.0	82.0	57.0	69.7	7	7	24	24	18	10	6	5	6	6	1	1	11	5.0
Jan., 1846,	62.0	71.8	67.9	79.0	54.0	67.2	3	3	28	28	18	17	8	8	1	4	4	3	10	4.6
Feb., "	63.3	73.5	68.4	78.0	57.0	68.4	10	10	18	18	16	14	10	10	0	1	2	3	10	3.0
March, "	63.4	75.8	69.5	80.0	56.0	69.5	18	18	13	13.15	14	6	8	4	4	6	5	16		6.6

DISEASES.—Asthma, croup, cutaneous eruptions, apoplexy, diarrhœa, dysentery, catarrh, dropsy, fevers, ophthalmia, influenza, inflammatory rheumatism, scrofula, syphilis, ulcers, consumption.

III. NAMES OF THE PRINCIPAL HAWAIIAN PERSONAGES FOUND IN THIS WORK.

Many names are significant or historical, designed not so much to mark the character of the possessor, as to perpetuate the remembrance of some event; for instance, the Queen being confined in a dark habitation on account of sore eyes, one of her friends called his infant son " *David Darkhouse.*" When she was ill and a brush was used on her skin, another named his son "*Gideon Skinbrush.*" To distinguish husband and wife, the people now sometimes subjoin *kane*, male, or *wahine*, female, to the name, but in oriental simplicity, they rarely use any term answering to *Mr.* and *Mrs.*

AI-KA-NA'-KA—*Man-eater.* A chief, the heir of Naihe of Kealakekua.

A-KU'A MA-KA-HI'KI—*God of the Year.* A deity whose image set up in a district would not remove till the tax was paid.

AU-WAE'—*Chin.* Chief of Wailuku.

BO'-KI—*Boat* or *boss.* Governor of Oahu, 1819—1829.

HA-A-LI-LI-O'. The friend, secretary, and ambassador of the king.

HO-A-PI'LI—*Joint partner, united companion.* Governor of Maui, 1836—40.

HO'PU—*Catch.* Native teacher.

HU-ME-HU'ME. G. P., Kaumualii. Insurgent, 1824.

I'I—*Stinted.* John, a counsellor and school inspector.

KA-A-HU-MA'NU—*Feathered* or *bird mantle.* Regent, 1824—32.

KA-E'O. King of Kauai, father of Kaumualii. A representative, 1845.

KA-HA-LA'IA. Governor of Kauai, 1824.

KA-HE-KI'LI—*Thunder.* King of Maui, 1773—1794.

KA-HU'HU—*Anger.* Capt. of the king's guard, 1829.

KAI-A-KO-I'LI—*Sea of Koili.* Headman of Koolauloa, 1834.

KAI-A'-NA. A high chief of Hawaii, and rival of Kamehameha.

KAI-KI-O-E'WA. Gov. of Kauai, 1824—40.

KA-I'LI—*The surface ; the skin.* A deity.

KA-LAI-PA-HO'A—*Daggermaker.* A so-called poison deity, p. 24.

KA-LA-KU'A. A wife of Kamehameha, and afterwards of Hoapili.

KA-LA'MA—*The flambeau.* Wife of Kamehameha III., 1837—47.

KA-LA-NI-MO'KU, } *Rent heaven.* Liholiho's general and prime counsellor of
KA-LAI-MO-KU', } Kaahumanu.

KA-LA-NI-O-PU'U—*Budding heaven.* King of Hawaii, 1778.
KA-MA-KA-HE-LE'I—*The eye a gem.* Queen of Kauai, 1799.
KA-MA-MA'LU—*The shade, umbrella.* Wife of Liholiho, 1818, 1824.
KA-MA-NA'WA—*The time.* A coadjutor of the conqueror.
KA-ME-E-IA-MO'KU. A high chief of Hawaii, 1778—1794.
KA-ME-HA-ME'HA—*Loneliness.* Founder of the present dynasty. (see p. 80.)
KA-NE-O-NE'O—*Desolation.* Chief of Kaui, 1778.
KA-PI-O-LA'NI. Daughter of Keawemauhili, and wife of Naihe, 1809—31.
KA-PU'LE—*Prayer.* Queen of Kauai, 1819—21.
KAU-I-KE-AO'U-LI—*Hang on the dark sky.* Kamehameha III., present king.
KA-U-MU-A-LI'I. King of Kauai (p. 154).
KA-WAI-LE-PO-LE'PO—*Filthy water.* Head man of Wailuku.
KE-A-LI-I-A-HO-NU'I—*The merciful chief.* Governor of Kauai, 1844.
KE-E-AU-MO'KU—*The boarding a fleet.* Father and brother of Kaahumanu.
KE-A'WE. Ancient king of Hawaii. A high chief of Kauai, 1778—95.
KE-A-WE-A-HU'LU. High chief of Hawaii, and coadjutor of Kamehameha.
KE-A-WE-MAU-HI'LI. King of Hilo, 1780.
KE-A-WE-A-MA'HI. Governess of KAUAI.
KE-KAU-LI'KE—*The equipoise.* King of Maui, and ancestor of the Maui
    family of chiefs, p. 80.
KE-KA-U-LU-O'HI. A wife of Liholiho, and of Kanaina. Premier, 1839—45.
KE-KAU-O-NO'HI. Daughter of Wahinepio, and a wife of Liholiho.
KE-O'U-A—*The rain-food.* King of Ka-u. A wife of Adams. A Gov. of Maui.
KE-KU-A-NAO'A. Gov. of Oahu, 1836—1847.
KE-O-HO-KA-LO'LE—*The hair the woven cloth.* Mem. of legislature, 1840.
KE-O-NI-A'NI—Derived from John Young. Son of Mr. Young, Premier, 1846.
KE-O-PU-O-LA'NI. Daughter of Kiwalao, and mother of two kings.
KE-KU-A-O-KA-LA'-NI—*The back* or *god of heaven,* champion of idolatry, 1819.
KE-KU-PU-O'HI. Wife of Kalaniopuu, 1779, a poetess, 1830.
KI-AI-MA-KA'NI—*Wind watcher.* Insurgent chief of Kauai, 1824.
KI-AI-MO'KU—*Island* or *ship watcher.* Insurgent at Kauai, 1824.
KI-NAU'. Dau. of Kamehameha and wife of Liholiho, 1819. Premier, 1832—7.
KI-WA-LA-O'. Son of Kalaniopuu, and rival of Kamehameha, 1780.
KO-A-LAU-KA'NI, KA-HO-LO-O-KA-LA'NI. Son of Kehekili, and gov. of Maui, 1794.
KO-NI'A. Wife of Paki, and member of the legislature, 1840—47.
KU-A-KI'NI, JOHN ADAMS. Governor of Hawaii, 1820—45.
LA-A-NU'I. Chief of Waialua, and brother-in-law of Kaahumanu.
LI-LI'HA—*Disgust.* Governess of Oahu, 1829.
LI-HO-LI'HO, I-O-LA-NI, } Son and successor of Kamehameha, 1819—24.
KA-ME-HA-ME'HA II. }
LI-KE-LI'KE. Wife of Kalanimoku.
LE-LE-I-O-HO'KU. Son of Kalanimoku, and governor of Hawaii, 1846.
LŎ NO—*Hearing.* A deity.
MA-NU'IA—*Fish bird.* Capt. of the Fort at Honolulu, 1825—29.
MA'LO— *Girdle.* David, a native preacher.
MA-NO'NO. Wife of Kekuaokalani, 1819.
ME'RE—Derived from *Mary.* Daughter of Gov. Adams.
NA-MA-KE-HA'. High chief of Hawaii. Insurgent, 1796.
NA-MA-HA'NA. Sister and wife of the king of Maui, 1770. Wife of Kame-
    hameha. Governess of Oahu, 1824.
NAI'HE—*The spears.* Chief of Kealakekua, acting governor of Hawaii, 1831.
NAI-HE-KU-KU'I—*The spears of candlenut.* The father of the present Queen.
NA-HI-E-NA-E'NA—*Raging fires.* Daughter of Kamehameha.
O-PU-KA-HAI'A—*Ripped abdomen.* First Hawaiian convert.
PA-KI'. Capt. of the fort, 1840. Member of the national council, 1840.
PA-LE-I-O-HO-LA'NI. King of Oahu, 1779.
PAU-A'-HI—*Fire destroyed.* A wife of Liholiho, and of Kekuanaoa.
PAU'LO KA-NO'A—*Paul the free.* A judge. Representative, 1845.
PU-A-A-I'KI. Bartimeus, the blind preacher, p. 481.

A RESIDENCE OF
TWENTY-ONE YEARS IN THE
SANDWICH ISLANDS

CHAPTER I.

ORIGINAL STATE OF THE NATION.

Tradition uncertain.—Origin of the race and of their *tabus.*—Character of their Religion.—Relation to other Tribes.—Prediction of a new Religion.—Parentage and childhood of Kaahumanu.—Discovery by Cook.—War of Kalaniopuu and Kahekili.—Deification and death of Cook.

DARKNESS covered the earth and gross darkness the people. This, for ages, was emphatically applicable to the isles of the great Pacific Ocean. But the voice divine said, "Let there be light."

The early history of the Hawaiian Islands being involved in great obscurity, the best efforts now to trace it must be attended with uncertainty. The nation had no written language, no records either hieroglyphic, syllabic, alphabetic or monumental, no ideas of literature before their discovery by Europeans, and, so far as appears, no tradition that their ancestors ever possessed any.

In the place of authentic history they had obscure oral traditions, national or party songs, rude narratives of the successions of kings, wars, victories, exploits of gods, heroes, priests, sorcerers, the giants of iniquity and antiquity, embracing conjecture, romance, and the general absurdities of Polytheism. These may be supposed to be mixed up with the confused impressions of their minstrels, or to be affected by the variations made by persons through whom the traditions have passed from generation to generation, or from one clan to another. With these various sources of uncertain history is connected the extreme difficulty of intercourse between the people of different islands, and of different clans on the same island, especially in the oft-recurring state of hostility to which they were long accustomed. To the actors and the narrators, exact information would in such cases be almost impossible, even had truth been their object, and much more so, where the desire and the temptation to misrepresent were strong; for flattery and slander naturally abound amid party strifes, where reverence for a holy God is unknown.

Destitute of high moral principle as idolaters of reprobate mind usually are, and by no means distinguished for forming in their own minds, or conveying to others by language, just conceptions of facts that came within the sphere of their observation; or for distinguishing between truth, falsehood, and fiction; or between conjecture, belief, and certain knowledge—the Hawaiians of former generations will not be injured if their oral traditions should be received with caution, or with many grains of allowance for fiction, poetic license, forgetfulness, and intentional misstatement.

History proposes to give just delineations of the characters of individual men and of governments, and to set forth the reasons and the consequences of their actions, for the purpose of warning, prompting, and guiding succeeding generations. It must therefore, deal, not only with outward facts, but with the motives of men and all the causes of the facts; and of course it must be conversant with the principles which governed, and with those which ought to have governed, the actors; for otherwise it can accomplish little or nothing for posterity. How imperfectly, then, were those stupid, unlettered, unsanctified heathen tribes furnished for making out a trustworthy history of their country for ages back or even for a single generation! If we would appreciate the difficulties which embarrass the traditionists of Hawaiian antiquity, let us consider how difficult it is even now for the intelligent readers of the various accounts given by tourists, residents, explorers, naval officers and missionaries, from the time of the bloody tragedy of Captain Cook, to the late and still more bloody French tragedy at the Society Islands; to trace out the causes, and the true and responsible authors of the more important transactions there, and to decide whether particular events and prominent measures are attributable to right or wrong intention.

Oral tradition alone, with all the advantages derivable from science and general history, could not be safely relied on to give to posterity in France, England, America, or the Pacific Isles, any just conception of the principal events in those islands, even since the discovery by Captain Cook, or since the introduction there of the Gospel. We need records carefully written by men thoroughly acquainted with the people, and friendly to the truth. With all the advantages of the pen and press, of science and Christianity, of wakeful attention and personal observation, we shall do well if we trace out the true responsibility, obtain a just view of facts and motives, and are able, in our estimate, to do justice to all classes concerned, and to decide what ought to be done in like circumstances. If modern writers, acquainted with the Bible, and with different heathen nations, find it difficult to convey, by the pen, just conceptions of heathen institutions, and their influence on human character, how vain it would be to expect that by the merely oral tradition of savages, through many generations, just ideas will be conveyed of what a heathen nation was, what it did, and what it suffered, ages or centuries ago, since which time, many terms have lost their meaning, and many tropes become unintelligible. Perhaps nothing is more difficult and at the same time indispensable in a missionary journal or narrative, than to convey to its readers just ideas of the heathenism, which is now to be met and removed among our deluded cotemporaries, who by the Divine arrangement have a high claim on our sympathy and beneficence.

With such views of the difficulty and importance of the task, I devote a few pages to the general history of the islands, previous to their discovery by Captain Cook, and a more particular history from that period to the introduction of Christianity, exhibiting the condition in which it found them, and the nature of the field to be cultivated. Further particulars of their manners, customs, laws, government and superstitions, will be incorporated with the narrative of the efforts to raise the character and change the religion and habits of the nation; to reform and purify society there, and to found and build up institutions adapted to bless the current and succeeding generations..

The origin of the Hawaiian race, of the first occupants of these islands, and of their system of religion, was involved, as might be expected, in difficulties which their descendants could not satisfactorily solve. Even wiser philosophers have found some difficulty in accounting for the peopling of these Islands,— so remote from the continents, and so distant, too, from the southern groups, with whom they are united by affinity of language, religion and customs.

There are indications in the traditionary history of the different groups, that the Hawaiians came from the south. Tahiti or Kahiki, is a term applied by the Hawaiians both to the principal of the Georgian or Society Islands, and to foreign countries in general. It is possible for the ancestors of the race to have come to the Sandwich Islands without much knowledge of navigation. Trees from foreign countries repeatedly land on their shores, probably from the American and Asiatic coasts. Several natives of Japan, leaving their country in Japanese junks, have fallen upon the Sandwich Islands since the arrival of our mission there, and others having approached in their lost and distressed state have been picked up and brought in by whaling ships. One crew made the Islands in great distress, sick and dying in their own little junk, which was brought to anchor on the N. W. part of Oahu, and then wrecked in the attempt to bring her round into the port of Honolulu. Another was taken by a whaler, from their unmanageable junk, not far distant, and brought into Lahaina, Maui. In 1840, a third crew, driven off in a single masted boat, was found at 170¼ E. and 34 N. 181 days out, and brought to the islands by the American brig Arguile, Captain Codman.

Junks, boats, or canoes, such as are still found in Polynesia, could pass in the variables, without the tropics, from the Asiatic coasts or islands; then, falling into the trades, they might come without compass, chart, or design, to the Sandwich or Society Islands. Or when the trade winds are interrupted by westerly winds that blow, for a considerable period annually, canoes with passengers might be driven thither from the west. As to provisions for a long voyage, we know that some nations are skilful in taking fish, and some eat one another on emergencies, as did the crew of the Essex, who, after being wrecked by a stroke from a whale in that great ocean, suffered extreme hardships for 90 days, till the survivors reached the American continent in boats. Two years before our mission commenced, Kotzebue found at the Radack group, a native of the Carolines, who, with three companions, had been driven eastward in a canoe, about 1500 miles.

Tradition represents the Hawaiian race as having sprung from two distinct sources; the two original occupants, Kahiko (the ancient) and his wife, Kupulanakahau, and the first two immigrants Kukalaniehu, and his wife Kahakauakoko. Wakea, the son of the former, and Papa, the daughter of the latter, became the progenitors of the Hawaiian race. Papa was considered as a goddess, and it was said of her that she brought forth the islands, and that an offspring from her head, became a god.

Wakea is regarded as the Patriarch of the whole tribe. Tradition represents him as consulting with a priest how he may commit incest with his first-born daughter, and escape the resentment of Papa, his wife. This gave occasion to the tabu system, the first prohibition of which forbids women the pleasure of eating with their husbands. The object of this first rule was the indulgence, unobserved, of a wicked passion. But the jealous Papa called the husband to account. Upon this he was angry, and forbade her the use of various kinds of food; such as in modern times have been tabu to women; degraded her—spit in her face, and put her away, and made a wife of his daughter. Hence the separate eating of the sexes uniformly; and the occasional separate lodging of husbands and wives, at the will of kings and priests; and hence the sanction of the separation at pleasure, of husbands and wives, and of the grossest pollution, incest, and fraud. The union of a brother and sister in the highest ranks became fashionable, and continued so till the revealed will of God was made known to them by our Mission.

Various times, places and things were placed under tabu, or declared to be sacred. To enforce the unreasonable tabu, the highest penalty was annexed, and it grew up into a bloody system of violence and pollution suited to the lust, pride and malice of the priests, who were often rulers at the same time, and who pretended to claim, in the name of the gods, the right to put to death, by their own hands, and to threaten with death by the power of their deities every subject that should break any of the senseless tabus. To favor licentiousness, and to punish women for jealousy, was, according to tradition, one of the objects of the system of tabu. How must the observance of it, then, debase the public mind, cherish the vilest passions, banish domestic happiness, and shield priests and kings in their indulgences and oppression! For a religion which is founded on the arbitrary will, and designed to favor the vilest wishes of a wicked patriarch, and a polluted and fraudulent priest, may lay claim to the earnings and even the heads of the people for sacrifice, if they can be led by sophistry, falsehood, or force, to yield to it. Hence the numerous offerings to Hawaiian priests, and the numerous capital offences in the tabu ceremonial. Polygamy (implying plurality of husbands and wives), fornication, adultery, incest, infant murder, desertion of husbands, wives, parents and children; sorcery, covetousness, and oppression, extensively prevailed, and seem hardly to have been forbidden or rebuked by their religion.

Natural conscience, which God implants in every human breast, to be the expounder of moral law, would have done far better alone than the stereotype and misguiding tabu. Conscience, doubtless, often opposed its cruelty on the one hand, and its licentiousness on the other; though the whole policy of Satan there, seemed to be, to *make that to be sin which is no sin, and that to be no sin which is sin.* Still, as God maintains the power of conscience for good to some extent, in all; the vile dogmas of a false religion, it is found, may be neglected or resisted by a large portion of the community, even where the antiquity and authority of the general system are acknowledged. Passion and private interest, too, in thousands of instances, will refuse obedience to some parts of an unwelcome system of restraints, whether right or wrong; and this was unquestionably true among Hawaiians.

The sense of guilt among the heathen generally, where passion violates conscience, makes sacrifices of some kind appear necessary, as "compensating contrivances" which Pharisaic formalists make for themselves in case of omitting the weightier matters of the law, or neglecting those duties which are more difficult for selfish moral agents to perform. Idolaters will give up certain things which they do not much value, if, in consequence, their love of pleasure, power and honor can be gratified, and the favor of the gods secured. But the guilt of violating God's law as written on the heart by the finger of God, or on the pages of his Word, and illustrated in the death of Christ, appears to the enlightened, so great, that no human service or sacrifice can be a compensation or atonement for it. The sense of guilt thus quickened and enlightened, makes the sinner hail the sacrifice of Christ as the only ground of peace and hope, destroys his pride of self-righteousness, and excludes all boasting. The heathen system, therefore, tends to immeasurable evil; but the Christian system to immeasurable good.

The priests of Hawaiian superstition, who were wholesale butchers of their fellow-men—the licensed murderers of numerous victims whom they put to death, or by sophistry or superstition persuaded to immolate themselves, seem more like fiends than anything else that walks the earth ; and though multitudes of Hawaiian mothers, because they were guilty or suspected of wantonness, or on account of poverty, imbecility, or love of ease, killed their own offspring, yet their crime, unnatural and inexcusable as it was, seems less diabolical than the practices of the priests of the Sandwich Islands under the garb of religion ; seizing men and women at pleasure, binding, strangling, or beating them to death, and offering them up in sacrifice to their malevolent deities.

Polytheism, which extensively prevailed at the Sandwich Islands, is always at variance with the will of God, and the principles of truth and virtue. The romance of heathen purity and felicity under such a system lives and flourishes only in minds where the length and breadth of the divine law are not perceived, the deep springs of heathen actions are unobserved, and the obligations of idolaters to the Creator and Benefactor of all are denied or misunderstood.

Let us examine the condition and character of the Polynesians, as all other heathen tribes are to be examined, with the light of the Bible to aid our judgment, and we shall see that Hawaiian pagans were by no means above the general degradation, wretchedness and vileness ascribed to the ancient heathen.

To get a just conception of their state before the Gospel poured in its purifying and elevating light, we need to take with us the graphic Scriptural description of the banditti before the flood, of the licentious in the days of Lot, of Pharaoh and Amalek, of Jezebel and Sennacherib, of Haman and Zeresh, and of pagan Rome.

Those who carefully investigate the mysteries, and fathom the depths of Polynesian heathenism, so as to be able to make an intelligible comparison of its characteristics with the inspired record and testimony concerning idolatry, recognize its forbidding lineaments, as face answers to face in water. The miserable captives of Satan, led by him at his will, sacrifice even themselves or their children to devils, being given over to a reprobate mind, because they change the truth of God into a lie, and worship the creature, rather than the Creator. Instead, therefore, of that pure, humble, diligent attempt to find and serve, and please their Maker, which is sometimes vainly ascribed to them, "their mouth is full of cursing and bitterness, their throat is an open sepulchre. With their tongues have they used deceit, and the poison of asps is under their lips. Their feet are swift to shed blood. Destruction and misery are in their paths, and the way of peace they have not known. There is no fear of God before their eyes."

In the place of being filled with love and reverence to the true God, and equity and benevolence towards his creatures, they are "filled with all unrighteousness, fornication, wickedness, murder, debate, deceit, malignity," being "whisperers, backbiters, haters of God, despiteful, proud, boasters, inventors of evil things, disobedient to parents, without natural affection, implacable, unmerciful." Such was the character of the famed "children of nature," or "children of wrath by nature," at the Sandwich, Society, New Zealand, and Marquesas Islands, while they had not been taught by inspired truth, to stand in awe of the holiness, power and justice of the Maker, Law-giver, Redeemer, and Judge of the world.

The process by which children, born of heathen parents, come to possess a character so odious, and so fearfully at variance with the laws of their Moral Governor, and with the design of man's creation, deserves our attention and care, especially if it be possible for us to arrest it. And the peculiarities of national character and condition, of the Hawaiians and other heathen tribes, ought to be studied and delineated in the process of evangelizing the world; in order to show the adaptation, and make the successful application, of the Gospel to the wants of idolaters, wherever they dwell.

Inasmuch as the natural disposition of our race is to indulge the sordid, selfish, sinful passions, it may be affirmed that no man is better than his principles, and no nation is better than its religion.

Looking back into the obscurity of Hawaiian history, to inquire respecting the character of the unknown islanders who have passed over the stage of earthly existence in preceding generations, we may estimate their corruption and debasement by the principles and religious practices in which they trained and left their children, and by the vile songs, and sports, the creeds and usages prevailing among them, and by the received narrative of the lives of their leaders. Their religion, their politics, their amusements, and the examples of rulers, priests, and parents, all tended to sanction and to foster lust and malevolence. The national history, so far as it was preserved and known by the people, must have continued, without the counteracting influence of a better religion than was known to them, to be debasing, instead of producing or promoting virtue. Violence, fraud, lust, and pollution, pervade the whole history from the oldest traditions of the origin of their race, and of their system of religion; and whether that history be true or false, its effects upon the moral sense, so far as it was relied on, were deadly. Even the story that cannibalism was once practised in the mountains of Oahu, does not show, as tradition relates it, that any king or chief cared to protect the people from the supposed devourers of men; or that any public sentiment, at the time, was expressed against it, any more than against human sacrifices to the gods, which it was believed the king and priests might offer and did offer at their pleasure.

In addition to this conceded power of the priests and rulers, it was claimed and believed, that by a species of witchcraft, incantations, and tricks of sorcery, or intercourse with malevolent spirits, the priests and sorcerers could, and would, in an invisible manner, accomplish the death of any that might fall under their displeasure ; and, therefore, every member of the community was deemed liable, and many felt themselves liable to perish any day, by the unseen agency of their fellow-men, who were above, or without law. How impracticable, in such a state, the enjoyment of the blessing of mutual confidence and love!

If, now, in addition to all this, it were possible for the mass of the people to believe that chiefs and priests, in all parts of the islands, possessed idol gods made of a species of wood so deadly, that a little dust scraped off and secreted in their food, would cause death at any time, and that their selfishness, misanthropy, and murderous training would dispose them to use that power where no law could touch them for it ; what an unfailing source of anxiety and of servile subjugation must it have been to the common people! But incredible as it may seem, their religion, in later generations, taught that such idols existed, and the people admitted that their priests and rulers did possess such horrid instruments of secret manslaughter, and were not slow to use them. The missionaries have been impressed with the evidence that malevolence and falsehood were the main features of Polynesian idolatry everywhere. And the bloody and lying character of the religion of Pagan Hawaii is well illustrated in the brief history of Kalaipahoa, one of their deities, called the Poison god—a history absurd enough to be at once rejected as fictitious, and yet so plausible, as to induce not only natives but white men, and even modern writers to admit the truth of its foundation. But I confess the tradition of this god of human manufacture, though not of ancient date, has quite overtasked my credulity, as it respects the existence of the *poison tree*, of which the images were supposed to be made.

It is maintained, that "a man of Molokai by the name of Kaneakama, dreamed that a singular tree of the mountains approached him with this message; 'Bring offerings and worship me; then cut me down and make an idol of my trunk, and it shall have power to kill whom you choose.' He, in obedience to the vision, cut down a singular tree on the mountains of Molokai, and carved out of its trunk an idol. He scraped off small portions of it, and concealed the dust in the food of men, and killed them at once. The idol became celebrated for its power and its subserviency to the will of the murderer. Chiefs and people came from the other islands, even the most distant, and carried away the branches and roots of this (Upas) tree, and converted them into idols that were scattered throughout the whole group; the scrapings of which were used by chiefs and sorcerers for killing all obnoxious persons, high and low."*

This tree, without predecessor or successor, " the only tree of the kind" ever known, probably never existed. Had any king or possessor of Molokai owned such a tree, would he have allowed *subjects* or *enemies* to come from all the other islands, and each freely carry away poison from this tree, enough to exterminate the whole population? But if it were a natural poison, so deadly, that a small particle of its dry dust concealed in men's food would be fatal, why did it need first to be worshipped to make it powerful? And why did those who professed to believe in its deadly efficacy, always use incantations, and the tricks of sorcery to perpetrate murder, when they attempted to destroy by the dust of the deified block? No small ingenuity must have been displayed in establishing the belief in the existence of such a deity, or poisonous tree, *sui generis ;* a belief that has outlived its annihilated power. But where the belief that such a secret and fatal poison was in the hands of chiefs, priests or sorcerers, and that they were ready to use it freely, was firmly established, the apprehension of the victim marked by the sorcerer that he was liable, any hour, to die by poison, would naturally produce depression of spirits, deter him from eating necessary food, and through his fears, hasten his death. Thus the murder could often be accomplished by a moral poison, where no *Upas* tree existed. Besides where malevolence was regarded as common, where mortality was great, disease or medical treatment so often fatal, and a false philosophy as to the causes and remedies of disease so prevalent, multitudes of the ignorant were doubtless led to conclude that death was frequently the consequence of sorcery or poison, though no such tree ever existed. It is remarkable that so much fear prevailed in respect to the power of a secret and mysterious poison, while the poisons often used in quackery were rarely or never allowed to be fatal. The fresh juice of the arum, and of the wild gourd, and other articles in their materia medica, given largely as a cathartic or enema, doubtless prove a fatal poison in cases, not a few, when used by quacks, professedly to cure or *prevent* disease. But these could not well be administered secretly. In the general mortality, and the general ignorance of the people, it would have been difficult to prove that the dry powder of *deified wood*, secreted in food, and not some of the various other causes of death, had proved fatal in any given case. But the purposes of a Satanic religion are accomplished without proof of the divinity of its objects of fear or adoration. What idolater loving darkness rather than light, would demand proof that the calves of Aaron and Jeroboam, the image of Nebuchadnezzar, or any other image, *ought to be worshipped ?*—When men wish to serve the

* See Dibble's History of the Sandwich Islands.

true God, they look for proofs of his existence and of his
infinite excellence ; and these are inscribed on all his works,
and fully demonstrated in his revealed Word. But, if, with
the light of reason, conscience, and nature, men prefer as
deities the workmanship of their own vile hands, or the vilest
objects in creation, or the viler creatures of their polluted imagination, they are judicially given over to blindness of mind and
hardness of heart. Then nothing is too absurd for them to admit,
and nothing too mean or worthless to command their homage.
Though the God of Heaven never leaves himself without witness,
never fails to exhibit to his creatures the evidence of his Godhead,
yet during the long and dark ages of the most absurd idolatry which
prevailed at the Sandwich Islands, if there was any effort to find the
true God, or to feel after him as the Creator and Benefactor of all,
so confused were Hawaiian minds as to his attributes, and so
low their conceptions of virtue, justice, power, goodness, and
holiness, that a divine revelation was indispensably necessary to
instruct, purify, and elevate them. But great as was the darkness of their minds, and pitiable as was the confusion or grossness
of their ideas of the divine attributes, still, every one of them was
created with conscience and freedom of thought and will, which
made them accountable to their Creator and Moral Governor.
They all had, moreover, a language capable of expressing truth
and falsehood, love and hatred, right and wrong, duty and sin,
moral excellence and moral turpitude, so as to afford a medium
for teaching a course of life far better than they pursued. The
phrase, " *God of Heaven*," was familiar to them ; and the following tradition, whether it record a fact or a fiction, exhibits evidence, not only that the terms which belong to the science of duty
were not wholly exterminated from the language, but that
the notion of a power above, which made a distinction between
virtue and vice, between the worship of God and impiety, respect
and contempt for parental authority, and equity and oppression in
rulers, was not wholly lost. The story, which I translate from
" Mooolelo Hawaii," may have been invented to rebuke some
abominable tyrant.

" One showing his head, and looking from a cloud, demanded—
' Who among the rulers of earth hath done well ?' Men replied,
' Kahiko, the ancient, was a good king, a wise man, a worshipper of
God, skilled in divination, attentive and active to secure the peace of
the land and the prosperity of his people.' ' What king,' the voice
demanded, ' has been distinguished for evil doing ?' Men returned
answer, ' Owaia, an impious man, unskilled in divination and war, neglecting the prosperity and happiness of his subjects, licentious, ava-
ricious, oppressive, and regardless of the dying charge of his excellent father.' "

Kahiko, the ancient, may have been Adam, the first patriarch of
our race, or Noah, the first post-deluvian.

The stupidity of the people, notwithstanding, was such, that absurd as it may seem, the most abominable priests gained credence when they claimed to be not only vicegerents of a higher deity but veritable gods, not merely as executing the will of the gods, but as acting in their person and character, and though full of malice and subtlety, came to be venerated and worshipped by their fellow worms. Bones, relics, and ghosts of the departed, monsters of the deep, birds and creeping things, were objects of their superstitious veneration. Yet much scepticism existed as to the truth and utility of many of their confused superstitions, and the prayers of one class were often directed against those of another, and addressed to different deities who were supposed to counteract each other.

To what other tribes or nations, it may be asked, are the Hawaiians most nearly related? They seem to have little or no affinity with the aboriginal tribes of the American continent, or with Japanese, Chinese, Africans, New Hollanders, or Europeans. But the degree of radical uniformity in the dialect, religion, and customs of the inhabitants of the Hawaiian islands, the Marquesas, the Society, the Samoa or Navigators, and New Zealand, and some others in the great Pacific, is so obvious and great as to prove them to have sprung from a common origin subsequently to the confusion of tongues. The resemblance or sameness of dialect is as obvious in the Sandwich Islands and New Zealand, distant as they are from each other, as in any two of the groups specified, though much more nearly contiguous. These Polynesian dialects, and the Malayan, appear also to have a common origin, though the affinity of the Malay to any one of these is by no means so great as that of each of these to the other. The Hawaiians, and their kindred Polynesian tribes, are probably descendants from the Malays.

But it is sometimes asked, Are not the Hawaiians the descendants of Israel, or a part of the lost tribes of that wonderful nation? A proud people like the Israelites, having had the earliest literature or the earliest histories of the world, and in their prosperity, the best code of laws in their own language, could hardly be supposed, while preserved themselves, and spread over a wide field like that of Polynesia, to have lost every vestige and tradition of their literature, and of their language, and of the names of their patriarchs, kings, prophets and heroes, and of their enemies and oppressors which are still found in authentic history. But among the Hawaiians not the slightest idea of the literature of their ancestors appears to be entertained; and no trace of the Hebrew language is clearly discernible in their tongue, though there is some resemblance in the structure and simplicity of the two.

The principal animals found among them were the unclean dog and hog, both of which they used freely for food. This might indeed have been the effect of necessity, or arisen from aversion to the Jewish restriction, had they descended from that stock.

They practised to some extent the rite of *incision*, instead of " circumcision." In their traditions, whether ancient or modern, they had a story corresponding in a remarkable degree with the Mosaic record of the family feud and reconciliation of Joseph and his brethren. Whether this story came to them from Egypt, through Jewish or Egyptian history known to their remote ancestors, or through some more modern wanderer acquainted with the ancient Scriptures, or originated in a similar fact, or a fiction, is uncertain.

They had places of refuge, or sacred enclosures for the security of non-combatants in war, which bore a slight resemblance to the cities of refuge for the man-slayer in Israel; but these were not *cities* or villages of permanent residence.

They have a tradition of the almost entire submerging of the islands by what they call " Kaiakahinalii," a term now used for deluge. This may be a tradition of the general deluge in the days of Noah, or an exaggerated account of a more recent inundation of their ocean abode, or of the sinking, according to some modern theorists, of a continent or vast countries in the Pacific, whose mountain-tops are supposed to be found encircled with coral reefs in great numbers. As the people are accustomed to live along the sea-shore, a great portion of the nation might, at any hour, be submerged by the rising of the tide as high as it does in some parts of the earth, or by such an agitation as the power of volcanic action could produce. Such a sudden rising and influx of the sea as the missionaries have witnessed in some places, would need to be increased but a little, and become general, in order to give rise to the origin of the tradition of " Kaiakahinalii."

But the most remarkable fact which I have observed in the archives of the oral history of the islands, the most wonderful which I gathered from the chiefs, is the *prediction* insisted on by a native prophet, *Kalaikuahulu*, of the generation preceding the introduction of Christianity, *that a communication would be made to them from Heaven (the residence of " Ke Akua maoli," the real God), entirely different from anything they had known, and that the tabus of the country would be subverted.* This, as Kaahumanu and other respectable chiefs assured me, Kalaikuahulu and his predecessors maintained. Could this be a tradition of some inspired prophecy of the Messiah, who was to introduce a new dispensation and a new revelation? Or did some shipwrecked voyager, from some partially enlightened part of the globe, convey to them the intimation that Mahommedanism or Christianity would take the place of the Hawaiian tabu? Or was it the spontaneous conjecture of some one of the more sagacious of the aborigines, who saw and felt the infelicity of their absurd religion, and ventured to express the hope or the opinion that it would be laid aside for a different if not a better system?

The latter is the more probable, and accords with the views of the late rulers. Dissatisfaction was undoubtedly felt, and some change looked for by different individuals among them, for several generations previous to the offer of the Gospel to them. The obscure prediction, or even vague expectation that their religion was to be radically changed, was doubtless favorable to the final prostration of their foolish tabus, and the introduction of Christianity. When the revealed Word of Jehovah was made known to them, Kaahumanu and others regarded the prediction of Kalaikuahulu as having a fulfilment.

Whatever may have been the sources of that prediction or expectation, it is an indication of the benevolent care of Jehovah over this portion of his helpless creatures, distant as they were from all the other nations of the earth, and immeasurably distant as they were from conformity with the will of their holy Creator.

To give my readers a clearer illustration of the condition and general character of the Hawaiians, in different states, ancient and modern, and of the process of the formation of heathen and Christian character, on the same field, I shall endeavor to trace the steps of prominent personages among them, whose early life was guided by heathenism, and whose later by Christianity. Numbers, born before the islands were known to Christendom, lived on till the New Testament was translated for them, and received by them, as the record of eternal life, which challenged their entire confidence. Among these, Kaahumanu, Queen of the Isles, may be presented as sustaining various important relations, living and acting in one age of darkness, and another of comparative light, and exhibiting in her life the results of widely different causes. The facts, in her case, will be the means of helping us to appreciate the transformations that take place in thousands of instances where the Gospel is published among the heathen.

Kaahumanu was born about the year 1773, at the foot of the hill Kauiki, on the eastern shore of Maui. Her father was Keeaumoku, subsequently a distinguished warrior and counsellor of the late conqueror.

Her mother was Namahana, the relict and sister of Kamehamehanui, and who, as his wife, and as the daughter of King Kekaulike, had been Queen of Maui. Kamehamehanui was the son and successor of Kekaulike, and the brother of Kahekili who governed Maui, as late as 1793, and of Kaeo, the father of Kaumualii, who, both father and son, were successive kings of Kauai and Niihau.

On the death of Kamehamehanui, King of Maui and its dependencies, his widow, Namahana sent for Keeaumoku (son of Keawepoepoe), who had been ordered to Oahu, and united with him; but appears to have fallen then into obscurity and neglect. They sojourned, for a time, with Kumukoa, at Molokai.

Paleioholani, then King of Oahu, invading Molokai, they went and dwelt for a season, as dependents on Puna, at Hana, the eastern district of Maui.

It was in these days of depression and adversity to her parents, that Kaahumanu was born. Her sister, the late Governess of Maui, says of her: " *He keike ia no ka wa ilihune o na makua o maua.* She was the child of the time of our parents' destitution."

Soon after her birth, at the request of their friends on Hawaii, they removed to that island, in the reign of Kalaniopuu. Here she twice narrowly escaped drowning in her infancy and early childhood. She was laid by her parents upon the *pola*, or top of a double canoe, wrapped in a roll of white *kapa* as they were sailing along by night, off the coast, to the southward of Kealakekua. Through the rolling and tossing of the canoe, she fell off into the sea, fast asleep. The roll of white kapa floating on the waves behind them, attracted the attention of her parents, who perceiving that their child was overboard, paddled quickly back, and drew her out of the water, as the daughter of Pharaoh did Moses.

Little did they or any human being then think of the rank she would hold, or the aid she was to render in Christianizing her degraded nation. When a little older, and able to tread a rough path with bare feet, she had a similar exposure and escape. Following her mother around the end of a canoe, lying near the sea, as many of them are often seen, immediately after a little voyage, or fishing excursion, she was caught by a huge wave rolling suddenly in, and in its recoil, carried beyond her depth. Some of the people cried out, " Dead ! O the daughter of Keeaumoku." A cousin of hers sprang in and rescued her.

The years of her childhood and youth, and those of her contemporaries, were years of violence and blood, while there were wars between Kalaniopuu, king of Hawaii, and Kahekili, king of Maui, and between Kamehameha and Kiwalao and others, and while the Hawaiians had their first intercourse with foreigners.

At this period, the celebrated navigator, Captain Cook, had the happiness and honor to bring the knowledge of the Hawaiian Islands to the civilized world, and to introduce civilized men to the pagan generation that preceded the introduction of Christianity there. There are indications that the islands had, before, been visited by foreigners or Europeans, and that thirty-seven years before the visit of Cook, a Spanish ship, captured by Lord Anson, had on board a chart, on which islands had been recently marked with a pen, in the latitude and longitude of the Hawaiian Islands. Captain Cook was sent into the Pacific, on a voyage of discovery, under the patronage of the Earl of Sandwich, and discovered the leeward part of the group, Jan. 18, 1778, on his way from the Society Islands to the North West Coast of America. He saw Oahu first, but being too far to leeward to visit it, he made Kauai, and brought his ship to anchor, off Waimea, on the south side, in the night. In the morning, the people on shore beheld this wonder, which they called by the same term as that used for island [*Moku*, to be cut, or broken off]. Their shouts of admiration, and their earnest inquiries were tumultuous. Some said, " What is that with so many branches ?" Others exclaimed, " It is a wood or forest that has moved along in the ocean." And some, greatly frightened, prognosticated danger and death. The chiefs Kaneoneo, and Keawe, being then in authority there, sent men, by canoe, to reconnoitre and report. The messengers, executing their orders, rejoiced to see the iron attached to the outside of the ship ; having before seen and learned to prize a little, which had floated to their shores, probably on pieces of wrecks. They climbed on board, and scanning the strange people, returned with the report, that their foreheads were white, their eyes bright, and their language unintelligible. They expressed astonishment at the size and structure of the ship, and the quantity of iron which they saw. One of the attendants on the chiefs, hearing of the abundance of iron, and desiring it, said, " I will go and seize it, for that is my inheritance or livelihood to seize property."* The chiefs said, " Go ;" and he soon commenced his work, and was shot down by the shipmen. Some of the natives proposed to fight the strangers. But Kamakahelei, a woman of high rank, proposed, like one of the enemies of Israel, a measure quite as fatal. She said, " Let us not fight *Lono*, our god, but conciliate him, that he may be friendly to us.' So she gave her own daughter, Lelemahoalani, to the commander of the expedition. Others of the company took other women, and paid in iron. That was the dearest bought iron, doubtless, ever bartered for guilty indulgences ; and thousands have been the victims of suffering and death, throughout the whole group, as the lamentable consequence of evils thus introduced, and not yet wholly eradicated.

It is a question in mental philosophy which different professors might answer differently, " How did *conscience* decide in the breast of him who attempted to rob the ship of iron, and of those who killed him for it, and of both the barbarians and the civilized who there bartered on terms no better than stealing or robbery ?"

Kaeo, a high chief of the royal family of Maui, the father of the late King Kaumualii not then born, and subsequently king of Kauai, here formed a friendly acquaintance with Vancouver, an officer of the squadron, which was renewed half a generation later.

The same year, returning from the North West coast of America, Captain Cook discovered Maui, Nov. 26, 1778. At that time, Kalaniopuu, king of Hawaii, with his chieftains and warriors, was engaged in a hostile attempt to wrest Maui from the dominion of Kahekili, the invincible sovereign of all the group except Hawaii. On the arrival of the ship, the natives having heard it described, seemed to recognize it, and carried off provi-

* The verb " *hao*" to seize officially, and the noun " *hao*," iron, are the same. So his thought was natural, ' It is *hao*, and I'll *hao* it, for that is my occupation to *hao*.'

sions to trade, from the shores of Hamakua. Kalaniopuu and his train went on board on the 30th, to gratify their curiosity, and his nephew, Kamehameha, then a youthful warrior (but subsequently a king and conqueror), showed his manliness by remaining on board with Cook over night, while the ship stood off to keep clear of the land. The old king is said to have supposed him lost. He was landed in the morning, and Captain C. passed on by the eastern part of that island, and discovered Hawaii. As he appeared off Kohala, some of the people scanning the wondrous strangers, who had fire and smoke about their mouths in pipes or cigars, pronounced them gods. Passing slowly round, on the east and south, and up the western side of Hawaii, Cook brought his ships to anchor in Kealakekua bay, Jan. 17, 1779, amid the shoutings of the multitudes who thronged the shores to gaze at the marvellous sight. Seeing so unusual a mode of traversing the ocean, and supposing the squadron to be the vehicle of the gods, setting at nought their tabus which forbid sailing on the water just at that time, they launched their canoes, and ventured out upon the bay to reconnoitre, and applied to the commander the name of a Polynesian deity, and rendered him the homage which they supposed would please him. The popular name of that navigator the missionaries found to be *Lono*, and to some extent it so continues to this day.

The following legend of one of the Hawaiian gods, professes to show the origin of the boxing-games of the Makahiki festival, and of the worship of Capt. Cook :—

In very ancient time Lono dwelt at Kealakekua with his wahine, Kaikilanialiiopuna. They dwelt together under the precipice. A man ascended the *pali* and called to the woman, " O Kaikilanialiiopuna, may one dare approach you,—your paramour—Ohea—the soldier ? This to join—That to flee—you and I sleep." Lono hearing, was angry and smote his *wahine*, and Kaikilanialiiopuna died. He took her up, bore her into the temple and there left her. He lamented over her and travelled round Hawaii, Maui, Molokai, Oahu, and Kauai, boxing with those whom he met. The people exclaimed, Behold Lono greatly crazed ! Lono replied, " I am crazed for her—I am frantic on account of her love." He left the islands and went to a foreign land in a triangular canoe, called Paimalau. Kaikilanialiiopuna came to life again, and travelled all round the islands searching after her husband. The people demanded of her, " What is your husband's name ?" She replied " Lono." " Was that crazy husband yours ?" " Aye, mine." Kaikilanialiopuna then sailed by a canoe to a foreign land. On the arrival of ships the people exclaimed, " Lo this is Lono ! Here comes Lono !"

When Captain Cook moved on the shore, some of the people bowed down and worshipped him, and others fled from him with fear. A priest approached him and placed a necklace of scarlet bark cloth upon his shoulders, then retreating a little, presented to him hogs, and other offerings, and with rapid incantation and prayer, did him homage; then led him to their sacred temple and worshipped him, as one of their long acknowledged deities.

About fifty days after his arrival from the north, the king of Hawaii returned from the war on Maui to Kealakekua. He treated Captain Cook with much respect, but finding the abominable practice on board which had been so unfortunately commenced at Kauai, attempted to restrain their licentiousness by forbidding the women to go on board. But in this he failed, for the measure induced the shipmen to throng the shore so much the more.

Kalaniopuu presented Captain Cook with some of his most valuable articles—brilliant feather mantles, and plumed rods, insignia of rank, of neat workmanship, and imposing form and aspect, for which he is said to have made little return. Priding himself on the honors shown him, and the influence he had acquired over these ignorant barbarians, and trusting to his naval and military skill and power, to resist or punish any aggression from the people, he ventured to assert rights which could not belong to him as a fellow-man. He not only received the religious homage which they ascribed to Lono, but according to Ledyard, who was with him, invaded their rights, both civil and religious, and took away their sacred enclosure, and some of their images, for the purpose of wooding his vessels, offering three hatchets in return. The effect was doubtless to awaken resentment and hostility. He sailed immediately on the 4th of Feb. But before he had passed Kawaihaè, finding one of his masts defective, he was providentially sent back to Kealakekua bay, where he anchored again, and engaged in the needful repairs. The men of the place were far less friendly than before, and finding that the foreigners had seduced the affections of some of their women, were disposed to oppose them. The shipmen became violent, fired on the people, and seized a canoe belonging to Paalea, a man of some distinction. He resisted, and was struck down by a foreigner with a paddle. Then his people threw stones. Paalea rising, and fearing he might be killed by Lono, the foreign chief, interposed, and quieted and drew off his men. But afterwards he stole one of the boats of the Englishmen, either for retaliation or indemnity. Captain Cook demanded of the king the restoration of the boat. But this was out of his power, for the people had broken it up to secure the iron in it for other purposes. Here was a real difficulty, though not sufficient for war or hostility of any kind. If Cook had been as ready to award justice to the injured people, and to Paalea who attempted to remunerate himself, as he was to exact restoration or remuneration from the king who had not trespassed on him, this matter might have been settled without the guilt of murder on either side. But disregarding the provocation which Paalea had had, though he mistook the course of duty in seeking redress, Captain Cook undertook to bring the king on board

with him, that he might compel him to restore the stolen boat. He
therefore on the 14th of Feb. blockaded the bay or harbor, landed
with an armed party on the north side of the bay, made a little
circuit, and came to the house of the king. He sent in his lieutenant, who invited and led the king out. The captain endeavored to persuade him to accompany him to the ship. They
approached the boat, which was waiting to receive them. A multitude of the people collected around, apparently unwilling that
their king should, in that posture of affairs, go off on board lest
they should lose him. Some, who apprehended danger, interposed to detain him. Among these was Kekuhaopio, who
had hastily crossed the bay in a canoe, having witnessed an
attack made by the English on another canoe crossing at the
same time, in which Kalimu, a chief and a relative, was
shot. The report of this outrage produced excitement in the
crowd around the king. Some urged an attack on the Englishmen. The king halted and refused to proceed. The armed
marines formed a line on the shore or at the water's edge. A
native approached Captain Cook with a dagger. The captain,
having a double-barrel gun, fired a charge of small shot at him.
Stones were thrown at the marines by the natives. Capt. Cook
then fired with ball, and killed one of the foremost natives. Stones
were again thrown at the marines, and returned by a discharge of
musketry from them and two boats' crews near the shore. The
crowd of natives received the fire with firmness, some holding up
mats as a shield against the whistling bullets. Their dauntless
men exasperated rushed on the marines, killed four and wounded three of them. Kalaimanohoowaha, a chief, seized Captain
Cook with a strong hand without striking him, thinking he might
perhaps be a god, but concluding from his outcry that he was not,
stabbed and slew him. The musketry continued from the boats
and cannon-balls from the ships, at length compelled the natives
to retire, seventeen being killed and others wounded. Two cannon shots were fired upon the people on the other side of the bay;
the effects of one upon the trunk of a cocoanut tree remained till
the missionaries arrived there. A skirmish took place between
the natives and the English stationed there, in which eight of the
natives were killed. Among the slain that day were two chiefs
acknowledged to have been friendly to the English.

The king and his people retired to the precipice that rises
abruptly from the head of the bay. They carried with them the
bodies of Cook and four of his men. On the heights of Kaawaloa,
they stripped the flesh from the bones of Cook and burnt it with
fire, preserving the bones, palms and entrails for superstitious
abominations. There were subsequent skirmishing and bloodshed.
The English demanded the body of their commander, burnt down
the village of Kealakekua on the south side of the bay, consuming
the houses of the priests and their property, including the presents
given them by the officers of the squadron. The bones of the com-

Village of Kaawaloa, on Keaiakekua Bay, where Capt. Cook was killed. Page 35.

mander were at length restored ; and were buried in the deep with martial honors. A reconciliation took place, and the two ships, the Resolution and Discovery, put to sea on the 22d or 23d of Feb., 1779, under the command of Captains Clerke and King.

In the intercourse between the natives and their discoverers, the late Queen Kaahumanu, Kekupuohi a young wife of Kalaniopuu, Kamehameha and their contemporaries, received their first impressions with respect to the civilized and Christian world. Kamehameha and others in their deep darkness endeavored to learn what advantage they could derive from intercourse with this new order of beings. The great and acknowledged superiority of Captain Cook and his associates over the natives would, had they taken the wisest course, have given them an enviable moral power for good, in making the earliest impressions from the Christian world highly salutary. Had this distinguished and successful navigator, conscientiously resisted, through jealousy for the honor of the Most High, every token of religious homage wrongfully offered to his own person by the infatuated natives, and with his party insisted on the propriety and duty of their leaving their horrid idols and vain oblations, and tabus, and acknowledging the living Jehovah alone as God, they might have prepared the way for the overthrow of the foolish and bloody idolatry of the land. But that was not the object of the expedition; and if the influence of it had been nugatory it might be passed by with little notice.

But we can hardly avoid the conclusion, that for the direct encouragement of idolatry, and especially for his audacity in allowing himself like the proud and magisterial Herod to be idolized, he was left to infatuation and died by the visitation of God.

How vain, rebellious, and at the same time contemptible, for a worm to presume to receive religious homage and sacrifices from the stupid and polluted worshippers of demons and of the vilest visible objects of creation, and to teach them by precept and example to violate the plainest commands or rules of duty from Heaven—to encourage self-indulgence, revenge, injustice, and disgusting lewdness as the business of the highest order of beings known to them, without one note of remonstrance on account of the dishonor cast on the Almighty Creator !

Had an inspired apostle, Peter or Paul, or an angel from Heaven in his celestial glory, instead of the lamented discoverer, visited these ignorant and debased sons and daughters of Adam, whom superstition was leading blindfold to ruin ; and had they proposed or attempted to sacrifice to him or to worship him, how promptly would he have rebuked them, saying with astonishment as that navigator ought to have done, "Not so—worship God, your Creator and Redeemer—I am his servant !"

But under the influence of a totally different example, the nation confirmed in superstition darker than before, and encouraged in adultery and violence more destructive, passed on another generation.

CHAPTER II.

WARS AND REIGN OF KAMEHAMEHA.

Death of Kalaniopuu—War of Kiwalao—Attack on the South of Hawaii—Invasion of Maui—Strife of Keawemauhili—Keoua's invasion of the North of Hawaii—Early visits of Portlock, La Perouse, and Mears—Metcalf's revenge —Capture of the Fair American—Vancouver's visit—Assassination of Hergest—Cession of Hawaii.—Death of the King of Maui.—Defeat of Kaeo—Treacherous destruction of Brown—Conquest of Maui and Molokai—Conquest of Oahu—Insurrection on Hawaii—State of the nation—Sandal-wood trade—Alliance with Kauai—Helpless moral condition.

AFTER the departure of the discoverer's ships, the old king, Kalaniopuu, left the bay and passed to Kau, the southern district of Hawaii, having in his charge the young Kaahumanu. He shortly after died there, leaving his warrior son, Kiwalao, to succeed him as first in authority. He was the father of Keopuolani, the present king's mother. To his son the dying king assigned three districts of Hawaii, Kau, Puna, and Hilo, and to a nephew, Kamehameha, the three remaining districts, Kona, Kohala, and Hamakua.

The son, prompted by his chieftains, undertook to convey the body of his father to Kona,—some say to deify his bones in the *Hale o Keawe*, at Honaunau; and others, to place it in Kailua as a pretext for landing a force there and taking possession of Kona, as a desirable part of his father's dominions. That he intended to rule there if he could, there is no doubt.

The funeral party proceeded by canoes from Kau and were met by Keeaumoku, who mingled his lamentations with theirs over their departed king. He then hastened to meet Kamehameha as he was returning from Kohala to Kona, and apprised him that Kiwalao was coming with a force to Kailua. Overtaken by a heavy rain, Kiwalao put in at Honaunau, and deposited the remains of his father in the house of the idols and bones of the Hawaiian kings. Kamehameha and his men prepared to dispute his further approach towards Kailua. They sailed down the coast and met Kiwalao near Kealakekua bay. The two rivals had a most singular interview. Kiwalao, alluding to the agency of one of his old chiefs, said to Kamehameha, "Where are you? This father of you and me is urging to a war between us. Two only, perhaps, you and I, will be slain. Commiserable both!"

What a pitiable contest does he seek, for the trial of strength, or for the settling of boundaries, without any specific complaint

to be urged, or principles of justice or equity to be supported !
Having made this declaration, he returned to Honaunau, and
proposed a division of the country among the chiefs who were
ready to acknowledge his supremacy. But Keoua, an able and
warlike chief, not only failing of his expected share, but getting
reproachful words instead, perhaps for his clamor or exorbitance,
was angry, retired with his men to Keomo, and without any apparent plan of action, more than to vent his spleen, felled a cocoanut
tree as a signal for strife, and slew one of Kamehameha's men.
A rude contest ensued, which continued, irregularly, two or
three days, when a decisive encounter of the principal chiefs and
warriors took place.

Kamehameha having among his chieftains, Keeaumoku,
Keaweaheulu, Kameeiamoku, Kamanawa, Kekuhaupio, and his
younger brother chiefs, confronted Kiwalao, Keawemauhili, Keoua,
and others. In the heat of the battle, Keeaumoku, being one of
Kamehameha's supporters, rushing upon the warriors of Kiwalao,
was thrown down by being hampered with a *pololu* or long spear,
and seized by Nuhi and Kahai, who wounded him with a *pahoa*
[dagger]. He was thrust at also with a *pololu* by one who taunt-
ingly said, " The weapon strikes the yellow-back crab." Though
in the hands of his enemies, overpowered, and weak with fatigue
and wounds, he still hoped that from his age and rank, their
king, who was near, might choose to capture rather than slay him ;
but hearing the voice of Kiwalao (instead of saying, as he supposed he ought, " save my father") giving this charge,—" Preserve
the ivory necklace ;" his indignation was rekindled, though he
momentarily expected the death-stroke. At that moment, Kiwalao was struck by a stone and felled, which arrested the attention
of these warriors ; and Keeaumoku, making an effort of desperation, approached him ; and instead of capturing him, as he supposed would have been right in his own case, seized him by the
throat, his hand being armed with sharks' teeth, and slew him.
Thus, in the utmost straits, he turned the scale of battle in favor
of Kamehameha, who then rushed on, overpowered and routed his
opponents.

Keoua returned to the residence of Kiwalao and became the
king of Kau. Keawemauhili passed over to Hilo, and for a considerable period, was king of Hilo and Puna, two of the six divisions of the island ; and Kamehameha was left in the
possession of the districts assigned him by the will of his uncle,
and which he had boldly defended against the encroachments of
Kiwalao.

Kaahumanu, then about eight years of age, having sought with
others an asylum in the sacred place of refuge at Honaunau, was,
after the battle, thence removed by her wounded father, who appears to have cherished the revenge of a savage against Keoua,
for years. What must have been the condition of Kekupuohi, a
young widow of Kalaniopuu, Keopuolani, the daughter of Kiwalao,

and other young daughters of Hawaii, at such seasons! Keopuolani was made a royal captive. The two rival chiefs, Kiwalao and Kamehameha, had each been proposed as a husband for Kaahumanu, in her childhood. The latter took her into his train immediately after the victory, and though he had other wives, he soon betrothed her to himself, and also made a wife of Keopuolani, the captive daughter of his fallen rival.

Far from being satisfied with his half of Hawaii, he strengthened himself for a time, and as soon as he could venture on it, made war on Keawemauhili and Keoua, who unitedly and successfully resisted him, and defended the eastern and southern divisions of that island from his grasp. His person was roughly handled by a company of fishermen at Puna. He received a blow on the forehead from one of their paddles, and narrowly escaped with his life. Returning to his own little dominions, he made preparation for a descent on Maui. He soon passed over to that island with an invading force, and made war upon Kalanikupule, the governor, a youthful son of Kahekili; his father, the king, being then at Oahu. A fierce battle took place in the mountain passes between Wailuku and Olualu, and many were slaughtered, so that the waters of the brook *Iao* were choked with the bodies of the slain. Kalanikupule, being defeated, fled to Oahu, and Kamehameha passed on to Molokai, meditating farther conquests.

Meantime, Keawemauhili of Hilo, and Keoua of Kau, fought with each other, and the former was slain. Keoua, exulting in his success, soon invaded, and attempted to possess the territories of Kamehameha; who, hearing of this invasion, turned back from Molokai, met and repulsed the invader. The latter, after two battles, at Waimea and Hamakua, retreated to his own dominions in Southern Hawaii, but not to enjoy them long undisturbed, as will be shown after glancing at the renewal of intercourse with foreigners.

After the tragedy, in which Cook, and four of his men, and some thirty natives fell, an impression of the ferocious barbarism of the islanders was so extensive in the civilized world, that no ships visited them for seven years. But as the lucrative trade in furs on the North West coast of America, first being suggested by that navigator, began to be prosecuted, different adventurers were called into those seas, who touched at the Sandwich Islands.

Captains Portlock and Dixon, of the King George and Queen Charlotte, the former having accompanied Cook, were the first. Being employed in the fur-trade by a British company, they visited Hawaii in 1786. Their vessels were surrounded with canoes, which brought off hogs and fruits, to exchange for bits of iron. Apprehending difficulty from insolent and troublesome natives, the commanders discharged their guns over them, and passed on to Oahu.

At that time Com. La Perouse, with two French frigates, was at Lahaina, Maui, the parties leaving the islands without knowing each other's visit. Though La Perouse appears to have been the first foreigner who landed on Maui, he omitted the formality of *taking possession* for his sovereign, having doubtless the common sense principle, that the mere seeing the domain of another, or setting foot on his soil, does not give possession, or the least claim to sovereignty. Kahekili was then King of Maui. Portlock and Dixon anchored at Waialai, east of Diamond Point, on Oahu, in June, 1786. They found among the people daggers, made by foreign hands, for the warriors of Hawaii, when Cook was there ; having probably been since taken in battle, at Maui.

In 1787, Captains Colnett and Duncan of the Prince of Wales and Princess Royal, visited the islands; and in 1788, Lieut. Meares and Mr. Douglass, in the Iphigenia and Felice, in the employment of British merchants at Canton. Kaiana, a distinguished Hawaiian chief who had accompanied Lieut. Meares to Canton, visited the American coast with Captain Douglass, and was brought by him to Hawaii. He took an active part under Kamehameha, in establishing his sovereignty in Hawaii, not without awakening jealousy.

Near the close of 1789, Captain Metcalf, of the American ship Eleanor, touched and traded at Hawaii and Maui, and left no enviable reputation. He gave an awful demonstration of what the sons of civilization could do with savages. In Feb. 1790, the Eleanor anchored off Honuaula, on the south-western part of Maui. Two natives from Olualu, a little farther westward, stole her boat moored under her stern. The watchman in it, being found asleep, they killed when he awoke, at some distance from the ship. The thieves having broken up the boat for the iron, returned to Olualu. Metcalf made a revengeful attack, first on Honuaula ; but hearing that the criminals were at Olualu, he brought his ship to anchor near that place, and offered a reward for *information* of the boat and the lost seaman. The information was given, and the promised reward was demanded by the natives. Captain Metcalf replied, "You shall have it soon." The people supposing he was satisfied, at least so far as they, who had taken no part in the theft and murder, were concerned, thronged around the vessel in their canoes, to trade. Having loaded the starboard guns with musket balls and nails, he *tabued* the larboard side, and the bows and stern of his ship, to prevent any of the canoes from lying there, thus making all take the fatal position unwittingly on the starboard side, in order to satiate his revenge. Then taking his stand in the gangway, to see the carnage of the defenceless, unresisting, and unoffending, he ordered the broadside fired into the multitude, and a volley of small arms, to complete or increase the slaughter ! More than a hundred of the poor people, according to the statement of Mr. John Young, who was then boatswain of the vessel, were thus killed, and many others wounded.

This same tyrant had flogged Kameeiamoku, a high chief of

Hawaii, the father of the late Hoapili, provoked his anger, and thus had led him to resolve to take revenge of the whites that should first come into his power. On the 17th of March, subsequently to the horrid *Metcalf massacre,* a schooner of 26 tons, the " Fair American," being a tender to the Eleanor, and commanded by a youthful son of Metcalf, but eighteen years of age, put into Kawaihae bay. The insulted and revengeful Kameeiamoku went on board, with some of his people, unarmed. He professed friendship, and informed young Metcalf that he might, that day, expect to see his father, who was near in the Eleanor. The defencelessness of the schooner and its crew of five men, the youth and inexperience of the commander, and the value of the vessel and cargo, united with the spirit of revenge in the breast of the savage, afforded reasons for attempting her capture, before she should join her consort, too powerful to be neglected. The strong chief seized the unsuspecting young captain and hove him overboard, where he was drowned. The man at the helm, Isaac Davis, snapped a pistol at the sea-robber, and was then himself thrown overboard. The other four men were killed. Davis, in his distress and helplessness, called out " *aloha.*" The natives taking that as a treaty of peace, spared his life, and the pirate assuming the control of his prize, set the captive sailor on shore. The Eleanor was at this time, leaving Kealakekua bay for China. John Young, who had gone ashore there from that vessel, was prevented from getting off to her by a tabu, laid on the canoes by Kamehameha, lest Metcalf, learning the capture of the schooner, should take vengeance as he had done at Maui.

Scarcely had the leading chieftain of Hawaii repelled Keoua from the north part of Hawaii, when Kaeo of Kauai, and his warlike brother, Kahekili, then at Oahu, united in a bold enterprise for the purpose of chastising or subjugating Kamehameha and his boasting warriors, for their invasion of Maui. They proceeded with their united forces, by way of Molokai and Maui ; and passed over the channel. The hostile parties met in their fleets of canoes, and fought, off Kohala. The allied brothers were repulsed. Many of their canoes being destroyed, they retreated to Maui, and reinstated themselves in the possessions of their father, Kekaulike, in 1791. Their repulse from the coast of Hawaii was ascribed to the effect of a swivel which the Hawaiian chief had obtained of Captain Douglass, who had mounted it for effective use on a large canoe. Kamehameha, to show his veneration of the gods, and to secure their favor, and strengthen his kingdom, engaged in building a great temple, at Kawaihae, for the worship of Kaili, and for offering human and other sacrifices. It was built on a hill, and called Puukahola. While he was engaged in the work of erecting this temple, which he consecrated with human blood, he sent some of his able warriors to Kau, to take possession of those southern and eastern districts, and to put an end to the sovereignty of Keoua. Kaiana, aided by Namakeha, led this expedition, and entered Kau, while Keoua was at Hilo. The latter hastened to repel him, by a rough way of fifty miles. Passing with his rude heathen warriors, by the great crater of Kilauea, he met, it is affirmed, with a most singular disaster. Halting there, for a night, they found the volcano in violent action; and supposing the presiding genius to be angry, tried their vain expedients to appease the deity, before they would venture to pass on to Kau. It may be briefly stated on the authority of natives who were contemporary with Keoua and Kamehameha, and who represent themselves as having been witnesses, that while they encamped, two days and three nights, at the crater, there were repeated eruptions, or the sending up of flame and smoke, cinders and stones. On the third day, they set forward towards Kau. The earth shook and trembled under their feet—a dense dark cloud rose from the immense crater—lightning and thunder burst forth over their heads, and darkness covered them, and a shower of cinders and sand, thrown high from the crater, descended on the region round about, and that a number of Keoua's men were killed, and were found there many days afterward, apparently unchanged, and were at first mistaken for a living company. The natives attributed their death to the anger and power of Pele, whether it were effected by lightning, or by steam, by heat or by deadly gases, from the dread laboratory. The inference of some of the people was, that the god of the volcano approved of the policy and the measures of Kamehameha, and opposed those of Keoua. The story of the death of any of Keoua's men, in these circumstances, while he was on his way to repel Kaiana, and while Kamehameha was erecting a great temple to secure the favor of the gods in establishing his sovereignty over the islands, would, whether correct or greatly exaggerated, or even unfounded, tend to confirm the superstitions of the people, and to induce them to conclude that Kamehameha could not now be successfully resisted. The greater the mystery, moreover, which the votaries of idolatry could throw around the catastrophe, real or alleged, the more would it subserve the cause of superstition.

Keoua passed on and engaged in several battles with his invaders; but becoming dispirited, and the expectation of maintaining his independence against the superior force and hostile intentions of his rival, failing him, he was induced to surrender himself to him at Kawaihae, in the north-western district of the island. Thither he repaired, with several of his friends and supporters, accompanied by two of his competitors, men who assured him that Kamehameha would receive him with kindness and honor. As they approached the landing at Kawaihae, the king and his chiefs stood on the shore, much interested to witness the arrival and surrender of so brave and formidable a rival as Keoua had been. Just as the bows of the canoe reached the land, Keeaumoku rushed into the shoal water, seized Keoua unresisting, and slew him. Nor was the long cherished revenge satiated by the treachery and violence by which this high chieftain fell. Several of his friends shared the same lamentable fate, from the same cruel hands.

Kamehameha stood by and saw the blood of murder flow freely at his feet, from a rival, who, under the assurance of friendship and protection, had cast himself on his clemency. He neither restrained nor punished the assassin. Apologists say, he was disposed to protect Keoua, but Keeaumoku was headstrong, and attempted to justify the deed by affirming, " If Keoua had not been killed, he would make further trouble." Was it for him to pass sentence and execute it for future offences of a vanquished chieftain ? " Their feet are swift to shed blood; destruction and misery are in their paths; and the way of peace have they not known."

Keoua and his slaughtered companions were laid on the altar of the new temple at Kawaihae, and offered to Kamehameha's abominable deities. Thus Kamehameha became master of the whole island of Hawaii, about 1792.

In March, 1792, Captain Vancouver, a distinguished officer of the British navy, commanding the sloop of war, Discovery, and attended by the armed brig, Chatham, Lieut. Broughton, visited the islands. This was fourteen years subsequent to his first acquaintance there, in company with Captain Cook. He touched at Kealakekua, where he was visited by two leading chiefs, Kaiana and Keeaumoku; the former claiming to share the sovereignty with Kamehameha. He touched also at Waikiki, Oahu, and at Waimea, Kauai, where he introduced to public notice, Kaumualii, the young prince, son of Kaeo and Kamakahelei, and subsequently king of Kauai. At that period, being supposed to be about twelve years old, he exhibited more mildness and vivacity than other natives, and gave promise of distinguishing himself among his barbarous and ferocious countrymen. The child was attended by a guard of some thirty men armed with iron daggers, and carrying muskets in bundles. Hostages were required of the commander for his safety when the young prince visited the ship.

In this visit, Vancouver was painfully struck with the evidences of the great depopulation of the islands which had taken place in half a generation, and with the demonstration of the disastrous consequences of the early intercourse of Cook and his men with the people.

Shortly after Vancouver left the islands for the North West Coast, the store-ship, Dædalus, Lieut. Hergest, touched at Waimea, Oahu, on her way to join him.

To procure water, Mr. Hergest and Mr. Gooch, an astronomer, and six sailors landed with some casks. The two gentlemen walked to the huts of the natives. A dispute soon arose at the watering place, between the sailors and the islanders, and a Portuguese was killed. The natives who were about the two gentlemen hearing of this, and fearing the vengeance that awaited them in case the two returned to the ship, stabbed Mr. Gooch with a dagger, knocked down Lieut. H. with a stone, and killed them both. The rest of the boat's crew escaped and returned to the ship. The next morning, a boat's crew, well armed, approached the shore and demanded the bodies of their murdered friends. They were attacked with stones from the crowd of natives, on whom they fired. The ship sailed the same day for the North West Coast. The sovereignty of Kahekili, king of Maui, was at this period acknowledged in Oahu.

In Feb., 1793, Vancouver revisited the islands. Anchoring off Kawaihae, Hawaii, to refresh his ship, he found the productions of the country were tabu and not to be sold except for arms and ammunition. Unwilling to encourage the war spirit, and desirous to promote peace among the rulers of the different islands, he firmly refused to purchase supplies with such articles as they eagerly sought with a view to further conquests. The chiefs at length yielded, as they did also in regard to various other tabus, when they were seen to stand in the way of their interest or gratification. It was then tabu for natives to sail on the sea, but four of the wives of Keeaumoku, to gratify their curiosity, managed to visit the ship in the *boats*, saying that it was their *canoes* only that were tabu. The ship proceeded to Kailua, where the king and his favorite wife, Kaahumanu, now about nineteen years of age, went on board, and were much gratified with unexpected presents, one of which was a long scarlet cloak decorated with tinsel. The ship passed on fifteen miles south, to Kealakekua, for a better anchorage, whither Kamehameha hastened to visit it again, going out to it with his train on board a fleet of canoes.

Vancouver, having before noticed the destitution of the islanders, kindly brought from California and presented for their benefit, a breed of goats, sheep and cattle, which proved serviceable. He took laudable pains to convince the Hawaiian chiefs of the inexcusable mischief they occasioned by their war spirit and plans of conquest. Appearing to respect his judgment, they are said to have authorized him to propose to the leeward chiefs a general peace, allowing things to remain as they were.

He passed over to Maui, and anchored near Lahaina, where Kahekili, the king, then supposed to be more than sixty years of age, with his chiefs, visited the ship. Vancouver discussed with them the two main points which required his attention—that of bringing to justice the murderers of Hergest and his astronomer, and of promoting peace with Hawaii, and if possible, put an end to the wars that were wasting the lives and possessions of the people, and consuming the products of the country. Kaeo, the brother of Kahekili, and king of Kauai, visited Vancouver and renewed the acquaintance he had formed nearly fifteen years before, at Kauai, on its discovery. He exhibited a lock of hair which Captain V. had given him, and now identified. It had been preserved as a charm—an object of veneration, or a token of friendship. The chiefs listened to Vancouver's arguments. Kaeo appeared especially pleased with the proposal of peace. Kahekili approved of the terms, and allowed Vancouver to signify it in a letter to John Young in the service of the Hawaiian king. But all were distrustful of the designs of Kamehameha, and thought the object could not be gained, unless Captain Vancouver would return to Hawaii for the purpose of securing what he had proposed. But this he could not well do. He had other engagements. He proceeded to Oahu. Kamohomoho was sent by Kahekili to assist him in the object of his visit there. The officer employed to arrest the murderers, not being able to find them, seized other men, and brought them to Vancouver, as though they had been guilty. Though they asserted their innocence, and protested against the charge, and the evidence of their guilt was very incomplete, they were shot.

The salutary impression intended to be made by the exhibition of justice in cleansing the land of the guilt of murder, was utterly defeated by the treacherous slaughter of unoffending victims. While we pity the victims, and the British officer, thus misled to participate with the base traitors, we would contrast his consideration with the madness of Metcalf and others, who would have readily fired on the multitude for a private theft or murder, for which they could not punish the guilty.

Early in 1794, Vancouver, commanding the Discovery, accompanied by the Dædalus and Chatham, made his last visit to the islands. He arrived at Hilo Bay, Jan. 9. Kamehameha, with several of his chiefs, went on board, and notwithstanding the tabu of Makahiki, forbidding the sailing on the sea at the New Year's festival, accompanied him around to the bay, where the tragedy of Cook had taken place. Here Vancouver, the second time, discharged cattle and sheep, which were tabued against being slaughtered under ten years.

Finding that Kaahumanu had been set aside by her husband for suspected intimacy with the aspiring Kaiana, he used his address and influence to effect a reconciliation, and was successful. His carpenters were employed to assist Kamehameha in the construction of a small schooner, for which he had collected timber from the mountains, relying on an English carpenter who had left some ship for his service, and John Young and Davis to build it; but who, on trial, were found unable to lay the keel. During this visit to Kealakekua, the king and chiefs endeavored to form an alliance with Great Britain, with the hope of securing the friendship and protection of that power. Reserving to themselves the sovereignty of the island, and the regulation of their relations with neighboring islands, and foreign traders; they, on the 25th of Feb., 1794, entered into some not well-defined agreement, in which, Vancouver says, " they unanimously ceded the island of Owhyhee to his Britannic Majesty and acknowledged themselves subjects of Great Britain, in the presence of George Vancouver and Lieut. Peter Puget." In the speeches made by the king and Keeaumoku,

Kaiana, and others, it was kept in view that their sovereignty, government, priesthood and religion were to remain as before the alliance. So the natives appear to have understood the transaction, and from that day, prosecuted their own plans of conquest, government and religion as before, even spurning the earnest advice of Vancouver to dwell in peace with neighboring islands. They were liable to insults from every armed vessel, and were led to hope for something like protection or friendship at the hands of King George, without considering that Great Britain gives protection only to those whom she rules, and who are expected to pay for being ruled and protected. Having secured the respect of the natives to an unusual degree, suggested the idea of a Christian mission there, and given them a partial promise of returning to reside with them, Vancouver took his leave of the Hawaiian chiefs, March 3, 1794, and touching at Maui and Kauai, returned to England, and there, early finished the voyage of life. His memory has been cherished in Hawaii by those who knew him, who, for some time, anticipated his promised return.

In the autumn of 1793, Kahekili having left Maui in the command of his brother, Kaeo, visited Oahu, and was conveyed by the Butterworth, Captain Brown, to Kauai, to regulate affairs there; and having confirmed Inamoo in the governorship of that island, and in the guardianship of Kaeo's son, Kaumualii, he returned to Oahu. Soon after this, probably in the early part of 1794, Kahekili died at Waikiki; while Kaeo had his quarters on the eastern part of Molokai.

The old king had once sent to the aspiring king of Hawaii, who was trying to wrest his country from him, this message, " Wait till the black kapa (bark cloth) covers me, then take my kingdom." This was a remarkable message, whether he meant to say, "'Tis vain for you to attempt to wrest my kingdom from me, while I live; when I am dead, take it if you can," or to intimate his purpose to disinherit his brave and warlike brother and ally, Keao, and his own sons, with a view to make his great rival his heir. Kamehameha made use of it, eventually, to establish his claim to the whole dominions of their late sovereign. Kaeo, soon after the death of his brother, left Maui and Molokai to return to Kauai, and on the way, visited Oahu. When on the point of embarking from Waianae, the western district of that island, he suddenly changed his purpose, saying he did not wish to die alone, and turning back, advanced towards Honolulu, and was met on the plains of Ewa, by his nephew, Kalanikupule, who gave him battle. Captain Brown, who had returned from China with the Jackall and the Prince Leboo, was induced, injudiciously, to allow his mate and several men with muskets and ammunition to take part with the Oahu chief against Kaeo, who fell in battle, with many others, according to his wish not to die alone. Kalanikupule and his party being victorious, maintained the appearance of friendliness towards

Brown, to whom they had pointed out the entrance through the coral reef into the harbor of Honolulu, not before known to the civilized world.

But, notwithstanding the aid which Captain Brown had rendered to Kalanikupule and his party, in defeating Kaeo, a plot was soon laid by them to cut him off, and capture the Jackall and Prince Leboo, the first foreign vessels that ever entered the harbor of Honolulu.

Captain Brown having apparently formed an alliance with Kalanikupule (if he had not stipulated to have the island ceded to him, as has been hinted), placed too much confidence in the friendship of these barbarians; and notwithstanding his exposure within a recently discovered reef harbor, he, on the 1st of Jan., 1795, employed most of the men of the two vessels in slaughtering and packing pork, on shore, and in procuring salt from a place at a little distance from his mooring. Armed natives, taking advantage of this, boarded the vessels, killed the captains and took possession. The ship-men on shore, and the boat's crew collecting salt, were by other natives assaulted and captured. These captives were shortly employed to fit the vessels for sea; under the immediate inspection of Kalanikupule and Kamohomoho, his prime agent, who had but a little before been commissioned by Kahekili to assist Vancouver in bringing to justice the murderers of Hergest, but who had now been the instigator of this barbarous piracy.

Scarcely had this now proud barbarian whom Kamehameha had driven out of Maui, been allowed to exult in his triumph over his brave uncle and his late friend and ally, Captain Brown, when the thought of making himself master of the group occurred to him. One of the boldest and wildest projects that a Hawaiian brain ever conceived was then attempted, which was, for Kalanikupule, availing himself of the aid of his foreign captives and a number of his people, to sail with the two vessels for Hawaii; to get Kamehameha on board, and into the cabin, as he would be expected to visit a foreign vessel that should come near his residence, and thus secure a most important advantage for taking his kingdom. In nine days the vessels were ready for sea, and a number of canoes. Flushed with recent, and confidently expected success, the haughty chieftain embarked according to his plan, selecting some, and with great pomposity rejecting others, who wished to embark with him.

The vessels were warped out of the harbor. The natives becoming sea-sick, the English rose upon them, and firing upon them, and beating them with the butts of their guns, drove overboard those who were on deck, and confined the king and queen and one or two attendants, in the cabin. The vessels being thus retaken, they stood out to sea till morning, then coming within five leagues of Waikiki, put their captives into a canoe and sent them ashore, and pursued their voyage, under the command of Messrs. Lamport and Bonallack.*

After the death of Kahekili and Kaeo, who for fifteen years had held in check the power of Hawaii, and the ambition of its rulers, Kamehameha and his aspiring chieftains, in Feb., 1795, passed over and ravaged Maui and its dependencies, spreading misery and destruction in their paths. Koalaukani, a son of Kahekili, whom Kaeo had left in the governorship of that island, unable without the co-operation of Oahu and Kauai, to withstand the whole Hawaiian army, 16,000 strong, fled to Kauai; leaving this distracted island to the disposal of the conqueror, who took possession, and made a new distribution of the territory and improvements among his people.

After three months, he embarked on board a large fleet of canoes, with his army, and invaded Oahu to subjugate its inhabitants. In this expedition, Kaiana, who had often shown his ambition, deserted the standard of Kamehameha, and landing on the opposite side of the island, united with Kalanikupule, to defend it. The hostile forces met between the village of Honolulu and the precipice of Nuuanu in the rear. Kaiana was slain in battle, with some three hundred men. The forces of Kalanikupule were defeated, and their leader fled to the mountains. Numbers attempting to escape through the narrow, precipitous gorge, are said to have been precipitated down the precipice, and killed by the fall. Thus Kamehameha became the sovereign of this important part of the inheritance of the sons of Kahekili.†

Distress and destruction swept over Oahu, and the miserable inhabitants who escaped death, felt the scourge of a victor's hand.

During a year's stay at Oahu, Kamehameha cherished the desire of subjugating Kauai and Niihau, and undertook to build a small vessel which he intended to arm for the expedition. Meantime, Captain Broughton, of the English discovery ship Providence, touched at Hawaii, and left the grape vine, and was supplied with provisions by John Young, and a blind chief, at Kealakekua. He touched also at Waikiki, Oahu, where the victorious chief proposed to salute him with his cannon, which he had

---

* The accounts of this transaction, given by the English, from Mr. Lamport's manuscript, by Mr. Jarves, and by Mr. Dibble, are all widely different from each other, and the diversity illustrates the difficulty of collecting facts respecting transactions fifty years ago, in such a state of barbarism as then existed at Oahu—a barbarism that seemed to forbid the establishment of a Christian mission there when Tahiti was first entered as a missionary field.

† Concerning the end of this haughty king of Oahu, Kalanikupule, there is some doubt. Some English writers and intelligent natives say "he was found dead in a cave." Mr. Dibble says, " he was sought out and killed." Mr. Jarves says, " he fell gallantly fighting for his inheritance till the last." A war tippet, said to have belonged to him, was presented to me by the present king, about forty-five years subsequent to this victory of his father. In respect to his ally, Kaiana, the natives have pointed out to the writer what they call his foot-prints, where he stood to throw his last spear before he fell. These prints have been kept visible by the practice of the natives, who, in passing, place their feet in them, and attempt to assume his posture.

purchased, and also to barter for arms and ammunition, both of which the captain declined. The king visited the Providence, dressed in European garments, and a splendid feather war-cloak. He importuned Captain Broughton for articles of rigging for his little vessel, which he was building at the harbor of Honolulu. He counted on the certain subjugation of Kauai, and, in love of slaughter and conquest, conceived the design of proceeding from Kauai, to subjugate the Society and Georgian Islands; an account of which he had received from some three or four Tahitians who had come to Oahu in a merchant vessel.

"Was not this world made for Cæsar?" is a question the spirit of which was very congenial with the feelings of this Hawaiian Julius. Captain Broughton's arguments to dissuade him from attacking Kauai availed nothing. Without waiting to finish his little 40 ton man-of-war, he embarked his army in canoes and boats, causing the live stock of hogs, on Oahu, to be destroyed, to prevent a revolt there in his absence, and also to guard against the retreat of his army before ·they should have taken the spoils of Kauai. Divine Providence defeated this bold and unprovoked attack which he thus undertook; and by a tempest drove him and his army back disappointed, to suffer with others from the destruction of provisions which he had himself rashly caused. Many, to relieve their hunger, pilfered from the chiefs, and were punished with great severity.

A revolt against Kamehameha occurred, at this time, at Hawaii, under Namakeha, one of his high chieftains, which became formidable At this period, the work of depopulation was rapid through the whole group, and distress general.

On a second visit of Captain Broughton, in July of the same year, Kamehameha boarded the ship, and entreated him to take him, with some of his principal men, to Hawaii. But this he refused, and passed on to Kauai, where the chiefs of the island appeared to be at strife among themselves. Keawe, a grandson of Paleioholani, appeared to have the control at Waimea. Koalaukani, who had been driven out of Maui, attached himself to the young prince Kaumualii, son of Kaeo, and heir to the sovereignty of that island, and opposing the claims of Keawe, was shortly after killed. The young prince, about sixteen, without power to rule, dwelt for a time with Keawe, who was also subsequently slain, leaving the sovereignty to Kaumualii.

Captain Broughton found it difficult to procure water, hogs and vegetables, except in return for arms and ammunition. By his resolute manner, he overcame the tabu on water, but passed on to Niihau to procure the other needed articles. Here, too, he met with difficulty. After two or three days' intercourse with the natives, two of his marines were killed by them. Broughton's party then fired on the people, destroyed sixteen of their canoes, burnt down their village, and departed, thus closing another scene in the Hawaiian tragedy.

Kamehameha returning from Oahu to Hawaii, suppressed the insurrection headed by Namakeha, who was slain. The undisputed sovereignty of Kamehameha was thus established over all the group, except Kauai and Niihau, in 1796.

It is supposed that some six thousand of the followers of this chieftain, and twice that number of his opposers, fell in battle during his career, and by famine and distress occasioned by his wars and devastations, from 1780 to 1796. Who can duly estimate the unnumbered wrongs, cruelties and distresses connected with the ten thousand murders perpetrated in these barbarian struggles? And what was the effect of such a course on the victors themselves? To Captain Broughton, "the conqueror and his chiefs seemed intent on seizing everything they could grasp, their success having effaced every disposition to liberality." Kemeeiamoku, he refused admittance on board the Providence, on account of his outrage on young Metcalf, whom he had drowned. But so far from showing any mortification or contrition, he avowed his determination to capture the next vessel that should fall into his power.

The leading chiefs at this period under Kamehameha, were Keeaumoku, the father of Kaahumanu, Kameeiamoku, the father of Hoapili, Keaweaheulu, the father of Naihe, and Kamanawa. In addition to these, were four others, deemed by the natives skilful, Kai, Kapaloa, Kaaloa and Kauakahi, who were sometimes consulted in public matters.

Claiming the right of soil throughout his realm, and the right to make and abrogate regulations at pleasure, and· using the privilege of a conqueror who could not endure to have others enjoy their just rights, Kamehameha wielded a despotism as absolute probably as the islands ever knew. Retaining a part of the lands as his individual property, which he intended should be inherited by his children, he distributed the remaining lands among his chiefs and favorites, who, for their use, were to render public service in war or peace, and in raising a revenue. These let out large portions of their divisions to their favorites or dependants, who were in like manner to render their service, and bring the rent; and these employed cultivators on shares, who lived on the products which they divided, or shared with their landlord, rendering service when required, so long as they chose to occupy the land. Thus, from the poor man who could rent $\frac{1}{8}$ or $\frac{1}{4}$ of an acre, up to the sovereign, each was, in some sense, dependent on the will of a superior, and yet, almost all had one or more under them whom they could control or command.

This, in a conquered, ignorant and heathen country, without the principles of equity, was a low and revolting state of society; where the mass could have no voice in enacting laws, or levying taxes, or appropriating the revenue, or in establishing a limited rent for the use of lands, fisheries or fish-ponds. To conceive of all as supremely selfish, and each superior as desirous to aggrandize himself at the expense of others, would do them no injustice.

With the limited knowledge and skill they possessed, it would hardly be expected that cheerful and productive industry would thrive, even in such a clime and soil, unless the principles of benevolence or a high public spirit could be engrafted in the hearts of the people, or that the population could multiply while the means of subsistence were scanty, clothing and lodging miserable, possessions utterly insecure, and all inheritance hopeless or uncertain.

The king, availing himself of his high position, engaged more extensively in commerce, monopolizing the chief sources of gain. The mountain forests being found to embrace the odoriferous and oleaginous sandal-wood which, during his reign, was in good demand in the China market, for incense and fancy articles, the conqueror, claiming it as his own, by heavy taxation, employed the people much in hunting out the trees, felling them, and cleaning the wood, and bringing down on their backs ship loads of it, from the mountains.

By this source of wealth, he was enabled to purchase boats, guns, ammunition, ships and cargoes. Hundreds of thousands of dollars worth of this wood, he bartered for goods, never to be used; but which, being stowed away in insecure and unsuitable store-houses, not to be given out or sold for the accommodation of the needy laborer, were allowed to perish. If the common people had been allowed to buy these articles, what could they have given him in exchange for them which he could not, without giving goods, take from their hands at pleasure? Tons of the sandal-wood were exchanged for such commodities as useless tobacco, and pernicious alcohol; and hundreds of tons for dollars. To increase his gains and compete with the traders to China, he procured and fitted out a ship, and loaded her with a rich cargo of the wood, and sent her to Canton. But the speculation was an utter failure; the charges for pilotage, anchorage, custom-house fees, and repairs, and the pay and extravagances of his English commander and officers amounted to some $3000 more than the avails of the cargo, which, probably, was not sold to the best advantage.

The knowledge he bought so dearly respecting port-charges and pilotage, induced him, from that time, to make port-charges on all foreign vessels entering his harbor, except public vessels, which were always free.

In the cutting and collecting of sandal-wood, he forbade the people to fell the young trees, which, before maturity, were almost valueless; but to leave them for his sons to inherit. This fact, and his charging his bird-catchers not to kill the little mountain bird, from whose wing they plucked two ornamental feathers, but to let them live for his children, struck the people as proof of a rare quality in a Hawaiian chieftain, and by his native biographers, are deemed worthy of special eulogium.

To avoid insurrection, he is said to have endeavored to keep the aspirants much about his person, and to have kept them poor and dependent.

To check the violence which existed in a disturbed country, he interdicted murder, theft, and robbery ; and so far, at length, restored the peace of the realm, that, as the people say in his praise, " the aged could journey, and sleep by the way."

He derived assistance in secular affairs, from the counsel of several white residents; particularly John Young, Isaac Davis, and Don Marin. But with all his facilities, he never encouraged or dared to allow a subject to rise to independent affluence.

Mr. Young, taking a female of rank for a wife, was himself promoted to the rank of a chief, partly in consequence of the services he had rendered in the wars of conquest, his strong attachment to the king, and his ability and readiness to serve him. He officiated for a time, as governor of Hawaii. Though at first detained there against his will, he at length preferred to stay rather than to return to England. He had two sons and three daughters, who at length came under the instruction of the missionaries. One of them has risen to the second rank in the kingdom. To the foreigners, during this reign, the improvement of the people, as to letters, morals and religion, appeared hopeless, if at all desirable. Those who took up their abode with them, easily accommodated themselves to the native customs, morals, and mode of living.

Provisions, wood, and water were supplied to ships on terms advantageous to the purchasers, who, for a few pounds of bits of iron hoop, could refresh their vessels. The reason for giving a good hog, or two or three barrels of vegetables for a piece of hoop, six inches long, was the cupidity of the trader, and the desire of the natives to make such an article into a small adze, to take the place of their stone adze of ancient time.*

Having remained at Hawaii four years, the king multiplied his canoes, passed over to Lahaina, where Kameeiamoku, the father of the late Hoapili, died, and repaired again to Oahu. Some seven years after his conquest of that island, he mustered an army of several thousand men, for a descent on Kauai.

With what show of equity he would have made war on the young and unoffending Kaumualii, who had but recently been established in the quiet possession of Kauai and Niihau, does not appear, and probably that question was not even agitated. A pestilence invaded his troops—cut off several of his counsellors—attacked his own person—weakened his forces, and sweeping through the whole

* The iron hoop adze, at length gave place to the bended plane iron, lashed to an adze handle, and which came to be one of the most convenient and common cutting instruments of the natives.

country, greatly diminished the population, and doubtless contributed to defeat the expedition.

The channel between Oahu and Kauai, being 75 miles wide, often rough, and far more difficult to pass and repass with canoes and open boats than the other channels, the conqueror had the sagacity to conclude it would not be an easy matter to retreat to Oahu, in case of disappointment and disaster; and he never again undertook the passage. Nor was it then or ever after necessary.

Kaumualii, to secure the peace of his little domain without a contest with one of superior power, having received assurance that he should be respected, visited Oahu, in person, on board an American ship, whose captain pledged him protection. He was well received by Kamehameha—made to him a nominal cession of his country, and returning home in the same vessel that brought him, he resumed, or continued the charge of his domain, as king of Kauai and Niihau.

He engaged in the sale of sandal-wood—purchased guns, ammunition, and other articles, but on a much smaller scale than Kamehameha. He erected a fort at the mouth of the Waimea river—no small achievement for such a people. In this, he had the assistance of Dr. Scheffer, a trader there, who had been an agent for the Russian governor, at Sitka, and whose movements gave some occasion for suspicion that he was plotting to get possession of Kauai. He was at length required to leave the country, and the prejudice he excited against the Russians subsided.[*]

After a residence of nine years at Oahu, Kamehameha took a business voyage to the windward, with his principal chiefs, on board foreign vessels, accompanied by canoes and other small craft. He touched at Lahaina, Kawaihae, Kealakekua; then at Molokai and Lahaina again; and finally settled at Kailua, where he resided about seven years. By this time nearly a generation of the race had passed away, subsequently to their discovery by Cook. How much of their strength had been exhausted by wars and the support of armies, and how much by new and terrible diseases, it is not easy to estimate. The population was greatly diminished, and the residue unimproved in morals.

Whether we contemplate the horrors or the glories of the rude warfare which wasted the nation, we are not to confine our views to the struggles of armed combatants—the wounds, the reproaches, and various evils inflicted on one another, but the burden of sustaining such armies deserves attention, and the indescribable misery of the unarmed and unresisting of the vanquished party or tribe, pursued and crushed, till all danger of further resistance disappeared, must not be forgotten. Especially do the domestic condition of women, and the influences employed in

* See Hawaiian Spectator, vol. i., page 48.

forming the character of the rising generation, demand our sympathetic regard.

Trained in heathenism, and on the battle-field, Kaahumanu, at the age of thirteen, was taken into the number of the wives of Kamehameha. The prowess of her father, his weight in council, and his successful influence in establishing the authority of Kamehameha, and her being the daughter of the Queen of Maui, previously to the reign of Kahekili, contributed to give her consequence in the nation, and in the eyes of her husband.

She became the favorite of the conqueror, though in his course, he had not less than twenty other wives, and many of them at the same time. By twelve of his twenty-one wives, he had no children, and by nine others, he had twenty-four. The amount and the kind of attention which a young wife, among many, could, in the circumstances of Kaahumanu, receive from such a pagan polygamist warrior, and his heathen family, must have failed of producing much domestic happiness as her share.

Subsequently to her accession, she had the mortification and vexation to have him take, successively, two of her sisters, younger than herself, Kalakua and Namahana. Still later, the daughter of one of these sisters by a former husband he numbered among his many wives, as one of peculiar beauty and sacredness in his esteem, and entitled to peculiar attention, when very young; one, who, after the king's death, became the wife of Liholiho, and, on the introduction of Christianity, the wife of Kanaina, and who has since risen to the second place in the government of the islands.

It was deemed lawful and respectable for a chieftain to have as many wives as he could get, and to turn any of them off at pleasure, and supply their place by obtaining the wives and daughters of others. The bond of marriage, if such their union could be called, in strict propriety, was of little value.

Although Kaahumanu was the favorite of the king, still she often had to endure his anger, and experience violence from his iron hands, as many a Hawaiian wife, less honored, and less firmly attached, can testify was customary, even where polygamy did not foster jealousy, envyings, bickerings, strife and cruelty.

At the time the reconciliation between Kaahumanu and her husband was effected by the address of Vancouver, she begged him to make Kamehameha promise not to beat her. Still she occasionally made manifest the natural independence of her character. In the early part of their residence at Oahu, after the conquest, some difficulty between them occurred, when she determined on making the passage to Kauai, by herself,—embarked in a beautiful single canoe, and nearly accomplished her design. She was, however, brought back to Honolulu, when she complimented Captain Broughton, of the Providence, with the present of the canoe in which she had made the bold attempt.

How it would be possible for a barbarian warrior to manage from one to two dozen wives—some young, and some old—some handsome, and some ugly—some of high rank, and some low, without martial law among them, or without resorting to despotic violence, or how he could regulate his own course among them, without hostile outbreaks, in reference to some parts of his numerous and complicated family, it would be impossible to show, and extremely difficult to conceive. It is certain that in fact he accomplished neither.

Kalakua, the late governess of Maui, who gave me much of Kamehameha's domestic history, says of him, " *He kanaka pepehi no ia ; aole mea e ana ai kona inaina.* He was a man of violence,—nothing would pacify his wrath." She said she was once beaten by him, with a stone, upon her head, till she bled profusely, when in circumstances demanding his kindest indulgence and care, as a husband.

An English resident, who enjoyed his confidence as fully and long as any foreigner, says, he has seen him beat Kaahumanu with severity for the simple offence of speaking of a young man as " handsome."

Captain Douglass speaks of his violent temper and rashness, judging that " those about him feared rather than loved him ;" and says, " Conceiving himself affronted, one day, by the chiefs who were on board, he kicked them all by turns, without mercy, and without resistance." His energy, ambition, and *success*, which gained admirers among natives and strangers ; his liberal attention to public vessels, after the establishment of his power ; his readiness to meet the views of foreigners in the pursuit of mercantile gains and low pleasures, under his protection, secured for him a higher reputation than his conduct and disposition would justify, when tried by the laws of morality. When multitudes in the nation who regarded him as an invader, tyrant, and oppressor, had perished before him, it was natural that those who escaped death, and were afterwards protected, should learn to respect and obey him, and that those whom he led to victory and to enlarged possessions, should highly honor him as a good chief, compared with predecessors and contemporaries, though there was much to be censured in his temper, his principles and his policy. When he added Kalakua to the number of his wives, she says, " Kaahumanu was angry." This may have been to her credit, if it is ever to the credit of a wife to be and to appear angry at the conduct of a husband. She was sprightly, beautiful for a Polynesian, and engaging, when young ; and Kamehameha was exceedingly jealous of her. His admirers speak freely of a peculiar edict which he put forth, and which gives a striking view of the state of society, that if any man should have illicit intercourse with Kaahumanu, however high his rank might be, he should be put to death. What an edict for a sovereign to spread before the nation, respecting a favorite wife by name ! And what an execution was that of one of his chieftains, under this singular edict, which made death the penalty for *one* of the guilty parties, though the same crime, in general, was to him, and the nation, of little or no account! But the severe and bloody penalty, the pointed specification, the jealousy, watchfulness, and partial love of the king, and the queen's love of influence, power, and reputation, and her attachment to her husband, all proved ineffectual as a safeguard, without *moral principle* or the fear of GOD. Naihe and other chiefs who feared their sovereign's frown, and knew not how soon they might feel its force, at his command, put their hands to the work of strangling Kanihonui, one of their compeers, who was alleged to have exposed himself to the action of that despotic edict.

Ruling Hawaiian chiefs insisted rigorously on the observance of the religious rites, put their own hands to the bloody and quivering human sacrifice, and charged their successors to sustain the system to the utmost. Nor did Kamehameha appear at all willing to abrogate or relax the ancient system of tabu, or discountenance the nation's dark and bloody superstitions. He would even seize and sacrifice men to prevent the fatal termination of the sickness of a wife, if a murderous priest recommended it, while nothing was done for the moral improvement of his wives or any other part of the nation.

Now, if such as has been described, were the condition and character of the favored daughter of one of the high and prosperous nobles of the land, and the favorite wife of the most powerful, successful, and intelligent chieftain the islands had ever known, what must have been the condition and character of the mass of the people, and especially of the wives and daughters of the subjects of such a master? How easily did the prince of darkness, who, entering Paradise, deceived and ruined the holy mother of the human race, triumph and rule over her deluded and debased daughters, driven far from the delights of Eden, and cast on the dreary and dark shores of Hawaii! These outcasts from the presence of God, being given over by him, how perfect the conformity of the disposition and circumstances of the rising generation, and their general character with the malevolent wishes of the destroyer! No pious mother watched with ceaseless care over their infancy and childhood. No untiring solicitude, or well directed paternal skill, was applied to curb the will and train the opening mind to filial duty. There was no moral teacher to instil sound first principles of action into their minds, and to array before them proper motives to virtuous feelings, well directed efforts, and benevolent achievements— motives which are indispensable, and which the Word of God presents to the children of Christian parents; no skilful tutor in the arts and sciences, to discipline their mental powers and put them on the stretch to understand the works and Word of God, and the character, duty and destiny of his intelligent creatures. Without these, or like influences, found needful everywhere, to mould, beautify, and elevate the character, how is it possible for a people to rise from the dust and abominations of heathenism ? While the tendencies of human nature are so decidedly and strongly downward as they are proved to be, its elevation in such circumstances must be impossible.   So forcibly have thinking minds been impressed with the stereotype character of the habits and religion of the Hawaiians, that they supposed Christianity itself could not change them for the better.   Even with the torch of Philosophy in their hands, and the lamp of Salvation before their eyes, they supposed the Hawaiians would refuse the offers of the Gospel as unwelcome and powerless.

If, then, a radical reformation, even with good instructions, good models, and good influences, diligently employed for years, was deemed so hopeless, what possible ground of hope for it could there be, when, instead of any aid of this kind, the minds and hearts of all were continually buried in the darkness and pollution of thickest heathenism ?   But if it were possible, it must, to the last degree, be improbable, though the knowledge of the exist- ence of God and of the falsity of idols is quite attainable from nature ; and, therefore, all who worship creatures are without excuse.   If any possible means in a single case (suppose that of Kaahumanu in her destitution) could awaken a desire, and prompt the intention, to rise from the course of superstition, sensuality, and crime in which parents, superiors, chiefs, and priests led the way ; how could the intention be successfully carried into execu- tion, without the precepts and motives of the Bible, while the soul was surrounded with ten thousand baleful influences, which pervaded the whole nation ?   Could a single heart become self- refined, while affected by its own sinful habits, misled by its own conceptions, and daily subjected to the pestiferous action of the mass of corruption all around, and to the hidden snares and open assaults of the arch tempter ?   How difficult for one of common powers, even with enlightened conscience, in such circumstances, to withstand a foe who betrayed, and with triumphant malevo- lence cast down one in the full vigor of a holy and highly intel- lectual mind, while in fellowship with God, and in a state free from the corrupting example of a gay, sinful, fashion-loving world, and from the influence of a gloomy and crushing superstition.

With this view of the helplessness of a whole nation, we can hardly fail to admire the benevolence of the injunction, " Go ye into all the world and preach the Gospel to every creature ;" nor can we too deeply deplore the fact, that the earliest intercourse of the representatives of Christendom with the heathen should so often have a decided tendency to confirm their vices, augment their pollution and misery, and complete their ruin.

CHAPTER III.

SIMULTANEOUSLY with the first impulses of foreign missionary feeling in the breasts of American Christians, in the current century, two tawny youths of the Hawaiian race, Opukahaia (Obookiah) and Hopu, from " a boy's notion," as O. said, but led by the hand of Providence, attached themselves to an American trader, Captain Brintnel, at the islands, and sailed with him to the United States. They landed in New York, in 1809. They were early taken to the theatre " to see the curiosity," as one of them called it; and like the mass of foreign seamen who then visited our cities without being improved in their morals, were for a time exposed to the evil of being confirmed in vice and ignorance, and in utter contempt of the claims of Christianity. The two youths accompanied Captain Brintnel to New Haven, Ct., where they soon attracted the Christian sympathy of some of the students, who offered to teach them, foremost of whom was Mr. E. Dwight.

Their prompt and successful efforts, their docility and grateful attention, promised soon to reward their teachers. Opukahaia represented himself as a homeless, miserable orphan, having seen both his father and mother bayoneted by a victorious party, in a bloody strife, " to see which should be the greatest."

In the course of a few years' residence, at different places, among Christian friends, he found a Redeeming Friend, and a Heavenly Father, and gave evidence of true conversion.

Acquaintance with these youth, and their readiness to avail themselves of Christian instruction, called attention to others who came from time to time from the same country. The friends of Christ were led to look upon these sons of Paganism, providentially brought to their doors, as having a claim for sympathy, care and instruction in the Christian doctrine, and attempting to meet this claim, they cherished the reasonable hope that suitable efforts to enlighten and convert them, would tend to the evangelization of their nation.

Early in 1816, the Rev. Messrs. A. Bingham and J. Harvey drew my attention to the work of training these youths for missionary service and conducting them to the Hawaiian field. But not having finished my collegiate course of study, and wishing to prosecute uninterruptedly, a three years' theological course, I declined the service which they commended to me.

Other youths, from other islands, and from several of the aboriginal tribes of the American continent, were found to be desirous of receiving instruction, giving similar promise of aid to the cause of improvement, among their respective tribes. Aiming to secure the salvation of these strangers, and to make their agency available in spreading the Gospel in heathen countries, the American Board of Commissioners for Foreign Missions established, in 1816, a school at Cornwall, Conn., for the sons of various heathen tribes, where they were taught the rudiments of an academical education and the doctrines and duties of the Christian religion, to which their superstition readily gave place.

The object of this school was, in its constitution, declared to be, "The education, in our country, of heathen youths, in such a manner, as, with subsequent professional instruction, will qualify them to become useful missionaries, physicians, surgeons, schoolmasters or interpreters, and to communicate to the heathen nations such knowledge in agriculture and the arts, as may prove the means of promoting Christianity and civilization."

This school embraced Opukahaia and several other Hawaiians, eight Cherokees, three Stockbridges, two Choctaws, two Oneidas, two Caughnowagas, one Tahitian, one Marquesan, and one Malayan. Here the hopes of the churches were encouraged by the progress of the pupils under the instruction of the Rev. H. Daggett, and especially by the evidences of piety and of mental capacity exhibited by Opukahaia, Hopu, Honolii and others from the Sandwich Islands.

The generous heart of Opukahaia, touched by Divine grace, glowed with gratitude to God and his people for the Christian privileges which he was allowed to enjoy, and melted in compassion for his heathen brethren, at his dark home, though their violence had made him an orphan. His ardent, growing desire to use his improved powers in conveying the Gospel to his perishing countrymen, gave high promise of his usefulness among them, if, in the providence of God, he should return to his native shores. While all was uncertain as to his return, and the sending forth of a mission to that dark field, Opukahaia, in his newly acquired and imperfect English, expressed feelings of confidence in God and of compassion for his countrymen, which drew the hearts of Christians more and more closely to him and his distant dying tribe. In a manner apparently childlike, he said,—

"God will carry through his work for us. I do not know what will God do for my poor soul. I shall go before God and also before Christ. I hope the Lord will send the Gospel to the heathen land, where the words of the Savior never yet had been. Poor people ! worship the wood and stone, and shark and almost everything their god. The Bible is not there, and heaven and hell, they do not know about it . . .   O what a wonderful thing it is that the hand of the Divine Providence has brought me from that heathenish darkness where the light of Divine truth never had been.   And here I have found the name of the Lord Jesus in the Holy Scriptures, and have read that his blood was shed for many.

" O what a happy time I have now, while my poor friends and relations at home, are perishing with hunger and thirsty, wanting of the Divine mercy and water out of the wells of salvation.   My poor countrymen who are yet living in the region and shadow of death, without knowledge of the true God, and ignorant of the future world, have no Bible to read, no Sabbath.   I often feel for them in the night season, concerning the loss of their souls.   May the Lord Jesus dwell in my heart, and prepare me to go and spend the remaining part of my life with them.   But not my will, O Lord, but thy will be done."*

He spent a little time among the Theological students at Andover, by whom he was instructed, and to whom he evinced a strong desire to understand the Word of God.   But the high hopes entertained by the friends of missions, that Opukahaia might be an humble apostle to his idolatrous countrymen, were soon buried with him in his early grave at Cornwall, Ct., and many felt the affliction.

Great as were the disappointment and grief at his departure, there were consolations in the reflection that the dear youth had himself been plucked as a brand from the burning, and made a trophy of redeeming mercy ; and in the hope that his timely conversion, his missionary zeal, his brief and consistent Christian life, and his affecting death, would fan the missionary spirit and hasten the promulgation of the Gospel on the shores that gave him birth.   Deeply as his unexpected death was felt, and loudly as we were called on by it " to cease from man whose breath is in his nostrils," it had no tendency to diminish the little ardor of the writer of this narrative, for evangelizing the Hawaiians, who had now lost such a friend and intended teacher.   Visiting the Foreign Mission school, during a vacation of the Theological Seminary, at Andover, and feeling a new impulse to become a pioneer in the enterprise of spreading the Gospel in that dark portion of the Pacific Isles, I freely offered myself to the American Board for that purpose, and was accepted by their Prudential Committee, in the summer of 1819 ; and soon after, Mr. Thurston, my class-mate, offered himself for the same work, and was likewise readily accepted.   We completed our course of Theological studies, at Andover, Massachusetts, in September, 1819. On the 29th of the same month, we were, at the request of the Prudential Committee, solemnly set apart, at Goshen, Connecticut, for the work of this ministry.   An unusual degree of

* Memoir of Obookiah.

enthusiasm prevailed there among the friends of the Hawaiian race, as many remember, and the missionary zeal of many was awakened or greatly increased. The language of the impulses of the Spirit seemed to be, " Go quickly to the rescue of the dying heathen, and I will go with you," and the Church responded, " Go quickly." Nearly simultaneously, twelve others, sons and daughters of the Church, offered themselves, and were accepted as assistant missionaries for that field. Their earnest language was,—" Here are we,—send us."

Within two weeks after the ordination in Goshen, the missionary company assembled in Boston, to receive their instructions and embark. There, in the vestry of Park Street Church, under the counsels of the officers of the Board, Dr. S. Worcester, Dr. J. Morse, J. Evarts, Esq., and others, the little pioneer band was, on the 15th of Oct., 1819, organized into a Church for transplantation. The members renewed their covenant, and publicly subscribed with their hands unto the Lord, and united in a joyful song.

> " O happy day that fixed my choice
> On thee my Savior and my God !
> Well may this glowing heart rejoice,
> And tell its raptures all abroad.
>
> 'Tis done—the great transaction's done,
> I am my Lord's, and he is mine ;
> He drew me, and I followed on,
> Charmed to confess the voice divine.
>
> High Heaven that heard the solemn vow,
> That vow renewed shall daily hear ;
> Till in life's latest hour I bow,
> And bless in death a bond so dear."

In these solemn and memorable transactions, the parties cherished the delightful expectation, that the prayer then offered by one of the Missionaries, " that this vine might be transplanted and strike its roots deep in the Sandwich Islands, and send forth its branches and its fruits till it should fill the land," would not only be heard in Heaven, but ere long, be graciously answered to the joy of the Hawaiian people, and of their friends throughout Christendom.

The object for which the missionaries felt themselves impelled to visit the Hawaiian race, was to honor God, by making known his will, and to benefit those heathen tribes, by making them acquainted with the way of life,—to turn them from their follies and crimes, idolatries and oppressions, to the service and enjoyment of the living God, and adorable Redeemer,—to give them the Bible in their own tongue, with ability to read it for themselves,—to introduce and extend among them the more

useful arts and usages of civilized and Christianized society, and
to fill the habitable parts of those important islands with schools
and churches, fruitful fields, and pleasant dwellings.   To do this,
not only were the Spirit and power of the Highest required,—for,
" Except the Lord build the house, they labor in vain that build
it," but, since he will not build his spiritual house, unless his
laborers build it, the preacher and translator, the physician, the
farmer, the printer, the catechist, and schoolmaster, the Christian
wife and mother, the female teacher of heathen wives, mothers,
and children, were also indispensable.   Nor could this work be
reasonably expected to be done by a few laborers only, at few
and distant points, and in the face of all the opposition which
Satan and wicked men would, if possible, naturally array against
them.

In conformity with the judgment of the Prudential Committee,
the pioneer missionary company consisted of two ordained
preachers and translators, a physician, two schoolmasters and
catechists, a printer and a farmer, the wives of the seven, and
three Hawaiians.

Mr. Chamberlain and his wife, in the prime of life, feeling the
claims of the heathen on them, were willing to leave their
friends, their pleasant home and farm in central Massachusetts, and
embark for the islands, with their five children, three sons and
two daughters, rather than to withhold their personal labors from
the heathen.

Christ undoubtedly requires all his followers to bear their cross,
and to forego or forsake whatever comes in competition with
rendering him the highest service, while, for everything sacrificed
with a right heart, for the purpose of honoring him, and extending
his gospel, he gives the unfailing promise of manifold more.
Many who admit that the Lord encourages and commands his
Church to give the Gospel to the heathen, decline the service, on
the plea that they are not qualified for it, forgetting that he, who
commands and calls, can give the grace that is needful, and that
qualifications may be increased while life and strength continue.
One of our pioneers, Mr. Whitney, though he had but just entered
on his Sophomore studies, at Yale College, felt so strongly
impelled to hasten to the Sandwich Islands, that with the consent
of his instructors, and the approbation of our Board, he concluded to forego the further advantages of that institution, and
embarking at once, in this enterprise, to prosecute his studies
on board ship, and in the field, and become a preacher to the
heathen when he could command their language,—and this he
accomplished.

The plan of taking females from this country to live or die
among the barbarians of Hawaii, appeared to many objectionable
and forbidding.   It was deemed advisable to send out the frame
of a house for the accommodation of the mission in their new
abode.   This was subsequently transported to the islands,

gratuitously, through the generosity of Messrs. Bryant & Sturgis, of Boston, prompted by sympathy for the females of the mission, for whose habitations they believed the grass-thatched huts of Hawaii would be unsuitable.   Such was the apprehension of these gentlemen that our families could not long remain among those barbarians, amid the privations and suffering to which they would be exposed, in so rude, so dark, so vile a part of the world as they knew the Sandwich Islands to be, that they gave their ship-masters visiting that quarter, instruction to offer them a free passage back to the United States.   While thousands treated the self-immolation of the missionaries, and the general plan of seeking the good of the heathen, at Christ's command, whatever it might cost, as truly commendable, tens of thousands regarded it as foolish or fanatical, an uncalled for sacrifice of comfort, property, and life.   By many, the missionaries were urged to a different course, because there was so much to be done at home, or because it would cost so much to complete the plan abroad, or because they did not think it of much importance that the heathen should ever hear the Gospel.   Nearly all the early missionaries from the United States, on resolving to devote themselves to the heathen, were strenuously opposed by their parents, relatives and friends. But those who opposed this cause, had either given too little attention to the pressing necessities of the heathen, and the ability and duty of Christians to give them the Gospel; or they were under great misapprehensions as to the detriment that might result to kindred, and country, and home, from foreign missionary efforts; or they had far too small a degree of regard to the authority of Christ, and the high claims, and holy principles of his religion, which require those who enjoy the Bible, to love their heathen neighbors, in such a sense as to be willing to visit them, or send them missionaries, and to make sacrifices to supply their wants.

The members of our mission, brought together from different parts of our land, feeling bound by the will of God to enter on the missionary work, subscribed to vows (it may be well to observe), similar in their nature and extent, to the public vows of all who properly join themselves to the Lord and his people. The specification of a design to convey the Gospel to a particular tribe, marked a difference from ordinary Church covenants, less than might at first glance be supposed; for all true churches engage, by covenant, to do the Lord's bidding.   The true convert is bound to observe the ordinances and to extend the influence of the Gospel, because Christ *requires* it, rather than because of his own *engagement*.   To know, to be qualified, to have opportunity, constitute the special call to do good.   And for aught that appears to the contrary, the Divine injunction to teach men universally to observe all the commands of the Redeemer, is a call to teach, extended by him to every son of Zion whom he qualifies **thus to serve him.**

That every church of Christ is bound to serve him with the same spirit of consecration and self-denial as any foreign missionary band, cannot reasonably be questioned, for whether we go up to the missionary field of battle, or tarry by the stuff, we have " one faith, one Lord, one baptism," one Bible, and one standard of Christian duty by which we shall all be judged. That a missionary laborer, or a missionary Church, ought to possess a degree of consecration far higher, and to practise self-denial far greater than what ordinarily appears in the churches, cannot be doubted. Still, God's claim on the missionary, the wealthy publican, the rich young man, the affluent Mary, and the poor widow, for the fullest revenue of honor which it is possible for them to render him, is equally imperative.

The mission received the public instructions of the Prudential Committee given by Dr. Worcester, on the evening of the 15th of Oct., at Park St. Church, when one of these pioneers preached " on the grand design of the Bible to promote benevolent action." In the course of an interesting week of final arrangements for the expatriation of our little Missionary Church, the members of it invited their fellow Christians to unite with them in renewing their oath of allegiance to the Savior at his table, and were in this solemn exercise, and in various other ways, allowed to mingle with sympathizing friends who took commendable pains to cheer them on in their untried course. Many churches, in different parts of the country, moved by the same spirit, engaged in special, earnest prayer for the success of this mission, and many a heart began to anticipate the happy result of the enterprise.

Mr. Evarts, the treasurer, having engaged a passage for the mission on board the brig Thaddeus, Captain Blanchard, for $2,500, exclusive of provisions for a long voyage, she was made ready for sea, by the 23d of October. In the forenoon of that day, Mr. Thurston gave the parting address of the mission to its friends, at Park St. Church, that monthly concert temple dear to many a missionary heart. They repaired together to the wharf, where they united in a parting hymn, pledging a close and permanent union though far and long separated ;—

" When shall we all meet again ?—
When shall we all meet again ?—
Oft shall wearied love retire ;
Oft shall glowing hope expire ;
Oft shall death and sorrow reign,
Ere we all shall meet again.

" Though in distant lands we sigh,
Parched beneath a hostile sky ;
Though the deep between us rolls,
Friendship shall unite our souls ;
And in fancy's wide domain,
We shall often meet again.

" When the dreams of life have fled ;
When its wasted lamps are dead ;
When in cold oblivion's shade,
Beauty, power, and fame are laid ;
Where immortal spirits reign,
There may we all meet again."

A fervent and appropriate prayer was offered by the Secretary
of the Board, and the mission was affectionately commended to
the grace of God, and immediately conveyed to the brig by a
barge furnished for the purpose by a U. S. Naval officer, they
being still accompanied by the Secretary and Treasurer and a few
other friends.   When these had given the parting hand and bene-
diction, they descended into the boat and began to move off.   The
tender and benignant look of Dr. Worcester, as the boat left our
vessel, turning his eyes upon the little band looking over the
rail, as if he would say, my love be ever with you, will not
soon be forgotten.   When they had reached the wharf, the brig
weighed anchor and set sail, and as we dropped down the stream,
they waved their handkerchiefs, till out of sight.   Though leaving
my friends, home and country, as I supposed for ever, and trying
as was the parting scene, I regarded that day as one of the happiest of my life.   But loosing from our beloved country, and not
expecting ever to tread its shores or look upon its like again, with
what intense interest did we gaze upon its fading landscapes, its
receding hills and mountains, till the objects successively disappeared in the distance, or sank below the horizon.

For the first month out, the sea was rough, and the winds not
favorable, and most of the passengers felt the inconvenience of
their new mode of life; and some suffered much and long from
sea-sickness.   In one instance, we were, for fourteen days and
nights (like Paul in Adria), driven up and down between 37° and
39° N. Lat., and, during a period of 24 days that we were tossing
and rolling, we made but five degrees toward the equator, and in
the meantime, shipped a sea that carried away the starboard
waist-boards and overturned the caboose.   The remark was then
made in our journal ;—

" November 17th. We cannot but conclude that he who controls
the winds and the waves and conducts the affairs of nations, is either
kindly withholding us from dangers and disasters at Cape Horn, or
operating changes at the islands favorable to the introduction and success
of this enterprise. He is inuring us to the hardships, and preparing
us for the trials of missionary life. He spreads our table on the face
of the deep ; gives us the comfort of returning health, teaches us to sit
with meekness at his feet, and learn his will, and trust in his all-sufficient grace."

The following day we were indulged with favorable winds, and
the rest of the voyage was, for the most part, agreeable and prosperous, allowing us generally several hours a day for study.

We entered the torrid zone, Dec 2d, 40 days from Boston ; crossed the Equator on the 13th, and spoke the ship Mary on the 15th, and sent by her a package of about 30 letters, to our friends, gratified to report progress. Jan. 4th, 1820, off the mouth of the Rio de la Plate, we experienced a gale from the north. Its violence rent several sails; we ran under almost bare poles, and learned what it is for mariners to " reel to and fro, and stagger like a drunken man." The tossing mountains around us " skipped like rams and the little hills like lambs." The foaming surges lashed the trembling sides of our little bark, and drenched her decks. The rain, like hail, pelted the poor sailors, as they clung to the rigging, through which the wind whistled ; and the spray swept over the face of the deep, like the driven snow in a northern winter's day. But he, who said to the raging tempest, " Peace, be still," afforded us protection, and gave us peace within.

We passed through the Straits of Le Maire, and on the following day, Jan. 27th, 1820, noticed the changeful weather in that forbidding region, and made some memoranda of what passed within and without, as follows ;—

Ten o'clock, A. M. With a fine morning and a fair breeze, which sprang up soon after the last evening's sacrifice, we find ourselves delivered from the dangers of Le Maire, and rapidly and pleasantly advancing towards our turning point, the place of hope and fear, while the pointed mountains of Staten-Land fall astern and sink below the horizon.

One o'clock, P. M. Every hour is big with interest. While at the rate of eight knots an hour the brig serenely cuts her way, the long looked for cape rises to our view, and all hearts leap for joy. But in the midst of congratulations, while we gratefully acknowledge that we are blest, not only with undeserved, but unexpected favors, and that our times and seasons are at the disposal of an All-wise Providence, it becomes us to rejoice with trembling, lest we should not sufficiently glorify God in view of his gracious smiles.

Two, P. M. The wind rises—dark clouds begin to hover round— an approaching whirlwind is announced. " All hands on deck." " The dead lights in"—the companion-way closed—the passengers imprisoned below deck.

Half-past two. For a moment, our Heavenly Father seemed to hold the rod over us. The wind subsides. A gentle rain descends—Light breaks in ; our Father smiles again ; we know that he who made Cape Horn and placed it here as a way-mark, which the tempests of sixty centuries have not been able to remove, can conduct us around it in safety ; nor shall whirlwinds or storms prevent us from erecting on it the Ebenezer of the Sandwich Islands Mission.

Three, P. M. The wind rises suddenly. " *All hands on deck*" resounds again. The waves lift themselves up ; the waters roar. Our little trembling bark, with her invaluable freight, yields to the opposing currents, and lightly bends her course toward the south.

Four o'clock. The sun breaks out in the clear western sky, while the dark tempest, passing on to the east, bears down upon the waters of the Atlantic, leaving us running briskly south, while the cape sinks behind a pleasant sea.

Six o'clock. The sun shuts in behind a dark cloud. A squall approaches.

Seven o'clock. The sun breaks out again and smiles.

Eight o'clock, P. M. While our vessel was lying to and tossing on the rising billows, her sails close furled, her decks drenched with a heavy spray continually breaking over her, and a strong west wind, as it roared through the rigging, drifted her reluctantly towards the south east, we assembled, as usual, at that hour, for evening prayers, read the 46th Ps., and sang the 83d hymn of the Selection, acknowledged " the good hand of our God upon us," in his past, undeserved favors, endeavored to lay ourselves peacefully at the feet of Divine Sovereignty, and to implore the kind protection, the sure guidance, the continued presence and blessing of him whose unfailing goodness constrained us to say, " Hitherto hath the Lord helped us." We sang, " Jesus lover of my soul." Through the evening, while his waves and billows seemed to go over us, we felicitated ourselves that this gale had not been commissioned a little sooner, which might have dashed us on the rocks of Staten-Land ; and we could say, " The Lord of Hosts is with us, the God of Jacob is our refuge."

During 24 hours, we went about two degrees to the eastward, and made about 50 miles southing ; most of the whole a loss. Our hearts were somewhat tried to be driven away from our course, and from our object, just at the moment when, with exultation, we seemed to be turning the goal, to bend our way north-westerly, directly towards our desired and destined field, and still to find ourselves in Lat. 56° 28', Lon. 65° 30'. Though we had passed almost a sleepless night, and the commotion of the elements continued through the 28th, we were not denied the comfort of a good degree of calm resignation, and unshaken confidence in the Captain of our Salvation.

On the 29th, our ground was regained, the Cape in sight as before, and our praises called forth to him " Whom winds and seas obey."

One of the happiest Sabbaths of the voyage was the 30th of January, when we passed the Cape, and we found the region of terror and danger to be the place of our special rejoicing, and we united in a grateful song, which was composed at the time, to celebrate the event, and denominated our

EBENEZER.

With joyful hearts and grateful praise,
Our Helper God, thy name we hail,
Our EBENEZER here we raise,
While round the stormy cape we sail.

Conducted by thy sovereign hand,
Mysterious, mighty, wise, and good ;
We left our friends and native land,
To toss upon the raging flood

When adverse winds our course delayed,
And dangerous currents rolled below,
Thy voice the roaring tempest stayed
And made the breeze propitious blow.

From want, from pestilence, and death,
Defended by thy gracious care,
To thee we raise our tuneful breath :—
Our Rock of Help forbids our fear.

This way-mark, source of boding fears,
Fixed by his hand who rules above,
The tempests of six thousand years
Have ne'er been able to remove.

So shall our grateful record stand,
" THUS FAR BY THY KIND AID WE'VE COME,"
So will we trust thy constant hand
To bring our souls in safety home.

During the week, from the 28th of Jan. to 4th of Feb., we ran
12 degrees westward, between 56° and 60° S. Lat. The days
were long, having about seventeen hours sun. The twilight
passing along the southern horizon, from west to east, under the
south pole, continued from sunset to sunrise, or seven hours. It
was mid-summer there, but the mercury stood but 12 degrees
above freezing poi..t, at the close of a long summer day, Feb. 2d.
Icebergs, or fields of ice were possibly not far distant. Winter
clothing was required to make us comfortable. From the 7th of Feb.
to the 7th of March, we ran 50 degrees to the northward, and 30
westward. It was the opinion of some of the officers that no vessel
ever passed more rapidly or pleasantly from Cape Horn to that
point, than that which conveyed our mission. On the 11th of
March we had an unusual visitor, against which missionaries at
sea should be on their guard. Several of the brethren and others,
having been many weeks denied the privilege, allowed themselves
the pleasant and healthful exercise of bathing in the ocean, when
nearly becalmed in the torrid zone. A few minutes after they
had returned safely on board, while a sailor was painting the bow-
sprit, with his feet in the water, a large shark approached him,
whose destructive jaws he narrowly escaped. The shark played
or raved round the vessel, with the boldness and fierceness of a
hungry tiger, and put up his nose to the side of the brig to smell
the track where the swimmers had ascended from the water. G. P.
Kaumualii and one of the officers, dexterously put a snare upon
him, as he passed under the main-chains. The vigorous flounder-
ing of this Leviathan made the sea boil. He seized hold of the
end of a pole with his teeth, by which, in connexion with the
rope on his flukes, the shipmen and passengers drew him up the
side of the vessel upon deck. It was found that he had swal-

lowed a bone, which the cook had thrown overboard while we were bathing, so that he must have been near at the time. The mingled emotions of gratitude for deliverance from danger, so recent, but then unknown, and so effective an admonition to be suitably on our guard, and of pity for a nation so degraded as to regard this monster as a god, and of confidence that he who had shut this lion's mouth, would hold in check all our enemies, and triumph over all the vanities of the heathen, cannot be easily described.

Somewhat similar emotions of gratitude and praise were awakened subsequently, by another singular occurrence, three days before we reached the islands. Mr. Whitney, for the purpose of getting needful bodily exercise, undertook to assist in painting the outside of the vessel, standing on a suspended plank, and endeavoring to secure himself, by grasping with one hand, a rope fastened above him. From this position he was thrown into the sea, and was left astern, calling for help, and struggling in vain to overtake the vessel, which was under full sail. Instantly, several buoyant articles were thrown overboard to aid him. With his self-possession, and skill in swimming, he was able to sustain himself, and to buffet the waves successfully, after one or two had broken over him, till he gained a bench which had been thrown out to serve him as a buoy. As he reached this, and found its aid, he raised and waved his hat, as a kind signal to his anxious but receding friends, and then composed himself in prayer, thus waiting to see what could be done for him. Never, before, did the mission family know how much they loved him. At the prompt orders of Captain Blanchard, the brig "was hove to," within the distance of about one-third of a mile from Mr. Whitney. In five minutes more, a boat was cleared away, lowered, and sent to his assistance, and in about 20 or 25 minutes from his fall, he was brought safely on board again. We had not forgotten the danger from sharks, nor were we insensible to the danger of drowning, even to a good swimmer, when so unexpectedly precipitated into the fathomless ocean. God had, we believed, something yet for our brother to do among the heathen, and we lifted up our thanksgiving for the speedy answer to prayer, in supporting and delivering him, as he once did Peter, on the sea of Tiberias. The promises were not only comforting to the Fishermen of Galilee, " When thou passest through the waters, I will be with thee,"— " Lo, I am with you always," but to us also, in traversing a seemingly returnless distance, amid the perils of the ocean. Such exposures and escapes were calculated to make us feel the need of present Divine aid, and of constant preparation for a sudden summons to depart.

Awake, in some measure, to considerations like these, we observed the next day, the 28th of March, as a season of fasting and prayer, that we might be brought safely to our field, and prepared to enter it with proper feelings of heart. The feelings which we deemed it necessary for us at this time, especially to seek and cherish, were, *confidence* in the government and providence of God, *penitence* for our own violations of his law, *gratitude* for the blessings of his Gospel, *compassion* for the wretched children of Paganism and superstition, *benevolence* towards all, and *faith* in the blood and promises of Christ with reference to the salvation of the heathen.

Two days later, at early morning, March 30th, to the joy of our expecting little company, the long looked for Hawaii appeared in the West. The lofty Mauna Kea lifted its snow crowned summit above the dark and heavy clouds that begirt its waist. Our natives eagerly watching, had descried it in the night, at the distance of eighty miles. As we approached, we had a fine view of about sixty miles of the N. E. coast of the island—the districts of Hilo, Hamakua, and part of Kohala; and as the sun shining in his strength dissipated the clouds, we had a more impressive view of the stupendous pyramidal Mauna Kea, having a base of some thirty miles, and a height of nearly three miles. Its several terminal peaks rise so near each other, as scarcely to be distinguished at a distance. These, resting on the shoulders of this vast Atlas of the Pacific, prove their great elevation by having their bases environed with ice, and their summits covered with snow, in this tropical region, and heighten the grandeur and beauty of the scene, by exhibiting in miniature, a northern winter, in contrast with the perpetual summer of the temperate and torrid zones below the snow and ice. The shores along this coast, appeared very bold, rising almost perpendicularly, several hundred feet, being furrowed with many ravines and streams. From these bluffs, the country rises gradually, for a few miles, presenting a grassy appearance, with a sprinkling of trees and shrubs. Then, midway from the sea to the summit of the mountain, appeared a dark forest, principally of the koa and ohia, forming a sort of belt, some ten miles in breadth—the temperate zone of the mountain.

As we approached the northern extremity of Hawaii, we gazed successively, upon the verdant hills, and deep ravines, the habitations of the islanders, the rising columns of smoke, the streams, cascades, trees, and vestiges of volcanic agency : then, with glasses, stretching our vision, we descried the objects of our solicitude, moving along the shore—immortal beings, purchased with redeeming blood, and here and there, the monuments of their superstition. Animated with the novel and changeful scene, we longed to spring on shore, to shake hands with the people, and commence our work by telling them of the great salvation by Jesus Christ. As we passed round the northern extremity of Hawaii, Maui rose on our right, at the distance of twenty-five or thirty miles.

Having gained the lee, or western side of Kohala, an officer with Hopu and Honolii, was sent by a boat, at 4 P. M., to make inquiry of the inhabitants respecting the state of the islands, and the residence of the king. Waiting nearly three hours, we hailed their return, eager to catch the sound of the first intelligence ; and how were our ears astonished to hear, as it were, the voice divine, proclaiming on their hills and plains,

> " In the wilderness, prepare ye the way of the Lord,
> Make straight in the desert, a highway for our God."

How were our hearts surprised, agitated, and encouraged beyond every expectation, to hear the report—" Kamehameha is dead—His son Liholiko is king—the tabus are abolished—the images are destroyed,—the heiaus of idolatrous worship are burned, and the party that attempted to restore them by force of arms has recently been vanquished !" The hand of God! how visible in thus beginning to answer the prayer of his people, for the Hawaiian race! But such is the known propensity of the human heart to follow the vanities of the heathen, that even the tribes of Israel, though trained to the worship of the true God, and made to acknowledge the oft repeated and wonderful interpositions of his power and mercy, were ever ready, we remembered, to relapse into idolatry ; and how much more did we fear these uninstructed heathen would do so, unless they could be speedily impressed with the claims of Christianity. Without this, there could be no security that the nation would not be scourged with atheism or anarchy, or with a species of idolatry more vile, bloody and fatal, than they had ever yet known.

To detail the circumstances of the departure and obsequies of Kamehameha, who finished his career at Kailua, and of the events that followed, I translate several passages from an account drawn up by natives and published in the Mooolelo Hawaii, 1838, which serve to illustrate the character of the religion in which he lived and died.

" The illness of Kamehameha became so great, that the native doctors could not cure him. Then said the priest, ' It is best to build a house for your god, that you may recover.' The chiefs, sustaining the advice of the priest, built a sacred house for his god Kukailimoku, and a kapu took place, at evening. The people, apprehending that the priest and chiefs were urging Kamehameha to have men sacrificed to his god for his recovery, were seen to fly, through fear of death, and remained in their hiding-places, till the tabu was over. Probably the king did not assent to the proposition, but was heard to say, ' men are tabu for the king'—alluding to his son. After the worship, the king's disease increased, and he became helpless. When another tabu day arrived for the new temple, he said to Liholiho, ' Go to the worship of your god—I cannot go.' Then was ended his praying to his feather-god, Kukailimoku (an image of Juggernaut-like form, made of net-work and feathers). But he assented to the proposition of another worshipper, who, having a bird-god called P-ia, said, ' The sick will be cured by it,' though the body of the god was the bird *alae*, that is eaten. Two houses were, therefore, erected ; but while occupying them, he ceased to take food, and became extremely weak. His wives, children, and chiefs, perceiving this, after three days, conveyed him to his dwelling-house. . . On account of the tabu of that period, there were six kinds of houses, a house of worship ; a front or eating-house for men ; an eating-house for women ; a sleeping house ; a rear house for beating *kapa*, and a house for the seclusion of women at certain periods. In the evening, the feeble king was borne from his sleeping-house to the front house, and took a mouthful of *poi* and a little water. The chiefs asked him for his final charge ; but he made not the least answer. He was lifted back to his sleeping-house ; and near midnight, brought again to the front house, where he took another mouthful of food with water. Kaikioewa then addressed him thus, ' Here are we all, your younger brethren, your king, and your foreigner; lay down for us your charge, that your *king* and *sisters* may hear.'* Not fully comprehending, he with difficulty inquired, ' What do you ask ?' The chief repeated, ' Your *charge* for us.' He made an effort, and said, ' Proceed only according to my policy, until—' not able to finish his sentence, he embraced the neck of the foreigner and drew him down for a kiss. Hoapili was another whom he embraced, and pulling him down, whispered in his ear, and was then carried back to his sleeping-house. In an hour or two, he was borne again, partially, into the front house, while most of his body remained in his sleeping-house. He was once more replaced ; and about two o'clock,—(May 8th)—1819, he expired. . . .

" Soon, the chiefs held a consultation, and without announcing his death, or even letting it be known abroad, one of the chiefs was heard to say, ' This is my thought—let us dissect him.' Kaahumanu faintly replied, ' Not, perhaps, for us is the body, but for the king (the successor)—our part the breath (his power to command us) has gone ; his body is the king's.'

" After this consultation, he was borne to the front house for the *uko* ceremony to be performed by the high-priest and the young king. When the *uko* hog was baked, the high priest made an offering to him who was dead; he was a god—the body without a soul lying there.† The king offered the consecrating prayer. The priest made an address to the king and chiefs, and said, ' I tell you of the human sacrifice for him here—to sacrifice now, it is one—but if we go out, and the sacrifice is made there, four men ; but if we carry him near the lua (pit), and the sacrifice be offered there, ten men are to die ; but if he is quite in the pit,‡ and the sacrifice be made there, fifteen are to suffer, and if this night should pass, and a tabu occur, should the human sacrifice be made then, forty are to die.' The ceremony of that priest closed. The high priest stood with the hog, and performed his ceremony, and smote the hog. His ceremony also ended. Then Hewahewa, the high priest demanded, ' Where shall the king (the

* In the native language, *your king*, here implies the relation of son, *your foreigner*, the relation of one adopted from another country—John Young. *Your younger brethren* meant the high chief men ; and *your sisters*, the high chief women.
† Ironical, now, like the words of Elijah, " He is a god."
‡ Probably the place of decomposition for detaching the bones.

heir) now dwell ?' The chiefs said, ' Where indeed ? You are the one that knows.' The priest said, ' There are two places, in one of which it is proper for the king to dwell, Kau and Kohala, but it is not proper for him to remain here, in Kona, for it is wholly polluted.'. . . Such was the tabu of that period concerning a dead body. If a king died, that whole district was polluted, and his heir went into another. When the body was disposed of according to custom, and the bones firmly bound in a bundle, the pollution ceased. But if the dead was not a king, to the house only the pollution extended—when buried, the pollution was ended.

" The chiefs agreed to the young king's residing at Kohala. The morning light arose, and Liholiho, with his servants and several chiefs, hastened thither. The chiefs and people indulged in frantic lamentations, and rioting and revelry, like maniacs and brutes, and their proceedings were too atrocious and revolting to admit of being described.

" As the chiefs were bearing the body to the place for detaching the bones, Keamahulihia, a friend of the deceased, met them, and desiring to die with him, perhaps on account of his affection, attempted repeatedly to leap upon them (apparently offering himself for immolation), but was repulsed by the chiefs. In like manner, Kalanimoku resolved on immolation, but was repulsed by Hookio."

These appeared to have offered themselves as victims, according to the declaration of the priests, but were both rejected by the chiefs. Multitudes indulged the apprehension that the king had been the victim of some unknown sorcerer, and professors of sorcery put their art in operation, and kindled their fires in vain, to destroy or detect the author of the king's death. The chief, Keeaumoku, brother of Kaahumanu, approaching intoxicated, broke the sorcerers' flag wand, which they had set up near the place of their fire. Then, people conjectured that Kaahumanu and her party had been the means of the king's death, and reviled them unjustly.

In the evening after the death of the king, a woman ate a forbidden cocoanut, and several men ate with women, contrary to the tabu, but this was rather attributable to the anarchy of the season of mourning for the dead; yet, as the gods did not bring on them evil consequences, it may have indicated the uselessness of the restriction.

After the bones of the king had been stripped and bundled according to custom, and some days had passed, Kaahumanu and Kalanimoku sent for Liholiho, at Kohala, to return to Kailua ; but he declined, because Kekuaokalani, his relative, more devoted to the gods than the dissipated young king, fearing he would break tabu and perish, objected. They sent again ; and the messenger, Eeka, said to Liholiho, " Thy guardians say, Return thou." He assenting, said to Kekuaokalani, " Let us both return," but the latter replied, " Let us both *remain*—there is fish at the sea-side, there is food inland ; death is afraid in the wilderness,"—(implying that they would be safer in their retreat than with the multitude at Kailua). Liholiho, however, returned to Kailua, and was inaugurated with ceremony and pomp; for which Kaahumanu had made arrangements.

" The chiefs and all the personal attendants of Kamehameha, with muskets, and the plebeians of Kona assembled at Kailua, in order that Kaahumanu might commit the kingdom to Liholiho. Then came forth Liholiho from the idol temple, robed in scarlet and a feathered mantle, with several chiefs on either side with *kahili* and spittoon, having on his head a princely hat from Britain. That day was Liholiho in his glory. Kaahumanu, (guardian of the realm), whom her husband had commissioned to take the kingdom and manage it herself, if his son failed to do it well, met her step-son, and (addressing him somewhat in the Chinese style by the title, Kalani, the heaven or the celestial) said, ' O Kalani, I report to you what belonged to your father—Here are the chiefs, and the men of your father—there are your guns, and this is your land; but you and I will share the land together.' Liholiho gave his assent, and was established over the kingdom."

On that occasion, Keopuolani, his own mother, proposed to him to eat without tabu, but was reproached for it by men. At evening, she induced his little brother, Kauikeaouli, a mere child, to eat without regard to the tabu. In August, 1819, the king and chiefs held a sacrifice at Kawaihae, and offered their prayers, and the people observed tabu; while drunkenness, heathen orisons, and amusements were intermingled, and baptism was given by the chaplain of a French ship, to Kalanimoku, who continued his heathen revelry. After this sojourn at Kawaihae, the king returned to Kona, and consecrated a temple to his god, at Honokohau; but made toilsome and unsuccessful efforts there, to accomplish what his senseless religion required. Owing to the confusion and impiety of his attendants, to whom the prayers of this dissolute youth, their kingly priest, doubtless appeared like a farce, they were not able to procure the *aha*, or to pronounce the prayer, unbroken or uninterrupted and availing. Before he left the place of these ceremonies, Kaahumanu, probably having little confidence in his prayers, sent a figurative proposition to him, somewhat ambiguous, but intimating that his god, to whom he was so vainly sacrificing, would not be worshipped at Kailua. The messenger said to him, " I am sent by your guardian, that your god may have a ki leaf covering, on arriving at Kailua." To this the king, bowing, assented, and immediately ordered a new supply of rum, and drinking freely, embarked in a boat, and for two days, drove about here and there, on the deep, off Kona, in his drunken revelry. During this time, preparations, without his knowledge, were made at Kailua, for discarding the tabu. At the close of the second day of the king's roving revelry, his boat being becalmed, he was sent for by the chiefs, with double canoes, and towed ashore. Here he drank rum, smoked, and ate with the chief women; and thus commenced the official renunciation of the ancient tabu system. A feast was soon made of articles tabu and free, and the king, and the male and female chiefs, openly and freely ate together, and the royal tabu was ended.

Messengers were sent as far as Kauai, to proclaim Liholiho's freedom from tabu. Kaumualii readily renounced tabu, and the ceremonial restraints on eating, smoking, drinking, and sleeping, were no longer enforced by the king and his supporters. The governmental sacrifices ceased, and licentiousness and revelry abounded. The high priest, Hewahewa, loving these indulgences himself, professing great love to the king, and being secure of his favor, and that of Kaahumanu, should he follow their wishes, readily concurred in the suspension of the public worship of idols, for he had, in fact, no more confidence in them, than Tetzel had in the power of purgatory to fulfil the promissory terms of the fraudulent indulgences which he bartered for the hard earnings of the deluded people, to enrich his speculating employers. The concurrence of the high priest in the great innovation, before it could be known that the people could be governed without the ceremonial tabu, was a rare and wonderful event, in God's providence. But neither the recklessness of the king, the pride of Kaahumanu, the indifference of the high priest to the honor of the gods, the general atheism of the higher chiefs, nay, even their suspension of the public religious rites, for the purpose of eating, drinking, gambling and revelling at pleasure during the brief remainder of life, without a sober thought of the future state, had any influence to change or purify the hard hearts of the nation, or to inspire respect to the true God, or the love of duty towards men. Multitudes, retaining still their superstition, disapproved of the innovations. Among these were Kekuaokalani, a high chief, and his adherents. He was angry at Kaahumanu and her party that they had encouraged Liholiho to eat unceremonially, and that their royal tabu was abrogated He desired it might be preserved, or rather restored and perpetuated. He withdrew to Kaawaloa, and some of the priests and some war-counsellers, deserting from the king, joined him. These encouraged him to maintain the tabu. They said, "No sin of ungodly rulers, by which they lost their dominions, is like this sin;" implying that Liholiho deserved to be deprived of his kingdom, and all his inheritance, for his unexampled, impious contempt of their religion. They awarded the realm to this chief, whose religion was still unaltered, and whose zeal and faith were rather increased than impaired. The country was in confusion, and the larger part of the plebeians, and some chiefs, concurred with Kekuaokalani; and the minority of the plebeians and chiefs concurred with Liholiho.

The step-mother of Kekuaokalani was sent to him to induce him to return to Kailua to renounce tabu, but he refused. The strong dissatisfaction of the plebeian adherents to tabu, broke out into violence, at Hamakua, and threatened immediate war. An officer being on that account sent thither by Liholiho was met by the insurgents, and killed by Kainapau, the leader of the insurrection. The chiefs immediately took counsel at Kailua, to send an army to Hamakua. But Kalanimoku objected and said, " It is not good policy to war there, for the cause of war is at Kaawaloa, that is the place to war. The strife at Hamakua is but the leaf of the tree : I go for the *trunk*. When that falls, the leaf will of itself wither."

Purposing to bring Kekuaokalani to terms, they despatched to Kaawaloa, an embassy of two high chiefs, Hoapili and Naihe, who were desirous to save him from taking arms against the king, and leading a civil war. They were accompanied by Keopuolani, the queen-mother, on her own responsibility. On meeting the supporter of the tabu, at the place where Captain Cook fell, Hoapili addressed him thus: " You are the son of my own sister, I have come for you. Let us return to Kailua. The plebeians are fighting, and the hostilities of the insurgents are charged to you ; and the charge accords with your remaining separated at a different place from the king. Come with me to Kailua, and dwell with the king. This evil will not rest on you, if you join him, and have personal intercourse with him. And it is still entirely with you to forsake tabu or not." He assented, but said, " wait a little, till I confer with Manono (his wife), then I will return : but I shall not discard tabu."

In the night the crier of that chief was heard, giving orders for the preparation of canoes to embark for Kailua. But in the morning, Kekuaokalani drew up his men, with guns and long spears in their hands, and sandals on their feet, and with them, appeared before the ambassadors. Hoapili said, " Are we now to go on foot ?" " Yes," replied the disaffected chief. " On board the canoes, let us all go," said Hoapili. The other rejoined, " I, with my people, who are all hungry, will go by land, where we can bake food and live." " Think not much of the people," said Hoapili, " yourself being on board the canoe, we will sail. Let the people then go by land. It is *thou* for whom I came." He replied, " I will not go by sea, but I and mine by land." Keopuolani, thinking herself in danger, and unwilling to parley, exclaimed, "Loose the cord, brother."

Thus the parties separated. Naihe advised Hoapili to land half way to Kailua, and meet Kekuaokalani. But Keopuolani advised to hasten to Kailua. On arriving there, meeting her son, and wishing to see something more effectual than an embassy of peace in the case, she said to him with falling tears, " A little more, and you had never seen me—I was on the point of being killed." This produced a sensation. " Where," demanded Kalanimoku, " is Kekuaokalani?" " Approaching by land," she answered,— " What of your embassy?" he rejoined. She said to him, " Seeking him as a relative is at an end ; what you counselled remains," i. e., to fight and crush him. He was ready to put in execution what he had before counselled, and to head a force to subdue him. That counsel now prevailed. That evening, arms and ammunition were given out, and the next day, Kalanimoku mustered a regiment, and the succeeding morning advancing to give battle, he gave the following laconic and spirited charge to his warriors, " Be calm—be voiceless—be valiant—drink the bitter waters, my sons,—turn not back—onward unto death*—no end for which to retreat." He knew something of the bitterness of the waters of battle, which even victors must drink, and of the use of martial valor, having often taken part with Kamehameha, after the death of Kiwalao; but he made here no allusion to any power but their own, and acknowledged no deity at all. Kekuaokalani sought the help of the idols—offered sacrifices and prayers, and paraded his war-god; though as yet he had fewer soldiers, and fewer arms than his antagonist, and little ammunition. Had it been his determination to make war, and had he drawn off to a distance, and given time for the friends of his cause to rally, his chance of success would probably have been more equal. Now the question of the dominion of the tabus and idols was to be tested speedily, by a savage fight, before the idolatrous party could have time to unite extensively for the support of their leader.

Apprised of the approach of the king's forces, Kekuaokalani, instead of sending proposals of reconciliation or submission, sent a scouting party, who met and fired on Kalanimoku, and killed and wounded several of his men. Taken thus by surprise, he retreated from this effective fire; but soon rallied, and finding the scouting party small, pursued them to Kuamoo, killing some as they retreated, and there joined battle with Kekuaokalani. He and his party courageously maintained their ground, till they were nearly surrounded by the forces of Kalanimoku on the land, and armed canoes, from Kailua, along the shore. Kekuaokalani, having early received a wound, was at length unable to stand,

" sat on a fragment of lava, and twice loaded and fired a musket on the advancing party. He now received a ball in his left breast, and, immediately covering his face with his feathered cloak, expired in the midst of his friends. His wife, Manono, during the day, fought by his side, with steady and dauntless courage. A few moments after her husband's death, perceiving Kalanimoku and his sister advancing, she called out for quarter. But the words had scarcely escaped from her lips, when she received a ball in the left temple—fell upon the lifeless body of her husband, and expired. The idolators having lost their chief, made but feeble resistance afterwards; yet the combat, which commenced in the forenoon, continued till near sunset."†

Kalanimoku's victory being complete, he immediately returned to Kailua. A pile of stones marks the spot where the rival chief, and his affectionate wife, his heroic and prime counsellor, expired; and near it, a larger pile marks their grave, over which the wild

---

* The death of one of the parties.   † Tour round Hawaii.

convolvulus creeps and blossoms, even on this dreary, lava waste. Around that grave, many piles of stones mark the spots where his friends and supporters were buried, who that day fell in the defence of idolatry, who, deluded and foolhardy as they were, may have been as correct in their principles and motives as their atheistic destroyers.

The custom of establishing by arms the supremacy of a successor on the decease of a king, aside from the dispute about the tabus, may have had no small influence on both parties, in leading to this war, which was wisely overruled for good.

Hoapili was immediately sent with a force to suppress the insurrection in the northern part of Hawaii. He met and vanquished the insurgents at Wiamea. The armed supporters of the tabus and idols being now subdued, the people acquiesced in the new government, without further outbreaks.

Whether the love of power, the love of idols, or rank atheism were the greater cause of this politico-religious war, the Ruler of the Nations made use of it to illustrate the impotency of the idols of Hawaii, which neither took vengeance on their leading despisers, nor favored their boldest champions. Atheism was emboldened. Governmental sacrifices ceased. The stone temples were deserted, and the frail thatched houses of worship burned. Some of the images were destroyed, and some hidden away in dens and caves, and some kept as matters of mere curiosity, or monuments of national folly. Irreligion, heathen amusements, licentiousness and revelry, abounded, and atheism took the throne.

Need the question now be repeated, "What occasioned this singular innovation in the national customs and religious rites handed down from former generations?" The brief narrative of the events among the people and of the movements for their help in the United States, is, perhaps, the best answer which I could give, though some differences of opinion on the question still exist. One reason for the observance of the tabu customs at all, was that "*such was the custom of the Hawaiians.*" Another was, that the principle of superstitious fear was a means of subjugation to rulers. Another was, their hope to preserve their own lives and to destroy their opposers. The idea that the gods they acknowledged *deserved* homage probably had no perceptible influence on their minds. The death of Kamehameha, their popular and powerful sovereign, whether it was regarded as the result of the neglect or the impotency of the gods whom he had served, or of the malice of others, was doubtless overruled to shake the superstitious confidence of those who had supposed him an object of the peculiar favor of the Hawaiian deities. The Providence of God, for some wise purpose of which Kamehameha had no conception, had allowed him to bring the country generally under his sovereign rule, and led him to allow almost equal authority to Kaahumanu, then a stout-hearted Pagan, at the head, we may say, of the powerful Maui aristocracy, embracing a large portion of the chiefs of the islands. This he had done without foreseeing the consequences, while he was persevering in his idolatry, and training his son, Liholiho, to maintain the tabus and the idol-worship of the land. But the high rank and magisterial authority of Kaahumanu supported by several chief women of noble blood, furnished the opportunity which had not occurred before, and which could hardly be expected to occur again, for a queen of such rank and power—such extensive influence over the whole group, to assert the rights of woman, unrestrained by a lordly husband, and to protest against the unreasonable disabilities under which they had been placed. To do this in her circumstances, would give to the tabus a mortal blow which Satan, when he framed the polluted system, had not anticipated.

This woman, with all her haughtiness and selfishness, possessed, perhaps, as true a regard for the safety of the state, as her late husband or his high chiefs, and with all her magisterial and consequential airs, had a degree of suavity and skill for managing the minds of others; and she often showed her address by the indulgences which she seemed to take pleasure in granting to the children of her late husband, when, looking ahead, she thought it could be safely done. They, therefore, had reason to expect their full share of personal gratification, if their guardian, the queen-dowager, were allowed to hold the rank and office assigned her by their father, and which she had partly inherited from the Queen of Maui and the leeward isles.

The compromise between Kaahumanu and Liholiho being in effect consummated, a modification or abrogation of the old tabus became almost indispensable. Kaahumanu desired equal privilege with *men*, in respect to eating and drinking, and, therefore, wished the termination of those distinctions and restraints which were felt to be degrading and oppressive to her and Keopuolani, and to her royal sisters, and royal step-daughters. Liholiho struggled on for months, between atheism and idolatry—between a regard to the onerous ceremonial of custom and the indulgence of his lusts unrestrained. His pride and love of liberty and pleasure impelled him to set his imperial foot on the neck of the gods of Hawaii, whom he accused of impotency or neglect, in not recovering his sick father. Believing that the people could be governed as much to his liking without religion as with, he was ready to turn from it as an engine of government, and rely on his guns and powder, and the support of the chiefs, who cared little for the gods. He, therefore, breathed out and acted out the spirit of irreligion—" Sooner let the *Akua* be destitute of his sacrifices and honors, than we of our pleasures."

The fact that the chiefs were fond of alcoholic drinks, but could not indulge freely in their use, without the unavoidable violation of the ceremonials of their national religion, both diminished their fear and increased their desire for the removal of its restraints and penalties. Kuakini had, from his boyhood, suffered from a defect, or disease in his limbs, which made it difficult for him to walk or stand.   From this, their *kahunas* took occasion to obtain from him many offerings, promising a cure.   He at length discredited them, withheld his offerings, grew better, rather than worse, and was on that account the more ready to turn away from the whole system.

The queen claiming her rights, and the king his unrestrained pleasures, and the high priest unwilling to oppose them—having himself a religion of custom, ceremony, and absurdity, rather than of conscience, argument, or vital power, concurring with their wishes, the main pillars of the ceremonial tabus were prostrated, and a new order of things suddenly sprang into existence.

Liholiho was now ambitious to have his reign distinguished as a kingdom free from ceremonial restraints, if not from *moral* also. The worship of images was prohibited, but the *private belief* of the people and their superstitious regard to the genius of the volcano, to the spirits of the departed, to the bones of their kings, and their *kini* of gods, the 40,000 deities on whom they had vainly called, were left to die a natural death, or to live on unrebuked till displaced by light from heaven.   No religious motives appear to have had any material influence on the minds of the innovators, the most sagacious of whom did not see, or even conjecture the result of their own experiment. Little did any of the actors in the drama imagine that the measures they attempted, either for or against the idols, were preparing for the introduction of a spiritual and holy religion, which should initiate both rulers and people into the service of the true God, and offer them a kingdom of ever-during felicity on high.   The influence of foreign visitors may have had some tendency to weaken the superstition of the rulers, but not more, perhaps, than in India and China.

But how conspicuous the wisdom and goodness of God to have provided a Christian mission for these islands, and to have brought it near their shores, at this auspicious moment!

The establishment, the long continuance, the bold infraction and final destruction of their bloody system of idolatry, must continue to be matters of wonder, when Christianity shall triumph over superstition in every land.

We were loudly called on, to go up, and "in the name of our God to set up our banner."   Nor could a doubt remain that he who created the light, and perfectly adapted to its properties the organization of the eye, had caused the movements in the two distant countries of Hawaii and the United States of America, to correspond for a benevolent end, though the agents were unacquainted with each other's measures and plans. We were certain he had ordered kindly for us, and were constrained to praise him for it. We felt a new impulse to tell the people how they ought to " praise the Lord for his goodness and for his wonderful works to the children of men."

1. The Family of KEKAULIKE, King of Maui in the middle of the 18th Century.

Wives.	Children.	Chil. in law.	Grand Children.	Gr. Grand Children.	Gr. Gr. Grand Children.
Kekuiapoiwa.	KAMEHAMEHANUI, King of Maui, 1772.	Namahana.	PALEIOHOLANI, King of Oahu, 1779.	{ Keeaumoku.	{ Kaneoneo, Gov. of Kauai, 1778. Keawe, Gov. of Kauai, 1795.
	Kalola.			{ Kiha.	
	KAHEKILI, King of Maui, 1773—93.	Kauwahine.	{ KALANIKUPULE, King of Oahu, 1794. Koalaukani, Gov. of Maui, 1794.		
Holau.	{ KAEO, King of Kauai, 1780—94.	Kamakahelei.	{ KAUMUALII, King of Kauai, 1795—1824.	{ Kepani. Kahekili. Kealiiahonui, Gov. of Kauai, 1845 Humehume, or G. P. Kaumualii.	Wahinekipi
Haaloo.	Namahana, Queen of Maui, 1772.	Keeaumoku.	(E.) KAAHUMANU, Q. Regent, 1824—32. Kalakua, Governess of Maui, 1841—2.	{ Kekauluohi, Premier, 1839—46. Kamamalu, Queen, 1819—24. Kinau, Premier, 1832—9.	{ Davida. Wm. Lunalilo { Moses. Lot. Alexander. Victoria.
			(Cox) Keeaumoku, Gov. of Maui, 1820. (J. A.) Kuakini, Gov. of Hawaii, 1820—1845. (L.) Namahana, Ac. Governess, Oahu, 1824.	Meri	
	Kuamanoha, Prince of Maui, 1775.	Kamakahukilani.	Kalanimoku, Commander of the army, 1819—24, & Prime Councillor of Kaahumanu, 1824—7. Boki, Gov., Oahu, 1819—30.	{ Leleiohoku, Gov., Hawaii, 1846.	
			Wahinepio, Governess of Maui, 1824.	{ Kahalaia, Gov., Kauai, 1824. Kekauonohi, Q.	

2. The Family of KALANIOPUU, King of Hawaii, 1778—1781.

Wives.	Children.	Grand Children.	Gr. Gr. Children.
Namahana.	{ Kiwalao, a King of Hawaii, 1781. Keoua, a King of S. Hawaii, 1781—92.	Keopuolani.	{ Liholiho, K. Kauikeaouli, K. Nahienaena.
Kekupuohi.		{ Pauahi, Q. & wife Kekuanaoa.	Ruth.
Kanekapolei.	Kaoleiaku.	{ Konia, wife of Paki Kanuha. Keolaokalani.	Bernice

3. The Family of KAMEHAMEHA, King of N. Hawaii, 1781, and of the Islands, 1795—1819.

Wives.	Children.	Children-in-law.	Grand Children.
KAAHUMANU, Regent, 1824—32.	{ LIHOLIHO KAMEHAMEHE II. King 1819—24.	{ Kamamalu, Kinau. Kekauluohi, Kekauonohi, Pauahi.	
Keopuolani.	KAUIKEAOULI KAMEHAMEHA III. King of the Islands, from 1824.	Kalama.	
	Nahienaena, Princess.	Keolaokalani.	
Kalakua.	{ Kamamalu. Kinau, Prem., 1832—9.	Kekuanaoa, Gov. of Oahu, from 1835.	{ Moses Kekuaiwa. Lot Kamehameha. Alexander Liholiho, Heir apparent. Victoria Kamehamalu
Kekauluohi, and 17 others			

CHAPTER IV.

FIRST YEAR OF THE MISSION, AND SECOND OF LIHOLIHO.—1820.

Missionaries' first intercourse with the natives.—Visit of chiefs to the Brig by double canoes.—Deserted Temple at Kawaihae.—Sermon.—Arrival at Kailua.—Villagers. —Visit and proposals to the king.—Royal Family.—High Priest.—Visit of Royal Family on board.—Admission of the Mission.—Debarkation of Mr. T. and Dr. H. —Arrival at Oahu.—Description of Honolulu, and adjacent country.—Governor Boki.—Intemperance,—Debarkation and location of Missionaries.—First Sabbath on shore at Oahu.—Visit of Messrs. Whitney & Ruggles to Kauai—Reception of George by his father.—Settlement of the Mission there.

On the 31st of March, a considerable number of the natives came off to our vessel, from the shores of Kohala, to dispose of their little articles of barter, and to look at the strangers. Their manœuvres in their canoes, some being propelled by short paddles, and some by small sails, attracted the attention of our little group, and for a moment, gratified curiosity; but the appearance of destitution, degradation, and barbarism, among the chattering, and almost naked savages, whose heads and feet, and much of their sunburnt swarthy skins, were bare, was appalling. Some of our number, with gushing tears, turned away from the spectacle. Others with firmer nerve continued their gaze, but were ready to exclaim, " Can these be human beings! How dark and comfortless their state of mind and heart! How imminent the danger to the immortal soul, shrouded in this deep pagan gloom! Can such beings be civilized? Can they be Christianized? Can we throw ourselves upon these rude shores, and take up our abode, for life, among such a people, for the purpose of training them for heaven?" *Yes.* Though faith had to struggle for the victory, these interrogatories could all be answered decidedly in the affirmative. At sunset they returned to their dark cabins, and we passed along a little further south.

On the 1st of April, as we were abreast of Kawaihae, Kalanimoku and his wives, and Kalakua (subsequently Hoapiliwahine) and her sister Namahana (sometimes Opiia), two of the widows of the late king, came off to us with their loquacious attendants, in their double canoe. It was propelled with spirit, by eighteen or twenty athletic men. Having over their heads a huge Chinese umbrella, and the nodding *kahilis* or plumed rods of the nobility, they made a novel and imposing appearance as they drew near our becalmed Mission Barque, while we fixed on them, and their movements, our scrutinizing gaze. As they were welcomed on board, the felicitous native compliment, *aloha* (good-will, peace, affection), with shaking hands, passed between them, and each member of the mission family, Captain Blanchard and others. Their tall, portly, ponderous appearance seemed to indicate a different race from those who had visited the vessel before, or a decided superiority of the nobility over the peasantry. Their weight has I think been overrated. The younger brother of these queens, on coming to maturity, balanced in the scales two peculs of their sandal wood, 266⅔lbs.—This was about the weight of Kalanimoku, and may be regarded as the average weight of the chiefs of the islands, male and female. Kalanimoku was distinguished from almost the whole nation, by being decently clad. His dress, put on for the occasion, consisted of a white dimity roundabout, a black silk vest, yellow Nankeen pants, shoes, and white cotton hose, plaid cravat, and fur hat."*   One of the bare-footed females of rank, soon threw off her printed cotton gown, to which she was unused, retaining a gingham shirt, and the customary Hawaiian robe for a female of rank. This consisted of ten thicknesses of thin unwoven bark cloth, three or four yards in length, and thirty inches in breadth, laid together, and tacked by single stitches, at several places, through the upper edge. It is worn by being wrapped several times round the middle, and having the upper or stitched edge turned over a little on the hip, to confine the outer end, and keep the whole from falling off. It would be difficult to say which party was most impressed with the novelty of the objects they beheld. Kalanimoku was much attracted by the *kamalii keokeo* [white children], and all were struck with the first appearance of civilized women.

Happy in so early and pleasant an introduction to personages of so much influence, we were assiduous in our efforts to impress them favorably, making them acquainted with our business, and our wish to reside in the country. But, notwithstanding our solicitude to obtain Kalanimoku's assent at once, he referred us to the king. As a token of friendship and confidence, he presented us a curiously wrought spear, a signal, we hoped, that their weapons of war were soon to be converted into implements of husbandry, and their warriors enlisted as soldiers of the Lord Jesus Christ.

Near sunset, our distinguished guests took leave and returned to the shore on their state vehicle—their double canoe, seated on a light narrow scaffolding which rested on the semi-elliptical timbers by which two large parallel canoes, each neatly carved from a tree, are yoked together, five or six feet apart. Their large canoes are two to three feet in depth, and thirty to fifty in length. The thin sides are raised by the addition of a nicely

---

* Articles of apparel had in some instances been given to the chiefs, or obtained by the late king in barter for sandal wood, but were in the main useless.

fitted waist-board. Additional pieces of thin wood, ingeniously carved, are attached at the ends, covering a few feet as a deck turning up some fifteen inches at the extremity, and giving the appearance of greater finish, beauty and utility.

The favored passengers on a Hawaiian double canoe sit three or four feet above the surface of the water, while the rowers sit on thwarts in the canoe with their feet below the surface and their faces forward. The steersmen sit in the stern. Their paddles have a round handle from three to four feet long, and a thin blade from twelve to eighteen inches long and eight to twelve wide, and are grasped by one hand at the extreme end, and by the other, near the blade, and are used by main strength.

The chiefs, on this occasion, were rowed off with spirit by nine or ten athletic men in each of the coupled canoes, making regular, rapid and effective strokes, all on one side for a while, then, changing at a signal in exact time, all on the other. Each raising his head erect, and lifting one hand high to throw the paddle blade forward beside the canoe, the rowers, dipping their blades, and bowing simultaneously and earnestly, swept their paddles back with naked muscular arms, making the brine boil, and giving great speed to their novel and serviceable sea-craft. These grandees and their ambitious rowers, gave us a pleasing indication of the physical capacity, at least, of the people whom we were desirous to enlighten, and to whose necessities we rejoiced to know the Gospel to be adapted. As they disappeared, the sun sank to his western ocean bed towards populous China, and the full orbed moon, brightly reflecting his light, rose majestically from the east, over the dark Pagan mountains of Hawaii, symbolizing the approach of the mission Church, designed to be the reflector of the sun-light of Christianity upon that benighted nation. Then, ere the excitement of the chiefs' visit was over, Mr. Thurston and his yoke-fellow ascended the shrouds, and, standing upon the main-top (the mission family, captain and crew being on deck), as we gently floated along on the smooth silent sea, under the lee of Hawaii's dark shores, sang a favorite song of Zion (Melton Mowbray), which they had sung at their ordination at Goshen, and with the Park St. Church choir, at Boston, on the day of embarkation.

" Head of the Church triumphant,
    We joyfully adore thee:
        Till thou appear,
        Thy members here,
    Shall sing like those in glory :
    We lift our hearts and voices,
    In blest anticipation,
        And cry aloud,
        And give to God
    The praise of our salvation.

While in affliction's furnace,
And passing through the fire,
  Thy love we praise,
  That knows our days,
And ever brings us nigher:
We clap our hands, exulting
In thine almighty favor ;
  The love divine,
  That made us thine
Shall keep us thine for ever.

Thou dost conduct thy people,
Through torrents of temptation ;
  Nor will we fear,
  While thou art near,
The fire of tribulation :
The world with sin and Satan,
In vain our march opposes ;
  By thee we shall
  Break through them all,
And sing ' the song of Moses.'

By faith we see the glory
To which thou shalt restore us ;
  The cross despise,
  For that high prize,
Which thou hast set before us:
And if thou count us worthy,
We each, as dying Stephen,
  Shall see thee stand
  At God's right hand,
To take us up to Heaven."

The next morning, our brig being in Kawaihae bay, I made my first visit on shore, landed on the beach near where Keoua and his companions had been murdered, and called on Kalanimoku at his thatched hut or cottage in that small uninviting village. With him, I visited Puukahola, the large heathen temple at that place, a monument of folly, superstition and madness, which the idolatrous conqueror and his murderous priests had consecrated with human blood to the senseless deities of Pagan Hawaii. Built on a rough hill, a little way from the shore of the bay, it occupied an area about 240 feet in length, and 120 in breadth, and appeared as much like a fort as a church. On the ends and inland side of the parallelogram, the walls, of loose black stone or fragments of lava, were 15 feet high, 10 feet thick at the bottom, and 5 at the top. On the side towards the sea, the wall consisted of several terraces on the declivity of the hill, rising from some 20 feet below the enclosed area, to a little above it. The frowning structure is so large and prominent, that it can be distinctly seen with the naked eye, from the top of Maunakea, a distance of about 32 miles. As a fortification of Satan's kingdom, its design was more for war against the human species than the worship of the Creator.

This monument of idolatry, I surveyed with mingled emotions of grief, horror, pity, regret, gratitude, and hope ;—of grief and horror at the enormities which men and devils had perpetrated there before high heaven ;—of pity and regret that the victims and many of the builders and worshippers, had gone to their account without the knowledge of the Gospel, which ought to have been conveyed to them ; of gratitude, that this strong-hold of Satan had been demolished and the spell around it broken ; and of hope, that soon temples to the living God would take the place of these altars of heathen abomination.

After this brief survey of this part of the field, Kalanimoku, his wives, and two of the widows of Kamehameha, embarked with us ; and as we together proceeded toward Kailua, the residence of the king, we engaged in public worship, and dwelt with pleasure on the glorious theme, the design of the Messiah to establish his universal reign, and to bring the *isles* to submit to him, and rejoice in his grace, as indicated by the language of the Prophet Isaiah, " He shall not fail nor be discouraged till he have set judgment in the earth, *and the isles shall wait for his law."*

Kalakua, a widow of Kamehameha, having little sympathy with the Evangelical prophet, and shrewdly aiming to see what the *white women* could do for her temporal benefit, asked them to make a gown for her in fashion like their own. Putting her off till the Sabbath was over, apprising her that unnecessary labor was on that day prohibited to all by the great Jehovah whom we worshipped, they cheerfully plied scissors and needle the next day, and soon fitted out the rude giantess with a white cambric dress. Thus, feeble, voyage-worn, having been long without fresh provisions, and withering under a tropical sun as they crossed the equatorial regions the second time, they began before we cast anchor, to secure favor by kindness and demonstration of their ability and readiness to make themselves useful.

As we coasted slowly along southward, we had a grand view of Hualalai, the volcanic mountain that rises some eight or nine thousand feet, near the western side of Hawaii, with its terminal crater, its forests, and apparently recent streams of lava. Becalmed in sight of the king's residence, we were once more allowed on the morrow to unite with thousands of our friends whose sympathies and supplications had followed us, in observing the monthly concert of prayer for the conversion of the world, mingling thanksgiving for our safe and opportune arrival, with petitions that an abundant entrance among these Gentiles might be ministered to us, and that our service for them might be soon and joyfully accepted.

On the morning of the 4th of April, 163 days from Boston, we came to anchor, abreast of the village of Kailua. Between our mooring and the shore, a great number of the natives—men, women and children, from the highest to the lowest rank, including the king and his mother, were amusing themselves in the water.

This large heathen village of thatched huts, though in a dry and sterile spot, is ornamented with cocoanut and Kou trees, which to the eye form a relief. A few miles inland, trees and plantations are numerous; then, still further back, rises the forest-covered Mauna Hualalai, with its lofty terminal crater, now extinct.

As we proceeded to the shore, the multitudinous, shouting, and almost naked natives, of every age, sex, and rank, swimming, floating on surf-boards, sailing in canoes, sitting, lounging, standing, running like sheep, dancing, or laboring on shore, attracted our earnest attention, and exhibited the appalling darkness of the land which we had come to enlighten. Here, in many groups, appeared a just representation of a nation of 130-000 souls, in as deep degradation, ignorance, pollution and destitution as if the riches of salvation, and the light of heavenly glory, had never been provided to enrich and enlighten their souls. There, with occasion for sympathy, and deep solicitude, the pioneer missionaries

> " Saw men, immortal men
> Wide wandering from the way, eclipsed in night,
> Dark, moonless, moral night, living like beasts,
> Like beasts descending to the grave, untaught
> Of life to come, unsanctified, unsaved."

Among the hundreds on the beach, where we landed, was the tall, portly, gigantic figure of a native chieftain, in his prime, Kuakini, the brother of Kaahumanu, and subsequently, the governor of Hawaii, who invited us to his house.

After a short call there, and another at Mr. John Young's, we eagerly sought the king, at his dingy, unfurnished, thatched habitation, where we found him returned from his sea-bathing. On our being introduced to him, he, with a smile, gave us the customary " Aloha."

As ambassadors of the King of Heaven, having the most important message to communicate, which he could receive, we made to him the offer of the Gospel of eternal life, and proposed to teach him and his people the written, life-giving Word of the God of Heaven. We made known to him the kind wishes of the American Board, and its friends, and asked permission to settle in his country, for the purpose of teaching the nation Christianity, literature and the arts.

He was slow to consent, as might have been expected. Having abolished the public rites of their ancient religion; and seen his sovereignty threatened by a powerful party, as the consequence, he could not know but that the followers of a new religion might as fearlessly oppose his will, or interfere with his pride and lusts, either to restrain them or to bring them into contempt. He and the leading chiefs had just begun an experiment, like what some equally vain philosophers have often desired, and sometimes recommended,—to rule a nation without any public recognition of religious obligation, or any respect to the religious views of the people to be governed. He might have been alarmed or made indignant by so bold and urgent an attempt by the people of a great nation, to introduce a new and uncompromising religion among his subjects. But he was willing, at least, to consider our proposition. We returned to our vessel, spread the cause again before the Lord, and the next day, renewed our efforts to gain the desired consent of the king and chiefs. We presented his majesty an elegant copy of the Bible, furnished by the American Bible Society (intended for the conqueror), which we had the happiness to convey and deliver to his royal son. It contained the laws, the ritual, and the records of the new religion—the grand message of salvation which we proposed freely to publish, and teach the nation to read, understand and follow. Thus commenced the kind and provident care of the American Bible Society for that benighted nation ; a care, which has continued to flourish to this day. The thought of such a present, to such a personage, at this juncture, by that noble institution whose fraternal co-operation with missionary societies, is so uniformly valuable, was exceedingly felicitous. The king seemed pleased to be thus complimented, though he could not read.

Bibles, furnished by friends for the purpose, were presented to the daughters of Kamehameha, and a good optical instrument from the Board to the king. Presents, in such circumstances, have doubtless a winning influence, as missionaries are taught by the patriarch Jacob, who understood well the power of a gift, as a pledge of peace ; for when he was about to meet his offended, warlike, and perhaps implacable brother, he, with supplication, painstaking, tokens of respect, and a *present*, " prevailed," and left the world a most impressive example for imitation, in uniting self-sacrifice, prayer, and appropriate means for winning souls, and elevating heathen nations.

At this time, we had not the means of knowing fully the standing and influence of Kaahumanu, and perhaps lost time and opportunities on that account ; but we soon learned to appreciate her importance in the nation.

The king and his four mothers, and five wives, and little brother and sister, constituted the royal family, if such a group can properly be called a family. Two of his wives, Kamamalu, and Kinau, were his father's daughters ; and a third, Kekauluohi, a half-sister of theirs, had been his father's wife.

Though in this royal family circle, and its honored connexions, there were natural powers, which, if they could be well directed, we believed were of great promise to the nation, to the world, and to themselves for the world to come, yet they and the nation had, on our arrival, neither book, pen, nor pencil for amusement or business, or for acquiring information, or communicating thought. They sat, like Turks or tailors, on mats spread on the ground, dipped their fingers in the dish to eat their fish, poi, and dog flesh, without knife, fork, or spoon. They stretched themselves at full length on the mats, to play cards, and otherwise kill time. Their water they drank from a gourd shell, and *awa*, the juice of a narcotic root chewed by others, and mixed with water in the chewers' mouths, they drank as their fathers had done, from a cocoanut shell, for the same purpose that other intoxicating drugs and liquors are taken.

Being a polygamist, as many of the chiefs were, the king doubtless felt what he expressed as an objection to our settlement ;—" If I receive and patronize these missionaries, I shall not be allowed but one wife." As our observed practice had probably suggested the objection, we allowed our practice for the time being to give the true answer. Another grave objection was urged, that the Government of Great Britain might not be pleased with the settlement of American missionaries at the Sandwich Islands. Captain Blanchard, of the Thaddeus, expresses the opinion that this objection came from Mr. John Young. To meet this, we referred to our public and private instruction as to the nature of our embassy. We alleged that our mission was approved by English missionaries, and their directors, that it was not our intention to interfere with the government or trade of the islands, that there was no collision between Great Britain and the United States, and if there were, it did not prevent American missionaries from engaging as missionaries even in the British dominions. These considerations seemed to satisfy the chiefs. Kamamalu interceded with her husband for us. Some of the chiefs proposed to Mr. Young to write to Great Britain, to prevent any misunderstanding there, in respect to the admission of American missionaries.

Hewahewa, the high priest, expressed most unexpectedly his gratification on meeting us, but, as he was, like his master, addicted to the excessive use of intoxicating liquors, awa and rum, we could have little confidence in his professions. But it was a matter of wonder that the bloody destroyer of his country-men, whose influence, more than that of any other man, we had dreaded, should be ready in any sense to welcome the teachers of a new religion. Still he seemed an object of pity, almost as hopeless as if he had been ready by a form of argument zealously to defend their ancient system of idolatry and ceremonial customs.

While the question of our settlement was pending, we invited and received the royal family on board the brig to dine. They came off in their double canoe, with waving *kahilis* and a retinue of attendants. His majesty, according to the taste of the time, having a *malo* or narrow girdle around his waist, a green silken scarf over his shoulders, instead of coat, vest, and linen, a string of large beads on his otherwise naked neck, and a feather wreath or corona on his head,—to say nothing of his being destitute of hat, gloves, shoes, stockings, and pants,—was introduced to the first company of white women whom he ever saw. Happy to show civilities to this company, at our own table, we placed the king at the head of it, and implored the blessing of the King of kings, upon our food, and on the interview. All assembled on the quarter-deck of the Thaddeus; and the mission family with the aid of a bass-viol, played by George P. Kaumualii, and of the voices of the captain and officers, sang hymns of praise.

Apparently pleased with this exercise, and with their interview with the strangers, our royal visitors gave us a friendly parting *aloha*, and returned with favorable impressions of the singular group of newcomers, who were seeking among them an abode in their isolated territories.

On the 7th, several of the brethren and sisters visited the king and chiefs, endeavoring to make their acquaintance and secure their confidence. On the 8th, we felt it necessary to ask of the king that a part of our mission might disembark at Kailua, and the rest at Honolulu, believing that it would be far better than for us all to leave the king, and go to Oahu, or for all to remain with him at Kailua, which he was proposing to leave ere long. So far as we could learn, Honolulu ought to be early occupied.

To this proposition the king replied, " White men all prefer Oahu. I think the Americans would like to have that island." This was disheartening; but for our comfort, he gave us permission all to land at Kailua, and offered us a temporary shelter in an extensive, barn-like, thatched structure, without floor, ceiling, partition, windows or furniture. We examined it to see if it were possible to lodge a mission-family of twenty-two individuals, in such a hovel, to make them reasonably comfortable there, where water for drinking and cooking would need to be brought four miles by hand, and at the same time, be all advantageously situated for doing the work for which we came. We hesitated. Captain Blanchard urged us to debark, the next day. We declined. We assured his majesty, that Jehovah has a tabu, once in seven days, and we were not permitted to remove our effects from the ship during his sacred time.

We improved the Holy Sabbath in endeavoring to encourage our hearts to meet, and turn to good account all the trials of our faith, which are appointed by Divine wisdom and goodness.

On Monday morning, the 10th of April, all the brethren repaired to the shore, to do what was practicable to get the royal permission to station part of the mission at Kailua, and the rest at Oahu. On renewing our application, the king said he should wait till the return of Kaahumanu. She had gone out on a fishing excursion. We sought again the co-operation of Kalanimoku, who had unexpectedly returned to the place. Quite beyond our expectation too, Kaahumanu, whose concurrence was indispensable, arrived in the afternoon. Keeaumoku, her brother also, who it was supposed would, were he present, favor our wishes, and, for whom solicitude had, for some days been felt, lest in a late gale he had been driven out to sea and lost, landed safely at Kailua. We could hardly help exclaiming, the Lord is on our side, and will now grant us our request.

With hearts burning with the desire to be advantageously and speedily settled down in our work, we seized such opportunities as from morning till 4 P. M., were afforded us, in various ways, for making ourselves understood, without rudely giving offence. We reasoned with individual chiefs, and requested an audience at their council. When several of the leading chiefs had assented, and we supposed the king and Kaahumanu were ready to attend to our business, which we came once more to lay before them, to our disappointment, two native dancers appeared near the king's dwelling, and a band of rude musicians, singing, and drumming on calabashes, probably by the king's order. As they commenced, multitudes thronged around to witness this heathen *hula* or out-door dance, which occupied the attention of the king and chiefs, and plebeians, for a time that seemed indeed long to us, and to our captain, who was impatient to prosecute his voyage.

Just at sunset, Kaahumanu and the king gave us the opportunity of freely stating to them our wishes. The whole subject of our location was reconsidered. The reasons for our coming to the country were recapitulated, the useful arts with which the missionaries were acquainted, were at the king's request enumerated. The considerations in favor of entering on our labors both at Hawaii and Oahu, were presented; the inquiries of their majesties, respecting our business, and our qualifications to promote their temporal good, frankly answered, and our hopes and wishes expressed, that they would give our proposal due consideration, and early grant us a favorable answer. This done, we gave them our *aloha*, and left them to hold a consultation among themselves by night.

Mr. Young told us we might think ourselves fortunate if they should decide in our favor in six months, and if they pursued their ordinary mode of doing business, we must not expect a definitive answer sooner. It was indeed to them a great question, entirely new, and of momentous and lasting consequences. Unwilling to wait six months for permission to debark, and locate ourselves in situations favorable for making our experiment, we on the morrow sought permission to take such situations for a *year*, a very short probation for such an experiment. This the king granted, not only permitting us to reside and labor at different islands, but offering us such a shelter as the grassy huts of the country afforded, and such protection as in their rude and degraded state he could give. This was as much as it was prudent to ask at the time. It was the pleasure of the king that our physician, Dr. Holman, one preacher, and two of the native helpers, should be located at Kailua, and the others at Honolulu, Oahu ; but that we should send for no more missionaries, till our experiment had been made and approved. This arrangement was hailed by the mission with thanksgiving, and no time was lost in carrying it into execution.

Thus, by a careful, persevering, and thorough consultation with the highest authorities, and their deliberate action after twelve days' intercourse, did our mission acquire the right to enter that field, and begin their work, with the formal and express approbation of the sovereign of the country, who himself designed to receive instruction from the missionaries, and commenced without delay. These facts will be seen to assume additional importance in the progress of events at the islands.

On the 12th of April, fourteen days from the time of our making the islands, we planted a detachment of the mission at Kailua, and set up a banner there in the name of our God. The king, having expressed so decided a wish to have our physician at his place, we could hesitate little as to his location there, though six men, five women, and five children of the family, were to proceed, some a hundred and forty-five miles, and some two hundred and forty-five miles, further, and notwithstanding the opportunities for inter-communication were unfrequent, irregular, and uncertain. Thomas Hopu, and William Kanui, were taken into the service and the train of the king. The choice of one of the two preachers to be stationed there was settled by the ballot of the brethren, and Mr. Thurston was, to the satisfaction of the parties, assigned to that station, to which, with little interruption, he has been thus far attached. The day was mostly occupied in selecting and dividing for them and removing to the shore such things as belonged or fell to them, and were needful for their immediate use. After tea, on board the brig, Mr. and Mrs. Thurston, and Dr. and Mrs. Holman, took a cheerful leave of the rest of the family, and debarked. I accompanied them to their lodgings. A small thatched hut was by the king's order appropriated for their accommodation, if such a frail hut, $3\frac{1}{2}$ feet high at the foot of the rafters, without flooring, ceiling, windows, or furniture, infested with vermin, in the midst of a noisy, filthy, heathen village, can be said to be for the *accommodation* of two families just exiled from one of the happiest countries in the world. Nor should it be thought very strange if some of them should soon cherish a desire to be a little further from such accommodations. In these untried, singular, and trying circumstances, they entered their new abode to commence their missionary work. They were then commended to the grace and protection of Him who had called us to his work, promised his presence to the obedient, and had guided them to that place, and they were left to the toils and privations and privileges of foreign missionaries, on a barbarous, heathen island, where no other Christian family or civilized female could be found.

Thomas Hopu and Wm. Kanui being accommodated by their countrymen, were pleased with their reception and location.

As I called to take leave of the king late in the evening, to go on board the Thaddeus, I was gratified to see that he was so soon ready to try to acquire the art of spelling and reading our language, though unable to speak it, or to read his own or any other.

Taking up our anchor, we sailed, and bore away to the north-west towards Oahu. Passing to the south-westward of the intermediate islands of Maui, Molokini, Kahoolawe, Lanai, and Molokai, we left them on our right, and reached Oahu in 36 hours. Early in the morning of the 14th April, that island rose to our view, and, as we approached rapidly, presented successively its pointed mountains, covered with trees and shrubbery, its well-marked, extinguished craters near its shores, its grass covered hills, and more fertile valleys, its dingy thatched villages, its cocoanut groves, its fort and harbor, and its swarthy inhabitants in throngs— the primary objects of our attention and concern. We cast anchor in the roadstead abreast of Honolulu village, on the south side of the island, about 17 miles from the eastern extremity. This we regarded as the termination of our voyage, whose length in time was 25 weeks, and in distance run, 18,000 miles.

By the blessing of God, almost beyond expectation, we had been brought thus far on our way unharmed.

With some of my associates I went early on shore, to call on the authorities, pay our respects, and to acquaint them with the arrangements already made with the king at Hawaii. Calling on the interpreter, Mr. Marin, a Spanish settler, we learned that Boki, the governor, a younger brother of Kalanimoku, was at a distant part of the island. We stated our wish to see him in respect to our landing, and our prominent design to teach the people Christianity.

Admitting that the " salvation of the soul was an important object," the interpreter soon despatched two Hawaiian messengers to make speed and apprise the governor of our arrival and of our design.

Meantime, we paid our respects to the second in authority at Honolulu. He appeared to be the commander of the fort or castle. This was a rude, quadrangular structure of loosely built walls, ten or twelve feet high, and about as thick as they were high. It enclosed an area of about one acre and three-quarters, mounted a considerable number of guns, and had a small magazine, and several thatched huts within it. It is situated at the brink of the harbor, and near the landing.

Passing through the irregular village of some thousands of inhabitants, whose grass thatched habitations were mostly small and mean, while some were more spacious, we walked about a mile northwardly to the opening of the valley of Pauoa, then

View of the southern side of Oahu from Ewa   Page 93

turning south-easterly, ascended to the top of Punchbowl Hill, an extinguished crater, whose base bounds the north-east part of the village or town. Its general form is a truncated cone, having a base of one third of a mile, a height of five or six hundred feet, and a concave or broad basin-like top, about three hundred yards in diameter. From the highest part of the rim we had a beautiful view of the village and valley of Honolulu, the harbor and ocean, and of the principal mountains of the island. On the east were the plain and groves of Waikiki, with its amphitheatre of hills, the south-eastern of which is Diamond Hill,—the crater of an extinct volcano, in the form of a cone, truncated, fluted, and reeded, larger, higher, and more concave than Punchbowl Hill, but of much the same model and general character. Below us, on the south and west, spread the plain of Honolulu, having its fish-ponds and salt making pools along the sea-shore, the village and fort between us and the harbor, and the valley stretching a few miles north into the interior, which presented its scattered habitations and numerous beds of *kalo* (*arum esculentum*) in its various stages of growth, with its large green leaves, beautifully embossed on the silvery water, in which it flourishes. Through this valley, several streams descending from the mountains in the interior, wind their way, some six or seven miles, watering and overflowing by means of numerous artificial canals, the bottoms of kalo patches, and then, by one mouth, fall into the peaceful harbor. From Diamond Hill, on the east, to Barber's Point and the mountains of Waianae, on the west, lay the sea-board plain, some twenty-five miles in length, which embraces the volcanic hills of Moanalua, two or three hundred feet high, and among them, a singular little lake of sea-water, abounding in salt crystalized through evaporation by the heat of the sun, the ravine of Moanalua, the lagoon of Ewa, and numerous little plantations and hamlets, scattered trees, and cocoanut groves. A range of mountains, three or four thousand feet high, stretches across the south-western part of the island, at the distance of twenty-five miles. Another range, from two to four thousand feet high, stretches from the north-western to the eastern extremity of the island. Konahuanui, the highest peak, rises back of Punchbowl Hill, and north by east from Honolulu, eight miles distant, and four thousand feet high, often touching or sustaining, as it were, a cloud.

The whole was to us a novel scene, not indeed like that presented to Moses when he ascended to the top of Pisgah, and surveyed the land of promise, with the earnest desire, but forbidden hope of entering it, even to exterminate its insufferable idolatry, and to establish there the seed of Abraham. It was to us interesting, partly from its novelty, singularity, and natural beauty, its volcanic character, its commercial importance, its peculiar location in the midst of the Pacific Ocean, its distance from the palaces of Zion and the abodes of civilization, but chiefly as the dwelling-place of some thousands of the heathen, to whom we were commissioned to offer salvation, and as the contemplated seat of government, and centre of operations for the nation. It was interesting, because, having been for ages past the battle-field of successive hostile bands of pagan warriors, till the last victory of Kamehameha, it was now to be the scene of a bloodless conquest for Christ, where his ignorant, debased, rebellious, and dying foes, were to be instructed, elevated, reconciled, and saved. With all its mental and moral darkness, and heathen pollution, like that of the whole group, it was contemplated as a scene of peculiar and thrilling interest, as a field of toil and privation, of various conflicts, and probably, of death to us, but of triumphs to the gospel, where heathenism was to be extirpated, and churches were to be planted, watered, and made to flourish, enjoying the presence, and reflecting the glory of the Redeemer of the nations, to whom the Hawaiian tribes, though they had not acknowledged his claims, or heard of his love, had long since been promised.

Who, among the true sons and daughters of Zion, looking upon such an open field, where Satan, by his varied malevolent agencies, had ruled and ruined generation after generation, would not exult in the opportunity of approaching these inhabitants with the varied Christian agency of the school, the pulpit, and the press, teaching, inviting, and persuading them to come under the protection, submit to the authority, and enlist in the service of the Prince of Peace? What evangelical local church in Christendom would not rejoice to employ an agent to rear there the altar and temple of the Lord, on the ruins of idolatry?

We returned at evening, presenting to the rest of our company fresh productions of the soil, and our report of the land of which we were to take possession.

It was not till the 16th, that Governor Boki returned to Honolulu; and he was then so much under the debasing and distracting influence of strong drink as to be unfit for business, except that of a speedy reformation, to which our business would call him. Intemperance among men without intelligence, and destitute of attachment to the charities and privileges of well regulated society, is as stubborn a foe as any species of idolatry. But this foe, emboldened by many foreign traders and visitors, showed his appalling front and gigantic strength wherever we approached, and for years stood dauntless to guard the field.

On the 17th of April, corresponding with the day when the persecuted Reformer stood before Charles V. in the Diet at Worms, we had an interview with the governor, who exhibited great but not unexpected indifference to our main object, gave permission to enter the harbor, but appeared in no haste to attend to the general orders from head-quarters, respecting our accommodations; and months elapsed before he furnished our promised lodgings. On the 18th we came with our vessel through the opening in the coral-reef—a singular gateway for ships, between the two disjoined parts, which extend along parallel with the shore, several miles each way. On these disjoined parts of the reef, the surf is constantly breaking with more or less violence, but they so effectually oppose the force of the heaving ocean, as at all times to afford protection from its waves to vessels that fully enter.

Here we dropped anchor in the peaceful waters of this safe and commodious harbor, the best in this part of the world. It is sufficiently large to admit 150 sail, of the capacity of 100 to 700 tons. The depth of water at the bar, or mouth of the harbor, being little more than twenty feet, and little affected by the tide, the largest class of ships could not pass in and out with safety, without under-girders, or camels, to buoy them up.

The wives of the missionaries soon accompanied their husbands on shore, to look at the thatched cottages that had been offered by foreigners, for our temporary accommodation.

White women were, as might have been expected, objects of great curiosity to the chattering natives, who thronged around them, as they walked along, to gaze at their costume, their white hands and faces, running before them and peering under their projecting bonnets, laughing, shouting, trotting around with bare feet, heads and limbs, men, women and children, and singing out occasionally, "*A-i-oe-oe*," a phrase signifying long, protruding neck. This term they doubtless applied from the appearance occasioned by the large, projecting fore-parts of the bonnets, in the fashion of 1819, so widely different from that of Hawaiian females, whose heads were usually bare, but occasionally ornamented with a simple chaplet of natural flowers, or small feathers.

The arrangement being now completed for it, on the 19th of April, the missionaries disembarked from that floating Bethel, which had been the home and sanctuary of our little missionary Church for about six months. Committing ourselves to the care and protection of our ever-watchful Heavenly Father, and putting ourselves into the power of strangers and pagans, untutored, and destitute almost of the feeling of moral responsibility; intemperate, lewd, and thievish, as they were, we unhesitatingly entered on this new mode of life among them, and as missionary pilgrims, cheerfully took up our abode in that dark, ruined land, which we looked upon as the place of our sojourn and toil while on earth, and as the resting-place of our bones, when our brief pilgrimage should end. We were sheltered in three native-built houses, kindly offered us by Messrs. Winship, Lewis and Navarro, somewhat scattered in the midst of an irregular village or town of thatched huts, of 3000 or 4000 inhabitants. After the fatigue of removing from the brig to the shore, Captain Pigot of New York considerately and kindly gave us, at evening, a hospitable cup of tea, truly acceptable to poor pilgrims in our circumstances, so far from the sympathies of home. As soon as the bustle of debarking

was over, and our grass-thatched cottages made habitable, we
erected an altar unto the Omnipresent God, and in unison with
the first detachment of the mission, presented him our offerings
of thanksgiving and praise for his goodness to us, and his wonderful providences in respect to the Pagan sons and daughters of
Hawaii, among whom he had granted us so propitious an
entrance.

We had some repose the first night. The heathen garrison, at
the fort, some thirty rods distant, having an hour-glass for a time-
keeper, about once an hour during the night, struck a bell,
and gave a loud shout, in a mongrel dialect, signifying " All's
well !"

We rose on the 20th, for the first time from our couches spread
on heathen ground, under new obligations of gratitude to the
Watchman of Israel, who kept our frail habitations in peace, our
minds from agitation, and our hearts from despondency.

With very little furniture of any sort, having scarcely more than
one chair among us all, the brig having been too much crowded
to carry them, and there being none in that market, and scarcely
one in the whole nation ; with neither floor nor ceiling, neither
chimney nor fire-place in our habitation, we commenced house-
keeping at once, accommodating ourselves cheerfully to our circumstances, and aiming to improve them as we should find
opportunity, applied ourselves to the great business for which we
had been sent thither.   Had there been a boarding-house at hand
suitable for our families, we might, perhaps, have done well to
avail ourselves for a time of its advantages.   But as everything in
the way of civilization, as well as religion, was to be taught the
people, both by example and precept, and as there was no time
to be lost in beginning, our cooking-stove was set up out of doors,
in the yard near one of our houses, surrounded with a light fence
or paling of slender poles set perpendicularly in close order in
the earth, having two horizontal ranges of poles tied to them with
bark or vines, or strings made of a strong grass, one a foot, and
the other four feet from the ground.   Through this paling
from fifty to a hundred natives, standing around without, might,
from time to time, be seen looking leisurely, to gratify their curiosity, especially when any of the missionary females found it
necessary to be employed about the stove, either for cooking,
or heating smoothing-irons, for ironing clothes.

Destitute of table furniture, as well as of many other articles
which were needful, we had this consolation, that a full supply,
without a house, cellar, or store-room, would have been a burden,
and a means of exposure to thieves and robbers.   A small crate of
crockery sent out with us, supposed to be good, was found to be
wholly refuse, embracing no whole article, but still, in our destitution, better than nothing, and less likely to provoke envy, or
excite the cupidity of rogues, which was too often called into
exercise by the few good things which we did possess.

Soon the Sabbath morning sun, having always a peculiar charm, rose upon us in unusual splendor, and arrangements were made for the public worship of Jehovah, whose claims we came to present.

With what comfort and courage did we seize on the opportunity afforded us, to bring to the notice of the people the sacred day of God, and on the first Sabbath that dawned on us in our new abode, to announce to those, who, both native and foreign, assembled at our call, the general object of our mission, adopting the language of the heavenly messenger to the shepherds of Judea: "Fear not, for behold I bring you good tidings of great joy, which shall be to all people."

The theme, the occasion, the cheering prospect of success, the dawning light of a brighter day, the Sabbath songs of Zion, now *beginning here*, and the momentous announcement, as from Heaven, of the glad news of salvation to our race, now first reaching the inhabitants of this dark heathen isle, inspired our souls with new ardor and joyousness. He who was born in the city of David, a Savior, favored us with his presence, in fulfilment of his promise to the propagators of his Gospel, " Lo, I am with you always."

On the succeeding Sabbath, a similar opportunity occurred, when the songs of Zion, with the presence of Zion's King, drew tears from a veteran resident, a self-expatriated American, who had not heard them before for twenty years, and who had a native wife, and a family of sons and daughters around him there, now to be taught the things of the world to come.

In these sacred songs, George P. Kaumualii assisted both by his voice and the bass-viol. They appeared attractive to native ears, as well as to the naturalized foreigner, who had seen better days.

Young Kaumualii was in haste to meet his father, and we as much to enlist him in our cause. It was quickly agreed that a detachment should visit that part of the group of which we regarded him as sovereign, a hundred miles to the north-west of Honolulu. In conformity with the reasonable wishes of George, properly expressed, Messrs. Whitney and Ruggles, with the concurrence of their associates, leaving their wives at Honolulu, embarked with him, and accompanied him to his father, to make known to him our object, explore that part of our field, and secure the friendship and co-operation of its chieftain. George took leave of the family with tears, though we had no good evidence that his heart was interested in religion, more than thousands of the gay youth of our country, who unduly rejoice in their freedom from the restraints of covenant religious vows. He was often courteous and affectionate in America, while at school. His tears on this occasion were, I think, tears of affection for his friends, who had shown him kindness; of hope of soon being restored with welcome to his father, from whom he had been separated in his childhood; and, perhaps, of struggling apprehension that he would not be permitted long to enjoy the society of his father, or at all to succeed him in the expected possession of his rank and estates. He felt strong dissatisfaction with the influence of an American, who had brought his father to Oahu long before. They embarked on board the Thaddeus, and sailed for Kauai, May 2d, 1820.

George was received by his father with affection and congratulation, and with as much respect as the pride of his own heart, or the wakeful jealousy of other chieftains, would safely permit. He introduced the brethren kindly, but characteristically, to his father, as friends who had come from America to accompany him home. The old king embraced them, and early applied to them the term "Aikane" [privileged friends], an honorary heathen title, implying some privileges which they did not covet. On a short acquaintance with their character and their objects, which they made known to him, he earnestly desired them to take up their permanent residence there. He expressed an unexpected degree of gratitude for the support, education, and return of his son, which had been assumed by the American Board after the man who carried him away had failed to fulfil his contract.

He professed a readiness to make such return as he could, by kindness and aid to the missionaries. As an expression of his gratitude to Captain Blanchard, master of the brig in which George returned, he furnished valuable supplies, freely, for the vessel, and gave him sandal-wood, valued at $1,000.

But we were particularly interested in the gratification he manifested, on receiving the elegant Bible, presented him by the American Bible Society, the contents of which he often desired the missionaries to read and explain to him, and which he, and his wife, and son, seemed inclined to learn at once to read.

He offered to give the use of land to aid in the support of the teachers, and when he feared they would not stay with him, said, on one occasion, "Why, you no stay here? We like you very much. My people all like you. We want missionaries here, as well as the other islands."

Having explored portions of the island, finding the people scattered, poor, debased and neglectful of their fine soil, these brethren returned to Oahu, after an absence of eight weeks—made a report of their welcome reception, and incipient labors, having brought with them, as proofs of the kindness of the friendly king and his heathen queen, Kapule, a present of cocoanuts, calabashes, oranges, pine-apples, fans, fly-brushes, spears and shells, thirty mats, one hundred kapas, and three hogs.

Though there was work enough, and more than enough, for all our laborers, either at the single station of Kailua or Honolulu, yet, for various reasons, and especially the injunction which requires the Gospel to be announced to all without exception, we could not hesitate to meet the wants and wishes of the king of

Kauai and others there, and of Kalanimoku at Kawaihae, so far as to give them teachers. If we would see the Gospel take effect on a nation, its light should be diffused over the whole nation. The mass must have opportunity to see it simultaneously, in order to the fullest impression. Christianity should be made by precept and example to radiate from many different points so extensively, that all the tribe or nation may have the means of judging of its merits and availing themselves of its advantages. To teach a single village, only, in each heathen country, or to limit missionary influence to a few of each nation, while all the rest of the inhabitants are left to the darkness of unmitigated superstition and ignorance, would require an age to make any perceptible diminution of the mass of heathenism in that country, even with an ordinary blessing on the preaching of the word. It was obvious that all ought to have access to the knowledge of the Savior in the shortest possible time.

Arrangements were made by the 23d of July, for Messrs. W. and R. and their wives to take up their residence at Waimea, on Kauai. On the eve of their departure from Honolulu, eleven of our number united in celebrating the dying love of our exalted Redeemer, for the first time on the shores of the Sandwich Islands, and found the season happy. Probably the Savior's death had never before been set forth in this ordinance in those islands. We were joined in this solemn and delightful service, by an American gentleman, Mr. Charles Carey, of Chelsea, Mass., master of the ship Levant, who had recently put into the harbor, on his way from the Oregon to New York.

The next day, he received on board his ship the detachment for Kauai, and gratuitously conveying them thither, landed them at their new station, where they were welcomed by the king, and applied themselves with gladness to their work.

Mr. Loomis'hastened to Kawaihae and engaged in teaching Kalanimoku and his wife, and a class of favorite youths whom he wished to have instructed. Thus to facilitate the diffusion of light over these islands, we were quickly and widely scattered and more or less exposed. We all regarded it as unsuitable, during several years of our early missionary life, to expose our women, by leaving them alone at any time, but less hazardous for the men to travel, lodge, and sojourn singly. Whether alone or in each other's company, there were dangers from which the Divine hand only could effectually guard us. The exposure of the females of the mission, so widely scattered, where there were no other civilized females, and scarcely civilized men, and no physician to be relied on, was among the trials of missionary life. Aside from the loss of the society of friends and relatives, this became, as in all new fields, a source of no small solicitude.

But trials, privations, and dangers, we knew should not prevent the prompt performance of the services to which we are obviously called by the Captain of Salvation. There is no method, known to us, of conveying the Gospel vigorously and speedily to the heathen world without the hazards attendant on voyages, changes of climate, and the opposition of the enemies of truth, either barbarous or civilized.   Never has the Prince of Darkness yielded any portion of his territory for the purpose of giving the Messiah possession there, without involving the soldiers of Christ in personal danger, and never have they carried their conquests very far, without much self-denial, cross-bearing, and personal exposures.

The compassionate Savior says to his heralds, "I send you forth as lambs among wolves, but take neither sword, nor staff, nor purse, nor scrip," as though he would compel them to trust his providential support and protection; and again, to warn them of danger at hand, and to impress them with the importance of being on their guard, he says, "He that hath no sword, let him sell his coat and buy one;" and again, lest they should take occasion thus to harm their opposers, he adds the admonition, "He that taketh the sword shall perish with the sword."

In entering, as missionaries, almost singly into the midst of a barbarous or heathen people like the Polynesians, it is well for the safety of life to be destitute alike of the means of personal defence by force, of warlike aggression, and of affluence. For in that case, more confidence in God's protection is manifested, more reliance on argument with the people is implied, and less provocation is given to heathen cupidity, jealousy, and violence.

CHAPTER V.

Instruction commenced with difficulty—First sermon to the king—Hopu's father—
First school at Honolulu—Claims for the use of the needle—Objections to the
mission—Boki and his partisans—Co-operation of foreigners in aid of the school
—Boki's stammering teacher—Ejection of aliens—Kaumualii and his school—Examination of the school at Honolulu—First houses of the mission at Honolulu—
Native style of building—Correspondence with Governor Reickord—Grateful notice
in the United States of the reception of the mission.

THE whole population of the Hawaiian Islands, amounting to
about 130,000, in their deep darkness and degradation, were cast
upon these few and scattered missionary laborers, to be instructed
in almost every branch of useful knowledge suited to their circumstances. None of them had even the alphabet of learning or of
true religion, or of sound morals.

Having assured the rulers, from the beginning of our intercourse with them, that if permitted, we could teach them and
their people, Christianity and the arts, we now made it a daily
object to gain their confidence, to make ourselves acquainted with
their language, habits, and modes of thinking, and the best means
of access to their minds and hearts, and, if possible, adapt our
instructions to their capacities and most urgent wants.

But how shall a rude nation be speedily instructed without
books, or the use of the press? True, the missionaries had books,
English, Latin, Greek and Hebrew, but neither they nor the
nation had any books in the language of the country, or in any of
the Polynesian dialects. Our ignorance of the language of the
people, and their ignorance of ours, was, of course, an impediment
in the way of intercourse between the teacher and the pupil, at
first very great; and the absolute destitution of suitable books for
the work of teaching the nation, was an embarrassment rarely or
never to be found among Asiatic tribes—an embarrassment similar
to what the pioneer missionary, J. Williams, found in attempting
among barbarians to build a missionary ship, on a heathen islet,
with neither tools, materials, nor competent artisans.

Desirous to teach them thoroughly, through the best medium
then available, we undertook with the English, with zeal, and
with some success, in the case of a very limited number. But our
object was not to change the language of the nation but to bring

to their minds generally, the knowledge of the Christian religion, and induce them to embrace and obey it.   The sounds of the English being so different from their own, and so much more difficult of utterance, their ignorance of the meaning of English words, and the impracticability of learning them from English dictionaries, together with the intricacies of English orthography, presented insurmountable obstacles to the speedy accomplishment of the main object of a Christian Mission, if the nation were to be confined to that medium. What could French Protestant missionaries do in teaching English and American seamen the doctrines and duties of the Gospel, through the medium of the French alone ? Clearness, accuracy, and force in religious teaching we deemed so essential to success, that the vernacular tongue, or a language understood by the learner, must needs be employed to be successful ; for a miracle is required to give sense and cogency to unknown words and phrases, before they can enlighten the mind or impress the heart in respect to the will of God.

The Hawaiians might indeed have been taught to cross themselves, repeat *Pater nosters* and *Ave Marias* in Latin, to dip the finger in water, gaze on pictures, bow before images, and buy indulgences with great formality and punctuality, and still have been as ignorant of the volume of inspired truth as the Aborigines of California and South America, or the youthful Spanish Franciscan monk, now a protestant missionary at Gibraltar, who, at twenty-five years of age, though studying for the priesthood, had never seen the Bible, and did not know that such a book existed : and they might, moreover, have been still just as idolatrous as their fathers were in the days of Cook, and as ready to visit with poison, fire, or bonds, any who should oppose or ridicule their folly.

The plan of teaching the mass of children *exclusively*, while neither children, adults, nor rulers knew the practicability and utility of learning; and the plan of teaching children exclusively in a language unintelligible to their parents, and the mass of the community around them, would have been chimerical ; and a perseverance in such an attempt would have given over the adult and aged population to incurable ignorance and hopeless degradation, or left them to rush *en masse* to pagan or papal polytheism, and thus have defeated the education of the children and the education of the nation.   To have neglected the rulers, and taught the children of the plebeians a new religion in a language unknown to the nation, would have arrayed prejudice and opposition against us in high places, and thus defeated our cause, or greatly retarded our success.

To change the language of a people is a work of time. Even in a conquered province, with the favoring influences of colonization, commercial intercourse and literary institutions, with an impulse from a new government and fashion, such a thing is effected but slowly and imperfectly.   With how much less hope of success could a few missionaries, with no help from circumstances like these, attempt it. The progress of a generation or two may so alter the circumstances of the nation as to make the use of the English more feasible and useful. This, then, is our answer to the oft-repeated and not unimportant question, " Why did you not teach the nation English, and open to them, at once, the rich stores of learning, science and religion, to be found in that language?" and here we show our warrant for applying ourselves to the acquisition of the Hawaiian language, reducing it to a written form, and preparing books of instruction in it, for the nation, and teaching all classes to use them as speedily as possible.

In connexion with this general mode of instruction, we could, and did teach English to a few, and have continued to do so. We early used both English and Hawaiian together. For a time after our arrival, in our common intercourse, in our schools, and in our preaching, we were obliged to employ interpreters, though none except Hopu and Honolii were found to be very trustworthy, in communicating the uncompromising claims and the spirit-searching truths of revealed religion. Kaumualii, Kuakini, Keeaumoku and a few others could speak a little barbarous English, which they had acquired by intercourse with sea-faring men. But English, as spoken by sailors on heathen shores at that time, was the language of Pandemonium ; and the thought of making young men and women better able to comprehend and use that language, while subjected to the influence of frequent intercourse with an ungodly class of profane abusers of our noble English, was appalling. We could not safely do it until we were able to exert a strong counteracting influence. It is worthy of a grateful record that King Kaumualii, though accustomed, like other heathen who stammer English, to use profane language, on being faithfully taught that it was wrong, broke off, and abandoned the vile habit. How chilling to a missionary's heart, to hear a heathen father curse his own little child in profane English, and to hear his own fellow-countrymen teaching the heathen that awful dialect, by which profane men anathematize one another, and insult their Maker !

That the sudden introduction of the Hawaiian nation in its unconverted state, to general English or French literature, would have been safe and salutary, is extremely problematical. To us it has been a matter of pleasing wonder that the rulers and the people were so early and generally led to seek instruction through books furnished them by our hands, not one of which was designed to encourage image worship, to countenance iniquity, or to be at variance with the strictest rules of morality. It was of the Lord's mercy.

With the elements of reading and writing we were accustomed, from the beginning, to connect the elements of morals and religion, and have been happy to find them mutual aids.

The momentous interests of the soul were the commanding reason for learning what God has caused to be written for its salvation, and for regulating its duty to him. The initiation of the rulers and others into the arts of reading and writing, under our own guidance, brought to their minds forcibly, and sometimes by surprise, moral lessons as to their duty and destiny which were of immeasurable importance. The English New Testament was almost our first school book, and happy should we have been, could the Hawaiian Bible have been the next.

At the station at Kailua, the king and his little brother, Kauikeaouli, five years old; two of his wives, Kamamalu and Kinau, Kuakini, and a son of Mr. J. Young, two youths, James Kahuhu, and John Ii, and others, were instructed by Mr. and Mrs. Thurston and Thomas Hopu, being assisted for a time by Dr. Holman. Their dwellings, for months, were daily surrounded by scores of men, women, and children. Many came from distant parts of that island, which is nearly three hundred miles in circuit, to see what sort of beings white missionaries were.

Though the heathen revelry of the king and others often disqualified them from making progress in study, or proved unwelcome hindrances, still, during the time which they did devote to instruction, though taught chiefly in a foreign tongue, they made such advances, that in three months the king was reading a little in the New Testament, and five of the others in the easy reading lessons of Webster's spelling book. The young prince, a promising pupil, though a mere child, on whom the cares and responsibilities of government were at length to rest, could spell English words of four syllables. But their studies in English were wearisome, and ere long chiefly suspended.

Much of the time of Dr. Holman, while he remained at the station in connexion with the mission, was occupied with the duties of his profession. Never, perhaps, had a medical man a better opportunity to make a good impression as a pioneer of science, civilization, and Christianity, than he enjoyed. He was very successful in the treatment of diseases, and might soon doubtless have possessed the confidence of the highest families in the nation, had he not cherished a premature desire, with his wife, who deeply felt her privations, " to return to the country whence they came out."

After three months of toil amidst the darkness, confusion, and pollution of that heathen village, Mr. Thurston secured the opportunity of preaching a formal sermon to the royal family. By the aid of Hopu, as an interpreter, he urged on them the claims of Jehovah, from the impressive words of the prophet, " I have a message from God unto thee." His little audience kneeled in prayer. Assisted by Hopu, he preached from Sabbath to Sabbath, to small circles, either at the school-room or his own residence, with the hope that the seed would not prove to have been scattered wholly in vain, in the stony places of Kailua.

In the good Providence of God, it was so ordered, that Thomas Hopu found his own father alive at Hawaii, and at his instance, willing to remove with his family from another part of the island, and come to Kailua, and receive religious instruction; and that Hopu should have the opportunity of reading the Scriptures to them daily, and praying with them morning and evening, for a time. What a privilege to a long absent son, who, in his heathenism, had wandered away to the ends of the earth with Opukahaia, and having found the Savior, to return, with the Bible in his hand, to enlighten the dark hovel of his father, and to aid in dispelling the gloom that had so many ages hung over his tribe and his country! His hands and his heart were full, and with earnestness and fidelity he applied himself to his work. But his labors for his father were ere long broken off, for with his fading contemporaries, he scarcely came to know and apparently to approve the leading doctrines of Christianity, before he died.

Notwithstanding the difficulties and embarrassments experienced at Honolulu, in establishing ourselves among so degraded a people, we were allowed to see a school opened in May, the month after our arrival, and daily instructed. The want of a suitable place to meet a school, was not among the least embarrassments which an American female would feel in beginning this work. Then, to the absence of suitable books and school apparatus, was added the want of a convenient medium of intercourse between the teacher and pupil, and the difficulty of securing a regular attendance.

It was a question with us, as it has often been with our friends —how could scholars be found, and induced to come together to attend to instruction and study for the acquisition of knowledge of which they could not know the value, and of the process and means of gaining which they had no just conception? . But, intent on engaging early in this part of missionary work, none of the many embarrassments could we regard as insurmountable. Uncouth and indifferent as were the adults in general, and wild, shouting, and thoughtless, as the children appeared when we attempted to approach them at first, though they oftentimes thronged around us in their merriment to gaze and laugh, there was found, here and there, one more confiding, who could be induced to come to our dwelling for a trial. Ingenuity and kindness were tasked to give interest enough to the school exercises to induce those who came once to come again, day after day, when the sun should reach a certain elevation, pointed out in the heavens, instead of uselessly naming the hour of the day or the time by the clock.

Whatever of hostility may have been manifested against the spiritual claims of the Gospel by foreigners and others, we were encouraged in our efforts to commence a school by several residents, some wishing their wives, and others their children to be instructed. Among these, were Messrs. Holmes and Navarro (American), Marin (Spanish), Harbottle, Woodland and Beckley

(English), and Allen, a refugee from New York slavery before its abolition, who resided at Waikiki, lived as comfortably, and treated us as courteously, as any who had adopted that country before our arrival. These cherished a desire that their long neglected children, whose morals, habits, language and manners differed little from their contemporaries—the children of aboriginal fathers—might now, at length, if they wished it, have the advantage of a school for their improvement. Allen from Schenectady, and Woodland from Port Jackson, wished to have their children " christened." The latter said ' he had done it himself, as well as he could, but wished it might be done over again better.'

During the first year, no suitable system of orthography was fixed upon for writing the language of the country. It was difficult, even, to write out in native, the meaning of words and sentences of English lessons. It was no small labor, not only to teach simply the enunciation of a lesson, but to teach the meaning of a column of words, or a page of sentences constituting their English lesson, which, without such an interpretation, must have been, to such pupils, too forbidding. But this was so far accomplished as to make the school pleasant to most of those who attended, partly by means of the slate, and partly by writing out short lessons on paper, with an imperfect orthography.

There was a frankness and earnestness on the part of some, in commencing and prosecuting study, which agreeably surprised us, and greatly encouraged our first efforts. On the Sabbath, very soon after our arrival, Pulunu came to attend our public worship, and brought two shy, but bright looking little daughters, (less tinged with copper and olive than their fellows), and after the service, she desired us to take them under our instruction. We readily consented ; and both mother and daughters became interesting members of the school. In a few weeks the mother conquered the main difficulty in acquiring an ability to read and write, and the others before many months. On the 1st of August, the slate was introduced, and by the 4th, Pulunu wrote on her slate, from a Sabbath School card, the following sentence in English ; " I cannot see God, but God can see me." She was delighted with the exercise, and with her success in writing and comprehending it. The rest of the pupils listened with admiration as she read it, and gave the sense in Hawaiian. Here was a demonstration that a slate could speak in a foreign tongue, and convey a grand thought in their own.

A lad, quite young and small, but with features more than ordinarily pleasing to the physiognomist, was seen standing one day, towards evening, looking at us through the light paling that surrounded our premises, where successive companies of all ages, from day to day, indulged their curiosity in marking the novel movements of their strange visitors ; and the question was put to him, " Would you like to live with us, and learn to work and read ?" " *Ae*," was his pleasant and unhesitating affirmative ;

and without further ceremony he was taken in, covered, fed, lodged, and instructed.   He became a docile and successful pupil, laboring to pay his board and making very rapid improvement; so that in a few months, he could read intelligibly several portions of the English Bible.   He expressed a desire to instruct the people, and early became a useful teacher even in his boyhood.   Some who were desirous to attend school were held back by the stupidity and prejudices of their friends, who looked upon us with jealousy or hostility, and some, though desirous to learn, were engrossed with other concerns which prevented their attending to instruction.   A young and sprightly native, J. Banks, who had been the commander of a schooner, then recently stranded, came to us one day, and said with some earnestness, " I goin to live with you now, I want to learn to read, and learn navigation. I like take the sun, sail out o' sight o' land, and go to any part o' the world."   He had been to China.   He told us that before the fatal blow was struck upon the worship of idols, he thought the tabus were unreasonable and the idols vain, that the priests were ignorant men and unworthy of confidence, as they could show no authority.   He professed to have said to Kalanimoku, that it would be well to disregard the tabu.   He had heard some pretend that we had come to take the country.   He said to them, " Where are their guns ?   And if they fight with us, what will they do with their women?"   His reasoning indicates that defenceless and non-combatant missionary women may be a safeguard to their husbands among the heathen, in matters of great importance, as well as an efficient aid in imparting instruction by precept and example.

The next day, Banks came with Boki and others to public worship, in which he appeared to be interested.   The hearers were called on to " behold the Lamb of God that taketh away the sin of the world."   Boki tarried after the service, made some inquiries, and expressed a desire to be able to read and understand our Bible, and, moreover, consented to be daily instructed in it.   I presented him a copy, and from time to time endeavored to make him and his wife Liliha acquainted with its contents.   The services of Banks were soon required by his superiors, and his design to get an education was defeated.   The lovers of rum-selling and dram-drinking plied him with their charms, from whose influence he never escaped.

Many of the chiefs had various engagements of business, gambling, revelry, and jaunting about from place to place with their retinues, which were unfavorable to their attention to the means of improvement offered them.   Liholiho, moreover, when he learned with what promptness we could teach reading and writing, objected to our teaching the common people these arts before he should himself first have acquired them.   His self-respect thus manifested was on the one hand encouraging, for we wished him to take the lead, and on the other, embarrassing, for we wished to bring the multitude under instruction,without reference to the distinctions of birth or rank. Kaahumanu too, for many months, was either heedless in regard to Christianity, or scornfully averse to our instructions, and at the same time not a little annoyed by the profligacy of Liholiho and his boon companions. Some were watching to despoil us of our few goods, or to expel us from the islands,and others to nullify our influence by slander and misrepresentations.

Watchfulness, on our part, was demanded not to provoke needless hostility or to wound unduly the self-esteem of the grandees, and at the same time not to omit to do good to them and their needy people according to the explicit commands of the Bible.

Some, before they could appreciate the greater good which we hoped our mission would confer on them, preferred claims for minor things which might have been rejected as unreasonable, had we not desired to encourage attention to improvements in their wardrobe, and to give them time to consider their ways and to find out the nature of our main design, and to appreciate it, instead of startling, disgusting or repelling them by abruptness or impatience.

The scarcity of wood and water was at that time felt in our domestic arrangements. Our fuel for cooking was obtained by barter at a high rate, being brought four or five miles on the shoulders of men. Before wells were used in Honolulu, our water for drinking and cooking was brought in calabashes a considerable distance. Embarrassments of this sort, almost too small to be mentioned at all, were particularly felt, when, among many things demanding attention in getting under weigh, the clothes of a six months' voyage were to be washed and ironed—a service, like other domestic labors, to be performed by the hands of the wives of the missionaries. While numbers of the natives were disposed to gaze to see the operation, not one could be found both willing and able to do this service. Our females tried the experiment of going back to the stream in the valley, to do their washing. This was done cheerfully. The novelty and even ludicrousness of their appearance and circumstances, off at what some of them called a "heathen brook" in the open country, while the tropical sun was withering their physical powers, and literally blistering their arms, seemed partially to sustain their spirits, while they rejoiced in the Divine goodness, which daily supplied the needful strength for these new scenes and untried labors.

Before this service was fully accomplished, they were required to do what at a more convenient time they would more gladly have done—to make a dozen shirts for the grandees, cut and make a full suit of clothes of superfine broadcloth for Naihekukui, the father of the present queen, and similar garments for Boki. In this, and especially the more difficult parts, Mrs. W. and Mrs. R., before going to their station on Kauai, took a leading part.

Soon after Mrs. Bingham had got her school in operation, the king sent Hopu to Honolulu with a piece of fine shirting to have Mrs.

B. make for his Hawaiian majesty five ruffled shirts with plaited bosoms, to be sent back to him at Kailua by the vessel returning in a few days. Such demands from the king, his wives, and other chiefs, male and female, in our destitution of not a few of the daily comforts once enjoyed, and an anxious desire to give full satisfaction, required some sacrifices, and caused, during the first years, some expenditure of health and strength on the part of those who were willing thus to toil, in connexion with their more important labors for the moral and intellectual improvement of the people. Before the people could appreciate the latter, and before their language was familiar to us, a courteous welcome given in season and out of season, the making or fitting a new garment, or the offer of a seat at table to those who sought our acquaintance, had its appropriate influence, as well as our more direct labors in teaching letters, and inculcating the doctrines of Christianity. Our female helpers, by conscientiously doing both, in the midst of infirmities and family cares, doubly proved their interest in the well-being of the natives, and showed a steady and loyal desire to deserve their approbation. They had the opportunity, of which they availed themselves, of showing the spirit of self-denial for the sake of another's good, which is the best logic to convince the heathen, and of illustrating the unreasonableness of overtasking the poor and the stranger, especially when heathen exorbitance crowded too freely on Christian kindness.

Some three or four years after the mission was commenced, a woman of rank, calling on the wife of a missionary, requested her to make a dress for her. The request was readily granted. She soon called for a second. This also was done, without demur or compensation. She then called for another. The third was promptly and gratuitously made by the missionary's wife, who wished still to oblige. The fourth was ere long asked for by the same exorbitant woman. The lady, perceiving not only that the demand was unreasonable, but that meeting it would not satisfy, and wishing to teach reason where it was wanting, said kindly, " Would it not be well for your own girls (whom I have taught to sew) to make this, if you need the fourth?" The chief woman replied, " It is but little for *you* to make it; you can do it so quickly; but my girls are all lazy, and would be long about it." The lady, glancing at the other side, said, " I am here alone in feeble health. I sew clothes for myself and family. I have not a company of servants about me to go and come at my bidding. Much of my cooking and other work I must do myself. I have a number of scholars to teach every day. I have made for you three dresses, and taught your girls how to sew. I appeal to you to say whether I ought now to do the fourth." She felt the rebuke, and waived her request. Others, however, were found ere long to be looking with equal eagerness to their missionary friends to help them to adorn themselves with good works, and to gain possession of the ever during heavenly robes.

There was not perhaps a wider difference of opinion among the natives, in respect to the influence of the mission, than among foreigners. It was obvious that some apprehended that success in our undertaking would modify the nature of the trade at the islands, to their disadvantage, and, moreover, bring into disrepute some things which had been deemed reputable and fashionable. It has been said that the interests of the mission, and the interests of commerce, were so diverse, or opposite, that they could not flourish together. And though it was admitted to be customary for traders to offer the profligate king a variety of tempting liquors, when a bargain with him was sought, lest others, by this kind of liberality, would secure too large a share of custom, we were cautioned not to instruct either Liholiho or Kaumualii in the cost of foreign merchandise, or in respect to the mischiefs which might come upon the nation by bargains made under the influence of intoxicating drinks.

It was on our part publicly announced that it was our intention to give a thorough education to such as would make the reasonable efforts to acquire it, and to introduce as we were able, the arts and usages of Christian society; and that the gospel, which we had come to propagate, was intended by its Author for all people, as a guide in the way of righteousness, temperance, and salvation, and that it must not only be proclaimed freely, with all its claims, proffers, and promises, but that it must also command respect and obedience among all nations, according to divine predictions. Our influence over the chiefs, when apparently very small, excited an unexpected jealousy, which was manifested especially in respect to the governor of Oahu.

Boki, who had but recently been appointed to the governorship of Oahu, had, as a public officer, but little experience. He was above the middling stature, but appeared at times like one stupified with alcohol, tobacco, and *awa*. Though in his prime, he was intemperate, and slow to do good; but he occasionally appeared desirous of distinction and honors. He had not sagacity enough to see what party it would be safest to follow, nor independence and integrity enough to mark out for himself, and follow, a steady and honorable course suited to his responsibilities. He must please his superiors, or lose his place, which was desired by Naihekukui, and others. He must please that class of foreigners who love their indulgences, or fail of their flattery and co-operation; and he must favor the missionaries, or himself and people lose the advantages which they offered, and which some were striving to obtain. To do all this, and yet indulge a vile heathen heart, and secure his ulterior ends, was no easy task, even if he had possessed the sagacity of Solomon. With his permission, we selected a location for our residence, in the rear then of Honolulu village, or town, within the limits which he specified,—a place, where, by means of irrigation from the waters of the valley, we might have the comfort of gardens and verdure.

But this he was induced, doubtless by others, to refuse. Had he
granted it then, there were some who would have contributed for
the erection of houses for the mission.

Waiving our claim both to the chosen site, and the proposed
aid, we wished still to unite such foreign influence there as could
be enlisted in the cause of the mission. The residents and others
were consulted, and a subscription paper, supposed to be
unobjectionable, was immediately circulated among those to
whose consideration our attention to the children of foreigners
and others equally needy, had already commended the mission.
It was as follows:—

" While the friends of Humanity and of Zion, in Europe and
America, are uniting their influence, and contributing their substance to
meliorate the condition of the wretched, and to give the Bible and the
blessings of the Gospel to the long neglected heathen; and, while some
are sacrificing the comforts of home, and devoting their talents, their
possessions, and their lives, to the diffusion of the light of science and
Revelation, in the dark places of the earth, we feel it to be a pleasure
as well as a duty, to promote the grand design of civilizing and
Christianizing the natives of the Sandwich Islands.

" Believing that American and European residents, gentlemen of
business from different countries, masters and officers of vessels of
different flags, as they visit these islands, will co-operate in a systematic
effort to provide for the comfort and education of orphan children (of
whom many may be found here) by donations in money, or articles of
trade, or the productions of the country, or other substantial means of
doing them good, we, the undersigned gentlemen, from different
countries, cheerfully agree to give to the mission established in these
islands, the donations severally annexed to our respective names, to
constitute a school-fund for orphan children, to be used by the mission
for the benefit of such children, in training them up in knowledge and
virtue, in the useful arts of civilized life, and in the principles of the
Christian religion, that they may be grateful to their benefactors,
useful to their country, blessings to the world, and fitted for heaven."

This was our treaty of peace with the foreigners. A respectable number signed it, within a year and a half from its
commencement. In the circulation of this paper we were aided
by J. Hunnewell, Esq., who, though he had no connexion with
the mission, and no personal interest in the school, has, from that
early period to the present, uniformly befriended the mission,
avoided collision with the rulers, and rejoiced in the prosperity of
the missionaries, and the progress of the nation. We are happy to
say, we have always had among foreigners at the islands some
friendly and honorable advocates of our cause. And we believe
that others there would gladly have shown us kind civilities, had
their moral courage been equal to their kindness, or to their convictions of what was right, or sufficient to enable them to face the
frown of the anti-missionary spirit when it grew strong by
numbers and concert, among those who resisted the attempts of

missionaries and chiefs to establish a system of Christian tabus, denominated " *Chastity, temperance,* loyalty, and Sabbath consecration."

Boki at length, by the order of the king, gave the mission a building spot for the Honolulu station, on the arid plain, about half a mile east of the landing, then some distance from the village, but now included in it. After a few months, he erected there temporary habitations for the mission family, residing on that island. Meantime, an English resident undertook to teach him the English language by books, but found it impracticable. This indeed was no matter of wonder; for, making due allowance for rum and revelry on the part of the pupil, and the ordinary difficulties which the natives find in pronouncing sibilants and double consonants, and in comprehending the orthography and structure of English ; and for the want of tact and zeal on the part of the teacher, which, if they existed, should have been tried long before ; it may be added, that had he succeeded in making the pupil copy the master perfectly, as an elocutionist, he would have made him one of the most barbarous stutterers that ever tortured " the king's English." It is said of him, that when an accident occurred on board a vessel of which he was an officer, he hastened to apprise the captain, and making a great effort, utterly failed. The captain, eager to know what was still struggling in vain for utterance, and understanding how he might be helped, earnestly bade him " *sing* it out." He immediately commenced singing the news, " The cook has tumbled overboard." In this he was more successful than in his attempt to enlighten and reform the governor, by teaching him to stammer English, which, after a trial, he relinquished, saying, " B—bo—Boki, you know, sir, is ve—ve— very, you know, sir,—ve--very--te--te—jus--you know,—sir."

This allowed us to apply again what tact and patience we possessed, to bring him forward with others. But Honolulu, the place where Neptune and Pele once strove to settle boundaries, has seemed destined never to be long quiet at a time.

In August, John Rives, a sort of clerk of Liholiho, came from Kailua to Honolulu, professedly to expel from the country such foreigners as did not belong to the king or to Kalanimoku. The right and practice of denying a residence to foreigners, which was here boldly and rashly advocated by a Frenchman, will be seen in the course of events, to have had some influence on the relations between the islands and France. Governor Boki immediately summoned the foreigners, not excepting the missionaries or their wives, to assemble at his house to hear the orders. Mrs. L. was too ill to go. Mrs. B. and Mrs. C., though meaning to be loyal, sent their apology to Boki, that they were engaged, making garments for the king, and presumed their presence would not be needed at the assembly. This he accepted ; and he moreover decided that the king's grant to us of permission to reside in his dominions for a year at least, exempted us from the orders to depart. We, therefore, proceeded with our work, not regarding ourselves as *belonging* to any of the rulers, but as American citizens, and while conforming to the laws of the country, entitled to the protection of both the United States and the civil power of Hawaii. Others have affected to regard us as beyond national protection, and our lives, liberty, goods and reputation as a prey to the violent and lawless.

At this time, the king of Kauai, after three months' instruction, addressed to me a letter, expressive of his high satisfaction in the missionaries that had " *come to do him good,*" and his gratitude for what had been done for his son, George. What would naturally be written in ten lines, he, in his early efforts, and unformed hand, like many other young Hawaiian pupils, spread over a folio page, as follows ;—

" Dear Friend. I feel glad that your good people come to my islands to do me good. I thank you. I love them. I give them eat, drink, and land to work on. I thank all American folks, they give my son learning. He know how to read, write all America books. I feel glad he come home. He long time in America. I think he dead. But some man speak ' no.' I very glad you good people. I love them. I do them good. I hope you do good Hawaii, Oahu and all the islands.

" Except this from your friend, Tamoree."

He used a bad orthography for his name at that time, for which is now substituted Kaumualii.

The readiness with which the rulers, generally, allowed their people to learn to read, and attend to religious instruction, after the mission had acquired their confidence, is not among the smallest matters of wonder in their history. The same summer, King Kaumualii wrote to the Secretary of the American Board, in his imperfect English, a simple expression of what we believe were the honest views and feelings of that chief on the importance of religion, and general education among his people.

" Atooi [Kauai], July 28th, 1820.

" Dear Friend : I wish to write a few lines to you to thank you for the good book you was so kind as to send by my son. I think it is a good book, one that God gave us to read. I hope all my people will soon read this, and all other good books. I believe that my idols are good for nothing, and that your God is the only true God—the one that made all things. My idols I have hove away—they are no good—they fool me—they do me no good. I give them cocoanuts, plantains, hogs, and good many things, and they fool me at last. Now I throw them all away. I have done now. When your good people learn me, I worship your God. I feel glad your good people come here to help us —We know nothing. I thank you for giving my son learning. I thank all America people. Accept this from your friend, King Tamoree."

How generous the feelings of this chief towards his subjects and their teachers, and how different from the feelings of Pharaoh towards the people of Israel while under his despotic power! He wishes his people to read the Book of God, and all other good books. He knew enough already of the work of education, to see that it must cost time and labor by no means small, and unless they were allowed time, and encouraged to perform the labor, they never would possess these advantages.

George, his son, for a time cherished the feelings of respect and gratitude towards the mission and his American benefactors, and some desire for the improvement of his country; though his efforts were desultory, and of doubtful tendency. He was not disposed to apply himself much to study, or any means of general improvement, but early felt the strong downward tendencies of a heathen community.

Kaumualii and his wife, Kapule, his son, Kealiiahonui, and an interesting school of thirty children and youth, under the direct and efficient patronage of that high chieftain, were taken under the instruction of Messrs. Whitney and Ruggles and their wives. In this school of children, with and by the advice and consent of the king, the discipline of the district schools in New England was introduced, and the unruly, disobedient, and refractory, were subjected to corporeal punishment. But this was an exception to the general practice in the islands. The superiority of the missionaries was quickly seen and acknowledged at all the stations, and the evidences of their kindness were so obvious, as well as their aptness to teach and to control the minds of pupils, that the love and respectful obedience of most of those who came daily under their care, were shortly secured without the rod. Throngs of spectators, who, from different parts, came to gratify curiosity, were favorably impressed; and some, by intercourse with the pupils at home, learned what we were teaching. To make a favorable impression on the pupils and on the public mind in reference to our object, a quarterly examination of Mrs. Bingham's school was held at Honolulu. It had been in operation three months, and, having commenced with ten or a dozen children and adults, now numbered forty regular scholars, attending five or six hours daily. One of their exercises on this occasion, particularly engaging to pupils and spectators, was the cantilating, in concert, and with a degree of Hawaiian enthusiasm, one of their lessons committed to memory, and which they were accustomed to teach to their acquaintances, at their places of abode. No one could, in these circumstances, hear these simple truths, and simple, monotonous notes and numbers, from their untutored voices, without being interested, as they, in exact time, cantilated aloud, in the *Hawaiian language*—

" In the beginning, God created the heavens and the earth.
" Jehovah is in heaven, and he is everywhere.

" Jesus Christ, the good Son of God, died for our sins.
" We must pray to Jehovah, and love his word.
" God loves good men, and good men love God."

That so much proficiency should have been made in so short
a time, in such circumstances, furnished evidence of the capacity
of the natives, and of the ability of the mission to elevate the
people by education—a demonstration of the practicability of the
enterprise we had undertaken.

The day after this examination, in which the pupils and teachers took as much interest and pleasure as is usually found in the
long expected quarterly or annual examination of an academy in
Christian lands, we took possession of the premises assigned us
by the government, and the buildings which had been chiefly
erected by Boki, in the course of four months from our landing.
These houses, cottages or huts, tabernacles, barns or sheds, for it
is somewhat difficult to say what term would give the true idea of
the structure, were built in the usual style of Hawaiian architecture, by natives; the light timbers being brought on their shoulders
some 14 miles, and the grass three.   Had we paid for them, as they
came from their hands, they might have cost us sixty dollars
each.   To describe them justly, would be to describe, in the main,
the habitations of the whole nation—which may, perhaps, as well
be done here as anywhere.

The Hawaiian mode of building habitations was, in a measure,
ingenious, and when their work was carefully executed, it was
adapted to the taste of a dark, rude tribe, subsisting on roots,
fish, and fruits, but by no means sufficient to meet their necessities, even in their mild climate.   Round posts, a few inches in
diameter, are set in the ground about a yard apart, rising from
three to five feet from the surface.   On a shoulder, near the top,
is laid a horizontal pole, two or three inches in diameter, as a
plate; on this, directly over the posts, rest the rafters.   A point
of the post, called a *finger*, rises on the outside of the plate, and
passes between two points of the rafter projecting over the plate
and below the main shoulder.   The joint thus constructed is held
together partly by the natural pressure of the roof, and partly by
lashings of bark, vines, or grassy fibres beaten, and by hand
twisted and doubled into a coarse twine, and put on manifold, so
as to act as four braces—two from the post, and two from the
rafter, extending to the plate, all being attached six to twelve
inches from the joint.   Three poles or posts, about three times
the length of the side posts, are set in the ground, one in the
centre of the building, and the others at the ends, on which rests
the nether ridge pole, supporting the head of the rafters.   These
crossing each other, the angle above receives the upper ridge
pole, which is lashed to the nether and to the head of the rafters.
Posts of unequal length are set at the ends of the building, sloping a little inward and reaching to the end rafters, to which their

tops are tied.   A door-frame, from three to six feet high, is placed between two end or side posts.   Thatch-poles are tied horizontally to the posts and rafters, from an inch to three inches apart, all around and from the ground to the top ridge pole.   At this stage the building assumes the appearance of a huge, rude bird cage.   It is then covered with the leaf of the ki, pandanus, sugarcane, or more commonly (as in the case of the habitations for us) with grass bound on in small bundles, side by side, one tier overlapping another, like shingles.   A house thus thatched assumes the appearance of a long hay stack without, and a cage in a hay mow within.   The area or ground within, is raised a little with earth, to prevent the influx of water, and spread with grass and mats, answering usually instead of floors, tables, chairs, sofas, and beds.   Air can pass through the thatching, and often there is one small opening through the thatch besides the door, for ventilation and light.

Such was the habitation of the Hawaiian,—the monarch, chief, and landlord, the farmer, fisherman, and cloth-beating widow,—a *tent* of poles and thatch—a rude *attic*, of one apartment on the ground—a shelter for the father, mother, larger and smaller children, friends and servants.   Such a habitation, whose leafy or grassy covering readily contracted mould, dust, and vermin, was insufficient to secure the inmates from dampness and the oppressive heat of the vertical sun.   Such houses, snugly built and in prime order, and much more, thousands of the same model, small, indifferently built, or falling to decay, by the force of wind, rain, and sun, or the rotting of the thatching, flooring, and the posts in the ground,—are ill adapted to promote health of body, vigor of intellect, neatness of person, food, clothing or lodging, and much less, longevity.   They cannot be washed, scoured, polished, or painted to good purpose, nor be made suitable for good furniture, pantry, or wardrobe, nor for the security of valuable writings, books, or treasures.   Nothing, therefore, would be more natural than that a heathen people occupying such habitations, and going bare-headed in the sun, should feel a depression or heaviness,—a tendency to listlessness, and even lethargy, which demands the stimulus of tobacco, rum, or *awa*, to give a temporary relief, or to add a zest to the few low pleasures within their reach.

Such habitations being erected for the pioneer missionaries, they introduced some improvements—partitions, window-frames, shutters, &c. (which have been copied to some extent), and afterwards gave them better models.   About as destitute of chairs, at first, as any of the natives, we made long seats of plank by the sides of one room, which we used for a school and for social and public worship for a time.*

* Of the other apartment in the same structure, the following description was, at the time, penned by a true helper's hand for private use:—"My little room is now so much in order as to incline me to wish my sisters to take a view of it, which, could my pen open the door, should be presented them.   The size is twenty feet by

The first Sabbath after entering our new houses, the school-room being well filled, at public worship I endeavored to show that God's gracious agency is essential to our success ; that still he will not build the house, nor the wall of Zion, unless his laborers build it, but will graciously prosper his servants when they build for him.

Sabbath school instruction was resumed here with increasing satisfaction. One of the exercises from Sabbath to Sabbath, at that time, was the reading and interpreting of successive portions of the memoir of Henry Opukahaia. As the closing scenes of the life of that interesting Hawaiian Christian, the first of the tribe known to have embraced the Gospel, were clearly exhibited to our pupils, who had listened to the narrative with increasing interest, many of them tenderly wept. It was highly encouraging to us to see, in less than half a year, such evidence of the susceptibility of the natives to receive impressions when their attention and confidence were secured, and that, notwithstanding the debasing influence of heathenism which they had felt, and the existing obstacles to gaining access to their minds and hearts, they were beginning to show serious regard to matters connected with the soul's well-being in eternity. The conversion and triumphant departure of Catharine Brown, a pupil of the mission among the Indians of the West, when made known to our pupils, appeared to be encouraging to them; partly because she had been in circumstances similar to their own. With the permission of one of our adult pupils, who took an interest in such communications, a public religious conference was repeatedly held at

ten. Mats, something like your straw carpets for chambers, but of a ruder texture, constitute the flooring. The mats which form the partition and the lining of the walls, are more curiously wrought than common. These were presented, in part, by the king of Kauai. They have a colored straw woven in, which gives them, particularly in the evening, the appearance of neatly papered walls. Two doors,—one opening into the school-room, the other into the *lanai*,—a covered entrance which extends over the rear doors of our three houses, which, being nearly contiguous, stand in a line. One window, looking southward upon the sea—no sash or glass, but a little white curtain, having a Venetian blind *promised*. Its furniture consists of a bed, high bedstead, and curtains, put together for me by my friends in W——; by the side of which are two yards of carpeting spread down, and a toilet, covered with a pretty mat, and curtained with furniture calico, having on the back part a row of neatly bound Andover books, and on the front a little desk, containing our writing establishment; and above this, near the window, and partly covered with the window curtain, is my looking-glass, three inches by four. On the end of the room, opposite the bed, a shelf filled with a neat row of good books, principally presented by choice friends. In a corner, at the same end, a little cupboard, which contains some of the best china-ware and glass, presented us by Mr. G. The remainder, two neat little chests, one containing a choice store of medicines, a little cricket stuffed and covered with seal skin, and my *maikai* rocking chair—all the work of my husband. Added to which has been a sofa, to-day, of common dimensions (the frame of pine joist), set in a place just of a size to receive it, from the same kind hand. On one side of the room hangs Mr. B.'s watch, measuring the pleasant hours as they pass. There, dear sisters, you have the dwelling-place of S. and her husband, on missionary ground. It is the humble scene of much sweet enjoyment, while many things, in accents loud, declare,

' This is not your rest.' "

her house, where the missionary stood by a lamp and Bible on the stand, and familiarly instructed such as were willing to attend. A hymn was sung and interpreted, and a prayer offered, while all kneeled quietly in their places. At one of these meetings, after the story of the prodigal son had been read, interpreted, and applied, one of the hearers, an adult female pupil, expressed her fears that she could not go to heaven, because she had sinned so long and so much; but said, "I thank the missionaries for coming here to tell us about God, and the right way to heaven."

Our pupils were soon taught the Ten Commandments, Watts's Catechism for children, and other things of like simplicity and importance, which were laid up in their minds before books in their language were prepared. And often out of school, they rehearsed select passages, by which they not only brought truth to the minds of others, but retained it better themselves. Thus the ideas of God, the soul, heaven, and retribution,—the grand ideas that lie at the foundation of all improvement in morals and civilization, began to find a lodgment in the minds of the people, and to produce their effects. This, in connexion with Divine promises, led us to look for an early, rich and ripened harvest, though those who sow and those who reap are as nothing; and, though the highest rulers, as yet, acknowledged not the authority of Jehovah.

Before the second quarter of the school, thus successfully begun at Honolulu, had closed, several Americans, having native women and children in the school, feeling themselves crowded upon by J. Rives, removed to the uninhabited Fanning's Island, situated 4° 10′ N. L. and 160° W. L., and taking their families with them, drew from the school, and from the dawning light of salvation, nine promising pupils. These, on the day of their departure, came to the bedside of Mrs. Bingham, then temporarily ill, on whose instruction they had attended, and tenderly bade her farewell, thus evincing the sincere and lively interest which the natives were then capable of feeling and manifesting towards religious teachers.

During the agitation of the question of our permanent settlement at the islands, and the attempt to deny a residence to certain foreigners, it was deemed prudent to apprise the Russian governor of Kamtschatka of our position, and the state of things at the islands, and to ask him if we could find protection and employment as Christian missionaries in that quarter of the world, if we should be driven from the Sandwich Islands. A prompt, courteous, and cheering answer was brought to us, by the hand of Captain Pigot, a trader, who, returning from the north through Behring's Straits, in fair weather, had a fine view of the two great neighboring continents at once. It is as follows;—

"Kamtschatka, St. Peter's and St. Paul's, Sept. 5th, 1820.

"Rev. Sir.—With exalted sentiments of Christianity, I had the happiness to peruse your evangelical epistle, which was handed me by Mr. Clark. I cannot help observing that its date, with the important contents, and the auspicious events of the Sandwich Islands, which prepared the way for your great work, appear to me to be stamped with something marvellous. The deep impression which this glorious event has made upon my mind, continues yet to occupy my imagination; and I firmly believe in the interposition of Divine Providence in behalf of your great undertaking.

"I beg you will accept my warmest thanks for the favor you have done me, in communicating news so gratifying to my feelings, and you shall have my fervent prayer unto our Lord, for the preservation of your precious life, consecrated for the happiness of the people, where you have devoted yourself to pass the remainder of your days, and where all your enjoyments and labors are closely connected with eternity.

"You wish to know, honored Sir, the moral condition of the people of Kamtschatka. I have the satisfaction to inform you, that, except a few wandering tribes, all the aborigines enjoy the sweet blessing of the gospel of our Lord, and even these wandering tribes are visited by our priests, to recommend to them the principles of Christianity; but, since, through all the extensive empire of our much beloved sovereign, so justly styled by you the 'great patron of benevolent institutions,' the character of the pious and devoted missionary stands so high, that they need not doubt his protection, but rather command it, wherever the sacred name of Alexander is pronounced. I should be very happy to receive any missionaries who would choose to visit the peninsula of Kamtschatka, and offer them all the assistance in my power.

"I have the honor to inform you that I am now about to send our post away to St. Petersburgh. A copy of your epistle is prepared to be transmitted to our minister, and the president of the Bible Society, Prince Galitzin, who will not fail to present it to our Emperor. I am quite proud of the idea that Kamtschatka's post, barren of itself, will announce this time, to all Christendom, the most glorious event for the kingdom of our Lord of Heaven and earth.

"With sentiments of high esteem:
"Yours faithfully,
"PETER REICKORD."

His mail left Kamtschatka for St. Petersburgh, perhaps by reindeer speed, when ours, by the Levant, was two months on its way to New York, through the China Sea, both hastening to announce to Christendom the new era at the Sandwich Islands. Notwithstanding their early start and desirable speed, before they reached their destination, the question of our residence appeared to have been quietly settled, and we had brought under immediate instruction about one hundred pupils, differing in age, sex, and condition —kings, queens, chiefs, plebeians, and orphans, had begun to make important attainments, and, with thousands of others, had become convinced that the mission could be useful to the nation.

The report of the arrival and reception of the mission reached the United States, in March, 1821, seventeen months after its embarkation from Boston. Multitudes, who had been aiding it by their prayers and contributions, and so long waiting to hear how it sped, received the intelligence with joy and devout thanksgiving, which it is believed will be renewed at length in heaven, and felt a new impulse to missionary zeal and activity : and others, who had been indifferent to the claims of Christ, were by these events led to engage in his service. As a specimen of the feelings and reflections of the intelligent friends of the Redeemer's cause in Europe and America, on hearing of the change of the tabus and the introduction of the mission, the remarks of the honored Secretary of the American Board at a monthly concert for prayer at Park St. Church, Boston, deserve a record at the close of this chapter. A large concourse from different churches were there assembled to hear, and pray, and give thanks, whom, after alluding to our voyage and to portions of our journal which he was about to read to them, relative to our reception, he thus addressed ;—

" Let us contemplate the circumstances in which this vessel was approaching these islands of the great Pacific.

" Here was a people numerous, and in many respects interesting, on whom no ray of the Sun of Righteousness had yet fallen ; but who had been groping their toilsome way, for unknown generations, probably from the very origin of idolatry among Noah's descendants, in all the darkness and gloom of a horrible superstition—a superstition which, under various modifications, but always essentially the same, has enchained so great a proportion of the human race, and of which the prominent characteristics are ' impurity and blood.' Here, from the days of the remotest tradition, human sacrifices have been offered. Here, the strange mummeries of idol-worship, which the worshippers themselves did not pretend to understand, served only to perplex and terrify the darkling mind, without affording even a momentary comfort, or having the least tendency to restrain from sin. From the discovery of these islands, more than forty years ago, a frequent and continually increasing intercourse with Europeans and Americans may have occasioned the rigor of heathen observances to be in some measure relaxed : but still no light shone from heaven ; there was no just knowledge of God, of Christ, and of salvation. Still, the unvarying testimony of voyagers was, ' These people are so addicted to their pagan customs, that they will never give them up. They will not abandon their taboos, and their sacrifices. You may attempt to teach them better, but you will never succeed.' Thus reasoned the world. The Christian knew such reasoning to be unsound ; but what Christian could have imagined, in his most sanguine moments, that such a change should have taken place, as the recent history of these islands discloses ? In the forcible language of our missionaries, ' By a single stroke of Jehovah's arm, the idols and the temples were crushed into the dust.' The priesthood deserted their altars of abomination ; and, in a single day, lost their proud and tyrannical pre-eminence. The spell of diabolical enchantment was broken ; the inveterate customs of three thousand years were

abolished.   Still, at the close of these wonderful, unparalleled, unex-
plained transactions, all was darkness; all was ignorance of what it
most concerns immortal beings to know.   The prison walls were indeed
levelled with the ground; and the manacles were knocked off: but how
could the prisoners walk, when they were both lame and blind?

" At this conjuncture, a vessel heaves in sight.   She has travelled
18,000 miles over a wide waste of waters, and has a select number of
passengers, who have come on a peculiar errand.   What is it?   It is to
proclaim the tidings of God's love to a perishing world; to offer salvation freely to all who repent and believe; to teach these benighted pagans
the way to heaven.   The heralds, who have cheerfully gone to make
this Divine proclamation, are our brethren.   From the doors of this
sanctuary they commenced their voyage of benevolence.   With strong
attachment to their native country; with prospects of usefulness and
respectability at home; with health and friends, and all that could
make this life desirable; they deliberately renounced the whole, and
counted all things but loss, if they might enjoy the privilege of preaching Christ to these perishing islanders.   Even delicate females, educated in all the tenderness which distinguishes a Christian country,
accustomed to polished and refined society, could willingly forego their
enjoyments, bid adieu to their dearest friends, submit to the inconveniences and perils of a six months' voyage in a crowded vessel, with
the single hope and aim of settling among barbarians, enlightening
their dark understandings, and communicating to them that ' Gospel,
which is the power of God and the wisdom of God to all them
that believe.'

" Were you present, my brethren, at this point of time, what would
be your feeling?   Did you see the islands, with their perishing thousands on the one hand, and the little company of missionaries, their
breasts heaving with the magnanimous, the high and holy purpose to
which I have barely alluded, on the other, would you not wish them
God-speed?

" Suppose the living worthies, who have done most to meliorate the
condition of man, and have given most evidence of their having partaken of the spirit of Christ, to be assembled for the purpose of behold-
ing such a spectacle.   Imagine the pious and philanthropic Wilberforce,
and the venerable Scott, and the honored Teignmouth, and the laborious and beloved officers of the Missionary and Bible Societies in
Great Britain, and the indefatigable Bogue, and the enraptured Chalmers, and Mrs. More, elevated almost above the confines of mortality,
and the aged Swiss Baron, with his equally venerable associate, and
Marshman and Carey from presiding in their schools, and Morrison
rising from his Chinese Bible, and Marsden the founder of Christian
society in New Holland: nor would they disdain the presence of their
younger brethren, and of those less known to the world, but belonging
to the same class, and delighting in the same employment.

" There you might see, mingled with other active laborers in the
Gospel harvest, our own Hall, and Newell, and Richards, restored from
the grave to witness so goodly a sight, and Kingsbury, forgetting his
Indians for a season, and Fisk and Parsons, with their eyes averted even
from their beloved Palestine.   In such a company, on such an occasion,
what would be the tone of feeling?   Would not the whole assembly,

as moved by one impulse, fall on their knees, and pray most importunately, that God would open an effectual door among the heathen, and give access to the princes and the people; that he would preserve this little band of pilgrims, and make their way prosperous; that he would glorify his own name, by the salvation of a countless multitude of souls, in the present generation, and through all succeeding ages.

"Though the actual condition of man upon earth does not allow of such a meeting as this; and though continents and oceans here separated those who are closely joined in purpose and affection; there is nothing in reason or Scripture to forbid the supposition, that the spirits of just men made perfect take a lively interest in the concerns of the Church below; and that they may be the delighted spectators of those movements, which bring salvation to their kindred, or light and joy to the dark places of the world. With what rapture, then, would the departed members and friends of the Society, under whose auspices this mission was sent forth, hail the day when the missionaries descried Hawaii, and spread forth their hands to its inhabitants, in the attitude of invitation and entreaty, beseeching them to hear the message from heaven. With what holy exultation would the sanctified and glorified minds of Dwight, and Spring, and Huntington, the father and the son, and Mills, and Warren, and Harriet Newell, and Opukahaia again visiting his birth-place, witness these overtures of mercy: and how would Eliot and Swartz, Brainard and Martyn, Vanderkemp and Thomas, with multitudes of others, possessing the same character, and having devoted their lives to the same ennobling employments, join in mutual congratulations, and in ascribing the most exalted praises to God and the Lamb.

"And what object would more naturally arrest the attention of ministering angels, on visits of kindness to the redeemed from among men; with what accelerated flight would they return to the regions of celestial glory with the ravishing intelligence!

"But, to whatever inconceivable height of heavenly joy and sympathy created spirits, all in their several ranks and orders, may have been excited on the occasion, and however numerous the assembly of saints and angels, there was still a more august Witness of the scene; and we have reason to believe that He regarded the enterprise with infinite benignity and love. This glorious Personage said, and not one of his declarations shall fail of accomplishment, 'Other sheep I have, which are not of this fold: them also I must bring, and they shall hear my voice: and there shall be one fold, and one Shepherd:' 'Go ye into all the world, and preach the Gospel to every creature.' 'Lo I am with you always, even unto the end of the world.'

"Let us then, my brethren, elevate our minds to the occasion, and learn to regard these transactions as they are regarded in Heaven."

Oh could the friends of Christ throughout Christendom but learn to regard his gracious designs towards the heathen " as they are regarded in Heaven," how soon would the sound of salvation reach all the ends of the earth !

CHAPTER VI.

SECOND YEAR OF THE MISSION, AND THIRD OF LIHOLIHO.—1821.

The Hawaiian Hula.—Removal of the Royal Family.—Insolent Priest.—Suspension of Kailua Station.—The King's visit to Honolulu.—Death of Likelike.—Wailing and Amusements.—Nuuanu and Palikoolua.—Arrival of Kaahumanu and the Royal Family at Honolulu.—Commodore Vascilieff.—Excursion to Kauai.—First Church at the Islands.—Visits of Whale Ships.—Proposed Voyage to Tahiti.—Sporting in the surf.—Liholiho's Voyage and Visit to Kauai.—Liliha's Canoe Voyage.—Excursion on Kauai.—Removal of Kaumualii.—His Union with Kaahamanu.—Her Illness.—Visit of the Russian Exploring Squadron.

WHILE some of the people who sat in darkness were beginning to turn their eyes to the light, and were disposed to attend our schools and public lectures, others, with greater enthusiasm, were wasting their time in learning, practising, or witnessing the *hula*, or heathen song and dance. This was intended, in part at least, as an honor and gratification to the king, especially at Honolulu, at his expected reception there, on his removal from Kailua.

Notwithstanding the self-indulgent and overbearing course of their monarch, the show of loyalty, feigned or real, was very general. For many weeks in succession, the first sound that fell on the ear in the morning was the loud beating of the drum, summoning the dancers to assemble. Some of our pupils were required to attend and perform their part. Day after day, several hours in the day, the noisy hula—drumming, singing, and dancing in the open air, constituted the great attraction or annoyance. The principal scene of the *hula*, at Honolulu, was a large yard contiguous to the house of the governor. The ground was covered with fresh rushes brought from a neighboring marsh, slung on the backs of the dancers, chiefs, and plebeians, men, women, and children, who, in such cases, walk in single file, precisely like the aborigines of North America. In the *hula*, the dancers are often fantastically decorated with figured or colored *kapa*, green leaves, fresh flowers, braided hair, and sometimes with a gaiter on the ancle, set with hundreds of dog's teeth, so as to be considerably heavy, and to rattle against each other in the motion of the feet. Notwithstanding these decorations, much of the person is uncovered; and the decent covering of a foreign dress was not then permitted to the public dancers. They were arranged in several equidistant ranks of considerable length, and at the sound of numbers, moved together, forward, backward,

to the right, and to the left, and vertically, giving extended
motions to the hands and feet, arms and legs, much like the
Shakers, without changing their relative position. The musicians
who sung without dancing, played on various unharmonious
instruments, the drum, the long gourd-shell, or double calabash,
and the long hardwood rod. Their wooden drum, with one shark-
skin head, is beaten by the fingers of the musician, sitting cross-
legged beside it as the uncovered end stands on the ground.
The long double calabash standing upright on the ground, is
beaten and often raised by the hands of the musician, sitting on
his heels, pressing the ground with knees and toes, and resounds
both by the strokes of the hands on the sides, and by its repeated
and forcible thumping on the earth, or the pad laid down for the
purpose. The long hardwood rod, used as a most simple drum,
is held in the left hand, the fore end pointing obliquely downward,
to help keep time, and increase the clatter, is beaten with a small
stick held lightly by the thumb and fingers of the right. The
numbers heard on these instruments, are sometimes difficult to
imitate or describe, and sometimes are more simple and orderly.
I have heard on them somewhat simple and natural numbers,
corresponding to what American boys call, " Bean porridge hot ;"

[musical notation in 2/4 time]

and similar numbers and measures without the first rests ;—

[musical notation in 2/4 time]

This also among many others :—

[musical notation in 2/4 time]

Two blacksmiths beating the same iron, and making similar
music, sometimes hit off numbers similar to the first and second
strains, the rests occurring while the two hand hammer is making
a circuit over the head of one of them, to acquire momentum,
then, that motion being changed, they give some seven or fifteen
strokes of equal time. Such toilsome exercises need the aid of
numbers. All parts of the *hula* are laborious, and under a
tropical sun, make the perspiration roll off freely from the
performers. Sometimes both musicians and dancers cantilate
their heathen songs together. Occasionally a single female voice
carries on the song, while the rest are silent, and sometimes
hundreds of voices are heard together. Melody and harmony are
scarcely known to them, with all their skill and art. The whole

arrangement and process of their old *hulas* were designed to promote lasciviousness, and of course the practice of them could not flourish in modest communities. They had been interwoven too with their superstitions, and made subservient to the honor of their gods, and their rulers, either living or departed and deified. Liholiho was fond of witnessing them, and they were managed to gratify his pride and promote his pleasure.

The royal family leaving Kailua towards the close of 1820, passed over to Lahaina, and thence, in the early part of 1821, with no little confusion, to Honolulu. Kalanimoku and his family school in charge of Mr. Loomis, at Kawaihae, and Naihe and Kapiolani of Kaawaloa, where Cook fell, removed to Honolulu about the same time, leaving Adams Kuakini as governor of Hawaii. Doctor and Mrs. Holman had previously left their station at Kailua, and thinking the privations and trials of the new field too severe to be welcomed during life, were seeking an early opportunity to return to the United States. William Kanui, who had been placed at Kailua, having in a few short months violated his vows by excess in drinking, which he attempted to justify, was excluded from Christian fellowship, but still performed some service for the chiefs for a time, then became a wanderer for many years. Mr. and Mrs. Thurston being no longer considered as reasonably secure at Kailua, were invited to repair to Honolulu, and soon removed. Before they left Kailua, and previous to the king's removal, they were annoyed and insulted by a vile heathen priest, who roughly laid hands on Mrs. Thurston while her husband was in school. Instantly breaking away, she fled, and sent for her husband and protector, who quickly joined her. Scarcely were they seated in their frail dwelling, which seemed but a miserable castle for protection, in such a land of confusion, before the priest, who had made off a little, re-entered the house, when Mr. Thurston, "himself a host," as many of his fellow students well remember, with a cane, showed the insolent intruder the way out again. It should be gratefully recorded, that from the entrance of our band into that field, Divine Providence has thrown such a shield over it, that, how much and often soever our families have been exposed, no other insult is known to have been offered by natives to ladies of the mission.

Mr. and Mrs. Thurston, for a season, left Kailua, and in circumstances singularly straitened, passed over to Lahaina, in a crowded brig, having, besides various inferior animals, 475 persons on board, occupying the hold, the steerage, the cabin, the deck, the rigging and the tops. Sojourning about a month at Lahaina, they proceeded, and arrived safely at Honolulu, Dec. 21st, where being most cordially received, they united in the labors of that station.

While at Maui, poor Hopu wrote for supplies, saying "that he had but one meal a day, and his shirts were rags, and he could get but little of King Liholiho, for he was always drinking rum."

But Hopu's zeal seemed not to flag for this neglect by his patron or its lamentable cause. Mr. Thurston, also, in his loneliness, feeling himself almost lost in the extent and darkness of the field, and lifting up his voice for helpers from home, thus wrote ;—

" We want men and women who have *souls*—who are crucified to the world and the world to them—who have their eyes and their hearts fixed on the glory of God in the salvation of the heathen—who will be willing to sacrifice every interest but Christ's—who will cheerfully and constantly labor to promote his cause—in a word, those who are pilgrims and strangers, such as the Apostle mentions in Heb. xi.—Men like these we want. Many such we need to complete the work which God, in his Providence, has permitted us to commence. The request which we heard while standing on the American shores, from these islands, we reiterate with increasing emphasis,—*Brethren, come over and help us.*"

The king, having purchased on credit, the celebrated Cleopatra's barge, built at Salem, Mass., and sold at the islands by Captain Suter, hastily embarked on board her at Lahaina, and sailed for Honolulu, about the 3d of February, 1821. Unexpectedly at Honolulu, the firing of the guns at night in Waikiki Bay, announced the king's approach, and our village was soon in uproar. The loud roar of cannon from the Cleopatra's barge, from the fort, and Punch-bowl Hill—the successive flashing of their blaze on the dark curtain of the night, and the reverberating echoes from the hills and valleys of their report—the shouting of the noisy natives, and the voice of the crier demanding hogs, dogs, poi, etc., to be gathered for the reception of his majesty (who was in his cups), formed a combination of the sublime and the ludicrous not soon to be forgotten by the missionaries. The king landed Sabbath morning, amid the continued noise, which was now increased by the yelping and crying dogs, tied on poles, and brought in for slaughter. Calling on the king at evening, to show proper respect, Mr. Thurston and myself found him in a mood not sufficiently companionable to speak to us. We were struck, however, with the ingenuity of Kamamalu, his favorite wife, who, in the dilemma, unexpectedly lifted the nerveless hand of her lord, that he might receive the salutation of his missionaries, before they returned to their house.

During his stay of a week, we besought him to allow us to erect for ourselves a more comfortable and durable house, the frame of which had been sent us by the American Board.

Mrs. B. had evidently suffered a severe illness from her exposure to the damp ground, after a confinement, without a floor, and we urged the danger to our wives as an important reason for permission to provide ourselves more comfortable accommodations. He replied, " My father never allowed a foreigner to build a house in his country, except for the king."

Kalanimoku, having come from Lahaina to induce the king to

return thither, called on us, caressed the children, and encouraged us to persevere in persuading the king to allow us to build. He listened to the cantilation of a Sabbath school lesson by the pupils, and of a rude translation of the hymn, " Come, Holy Spirit, heavenly Dove"—taught them by Honolii. On renewing our application to the king, he consented to our building, but bade us defer the work till he should return from Maui. He and Kalanimoku hastily sailed for that island, whence, in about a month, they returned to Honolulu to reside.

Laboring to master the language and to teach and preach as we had opportunity, Mr. Thurston and myself stood shoulder to shoulder, witnessing the confusion and ruin around us, and looking together for aid from on high.

How often have the chiefs and people of the Sandwich Islands been represented as easily influenced and moulded to one's will! Their ready compliance was doubtless in reference to what was agreeable to perverse nature, or with reference to that which they had not physical strength to resist. But in respect to the course the Bible marks out, the case was different. The missionaries found that the conflict between the light of Christianity and the darkness of heathenism was no momentary struggle. Even those who were desirous to be instructed, clung with great tenacity to their heathen customs, and their heathen pleasures. Multitudes passed away quickly to the grave before much impression could be made on them, and others resisted for years all the endeavors of missionaries to reclaim them.

Among those who, on removing from Hawaii to Honolulu, called on our family there, was Likelike, the favorite wife of Kalanimoku. Scarcely had she given proof of her desire and ability to learn, when the birth of an heir of Kalanimoku, and son of Likelike, was announced by the roar of cannon and musketry. Some two hundred pounds of powder, it was supposed, were consumed on the occasion, much of it at the door of her hut. Nor was it strange that the babe which had been complimented with such noisy honors, died in twenty-four hours; nor that the mother, though accustomed to the confusion of war, and to a rude heathen life, was unable to go through all this with safety. In a few days the sound of wailing from her house, reached the ears of the missionaries. Two of us, repairing to the place, found the poor, sinking Likelike shrieking and writhing, in the agonies of death, beyond the reach of human skill or help. Oh, how different the death of a heathen from that of the Christian! What horror appeared to hang over the grave! For four nights in succession, at her earnest solicitation, her friends had carried her out and immersed her, to cool the burning fever, with the hope of prolonging her life till her husband should arrive. But now the hour of her departure had come. Boki, who had called us to sit near her, finding that her breath had ceased, and every sign of life was gone, turned his face upwards, and set up the loud heathen wail, which soon became general and deafening, from a multitude of voices. We retired from the crowd, while some stood wringing their hands in anguish, crying with loud and lamentable tones and cadences, while floods of tears ran down their swarthy faces. Others uttered piteous moans, without tears, and a few, after a little time, sat in silent sadness. Not a ray of Christian consolation, probably, fell upon the group.

The husband of the deceased had taken her from his brother, Boki, who, to supply her place, had taken Liliha from his nephew Kahalaia.

Kalanimoku, at an earlier period, on being deserted by a former wife, is reported to have said, in his anger, to Kamehameha, "I want to burn up the world," to which the old king replied, "Burn." Like a madman, he set fire to the village of Honolulu, destroying a considerable number of habitations.

On repeated visits to this house of mourning, for a few days, we had impressive lessons concerning the customs and tastes of the people. Some were cutting off each other's hair, close to the skin, on the sides of the head, leaving the rest long, and indulging in loud laughter. Some were lying on their faces, uttering loud wailing, with tears, while others lay in a state of intoxication, suffering the time to pass unconsciously away. Some were burning semi-circular scars on their skin, with semi-cylindrical pieces of bark on fire. Others were seen cheerfully employed in playing cards, and other games. Kalanimoku himself, arriving from the windward, engaged in their favorite game of *Puhenehene.**

How incongruous and revolting, to bring revelry, gambling, and the mirthful, giddy dance of the ungodly pleasure-seeking throng, into the midst of death and mourning! Earnestly did we for several days plead with Kalanimoku and the king, to substitute for these, at least for one Sabbath day, or for an hour of it, an appropriate funeral service.

Kalanimoku at length consented to have a funeral sermon on the Sabbath, at his house, and listened with others, while some of the strange doctrines of " Jesus and the resurrection," were set forth, as connected with the sin and death of mankind. He wished us to tell him, if his departed wife had gone to *heaven.*

After this service, we sought and found the king, whose

* The instruments for playing this, are five pieces of folded bark-cloth, which, laid side by side, cover about a square yard, a stone, to be hidden, and sought under them, and for each player, a neat and slender wand, having a shred of a leaf or cloth drawn at right angles, into a hole at the tip. The players, usually from four to ten, each with his wand in hand, sit like Turks, upon their rush or pandanus mat, around the quintuple heap of *kapa.* One of the players, taking the pebble, passes his hand and naked arm under the five pieces of *kapa,* leaving it where he supposes the opposite party will be least likely to guess it to be. That party, chattering awhile about the position of the hidden stone, strike forcibly with their wands, two of the five parts of the heap, the chance of hitting right being two to three, and a little more they think. This operation, pursued by rotation, gives each party an equal chance to win the stake, by finding the stone most frequently in a given number of trials.

attention we called to the institution and obligations of the Sabbath, and urged him to suspend the public Sabbath dancing. He replied, " This is the Hawaiian custom, and must not be hindered." Several of our pupils expected to be called on by the governor to dance on the Sabbath ; and fearing that their newly instructed conscience, and inexperienced heart, could not withstand such a call, we interceded with the king to excuse those who wished to attend our Sabbath school, instead of the *hula*. " I wish to see them dance to-day," was his reply ; and the drum beat to summon them. His consent was then asked, and gained, to allow the daily dance to be suspended on the following Sabbath. When Boki heard this, he said with magisterial and atheistic air, " Dance we will—no *tabu*." Several of our pupils, however, resolved to attend the Sabbath school rather than dance.

Believing the dance to be connected with idolatry and licentiousness, and wholly incompatible with Christianity, we spoke to Liholiho and Kamamalu, of the appearance of idolatry, who affirmed that it was *play*, and not idol worship. One of the officers of Boki asked us to pray to Jehovah to give the king a new heart, and make him stop drinking rum.

At the close of the week, as the missionaries visited his Majesty, he earnestly demanded, " Why did you not come to my dinner to-day ? This is my great day. By good eating and drinking, and firing many guns, I commemorate the death of my father." Expressing our regard for his father, and his successor, we signified our readiness to improve the occasion, by giving an appropriate discourse, the ensuing day,—the Sabbath. " Had you done it to day," said he, " I should have liked it. To-morrow I go to Maui." Seeing a rum-drinking resident enter that moment, he instantly called for a bottle, and stepping forward, said, " I give you this bottle of rum, take it, and go home ;" then with the same kind of grace, drank off a tumbler of the like beverage, to the health of the missionaries.

As the Sabbath arrived, we again sought his ear and his conscience. He was looking for a fair wind, to embark for Maui, and was very loquacious. When asked if he would not defer his embarkation, if there should be head wind, and attend Divine service with us, as it was the Lord's day, he said, " If a head wind blows, I will beat this way and that, and go up quick," suiting the action to the word. Being then affectionately entreated to abstain from rum, he said, " By and by,—by and by—not now. I go now to my house to pray to God. Pray ye to Jehovah to give me a good wind ;" and suiting the action to the word again, said, " I don't want it to blow from this quarter, but from that." He persevered and embarked the same day, with a great company, on board several vessels, but he returned before many days.

In a short vacation of our school, about the middle of March,

I made an excursion to Koolau in company with Mr. Thurston, taking with us a troop of our boarding and other scholars, and Honolii to assist in addressing the people. Directly in our course we crossed the natural curiosity, the *Pali*—the precipice or Alpine pass of Nuuanu. Travelling north from Honolulu, we gradually ascended the left branch of the valley about eight miles. Our narrow foot path led along by the streams and numerous kalo beds about half the distance, when we passed the celebrated battle-ground; then (as the valley becomes contracted between two steep mountains), among shrubs, ferns, wild vines and trees, hills and dells and murmuring brooks, and the last mile and a half, through a wood. The scenery on the right and left is exceedingly picturesque. The mountains on either side about one hundred rods distant, rising higher and higher as we passed along up the valley, presented a well-defined outline against the sky, sloping from their summits in the middle of the island almost to the sea on the south. The luxuriance of the vegetation, the great variety of shade and form of the foliage, the little cascades rushing merrily down the steep mountain sides, the densely shaded brooks seeking a passage through the thicket into the open country, presented a fine contrast to the naked sides of the Punch-bowl crater, and the arid plain at its base near our residence. In the wood at the foot of a water-fall, at the base of one of these mountains, we were told, " *Ke-akua-moo*," the reptile god, who devoured men, once resided.

Emerging from a thicket, we at length found ourselves on the brink of the *Pali*, or precipice, eleven hundred feet above the level of the sea, overlooking the district of Palikoolau. The sudden bursting on the vision as by magic, of this district—its broad, quiet valley spread out like a map beneath our feet, its vast amphitheatre of mountains, and beyond it, the heaving, white fringed ocean, rising in the distance to meet the sky, in their united beauty and sublimity, make a powerful impression on the senses, while one is balancing on the verge, and holding his hat to prevent it from being whirled high in mid air by the force of the trade winds rushing through this gorge, as if demanding a wider passage. To heighten the grandeur and beauty of this view, which is rarely surpassed by any scene in nature, the lofty peak of Konahuanui, very near on the right, towers about 3000 feet above the precipice, and on the left, and equally near at hand, the more precipitous, perpendicular, rocky, needle-pointed Nuuanu rises almost to an equally lofty height. It is nearly perpendicular on the north, where it forms a part of the stupendous wall of the valley, but, like Konahuanui, slopes gradually to the south. From its steep basaltic side, half way to the summit, the whitish tropic bird sailed off over the valley as it lay basking in the summer sunbeams, stretched out in the giant arms of the mountain, which, in their ample sweep, reached and touched the white fringe of the ocean's broad mantle.

The people who could be seen below the precipice, appeared like the fabled Liliputians, and as slow in their motions, as diminutive in their size.

The interest of the visit to this place is, if possible, heightened by the reflection that in the days of heathen warfare, a portion of the united forces of the haughty Kalanikupule and the aspiring and traitorous Kaiana, flying from the victorious warriors of Kamehameha, were, in their haste, precipitated down this steep and destroyed.

Imagination was here put upon the stretch to conceive how this grand panorama had been formed ; whether its grand and singular features had been given it at the creation, by the hand that weigheth the mountains in scales and the hills in a balance, or at the breaking of the bars of the great deep, they were shaped by the same hand that now stays the proud waves of the wide sea, or in later ages, by volcanic agency long and obviously employed by the same Almighty power in different parts of the whole group. Did this grand semicircle of mountains seen from the pali, once constitute half the rim of a stupendous active crater some thirty-five or forty miles in circumference ? And has the other, the northern half, been, by some terrific convulsion, rent away and thrown down with awful detonations, and with indescribable commotion of the elements, buried for ever in the depths of the ocean ? Has the enclosed area, now the place of streams, green hills and lawns, been in ages past, half the surface of a fiery lava-lake in fearful ebullition, but extinguished by the voice of the Almighty, and long quiescent and decomposing, become the dwelling-place of a portion of the Hawaiian race, now waiting for the Messiah's law ? Who can tell ?

Whatever may be the true answer to these questions, not easily solved, it is affirmed by travellers that of all the natural scenery they have witnessed this presents decidedly the finest view.

To descend or ascend the precipice on which we stood, seemed extremely difficult, and to scale the lofty summits on the right and left, impossible ; but modern discoveries and improvements in the passage with a little experience, make the former quite feasible, and further improvements might make it passable for horses or mules.

After feasting our eyes awhile with the charming scene, we descended into the valley beyond the dense wood at the foot of the precipice, collected a few of the inhabitants, and for the first time, preached the Gospel to them. Extremely ignorant, destitute and debased, they appeared wild as the young ass's colt upon the mountains, and some of them, even frightened at the voice of the preacher and interpreter, as though they apprehended they were to be laid on the altar, or prayed to death, as they believed the victims of the priests of their superstition had been.*

* A missionary station, at Kaneohe, has since been established in that valley.

After the sermon, retracing our steps with some difficulty, we climbed the *pali* with our little group, who were pleased with the excursion, though they did not wholly escape bruises ; and gazing once more at the grand panorama seen from the *pali*, we cheerfully returned to Honolulu.

Early in the month of April, 1821, Liholiho, Kaahumanu, and the rest of the royal family, came to Honolulu to reside, and were received with some noise and commotion.

The next morning the king called on the mission family.. Without ceremony he threw himself upon a bed, and in his merry mood, rolled from side to side to prove its quality. Kamamalu entering Mrs. Bingham's room, which was lined with mats, and gazing at its order and finish, lifted both hands, and exclaimed " *Maikai !*" excellent ; then snatching her sleeping first-born from its quiet cradle, and pleased with its dress, complexion and smiles, hastened to another house to present it to the king, and returned with him. He bade the mother good morning, and gazing a moment at her apartment, passed from it into the school-room, and heard a lesson rehearsed with spirit by our boarding scholars at his request, and pronounced it *maikai !* Giving a laconic *aloha* to the missionaries, he mounted our hand-cart at the door, and was wheeled off with speed by his servants, a troop of attendants, two of his five wives, and an armed guard, running to keep him company.

The same day we received a very polite call from Commodore Michael Vascilieff, of the Imperial Russian Navy, his aged chaplain of the Greek Church, with a long white beard hanging down upon his bosom, and thirteen of the officers of the Exploring Squadron, all in their appropriate uniforms. They showed the mission repeated kindnesses, which were very grateful.

The first anniversary of our landing at Honolulu,—the 19th of April, was observed as a day of thanksgiving and prayer, as it has often been since, by an examination of schools on Oahu, and review of our progress. Our Sabbath congregation soon increased, prejudices yielded, and a more friendly aspect was assumed by the chiefs. The king invited us to a public dinner, at which he presided, and in his uniform, or military dress, appeared with unwonted dignity. The next day, with several chiefs, he visited our families ; and, on being assured anew of our unvarying intention to do him good, and not evil, to elevate the nation, and promote their prosperity and salvation, he confirmed the original permission granted us, to remain and labor as missionaries, approved of our erecting a permanent house for our accommodation, and requested us to aid him in building a palace three stories high ; the upper story of which, he said, should be devoted to the worship of Jehovah. In token of his confidence and friendship, he gave us a hog and ninety pieces of bark cloth. In like manner, Kaahamanu, Kalanimoku, and Kalakua, visited our families soon after, and gave still more liberally, useful supplies. Kaahamanu, far from being satisfied with the profligacy of Liholiho, seemed to turn her thoughts to the possible aid that might be obtained from a higher power, and asked us to pray for the king. She did not pretend to pray herself, or to obey the divine commands; nor had she yet shown the least desire to learn to read or write. Kaumualii exceeded them all.

At this time, with Mrs. Bingham, I visited the station at Waimea, Kauai, and found it prosperous, preached a few times, baptized the children of Mrs. W. and Mrs. R., and encouraged the king, whom I found teachable and friendly. As I proposed to return from Kauai to Honolulu, Kaumualii took a handkerchief, and bound my hands and drew me near his side, thus emphatically signifying his wish if not his purpose to detain me as his missionary.

We shortly returned to our post, leaving Honolii to assist the brethren, at Kauai. He soon sent me the following report of one of his efforts to instruct the king.

" On Sunday morning the king and queen came into the meeting, with his few people. Then Mr. Whitney read about Jesus Christ on the cross, and the Ten Commandments, and I explain them, in our tongue, and make prayer, and after that, I sit down. I ask the king, ' How you like the meeting ?' He say then, ' I like the meeting very well, sir.' Mr. Whitney ask him—' You understand what John tell you about ?' ' Yes, sir.' Then he say, ' I not understand what you say before, but little ; now I hope I do understand more ;—more by and by.' I, John, told the king, ' Your peoples—they have *hulahula*, [dancing] on this day ?' King say, ' Yes.' Then I ask him, ' Can you wait *hulahula*, on this day ? Your peoples may hulahula [dance] on Monday.—This day, it is holy.' And the king say, ' We may stop hulahula on another Sabbath day.' "

Within two months from our first anniversary, our place of worship was quite too strait for us, and on the 25th of June, a subscription was opened for a church, to which chiefs and foreigners subscribed. An amount sufficient for a frail, thatched house of worship, fifty-four feet by twenty-one, was soon obtained, and the work of building it by native hands hired for the service, was in a few months accomplished. Plain doors, a pulpit window, and a decent pulpit, surmounted with astral lamps, were added by foreign workmen, which, though cheap and rude, were adapted to the cheap, frail building, and gave it somewhat the air of a house of God.

On the 15th of September, Mr. Thurston preached the dedication sermon, from the words, " And the children of Israel, the priests and the Levites, and the rest of the children of the captivity, kept the dedication of this house of God with joy." The next day, the public services of the Sabbath were performed and highly enjoyed in the new sanctuary.

Scarcely had the solitary missionaries been thoroughly initiated into their work in those islands, where they had contemplated an almost absolute seclusion from all the rest of the world, when the whaling ships from different countries, but especially from the United States, were in rapid succession and considerable numbers, attracted to that quarter. This was in consequence of the discovery in 1820, made and published by Captain Joseph Allen, of the ship Maro, of Nantucket, that the North Pacific off the coast of Japan and Niphon, abounded in sperm whales. He visited Oahu the same season, and as a sympathizing " Friend," ministered to the wants and secured the gratitude of the mission family. The Sandwich Islands becoming a safe and convenient place for watering, refitting, and procuring refreshments, the calls both of merchant vessels and ships in the whaling service, chiefly from Nantucket, New Bedford, and New London, became common, especially at Honolulu and Lahaina. The faces and the names of several masters, Allen, Arthur, Bunker, Swain, Weeks, Sayre, Gardner, Coffin, Stetson, Brayton, Turner, and others from the United States, and Starbuck, Best, Green, and Morgan from Great Britain, became familiar and pleasant, and though their home was sixteen or eighteen thousand miles distant by sea, we looked upon them as *neighbors*, whom we were glad to meet on their long and toilsome voyages. From such men, in the whaling and merchant service, we received repeated tokens of kindness, which alleviated the trials of our early exile, while we were allowed to promote their security among the people who furnished them supplies, and to call their attention to the pearl of great price, by which we were seeking to enrich the sons and daughters of long neglected idolaters.

While many masters and mates, in the Merchant, Whaling, and Naval service, have proved themselves honorable and courteous, it must not be inferred that the influence of their crews, and of a large class of other captains and officers, was always favorable to the peace, reputation or success of the missionaries, or their native helpers.

Early in the summer of 1821 a voyage was planned by the friendly king of the leeward Islands to open an intercourse with the Society and Georgian islands. He proposed to send the brig Becket, one of the vessels which he had recently purchased of American traders, and to allow two of the missionaries the privilege of a passage thither.

This being made known to the missionaries, they deemed it advisable that one from Honolulu and one from Kauai should avail themselves of the king's generous offer of a passage, for the purpose of consulting the missionaries who had for years been successfully employed in the South Seas. We were very desirous of obtaining copies of all their publications, and the results of their experience in the difficult work of evangelizing a tribe of the heathen possessing great similarity of character, habits, language, customs, condition and religion, and thus securing important means for the furtherance and consummation of our missionary enterprise.

It was deemed very desirable to have the concurrence, if not the active co-operation of Liholiho, Kaahumanu and Kalanimoku, in this undertaking, that no jealousy or rivalry might find occasion to defeat the object. They were consulted, and offered no objections. Kaahumanu entered into it in a more business-like manner than the others. When we called upon her to know her pleasure in regard to it, we passed an hour with her pleasantly, and made known our plan and wishes. She received us kindly, entered into our views with unexpected readiness, and, at our request, designated a man to accompany us, and said she would come to us and finish what she had to say about it.

The next day, as Mr. Ruggles and myself were about to proceed to Kauai to complete our arrangements for the Tahitian voyage, Kaahumanu came to the mission house with Mr. Marin, the interpreter, and commissioned us to give her salutations to Pomare, the king of Tahiti, and to convey to him, as her present, some native bark robes, and a splendid war-cloak of net work, neatly covered with small, bright and beautiful feathers, and to bring for her, sea-shells, cocoanut shells polished, a royal surf-board, and seeds of the productions of that country to plant in her own. At our request, she consented to our taking with us John Ii besides her servant, whom she had designated to accompany us.

As we left the wharf at Honolulu, she and Kalanimoku came and gave us the parting hand—a great condescension, and an indication of increasing interest, particularly in the case of the haughty queen.

Her sister, Kalakua, having embarked the day before for Hawaii on board the king's brig, was providentially driven back into the harbor, and, immediately changing her plan, embarked with us for Kauai. Going together on board the ship Tartar, Capt. Turner, who obligingly gave us a passage, we set sail July 8th, and in twenty hours came safely to anchor in Waimea roads. Kaumualii quickly sent his double canoe, and conveyed the missionaries and their families on shore. He received us in person on the beach, and as I saluted him with a kiss and a hearty *aloha*, he gave me his friendly hand, and said, with a dignified smile, " I *very glad to see you.*"

He was already directing the labors of some twenty men in preparing a feast for the honored relict of Kamehameha, having ordered the slaughter of the requisite amount of hogs, dogs, and fowls for the purpose. Early in the afternoon, Kalakua and attendants landed from the Tartar, just in front of the mission house, which then stood directly between the fort and the sea.

Kaumualii and his queen, Kapule, and their attendants, met her near the water side; and, with the ancient etiquette, they embraced each other, joined noses, and, reminding us of Jewish manners, lifted up their voices and wept ; then sat down together on the sandy beach, and in remembrance of past sorrows, or in proof of friendship, continued crying for a time.

The king, having his house prepared for the occasion by spreading its area and the court in front with his best grass carpets or figured Niihau mats, introduced his royal guest. When the dinner was prepared, the king assisted to set the feast before her, and after dinner resigned the house to her and her company, proclaimed a tabu forbidding the people of Kauai to enter its court unbidden, and retired himself to a more ordinary habitation.

The royal parties, the next day, amused themselves awhile by trimming and stringing the bright, yellow, polished nuts of the Pandanus for coronets and necklaces, and decorating their own and each other's heads and necks, with this much esteemed but rude ornament. After this, they resorted to the favorite amusement of all classes—sporting on the surf, in which they distinguish themselves from most other nations. In this exercise, they generally avail themselves of the surf-board, an instrument manufactured by themselves for the purpose. It is made of buoyant wood, thin at the edges and ends, but of considerable thickness in the middle, smooth, and ingeniously adapted to the purpose of sustaining a moderate weight and gliding rapidly on the surface of the water. It is of various dimensions, from three feet in length, and six or eight inches in breadth, to fourteen feet in length, and twenty inches in breadth. In the use of it, the islander, placing himself longitudinally upon the board as it rests upon the surface of the water, and using his naked arms and hands as a pair of oars, rows off from the sand-beach a quarter, or half a mile into the ocean. Meeting the succession of surges as they are rolling towards the shore, he glides with ease over such as are smooth, plunges under or through such as are high and combing, allowing them to roll over him and his board, and coming out unhurt on the other side, he presses on till his distance is sufficient for a race, or till he has passed beyond the breaking or combing surf. After a little rest, turning around and choosing one of the highest surges for his *locomotive*, he adjusts himself and board, continuing longitudinally upon it, directing his head towards the shore, and just before the highest part of the wave reaches him, he gives two or three propelling strokes with his spread hands. The board, having its hindmost end now considerably elevated, glides down the moving declivity, and darts forward like a weaver's shuttle. He rides with railroad speed on the forefront of the surge, the whitening surf foaming and roaring just behind his head, and is borne in triumph to the beach. Often in this rough riding, which is sometimes attended with danger, several run the race together. Formerly, this was usually done on a wager. The inhabitants of these islands, both male and female, are distinguished by their fondness for the water, their powers of diving and swimming, and the dexterity and ease with which they manage themselves, their surf-boards and canoes, in that element. Their divers can stay under water five or six minutes.

The adoption of our costume greatly diminishes their practice of swimming and sporting in the surf, for it is less convenient to wear it in the water than the native girdle, and less decorous and safe to lay it entirely off on every occasion they find for a plunge or swim or surf-board race. Less time, moreover, is found for amusement by those who earn or make cloth-garments for themselves like the more civilized nations.

The decline or discontinuance of the use of the surf-board, as civilization advances, may be accounted for by the increase of modesty, industry or religion, without supposing, as some have affected to believe, that missionaries caused oppressive enactments against it. These considerations are in part applicable to many other amusements. Indeed, the purchase of foreign vessels, at this time, required attention to the collecting and delivering of 450-000 lbs. of sandal-wood, which those who were waiting for it might naturally suppose would, for a time, supersede their amusements.

On the 20th, Mr. Jones, the United States Commercial Agent, arriving from Oahu, called on us, and spoke of some opposition to the proposed voyage to the Society Islands. He said, " the objections urged against it by the traders were, that it would be injurious to bring speculators from the Society to the Sandwich Islands ;—that the honor to the American people (so young, and so recently independent), of sending out first, and establishing so large and important a mission, at these islands, would be diminished if we should now apply to English missionaries for aid, for it would be said in England, we could not succeed without their help ;—that it would not be well for the mission to be laid under so great an obligation to Kaumualii as the favor contemplated would impose ;— and finally, that there was such a total dissimilarity between the two languages, that the procuring of books and translations would be of little or no use." Such was the array of reasons presented by Mr. Jones in behalf of American traders, against a harmless visit to English Protestant missionaries, to obtain their advice and their publications. The benevolent notion of Mr. Jones and his friends, that missionaries ought not to be laid under great obligations, deserves to be remembered in the progress of the work. The objections of Mr. Jones are the more remarkable, placed beside his own reasoning on the other side, when *Catholic* missionaries, both English and French, came to the islands, backed by the power of France and Rome, not to aid the American mission, but to defeat it. The traders, who had some claims on Kaumualii, had, doubtless, other objections to his sending away his brig, and the king was discouraged or dissuaded from the enterprise, and we failed of the advantage contemplated, and commenced writing and printing the Hawaiian language without. Subsequently, we were favored with an interview, to be mentioned in its place, which promoted the object sought without our further incurring the displeasure of our neighbors.

At this time, Liholiho, wishing to visit Kauai, which his father had never accomplished, concealing his plan, chose an open sail-boat, instead of one of his brigs, and embarked from Honolulu, July 21st, with Naihe, Kapiolani, Boki, and about thirty men, professedly for Ewa, a few miles west. But contrary to the expectations and wishes of his attendants, he refused to land at Ewa, or to enter its deep lagoon, and passed round Barber's Point. Then, to their great surprise, he ordered the helmsman to steer for Kauai, nearly one hundred miles distant. All but himself were afraid to attempt it. They remonstrated, and urged him to refrain and return ; but in vain.

Destitute of water, provisions, compass, chart or quadrant, embarked in an undecked sail-boat, built by a Hawaiian, crowded with passengers, stretching out to sea, over a rough channel, having the strong trade-winds abeam, as the night was approaching and shutting down upon them, how presumptuous to attempt to reach Kauai, far beyond their sight! But the king, half intoxicated, and fearless of dangers of that sort, and totally regardless of the reasonable apprehension of others, who had a right to his consideration and protection, would neither listen to advice, nor allow remonstrance to have the least influence. Neither their utter destitution as to preparation for a voyage, should they miss their object, or be driven out of sight of land, nor the danger of speedily foundering in mid-channel, where they must all have perished, nor the possible hostility and resistance of the Kauaians could alter the determination to proceed of this headstrong, indomitable monarch of the isles. He assumed the character of sailing-master or pilot of his little home-built vessel; and, in his merry mood, spread the thumb and fingers of one hand, and facetiously called it his compass, and considered their diverging points as representing several of the different points of the compass, which, to native ears, he attempted to explain, or express in broken English, and calling one of them " nor'-west," the supposed direction of Kauai, thus gave the course and directed his frail barque.

Thrice they were nearly capsized, and the sea broke over them, to the amazement of his friends, and the hazard of swamping. His attendants exclaimed, " *E hoi kakou—o make !*" Let us return lest we perish. " No," said the king, peremptorily (and " where the word of the king is there is power"), " dash out the water and go on." With a spice of that spirit, perhaps, which dictated the proud, artful, and animating address of the dauntless Roman to his boatman in time of danger, " Fear not, for thou carriest Cæsar," he added, "If you return to Oahu with the boat, I will *swim* to Kauai, in the sea." Heaving out the water with gourd shells, as their manner is in freeing their canoes after taking a sea over them or admitting water by a leak, they continued their

course at his stern command. They steered too far to the northward, fearing, perhaps, the falling too much to the leeward ; and
running rapidly, they descried the island in the distance, under
their lee bow ; then, veering to the westward, with great hazard
and inconvenience from the successive breaking of the sea over
them in mid-channel, they reached Waimea roads before the dawn
of day, in a condition about as defenceless as the unarmed missionary as he travels on foot over their mountains and ravines, or
passes in their small craft, from island to island, in the prosecution
of his peaceful work. Liholiho threw himself entirely into the
power of king Kaumualii. No roaring cannon opposed or welcomed his approach. Kaumualii being apprised of his arrival in
the roads, rose, and with composure dressed himself, and taking
with him two or three unarmed servants as proof of his pacific
disposition, went off in a canoe and put himself equally in the
power of Liholiho. They, in mutual compliments, interchanged
the expressive *aloha*, and joined noses. The company on board
expressed much satisfaction at being allowed to see Kaumualii
in peace, and were soon kindly welcomed on shore.

Liliha, the wife of Boki, followed her husband and her king, in
a single canoe, one hundred and twenty miles, from Honolulu to
Waimea. As we saw her frail sea-boat come in, with its little
white sail, and four rowers with broad paddles, bringing her safely
from the perilous channel, the king exclaimed, "*Aloha ino !*"
The broad, rough channel between Oahu and Kauai, is the most
difficult of the Hawaiian channels to pass with a canoe. It might
be deemed by a New Englander quite impracticable to sail such a
distance over the rough Atlantic in a hollow log or canoe carved
out of a single trunk, so liable to be overturned by wind and
waves, or to be overwhelmed by the combing surges. But the
ingenuity with which the Hawaiian shapes and rigs his hollowed
tree trunk, and the dexterity with which he manages it in all circumstances, *on* or *in* the water, make these voyages, which would
be hazardous to us, quite practicable to him.

The canoe is wrought with skill, the sides being made smooth
and thin, the ends light, pointed and partially decked over. If it
meets a large wave endwise, it quickly rises and easily mounts over
it. It has neither keel nor helm, but is steered by a common
paddle, put down by hand beside the stern. The device for preventing the narrow, round-bottomed vessel from being capsized in
rough weather or insufferably unsteady in smooth water, consists
of an out-rigger—a piece of buoyant wood, about half or two-
thirds the length of the canoe, round, slightly curved in the
middle, and turned up at one end like a sleigh runner, and at the
other end raised a little, and perpendicularly flattened, and terminated somewhat like the breach of a musket. It rests and runs
on the water parallel with the canoe, and at the distance of
five to ten feet from it. It is attached by two curved yokes,
lashed at one end with cinet to the top or upper edges of both

sides of the canoe, and at the other to the outrigger where the yokes bend down to meet it. The buoyancy of the corky outrigger prevents the canoe from falling in that direction, and the weight of it and of the yokes prevents it from falling over in the opposite direction. But if a mast and sail are raised on the canoe, and the wind tends to careen it too much, the passengers incline to the opposite side to balance its force. In case they are swamped or upset by the violence of the wind or waves at sea, all on board have ready recourse to their dexterity in swimming; and while some attend to the articles liable to be lost, others, bringing the canoe right side up though full of water, throw their weight upon one end of it and depress it, while the other rising above the surface, causes a portion of the water to flow out; then, throwing themselves suddenly off, the emptied end falls upon the surface and the other rises, when one of the mariners springs in, and with his calabash, briskly throws out the remaining water; the rest resuming their places, with what they may have preserved, they again joyfully pursue their course. They are, however, sometimes overtasked, chilled, or exhausted, or driven off by storms and lost.

Liliha, on landing, was greeted by her friends, and the two kings soon attended to business.

Kaumualii, wishing to know the pleasure of Liholiho, proposed to give up to him his country, vessels, fort and guns. When the generous proposition was fully made, there was, for a little time, a profound stillness, the parties waiting with deep interest to hear the reply of Liholiho, on which the fortunes of Kaumualii and his family, and of others, seemed to be suspended. At length, his majesty Liholiho replied, "I did not come to dispossess you. Keep your country and take care of it as before, and do what you please with your vessels." To this succeeded a shout of cheerful approbation from both parties, and Kaumualii retired from the consultation with a peaceful smile. In this very singular transaction between the " *emperor and king*"—as Liholiho sometimes styled himself and Kaumualii, it is difficult to say which of them showed the greatest degree of sagacity or magnanimity.

In two days, the five wives of Liholiho arrived from Oahu on board the Cleopatra's barge. The two kings and the principal chiefs present, soon set out on a tour round Kauai, to see the country and enjoy the fruits of the land.

During their absence of more than forty days, Mr. Whitney and I crossed over the island to visit and instruct them and the people in their dark places of abode. Taking with us a guide and a son of Mr. Chamberlain, we ascended gradually from Waimea northward to the mountains. We found no inhabitants residing in the upland country. The land, as it rises several miles from the sea-shore towards the forests, is not well watered, except in the deep, narrow valleys, through which streams from the mountains flow towards the sea, and where the principal cultivated productions are found. The fire had run in the withered grass over some tracts, making it black. The face of the country exhibits marks of former earthquakes, and of other volcanic agency. A variety of forest trees, besides the sandal-wood, grow in the interior, some suitable for building, and some for cabinet-work, but none like the trees of New England.

About one o'clock P. M., it began to thunder, and we were soon enveloped in a cloud on the mountains. At two, a heavy shower of rain commenced. We took shelter in a temporary booth built by the sandal-wood cutters, where we experienced and had occasion to record the preserving care of Omnipotence, who made his lightnings play and thunders roll harmless around us. At three, the shower appeared to be principally over, and as we were anxious to reach, if possible, the opposite side before dark, we pressed on; but to our disappointment, the clouds gathered more thickly, and the rain came down copiously, and streams fell from the points of our half-sheltering umbrellas, as we trudged along in a narrow, winding, slippery foot-path, sometimes on sharp ridges, here ascending and there descending rugged steeps.

In the deep solitude of these dreary mountains we came to two little temporary sheds left by the sandal-wood cutters on the bank of a swift mountain torrent, swelled by the rain. Into these we crept to seek a partial shelter. Solitary, damp and cheerless as they appeared, we thought it expedient to make them our lodging for the night, as we could not, without daylight, proceed with safety to the nearest settlement on the other side, and the day was now too far spent to attempt it. Our attendants struck up a fire, and collected fuel to feed it. We partly dried our clothes. The rain abated. The thunder ceased, and the stars appeared. Offering our evening sacrifice, and spreading down upon the damp leaves a large cloak, we laid ourselves down to rest under the care of the Watchman of Israel. The night passed quickly away. The rising day dawned upon us in peace, and invited us to proceed. Our path was still wet, rugged and slippery, leading up and down successive steeps, through miry places, and over a tract of high table-land; while the singing of birds cheered the forests which never feel the frosts of autumn, or the icy hand of winter. About nine o'clock, A. M., we came suddenly to the verge of Maunahina, a high and steep mountain which overlooked the northern part of the island. The clouds were literally spread under our feet, completely bounding the view below us, though we had the clear and bright sunshine where we stood, but breaking away occasionally before we began to descend from this giddy height, allowed us to see the white surf of the Pacific, rolling upon the shore, at the distance of seven miles; while majestic and lofty mountains on the right and left, presented scenery of peculiar grandeur and beauty. Down this awful steep on which we stood, four thousand feet in height, with the toil of three hours, we descended on a very sharp steep ridge or rib, extending from the top to the base of the mountain, and so nearly perpendicular, and in many places so difficult to pass, that we were obliged to go backwards, clinging to roots of trees, and shrubs, and crags of rocks, our guide going before and showing us where to place our feet, and where to hold with our hands.

The vapors condensing upon the rocks and cool earth, and trickling down, and frequent showers of rain, form various little streams and cascades in different parts of these mountains, which descend and unite in forming the river Wainiha, and thus, with short and rapid course, roll to the ocean no mean volume of water.

Descending a little from the verge of the mountain—the border of the table-land, we came below the cloud, and enjoyed a more clear view of the country, the rivers, the perpetual verdure of the mountain sides, the plantations and huts of the heathen inhabitants of this part of Kauai. Finding ourselves, at length, safely arrived at the foot of the mountain, we gladly cast down our weary limbs on a mat, in the first house to which we came. The friendly natives rubbed and pressed with their hands the muscles of our limbs, in order to relieve them. No custom is more common among the Hawaiians than this operation, called *lomilomi*, the kneading and pressing the muscles in case of fatigue or illness.

Following down the river Wainiha, we crossed it five times without a bridge or boat, sometimes leaping from one rock to another, which rose above the surface of the water, and sometimes wading. The inhabitants along the banks saluted us with their *aloha*, adding the compliment, *mama* (nimble), with reference, doubtless, to what we had achieved, rather than to our apparent activity. Near the head of this river, as in many other mountainous parts of these islands, are found bananas of spontaneous growth, and a sort of wild apple, and a plant somewhat resembling hemp, especially in its bark, which the natives manufacture into excellent twine, fish lines, nets, etc. The bananas grow along up the sides of the mountains, and though very luxuriant, appear to be far less fruitful than when cultivated in the valleys. Dragging our weary steps along till just before night, we came to the place on the sea-shore, about half a mile west of the mouth of the river, where the two kings and their party were encamped. Kaumualii was sitting with his family in his wagon-box placed on the ground, and defended from the fresh trade-winds by a large mat supported by poles. He very kindly ordered a good supper for us, but said he had no house for us or himself to sleep in, as the houses of that place were all occupied by Liholiho and his company ; but that a temporary booth [composed principally of slender poles ingeniously covered with green leaves] was then building for himself and family, in which he would give us a lodging. Spreading down their mats on the green grass they made us a comfortable bed, then five sheets of beaten bark cloth were presented each of us for bed-clothes.

The next day we visited the neighboring district of Hanalei, one of the best in the island, having a good tract of land, and a considerable river, sixty or eighty yards wide.   The people, in their original state, treated us with such as they had.   One ascended a cocoa-nut tree and threw down a nut.   Another tore off with his teeth, the thick, fibrous husk, then cracked the shell with a stone, to give us drink.   The head man gave us a coarse dinner. A pig, baked with heated stones covered in the ground, was set before us on a large, shallow, wooden tray.   Kalo, baked in the same manner, and beaten, was laid on large green leaves instead of plates, on the ground.   Of knives, and forks, and spoons, the people were then universally destitute.   Water was given us in a tumbler consisting of the neck of a gourd-shell, and bananas, ripe, rich, and yellow, were put into our hands singly.

The mountain scenery, viewed from the hill at the mouth of this river, is singularly grand.   I called the attention of the untutored natives to the works of nature, and asked them concerning their Creator.   "We know not," they replied.   We spoke of Jehovah, the God of Heaven.   They said, "It is your God, is it not?"   "Yes, and is he not *yours* also?"   "No," they replied, "our gods are all dead."   Having exhorted them to worship Jehovah, the Maker of all things, we re-embarked on board our double canoe, and by the aid of a sail and fair wind, ran briskly back from Hanalei, to the mouth of Wainiha, and passing through the surf, landed safely.

Liholiho and his party, we found encamped for the night in a grove of the Pandanus, or screw-pine, which was illuminated in the evening by large flaming torches of the candle-nut, presenting a truly novel and romantic scene.

Seizing the lucid hour which the reckless monarch seemed to enjoy, I sat down by him and attempted to direct his energies and influence to the right objects.   The rude lodgings of the kings, chiefs, and people,—some under the trees, some in booths, and some stretching themselves to sleep on the green grass, in the open air, with no canopy over them but the starry sky, reminded me of the early missionaries, sleeping among the New Zealand warriors, who stuck their spears in the ground around them.

The next morning, the kings started on their way eastward, and we returned by double canoe, around the north-western end of the island, where the mountains are very bold, some rising abruptly from the ocean.   At one place, the pointed and lofty peaks, and sharp ridges and spurs, are cast in fantastic forms, and being crowded together, resemble in their sharpness and closeness, the lobes of honey-comb in an upturned bee-hive.   At another part of this precipitous coast, we landed where there is a small tract of sterile ground, partly environed by a stupendous precipice, nearly perpendicular, forming at its base a semicircular curve which meets the ocean at each end. This vast rock rises at the ends of the curve about 300 feet, and in the centre nearly 2500 feet.

Commencing the ascent by a rude ladder that hangs over the sea, natives sometimes climb for amusement to the summit, to exhibit their simple fire-works, and throw off torches, so constructed, that they will reach the sea. Near one end of the curve, the rough face of the rock projects gradually forward some fifty feet, so as to cover a little hamlet built under its shelter, where the frail houses of the poor inhabitants are generally defended from the rain, and always from the direct rays of the sun, till afternoon. The cool shade of this rock, at half-past ten, in mid-summer, extended more than one hundred feet from its base. Never was I so impressed by any natural scenery with the forcible figure by which Isaiah sets forth the Messiah as " a hiding-place from the wind and a covert from the storm,—the shadow of a great rock, in a weary land."

Near this settlement, a party of natives—men, women and children, were engaged in fishing in a singular manner still in vogue. Diving down, they place among the stones a native plant—the *auhuhu,* called a poison, which appears to intoxicate the fish. The natives then dive or swim after them, and take them in their hands, or sitting in canoes, or standing near the shore, take them easily in scoop nets.

It was amusing to see our attendants, as we passed along, join in the sport, diving off from our double canoe, first on one side, and then on the other, and seizing the bewildered fish, turned on the side, swimming near the surface, and struggling in vain, like the inebriate, to avoid the destroyer.

Pursuing our way around the south-west point of the island, leaving Niihau some fifteen or twenty miles on our right, and directing our course eastward, we had a view of a more level country which lies to the south, and includes Mana, Makawele, and Hanapepe, and the village of Waimea, where we left our families.

The fort, the vessels in the roads, the village of a hundred habitations, including the mission-house, appeared in succession as we swept along the coast, the paddles moving more briskly as the terminus of our thirty miles' sail cheered our weary rowers. As the evening set in, we entered the mouth of the Waimea river, and found ourselves welcomed home.

Governor Cox was then at the place, and with his people attended on the preaching of the Gospel on the Sabbath. He was able now at the close of a meal to say, " I thank God I am now full," and to tell those around him that " Jehovah is the true God, and that he made the heavens and the earth, and gives us our daily food."

As the two kings and their company proceeded eastward to Puna and halted, Mr. Ruggles went over and spent a Sabbath with them. His visit was seasonable and salutary. The monthly

commemoration of Kamehameha's death recurring on that Sabbath, the customary feasting, and firing, and drinking, were, at Mr.
Ruggles' request, postponed in deference to the Christian's God,
and to the wishes of the missionary.

On the 5th of September, 1821, occurred the first annual examination of the mission school at Kauai, which had been, by rotation, taught a year by Mr. and Mrs. Whitney, and Mr. and Mrs.
Ruggles.

It then consisted of thirty scholars, one-third of whom had, for
the most part, been in the family, enjoying its Christian kindness
and influence, being fed, clothed, and watched over, while, with
others, they were acquiring the rudiments of learning, and the
knowledge of the Bible, and of useful arts. They exhibited
gratifying proof of their capacity and desire to learn, and of the
diligence and aptness to teach of their instructors.

The day following the examination, the kings returned from
their tour of forty-two days, their company being considerably
enlarged by the arrival of Liholiho's guard from the windward,
and by the Kauaians who were attracted by their movements.
Mr. Ruggles and myself called on them to know what advice and
encouragement they would now give respecting our proposed voyage to Tahiti. Liholiho said, " It is well for you to visit Tahiti, but
don't be in haste to go." To Kaumualii I remarked, " You
requested me to come down from Oahu, proposing to give me and
Mr. Ruggles a passage in your brig, to Tahiti. I have come, and
am ready. I have waited a long time. I very much desire now
to go." He promptly replied, " You are most gone. Six days
more, you go. The young king, he go to Oahu. You go with
him, then, go from there to Tahiti." " Where are the provisions ?" " I take care," he replied ; " I will put them
aboard." To secure their joint attention to this subject for a
quiet hour, that we might learn from them together, what we were
to rely upon, we engaged them to dine with us, with that understanding. They came at the moment when dinner was placed on
the table. Liholiho, as soon as he was satisfied, spoke of the heat
—turned hastily from the table, and said he must go and bathe ;
but recollecting that thanks to Jehovah had not been audibly
returned, resumed his seat till that was done ; then, with the rest
of the party, made a hasty exit, giving us an opportunity to
exercise our patience a little longer. His disposition to range
about seemed to us hardly less than that of the aborigines of
America, which made the wonder the greater that on our arrival in
his country, he so soon made up his mind to favor our settlement
as missionaries. But this incessant roving affecting large classes,
greatly hindered his own improvement and that of his wives and
friends, and the missionaries felt that so far as they were bound to
educate them, they were like the Israelites when required to
deliver the full tale of brick, and find their own straw where they
could.

On the Sabbath, September 16th, we invited the two kings to attend public worship, but both declined. Queen Kamamalu, who was desirous of availing herself of instruction more than she was allowed, attended with the scholars, and listened with care to the intelligible language fluently delivered by my interpreter, Mr. J. Going, as line upon line of evangelical truth was proclaimed.

The two kings amused themselves with a Sabbath sail on board their respective brigs, coming to anchor at evening. Kaumualii going on board the Cleopatra's barge, at the word of Liholiho, at 9 p. m. orders were immediately given for the brig to sail for Oahu. No previous notice was given of such a destination, nor reasons assigned for this singular movement. The next morning the people, finding their friend and protector had disappeared, were in great agitation. Haupu, the head man at Waimea, expressing the feeling of many, exclaimed in his sorrow, " Farewell to our king—we shall see him no more." As the chiefs, the wives of the king and others of his retinue, were about to set off to follow him, we had the pleasure of seeing an early indication of religious concern in the case of John Ii. He had swum off to the king's boat, as he embarked from Honolulu, and crossed the channel with him to Kauai, and was now required to follow him, though he desired to stay, to pursue his studies with us. Before leaving Kauai he came to me, and in his pleasant confiding way, said, " I am come near to going away from you. I want you to pray with me first." Taking him to my room, we kneeled down together, and I commended the dear youth to the care of the great Jehovah, and to the word of his grace. Being in turn requested to pray with me, he replied modestly, " I do not know how to use the words, but I pray in my thoughts." " God can understand your thoughts," I added, " when your words are few or broken, or even without words; but it is well to express your thoughts sometimes in words." After a little reflection, he kneeled with me again, and in an earnest childlike manner, offered a short prayer of this import;—" Our Father in heaven, we love thee. We desire thee to take care of us. Take care of the king and all the queens. Make all the people good. Take care of the land. Make the devils give it up. We thank thee that the missionaries come here. Take good care of the missionaries here and at Oahu, and of all good people. May we go to heaven. Amen." Such were, at that period, the lispings of this youthful pupil, once a heathen lad of some rank, intrusted with the lighting of the king's pipe, and who at length became an able counsellor in the affairs of state, and an eloquent advocate of the cause of Christ.

The kings crossed the channel to Waianae, the western part of Oahu. Whether Kaumualii was regarded as a king or a captive, it was not easy to decide. He still retained his title and responsibilities as the head of Kauai, as subsequent transactions proved; though Cox appeared for a time to hold a sort of superintendence over that island. It must be confessed that the government of the Sandwich Islands was not easily definable, or made intelligible to a stranger, at that period, if indeed it was fully understood by the people themselves.

During this most singular movement of Liholiho and his people at Kauai, the state of things at Oahu was exceedingly unquiet. The unsettled state of affairs tended to sour the minds of those foreigners who had large contracts to settle there, which may account in part for the foreign opposition to the proposed visit to Tahiti, and to the cause of the mission. Among the people, incipient efforts to find a Savior appeared sometimes in striking contrast with the ebullitions of the heathen heart. About the middle of August, Holo, a chief of low rank, being very ill, was visited by Mr. Loomis and Hopu, to whom he gave some evidence that he believed the truth and loved it. Hopu at one time, finding an English Bible, which, though unintelligible to the sick man, was lying on his bosom, asked him the reason for it. He replied, "I love Jehovah, and wish to be with him."

As Mr. Loomis was once on his way to visit this languishing inquirer, his attention was attracted by a crowd and bustle of the natives. He heard an outcry, and saw the crowd suddenly disperse as sheep frightened by a dog or wolf, and soon collect again and carry away a dead man. An inferior chief, in a fit of rage and partial intoxication, had seized a club at hand, and given him a death blow on the head. He was arrested—kept in manacles one day, and sentenced to deliver to the government one hundred piculs of sandal wood—a fine equal to seven or eight hundred dollars. Holo, of similar rank, once as reckless as he, was evidently feeling after GOD, the Creator and Redeemer of men. He professed to love him, and daily to pray to him as his GOD and deliverer. The following is a specimen of one of his prayers, preserved by Hopu. "My Father in Heaven, hallowed be thy name, thy kingdom on earth come. My Father in heaven, cover me with thy power. Jehovah, holy King, make righteous and take me, O Jehovah, into Heaven when I die." He was visited by chiefs and people while he exhibited this concern for his salvation, and acknowledged himself a helpless sinner and willing to be at GOD's disposal. Hopu, who devoted much attention to him, thought very favorably of the evidences of his conversion. It is obvious that with so brief and imperfect a knowledge of the provisions and invitations of the gospel, and of the extent and spirituality of the divine law as the people then possessed, it would be no easy matter for them or their teachers to form a well grounded opinion of the presence or absence of a work of saving grace in individual cases of seriousness. Though human nature is the same in all climes and ages, and conversion from sin to holiness, from the service of Satan to the service of God, from the love of self and the world to the love of the Father, must be radically the same in all cases, yet the forms of manifestation may be widely different in different circumstances. Some missionaries would have readily baptized Holo, John Ii, Puaaiki, and Kaumualii, at that period.

Returning from his excursion to Kauai, Liholiho arrived at Honolulu in the afternoon of the Sabbath, and as he met the foreign teachers, pronounced the missionaries all *maikai*, and expressed his approbation of the proposed visit to Tahiti. While they were conversing, Don Marin, the Spanish interpreter entered with a message from Captain D——, requesting the king to come and drink rum with him—a challenge which he instantly accepted. Efforts of this kind often repeated, did us and the poor people much evil.

Kaumualii having been landed at the western part of Oahu, reached Honolulu, Oct. 5, 1821. There was in his countenance an appearance of dejection, or sadness, which called forth the sympathy of his missionary friends, and others. But he seemed disposed to make the best of it. He came to Oahu, he said, to return the visit of Liholiho to Kauai.

On the 9th, the windward Queen and the leeward King were united, and thus the alliance between the two parts of the group was cemented. None could greatly censure Kaumualii for leaving Kapule (who preferred Kealiiahonui), and uniting with another. Nor could he be much envied in leaving the occupancy of his own island and putting on such a crown. That he might prove to the windward chiefs that he was *maikai*, blameless, was one of the objects for which he was reconciled to his separation from Kauai, his home. The missionaries at his island felt his absence; confusion increased, and one of the savage chiefs there killed his own wife.

About two months after the union of Kaahumanu with Kaumualii, she had a severe trial and admonition. Sickness, so much deprecated by the high and low, in Christian and in heathen lands, is often the messenger of mercy to the proud and gay lovers of the world, to make them feel the need of a friend in adversity, and to apprise them of the frailness of the tenure by which they hold their cherished share of earth, and to remind them of the necessity of something more satisfying and enduring. Never perhaps was such an unwelcome messenger of mercy more opportunely sent to a haughty ruler, than in Dec. 1821, when the hard and lofty-hearted Kaahumanu was laid low and brought to the borders of the grave. Repeatedly we called on her during this illness, and endeavored to secure her confidence and to do her good. So severe were her paroxysms, December 15th, that much apprehension was entertained that she would not live through the day. Two skilful physicians connected with the Russian ships of discovery, before mentioned, under Commodore Vascilieff, now returned, prescribed for her. On the evening of the 16th, Mrs. B. and myself visited her, when she returned our salutations with unwonted cordiality, and as I said to her, " I trust you are thinking seriously of the great God and our Savior," she replied, " I think more about him in my sickness." I endeavored to assure her that the blessed Savior who died for sinners could preserve her body and her soul; that he could restore her to health ; or, if she trusted in him, he could take her ransomed soul to Heaven, if her body should be laid in the grave. To which she replied, " *Maikai*," it is well. When prayer was proposed, she gave her full consent, and required a general silence. When I had commended her and the interests of the nation to our great Helper and Deliverer, at the close she subjoined, " It is well." She united with her husband in requesting us to come again. On the following evening, as we entered the room, her sister, Namahana, said, " Here comes the *kahunapule*" (master or leader of religious worship)—" I hope we shall hear him pray." The sick queen appeared in some measure relieved ; but yet not free from anxiety. She seemed gratified by our attentions. After pointing her to the Lamb of God that taketh away the sin of the world, I was requested by her to pray, before leaving her. At her direction that conversation should be suspended among the group around, there was a solemn stillness (altogether unusual in such an assemblage of natives, chiefs, and foreigners), while a minister of Christ kneeled by the couch of the sufferer, and implored the health-giving mercies of God upon her body and soul. She was soon restored, and with her friends set a higher value on the religion which we were endeavoring to inculcate. There was from this period a marked difference in her demeanor towards the missionaries, which became more and more striking, till we were allowed to acknowledge her as a disciple of the Divine Master.

Rarely has a missionary a more favorable opportunity to exert an influence on a whole nation, than was here afforded in the circle of the highest chiefs of these islands, balancing, as they were, between idolatry, atheism, and the service of the true God. Rarely has a Christian female, in any circumstances, a better opportunity to make an impression, powerful and salutary, than in attending a missionary husband at the couch of such a patient, surrounded by such a circle of relatives and dependants. As Mrs. B. sat down by the side of the sick queen, and with unfeigned sympathy for her sufferings and danger, bathed her aching temples, she bound a silken cord around her heart, from which I think she never broke loose while she lived. Kaumualii not only desired me to repeat my visits to instruct her and pray for her, but when I requested him to teach her and guide her, he said, " I have told her some things about God, and I like to tell her what I understand." His rank and weight of character, his abstinence now from profaneness and intemperance, his confidence in the missionaries, and in what he had learned on the subject of religion, enabled him to exert a good influence in his new, though not altogether the most welcome circumstances.

Before the next morning rose, Liholiho, who had revisited Hawaii, arrived in the Cleopatra's Barge, and was received in the morning by a salute from the fort, and by the loud wailing of the multitude that might be heard at the distance of a mile or two. He and his wives soon came on shore and repaired to the sick room of Kaahumanu, and with flowing tears expressed their sympathy and affection for their afflicted step-mother. Most of the chiefs gathered around her, fearing commotion, perhaps, in case of her decease.

· Commodore Vascilieff, of the Russian Exploring Squadon, in his visit to the islands, this year, besides allowing the aid of his physicians in her illness, treated the rulers and the missionaries very courteously, gained their high esteem, and aided their cause. He read a letter to the king from Governor Reicord of Kamtschatka, favorable to the independence of the islands, proposing to acknowledge the Hawaiian flag. He assured the chiefs he should report to the Emperor Alexander the happy arrival and favorable reception of the mission established there, and the good system of instruction which the missionaries had commenced among the people.

The civility and kindness of the Commodore and his officers to the mission family, manifested in various ways, are well illustrated in the following note, in Russian and English ;—

"H. Imp. Maj. S. Otkritie, Dec. 19th, O. S. 1821.

"DEAR SIR—I thank you from all my heart and soul for the opportunity given me and the officers under my command, to be sharers in promoting the business of this Christian mission. The collection of seven golden ducats and eighty-six Spanish dollars I take the pleasure of sending with this letter, of which you will make use as you think proper.

"Please to receive our most sincere wishes that your good intention and the glorious design in which you are engaged may be prospered and increased. Remaining, with my respects to you and your respectable society,

" Your humble servant,
" MICHAEL VASCILIEFF."

This was at the time when the Emperor Alexander and Prince Galitzin were so laudably engaged in promoting the circulation of the Holy Scriptures, against which Popes and Jesuits used their intrigues with but too disastrous assiduity.

Kaahumanu being distinctly apprised of what this Russian officer had said and done in favor of our mission, appeared interested, and was encouraged by it to look the more favorably on our cause. We could hardly avoid calling on the patrons and friends of missions to take courage with us in efforts to propagate the Gospel, from the labors and success of some of the rulers of Russia in introducing Christianity into that vast empire, particularly of the grand Princess Olga, in the tenth century, and her royal son Vladimir, who so successfully used his influence to bring his subjects to the adoption of Christianity, though not in its unobscured glory. How vast the spiritual interests of many millions of souls in each succeeding generation of the Russians! Now a distant but distinct ray of evangelical influence from the Sun of Righteousness, reflected by Constantine VI., who instructed that princess in religion, who, in her turn instructed Vladimir, now reflected again by Vascilieff and his fellow subjects of Alexander, falls on the mind of Kaahumanu and her associates at the Sandwich Islands, combining with the influence of the mission to illuminate and convert the nation to Christ. Of what amazing consequence was it that Kaahumanu should be a believer and advocate of Christianity! Who would not covet the privilege of giving a right impulse to the mind and heart of one so high in rank, possessing her mental powers and occupying a position so favorable for exerting influence over a nation? The Lord had a great work for her to accomplish, and was now recovering her from dangerous illness, and ordering circumstances and applying influences favorable for making her what her Christian friends desired her to be and what she was at length to become—a humble disciple of Christ, and a reformer of her nation.

But, rising from her illness to comfortable health, she was still too proud, too independent, too fond of pleasure, gaiety, honor, and amusement, to take the place of a cross-bearing servant of Christ. Not many rich, not many noble are yet found among the ranks of those who are weaned from earth, and made to fix their hearts on the treasures above. How can they believe the humbling doctrines of Christ who receive honor one of another? How hardly shall they who love earthly riches and distinctions enter into the kingdom of God! Alas! if the salvation of the ten thousands of the poor Hawaiians were to depend on the reformed and holy life of the licentious Liholiho, or the humble, broken-hearted piety of the haughty Kaahumanu, both of whom, for a time, seemed among the least likely to yield their hearts to the Divine claims, how much reason there was to fear that the nation would sink down together to ruin. He was rapidly wasting the days and energies of his prime by his debaucheries. She, having now been proved to be as vulnerable to the shafts of disease as any of that fading nation, was advancing to the period of threescore years, without appearing to entertain any desire or thought of learning to read the Word of God, and thus making herself wise for eternity. How immeasurably important that, in the case of both, the right kind and amount of moral influence should now be applied!

CHAPTER VII.

SOME notice may be expected of the character of the Hawaiian
language, and of the manner of first acquiring and writing it,
and making it available in books for the use of the nation, for
the purposes of business, education, and religion. It may well
be conceived that there were difficulties to be encountered, which
are not necessary to be detailed.

The variety of vowel sounds in the language is small; but
small as it is, the recurrence of vowel sounds in speaking it, is
much more frequent, in proportion to the consonants, than in the
English—the proportion in the latter being about two vowels to
three consonants, and in the former, three to two.

To one unacquainted with the language it would be impossible
to distinguish the words in a spoken sentence, for in the mouth of
a native, a sentence appeared like an ancient Hebrew or Greek
manuscript—all one word. It was found that every word and
every syllable in the language ends with a vowel; the final vowel
of a word or syllable, however, is often made so nearly to coalesce
or combine with the sound of the succeeding vowel, as to form a
dipthongal sound, apparently uniting two distinct words. There
are, on the other hand, abrupt separations or short and sudden
breaks between two vowels in the same word. The language,
moreover, is crowded with a class of particles unknown in the
languages with which we had any acquaintance. There were
also frequent reduplications of the same vowel sound, so rapid,
that by most foreigners the two were taken for one.

To avoid all arbitrary spelling, all silent letters and the representation of the same monosound by several different letters, and
many sounds by the same letter, as in the English, seemed to be
due even to the philosophy of the unlettered Hawaiians. To make
the spelling and reading of the language easy to the people, and
convenient to all who use it, was a matter of great importance,
almost indispensable to our success in raising the nation. It was,
therefore, a part of our task to secure to the people a perfect

alphabet, literal or syllabic, of all the sounds which were then in use, and which would need soon to come into use in the progress of the nation. Those who had attempted to write the names of places and persons in the islands, had materially failed, even in the most plain and common. No foreigner or native, at the islands, could illustrate or explain the peculiarities and intricacies of the language. Though we obtained a few words and phrases from Wm. Moxley and others, we found the dialect in use by foreigners often materially misled us, so that none could be trusted as to accuracy; and it required time to detect and unlearn errors. In the oft recurring names of the principal island, the largest village, and of the king of the leeward islands, " Owhyhee," " Hanaroorah," and " Tamoree," scarcely the sound of a single syllable was correctly expressed, either in writing or speaking, by voyagers or foreign residents. Had we, therefore, followed the orthography of voyagers, or in adopting an alphabet, made a single vowel stand for as many sounds as in English, and several different vowels for the same sound, and given the consonants the ambiguity of our *c, s, t, ch, gh,* &c., it would have been extremely difficult, if not impracticable to induce the nation to become readers, in the course of a whole generation, even if we had been furnished with ample funds to sustain in boarding-schools, all who would devote their time and labor to study.

Have not American philanthropists sufficiently demonstrated, in the course of two centuries, the difficulty of inducing the aboriginal tribes of this continent to use our literature? and is not our anomalous, intricate, and ever dubious orthography a prominent cause of failure? But the philosophical, syllabic alphabet of the sagacious Choctaw GUESS, enabless the men, women, and children of his tribe to read their own language with facility.

Aiming to avoid an ambiguous, erroneous, and inconvenient orthography, to assign to every character one certain sound, and thus represent with ease and exactness the true pronunciation of the Hawaiian language, the following five vowels and seven consonants have been adopted: *a, e, i, o, u, h, k, l, m, n, p, w.* These twelve letters, and possibly eleven, omitting either *u* or *w,* will express every sound in the pure Hawaiian dialect. The power of the vowels may be thus represented :—*a,* as *a* in the English words *art, father ; e,* as *a* in *pale,* or *ey* in *they ; i,* as *ee* or *i* in *machine ; o,* as *o* in *no ; u,* as *oo* in *too.* They are called so as to express their power by their names—*Ah, A, Ee, O, Oo.* The consonants are in like manner called by such simple names as to suggest their power, thus, following the sound of the vowels as above—*He, Ke, La, Mu, Nu, Pi, We.*

The slight variation in quantity, though not in quality, of sound in the vowels requires no mark of distinction, any more than the variation of the sound of *a* in the English words *art* and *father.* Here the quantity may differ slightly though it is not necessary to put a distinctive mark, or make a different character,

In the few dipthongal combinations *ae, ai, ao,* and *au,* whether more close or more open, each letter retains its original mono-sound. *A-i,* when sounded in quick succession, resemble the sound of the English pronoun *I,* and *a-u,* in quick succession, the sound of the English *ou* in *loud ;* so the Hawaiian word *hau* (hibiscus) resembles the full, round, English interrogative *how.* In the name of the island, second in size in the group, whether pronounced Mau-i or Ma-u-i, there is no such difference as to cause a mistake in a native hearer.

Consonants are not doubled, and never end a word or syllable. Double or triple vowels are never used to express a single sound, and where they occur, are sounded separately, as *a-a, e-e, i-i, o-o, u-u.* The accent being generally on the former, the latter is a sort of echo, as in the name Ha′-a-li-li-o′, but sometimes the reverse, as Ka-a′-hu-ma′-nu.

The convenience of such an alphabet for the Hawaiian language, undisturbed by foreign words, is very obvious, because we can express with simplicity, ease, and certainty, those names and phrases with the sound of which former voyagers were utterly unable to make us acquainted by English orthography. Though it were possible to spell them with our English alphabet it would still be inconvenient. A few names may illustrate the reasons for our new orthography.

The Old.	Corrected in English.	The New, or Hawaiian.
Tamaahmaah,	Kâh-mā′-hâh-mā′-hâh,	Ka me′ ha-me′ ha.
Terreioboo,	Kâh-lâh′-nў-ō-poo′-oo,	Ka la′ ni o pu′ u.
Tamoree,	Kâh-oo′-moo âh-lee′-ee,	Ka u′ mu a li′ i.
Owhyhee	Hâh-wўe′-ee,	Ha wai′ i.
Woahoo,	O-âh′-hoo,	O a′ hu.
Attooi,	Cow′-eўe′,	Kau′ ai′.
Hanaroorah,	Hō-nō-loo′-loo,	Ho no lu′ lu.

The name of the largest and most frequented village in the group had three *a's* in three distinct syllables, though no sound of *a* belongs to the name. Shipmasters and learned men agreed in calling the king of Kauai and his son in America, Tam′oree, a name of three syllables, with only three vowel sounds, and making the *m* the final and emphatic letter of the first syllable, whereas the *m* should commence the third syllable, and the name contain six vowel sounds in six distinct syllables, for it is composed of a significant phrase of that length, and is unabridged—*ka,* the ; *u-mu,* oven or pit for baking ; and *a-li-i,* chief or king, here expressive of the thing to be baked : thus, Ka-u-mu-a-li-i, the-chief-baking-oven.

It could hardly be possible to write any language in the world with a more simple or limited alphabet, and at the same time equally intelligible to the children who use it. A syllabic alphabet of ninety-five characters would have been tolerably convenient for all native words, but not so simple or convenient as the alphabet adopted.

There were some difficulties to be encountered in distinguishing several consonant sounds, and to determine which of two characters in the Roman or English alphabet to adopt for certain sounds that appeared somewhat variable in the mouths of the natives. The following appeared sometimes to be interchangable : *b* and *p*, *k* and *t*, *l* and *r*, *v* and *w*, and even the sound of *d*, it was thought by some, was used in some cases where others used *k*, *l*, *r*, or *t*. For purely native words, however, *k*, *l*, *p*, and *w* were preferred.

Though five vowels and seven consonants would well express the Hawaiian language, unmixed with foreign terms, yet there were reasons for introducing other letters, abounding in kindred Polynesian dialects, and in the names of persons, places, and things in other countries, with which the Hawaiians needed to become acquainted. Eleven or twelve letters must be too limited to be the representatives of general knowledge. To preserve the *identity* of foreign or scripture names, was deemed of some importance. We could not, in good conscience, throw out every consonant in the names of Obed, Boaz, Ruth, David, Ezra, Russia, and Gaza, and nearly all out of such names as Sabbath, Christ, Moses, Joseph, Boston, and Genessaret, simply because such consonants could be dispensed with in writing the words familiar to the people. The following additional consonants, therefore, were adopted : *b, d, f, g, r, s, t, v*, and *z*. These form the third class of letters in the Hawaiian alphabet, which is arranged according to ease and importance, allowing the native pupil to learn to spell and read pure native words first.

Compound consonants, recommended by J. Pickering, Esq., for writing the Indian languages, are not adopted in the Hawaiian, though the basis of his alphabet, in respect to vowel sounds, is followed. C, J, Q, X, and Y we omit. To preserve the identity of a foreign name embracing a compound consonant which cannot well be omitted, we take the more important or practicable part of the power—as *p*, for *ph* or *phi ; t*, for *th* or *theta ; k*, for *ch* or *chi*, &c. When two consonants joined in a foreign word, need both to be preserved, we interpose the vowel *e*, and after a final consonant add usually the vowel *a*—as Bosetona for Boston.

Sibilants and compound consonants are exceedingly difficult, if not impracticable, to the unlettered Hawaiian. Had we made the Hawaiian people, as we found them, pass through the Israelitish ordeal of distinguishing and pronouncing correctly the words *Sibboleth* and *Shibboleth*, to save their lives, it is not probable that one in a thousand would have succeeded, even if each had been allowed a whole day, with patient instruction, in the trial to adjust and control the vocal organs right.

Pronouns—personal, relative, and adjective—have no distinction of *gender ;* but *number* in the personal pronouns we found to be distinguished with a philosophical precision which surprised us. For instance, there are, in the first person, four plurals, or two duals and two plurals, *kaua*, thou and I; *maua*, he or she and I; *kakou*, we, more than two, the party speaking and the party addressed; and *makou*, we, more than two, but excluding the party addressed. Here are four nicely distinguished classes, each of which is in English, less definitely represented by the word *we*. But I must not here detain the reader with extended remarks on the structure of the language.

On the 7th of January, 1822, a year and eight months from the time of our receiving the governmental permission to enter the field and teach the people, we commenced printing the language in order to give them letters, libraries, and the living oracles in their own tongue, that the nation might read and understand the wonderful works of God. The opening to them of this source of light never known to their ancestors remote or near, occurred while many thousands of the friends of the heathen were on the monthly concert, unitedly praying that the Gospel might have free course and be glorified. It was like laying a corner stone of an important edifice for the nation. A considerable number was present, and among those particularly interested was Keeaumoku, who, after a little instruction from Mr. Loomis, applied the strength of his athletic arm to the lever of a Ramage press, pleased thus to assist in working off a few impressions of the first lessons. These lessons were caught at with eagerness by those who had learned to read by manuscript.

Liholiho, Kalanimoku, Boki and other chiefs, and numbers of the people, called to see the new engine, the printing-press, to them a great curiosity. Several were easily induced to undertake to learn the art of printing, and in time succeeded. Most of the printing done at the islands has been done by native hands.

When the king first examined the press, a sheet of white paper being laid on, he pulled the lever round, and was surprised to see the paper instantly covered with words in his own language. He had some shrewdness, and, for a Hawaiian, an uncommon share of confidence in his own attainments and abilities. Being once asked whether *L* or *R* ought to be used in spelling his name, he attempted earnestly to ring the changes on the two letters, and at length gave the preference to *R* and used it, though *L* is doubtless the better representative of the initial sound in his name. Not a few foreigners coincided with him. But for the ruinous effects of self-indulgence, particularly in the use of intoxicating liquors, this high born chieftain, having renounced idolatry, and escaped its spells, might have become a man of energy of character and respectable attainments, in some sense corresponding with his tall, portly, physical frame. But like multitudes of the self-pleasing around him, he was slow to hear the Gospel.

It was difficult to collect an audience on the Sabbath, or to induce the natives to assemble at a suitable hour for public worship; and it was needful for the missionaries to go out on Saturday, and apprise the people and their leaders who were accessible, that the morrow would be the sacred day of Jehovah, and invite them to attend his worship. Sometimes on the Sabbath morning, we called on the chiefs with a similar message, " We are about to meet to worship God at his house, to pray to him, proclaim his truth, and praise him for what he has done ; will you join in the service which God requires of men ?" Some would comply; some would refuse without any reply, and others offer various excuses.

On the Sabbath, January 20th, about sixty natives, including Cox Keeaumoku, and Adams Kuakini, and some fifty foreigners, attended public worship, and listened to the story of redeeming love in two languages, the English being forcibly interpreted by Thomas Hopu. The following Sabbath, we endeavored by invitation and intreaty to secure the attendance of Liholiho and the chiefs. The king said, " I am tipsy, and it is not right to go to church drunk ; when I have got through, I will come." Adams said, " When the king attends, I will attend." Kalanimoku, engaged in gambling, offered an excuse unrivalled as to its frankness, ingenuity, and courteousness, from a heathen or a gambler, saying, " I have business and cannot go—my heart will be with you, though my body is here." A number of our pupils and others, attended, and among them Governor Cox, though his superiors, the king, Kaahumanu, and Kalanimoku, all declined. On the succeeding Sabbath, with the same solicitude, we repeated our efforts to secure the attendance of the rulers, for their own sake, and for the sake of the people, and for the honor of God whose laws they were still making void or trampling under their feet. Kaahumanu being slightly ill, and having little regard for the authority or duties of the Sabbath, or love for the house of God, could hardly be invited to come. Her husband, a man of peace, on whose attachment to our cause we then relied more than on any other chief, said, " Kaahumanu is ill; I cannot leave her to go to church, lest she should be angry with me."

Kalanimoku and Governor Boki excused themselves under the pretext that they must wait on Kalakua, who had just arrived from Hawaii. Her own brothers, however, Cox and Adams, notwithstanding her arrival and the illness of the other sister, Kahumanu, both attended church, with other natives, a goodly number, for those days ; and we pressed on their attention the duty, divinely enjoined, " Be wise now, therefore, O ye kings, and be instructed, ye judges of the earth." The next day, Adams sent for the lessons we had printed in his language, and was quickly master of them. But a few days passed before I received a letter from him, which I immediately answered in the Hawaiian, under date of Feb. 8th, 1822, one month from the first printing for the nation. Epistolary correspondence, thus commenced in that language, suddenly opened to the chiefs and people a new source of pleasure and advantage, of which hundreds soon availed themselves.

Early in the same month, this high chief and his brother, uniting with others in the worship at the sanctuary, Mr. Thurston urged their earnest attention to the interests of the soul from the impressive interrogatory of the "Great Teacher," who best knew the extent of the contrasted claims, "What shall it profit a man if he gain the whole world and lose his own soul?" This discourse having been written out in English, and twice read distinctly and deliberately, to John Honolii, before its public delivery, was well interpreted by him, as it was delivered.

On the succeeding Sabbath, an interesting assembly, at Honolulu, listened to a discourse on the great commission given by Christ to his disciples to proclaim his Gospel and teach all men to observe his commands, as the grand reason for our coming to teach them their duty and the way of life, and for their attending to the message of his ambassadors.

Thomas Hopu, having had my manuscript a week, to study out the translation, was able, with peculiar freedom and force, to give the sense as it was delivered from the pulpit, sentence by sentence, while the people listened with unwonted attention. In the afternoon, the same discourse was delivered at Waikiki in a similar manner, before the king of Kauai and Kaahumanu and their people. The king seemed feeble. He had been several days ill, and requested me to pray for him that he might recover from his great weakness. He appeared calm, contemplative, and sober-minded. Such a request and such expressions of gratitude as followed were indicative of his views of the reasonableness and efficacy of prayer, and of the privilege of approaching the throne of mercy. His devotions were sometimes cruelly opposed by his wife, who, in one instance, angrily threw a heavy dish at his head when he was imploring a blessing on his food. The intended blow was warded off by the arm of a mutual friend. He, however, regarding the authority of God as paramount, from this period, persevered in acknowledging him.

How differently did Liholiho, in what he regarded as his unbounded freedom, demean himself! He looked at the claims of God, and saw that they were reasonable. His conscience coincided; but the temptations around him, his rebellious lusts, his long continued habits, the power of Satan which he admitted, all stood between his conscience and his duty, between his soul and God. Attending once, about this time, our morning family worship, he said in English phrase, "Jehovah—he's good—I like him—the devil I no like." Passing on to Waikiki, he continued his revelry, though he professed not to like the instigator of it. Many of the chiefs were quite too ready to join him in it. They occupied a number of huts and booths in a grove of some thousands of cocoanut trees, near the sea-shore, convenient for fishing and bathing and playing in the surf of Waikiki bay.

In a few days, the alarm was given, that the king was dying at Waikiki. I hastened with Hopu to the spot. A great multitude of the people went out weeping to see him, or to be near him. His guards assembled around him, with swords and muskets; and the multitude surrounding the grass thatched habitation where he lay, made the groves resound with their loud and bitter wailings. His mother, Keopuolani, his step-mother, Kaahumanu, his five wives, and his particular friends, Hopu among the rest, gathered around his mat in tears.   No wonder they should have been alarmed by the singular symptoms, in rapid succession—great redness of skin, rigidity of muscles, convulsion, difficulty of respiration, emission of blood from the mouth, etc.—the result, doubtless, of his excesses.   I gave him medicine, and stayed with him through the night, and the next morning sailed with him, in a double canoe, to Honolulu, with thirty-five persons on board.   He recovered in about two weeks.   Then, inviting me to sup with him, he requested me to implore a blessing and give thanks at his table.

On a Sabbath of the same month, the king, five or six of the high chiefs, and an increased number of the people, with our pupils, seamen in port, and residents, in all about three hundred, attended the service of the sanctuary.   Mr. Thurston urged on them the impressive invitations of the gospel.   They listened with attention, and while there were indications that the truths of God were exerting some influence on the minds of the people, there were not wanting efforts to draw the king from the sanctuary to banqueting and revelry, and to catch away the word.   Within a month from the commencement of printing in their language, the missionaries thus reported to their directors their progress and position.

" To give you a brief view of the state of the mission families and schools.   The present number of native children in the family is twenty-two, fifteen boys and seven girls, which, with Hopu and Honolii, and a hired laborer, makes our number forty-three.   Mrs. Chamberlain takes the principal charge of providing our meals, which is no small task.   The number of pupils at the station, exclusive of a few of high rank, occasionally taught, should be reckoned forty.   The Sabbath school is interesting and promising.   At Kaui, there are ten native children in the family, besides three adult male domestics who have wives, making their number twenty-two in the family,—their pupils from twenty to thirty, since the absence of Kaumualii.   The total in the families at both stations, sixty-five, about equal to the present number of regular pupils.   You will see, therefore, that the mission, on its present plan, cannot be sustained without involving considerable expense to the Board.   You are doubtless well aware that on account of the vacillating state of the nation, the deep subtlety of the arch enemy to discover and thwart our plans, the withdrawal of part of our number, the laborious business of making books and translations of the Bible in this difficult, unwritten tongue, and the terrible influence of profane and licentious outlaws and others, more to be deprecated than the absurdities of superstition, the exigencies of this mission demand the aid of no ordinary talents. A considerable number of laborers who are emphatically prudent, tried, and faithful, of such qualifications and for such purposes as have been heretofore specified, could now, we believe, be very advantageously employed in this field; and we repeat our request that as in the wisdom of the Board, and the Providence of God, it may be allowed, they may be sent to our aid, and to the help of the nation. We desire still further, that among the missionaries of the Board, our case may be regarded as in a very important sense peculiar, and as having peculiar claims. Your missionaries at Bombay and Ceylon always enjoy the personal advice and co-operation of able and experienced men, in the prosecution of their plans. Your missions in America are visited by officers of the Board and others competent to give important advice and aid. We alone are denied that salutary aid. They labor among a people whose character and history are known. We are among a people almost unknown. Their plans of operation are matured and tested by successful experiment. Here, new plans are to be adapted to the character and condition of a singular people. There, civil institutions are already established. Here, the laws of society and of the State are yet to be formed, not directly by the missionary, but indirectly by the increase of light. Your missionaries to Palestine find friends, instructors, guides, and helpers, wherever they go. How widely different the character of those we meet with in general. How inconsiderable the comparative aid they are willing or able to afford. We deeply feel the need of able counsellors ourselves, and of able teachers for the people. We therefore earnestly entreat the Board to endeavor to meet the special exigencies of the mission, by appointing to its aid (among others), one or two able preachers, possessing richly those qualifications implied or expressed in the terms, " Wise as serpents, harmless as doves, patient in tribulation, apt to teach, always abounding in the work of the Lord."

The introduction of printing in the language of the country, not only awakened curiosity among the chiefs and people, but gave a new and decided impulse to our schools and the cause of education. From sixty to seventy pupils were at once furnished with copies of the first sheet, as they could not wait till the work was finished. They found the lessons easy. They not only soon mastered them, but were able to teach them to others. In a few months, there were not less than five hundred learners. The mission family at Honolulu, including our boarding scholars, was large, and we found it difficult to procure a comfortable supply of the necessaries of life without offering extravagant prices, which we could not do without reluctantly embarrassing our Board, and unduly encouraging exorbitance or cupidity among the people whom we wished to lead in the paths of wisdom, piety and salvation. A stranger could hardly conceive how difficult it must have been for the missionaries properly to urge a destitute and degraded people to endeavor by their own well directed efforts to rise from penury to affluence, and at the same time effectually to guard them against the cultivation or the indulgence of a sordid spirit. The greatly increased demand for the productions of the country for the supply of foreign ships, and the growing desire of the people to possess themselves of money and articles of foreign manufacture, combined to raise the prices of supplies, far above the trifling and wholly inadequate compensation, which had formerly been given them, when a bit of iron hoop was bartered for a hog, and a fish-hook for a fowl. Now the natives demanded a quarter of a dollar for a fowl, two or three dollars for a barrel of potatoes, and six or eight or ten for a hog, weighing two hundred pounds on the foot.

Having failed to visit the Society Islands, our mission was providentially favored with a visit from Mr. Ellis, a missionary from that field, and Messrs. Tyreman and Bennet, who had been sent thither as the deputed agents of the London Missionary Society. Without their contrivance or ours, they, while seeking to convey and accompany teachers from the Society to the Marquesas Islands, found an opportunity to touch at the Sandwich Islands in their course. Long before this, Vancouver of the Royal Navy had given the former king of the Sandwich Islands reason to expect that a vessel would be sent him by the king of Great Britain. At length, a small schooner, the "Prince Regent," built at Port Jackson, and intrusted to Capt. Kent of the Mermaid, was sent and delivered to Liholiho. Touching at the Society Islands on his way, and finding these gentlemen there wishing to proceed to the Marquesas with native teachers, Capt. K. offered them a passage thither, on his way to the Hawaiian Islands, and they embarked with him. Then, contrary to their plans, he concluded to visit the Sandwich Islands first. They, with several South Sea converts, arrived at Hawaii on the 29th of March, and at Honolulu on the 15th of April, and were welcomed with gladness by our mission and by the rulers. The plan of their mission to the Marquesas was materially obstructed or deranged by the defection or seduction of the wife of one of the native Tahitian teachers. The company was, moreover, detained at Honolulu beyond expectation by a trip which their captain was induced to make, before he could restore them to the Society Islands, and for four months they made their abode with us.

The king was gratified with the royal present of the "man-of-war" schooner, with her armament of six smart little guns, to be added to his fleet of seven or eight vessels, several being of a larger class, and equally armed. John Ii, one of our engaging pupils, was speedily promoted to the command of this pigmy battle ship. In navigating it around the shores and across the channels, from island to island, he exhibited commendable loyalty, skill and energy. Auna, a Tahitian *Raatira*, who, as a teacher, had been designated to the Marquesas, was, with his wife, *Auna wahine*, hospitably received at Honolulu by Kaumualii and Kaahumanu, and even invited to remain. Auna was regarded as

pious and exemplary. He was of a tall, commanding figure,
placid and benignant countenance; sober, discreet, and courteous;
and soon capable of imparting rudimental instruction, and making known the Christian doctrine. He gave important testimony
respecting the course of events at the Society and Georgian
Islands. He had been with Pomare in a battle at Tahiti, in the
last struggles of the heathen party there to keep off or exterminate Christianity, when the king and the Christian party, standing on the defensive, and calling on the name of the Lord of
Hosts, proved triumphantly successful in resisting and repelling
their attacks and maintaining his ascendency. Having witnessed
the success of the Gospel among those of his countrymen who
had received it, and the downfall of the foolish gods that Tahiti
worshipped, and having, with many others, shouted the triumphs
of Jehovah there, he was now willing to devote himself, for a
time, to the business of acquainting the Hawaiians with what
he knew, so far as he could make their language available. For
this purpose he and his wife, who was a help-meet, tarried a year
before they returned home.

Mr. Ellis preached to his Tahitian people at Honolulu in the
Tahitian dialect. They sung Tahitian hymns, in a manner
gratifying and encouraging, and numbers of our people attended.
He introduced gradually into his discourses the changes required
to make them intelligible to the Hawaiians, as well as to the Tahitians. This exercise facilitated our progress, as well as that of
the Tahitians, in acquiring the use of the Hawaiian.

Kaahumanu, with her husband, made a tour through the windward islands, with a large retinue, including her sister Namahana,
her brother-in-law, Laanui, and Auna the Tahitian teacher.
Neither attempting to learn to read, nor consenting to refrain,
even on the Sabbath, from her amusements, she set herself against
the foolish gods of Hawaii; and while on this pleasure-seeking
tour, searched out and destroyed many idols. On the 4th of
June, she sent for Kamehameha's image of Kalaipahoa, the so
called poison deity, and caused it to be publicly burnt, with nine
other images. On the 26th of the same month, one hundred and
two idols, collected from different parts of Hawaii, where they
had been hidden "in the holes of the rocks and caves of the
earth," were, by her authority, committed to the flames. In her
new war with idolatry, she gave a new demonstration of her
energy, which, if it should ever be sanctified and brought under
the sway of the love of Christ, seemed likely to make her a burning and shining light among her people.

While, as the haughty Kaahumanu, she was performing this
tour, great numbers of dogs, hogs, fowls, fish, and *kapas* were
laid at her feet. She and her company returned to Honolulu in
July. Meantime, Messrs. Tyerman, Bennet, Ellis, and myself,
attended by Honolii, and a guide furnished by Liholiho, made a
tour through Oahu, communicating with the people, surveying

the field, and imparting some knowledge of the great salvation. The demand for our labors increased on our return. Our utmost exertions and best influence being required, our weekly efforts among the chiefs and people were multipled, and five or six public Sabbath services were held. Keeaumoku, with concern, told us, that in a dream he had seen the islands all on fire, and was greatly alarmed, but was unable to find a way to escape, or a place to hide himself from the terrible conflagration. Dreams being influenced by waking thoughts and the power of association, such a dream was very natural for a man who had been brought up over a volcano, and had witnessed its tremendous power in shaking the earth and deluging portions of it with torrents of melted lava, and who had begun to learn that the soul, without a Divine Refuge, is in danger of eternal destruction. Being urged to seek the gracious Savior, he now manifested an earnestness to be instructed, and conceiving that the knowledge of letters and the possession of religion were valuable and attainable both for himself and friends, he urged his haughty sister, Kaahumanu, to unite with him in building a school-house, and to attend diligently to the instruction of the missionaries. She demurred; but he, to avail himself of our aid, opened his own house for the worship of God and for the school instruction needed for himself and others.

Kamamalu applied herself also with renewed vigor to learn, both in English and in her own language, and exerted an influence, on the whole, favorable to the cause of instruction, and soon had a school-house built for the benefit of her people. Liholiho requested a hundred copies of the spelling-book in his language to be furnished for his friends and attendants who were unsupplied, while he would not have the instruction of the people, in general, come in the way of their cutting sandal-wood to pay his debts.

Four or five hymns having been prepared in Hawaiian by Mr. Ellis, were introduced into public worship with manifest advantage. On the 4th of August, these were read and sung, and I addressed the throne of grace in the language of the country. In my early efforts to do this, it seemed that an invisible power granted the needed assistance. The language was found to be favorable to short petitions, confessions, and ascriptions of praise and adoration. On the next day, while many of our friends, over oceans and continents, were remembering us at the monthly concert, the king and his attendants applied themselves to their new books. A number of natives, already able to teach them, joined with the missionaries as teachers, and we rejoiced to see the king's thatched habitation, under the guns of the fort at Honolulu, become a primary school for the highest family in the land. Naihe, Kapiolani, Namahana, and Laanui, at their own houses in the village, were endeavoring to learn to read and write.

But the female of highest rank had not yet deigned to give her attention to a book, though many others were in earnest to learn

without her requiring it; and it was still very doubtful whether
she would condescend to learn the alphabet. She was nearly
fifty years of age. She was tall and portly, but not so tall and
gigantic as her sister Kalakua, nor had she the unseemly obesity
of her sister Namahana. She had black hair, a swarthy complexion, a dark, commanding eye, a deliberate enunciation, a
dignified and measured step, an air of superiority, and a heathen
queen-like hauteur; yet, sometimes, a full length portrait of her
dignity might have presented her stretched out prostrate on the
same floor on which a large,black, pet hog was allowed, unmolested, to walk or lie and grunt, for the annoyance or amusement of the inmates. She would amuse herself for hours at
cards, or in trimming and stringing the bright, yellow nuts of the
Pandanus, for odoriferous necklaces or rude coronets, listen to
vile songs and foolish stories, and sometimes make interesting
inquiries. Her stiffness towards the missionaries, to whom her
little finger, instead of a right hand, had been sometimes extended, had unbent from the time of her severe illness, and there
was reason to hope that continued kindness and God's blessing
would bring her over, and make her a friend and coadjutor.
Deeming it of great importance to induce her, if possible, to substitute the reading of divine truth for her heathenish or trifling
engagements at this period—more than two years after commencing
our work—Mrs. B. and myself called at her habitation, in the
centre of Honolulu. She and several women of rank were
stretched upon the mats, playing at cards, which were introduced
before letters. It was not uncommon for such groups to sit like
tailors, or to lie full length with the face to the ground, the head
a little elevated, the breast resting on a cylindrical pillow, the
hands grasping and moving the cards, while their naked feet and
toes extended in diverging lines towards the different sides or
extremities of the room. Being invited to enter the house, we
took our seats without the accommodation of chairs, and waited
till the game of cards was disposed of, when the wish was expressed to have us seated by her. We gave her ladyship one of
the little books, and drew her attention to the alphabet, neatly
printed, in large and small Roman characters.

Having her eye directed to the first class of letters—the five
vowels, she was induced to imitate my voice in their enunciation,
a, e, i, o, u. As the vowels could be acquired with great facility,
an experiment of ten minutes, well directed, would ensure a considerable advance. She followed me in enunciating the vowels,
one by one, two or three times over, in their order, when her skill
and accuracy were commended. Her countenance brightened.
Looking off from her book upon her familiars, with a tone a little
boasting or exulting, and perhaps with a spice of the feeling of
the Grecian philosopher, who, in one of his amusements, thought
he had discovered the solution of a difficult problem, leaped from
the bath, exclaiming " *Eureka !* I have found," the queen ex-

claimed, " *Ua loaa iau !* I have got it", or, it is obtained by
me.   She had passed the threshold, and now unexpectedly
found herself entered as a pupil.   Dismissing her cards, she accepted and studied the little book, and with her husband, asked
for forty more for their attendants.   The next day, securing the
co-operation of Kamamalu, we invited her to accompany us to
church.   Hawaiian etiquette would hardly allow her to turn off
the daughter unheeded.   Directing her plain, American-built
wagon, with unpainted covering, to be brought to her door, though
she had no trained steeds or coach-horses to draw it, she mounted
it, and drawn by her willing servants, was conveyed half a mile,
to the place of worship.   Numbers, at the same time, moved on
over the plain, at the sound of the church-going bell, and came to
the house of God in company, and listened to the teaching of
Divine truth.   The following Sabbath, the church was full.   The
Gospel was proclaimed, the Savior's dying love was commemorat-
ed at his table, and the praise of God resounded in the songs of
Zion, and all our hearts were encouraged by the decisive evidence
of a new and important impulse being given to our cause.

The need of a great increase of native teachers and of the
labors of a native ministry was now apparent.   Hundreds, had
they been qualified, might now have found employment.

Among the various objects of interest and attention for Thomas
Hopu, there were two of special importance in his estimation,
the possession of a good wife and of a license to preach the
Gospel.   It may well be conceived that there were not wanting
difficulties in both cases.   His license, the gentlemen of the
Deputation from England recommended.   But their standard of a
missionary preacher, and their views of employing *lay* laborers,
were somewhat different from those of our mission.   Their deliberate opinion on this subject was, that pious artisans, physicians,
etc., as laymen, if required by natives, should find their support
among those for whom they labor, and not from the funds of Missionary Boards ; but if Missionary Boards wished to introduce the
arts among nations like the Polynesians, they should employ
preachers with qualifications to do it.   " A missionary," they say,
(a preacher of the Gospel sent abroad), " will do more towards
promoting civilization by a well cultivated garden, a neat house,
with decent furniture, with suitable and becoming clothing, and
with the ability to instruct those around them how to make any
article of furniture which may attract attention, than fifty artisans
who might be sent for the express purpose of teaching the heathen
their arts.   Nor let it be imagined that it lessens a missionary in
their eyes, to know that he is able to work at any of the mechanical arts.   It has the opposite effect.   They are not able to appreciate his knowledge of the classics or what is called learning,
but they can appreciate the talents of a man who can build a
house or make a coat better than they can.   By such means a missionary establishes, in their view, his superiority over them.   This

being done, they will listen to his religious instructions with deference, and feel confidence in him as a teacher."

But a more full delineation of the general qualifications of a missionary laborer, by that Deputation, in their friendly letter to our Prudential Committee, may be found in the following paragraph ;—" As the resources of our societies are limited, economy in the expenditure of our finances is of indispensable importance, and hence the question arises, how shall we most effectually and the most extensively promote the Redeemer's cause with the means which are put into our hands ? Or, in other words, what description of characters are likely to be the efficient instruments in promoting at once the interests of religion and civilization ? Our opinion is made up. We think that they should be those only who possess such talents as qualify them for instructing the heathen in the knowledge of the Gospel, and also for promoting among them an acquaintance with the arts of civilized society ; *and these talents should meet in the same person.* While we think it highly desirable that some missionaries should be sent into such parts of the world as these, who have received a liberal education, with a view to the translating of the Scriptures, we do not think it necessary for all who are intended to preach the Gospel among the heathen. A competent knowledge of their own language, some general acquaintance with the most popular sciences, an ability to work at some mechanical business and to instruct others, with a talent to adapt his exertions to any and every necessity which presents itself in the mechanical arts, which we call *handicraft*—these qualifications, in connexion with genuine religion, a heart glowing with zeal for the salvation of souls, an aptness to teach, a readiness to acquire a foreign language, an intimate knowledge of human nature, a prudent, patient, and persevering mind, will make a young man of twenty, or one or two and twenty years of age, a valuable missionary in such countries as these."*

Our views of the importance of consistency and weight of character in an ambassador of Christ, of knowledge and skill in the evangelist to wield the Sword of the Spirit, in the circumstances of our mission, at that time, and the abundant and favorable opportunities for the labors of well-disposed laymen, several of whom, then in the mission, were better qualified to be preachers than Hopu, led us to decline giving him a formal license. He labored on as a layman. The other object of Hopu's desire, and to which he had as good a right as any of his countrymen, was granted. A young maiden selected by him from the women of Hawaii, was instructed in the family of Mr. Thurston, received the name Delia, made respectable progress, appeared unusually quiet and seriously disposed, and finally proved herself a companion worthy of him. The consummation of his wishes in this case

* Missionary Herald.

we endeavored to make available for the introduction of the general practice of Christian marriage at the Sandwich Islands, where
such a thing had never been known, and where the nation, even
in its highest circles, had been at a great remove from its sanctity,
its rights, and its happy influence. To give it due consequence,
the marriage was solemnized at the close of public worship, in the
presence of the congregation composed of natives, rulers, and
foreigners. To make it appear still more sacred and indissoluble,
a blank book being provided for a marriage record, the parties
subscribed their own names under a note inserted on and for the
occasion, with witnesses in great particularity and formality—
thus ;—

" *Married, by the Rev. H. Bingham, August 11th,* 1822.

	Daniel Tyerman.	THOMAS HOPU.
Witness,	George Bennet.	DELIA."
	James Kahuhu.	

This first female who, in Hawaii, took the vows of Christian
marriage, proved herself to be an affectionate, obedient, faithful
wife, where little of these qualities had been before known
among her countrywomen, but where many since have deserved
the same commendation.

Before the departure of the English visitors, an invitation,
through our friend, Kaumualii, was given to Mr. Ellis, whom we
were desirous to retain, to bring his family from the Society
Islands and settle in our field, in which other chiefs, particularly
Kalanimoku, and our missionaries, concurred ; and we were cheered by having this arrangement made with the cordial approval of
the Deputation. Having made a very opportune, acceptable, and
useful visit, of more than four months, they took an affectionate
leave, on the 22d of August, and sailed for the Society Islands.

Their talents, experience, kindness, and courtesy, rendered the
Christian intercourse of these brethren with our missionaries, so
isolated and secluded from civilized society, a peculiar privilege,
long to be remembered with pleasure. Prejudices had been allayed,
and the confidence of the rulers in our cause, increased. Mr.
Ellis, being some four years in advance of us, in acquaintance with
missionary life, among a people of language and manners so simialr
to those whom we were laboring to elevate, and being peculiarly
felicitous in his manner of communication with all classes, greatly
won our esteem, awakened a desire to retain him as a fellow
laborer, and made us grateful for the providence that kindly made
the arrangement, for a season, by which the language was sooner
acquired, and our main work expedited.

From the newness of our situation, and our circumscribed
quarters, our complicated family being lodged in one small house,
having native boarding scholars, and scanty means, we were not
in circumstances to make such provision for the daily comfort of

our welcome guests, during four months, as our feelings would
have dictated; but neither they, nor we, expected luxury or ease
on missionary ground, and remembering the injunction, " Be content with such things as ye have," we shared our privations and
comforts in common, and enjoyed the happiness peculiar to the situation in which the hand of Providence is seen to " give us, day by
day, our daily bread."

Our little isolated band was cheered also, about this period,
with the courtesy and kindness of Capt. De Koven, of Connecticut, an Episcopalian gentleman, who, on his way from Macao to
the United States, visited us; and also by the sympathy of an American gentleman in China, who sent us a seasonable present of
table furniture and other articles, which subserved our convenience and comfort, beyond the expectation of the donor, especially
while our English guests were with us.   Its value was enhanced
by the sympathizing and cheering letter, which accompanied it,
modestly signed " O"—from which the following is an extract,
sufficient to show its spirit.

" An opportunity offering for the Sandwich Islands, I avail myself
of it to send you some articles, which I hope may be serviceable to
your society, and grateful as a token of Christian remembrance and affection.   If they, in any degree, administer to your comfort or convenience, the privilege of dispensing it is one for which I cannot be
sufficiently grateful.   Who that has tasted the Saviour's love, but must
wish to express it ?   And to whom shall he express it, if not to those
who have renounced their homes, that they may labor for the good of
their fellow-men to bring them from the wretchedness and degradation
of their darkness, to that Saviour, and the blessings of his grace ?

" May your hearts be animated with frequent thoughts of, and
prayers for, China.   How important may your labors be in regard to it,
—perhaps more so, than for those for whom you are more immediately
engaged.

" I bid you farewell, praying with the spiritual Brown, that as you
have been called to labor for our common Lord, in the Isles of the
Ocean—'You may for ever stand on the Rock of Ages, on the sure
bottom of divine purposes and promises ; and may the ocean of Redeeming love surround, protect, wash, and fructify all your powers.
While you inhabit time, that almost invisible island, thrown up in the
ocean of eternal duration, may eternal things be your prospect, your
refreshment, your all in all.' "

At this period, we were also encouraged in our progress, by
being able to teach and preach, and conduct divine service,
without the intervention of interpreters.   But notwithstanding
these encouraging circumstances, and the proposal of our Board
to send us a large reinforcement soon, there would have been
room for despondency, but for the divine promises and predictions,
which cannot fail.

Our third year was passing away, the bones of our valley were
yet exceedingly dry.   We longed to see them move and live, and

stand up, an army to praise God, a civilized and Christian nation. But 'how can a nation be born at once, or the earth made to bring forth in one day?' To save their souls was the main object, but that object was not to be singly and constantly pressed on the attention of such a people. Their uncouth and disgusting manners were to be corrected, their modes of dress and living to be improved, their grossness, destitution, and wretchedness, if possible, removed; and taste, refinement, and comfort, substituted. In attempting this, we were sometimes amused, and sometimes pained, to witness the efforts of some of the noble women, Kamamalu, Kapiolani, and others, attempting to put off their heathen habits, and assume a more civilized air. To give them a just taste at once, and the skill and means of gratifying it, was impossible; and if their honest efforts to make the desired changes should result in grotesque and ridiculous combinations, not a whit better than the ordinary native costume, except in the texture of the material, it might be regarded as a matter of course; and even if a facetious fancy should put forth its efforts designedly to amuse by novelties, it was no matter of wonder. Very little, of course, could be said from the pulpit, in favor of improving the fashions without interfering with the weightier matters of the law, or without giving to the forms of dress, a religious aspect on the one hand, and provoking vanity, pride, and envy, on the other. To improve greatly a heathen's dress, furniture, or habitation, before changing the taste, manners and morals, accomplishes little or nothing in the real work of reform, and leaves the main business of inducing self-denial, repentance, humility, faith, and a desire for divine and heavenly things, as difficult and distant as when you began. And how many articles, and touches of skill and taste, must be required, to metamorphose a heathen hut, and its inmates, into a well furnished mansion, a civilized, intelligent, tasteful, courteous, orderly, and happy family. It is the work of an age; and if those who undertake it should sometimes feel discouraged, it would be very natural.

How difficult the process, how great the number of strokes to be given, and the extent of the mass to be moved, in order to do this thoroughly in one case, where disease and death were so fearfully mowing down by annual thousands those for whom the work was undertaken, and where, in the commencement, there was not a single female in all the land, who had the skill, or the motive, or the courage to begin aright! What a figure would a band of foreign bachelors have made in attempting this part of the work for the females of the Sandwich Islands, or for the children surrounded by heathen mothers, and at the same time struggling to keep their own persons, clothes, furniture, table, and habitations, in good order as models, besides the work of translating, preaching, and inculcating religion for the whole nation, or a community large enough for ten times their number to instruct! It was difficult even for educated females to make a beginning, to show what was needed, and to enlist any material effort even in those most disposed to improve.

Just look into the straw palace of a Hawaiian queen, the first or second year of our sojourn among them, and see a missionary's wife waiting an hour to get her to turn from her cards to try on a new dress for which she had asked. Then, on trial, hear her laconic and supercilious remarks, "*pilikia—hemo—hana hou*" (too tight—off with it—do it over) ; then, see her resume her cards, leaving the lady, tired and grieved, but patient, to try again ; and when successful, to be called on again and again for more.

Look again, as another year passes on, and you may see the same woman at her writing desk, her maidens around her, under the superintendence of the same teacher, learning to ply the scissors and needle, making silk dresses for her majesty, and a pet hog, like a puppy, shaking the folds of the silk for sport, and demonstrating how civilization and barbarism could walk hand in hand, or lie down together, in queens' palaces. Within another year, Kamamalu, Kapiolani, Kaahumanu, Kekauluohi, Kinau, Keopuolani, Kalakua, Kekauonohi, Liliha, Keoua, Kapule, Namahana and others, threw around them an air of rising consequence by the increase, not only of foreign articles of clothing, but of furniture —a chair, a table, a work-stand, a writing-desk, a bedstead, a glass window, partitions, curtains, etc., noticing, and attempting to imitate what, in the mission families, attracted their attention or appeared sufficiently pleasing, useful, and available, to induce them to copy.

But how difficult and long must be the process of learning to make use, or keep in order and enjoy the variety of useful articles which the arts of civilized life supply, had the chiefs and people possessed money or exportable products in abundance, to purchase the materials at pleasure! But not one in a thousand had the money or the exportable products at command, and while it seemed to us a difficult thing for the chiefs to pay for half a dozen brigs and schooners, for which they had contracted, and to build and furnish houses for themselves, it seemed equally difficult for the common people to supply themselves, who had not the means to purchase the soil they cultivated, if they had been allowed to buy it, nor the capital to put a plough, a pair of oxen, and a cart upon a farm, if farms were given them in fee simple ; nor the skill and enterprise to use them advantageously, if every hand-spade-digger of kalo and potatoe ground had been gratuitously furnished with land, teams, and implements of husbandry, like the yeomanry of New England.

Want of skill and self-confidence, therefore, until morals and intelligence could be greatly increased, must be a grand barrier to useful accumulation, or the possession and enjoyment of what we call a competence, even if the people had as full confidence in the government as is common in other countries.

Whence, then, were they to obtain the requisite skill ? By what means shall the knowledge of the arts and sciences be acquired by a nation so stupid and ignorant, whose destitution seemed almost to forbid their progress, while it imperatively required it, and whose spiritual wants, first to be met, demanded more attention than the missionaries could give ?

How difficult, during the first years of our labor, to displace the notion entertained by the more intelligent rulers, that the earth is a stationary plain, around which the sun, the changeful planets and stars revolve. Laboring, occasionally, to teach by means of a watch, the divisions of hours, minutes, and seconds, and of days and weeks, by the artificial globe, using the common arguments for the globular figure and diurnal motions of the earth, we were met by their objection, that everything would fall off if the earth were to turn over. The king himself laughed at our astronomy, and maintained that sailing round the earth was like sailing round one of his islands. But he at length yielded to the force of argument in favor of the globular form and diurnal motion of the earth; yet many others were far less teachable. After a period of daily and successful toil in teaching him, it was painful to see him lock his writing-desk and turn away from study, for Saturnalian revelry. What a task was still to be accomplished for the nation! But one thing after another, "line upon line," stroke after stroke,—the fire, the hammer, the file, the burnisher, will in time succeed. The rude iron, copper and zinc ores, gypsum, quartzy sand, and porcelain clay, are capable of being wrought by skill and persevering labor, into time-pieces of beautiful forms and exquisite machinery, which gratify the eye and the ear; and by whose uniform and exact motions, under divinely established laws, the business of communities may be regulated, the flight of the great ships from clime to clime be measured, and the admiration of the beholder attracted to the wisdom and agency of Him who made and directs all things. So, from the rudest materials of a destitute and degraded heathen nation, He can mould, reform, polish, and put in motion, for a long eternity, instruments of his exquisite workmanship, to show forth to the inhabitants of heaven and earth, the high praises of Divine wisdom and grace. What a privilege, then, to have a part in bringing forward the ore for the Founder and the " Finisher ;" in preparing thousands of instruments for God's everlasting praise, or even to witness the demonstrations of his skill, power, and goodness, in accomplishing this wonderful work !

By this time Liholiho, notwithstanding his dissipation and irregularities, had become able to write a letter of business or of friendship, and he availed himself of it by addressing a note to the king of Huahine, one of the Society Islands. The following is a translation, with the exception of the signature, which, as to name, title, and orthography, is strictly his own :—

" Hawaii, August 16th, 1822.

" O Mahina—I now make a communication to you.　I have compassion towards you on account of your son's dying.　Love to you and the *alii*, chiefs of your islands.　I now serve the God of you and us. We are now learning the palapala.　When I become skilful in learning I will then go and visit you.　May you be saved by Jesus Christ.

" RIHORIHO, TAMEHAMEHA 2d."

Having just begun to learn to read, Kaahumanu, about this time, embarked with her husband, and visited his islands with a retinue of some eight hundred persons, including several chiefs, and Auna, and William Beals, whom the queen requested us to send as her teacher.　They left Honolulu harbor in four vessels, three of which belonged to Kaumualii, but which, with their possessor, were probably counted by the Cleopatrian pride of Kaahumanu, as all her own.

On their arrival, the next day, at Waimea, they gave a new impulse to the desire among the people to be instructed, much to the surprise and gratification of Messrs. Whitney and Ruggles, who said their house for several days was thronged with natives pleading for books.　They immediately took three hundred under instruction.　Their former pupils were now demanded as teachers for the beginners.　Kaahumanu, spurring on these efforts, soon sent back to Kamamalu at Oahu the following characteristic letter.

" This is my communication to you: tell the *puu A-i o-e-o-e* (posse of Long necks) to send some more books down here.　Many are the people—few are the books.　I want *elua lau* (800) Hawaiian books to be sent hither.　We are much pleased to learn the *palapala*.　By and by, perhaps, we shall be *akamai*, skilled or wise.　Give my love to Mr. and Mrs. Bingham, and the whole company of Long necks."

The little half cast lad (not yet in his " teens"), who had been sent as her domestic teacher, after he had been instructed about two years, and who had been encouraged to prosecute his juvenile studies at the same time, and also keep a journal, showed at this time his mental capacity, his activity, progress, affection, and maturity, by a report of himself, neatly written in his newly acquired English, and addressed to his teacher.　It is as follows :—

" My very dear Mrs. Bingham—I long very much to see you.　I am in hopes I shall see you in a couple of months.　I hope that you are well and Mr. B. and little Sophia.　I long very much to see her.　I think about her every day, and how she used to play with me.　I wish kiss her for me.　You might be pleased to hear I have a school twice a day.　I have thirty-five scholars, boys and girls, and the remainder of the time I take to teach the king and queen, so I have no time to write my journal.　Once in a while, when they are out in swimming, I have a little time to write it.　I would thank you to send down some books, for there are some scholars who have none.　You have mentioned in your letter, for me to live with Mr. Ruggles and to sleep there. But it is inconvenient for me to cross the river. But once in a day I can get across when I says my lesson regular before Mr. Ruggles. I would thank you to let me know whether I sleep there or not I am going to Niihau in the Tartar, and my scholars are going with me, so I teach them there. Mr. Whitney is going with us to Niihau. He says he will hear my lesson any time. I thank you to give my love to Mr. and Mrs. Chamberlain and to all the family children. Tell them they must all be good children. Give my love to John Honolii and James. King Kaumualii give his love to Mr. B. and to you, and queen Kaahumanu too. They say they like the *palapala.*

"Do not forget to pray for me—I am your child,

"WILLIAM BEALS."

The adaptation of this lad to a post so difficult, and his marked success in filling it, even for a short period, were some of the fruits of the early boarding-school efforts of the mission. Such efforts, without the efficient aid of missionary females, would hardly have been attempted, even if without their presence and co-operation, the table, health, and reputation of the missionaries could have been properly maintained in a land of ignorance, destitution, confusion, jealousy, and pollution so great, that with all the facilities we possessed, and all the sanctions of the Word of God, it was almost impossible to save from reproach and ruin, the native assistants, who had been instructed and hopefully converted in the United States of America.

CHAPTER VIII.

THE first day of 1823 was observed by the missionaries as a
day of fasting and prayer, in reference to the cause of religion;
and on the first Monday of that year, inviting the people to join
them, they united with the friends of missions in the monthly
concert of prayer for the conversion of the world. Though few
and feeble, they felt encouraged to lay hold on the great and exceedingly precious promises, and to expect a blessing to crown the
means daily employed according to divine appointment.

By this time, we had among our pupils, besides Liholiho and
the young prince, twenty-four chiefs, twelve male and twelve
female, who, in some sense, acknowledged Christianity. While
some of these seemed to be seeking the things above, others clung
to their vices as firmly as ever, and not a few in the nation were
evidently hankering after their old idolatry, or felt themselves
bound by its long-riveted fetters.

At the decease of the wife of Cox, at Kauai, towards the close
of the year, her friends for seven days performed their heathen
rites, using incantations, offering sacrifices of hogs, dogs, and
fowls, so sickening to the missionaries, so offensive to God, and
so degrading and ruinous to the people. Heathen burials were
suited to the hours of darkness; and the Hawaiians chose that
time to put their departed ones out of sight, without coffins, into
a cave or under the surface of the ground just where the spirit
left its clay. This they did, it is said, to escape the coarse and
unkind remarks which they feared from spectators.

In the place of the gloomy scenes of heathen burial, Divine
Providence, by a tender bereavement in the mission family, called
on us to set the example of a Christian burial, which, while it
awakened sympathy in the breasts of stout-hearted rulers, became

the means of introducing a custom long to exert a humanizing and salutary influence. The little L. Parsons Bingham, at the age of sixteen days, passed away suddenly, as did the dear missionary in Alexandria, whose name he was expected to bear, and by which he had been baptized. The principal personages to whom we had been attentive, manifested some sympathy. Kaahumanu, Kamamalu, and Kaumualii, early made us a visit of condolence, noticing the evidences of grief and submission, the acknowledgment of God's hand, and the manner of preparing for interment.

As strangers and sojourners with the people of a heathen land, we felt the affecting necessity of asking of the rulers a burying-place among them. A spot of ground near the church was, according to our wishes, readily granted us. There, with mournful but not desponding feelings, we broke the ground to deposit the beautiful flower that had fallen, where we expected the mission family would, one after another, be gathered around it, and where we should choose to be buried when our work is done. The funeral services and burial took place on the Sabbath, the 19th of January. The king and his principal chiefs, male and female, several foreign residents and others, assembled at the mission house and walked in procession to the church, where Mr. Thurston preached an appropriate sermon. We then drew around the grave, and with tenderness laid the little sleeper in its lonely, silent bed, where the ocean and the volcano had, at some former period, struggled for the mastery.

So rich and strong were the consolations of the Gospel, so glorious did the Savior appear in offering himself a sacrifice for the sins of the world, providing a balm for every sorrow, a home in heaven, at his own right hand, for his people, and receiving little children to his kingdom, that we rejoiced to avail ourselves of these new circumstances to tell a heathen nation of the preciousness of Christ, and felt a new and strong impulse to be ready for any toil or sacrifice by which his great salvation could be the sooner made universally known for the rescue of earth's millions from temporal suffering and from everlasting death.

Three days subsequent to this funeral, a young relative of Liholiho, whom he called sister, died at Honolulu, when our sympathies and attention were readily returned. The king and Kamamalu made a particular request for funeral services like those at the burial of the little L. Parsons. Kaahumanu, believing that the soul of the child still existed and might be benefited by prayer, requested us to pray that it might go up to heaven. We had yet to teach them that probation ceases when the soul leaves the body. The king specified a particular time when he thought it would be proper to give his departed sister to Christ, as though the mere mass of clay were to be consecrated to the Deity instead of the soul and body as "a living sacrifice." He had some serious reflections, and was quite as ready to do what God had not commanded as what he had. It was the living sacrifice which we endeavored to convince him and his people ought to be consecrated to God without delay. The occasion was seized on to direct the minds of the bereaved friends to look at things eternal, and to prepare for the world to come. The remains of the honored child, dressed for the grave, were laid in a coffin at the house of Kalanimoku. The king and his wives, and principal chiefs, of both sexes, the missionaries, and others, assembled there, and offered a prayer, formed a procession, and moving with the corpse to the church, there respectfully attended to the unfolding of this lesson of inspired instruction : " As it is appointed unto all men once to die, and after that the judgment, so Christ was once offered to bear the sins of many, and unto them that look for him, shall he appear the second time without sin unto salvation." The procession being again formed, proceeded to the fort, within whose walls, and near the lofty national flagstaff, the remains of this juvenile chieftain were respectfully lowered into the " narrow house." Over the closing grave the missionary endeavored to plant the thought in the minds of the beholders, that this was the resting-place for the lifeless body till the morning of the resurrection, "when the dead, small and great, shall rise and stand before God." For a few days there were indications of seriousness among the rulers.

Liholiho quickly hurried off to Puuloa, at the opening of the lagoon in Ewa, which lies some fourteen miles west of Honolulu. His retinue, Kaumaulii, Kaahumanu, and others, soon gathered there. To keep our hold of him, and follow up a good impression, was deemed important, not only for his own sake, but for the sake of thousands whose temporal prosperity, and whose attention to the claims of the true religion, might be promoted by a wise and Christian-like course of their king, and whose interests might all be jeoparded by the reverse; and on that account, leaving my family, I followed him, in compliance with his wishes.

The mean habitations of the hamlet at Puuloa were put in requisition, and temporary booths added, for the wretched accommodation of the visitors.

In the house occupied by the king, a space six feet by three, having a mat spread on the ground, was, by his order, partitioned off for my lodging place as his teacher, the occupancy of every inch of which was stoutly disputed by the *uku-lele*. Dark and comfortless as was our encampment, the great inconveniences as to food, lodging and study, were overbalanced by the opportunities afforded there, for preaching the Gospel to those who would not otherwise hear it, and for directing the studies, answering the inquiries, and urging the duties of these wanderers. While encouraging here the early efforts of Kauikeaouli, the young prince, I marked with peculiar pleasure, the promise of his childhood, though many and strong deleterious influences were still thrown around him. While some of his honored superiors were given to revelry, and many adults seemed almost idle, this child would, sometimes, sitting by himself with book in hand, be heard reading his lesson with animation, and elevated voice.

I one day accompanied the king and others by boat to see the reputed habitation of a Hawaiian deity, on the bank of the lagoon of Ewa. It was a cavern or fissure in a rock, chiefly under water, where, as their traditions teach, and as some then affirmed, a god, once in human form, taking the form of a shark, had his subterraqueous abode. Sharks were regarded by the Hawaiians as gods capable of being influenced by prayers and sacrifices, either to kill those who hate and despise them, or to spare those who respect and worship them. It had been held that, when a mother gave her offspring to a shark, the spirit of the child dwelt in it, and the shark becoming an *akua*, would afterwards recognise and befriend the mother on meeting her, though ready to devour others. As we talked over these matters, the king laughed at the folly of worshipping such a monster. This afforded a good opportunity for recommending a more rational worship and the observance of God's ordinances.

Calling the chiefs and people at Puuloa together, on the Lord's day, I preached to them on the sanctity and duties of the Christian Sabbath, as a divine institution, and urged them to regard it as a season of holy resting from secular labor and amusement, a day for Christian instruction, and the public and private worship of Jehovah. The same subject was, at the same time, earnestly pressed by Mr. Thurston on the attention of Kalanimoku, and other chiefs and people, at Honolulu, where the attendance at the sanctuary was scarcely diminished by the absence of the king's company. On the evening of the next day (being monthly concert), the government herald proclaimed the order, that the Lord's day was sacred, and that the people must, on the Sabbath, abstain from work and play. This was an important step, in advance of what they would do or allow when dancing, revelling, sailing from port, and firing salutes on the Sabbath, were, in the estimation of the king and chiefs, among privileges not to be denied them by any authority.

The acknowledgment of the sanctity of the Christian Sabbath resulted in the almost universal suspension of kindling fires and cooking food on that day by the natives. The reason for this may be seen, partly in the terms of the divine command, to do no work, and partly in their modes of cooking and eating, which may have helped to produce in the Hawaiians a commendable peculiarity in their observance of the Lord's day. Their usual mode of cooking is to excavate a place in the ground, sufficiently large for a bushel or two of the large bulbous roots of arum or kalo, which are brought fresh from the patch or field, for the occasion; procure and put down at the bottom of the pit, the requisite amount of fuel, wood, or other combustibles, and raise upon it a heap of small stones, which are heated thoroughly, as the fuel burns out.

The arum roots, or whatever articles are to be baked there, are placed compactly upon the heated stones, and covered with leaves and grass, to keep them clean, and prevent the heat from escaping into the air.   A little water is then thrown upon the mass, and the whole covered quickly with earth, like a little coal-pit, as closely as three or four inches' depth of earth will make it.   The water coming gradually in contact with the hot stones and coals, is converted into steam, which, with the radiating heat of the stones, in the course of two or three hours, accomplishes the object.   Then this hemispherical little mound or ground oven is opened, the covering of earth, leaves and grass, is carefully removed, and the contents taken out.   The arum roots are washed and peeled, and usually are pounded on a large thick wooden platter, with a stone pestle, some four or five inches in diameter. When thoroughly beaten, the mass resembles dough.   It is sometimes eaten in that state ; but usually, being mixed with water, it is made into a paste called *po-i*, which would serve well for bookbinder's work, and is eaten cold and unseasoned.   The people sometimes sipped it from the rim of the dish, but most commonly dipped the fore and middle finger into the paste, moving them in small circles ; then, with appropriate manipulations, conveyed to the mouth so much of it as adhered to their fingers, and sucked, or slipped it off by the earnest action of the lips.   They think it relishes better from the fingers than from a spoon.   This has long been the principal article of daily food for the mass of the Hawaiian people.   The article of food next in importance with them, is fish, raw, dried, roasted or baked.   It is eaten in moderate quantity, with the arum paste.   Fowls, ducks, turkeys, goats, hogs and dogs, are, like the arum, baked in the ground-oven occasionally.

Such cooking and preparing food being obviously unsuited to the sacredness and duties of the Sabbath, that labor was required to be done previously.   The unusually numerous smokes rising from different parts of a village or valley, on a Saturday morning, became at length a pleasing, noiseless signal of the approach of the sacred day, and of preparation for it, as the people came to recognise its authority.

In my sojourn at Puuloa, waking one night, rather than sleeping on my comfortless bulrush mat, and perceiving the king to be awake, and sitting by himself near a light kept burning, I rose, and seating myself quietly near him, drew him easily into a midnight conversation ; and feeling my heart inclined to win his soul, if possible, I called his attention to the duty of personal and decided piety, and urged the necessity of immediate repentance. "I cannot," he said, "repent at once.   *He nui loa kuu hewa*, my wickedness is very great ; but in five years, I will turn and forsake sin."   "But you are not sure of five years, or five months, or five days.   You can gain nothing by delay.   You ought to repent now, of all your sins, and enter at once upon the service of the great God of heaven, that your soul may be saved through

Christ." Either wishing to evade the duty wholly, or preferring to try the gradual surrender of one sin after another, and yet assure me that he meant eventually to be a Christian, he made this statement: " When I saw my little sister lying dead, I thought of her soul. I meditated alone. I said to Jehovah, 'in five years I will turn and be a good man ; the Lord's servant, that then he might look at me, and if good, preserve me ; and if not, send me to the place of punishment.' " Whatever of sincerity or pretence, compliance or evasion, may have been in this, it seemed like *bartering with God for further indulgence in sin.* Like Felix, and uncounted multitudes of other sinners, he probably hoped and intended at some future, convenient time, to give heed to God's claims, but could not yet make up his mind to *give up the world,* which some in Christian lands, and even among professors of the Gospel, affirm " is not expected of Christians, at the present day."

" What, then," it might be asked, " must all hope of the conversion of the nation be relinquished because the sovereign is unwilling to repent and reform, when the claims of Christ are made known to him?" By no means. Great as his influence might be for good or evil, in his position, yet the nobility could be as easily converted as the sovereign, whether he were converted or not, and the peasantry as easily as the nobility, especially if they were allowed to be as thoroughly instructed. But how often has the religious aspect of the Sandwich Islands been looked upon as the result of the official influence of the rulers, who are admitted to have become Christians ; as though the same religious truths, the same divine authority, the same heavenly influences which were competent to subdue and control, at length, the proud, domineering, self-indulgent rulers, were not equally competent to subdue and guide their subjects. Though "not *many* noble are called," not many rich, proud, and mighty, yet among subjects, poor or oppressed, multitudes have found through the Gospel, " the pearl of great price." In the present instance, Kanepaiki, a subject who witnessed the conversation between the missionary and the king, saw the unreasonableness of his sovereign, and soon declared himself on the side of the Gospel.

Multitudes were, at length, led to consider and deplore the great mistake of their king, and not a few, learning from his example, have taken warning to avoid the danger which he incurred. No one thing has, perhaps, been more effectual to enforce the lesson we labored long to teach the people—a lesson which the sons and daughters of Hawaii, not more, perhaps, than of some prouder countries, have been slow to learn, that they are *personally* responsible to God, whatever rulers may do or say, and in their worship of him and their care of the soul, they must at once obey his commands, and not wait for the example, or commands, or permission of earthly potentates or pontiffs.

The demon of intemperance, so terrible in heathen nations, still held a cruel sway, and threatened ruin to many, but to none, perhaps, more than the monarch of the isles. So disgusting and abominable were the doings of the destroyer, even in the family of the king, and so determined were a class of human agents (who knew better) to encourage and confirm the king in his drinking habits, that the missionaries, anxious for him and those who hasted with him in this way to ruin, could have taken their lives in their hands to lay siege to this stronghold of Satan. Some chiefs had begun to see the wickedness and danger of this vice, and to reform, while Liholiho and his favorites, regardless of the disgrace, the crime, and the hazard connected with the practice, often repeated their excesses. Our hearts yearned over him when we saw the snare laid for him.

On one occasion, soon after our return from Puuloa to Honolulu, as I was attending on the king as a teacher, and sitting with him and others upon a mat, in the mild open air towards evening, a native brought a square bottle of spirits and dropped himself down upon his hams by my side. Supposing this to be intended to tempt the king and to defeat my purpose of teaching and reclaiming him, I gently took the uncorked bottle, and offering it to the earth rather than to his majesty, turned it bottom upwards on the mat. Though the liquor did not escape, the king, who had doubtless ordered it, was offended, and muttered indignation in terms which I did not fully comprehend. Kakuanaoa (now governor of Oahu) and others thought me in more danger, for a moment, than I myself apprehended from his wrath, which, when roused, was fearful. Kamamalu assured me it would be prudent to go out of his presence, which, after being urged, I did, but soon joined the circle again; and no harm appeared to result from my attempt to thrust aside a deadly weapon aimed at the king.

A little before this, a subordinate chief, familiar in the king's family, had become the victim of his jealousy, and, by his sovereign's order, had his head chopped off with an axe by Kahalaia, while he lay at night asleep upon his mat. How unfit such a ruler to be the leader of a nation! But it may be observed, that in thus acting out the feelings of a heathen tyrant, he had imitated the example of his father in putting to death Kanihonui; and that other chiefs, to court his smile or shun his vengeance, concurred in this dark deed, the repetition of which it was hoped the Gospel would for ever prevent.

What but a power Divine, exerted in great condescension and mercy, could effect a radical reform or produce holiness of heart and life in beings trained in heathenism, as the king and his contemporary chiefs had been? What other power could have effectually shielded the missionaries?

Kaahumanu and Kalanimoku, hearing of my prompt and strong protest against the intemperance of the king, were led the more carefully to consider whether I had not reasons to warrant it; and the more quickly and decidedly, it is believed, they became advocates and promoters of the temperance reform at the islands.

On the 4th of February, 1823, the Rev. Mr. Ellis and family from the Society Islands, as had been expected, arrived at Honolulu on board a small vessel, the Active, Richard Charlton master, and were kindly welcomed both by the missionaries and the rulers. They were accompanied by three Tahitian teachers, Kuke, and Taua, having their wives with them, and Taamotu, an unmarried female.

Mr. Ellis entered at once into the labors of the mission, and with much satisfaction, we could unitedly say, " Let us see the great work done in the shortest possible time."

The Rev. George Burder, the honored Secretary of the London Missionary Society, had before, in his correspondence with his transatlantic brethren, expressed the well timed and anti-sectarian sentiment; " It is not of the slightest consequence who does the work of evangelizing the world." This sentiment, respecting the great work, and especially, with the proviso, " if it be done *seasonably*," must be appreciated by missionary directors, who feel unable to provide for one hundredth part of the heathen world, during a whole generation, by all that is put into their hands. Nor will it be less appreciated by true missionaries, crushed down with the responsibility and labor of overthrowing long established superstitions and vices; of sowing the good seed of the kingdom ; of guarding against formidable errors and prejudices, and of offering the various, needful means of grace and salvation, to thousands and millions of their fellow-sinners, dying around them. A right view of this subject, and a proper degree of love for souls, would render easy the *union* or *co-operation* of Christ's ministers, from different parts of the world, for the speedy consummation of the missionary enterprise. The Tahitian teachers readily found useful employment, and applied themselves with becoming promptitude and sobriety.

Mr. Ellis, on the first Sabbath after his arrival, choosing as his theme, a part of Peter's address to Cornelius ; " Therefore came I unto you as soon as I was sent for : I ask, therefore, for what intent ye have sent for me," improved the excellent opportunity for exciting, and meeting the inquiries of the people, respecting the duties of the missionary, and the intent for which he had come. On the following Sabbath, I preached to the rulers and people, from a part of the answer of Cornelius to Peter's question : " Thou hast well done, that thou art come ; now therefore are we all here present before God, to hear all things that are commanded thee of God," illustrating and enforcing the duty of the people to come before God, and hear, and observe whatever the ambassadors of Christ are commanded by him to teach. Rarely, if ever, in any clime, has the attention of a nation to this duty been more speedily or extensively secured, than at the Sandwich Islands.

On the 28th of February, the Hawaiian Clerical Association was formed by the ordained missionaries, for mutual improvement, and mutual aid in laying the foundation, and maintaining the order, and rearing the superstructure of the house of the Lord in the Sandwich Islands. This came, eventually, to embrace nearly all the preachers of the Gospel, in those Islands, up to 1840. Immediately, Mr. Samuel Whitney, who, for the cause of the heathen, had left his early collegiate course at Yale College, prosecuted his studies during the passage out, and while engaged in teaching the people, was examined by the association, licensed, and recommended to preach the Gospel. Entering on this work on the ensuing Sabbath, he officiated at Honolulu, was welcomed as another preacher added to the little band, and soon returned to his post.

Shortly after this, Mr. and Mrs. Chamberlain, having diligently and usefully labored three years for the establishment of the mission, were called, as we generally believed, to return to their native land with their six children. Their health had begun to suffer materially. The prospect of obtaining a farm, and the means of cultivating it to advantage, under the existing policy of the rulers, was not favorable ; and the Christian training of so large a family of children, in so rude and ruined a state of society, appeared to them hardly practicable. They retired, having the cordial fellowship, high esteem, warm sympathy, and full concurrence of their associates ; and left the ground to be occupied by less encumbered laborers, then near at hand.

Waikiki, a place of frequent resort of the chiefs, and formerly a favorite residence of successive kings of Oahu, a few miles east of Honolulu, we often visited as an out station. It is distinguished for its extensive groves of cocoanut and kou trees, the ruins of a small heathen temple, and a unique, well-defined and extinct crater, called Leahi, and by foreigners, Diamond Hill ; a name loosely derived perhaps, from *lei*, a gem or bead, and *ahi*, fire or fiery. In one of these groves, Keopuolani pitched her tent, and sojourned for a time, in the spring of 1823, and frequently listened to the gospel. She showed unusual readiness of heart to attend to the things spoken to her from the Scriptures, and desired they might be repeated from Sabbath to Sabbath, while she, in feeble health, remained there. We were led to contrast her present with her former residence at Waikiki.

Sixteen years before, she, in her heathen state, had been dangerously ill at this place, and when various modes of treatment seemed unavailing, a bloody priest maintained that her sickness had been occasioned by the anger of the gods, from whom she had descended ; whose *tabus* had been violated by men who had eaten prohibited cocoanuts ; and that the sacrifice of the men would be the most certain means of appeasing the gods and preventing her death. Ten men were seized as victims, by order of Kamehameha and his priests. Her alarming symptoms abating, seven were liberated, and three only were slain and laid on the altar. Her life was spared to see that period of gross darkness, malevolence, and blood, pass away ; and to hear of the sacrifice of

Christ offered once for all. She reproved the wickedness of
some of the " dark hearted" chiefs around her, and when one of
them urged her to resist and forsake the Gospel and indulge in
drinking rum as formerly, she replied : " I will never return to
that evil course—I fear the everlasting fire." She, like many
other women in the land, had more than one husband at the same
time. When she became acquainted with the claims of Christianity, Keopuolani said in reference to her own case, " I have followed the custom of Hawaii, in taking two husbands in the time
of our dark hearts: I wish now to obey Christ, and to walk in the
right way : it is wrong to have two husbands, and I desire but one.
Hoapili is my husband ; hereafter, my *only* husband." To the
junior, she said, " I have renounced our ancient customs—the religion of wooden images, and have turned to the new religion of
Jesus Christ. He is my King and my Saviour; and him, I desire
to obey. I can have but one husband. Your living with me is
at an end. No more are you to eat with my people, or lodge in
my house."

She rejoiced that the knowledge of the great salvation had been
brought to the land before she closed her career; but exclaimed,
" Lamentable that the true religion did not reach us in our
childhood !" Having spent more than half a gloomy century in
the darkness, pollution, and cruelties of heathenism, now opening
her eyes to the dawn of Christianity, and thinking how many of
the chiefs, warriors, and peasants, the contemporaries of her
childhood, had departed without seeing it, and that those who
survived had come near to the close of life without its advantages, what a forcible appeal does this declining thoughtful chief
make to Christian sympathy to hasten the work of evangelization,
when she exclaims, " *Lamentable that the true religion did not reach
us in our childhood !*" She, at this time, expressed her earnest desire
that her two young children, the prince and princess, then able to
read and write, might be well educated, and particularly that
Nahienaena might be trained up in the habits of Christian and
civilized females, like the wives of the missionaries. She wished,
too, that the missionaries would pray for Liholiho.

The king now hastened to commemorate, by a feast at Honolulu,
his accession to the sovereignty. Anticipating the time about two
weeks, he chose the 24th of April, rather than the 8th of May, for beginning the annual festivities. The missionaries seized on the occasion to call the attention of the rulers and people to their deliverance
from the thraldom of their ancient superstitions and cruel tabus,
and to their opportunity and obligation to substitute the Christian
system and acknowledge the reign of Christ.

After divine service at the church, his majesty, attended by his
armed guards, repaired to a large booth, prepared for the occasion,
where a dinner table, about one hundred feet long, was spread
and furnished in a semi-civilized style.   At the head of this,
he seated himself, having his five wives and about a hundred

guests, chiefs, and favorites, a few missionaries, shipmasters, and residents, to dine with him.   Thousands of his subjects, men, women, and children, crowded at a little distance to gaze.   The armed guard stood around between them and the table; and some warriors of Kamehameha, promenading in their feathered war-cloaks and tippets, made a striking display of their brilliant military decorations.   Nahienaena, the princess, attended by persons of rank bearing imposing *kahilis*, was brought to the table, in the midst of the dinner, in a four-wheeled carriage, fantastically decorated, and drawn by her friends and servants.   As the carriage drew near, the king, rising, lent his hand to draw it a few feet, then, bearing her on his back to the table, introduced her, saying, " This is my sister, the daughter of Kamehameha ;" then seated the child by the side of Kauikeaouli, the young prince, with whom she then held equal rank.   Kamamalu, on this occasion, in a black satin dress, decorated according to her own taste with gold or mock lace, was active and attentive to the arrangements of the table, and the accommodation of her lord and his guests.   The Divine Author of all mercies was acknowledged on this festive occasion, where heathenism and Christianity displayed each a banner.

The festival was not wholly closed till the 8th of May, when the king consummated his annual celebration of his accession to the supreme ·magistracy.   The ceremonies and ehxibitions of this day were chiefly Hawaiian, quite imposing, in part at least, and as a display of aboriginal taste and customs, were striking and interesting.   Great efforts were made to honor the wives of the young monarch, and his brother and sister.   The females of rank at the islands, and even those without rank, have, by some means, secured to themselves a high degree of attention and respect from their husbands and others, though the spirit of des-potism was often manifested towards them by what are called the " lords of creation."   On this occasion, the favorite queen, Kamamalu, was borne in state by about seventy subjects, upon a singularly constructed carriage—a whale-boat upon an extensive wicker-work scaffold of transverse poles and light spars lashed together, and supported on the heads, hands, and shoulders of a column of men in their martial dress.

Seated as a Cleopatra in the middle of the boat, having a scar-let silk robe around her waist, a coronet of brilliant feathers on her head, and a large and superb umbrella of scarlet silk, fringed and tasselled, supported over her by a warrior chief, who was girded with a scarlet girdle, and had on a lofty feathered helmet, she rode, a queen, above the heads of the admiring multitude.   Towering above this canopy, were two lofty *Kahilis*, their ancient and splen-did standards, supported by two of the queen's friends and public counsellors, Kalanimoku and Naihe, on either quarter, in their imposing feathered helmets and scarlet silk girdles.   This strik-ingly symbolized the difference between the condition of the queen and statesmen on board the boat, and of the waters upon which it was borne.

Two other wives of the king, Kinau and Kekauonohi, were borne in procession, much in the same manner, on board double canoes, taken from the common element, and carried, as was the whale-boat. Pauahi, another of his wives, after being borne in state in the procession, upon a couch ornamented with showy and expensive decorations, alighted and set fire to them; then, in haste, consigned her dress to the flames, retaining but a single article; and was imitated at once by her attendants. Thus, quantities of native and foreign cloth were consumed, to commemorate her deliverance in childhood, from a conflagration occasioned by the accidental explosion of gunpowder, by which she was greatly exposed. This destruction of native and foreign cloth, among a people oppressed and indigent, seemed inexcusably prodigal. But it is but one case among millions, of the injudicious expenditure of the bounties of Providence, which might be more discreetly used, if the possessors were truly wise and good.

The young prince and princess were borne in state, seated on a singular carriage, consisting of four neat, imported field-bedsteads, lashed together side by side, and fantastically decorated with bark cloth, and a yellow figured moreen covering and drapery, and, like the others, supported by the bones and muscles of willing subjects.

As an impressive acknowledgment of distinction by birth, and a lesson deemed of much importance for the nation to comprehend, two aged and noble chieftains, Gov. Hoapili, the step-father of these children (the one seven and the other five and a half years old), and Gov. Kaikioewa, the guardian of the prince, attended them in the humble character of menial servants—the one bearing calabashes of raw fish and arum paste, and the other a dish of baked dog, then, and for some years later, a favorite article of food among the gentry. A woman of high rank made a singular display by putting on an unwieldy robe of some seventy yards of foreign cloth, wrapping about one half round and round her waist, and having the remainder carried by her women, thus illustrating the labor and the inconvenience of appropriating foreign manufactures to Hawaiian use.

The vast assemblage of people, the variety of dress and colors, the splendid war cloaks, tippets and helmets, consisting of linen network, covered with uncounted, smooth, bright, short feathers of various colors, the wreaths of flowers and leaves, the coronets of small bright feathers, the necklaces of black, braided hair, with the ornamental, ivory hook attached as an amulet upon the breast, being displayed in the various movements of the day, and the hilarity, songs, and shouts of the multitude, altogether presented a scene interesting both to the native-born Hawaiians, high and low, and to the intelligent stranger.

Whether the entertainments of the festival had been continued too long, or the excitements of the occasion, or the intoxicating influence of rank and power, or artificial stimulants, proved too much for royal nerves, the king certainly did not appear at all to good advantage towards the close of these ceremonies. He never renewed them, and probably his successors never will. As a demonstration of the ingenuity of some of their ancestors, and as a remembrancer of the glory of departed chieftains, this exhibition may have been, in some sense, useful, though "vanity of vanities" was inscribed on all. And the thousands who retired from these fading pageants to their comfortless, unfurnished, grass-thatched habitations, and with or without a candle-nut torch, laid themselves down upon their rush mats spread upon the earth, might have reasonably sighed, "vanity of vanities." But the missionary saw here both the material and the occasion for the missionary work.

The last Sabbath in April, 1823, was made peculiarly joyful to the missionaries and their Hawaiian friends, by the safe and opportune arrival of new fellow-laborers, the first reinforcement of the mission from the United States. The ardent, grateful, and aspiring missionary feeling in the American Board and its supporters, which was, in part, called into exercise by the wonderful interpositions of Providence connected with the introduction of Christianity at the islands, did not exhaust itself in exultation or in notes of thanksgiving and congratulation : but it more efficiently showed itself on the part of some who said, " Let us hasten to enlighten Hawaii," and on the part of others who said, " Go, and we will provide for the expenses of the enterprise ;" and on the part of others still by their care, wisdom, and energy in selecting, arranging, fitting out, and promptly sending forth such laborers as, in their judgment, were demanded, and as would be likely to be welcomed.

The new missionary company, Messrs. Richards, Stewart, Bishop, Chamberlain, and others, assembled at New Haven, Ct., with many members and coadjutors of the American Board, and thence embarked in the autumn of 1822, amid the varied demonstrations of the sympathy of the friends of Opukahaia and of the heathen. President Day addressed the people, and Rev. Mr. Bardwell the missionaries ; Mr. Evarts delivered the instructions of the Prudential Committee, and Mr. Richards preached from the text, " Surely the isles shall wait for me." The kind people of New Haven endeavored to cheer on the laborers in various ways, and contributed for their outfit $1334,00. The missionaries, their directors and relatives, and many of the people of the city assembled on the wharf, and there poured forth their earnest aspirations for the salvation of the Hawaiian race, and their loud hallelujahs to their Redeemer in the strains of a prophetic song anticipating the speedy conversion of the islands.

" Wake, isles of the South ! your redemption is near,
    No longer repose in the borders of gloom ;

The strength of his chosen in love will appear,
And light shall arise on the verge of the tomb :
   Alleluia to the Lamb, who hath purchased our pardon,
   We will praise him again, when we pass over Jordan.

" The billows that girt ye, the wild waves that roar,
The zephyrs that play where the ocean storms cease,
Shall bear the rich freight to your desolate shore—
Shall waft the glad tidings of pardon and peace.

" On the islands that sit in the regions of night,
The lands of despair, to oblivion a prey,
The morning will open with healing and light,
And the young Star of Bethlehem will brighten to day.

" The altar and idol in dust overthrown,
The incense forbade that was hallowed with blood,
The Priest of Melchisedec there shall atone,
And the shrines of Hawaii be sacred to God.

" The heathen will hasten to welcome the time,
The day-spring the prophet in vision once saw,
When the beams of Messiah will illumine each clime,
And the isles of the ocean shall wait for his law.

" And thou, Obookaiah, now sainted above,
Wilt rejoice as the heralds their mission disclose,
And the prayer will be heard, that the land thou didst love
May blossom as Sharon and bud as the rose.
   Alleluia to the Lamb, who hath purchased our pardon,
   We will praise him again, when we pass over Jordan."

This ode of a youthful American poet—Wm. Bingham Tappan—embodying much of the feeling of the churches at that period in respect to Hawaii, was written while the pioneers of the mission to that field were on their voyage thither, and before the events there of 1819 and '20 were known in the United States. Many a heart thrilled with emotion, as the vision brightened, and as the joyous hallelujahs of lofty praise ascended, on this occasion, to the Most High. Fathers and mothers cheerfully gave up sons and daughters to go to the rescue of the heathen, praising God for allowing them to labor in that cause. The thoughts of the multitude were led in prayer by the Rev. Mr. Merwin, and the missionaries were commended to the guidance and protection of Him who rides upon the whirlwind and directs the storm. They embarked on the 19th of November, on board the Thames, Capt. Clasby ; and enjoying favorable weather, and the kindness of the captain and officers of the ship, through the voyage, they came to anchor in Honolulu roadstead, April 27th, 1823,—158 days from New Haven.

Some of them soon came on shore, and were met and welcomed

by Kamamalu and some of the resident missionaries. Several of the high chiefs, who that day attended public worship at Waikiki, sent salutations to the newly arrived laborers, inviting them to join them in the afternoon service at that place. Messrs. Richards, Stewart, and Bishop, after being received at the mission house, complied with the invitation, and were cordially welcomed. I called the attention of the assembly to the scriptural appeal, " Arise, shine (be enlightened), for thy light is come, and the glory of the Lord is risen upon thee." The occasion was gladly improved to encourage the rulers and people to avail themselves of the blessing of the Gospel, and to rejoice in the increasing light from heaven now beaming upon them. After the service, Kaahumanu bidding the new missionaries welcome to the islands, said, " Our hearts are glad you have come, very glad. We are glad you come on tabu day, and have been with us in worship. Give our *aloha* to all the new teachers and their *wahines*." Nor were Keopuolani and Kalanimoku less gratified with this accession of missionaries.

The Thames was towed into the inner harbor on the 29th, and at the king's request, the new missionaries were introduced to his majesty, the royal family, and the principal chiefs of the nation. The reception room was a new thatched house, recently erected for the king, on the stone quay at the harbor; under the guns, and within a few rods of the wall of the fort. Its earth floor was spread with handsome mats. It was furnished with lattice windows, tables, sofas, and chairs, and ornamented with chandeliers, engravings, mirrors, etc. ; much in advance of the place where the first missionaries pleaded for admission into the new field. The papers of the missionaries, their commissions, and certificates of American citizenship, were presented, and the king and chiefs, by the reiterated expressions of " *aloha* " and " *maikai*," evinced their approval and congratulation.

" All the principal personages of the kingdom, including the party from Waikiki, having assembled, made a highly respectable appearance, especially the favorite queen Kamamalu. She was seated on a sofa, at the middle of a long table, having a writing-desk open before her, and a native secretary at each end of the table, recording the names and taxes of the inhabitants of a district, who were paying tribute.* Her dress was a loose pink slip. She left her writing-desk on the entrance of the missionaries, but immediately after receiving them, resumed her seat. Her manners were dignified and graceful, and her whole appearance that of a well-bred woman, having an unaffected expression of conscious and acknowledged rank. Kaahumanu is one of the most powerful of the female chiefs. She entered the house with much real majesty in her step and manner. She was dressed in the native female costume. The *pau*, or under garment, consisted of about twenty yards of yellow satin arranged in loose and graceful folds, and hanging neg-

* About $5000 are said to have been collected, on the king's entering this house.

ligently in front. The upper robe was of purple satin, in a profuse quantity. It was cast over one arm and shoulder only, leaving the other exposed, and flowed in its richness far on the ground behind her. Her hair was neatly put up with combs, and ornamented by a double coronet of exquisite feathers; colors bright yellow, crimson, and bluish green. She appears to be between forty and fifty years of age, is large and portly, still bears marks of the beauty for which she has been celebrated, but has an expression of greater sternness and hauteur than any other islander I have yet seen. Kaumualii has a fine figure, though not so large as his fellow chiefs, with a noble Roman face. His dress consisted of a black silk velvet coat and pantaloons, buff kerseymere waistcoat, white silk stockings, splendid gold watch, with seals and rich ornaments. Kalanimoku is a man of very superior powers and great political sagacity, is a fine-looking man, apparently between fifty and sixty years of age, and was dressed in a suit of lead colored silk camlet, with white Marseilles waistcoat, and white stockings. He avows his belief in the true God, and uses all his influence as an officer of government, in favor of the external observance of Christianity.*"

It was the pleasure of the king and several of the chiefs, who welcomed the reinforcement, that some of the missionaries should labor on Hawaii, and some on Maui, which coincided with the views of the mission.

The old Hawaiian pontiff, Hewahewa, not yet cleansed from his idols, *awa* and *rum*, being introduced to the new missionaries in the course of a few days, approved of their coming, and expressed the conjecture that the people would become enlightened. Aware that his bloodshot eyes appeared somewhat injured, he said they were made sore by drinking rum, which had been occasioned by his great love to the king.

His majesty, on the day of the reception of the missionaries, did not appear to as good advantage as when, with his portly and noble form, dressed in a fitting broadcloth suit, and sober and well, he met them in civility, or on the Sabbath attended, with them, the services of the sanctuary. Nevertheless, much to his credit, he remitted the harbor dues, chargeable to the ship that brought them, and commending the captain for the service he had rendered, sent him the following laconic note:

" Capt. Clasby.—Love to you. This is my communication to you. You have done well in bringing hither the new teachers. You shall pay nothing on account of the harbor—nothing at all. Grateful affection to you. LIHOLIHO IOLANI."†

On the 5th of May, the reinforcement were united with the

---

* Stewart's Residence in the Sandwich Islands.
† E Capt. Clasby: Aloha oe. Eia ka'u wahi olelo ia oe. Maikai no oe i kou haawi ana mai i na kumu hou. Aole oe e uku i ka awa—aole akahi. Aloha ino oe."

mission church.   As in all missionary communities, while the
speedy elevation and conversion of the people were so far above
all private interests and personal preferences, it was a matter of
concernment to secure the greatest possible efficiency of the
whole body, and the advantageous location, and mutual satisfaction of all its parts.   The making of rightful and judicious arrangements for this, constitutes an important part of missionary
work, which puts in requisition the wisdom and benevolence of
such communities, newly thrown together into new circumstances;
where, by some, it might be thought that the comfort and usefulness of a life might be materially affected, by a particular location,
or close association with others.   The chiefs took a commendable interest in this matter, and manifested not only a readiness to
favor the enlargement of our plans, but a concern to have a proper
distribution of their teachers, on the principal islands of the group.
    Oahu, with more than 20,000 inhabitants, embracing the station
at Honolulu, required at least two of the preachers and the
secular agent; Kauai with 10,000, one or two; Maui, with 25,000,
two; and Hawaii, with three times that population, three or four.
    Messrs. Ellis, Thurston, Bishop and Goodrich, being deputed
by the mission, and accompanied by Mr. Harwood, made a tour
through, and round Hawaii, for the purpose of exploring the
ground, preaching to the people, making them acquainted with our
object, and reporting the comparative claims and advantages of the
different parts of the field for missionary labor, and for new stations.
This service was, in the course of the summer, accomplished with
care and toil, and manifold advantages, the narrative of which was
soon given to the public, in an interesting volume, chiefly drawn
up by Mr. Ellis.
    Keopuolani, the king's mother, whose heart the Lord had opened,
leaving Waikiki, and being about to embark from Oahu with Hoapili and the young princess, for a residence at Lahaina, apprised
us that she must have a missionary to speak the good word and
pray with her.   Kalanimoku, Cox, Keoua and others, desired that
missionaries might be located at Lahaina.   The mission immediately assigned Messrs. Stewart and Richards to that post.   Being
offered a free passage by the chiefs, they and their families embarked from Honolulu, with the king's mother and her party, on
board the Cleopatra's Barge, or " *Haaheo o Hawaii,*" Pride of
Hawaii, of which Kalanimoku, in courtesy to the queen-mother
and the missionaries, took the command for this service.
    The king and other members of the royal family, and several of
the missionaries, assembling with this detachment on the quarter
deck of the brig, united in a parting hymn and prayer, and returned on shore.   The party, accompanied by Mr. Loomis, to aid
the establishment of the new post, sailed May 28th, and reached
Lahaina, on the 31st, after a rough passage of a little less than
one hundred miles.
    The chiefs not being able to accommodate their teachers at

once with a convenient shelter, desired them to find temporary quarters with Mr. Butler, an American, whose residence was about seventy or eighty rods in the rear of the landing. They were received with civility, by Mr. B., and for a little season, were quietly located in his thatched cot, where they say, " The thick shade of the bread-fruit trees, which surround his cottage, the rustling of the breeze through the bananas and the sugar cane, the murmur of the mountain streams encircling his yard, and the coolness and verdure of every spot around us, seemed, in contrast with our situation during a six months' voyage, and four weeks residence at Honolulu, like the delights of an Eden ; and caused our hearts to beat warmly with gratitude to the Almighty Being, who had brought us in safety to the scene of our future labors, and had at once provided us with so refreshing an asylum."

On further acquaintance with Lahaina, B. Stockton remarked, that though it had been compared to Eden, she thought it more like the land " *East of Eden.*"

On the morrow after their debarkation at that place, the queen, the young princess, Kalanimoku and other chiefs, and their attendants and others, amounting to some hundreds, assembled for worship in the open air. The brethren with Taua, a Tahitian teacher attended with them, delighted with the privilege of erecting a public altar there under circumstances so encouraging, which they wished their Christian friends could have witnessed, on that interesting Sabbath.

Kalanimoku soon offered them a site for building. A few cultivated patches were given them to aid their maintenance, and fresh provisions, fruit, fowls, pigs, etc., were occasionally sent them by the queen mother.

In a few days, she asked William K., their helper, "Have they any pork?" He replied, "Yes." "Have they any dog?" " *No eat dog.*" " Any potatoes?" " No." " Any melons ?" " No." Sending two men loaded with potatoes and melons, she quickly supplied this deficiency. So full and frank were the tokens of kindness, that they say, " No Christian congregation in America could have received a clergyman, coming to minister the Word of Life to them, with greater hospitality or stronger expressions of love and good will." Two houses, in Hawaiian style, each twenty-three feet by fifteen, were soon built for them by the natives ; and within a month of their landing there, a temporary house for public worship was commenced by Kalanimoku, Keopuolani, and Keoua, the acting governor of Maui. Their dependants being called out to do this work, performed it with apparent cheerfulness and good will, as a far more happy service than the building of temples for heathen gods ; and among the chattering laborers were often heard the short emphatic phrases, " Ka hale o ke Akua—ka hale pule—maikai—maikai nui," (The house of God—the house of prayer—good, very good.)

Kalanimoku, during his short stay, continued his efforts already happily begun. He said to the missionaries, "I am growing old. My eyes are already dim. I may soon be blind. I must learn in haste, or I shall never know the right way. I greatly desire to be like Keopuolani and Opukahaia. Come, therefore, to my house daily and teach me, for soon my eyes will see no more." Nahienaena, the young princess, though in her childhood and surrounded with heathen pollution, was an interesting pupil. The missionaries and their wives earnestly desired to withdraw her from the scenes of heathen corruption, and throw around her daily the protecting shield of Christian families. But this could be accomplished only in part, as in that state of the nation she could not well be detached from the native community.

Keopuolani, her mother, notwithstanding her infirm health, was equally interesting and promising as a pupil, and even more so on account of the readiness with which she received spiritual instruction for the benefit of her soul. She needed no earthly sovereign to require her to listen to the Word of God, whose own challenge to attention, made known by his messengers, was far better for her. And having once commenced a Christian course, she encountered opposition with meekness and firmness. A chief, unfriendly to Christianity, said to her, "You are old, and ought not to study so much." She replied, "I am old, and perhaps near to death, and therefore must learn soon, or never find the right way." "You have built two houses," he said, "for the missionaries, and a house of prayer, and are about to build a schoolhouse; it is not right." "Kalanimoku," she replied, "says it is right, and so does my teacher; it is right; that is my opinion." He added, "The missionaries are not right in denying us our pleasures, telling us to leave off rum and revelry, and to sing and pray, which can do no good. Send them away, and let us drink rum and be merry, as formerly." From what school of infidelity did this heathen learn these objections to piety and a Christian life? She said to him, "My teachers are good; I will follow their instructions. Go with me." Others said, "It may be well for us to learn the *palapala*, but prayer and *tabu* days will not enrich us." The opposition which early converts encountered shows the basis of the obloquy and opposition which the sons of the Puritans meet, in propagating a religion that holds no compromise with the vile pleasures and criminal indulgences of those who love darkness rather than light.

Liholiho and Kamamalu came to Lahaina, and visited his mother. Being then at Lahaina to aid the labors of the station, I secured their attention to books for a short time. He, however, was quickly off to the other side of the island—Mr. Richards and myself seeking him, and William Kamahooula, who was wandering with him, crossed over the low isthmus between the lofty mountains which rise in the western and eastern parts of Maui. We passed through Waikapu in the middle of the isthmus, the birth-place of Bartimeus. Between this place and the northern shore, we walked over a bed of sand (a part of an extensive plain), mingled with the bones of former generations, and subject to constant changes of position by the action of strong trade winds. These bones may have been once in the heathen armies of Kalaniopuu, Kahekili, and Kamehameha. We found his majesty and the wandering youth at Wailuku on the sea-shore, and after one night in that place, at that time apparently comfortless, returned with William to Lahaina.

Soon, Kaahumanu, Kaumualii, Naihe, Kapiolani, Namahana, Laanui, and other chiefs, with a numerous retinue, arrived there from Oahu, on board three brigs and two schooners, exceedingly crowded. Passing from their vessels to the shore, one of their double canoes was swamped in the surf, without much damage. After landing, their supper scene along the beach exhibited a good specimen of the rude customs of the nobility, to which the mild atmosphere and clear sky of their evenings, on the leeward parts of their islands, were favorable.

On the arrival of such a party, hogs, dogs, and poultry, are slaughtered and baked in the ground with heated stones, and a repast of a few simple articles in profusion is prepared. Slaughtered animals, larger and smaller, baked whole, are set forth in full size on heavy wooden platters, placed on the ground or mats. At intervals are set calabashes of *poi*, and other dishes of vegetables and fish. The company sit or recline around upon mats. A strong man down on his knees or hams, with naked arms, sets to the work of dividing, by cutting and pulling. The guests, not missing knives or forks, dipping their hands first in a dish of water, lay hold with fingers of what comes to hand,—meat, fish, *poi*, potatoes, cresses, sea moss, and fruit.

Here, at eight or nine o'clock P. M., in the light of many large torches of the multiplied strings of kukui-nuts, Kaahumanu's numerous party, hungry from the voyage, made their genteel repast, some of them having tea and ship-bread added to their ordinary dishes. The rest drank cold water from gourd-shell bottles.

In many cases, the host sits by, while travelling guests make their meal and stow for subsequent meals the residue of what is set before them. In this case, Kamamalu sat at her writing-table, in the open air, by the light of the glaring torches, writing a letter, to announce to her lord on the other side of Maui, the arrival of Kaahumanu and her party. Before the evening closed, the missionaries led the multitude in prayer to the Christian's God, whom they had begun to acknowledge, though Namahana afterwards said of herself, what each of her compeers might have said, " I lived in the house of mirth and feasting till near destruction."

The new church being erected within three months from the location of the missionaries there, preparations were immediately made for dedicating it. It was of moderate dimensions, of ordinary structure, and frail material; but in its spiritual design, it was not inferior to the most costly and superb churches of Christendom.

Most of the nobility favorable to the mission, chiefly the grand-children and great grand-children of King Kekaulike, assembled with the people, August 24th, to dedicate this humble temple to Jehovah. The dedication sermon was founded on the language of the devout and admiring patriarch awaking from his delightful vision of angels ascending and descending between earth and heaven. " This is none other than the house of God, and this is the gate of Heaven." We sang Tappan's Ode, " Wake, Isles of the South," and a Jubilee hymn,

> " Blow ye the trumpet, blow
>   The gladly solemn sound,
> Let all the nations know,
>   To earth's remotest bounds,
> The year of Jubilee is come,
>   Return, ye ransomed sinners, home."

I had never more freedom or pleasure in attempting to address the throne of grace in the unaccustomed accents of the Hawaiian language, than in offering the dedicatory prayer in opening this house of worship. The high chiefs and others appeared to take pleasure in the solemn service. " Seldom," said the resident missionaries, " have we seen a house filled with a more crowded and interesting audience," and our hope was, that many an audience equally attentive and interesting, might, on these long neglected shores, listen to the joyful sound of salvation.

The queen-mother, who had aided in the erection of this little temple, did not much longer require the accommodation of temples made with hands. Her illness increased, and soon became alarming. Doctor Blatcheley, our physician at Honolulu, was sent for by the king, and hastened to visit her. Meantime Kaua and Auna, Tahitian teachers, were, in connexion with the missionaries, attentive to her, and apparently highly useful. She earnestly requested baptism and said, " I have given myself to Jesus Christ, I am his and wish to be like his people." Convinced that she must die, and fearing that the people might renew the abominations which she had seen on the death of chiefs of her rank, she took care to guard against them by her dying counsels. The feelings she expressed respecting her friends who had left the stage before the true light arrived, and those whom she was about to leave to be guided by it, indicated the power which the Gospel had begun to exert at this period. She had never seen a Christian die. But without such a pattern or model, she seemed to be taught of the Spirit to lean on the great Shepherd's arm, as she descended into the valley, and to adorn his doctrine as she passed through.

To Kalanimoku, her friend, she said, " Great is my love to the Word of God. It is true—it is good. A good God is Jehovah.

The gods of Hawaii are false.   My attachment to them is ended ;
but I have love to Christ.   I have given myself to him.   I do
not wish the customs of Hawaii to be observed when I die.   Put
me in a coffin, and bury me in the earth in a Christian manner,
and let the missionaries address the people.   I remember my
grandfather, Kalaniopuu, my father, Kauikeouli (Kiwalao), my
former husband, Kamehameha, and other relatives, who trusted
false gods, and died without the knowledge of the true God.
Great is my desire that my children may be instructed in the religion of Christ, and know and serve God, and that you watch
over them and counsel them to avoid evil associates, and walk in
the right way.   Forsake not yourself the worship of God.   Observe the Sabbath.   Do no evil.   Love Jesus Christ, that you
and I may meet in heaven."   She expressed to her husband
her solicitude for his proper attention to her people and
the young princess, assured him of her confidence in the mercy
of Christ towards her as a sinner, and her hope that he would
take her to his own right hand ; and, as an intelligent and pious
wife would naturally have counselled a husband not fully established in the faith, said," Cast not away the Word of God, neither
fail to love Jehovah, that he may love you, and we two may meet
in heaven."   To others around her she said, " I am about to die,
and leave my children, my people, and these lands."

She then gave the king a charge, which was motherly and judicious, and worthy of his regard.   " This is my charge to you:
Befriend your father's friends and mine.   Take care of these lands
and the people.   Kindly protect the missionaries.   Walk the
straight path.   Observe the Sabbath.   Serve God.   Love Jesus
Christ.   Obey God's Word, that you may prosper and meet me in
heaven.   If the people go wrong, follow them not, but lead them
yourself in the right way, when your mother is gone."   To the
chiefs in general she said, " Protect the teachers who have come
to this land of dark hearts ; give heed to their instructions ; reject not the commands of God.   Love him—obey his word.
Give heed to the Sabbath and the *palapala*, and neglect not to
pray to God.   He is a good God.   Our former gods were vain.
But Jehovah is the God by whom we may have eternal life in
heaven."   How different the circumstances of a dying chieftain,
calmly contemplating, by faith, the world of eternal light and
glory as her future inheritance through Christ, from the gloom
and horrors of heathenism which sometimes appalled her warrior-
hearted ancestors, and their contemporaries, as they went down
to the darkness of the grave.   She could say as she approached
the tomb, leaning on the Savior, " It is not dark now."

Messrs. Ellis and Ruggles arrived at Lahaina in her last hours,
too late to instruct her, but in season to render important aid to
the minds of others on the occasion.   At the earnest solicitation
of the king and chiefs, Mr. E., with the concurrence of the other
missionaries, baptized her in her dying hour.

She finished her course on the 16th of September. Considerable alarm was momentarily felt, and was increased by the representations of foreigners from Honolulu, lest the horrid excesses of heathenism would break forth to the exposure of all classes; but, with the exception of the wailing, order prevailed in striking contrast with the confusion and excessive indulgences of the vile passions, which had been customary in the darker days of heathenism.

At evening, after her decease, the missionaries visited the apartment where lay her remains surrounded by her bereaved and afflicted friends. They were comparatively quiet. The solemn evening sacrifice on this occasion was peculiarly interesting. The bereaved husband and the two children, the prince and princess, wept much. Her friend, Kalanimoku, who, on the loss of his own wife, Likelike, two years before, had sat down to amuse himself at the heathen game of *puhenehene,* was now convulsed with grief at the departure of this mother of kings, whom he now esteemed as a Christian.

Loud and repeated wailings were heard among the multitude for several days. They burst out with great violence on the arrival of Gov. Kuakini from Hawaii, just before the interment. It may have been partly from sympathy, partly as a profession of sincere regard to the deceased and her relatives, and partly to disarm or soften any one who, on the occasion of such changes, might be disposed to assert unwelcome claims, or commit violence. The motives which influence the heathen mind, and the specific reasons on which heathen customs are founded and sustained, are not easily ascertained. Pagans often do things for which themselves cannot or will not assign any reason, further than to say, " Such is the custom of the country."

On the 18th of September, a great concourse of people, including the chiefs and their attendants, the missionaries and foreigners, the children and relatives of the deceased, and thousands of the peasantry, assembled under the kou trees, near the beach, for the funeral services.

A stage, or low platform, was provided, on which the speaker and other missionaries were accommodated. Not a few of the people put on some badge of mourning for the dead, to the use of which a tendency, as in most nations, was manifest among the Hawaiians. The wailing which had been so mournful and incessant, from the hour of her death till the public Christian services were about to commence, was suspended, and good order prevailed. The better instructed, or more intelligent, part of the immense concourse listened with attention to an appropriate discourse by Mr. Ellis from Rev. xiv., 13 : " Blessed are the dead which die in the Lord." A procession of about four hundred, was formed to attend and convey the honored remains to the tomb. It moved in solemn order as follows : First, gentlemen from foreign countries who happened to be present and wished to show their respect; then the missionaries in mourning, followed by the favorite attendants of the deceased ; next, the remains on a bier borne on men's shoulders, and six pall-bearers, embracing four wives of Liholiho and two principal women bearing each a *kahili*, or rod of plumes, such as the highest chiefs delighted to have held over them as graceful nodding badges of distinction.   The mourners followed, two by two, the prince and princess, the king and Hoapili, Kalanimoku and Governor Boki, Kaumualii and Kaahumanu, Governor Adams, Opiia and Wahinepio, Governor Kaikeoewa and Keaweamaki, Naihe and Kapiolani, succeeded by their attendants.

Thousands stood on both sides of the way to gaze at the solemn pageant as it passed, to most of them new, and to many an affecting proof that they had lost a friend and patroness, whose departure was not the less afflicting because she had but so recently shown any true concern for their best interests.   The missionaries were not among the least afflicted and sincere mourners.   But while in sorrow unfeigned, they committed " dust to dust, ashes to ashes," the evidence that the Gospel was taking root, and that the soul of this Hawaiian convert had gone to a better country, and left the proof of her reform to aid their cause, afforded them strong consolation.   Nay, they exulted in the confidence that the same causes which were adequate to arrest her attention and lead her to penitence, prayer, and faith, and to put her in possession of the blessings of salvation, were equally adequate to bring tens of thousands of her countrymen to the same inheritance.   With invigorated courage, the whole company of missionaries addressed themselves anew to the main business of enlightening the nation in the doctrines and enlisting them in the duties of Christianity.

The relatives and friends of the deceased brought stones from the ruins of an old neighboring heathen temple, and laying them up into a wall, enclosed the tomb where they had deposited their friend.   Though performed in a manner more gay and trifling, or more rude and toilsome than the best taste or philosophy would have dictated, for men and women of rank carried heavy stones in their arms, or on their shoulders, attended by servants carrying their plumed rods, still, this labor was a rational and commendable testimony of affection and respect.   And if this was reasonable for half enlightened natives in respect to the dead, how reasonably might enlightened men from Christian lands, have been expected to take an interest in the true welfare of her living children, and in keeping Liholiho to his pledge of abstinence, which he had for a time observed.

How deeply grieved were the missionaries to find a gentleman of standing from the United States, assiduously enticing the king into intoxication, and boasting of his success !   Though for a time, the king, having been touched with the sickness, death, and exhortations of his mother, and the solemn religious services connected with them, endeavored to avoid the snare which he thought was laid for him, he fell too easy a prey to the wicked, who, after several trials, prevailed by the artful offer of cherry brandy, accompanied with the assurance that it would not harm him.

After this inglorious triumph, the missionaries called at the king's, and found him under the power of intoxicating drink, and encouraging revelry. He, like other lovers of the world, still looked for consistency in Christians. He demanded, "Why do you come here? You are my friends, but this is the place of the devil. —You are good men, and ought not to be here." Kindly expostulating with him, they passed on, but seemed not to get out of the same usurper's territory by coming to the lodging-place of Governor Adams, where there were foreigners industriously engaged in attempts to encourage him also to contemn religion, and to join with them in the lowest vulgarity and folly.

What injuries were inflicted by civilized hands upon the rulers and people, every week, while drunkenness, lewdness, gambling, Sabbath-breaking, and blasphemy, were countenanced and practised by men who claimed an elevation in rank, education and religion, somewhat above the common class. Two of these, a Yankee and a Frenchman, claiming considerable precedence, and considering the sentiments of the missionaries too illiberal for that quarter of the world, where more indulgence to the passions, they supposed, ought to be allowed than would be proper in enlightened and Protestant countries, undertook to conduct a Sabbath meeting at Honolulu, soon after the mission was fairly established there. Of this none complained. Naihe and Kapiolani, thinking, perhaps, that these men had begun to reform, and were disposed to promote the worship of God, were drawn once or twice to attend their meeting. But judging the efforts of the gentlemen to be mimicry or burlesque, soon stood aloof, and though but little instructed, thought the doctrines and practice of the missionaries more trust-worthy and better adapted to their necessities.

The gentlemen conducted the meeting by rotation for a time, till on a certain Sabbath, one of them being too much disabled by artificial stimulus to perform his part, the course was broken up. But both became more distinguished by their advocacy of the intrusion of the exclusive ecclesiastics of Rome, than of piety or purity, or subordination to rulers, human or divine.

The champion of liberal sentiments in the United States has said, "A man of only ordinary goodness, who puts himself forward in this work, throws a suspiciousness over the efforts of better men, and thus the world come to set down all labor for spreading Christianity as a mere pretence. The heathen abhor our religion because we are such unhappy specimens of it."*

On the arrival of the reinforcement already noticed, measures were taken for the re-occupancy of the station at Kailua. Kuakini,

* Channing's Essays.

the governor, residing there, had been encouraged by the missionaries to expect it, and had commendably exerted himself to prepare the way for it, by keeping up a school, and erecting a house of worship. Mr. and Mrs. Thurston, having waited for new helpers to be associated with them in resuming their labors there, found them especially to their choice in Mr. and Mrs. Bishop, and preceding them a little, embarked from Honolulu, October 24th, 1823. They, with their two children, Persis and Lucy, were accompanied to the water-side by their fellow missionaries, where, after the little company had joined in a hymn and prayer, they set sail with mingled emotions, to rear anew the standard of the cross at the important spot which they had for a time been called to leave.

In a crowded vessel of the natives they reached Lahaina on the fourth day. Here they tarried about a week. Mr. Thurston preached several times to full and attentive congregations. Refreshed by Christian intercourse, and encouraged by what appeared to be the Lord's doings there, they passed on to Kailua, where, on the second day, they arrived in safety and were kindly received.

Liholiho, arriving by another vessel, on what proved his last visit to that place, landed simultaneously with the missionary. As the king appeared on the beach, says Mr. T.—

" The assembled multitude of subjects commenced a wailing. The king stepped from his boat, advanced a few steps, and standing in the centre of the circle, lifted up his voice for nearly twenty minutes, wailing with the multitude in the cry of aloha. Well might emotions of tenderness take possession of his heart, on returning to witness the scenes of his childhood and youth, and the house sacred to the remains of his venerated father, who, with all his power and greatness, had no better god to worship than the neglected idol, which still stands, and is now hooted at by the passing boy as a senseless block."

After a repast ordered by Mr. Young, and an interview with the king, he says,

" The next day, the governor furnished us, for our present accommodation, with a large house, which had been built and occupied by Kaahumanu. He also offered the use of one of his sail-boats, and men to assist in removing our effects from the vessel.

" Thus have I been called to return, and again sit down on this barren spot, where the first seven months of my missionary course were spent, where I labored and where I wept. But with all its rudeness and barrenness, it is a most interesting field for missionary exertion. Within thirty miles of this place, there are not less than 20,000 inhabitants who live clustered in villages. In this village there are about 3000 inhabitants.

" This place is the permanent residence of the governor. He daily takes tea and coffee at his own table, is fast rising in civilized habits, and speaks the English language intelligibly. He has lately purchased a framed house, brought from America.   This house adds much to the appearance of his establishment, which he has been enclosing with a wall ten or twelve feet high, and about the same in thickness.''

While providing and ramparting a ceiled house for himself, the governor had been equally prompt in erecting a church, sixty feet by thirty, in advance of the missionary, and enclosing it with the ruins of a heathen temple.   Of its completion and dedication, Mr. T. thus writes to the Secretary of the Board :—

" As erected by a heathen ruler on heathen ground, encircled by the ruins of a fallen Heiau, where so lately were offered human victims, it wants neither gold nor carved work to induce the benevolent mind to contemplate it with interest.   There may the mighty God vouchsafe his presence, and repenting sinners give joy to angels.   During one month after reaching this place, public services were attended on the Sabbath beneath the shade of some *kou* trees in the king's yard.   But the house being completed December 10th, the chiefs and people of Kailua assembled for the solemn services of dedication.   These were commenced by reading a part of Solomon's prayer at the dedication of the temple translated into the Hawaiian language.   We then sang the Jubilee Hymn, ' *Pupuhi i kapu oukou.*'—' Blow ye the trumpet'   I preached a sermon on this occasion from Haggai i : 7, 8 : ' Thus saith the Lord of Hosts, Consider your ways.   Go up to the mountains and bring wood and build the house, and I will take pleasure in it, and I will be glorified saith the Lord.' "

Eight weeks later he had the happiness to say :—

" The congregations which usually assemble are from six hundred to one thousand, who listen with a good degree of seriousness.   During the two past months, by the particular request of the governor, either Thomas or myself has conducted family worship at his house, morning and evening.   This practice has also been introduced into the families of other inferior chiefs.   During seasons of public worship, one woman of considerable distinction, whose head is silvered with age, is ever seen sitting on the mat, leaning on the end of the foremost form, seemingly regardless of everything but what falls from the mouth of the speaker. We have had several interviews with her.   She called on us one evening after meeting, expressing, with much feeling, her desire to know and worship God aright, before going to the grave.   Hopu taught her a short prayer, which she and her train repeated till fixed in their minds, and then returned home, repeating it as they passed along.

" Kapiolani, Naihe, and their train, have several times come sixteen miles from Kaawaloa to this place, for the sake of hearing the Gospel. Ever since missionaries arrived, Kapiolani has constantly been situated near them, and for nearly two years has listened to the words of eternal life in her own language.   In consequence of her being separated from the other chiefs, Kalanimoku asked her, by letter, if she was not *lonely*. The purport of her reply was, ' Lonely ! No. If I am separated from my friends, here is God ; and with him I have communion.   Besides, on these shores, there are two gates of Heaven (alluding to this meeting house and the one they are building at Kaawaloa), in consequence of which blessings will descend.'

" Kamakau, an elderly chief, residing at the same place, appears in a still more interesting manner. He too, with his wife and train, have several times come to this place on Saturday, that they might have opportunity of enjoying the privileges of the sanctuary. The last time he came he remained through the week and over the next Sabbath, that he might from day to day be favored with instruction. On the morning of the last Sabbath, on hearing the second bell ring for meeting, he started to go ; but it was suddenly impressed on his mind with great force, ' Pray, pray, before you go to the place of worship,' and he stopped short, kneeled down, and breathed out the following prayer ; ' O Jehovah, here we are, going before thy presence on this sacred day, with the common people ; may we meet with the presence of thy Son, Jesus Christ, in thy house of prayer.'

" He expressed much satisfaction in the truths which he heard, and longed to become acquainted with the whole Word of God. The last time he saw us he appeared much animated. Everything he uttered, the very expression of his countenance, conveyed feelings to the heart, which would warm the bosoms of angels. The morning of his return he called on the governor, and, on being requested, readily engaged in prayer with him and his family. After walking to the beach with his people, and before stepping into his canoe, he kneeled down and offered up a short prayer to God for protection on his way home. ' A great minister,' said the governor, as he stood reflecting on the prayers and conversation of this man ; and seeing him sail away, he added, ' A great missionary.' At his own place he forbids his people working or bathing on the Sabbath, and regularly assembles them twice to pray and converse with them on religious subjects. He seems to have been searching for truth as for a hid treasure. I once heard him pray in his own family, and I was surprised at the simplicity, fervency, and apparent sincerity which were manifested, as well as with the correctness of religious sentiment which the prayer contained.

" On this important, long neglected island, two standards of the cross are now erected, and throughout its borders the Gospel trumpet has been blown. With my associates I have travelled and searched out the land. These eyes beheld the miseries of the people. Full seventy-five thousand are sunk in all the pollution of sin, and groping their way through life in all the darkness of nature. As we passed from place to place, we told within the cottage, beneath the shade tree, and by the wayside, of a God and of a Savior. Thousands listened to the words of salvation for the first, and many for the last time.

" Already some have gone down to the grave. Yet who can limit that mercy which gave to our race a Savior? It may have guided souls to heaven through the instrumentality of a single sermon. But what is to be done for those who survive? A single soul ! Who can speak its value? Who estimate the happiness it will enjoy if saved; or the misery it must for ever endure, if lost. Disciples of Jesus, you who have been nurtured in the cradle of piety, whose souls have been redeemed by the blood of the Son of God, and are soon to stretch the wing for immortality, think of these perishing immortals."

The same autumn a new movement was made. Liholiho, having been assured of the friendly regards of George the Fourth and the President of the United States, cherished a desire to make the acquaintance of these personages, and to visit their countries, and having a propensity for roving, hastily resolved on making a voyage to England and America. The hearts of kings are deep, and it is not easy to decide what were the primary objects of this voyage, so prematurely and injudiciously undertaken, without any intimation to the authorities of those countries of such an intention, or any assurance from them that a visit would be well received.

His restlessness and homelessness in his own country, the conception that his pleasures might be increased, his political and commercial knowledge promoted, his alliances strengthened, and some special favor from King George secured to himself as a brother monarch, were doubtless among the reasons which led him to this step. It is possible that he intended it as an experiment to break from polygamy. Capt. Starbuck, an American master of an English whaleship, L'Aigle, who had shown us kindness, touching at the islands this season, homeward bound, offered the king and his suite a free passage to England, which he readily accepted.

The more sagacious chiefs were not without their apprehensions that evil would befall him or them, if he should pursue his plan without a competent and trustworthy interpreter and instructor: and therefore, to meet the case, they, in concurrence with the king and Kamamalu, interested themselves to secure the services of Mr. Ellis. He, willing to attend him as a Christian teacher and interpreter, and desirous to remove Mrs. Ellis to England on account of her severe and protracted illness, made known his readiness to accept the service, provided his family could accompany him, under the care of Dr. Williams, the surgeon. The rulers offered to pay Capt. S. for their passage, but he objected—first, because he had not room. His surgeon, Dr. Williams, sympathizing with the missionary family, offered to give up his state-room for their accommodation. The captain then affirming that he was not allowed to carry passengers to England for money, and that to overcrowd his ship might affect his insurance, persevered in declining.

The expedient of fitting out the Cleopatra's Barge, for the accommodation of the party, including Mr. Ellis and family, was considered by the king and chiefs. But either skill, courage, cash, or time failed, and the king, foregoing the aid of Mr. E., concluded to dash ahead, as in his visit to Kauai. From among his wives he selected Kamamalu to attend him, who was not only a favorite and the most interesting, but had been charged by their common father with special duties towards her fraternal husband. For his suite, he selected Governor Boki, and his wife, Liliha; Kekuanaoa, subsequently governor of Oahu; Naikekukui, of similar rank; Manuia, and a son of Mr. Young, by a native woman of rank. Nominating his little brother as his successor, in case he should not return, which he ought to have considered, and perhaps did consider, extremely doubtful, he left him and the government in the hands of Kaahumanu and Kalanimoku.

The party embarked from Honolulu on the 27th of November, 1823. Novel and interesting to the nation was the embarkation of their sovereign and his suite on board a foreign ship, for a long voyage, putting himself into the power of an irresponsible foreigner to visit distant countries, as tradition represents Lono, one of their former gods, to have done. They could not, of course, tell what might probably befall their king and his company, in whom many were interested as relatives, nor whether they should be likely to see them again; nor whether the government could stand unshaken without a present king, to whom all acknowledged allegiance. They, like ancient Asiatics, lifted up their voice and wept. That parting scene was touching, even to strangers, and particularly to us, who then had our last interview with several of the number, over whom we had, for more than three years, been striving to exert influence for their instruction and conversion.

It had not been wholly in vain. The king, as he had done before, again recommended attention to the instruction of the missionaries; and Kamamalu distinguished herself as she was wont to do. This Amazonian lady, about twenty-six years of age, tall and portly, of queen-like air, yet affectionate, filial, courteous, patriotic, and friendly to the missionary cause, breaking away from mother, sisters, home, and native land, appeared exceedingly interesting in taking leave of the nation. Few educated ladies could have been more so, had they been called to leave their home, with the expectation even of never seeing it again. Standing on the stone quay near the boats, looking around with open countenance, she, in a tender and plaintive strain—an elevated and poetic impromptu, poured forth eloquently her parting salutation—her last farewell:

" O skies, O plains, O mountains and oceans,
O guardians and people, kind affection for you all.
Farewell to thee, the soil,
O country, for which my father suffered; alas for thee !"

Then, with a bold transition and strong apostrophe, she addressed, in similar style, her deceased father, Kamehameha; and renewing her professions of regard to his authority, her persevering adherence to his charge to follow her husband faithfully, she said,

" We both forsake the object of thy toil.*
I go according to thy command:
Never will I disregard thy voice.
I travel with thy dying charge,
Which thou didst address to me."

* The conquered country.

What an ornament to her nation might this noble woman have become had she from her childhood been trained in the Christian religion, or had she been indulged with some years more of thorough instruction in the most useful knowledge, attended with the divine blessing!

As the company entered the boat and shoved off, the people thronged the shore and uttered their affecting response. Their loud weeping and parting salutations mingled with the roaring of the cannon on the walls of the fort, while the voyagers spread the sails of their ship and took their departure. Their persons were soon beyond our ken, and the hull and sails and masts soon disappeared behind the rolling billows.

There should have been some good and important object to justify such a movement, and it should have been so far declared, that the nation might have had the satisfaction of acquiescing intelligently. It was, perhaps, one indispensable link in the chain by which the true interests of the nation were to be secured, though he may not have meant so. The sinking of the masts of their king's ship and his departure were, to the minds of some of the people, like the letting him down in a coffin into the grave. Doubtless the hand of Providence was, in this event, moving in mercy to the people for their salvation; for how far soever it might have been from the calculations of the adventurous monarch, it opened the way for the introduction of a policy far better than he had pursued.

Kaahumanu, alluding to this movement in addressing the chiefs and people assembled at Kailua, some two years later, and affirming what I never heard contradicted by any Hawaiian, friend or foe, though conceited, interested, and ill-designing men, of foreign blood, have attempted to give a different view of her standing, said: "My husband, the departed, was correct according to the former system. The country remains. Men depart. My husband diligently sought the true policy. He left me the charge over his son. We took charge, but he would not hear. He forsook his father's policy, and went to Britain to seek a *hakuaina*, a landlord. He fled from me and forsook me. You and I abode by the ancient policy till he departed. This is Kaahumanu who speaks. Make good your heart, and obey the Word of our Lord."

On board the same vessel, the Frenchman, J. Rives, took a secret passage, a small circumstance by itself, but connected with greater events yet to be noticed—events of unhappy consequence to the Hawaiian nation, and to individuals of other nations,—French, English, and American.

The ship passed round Cape Horn, and put in at Rio Janeiro for repairs and refreshments. The king and his suite there received respectful attention from the British consul-general and the constituted authorities, and passed on for England, where we leave them, for the present, to notice what immediately followed at home.

The departure of the king, and the opportunity thus afforded Kaahumanu as superior, and Kalanimoku as second, to hold the reins of government, formed a new epoch in the affairs of the nation. Many of the chiefs, from different parts of the islands, being assembled at Honolulu, on the occasion of the departure of the king and queen and Gov. Boki, not perturbed or disconcerted, but rather feeling more at liberty to breathe easily, remained together a few days. No disorders appeared to arise in consequence of so singular and material a movement. On the other hand, Kaahumanu, and Kalanimoku who took charge of affairs at Oahu, and in general acted as the right hand man of the queen, with the co-operation of Keeaumoku, Adams, Kaikioewa, Hoapili, Kekauluohi, Kapiolani, and Naihe, made special efforts for forwarding the cause of schools, and the observance of the Christian Sabbath, and a general attention to missionary instruction. Some were, however, disposed to suspend their opinion on the subject of religion till they should hear a full report, through the voyagers, from England—the land of Christianity and Christian rulers. They were not yet willing to take up any heavy cross, or deny themselves much for the good of others, or for the glory of God.

Keoua, the acting governor of Maui, who had been some time instructed and was favorably disposed, died at Honolulu on the day of the king's departure, and was interred the following day. Wahinepio, a woman of stern heathen character, the sister of Kalanimoku and Boki, and cousin of Kaahumanu, succeeded him for a time. But Kaahumanu eventually appointed Hoapili, her brother-in-law, to that office, which he sustained with dignity till the general triumph of Christianity in the islands

At the breaking up of the consultation, five days after the king's departure, the chiefs, who had come to Honolulu from other islands, repaired with their retinues to their several homes or posts of duty. Embarking on board eight brigs and schooners, mostly owned by them and under native commanders, leaving the harbor in regular and quick succession, and spreading all their white sails to the six knot N.E. trades, and stretching over Waikiki Bay, in full sight from the mission houses, they gave us a beautiful and striking illustration of their advancement in navigation, and of the facility, safety, and comfort, with which they could pass from island to island, for pleasure or business, instead of depending on their frail canoes. This peaceful and apparently commercial scene, not only showed their ability to make progress towards a state of civilization, but was symbolical of the liberty and facility now expected to be extended to those who desired it, to acquire the knowledge of letters and of salvation, and to practise the duties and enjoy the privileges of the Gospel.

CHAPTER IX.

It was now time to occupy a new post on the largest island of the group. The wide and open field in the eastern part of Hawaii having been carefully explored by the missionaries, and found to present peculiar claims, the mission took a station there in the early part of 1824. To accomplish this at some sacrifice, Mr. and Mrs. Ruggles, freely leaving Kauai, where they had happily labored three years, and Mr. and Mrs. Goodrich, of the reinforcement, were associated and employed to commence the new station at Waiakea, central for the large districts of Hilo and Puna, which extend along the seaboard about eighty miles. They embarked from Honolulu about the middle of January, on board the schooner Waterwitch, a vessel of thirty tons, owned by J. Hunnewell, Esq., who kindly volunteered to accompany them, and navigate the vessel for them. They were accompanied by Dr. and Mrs. Blatchley, for a temporary stay, by Messrs. Ellis and Chamberlain, on a missionary excursion, and Mr. and Mrs. Ely, bound to Kona. The little schooner, deep, full, and overflowing, accomplished the passage to Hilo in ten days, being nine days at sea. On their way, they touched and spent the Sabbath at Lahaina, where Mr. Ellis preached to a great concourse, and were encouraged by decisive evidence of progress. This company of thirteen arriving a little after midnight at this new station, and needing hospitality such as none in the place but the mission family could give, and several of these being at this time ill, put to the test the kindness and tact of Mrs. Stewart, who gave them a cordial reception, and as she was wont, cheerfully contributed to the comfort of her guests and fellow-laborers.

They had, while here, a striking view of the majestic Maunakea, distant about 120 miles, whose icy and snowy summit glittered in the morning sunbeams, beckoning them onward to the station beyond its south-eastern base. Refreshed by the hospitalities of this new station, they re-embarked on Monday morning, and beat out between Maui and Molokai, and during the week were favored with moderate trade winds, whereas, had they been met with such a gale as often blows there, at that season, they would probably have been forced back and had their decks swept. The morning and evening sacrifice was daily offered on board, and the spirit of accommodation strove to make all comfortable. Still, there were some privations, as the commander and some of the passengers were not below deck during the nine days and nights at sea. Passing to the eastward of Maui, and along the north-east part of Hawaii, they anchored in Hilo bay about sun-set, and landed before dark with a few necessary articles. They at once prepared their lodging in a large thatched building, seventy feet by thirty, designed as a shelter for canoes, timber, and other articles, and, by order of the chiefs at Oahu, appropriated to their use. It was without floor, partitions, or windows; and though the canoes were removed, a large pile of long timber still occupied the central part of the building, near the rude posts that supported the ridge-pole. Ushered into this new missionary *mansion*, Saturday night, they were allowed, without annoyance or assistance from the stupid inhabitants, to take care of themselves as well as they could. With a little salt pork, ship bread, and tea from the vessel, *kalo* and potatoes, and a single fowl procured of the natives on shore, a supper was soon prepared for the company of seventeen. The cooking was performed at a little fire kindled on the ground between the pile of timber and one side, and midway between the two extremes of the house. Around this Mrs. Ruggles and her native domestics, moving in the light of the fire and a taper,—a light insufficient to dispel the darkness from the immense building,—reminded the spectator at the wide entrance, of the tales of earlier times. On the other side, the rest of the company engaged in bringing in and putting up bedsteads, and cloth or mat partitions for their sleeping apartments. For their missionary table, two long, rough boards were brought from the vessel and put up, one end resting on the central pile of timber, and the other on boxes. Around this, when spread with their frugal fare, the company, with sharpened appetite after the abstemiousness and privations attending their voyage, cheerfully gathered, and with a peculiar zest, enjoyed their evening repast, reserving a portion for breakfast.

The next day, the duties of preaching and public worship engaged their attention. To favor this, Kaahumanu had offered the use of another building of similar structure. It was well filled by the people and missionary company, to whom Mr. Ellis preached. In the midst of the service, a large pet hog, black and fat, asserting equal or superior right to occupancy, marched in, swinging her head armed with huge tusks. The native crowd, not daring to resist her, gave way, forcing the preacher and his friends from their position. The murmurs of surprise and apprehension among the natives rose to boisterous shouting, and the congregation, retreating through the great doors at each end, left the hall of audience to the persecuting beast, whose rights were regarded, by high and low, as superior to those of the people, having been tabued, and often fed from the mouth of a native. Her feeder, more bold or skilful than the rest, approached the animal, and by repeated, gentle *passes* of the fingers on her bristly back, composed her to a sort of *mesmeric* sleep, more easily than leviathan is tamed. The congregation then resumed their places, and the preacher was allowed to finish his discourse. This hog was a tabu pet of Queen Kaahumanu, and bore her name.

Hawaiian females were not fastidious, in those days, in the choice of pets. The missionaries who visited Kapapala in Kau the year before, give an amusing anecdote of a curly-tailed favorite sleeping with two sisters in the neighborhood of the volcano.*

The schooner, on Monday, discharged the residue of the baggage of the two families, and of Dr. and Mrs. Blatcheley, who were to stay a few weeks; and soon proceeded round to Kailua, where Mr. and Mrs. Ely were disembarked, to enter on the work in Kona. The rest returned to Honolulu.

The laborers at Hilo commenced the work under some discouragements, if the ignorance, stupidity, and vices of the people, of all classes, might be regarded as circumstances of discouragement. But were it not for wickedness, stupidity, ignorance, or superstition, for what purpose would foreign missionaries need to go among them? Though our mission had now been in the islands nearly four years, yet some of the people of Puna and Hilo were as much afraid of the *palapala*, as they had been of Pele. Some retained their superstitious regard to the volcanic deities. Some, in their self-complacency, questioned or doubted whether any benefit equal to the trouble, could •be obtained by attention

---

* "Here," say the exploring missionaries, "we observed a species of favorite that we had not seen before. It was a curly-tailed hog, about a year and a half old, three or four feet long, and in tolerable order. He belonged to two sisters of our host, and joined the social circle around the evening hearth. The hog was lying by the side of them when we arrived. During the whole of the evening he closely followed every movement they made, and at supper put forth his nose and received his portion at their hands. According to custom, they washed their hands after their meal, and then passed the bowl to the hog. At the usual time for retiring to rest, these two ladies spread their mats and kapas on the ground in one corner, and, as is the usual practice, lay down to sleep with their clothes on. The hog waited very quietly till they had taken their places, when he marched over their kapas, and stretched himself along between them. The large kapa that covered them all was then drawn up by one of them to his ears, after which she reclined her head on a pillow by his side. Till this time we had maintained our gravity, but happening to look that way, and seeing the three heads all in a row, and the pig's black ears standing up in the middle, we involuntarily burst into a laugh. This disconcerted them a little. The hog lifted up his nose and grunted; and the host inquired the reason of our laughter. We told him the occasion of it. He said his sisters had a great attachment for the hog, having fed it from the hand ever since it was a few days old, and did not like to have it sleep with the other hogs out in the cold; adding, that if it were to be put out, it would make such a noise all night at the door, that no one in the house would be able to sleep."—*Tour round Hawaii.*

to missionary instruction. Some demanded what temporal advantages could be derived from listening to preaching. Some asked a *malo* or girdle a day ; others a shirt a week, as a compensation for attending school, allowing the missionaries to give their time and strength to teach them, and find themselves.

That temporal advantage should have been the first question with the poor peasant in the blindness of pagan Hilo, is not very strange, since the same spirit so often appears in the enlightened and affluent merchants and nobles, lords and kings of the earth. To the Hawaiians, as to the mass of mankind, that from which they could not expect worldly gain or pleasure, was as nothing. The natives of Hilo, when urged by the deputation, as they passed through, to attend to education and the worship of God, objected, on the pretence that it would interfere with their secular business. There was now no trustworthy chief or influential head man resident at Hilo. The intercourse, moreover, between Hilo and the other stations, to say nothing of other parts of the world, was difficult and unfrequent. Nor was there, besides the missionaries, a civilized family on that side of the mountains, or anywhere much short of a hundred miles ; and but one or two on the island; and the rough country between them could, for the most part, be travelled only on foot.

But dark and forbidding as Hilo was at that time, schools were commenced; native teachers, from other districts, came to their help; and chiefs, instructed at other stations, favored their efforts. In two months, a house was erected for the families, by order of Kalanimoku, and a church, the ninth erected in the islands, during our first four years' labor, was soon finished in the frail Hawaiian style, and the Gospel made known; and in a few years, a new face of things appeared, and from these small beginnings the work there has gone forward like a river.

The romantic might easily imagine Hilo to be a very inviting location, among barbarians, on account of the beauty, grandeur, and wonders of nature, which are there so interesting. Nay, it may too be thought, even by the sober, pious mind, to be now a desirable residence, because the wonders of nature and the wonders of grace are there united and so distinguished ; yet, to this day, no civilized family on earth is known to have chosen it for a residence, except those who are sent there to dispel the moral darkness, and to watch over the spiritual interests of thousands too indigent and too imbecile, with all the salubriousness and fertility of their rough country, to give a decent maintenance to their missionaries in their arduous labors of love. Such a location could hardly be chosen by a cultivated family, for the sake of its privileges, unless doing good to the needy be esteemed, as it justly might be, a privilege.

Another part of the same island was now to be supplied.

The chiefs, Naihe and Kapiolani, were, for more than a year after the arrival of the reinforcement, very solicitous to secure for themselves and people, a missionary to reside at their place, at Kaawaloa, on the north side of Kealakekua Bay. It was very difficult to spare a man from the other portions of the field, while it seemed almost indispensable that two families should be located at each of the occupied stations. Kapiolani seemed so deeply interested in this commendable object, that we generally encouraged her to persevere in her efforts, in the hope that she would, at length, succeed, when it should seem good to our Great Director. Having made applications, during a period of six months after the arrival of the reinforcement, she wept when she thought her importunity had failed, and she must remove from Honolulu, where she had been instructed in the best things, to her old heathen home, on Hawaii, without a *kumu* to lead her, her husband, and her people, in the paths of Christianity. How tardily do the churches of Christendom move to meet the wants of the perishing in heathen lands! She went mourning back to her place—the scene of strife between her predecessors and Captain Cook and his party—and there continued seeking and asking for a missionary, and with uncommon energy preparing the way there for the establishment of the Gospel.

Kamakau, Naihe's head-man, advanced in years, but interesting, inquisitive, and communicative, was ready to aid her. Alapai and Kuhio, stewards of Naihe and Kapiolani, appeared also to espouse the missionary cause. These five persons constituted, at that early period, a sort of mission for the promulgation of the Christian religion, in that region. They not only urged forward instruction in schools, but maintained religious worship on the Sabbath, in two or three different villages, where some of them would lead in prayer, read, sing, and exhort, and tell of the great salvation. In these cases they were heard with attention. Naihe and Kapiolani frequently sent a boat or canoe, on Saturday, to Kailua, some fifteen miles, to bring a missionary to preach to them on the Sabbath, and again on Monday to carry him back. So strong was the desire of these chiefs and their coadjutors to have the Gospel preached to them and their people, that they built a convenient house of worship, sixty feet by thirty, and continued their importunate request, to the mission, for a preacher. Meantime, the missionary on his visits preached to attentive congregations, under the spreading branches of a large *kou* tree, within a few paces of the place where Cook fell; and occasionally, to ruder hearers, on the opposite, or Kealakekua side of the bay, in a grove, where the mark of a ball from Cook's ship was still visible in the trunk of a cocoanut tree.

Their new church, built with care and neatness, in the Hawaiian style, being completed, Mr. Thurston, by invitation, preached the dedication sermon, March 29th, 1824. Great propriety of demeanor was manifested both by chiefs and people. A large assembly listened attentively to the Word; and the whole scene, as proof of progress, as a new offer of salvation to the multitude, and as a promise of the further and rapid advance of Christianity here, was exceedingly interesting. Moving steadily and energetically towards their object, to secure a preacher, Naihe and Kapiolani proceeded to rear, near their own dwelling, a good thatched habitation for the accommodation of a missionary family, whom they proposed to supply with fresh provisions, and water for drink, the latter to be brought two or three miles by hand.   They extended a pressing invitation to Mr. Ely, who was yet unsettled, to become their missionary.   Mr. Whitney being willing alone to take charge of Kauai with occasional help, till Mr. Ruggles, temporarily assigned to Hilo, could join him again, or additional helpers could be obtained from the United States, the means were more obviously at hand, for occupying Kaawaloa.   In April, Mr. and Mrs. Ely were welcomed at this interesting spot.   They had spent some time at Honolulu and Kailua in the study of the language, and they now took up their abode at Kaawaloa, in the house so generously provided for them, by those interesting chiefs, and entered into the work with pleasing prospects of an early harvest.

Having now six radiating points of missionary influence and Gospel light, each, for the most part, about one hundred miles from the other, and extending along about four hundred miles from the north-western to the south-eastern extremity of the group, we were in circumstances more favorable than before, for superintending the instruction of the whole population who might choose to be instructed, and for conveying the invitations of the Gospel to the mass of those who desired or could be induced to hear. Thousands had heard, and thousands showed some desire to hear, and some a desire to receive and obey the Gospel; yet a great proportion of the people were still enveloped in deep darkness. The dry bones of the valley were many and very dry.   But there was a motion, a slight shaking, a tendency towards moral life and action sufficient to show that the energy of the Divine Spirit was ready to give efficacy to the appointed means. The instrumentalities needed for effecting the desired changes, were the written Word of God, schools, the magistracy, the Christian ministry, and the arts of civilization.   The feudal policy of the rulers, and commerce so far as it had yet exerted influence, all unsanctified, seemed, at first, rather as hindrances than helps, and needed purifying in order to work well.

As the belief of Christianity gained ground in the minds of the rulers, we were happy to see a corresponding desire to do what seemed to them proper to do, towards enlightening and reforming the people.   When we urged them to undertake this, according to their knowledge and good pleasure, we refered them to the word and will of God as the standard, and desired them to follow it themselves, and use their best influence to have their dependents understand, adopt, and practice, the principles inculcated in the Bible.

In April, 1824, a special meeting was held in Honolulu, at a

school-house, which had been erected by Kamamalu, for the instruction of her dependants before her departure for England.
Kaahumanu, Kalanimoku, Kaumualii, and other chiefs, head-men,
and native teachers, and the missionaries, were present.   The
subject or matter of business was national reform.   It was new,
important, and difficult, for semi-barbarous rulers to manage, and
not very easy for missionaries.   Something was needed here, different from the arbitrary edicts of secular power, which could send
20,000 men to the mountains to cut sandal-wood for traders, who
were never heard greatly to object to that mode of using the prerogatives of Hawaiian sovereignty.   It needed something different
from the voice of a householder, who can say to his servants,
" Make ready my supper."   They hardly knew how to begin,
when they had come together, and none could easily tell them.
There was a difficulty, not easily appreciated, attending the attempt to induce the rulers to take the lead themselves, and at the
same time to exert their influence, not only rightfully, but to the
satisfaction of the people, without whose *voluntary* and *hearty* concurrence, little or nothing could be accomplished to meet our
wishes.   Providence had made them leaders, and it was suitable
for them to begin and do for the people and for themselves, what
now devolved upon them.

I asked Kalanimoku to state the object for which they had come
together.   He turned to his superior, Kaahumanu, and said, " Is
it not to make known our *manao*, resolution, concerning the *palapala* and the law of God?"   " It is," she replied, and added
" that it was her determination, to attend to the instruction of the
missionaries, and observe God's laws herself, and have her people
instructed in letters and the new religion."

Kalanimoku, who was forward of her in attachment to our cause,
encouraged by the earnestness and consistency of Keopuolani,
Kaumualii, and all the missionaries, whom he had seen and heard,
seemed now to be ready, according to his ability, to take a
leading part.   He made a stirring address, in which he happily
contrasted the old religion with that which was proposed to them
by the missionaries, and their former condition with the prospects
now opened before them.   He avowed his determination to apply
himself to the means of improvement now offered, to observe the
Sabbath, keep the law of Jehovah, and have his dependants and
people, generally, attend to missionary instruction.   He decidedly
recommended the adherence of the people to the system of religion now proposed to them, and demanded of the other chiefs,
and head-men, and teachers present, whether they concurred with
him.   Kaumualii, Kealiiahonui and others, promptly replied in the
affirmative, " *Ae.*"

Kalanimoku, gratified with apparent success, said, " This should
have been done before, but for the dissipation and distracting influence of the king, roving about, hurrying from place to place,
and diverting the attention of the people."   Obviously in this case,

subjects and subordinate chieftains were in advance of their sovereign, in their desire for reform.   They had been waiting for permission or opportunity for securing benefits from instruction, which
the habits and engagements of the king, and his unwillingness
that others should excel him, had, to some extent, denied them.
He had, however, doubtless to the public advantage, been induced to give his consent to the labors of the missionaries, and his
approval of their system of instruction, had himself heard them,
and like Herod, had done many things, though not with a perfect
heart.

On the adoption of this very gratifying resolution, which the
missionaries strongly commended as calculated to promote the
public good, they took occasion to urge on the rulers and the native
teachers, in their attempts to carry it out in practice, the importance of discountenancing among other evils, every species of
gambling.   For much of the time of the people was devoted to
games, in which money and articles of property were staked, the
chance of winning something forming the principal charm in all
their sports.   The evils of this practice, the indulgence and cultivation of covetousness and envy, which God forbids, and the increase of destitution and misery instead of wealth and happiness,
were pointed out.   Gambling was shown to involve the wasting
of that time, which, in the existing emergency, was needed for
moral and mental culture of a better character than any of the
engagements of heathenism afforded, and for the honest industrial
pursuits of life, which were indispensable especially for a people
so destitute.

So successful was the effort to make the change here contemplated, as probably to lay the foundation for the oft repeated allegation, that the missionaries had deprived the nation of their amusements.

The progress of Kaahumanu for two years had been highly
encouraging ; for, notwithstanding her age when the missionaries
found her, the doubts she so long entertained as to success, should
she attempt to learn, the slowness with which she began, the in-
completeness of the means of instruction, the infrequency of
opportunities for her successful application to study, as well as
the unfavorable influence of her former habits of life, she had now
conquered some of the difficulties in the way not only of learning to read and write, but also of declaring herself both a learner
and a friend of Christianity.

Proud as she had been of her rank and superiority, she was
willing now to appear with her subjects as a learner at a school
examination at Honolulu, on the fourth anniversary of the debarkation of the pioneers of the mission; and she availed herself of
the opportunity of expressing a thought of what she had learned
and valued, which interested many, though in any other circumstances it would hardly deserve to be remembered at all.   She
wrote, signed, and presented for inspection the following :—

" This is my word and hand—I am making myself strong—I declare in the presence of God that I repent of my sins, and believe in God our Father."

There were five hundred pupils present, among whom were several high chiefs besides Kaahumanu, viz., Namahana, Kinau, and Kekauluohi, who exhibited good specimens of hand-writing, ability to read, and some acquaintance with Christianity.

As an exercise somewhat peculiar to our schools, but falling in with the habits of the people, to them, at that time, pleasing and useful, was the joint and spirited cantillation of some Scripture passages, which some schools committed to memory. With this exercise the old queen seemed excited and delighted, more than we had ever seen her at a dance, or scene of mere amusement. Approaching the close, the interest appeared to rise; and as the pupils who were trained to it came out in exact time upon the last line, and with elevated and united voice, shouted, " *Hoolea ia Iehova,*—Praise the Lord," the queen, imagining that God was present, or was descending upon us, exclaimed, " *Ua ilihia au!* " expressing, as I supposed, the feeling described by Eliphaz, when he said,

> " The Spirit passed before my face,
> The hair of my flesh stood up."

She recommended to the people to forsake their former evil practices, and to walk in the new and the right way, to attend diligently to the means of instruction, and to obey the law of God. To those who heard her she kindly put the question, " Are you willing to unite with me in this good work?" Many at once shouted their assent, " *Ae !* "

Then she felt strong, and asked what hindered her from being baptized. She was, perhaps, led to this request now, because she had been told that a true disciple of Christ, in her standing, would use influence to have the people forsake sin and serve God. But however gratifying appeared her beginning, and how desirable soever it might be to have her baptismal vow, or solemn public pledge, given before the church and the world, to be on the Lord's side, we dared not authorize such a step till we had more decisive evidence that she had been born from above by the power of the Spirit of God. We had no confidence in baptismal regeneration, or the efficacy of consecrated water to wash away sin. Nor did we baptize any hearers of the Gospel, merely because they were hearers, or, as such, asked to be baptized. Kaahumanu stood, at that time, on the same ground with many others in the nation. The same truths, the same divine laws, and the same system of redeeming mercy which, united with the same missionary influences, were gaining her confidence, being presented with equal clearness and force to the minds of thousands, were, by the divine blessing, making, simultaneously, a similar conquest over multitudes, whom a careless spectator might have suspected of adopting the form of religion in obedience to the will, or in imitation of the example of Kaahumanu.

At any rate, *elementary* instruction in reading, writing, morals, religion, arithmetic, geography, sacred song, and sacred history, spread rapidly over the whole group, extending more or less (in the course of a few years from this important forming period) to a third of the whole population. In the meantime, the heathen sports of the nation nearly disappeared.

It was not a matter of wonder that any agreeable substitute, moral, literary, or religious, which should be generally adopted by the people in the place of gambling, or any influence that should speedily put an end to the practice of that vice, while our proposed substitute was openly and diligently, but kindly, urged upon the mass, should be supposed, whether correctly or not, to have nearly abolished the sports of all classes of the people throughout the Sandwich Islands. The experiment was interesting.

Whether anything like the early schools in the Sandwich Islands could be substituted for heathen amusements and follies, in unevangelized or apostatized countries, where there exists already a literature opposite in its tendency to the object of Christian education, may be a question much more easily raised than answered. It was easy for vain men to accuse us of interfering, unreasonably, with the amusements of the chiefs and people. It was easy for those who thought their sports foolish and injurious, to call in question our right to oppose them. And it was, moreover, not very difficult for good men to sneer at the shabby appearance of Hawaiian schools, the incompetency of the native teachers, and the magisterial patronage they enjoyed; and even to think those schools had soon accomplished all they could accomplish, and might, without loss, be abolished. But whatever unfriendly views might have been taken of missionary influence, and whatever want of adaptedness to the state of other countries might have been apparent or imaginary in Hawaiian schools; to us it was a consolation, in the toil of bringing a nation to an acquaintance with letters, morals, and the true religion, to find at length that a large portion of the people, of all ages, could b'. induced to collect in schools; and to have ourselves the exclusive privilege of furnishing them with reading matter, and putting into their hands, and bringing into contact with their minds, such books only as were designed to have a salutary tendency, or were, on the whole, favorable to the service of God.

This may have been one of the secrets of success among the Polynesian tribes, who have been taught, by Protestant missionaries, the knowledge of letters and the Word of God. Let spectators laugh at the wall which they think "a fox could break down," and despise the unfurnished and unsightly school-houses of grass and poles; yet we will rejoice in the immeasurable ad-

vantages of native schools, opened in rapid succession for the
benefit of 100,000 souls, heretofore without an alphabet; for
they were the centres of moral influence, the means of inculcating Christianity generally through the land, not only by
tracts, books, and the Scriptures, while the nation had no access
to the printed mummeries of superstition, or the literary blas-
phemies of atheism, but as affording important facilities for missionaries, pious rulers, and native teachers, to make known to all
assembled there the invitations, the claims, and promises of the
Gospel of salvation.

It is on the whole creditable to any people to find their churches
and school-houses as substantially built, and as carefully finished
as their own habitations. At this period Kaahumanu, at Honolulu,
and Governor Adams Kuakini at Kailua, had each a decent two
story framed house erected for themselves; but the mass of the
nation lived in their frail thatched huts.

It being deemed advisable, from the solitariness of Mr. and Mrs.
Whitney at Kauai, and the state of the island which they now
occupied alone, that I and Mrs. B. should join them for a time,
Mr. Stewart temporarily took my place at Honolulu, and united
with Messrs Ellis, Chamberlain, and Loomis, in the labors of that
station. On leaving my post, we called on our chiefs, at Kaahumanu's framed and ceiled house between the fort and the harbor;
and intimating my intention to visit Mr. Whitney, and travel round
the island of Kauai, we interchanged the parting salutations with
Kaahumanu, Kaumualii, Kalanimoku, Kealiiahonui, and others,
exhorting them to stand firm by the Word of God, and make themselves strong in his work. Kaumualii we found here, seated at
his desk, writing a letter of business. We were forcibly and
pleasantly struck with the dignity and gravity, courteousness,
freedom and affection, with which, on finishing his letter, he rose
and gave us his hand, his hearty *aloha*, and friendly parting smile,
so much like a cultivated Christian brother. This was our last
interview with him.

We embarked at 4 P. M., May 2d, on board the Washington,
Captain R. Swain, who kindly gave us a passage; and passing
Barber's Point, where Captain Barber had wrecked his ship, in
the days of Kamehameha, we crossed the wide channel by night,
and by eleven o'clock the next morning, reached Waimea roadstead. Captain Swain, Mrs. B., and myself, stepped into a boat
suspended on the davits near the quarter rail, and when comfortably seated, with our two children, were quietly "lowered"
till the boat rested on the water; then, rowing near to the shore,
took advantage of a good roller or wave, and ran in upon the
beach in safety, about one hundred rods west of the fort, where,
at almost all seasons, a whale-boat or canoe can successfully land.
We walked to the bank of the river, some eighty rods from its
mouth, and crossed to its eastern bank in a canoe, which Mr.
Whitney had provided for us, who, with his family, gave us a cor-

Village of Waimea, Kauai.   Page 217.

dial welcome.   His humble cottage and chapel were located on a narrow glebe, between the river's brink and a steep cliff, quite near. Before his door, or between his dwelling and the river, were several fine *kou* trees, affording a dense and cool shade, agreeable and ornamental.   In the rear, a grove of cocoanut trees, of unusual freshness and beauty, extended along under the cliff.   The beautiful river, formed of the limpid waters of two rapid streams, descending from the mountains in the north, here, for a mile, is broad, deep, and silent, and passed within a few rods of the missionary premises.   It glides almost imperceptibly along, while the sportive fish leap out from its smooth surface, or play incautious around the native angler's hook, till it meets the sandbank, thrown up at its mouth, by the never ceasing action of the sea.   There, through a narrow channel cut by its own force, its waters pass briskly into the sea, by pulsations, being unequally resisted by the waves from the ocean.   The surf often tosses itself to the top of the sand-bank, which stretches along between the sea and the valley, and is fifteen or twenty feet above the ocean level.   For a few moments, it beats back the river, which, as the wave recoils, pursues it again, and pours its torrent into the sea, till met by another surge, heavy enough to resist it again, as the turbid billows of a restless world rise successively to check the current of that blest stream, whose gentle and untiring flow " makes glad the city of our God."

This valley contains about four hundred habitations, including those on the sea-shore.   The numerous patches of the nutritious arum, and the huts or cottages of the people, were beautifully interspersed with the bread-fruit, the cocoanut, and the furniture *kou*, the medicinal Palma Christi, the oleaginous candle-nut, the luscious banana, and sugar-cane.   On each side of the valley, the country rises, with easy ascent, towards the interior, forming, at length, precipitous walls to the valley, or river-bed, which overlook the tops of the highest cocoanut trees, growing at their feet. On the east bank of the river, at its mouth, stand the fort and national banner.   In the distance, to the westward, appear Niihau, and the islets, Lehua and Kaula.

To a spectator from the missionary's door, or from the fort, or either precipice, is presented a good specimen of Sandwich Islands scenery.   On a calm and bright summer's day, the wide ocean and foaming surf, the peaceful river, with verdant banks, the bold cliff, and forest covered mountains, the level and fertile vale, the pleasant shade-trees, the green tufts of elegant fronds on the tall cocoanut trunks, nodding and waving, like graceful plumes, in the refreshing breeze ; birds flitting, chirping, and singing among them, goats grazing and bleating, and their kids frisking on the rocky cliff, the natives at their work, carrying burdens, or sailing up and down the river, or along the sea-shore, in their canoes, propelled by their polished paddles that glitter in the sun-beam, or by a small sail well trimmed, or riding more rapidly and proudly on their surf-boards, on the front of foaming surges, as they hasten to the sandy shore, all give life and interest to the scenery. But the residence of a Christian missionary, toiling here, for elevating thousands of the heathen, and an humble house of God erected by once idolatrous hands, where from Sabbath to Sabbath the unsearchable riches of Jesus were proclaimed, amid the ruins of the bloody temples of heathenism, gave the peculiar charm to the scene which it never had for ages of pagan darkness, and which Cook, when he gazed on this landscape, did not expect it would ever have. For it was the opinion of that navigator, that the fairest isles of the Pacific would never be evangelized.

When the golden sun, declining in the west, had sunk below the ocean horizon, and the short twilight had disappeared, I walked out with Mrs. B. to enjoy the evening scene, on the bank of the gentle river, which on a former visit had so cheered and delighted her. We united in adoring that goodness which had hitherto led us beside the still waters. The natives of the valley were gathered to their little cottages. The wind breathed softly through the foliage. The moon rolled silently her silver orb smiling on our evening landscape. The starry host glittered with tropic brightness, in the lofty blue canopy. The unruffled surface of the silent river, like a polished mirror, beautifully reflected the exact inverted image of the native huts, the shrubs and trees on the opposite bank, and of the spangled arch above. With such a view of the exterior of our little Waimea, the capital of Kauai, who would not have breathed the aspiration, that its spiritual aspect might soon be equally engaging! For this, the utmost efforts of the missionary were required.

As most of the leeward chiefs, and many of their effective men also, were at that time assembled on the opposite side of the island, being called there for a new lesson on the evils of intemperance; I started soon to meet them, and to explore and preach, and encourage schools. The lesson which some yet needed to learn more thoroughly, was, that if the free use of intoxicating drinks is allowed in kings, or commanders of nations, it must be equally allowable in commanders and mates of vessels, and if a ship cannot well be commanded by a drunken captain, much less a nation by a drunken ruler. But who could trust a fine vessel to an inebriate maniac; and what sane passenger could risk himself with him? But through the mismanagement of a drinking captain and crew, the beautiful Cleopatra's Barge, the favorite vessel of the monarch of the Hawaiian archipelago, was wrecked in the bay of Hanalei, and lay not far from the beach, dismantled and ruined. The people had assembled for the purpose of hauling her up, and saving what could be saved from the wreck. To reach them, I passed through Hanapepe and Wailua. The former lies six or seven miles east of Waimea. It is a pleasant, fertile, well watered valley, about 175 rods in width, along a mile or two from the sea-shore, diminishing in breadth and increasing in depth, as it recedes towards the mountains, till it becomes a very deep and narrow ravine, curving between precipitous and lofty cliffs, and grass-covered hills. A beautiful stream from the mountainous interior leaps down from high basaltic rocks, and forming a fine cascade at the head of the valley, flows through it to the sea. Like the Waimea river and others at the islands, it is, at its mouth, obstructed by sand, by which the surf seems incessantly endeavoring to prevent its entrance into the ocean. Where it is thus retarded in its flow, it is from ten to twenty rods in width and three or four feet in depth, where we cross it in a canoe, or on horseback. It escapes by a narrow channel, which it cuts through a sand-bank.

For the first half mile from the sea, the valley seems sterile, and is little cultivated, but has a pleasant grove of cocoanut trees. The rest of the valley, more fertile and more cultivated, is sprinkled with trees and shrubs, embracing a few orange trees, and being walled up on the east and west by bold, precipitous bluffs, rising higher and higher towards the mountains, from fifty feet to fifteen hundred, appears from one of the *palis*, like an extensive, well-watered plantation, interspersed with *kalo* beds and one hundred and forty cottages, and furnishes employment and sustenance to some seven hundred inhabitants. The immense and irregular precipices shut in by each other towards the interior, obstruct the vision of the spectator looking up the valley, but beyond the pleasant opening towards the sea, the eye reaches the distant line where the ocean seems to meet the sky.

Near one of these *palis*, about a mile from the ocean, Mr. Ruggles chose his station and built a temporary cottage, had a house of worship erected, and opened a school, with the expectation of having a preacher from America stationed there permanently.

Of his humble and now desolate cot, the walls, two feet thick and seven feet high, were built of the common stones of the valley, of irregular shape, laid up in mud and stubble, or broken grass; and the simple roof of poles was thatched with grass, and overlaid with mud. This perishable dwelling was surrounded by a pleasant court, in which grew bananas, grape-vines, pine-apples, cotton and Palma Christi shrubs, lettuce, and a variety of other plants, useful and ornamental.

Here, for a time, under Kupihea and Kiaimoku, the two chieftains of Hanapepe, Mr. Ruggles, with his wife and two children, resided as the shepherd of the valley, esteemed by many of its seven hundred inhabitants and of the ten thousand of the island.

Back of Mr. Ruggles' cottage, I ascended a steep hill, or high *pali*, that walls up the valley on its eastern side, and by a slightly circuitous route, passed over to Wailua, through a country of good land, mostly open, unoccupied, and covered with grass, sprinkled with trees, and watered with lively streams, that descend from forest-covered mountains, and wind their way along ravines to the sea. It is a much finer country than the western part of the island,

over which I passed to meet the kings. In the interior, I saw a
small herd of wild cattle. Some of them, as I passed, gave me a
stern look, and retreated, without annoying me as they had once
done Mr. Ruggles, by chasing him till his native attendants frightened them, by shouting and shaking their *kapas*.

Not far from the birth-place of King Kaumualii, I passed one of
the favorite places used by his predecessors, for the ancient sport,
hoolua—coasting, or sliding down hill, on a sled, without snow
or ice, such as New England boys prefer. A broad, smooth furrow is made from the height, down a steep declivity, and extended a distance on the plain, less and less inclined. This furrow is
lined or smoothly covered with a thin layer of grass, to prevent
too much friction. The gambling part, and the excitement of the
game, is much like that of a foot or horse race. The game is thus
performed. In the presence of the multitude, the player takes in
both hands, his long, very narrow and light built sled, made for
this purpose alone, the curved ends of the runners being upward
and forward, as he holds it, to begin the race. Standing erect,
at first, a little back from the head of the prepared slippery path,
he runs a few rods to it, to acquire the greatest momentum, carrying his sled, then pitches himself, head foremost, down the declivity, dexterously throwing his body, full length, upon his
vehicle, as on a surf-board. The sled, keeping its rail or grass-
way, courses with velocity down the steep, and passes off into
the plain, bearing its proud, but *prone* and headlong rider, who
scarcely values his neck more than the prize at stake. Gliding
with accelerated velocity for a time, then more and more slowly,
it at length stops, and another quickly succeeds in the same track.
The party that reaches the greater distance the greatest number
of times, wins the prize, or takes up the wager. Much time was
spent in such games before the introduction of schools for the elevation of the nation.

At the distance of about thirty miles from Waimea, I lodged at
the house of the chief of Wailua, who, years before, had murdered
two men in the presence of Captain Vancouver. After a coarse
and frugal supper, and a hymn and prayer, much fatigued, I
stretched myself on a rush mat spread on the ground, rather to
rest my weary limbs than to sleep for the night. Tortured incessantly, from evening till morning, by the skipping tribes, not of
the smallest dimensions, so hungry, multitudinous, busy, and poisonous, as to cover me with blotches from one dozen to two
dozen on a space as large as my hand, I found the hope of no very
distant escape from this species of cannibalism to be some solace,
while my sympathy was excited for the people, who seemed pretty
generally destined to suffer on daily and nightly from the same
source of annoyance.

On the third day, I reached the place of concourse at Hanalei
Bay, and was welcomed by the chiefs. In the midst of a group
seated on the beach, at the head of the bay, I found Kapule in a

neat, light chintz dress, Canton crape shawl, and lace cap, having her young, neatly dressed husband, Kaiu, by her side. I led the evening worship with her family, and that of the governess, Wahine. The next day the chiefs, after consultation, agreed to have public worship there on the Sabbath, and to favor the cause of instruction.

On the Sabbath, a large concourse, including eighteen chiefs, assembled in the open air for the public worship of Jehovah; when I proclaimed to them the goodness of God in the gift of a Savior to our lost race, and the duty of believing in him, in order both to honor him and to escape the doom of those who reject him. Notwithstanding the bustle of worldly business during the week, there was an increase of attention to instruction. Those who had been instructed before, were sought out. Hundreds of books were solicited, and the demand partly supplied. Four interesting boys, about fourteen years of age, were selected and commissioned as school teachers, for four districts, stretching along from Kipu on the north-east, to Haena on the north-west part of the island. After the people had, with commendable activity, brought on shore from the wreck, spars, rigging, and other articles, they attempted to draw up the brig itself. This furnished one of the best specimens of the physical force of the people, which I ever had opportunity to observe for more than twenty years among them—indeed the most striking which I ever saw made by unaided human muscles. They collected from the woods and margins of the river, a large quantity of the bark of the *hibiscus*, and with their hands without any machinery, made several thousand yards of strong rope, such as is in common use at the islands. Twelve folds of this they made into a cable. Three cables of this kind they prepared for the purpose of dragging up the wreck of the Cleopatra's Barge on shore.

These three cables were then attached to the mainmast of the brig, a few feet above the deck, leading some distance on the shore towards the mountains, nearly parallel to each other. At the sides of these the multitude were arranged as closely as they could conveniently sit or stand together.

The brig lay in about ten feet water, and partly on her side which was furthest from the shore, and very near to a reef of rocks rising nearly half way to the surface. Over this reef they proposed first to roll the vessel. Everything being arranged for their great muscular effort, an old but spirited chieftain, formerly from Oahu, called Kiaimakani [Wind-watcher], passed up and down through the different ranks, and from place to place, repeatedly sung out with prolonged notes, and trumpet tongue, "*Nu—ke—hamau i ka leo*, be quiet—shut up the voice." To which the people responded, "*Mai pane*, say nothing," as a continuance of the prohibition to which they were ready to assent when they should come to the tug. Between the trumpet notes, the old chieftain, with the natural tones and inflections, instructed them to grasp the ropes firmly, rise together at the signal, and leaning inland, to look and draw straight forward, without looking backwards towards the vessel. They being thus marshalled and instructed, remained quiet for some minutes, upon their hams.

A man called a *kaukau*, son of a distinguished *kaukau*, whose office it was to rehearse for the encouragement of the drawers, an ancient and popular song, used when a tree for a canoe was to be drawn from the mountains to the shore, rose, and with great rapidity and surprising fluency, commencing with an address to Lono, an ancient god, rehearsed the mythological song, of which the following are the better parts :—

" Give to me the trunk of the tree, O Lono—
Give me the tree's main root, O Lono—
Give me the ear of the tree, O Lono.
Hearken by night, and hear by day,
O Poihiihi—O Poahaaha—
Come for the tree, and take to the sea-side.

" My husband heard at the Pali,
Heard at the Pali at Kailua—
Koolau was filled with the stench of smoke
By burning men to cinders—
The dogs followed the scent.

" My feet have led on and are weary,
I am come from inland,
From the land of distress where I stayed.
My dwelling was on the mountain height,
My talking companions were the birds,
The decaying leaves of the *ki* my clothing."

These passages constitute about one tenth of the whole song, some of which is adapted only to a gross heathen state, and is unfit to appear in an English dress.

The multitude quietly listening some six or eight minutes, at a particular turn or passage in the song indicating the order to march, rose together, and as the song continued with increasing volubility and force, slowly moved forward in silence; and all leaning from the shore, strained their huge ropes, tugging together to heave up the vessel. The brig felt their power— rolled up slowly towards the shore, upon her keel, till her side came firmly against the rock, and there instantly stopped : but the immense team moved on unchecked ; and the mainmast broke and fell with its shrouds, being taken off by the cables drawn by unaided muscular strength. The hull instantly rolled back to her former place, and was considered irrecoverable. The interest of the scene was much heightened by the fact that a large man by the name of Kiu, who had ascended the standing shrouds, being near the main-top when the hull began to move, was descending when the mast broke, and was seen to come down suddenly and simultaneously with it in its fall. Strong apprehensions were felt on shore that he was killed amidst the ruins. Numbers hastened from the shore to the wreck, to see the effects of their pull and to look after Kiu. He was found amusing himself swimming about on the seaward side of the wreck, where he had opportunely plunged unhurt, when he was in imminent danger.

At this time the king of Kauai, then at Honolulu, was dangerously ill. The chiefs and people assembled to recover the lost brig, being apprised of it, soon dispersed, some to hasten to him, and some to return to their dwellings to wait the result.

The afflicted king settled his worldly business with composure. He willed his possessions to Kaahumanu and Kalanimoku for Liholiho, with the understanding that they should pay his debts —especially his contracts for foreign vessels.

As to his spiritual concerns, though he did not exhibit a high degree of joy in God, yet he showed that four years' instruction had not been in vain. To the missionaries, Messrs. Ellis and Stewart, who were attentive to him, he manifested a becoming humility, and in their view, a degree of calm reliance on the Savior. Mr. E. says: "The last evening of his life he observed, with visible satisfaction of mind, that he was resting on Christ; that he thought only and constantly of him, and that he believed he was not forgotten by him."

He requested that after his death his remains might be placed by the side of the departed queen-mother, Keopuolani, at Lahaina. "Let us both," he said, "have the same house." He expired about nine o'clock on the morning of the 26th of May, 1824, his last hours being very tranquil. The body was laid out in state. His splendid war cloak of close netting, covered with small, smooth, bright feathers, red, yellow, and black, laid on in fanciful patterns, and a tippet of similar fabric, decorated his couch, and a coronet of feathers encircled his brow. The body, partly covered with velvet and satin, was thus exposed to the mournful observation of his friends, then enclosed in a coffin, covered with black velvet. Chiefs, foreigners, members of the mission family, and others, assembled at the residence of Kaahumanu, where prayer was offered, hymns sung, and a sermon by Mr. Ellis, preached from the Savior's injunction, "Be ye also ready." His friends from Kauai arrived at Honolulu just in time to mingle their tears and lamentations over his departure, but failed to have an interview with their loved chieftain.

Kaahumanu, accompanied by Mr. Ellis and several chiefs, then conveyed his remains to Lahaina, and, in accordance with his wishes, placed them in Keopuolani's tomb. His death threw a gloom over Kauai. Any tribe, incapable of self-government, if suddenly deprived of its hereditary leader, would be thrown into confusion and distress. Here a strong spirit of jealousy and rivalry existed among surviving chiefs, and no one at Kauai was recognised as the rightful successor of their king. The ill-disposed had now the opportunity to work mischief unrestrained, and the ambitious to strike for supremacy. The limited extent to which the leaven of the Gospel had affected the mass of the chiefs and people of Kauai, was not to be relied on as a safeguard to the missionary families there, and their particular friends, or for the maintenance of perfect order. In their exposure, they believed it would be no great departure from Hawaiian customs if the wildest ebullitions of the vilest passions should burst forth around them in the forms of drunkenness, prostitution, revenge, and bloodshed, as on the death of former kings.

When Kapule returned to Kauai and landed at Waimea, she was met by a concourse of people, who thronged to salute her, join noses, and mingle tears with hers. The press increasing, she was borne above the crowd, as they lifted up their loud lamentations for their departed king. Though he had " exercised lordship over them," he was regarded by them as a friend and benefactor. One of his old stewards, who had received kindness from Gen. Washington in New York, learning that his king was dead, put on the rudest mourning, and said, partly in imperfect English, and partly in Hawaiian, "I feel very bad. *Make loa i ke aloha.* King Kaumualii, he have but one heart, and that was a good one. Some chiefs have two hearts—one good and one bad." The Hawaiian phrase, by which he described his sorrow, is so forcible as to make his English very tame. "I feel very bad: I have got no eat to-day," with all his mournful looks, and tones of grief, were but feeble expressions compared with his native phrase—" *Make loa i ke aloha*—I die with affection."

Kaumualii had more than answered the anticipations of Vancouver, who had been struck with the promising appearance of his youth. He had exceeded the expectations of his American friends, who had heard of him as the father of George, before the mission reached his shores. His conduct was becoming a prince in his standing. Far more intelligent than his predecessors, and attentive to the claims of the Gospel after he was made well acquainted with them, he was sedate, dignified, courteous in his manners, honorable in his dealings, respected by foreigners, highly esteemed by the missionaries, and beloved by his people. He was our patron, warm friend, and faithful coadjutor; and though he was called to leave us when his ability to aid us and the state of the field made us highly value his co-operation, yet were we consoled with the hope that he had found an inheritance infinitely above that which he had for ever left below. Much as arbitrary power may be dreaded, where a better government is practicable, the death of such a ruler was felt to be a loss not easily repaired. Strange as it may seem to American freemen, yet it is true that Hawaiians have appreciated the energy, providence, and protection of their hereditary leaders, because, without this, the common people must, from ignorance, imbecility, or ignorance, have been subjected to greater confusion, destitution, and danger.

Four days after the death of Kaumualii, the church at Honolulu was burnt down, probably by a native incendiary. It had before been attempted by a white man, who threw a lighted cigar into the tinder of the thatching in the hour of public worship. In two or three days, Kalanimoku gave orders to have it rebuilt. Namahana, having collected timber to build a house for herself, freely offered it, so far as it would go, to expedite the erection of a new "house of prayer." This promptitude of the chiefs, spontaneously meeting the emergency, was a pleasing indication of increased interest on their part. They thus exhibited to the people their decided friendship to the Gospel, and demonstrated to the incendiaries and other opposers, that the death of a friendly chief, or the conflagration of frail, thatched churches, would not defeat a cause which, in earlier ages, could not be checked by the martyrdom of its ablest friends and advocates. In two weeks, a large number of the natives, having brought the principal timbers to the spot, assembled to raise it and thatch it. Some came bearing bundles of slender poles, to be lashed horizontally across the posts and rafters, to support the thatching. Others brought enormous packs of materials for thatching, consisting of many bundles of long grass, bound together with cords, and borne on their stooping backs, the supporting bands passing before the shoulders. In a short time, a house, seventy feet by twenty-five, and capable of seating six hundred, which, in those days, was deemed a large audience, though not more than one-sixth of what later churches would admit, was completed.

Kalanimoku, who was then erecting an expensive house for himself, desirous that the house of worship should be soonest ready to be occupied, took off his own carpenters and employed them to fit in the doors, windows, and seats of the public sanctuary, and employed others to enclose it with a light paling. Numbers of the chiefs and plebeians, walking in Indian file, brought grass and rushes, and spread the floor of earth in the new temple, which they and their teachers were glad to see quickly opened for public worship.

Kalanimoku, while contemplating a visit to Kauai, to regulate its affairs, hastened to make his own stone dwelling-house habitable, in which he sought not only to provide for the comfort of his family and friends, but to aid in elevating the nation. He desired to be conveniently near the missionaries, who had already secured his confidence. In attempting to imitate a foreign style of building, he caused a deep excavation to be made for a cellar, and laid the foundation of his house on a bed of conglomerated coral, shells, and sand, in which he sank a well. In reference to this part of his house, in his somewhat usual strain of pleasantry, he said to some whose distrust had been obvious, "My cellar is larger than Binamu's." By this, he shrewdly satirized the puerile jealousy of those who had said that the cellar of the missionaries was made for purposes of war. On the floor of the second story, he had a commodious and pleasant saloon, or hall, with a verandah, four lodging rooms, and a school-room for the accommodation of the young prince and his friend Haalilio, whom he wished to be under my particular instruction. These six rooms were ceiled, painted, lighted with good glass windows, and comfortably furnished. About the 20th of July, he entered it, with the voice of prayer and praise. The superiority of this house or palace, as to its cost, dimensions, height, and finish, and my subsequent familiarity there as a teacher, procured for me the compliment of "living like a *nabob*." The workmen, however, it was found, had widened the building and greatly increased the thickness of the walls, just at the surface of the ground, which marred their strength, forbade their permanency, and in the end, occasioned material loss and disappointment.

Kaahumanu, somewhat softened by the death of her husband, took some considerate measures encouraging to the missionaries. She issued orders prohibiting murder, infanticide, thieving, and secular labor on the Sabbath, and encouraged attention to instruction, wherever teachers were employed. She addressed a brief, pertinent, and delicate reproof to Wahinepio, governess of Maui, who, Gallio-like, had not cared to correct some evils that came within her notice and jurisdiction, as follows :

"Love to thee, Wahinepio, this is my communication to you. I have to-day heard of the evil-doings of our people night after night; their noisy revelling, at midnight, among those who wish to sleep. Even the house of God is defiled by their evil-doings. I much regret this evil. We chiefs ought to counsel our people and oppose this evil-doing, and to regard with care, the house of God, built for the praise of Jehovah. My communication is ended.

" KAAHUMANU."

Among a people disposed to indolence and addicted to falsehood, fraud, and violence, it was important that the chiefs, as they acquired the requisite knowledge, should encourage industry and providence, and protect the ignorant from injurious imposition, and the weak from violence. The following attempt of Kaahumanu and her sister, to silence a false teacher, in the summer of 1824, illustrates the general policy of the rulers in opposing imposture, superstition, jugglery, and idolatry.

A pseudo prophetess belonging to Hawaii, visited Maui, and claiming authority from the god of the volcano, and even calling herself *Pele*, drew the attention of many to her vagaries. Her arrival in Lahaina caused an excitement among all classes; and some affirmed that she had been offended with the missionaries, who had rolled stones into her crater, and had plucked and eaten her prohibited *ohelos* without making offerings to her, and had dared to take away portions of her hair, and that she had come to induce the chiefs to dismiss the missionaries and suppress the *palapala*. Some seemed to think she would make some terrific display of power, unless the chiefs should yield to her demands. The day after she reached the village, she came to the chiefs with her insignia of office. Marching with haughty step, with long black, dishevelled hair, and countenance wild, with spear and *kahilis* in her hands, attended by her two daughters, bearing each a small flag, she attempted to make a display corresponding with her pretensions. As she approached, she was accompanied by an immense crowd, attracted some by curiosity, some by superstition, some with a desire to see her maintain her cause, and some to see her foiled by Kaahumanu and her coadjutors. Paying little attention to the throng, she drew near the chiefs, and exclaimed, " I have come !" Kalakua, who after the death of Keopuolani had married Hoapili, replied : " We are all here." " Good will to you all," said the prophetess. " Yes," said the chief, " good will perhaps." " I have now come to speak to you," said the impostor. " Whence are you ?" said Madam Hoapili. She replied, " From foreign lands, from England and America, whither I went to attend your king." Indignant at this falsehood, the chief rebuked her, saying, "Come not here to tell us your lies—what are these things in your hands?" " The spear and kahilis of Pele," she promptly replied. " *Lay them down*," said the chief. Unwilling to lose her honor in the eyes of the world, she demurred, and put on the air of sullenness, as if insulted. " LAY THEM DOWN," was sternly repeated, and she complied. The chief continued with well sustained dignity, " Tell us not that you are *Pele*. There are other volcanoes than those on Hawaii. They are all under the control of the great God of Heaven. But you are a *woman*, like one of us. There is one God, who made you and us. We have one common Parent. Formerly we thought *Pele* a god, and gave our hogs, dogs, and cocoanuts. Light is now shining upon us, and we have forsaken our false gods. This now is your business—go back to Hawaii, plant potatoes, beat kapa, catch fish, feed swine, and eat of your own earnings ; but demand not of the people this and that for Pele. Go to school and learn the *palapala*, and send also these your daughters. Books are our teachers. Now tell us, without falsehood, have you not been lying to the people ?" The impostor confessed, " I have been lying, but will lie no more." " Remember then your promise," said Madam Hoapili, " to lie no more. Go home, and observe my word and deceive the people no more." She yielded, burned her mysterious flags, and was about to burn the spear which she had called Pele's ; but one of the chiefs interposed, and claimed it to be used for tilling the ground.

A Tahitian present harangued the multitude on the vain pretensions of the hag, whom he called a *new devil*, and the folly of listening to any attempts to revive the worship of Pele. At the suggestion of Kaikioewa, a prayer was offered to Jehovah, and it is believed the bold and foolish movement of this pretended vice-gerent of Pele, was overruled for the promotion, not only of the cause of the *palapala*, but of the true religion. Who, then, can doubt that the silencing of such an impostor in that state of affairs, and among such an ignorant and superstitious race, was on the whole right?

The affairs of the late king of Kauai now required the attention of the chiefs. In taking preliminary measures for settling the government and public concerns of his dominions, George was allowed, after the interment of his father, to return to Wahiawa, not as the governor or viceroy of Kauai, but as the chief of his own little valley. If either of the sons of Kaumualii deserved the office of governor, it was doubtless Kealiiahonui. This, George and others probably well understood. But Kahalaia, the nephew of Kalanimoku, was appointed governor. He was young, well-formed, above the middling stature, fond of amusements and worldly pleasure, bold and ambitious, and more distinguished for energy than honor, sobriety, or love of equity and peace. But he was probably better qualified to take charge of the island, and do the bidding of his superiors than George, who had already conceived some prejudice against the windward chiefs, for what he thought their encroachments on the hereditary rights of his father and himself.

Kahalaia soon repaired to Kauai, and entered on the duties of his office. Early inquiring for the house of public worship, and learning that it was on the river bank, a quarter of a mile above the fort, he proposed to build one much nearer. Whether this was to make a show of respect for religion, or to avoid what he might consider the danger of attending public worship, at that time, so far from the guns of the fort, or because he thought the public good would be promoted by having the village church nearer the fort and landing, was not obvious.

The day after his arrival, he examined the state of the fort, which mounted about fifty guns, larger and smaller, and furnished a guard with muskets, bayonets, and swords, and put them in motion on different parts of the walls. The next day, as his appointment and arrival there occurred during my stay at that island, I waited on him in his castle. He asked me to dine with him, and at table, showing his respect for Christianity, he required silence among his attendants, and requested me to implore a blessing and give thanks.

The general course of instruction having been much interrupted at Kauai by the sickness and death of Kaumualii, Mr. Whitney and myself were anxiously watching for the favorable moment to renew it with vigor throughout the island. A thorough extension of school instruction through all the districts at that time, would have been a better safeguard against insurrection than the display of guns and bayonets, *in terrorem*, on the ramparts of a fortification. The question was put to the governor,

" When shall we unitedly prosecute the work of instruction
throughout this island ?" " *Aia pono lea makou*—when we are
regulated and secure," he replied. What was greatly needed as
the means of security he thought might be postponed till we had
obtained it. Thus the disaffected gained time to plot with
greater facility against his authority, if they were not diverted
from the peaceful pursuits urged by the mission, and provoked
to hostility by the military flourish he attempted to make.

Previous to his arrival there, I had announced to the people
that there would be an eclipse of the sun at mid-day on the 26th
of June, at fifty-seven minutes after twelve o'clock, and gave a
brief account of its extent and duration, with which the event
accorded. During its progress, this phenomenon, which they
had been accustomed to regard with superstitious awe and fore-
bodings of evil, I endeavored to explain as the mere passing of
the moon between us and the sun, so as to throw a shadow upon
us for a time. Some, supposing me to be able perhaps to take
the place of their old astrologers, demanded of me the *ano*, purport of the wonder, or to tell the event indicated by it. But I could
not, from that phenomenon, predict either *war* or *peace*, famine
or plenty, death or prosperity, as their pretending astrologers
had been accustomed to do. Some, however, prognosticated war,
and this was thought by others to be an indication that war was
desired, or was already meditated. The gloom of the moon's
shadow on the islands corresponded with the political gloom that
then hung over Kauai, while many of the inhabitants lived in
apprehension of evils, against which they had no competent protection. Some feared oppression from the windward chiefs,
should their control be undisputed. Others feared oppression or
destruction from Kauai chiefs, now divided into parties. Some,
decidedly favoring the new order, provoked the envy and hostility of those who disliked to yield to windward supremacy. The
want of integrity, and of the means of intelligence and intercom-
munication, magnified the difficulty ; and distrust, disaffection,
and danger, seemed to envelope the island in clouds.

During this period of solicitude and disquiet throughout Kauai,
though attended with considerable hazard to the missionaries, not
willing to let the malcontents know that we expected hostility
from them, I travelled about the island freely. I visited the disaffected George at his estate—the little secluded Wahiawa. It
was a small valley, running back from the sea to the mountains,
containing some twenty small habitations, about a hundred souls,
and some hundred acres, very little cultivated, yielding a scanty
amount of the common productions of arum, bananas, cocoanuts,
potatoes, sugar-cane, squashes, melons, and wild apples. At
the foot of this valley, I found George living much in the original
native style, in a dingy, dirty, thatched house at the sea-side, just
where the surf washes a small beach between two rocky cliffs.
His wife, Betty, was a daughter of a Hawaiian mother and Isaac

Davis, whose life was spared when, in 1790, the crew of the Fair American was cut off by the natives at Kawaihae, and who afterwards assisted Kamehameha in his wars. George might, therefore, have boasted of an alliance by marriage with Hawaii and Great Britain. Betty was more fair, of more European feature and slender make than most of her countrywomen at the age of 25 or 30 ; more taciturn, thoughtful, sedate, and retiring than others of equal rank and intelligence. She had derived some advantages from the instruction of the missionaries, and manifested some concern for her salvation. But her circumstances differed little from those of the wife of a petty chief of the lowest rank. They had one young daughter then in infancy, who grew up at length to womanhood. George had about him two or three worthless white men, and ten times that number of natives,— men, women, and children,—poor, ignorant, and comfortless as the mass of the peasantry at that period. To have the precedence, or to affect superiority over his countrymen, seemed far more to be his object, than to improve and elevate them. After he had lost the high confidence of his father and others, he once, with gentlemanly assurance, said to a young foreigner who had recently come to the islands from an unsuccessful enterprise in the South Seas, " If you feel inclined to take up your residence in Kauai, there is $70 a month for you for taking care of *my estates ;* or, if you prefer it, $40 a month for taking charge of the brig Becket."

Finding him now very uneasy, and cherishing, apparently, hostile feelings towards Kaahumanu and others, I endeavored, in a conversation of nearly two hours, to remove his difficulties. I was grieved to observe the incoherency and untrustworthy character of his statements as well as his reckless determination to resist the ruling powers, or to take revenge on some by whom he fancied or pretended that he had been wronged. In his undress or shirt sleeves, he sat in the middle of his comfortless cottage, on a stool which had one more leg than Alfred's—the seat of an old chair that had lost its back. He talked freely, somewhat at random, almost incessantly smoking tobacco, in a short, wooden pipe, of Hawaiian manufacture. He may have intended to be enigmatical, to conceal his own views or draw out mine; and there may have been more method in his madness than I was able to perceive. He said, " When I was at Oahu, I never expected to see Kauai again. The old woman gave me a dose; and I had the same sickness that my father had." I replied, " I understand your father had the *pleurisy,* and afterwards a diarrhœa. It was the latter, probably, that you had." " No. I think my father had not much of that. The old gentleman was *poisoned,* just the same as I was. I must have got it at Lahaina, where I ate once or twice with Kaahumanu. I have been up almost every night since I returned from the windward. Four nights ago, I and another chief sent out to meet a party from Waimea, who were coming to take us. I met them, and drove them back." "Did you go with the party ?" "No. I stayed here, and sent on the men. Kahalaia sent me a note requesting some fish. I sent them. He asked me what he should do. I sent him back word to collect all the arms into the fort, and not have any fighting ; but if they were going to rise, let us have as many guns as they."

I encouraged him to think that by a prudent, loyal course, quite practicable, he might secure the confidence of Kaahumanu and Kalanimoku, and have a post of trust, of honor, and emolument, suited to his rank, which would afford him full scope for all his talents. Leaving the abode of the once more promising prince, with some fears that he would wholly throw himself away, I passed on, and lodged among strangers at Koloa, near the south-eastern extremity of the island, since occupied as a missionary station. Thence I passed round to Wailua, once the residence of Kaeo. There I visited the sacred birth-place of Kau-mualii, a rocky nook, at the foot of a hill on which the sacrifices of heathenism had been offered. Following up the Waimea creek a little way from its mouth, I visited the fine falls at that place, equal in height to Niagara, though the volume of water is not large. The stream leaps from a well defined, perpendicular rock, 175 feet high, and falling into a basin, sends up a spray on which a rainbow is often beautifully painted amid the shrubbery and trees that grow on the steep banks on either side below the falls. I stood with several natives on the verge of the rock, and let down a stone with a line, to ascertain the depth. Subsequently I forded this river on horseback, with my family, above the falls, where the water was up to the skirts of our saddles.

Leaving the falls, and returning towards Waimea, I was met by a young native with two horses from Mr. Whitney, who wished to facilitate and hasten my return. We passed through the valleys of Wahiawa and Hanapepe before described. Enter-ing Hanapepe, occupied by Kiaimoku, a disaffected chief and coadjutor of George, I found, I confess, its beauty had faded since Mr. Ruggles had left it, and the care of Kaumualii had ceased. We hastened through it with unwonted speed, and not without conjectures that danger was near, and reached Waimea unharmed. But darkness thickened over the island. Incendiary attempts to burn the church near the mission house were reported to us. During these days and weeks of suspense and solicitude, the thoughts and voice of the mission family on that so lately peaceful river, were often occupied with the scriptural sentiments of Newton, by which we were prompted to our peculiar duties, and reminded of our ground of trust and rejoicing.

" Ye servants of God, your Master proclaim,
And publish abroad his wonderful name :
The name all victorious of Jesus extol ;
His kingdom is glorious and rules over all—
God ruleth on high, almighty to save,
And still he is nigh—his presence we have."

Looking some time in vain for intelligence and relief from the windward, we were at length cheered by the report that Kalanimoku, our friend, had come to the opposite side of the island. Leaving Honolulu in his own little schooner or pilot boat, the New York, he crossed the channel, accompanied by Kekauluohi, and touched at Waioli first, to look after the wrecked Cleopatra's Barge. Thence, on board the Tamahololani, a brig of the late Kaumualii, he passed around, and arrived at Waimea on the first of August, 1824. It is said that George prepared to meet and welcome him, but was dissuaded by older chiefs, who advised a different course. Kapule promptly launched her double canoe, and went off to the brig and conveyed the chief to the shore. As he debarked from the brig, the governor sent from the fort a file of soldiers, armed with muskets, to receive him. He landed some eighty rods west of the fort, and immediately called on the ex-governess, Wahine, whose husband had just died. Finding a number of chiefs there, and others, making lamentations, he expressed his regard for the departed and his friends, and recommended that their wailing should be suspended till the Sabbath day was passed; then inquired for a comfortable place to rest himself, and was conducted by Kapule to the cool shade of the large Kou trees, near the bank and mouth of the river, over against the fort, where they strewed the area beneath with grass and rushes, overspread them quickly with mats, and placed for him an armed chair. He pleasantly seated himself in the midst of the multitude, who were gathering from every quarter, to gaze on the old companion of Kamehameha, and prime agent of Kaahumanu. Kahalaia crossed the river from the fort, and respectfully welcomed his honored uncle.

It did our hearts good, in our strait, to see the friendly old chieftain. Still, much as we relied on his friendship, experience, and talents, we did not feel even now, that all was safe. He met and saluted Mr. Whitney and myself as we called on him; then, after we were seated, repeatedly turned to me with an affectionate smile, and grasping my hand anew, repeated his warm *aloha*. He spoke with interest of the burning of the church at Honolulu, and the erection and opening of a new one in its place, and of his progress towards completing his own stone house, where he hoped soon to dwell quietly by our side.

He attended public worship and heard a sermon from Mr. Whitney, and after the service took a seat under the pleasant shade of the kou trees before his door, and conversed kindly with the people who came around him.

On Thursday, of the same week, he called together the chiefs and head men of the island, and said to them, " I have come to acquaint you with the charge of the deceased, and to regulate the affairs of your state. This is the dying charge given me by the departed, ' that the son (Liholiho) of us two (Kaahumanu and myself) be over you (your sovereign)—and that the possessor of lands before, be confirmed in his possession, and he that was before poor, abide in his poverty.'" This was not satisfactory to that class who had not been well supplied with lands.

Kiaimakani [wind-watcher], an old chief originally from Oahu, thinking the existing order of things was unfavorable to his interest, demanded that the estates on the island should be thrown together and a new division made. To this, Kalanimoku objected, and said, "Let us abide by the charge of the late king." Kiaimakani, by no means satisfied with retaining the little inheritance which he had held under Kaumualii, nor with the control of the windward rulers, unless he and his party could be enriched by a new division of lands, persevered for two or three days in his demand. He gave some account of the strife for the sovereignty of Kauai before Kaumualii possessed it. He affirmed that Hikiki had slain Keawe, and taken the control of the island, and that Kaumualii and his supporters had opposed Hikiki, and slain him in battle, thus establishing the sovereignty of the late king, intimating, perhaps, that the established custom of settling questions of sovereignty by a trial of strength or martial prowess, was not yet to be set aside by the *palapala*, or the new religion. His arrogance in demanding a throwing together and dividing anew of the estates of Kaumualii's dominions, was sharply rebuked by one of Liholiho's men.

Leaving the scene of this earnest debate about sunset, Saturday evening, I came to the bank of the river to cross over, by canoe, to my family, hoping to embark with them and Kalanimoku for Oahu, early on Monday morning. As I was about to step into the canoe, Trowbridge, an active but erring young Englishman, ran to me to return a book which I had lent him.

Having found him sceptical, and wishing to turn his attention from one of the vilest of Byron's works, which I was sorry to find in the hands of a man who was searching for weapons of rebellion against the Sovereign of the world, I had lent him " Chalmers's Evidences of Christianity," and requested him to examine it. On returning the book, he commended the talents of the author, but said, " The Gospel requires men to love their *enemies*, but I do not think it *possible*." Being referred to the fact, that *Jesus loved his enemies*, and died that we might live, and by his resurrection proved the truth of his religion, he said, " I believe, and I don't believe." I said, " Here you have a Savior offered you, and here is the demonstration of the truth of his religion before your eyes. He is infinitely excellent, and worthy of all your powers and affections. Now give your heart to him and seek his favor and strive to make him your friend." He gave me his hand, saying, " I'll try," and went into the fort to lodge. I returned to the mission house ; but the island was unquiet.

Before the dawn of the next morning, August 8th, 1824, the confused noise of the battle of the warrior was heard pealing through the valley, from the fort.   The malcontents, surprising the little garrison, had commenced the work of blood.

Roused by the noise of battle so near, and hearing the balls whistle over us, what was our surprise and anguish to hear that George and his coadjutors were attempting to take the fort !   We trembled for our friend, Kalanimoku, and his party, and for George, too.   For ourselves and little ones, we looked to the Lord as our defence, while hostile insurgents were passing and repassing our door ; and we were not forsaken.

Some of the insurgents entering the fort, and hoping for a rush of the neighboring inhabitants to ensure the victory over the garrison, one of them stood on the walls and called aloud to the two divisions of the valley on either side of the river, " Ho Waimea ! —Ho Makawele!—come on—the Hawaiians are beaten—the Kauaians have the fort !"   Some of both parties rushed to enter, amid balls and bayonets.   Kahalaia and Niau, a royal chief, being on the opposite side of the river, started to cross the river to defend the fort.   The former was dissuaded by the latter on account of the personal danger.   But rushing into that danger himself, and meeting with Kiaimakani, he demanded if he were a friend, and was instantly shot down by an insurgent, who was then cut down by an attendant of the fallen chief.   Kiaimakani fled.

The noise of the battle continued about thirty minutes.   Meantime, Kalanimoku sent for Mr. Whitney and myself to come to him, then on the sand beach, a little distance west of the fort. As we left our habitations, Mrs. B. and Mrs. W. watched the steps of their husbands till they passed near the fort, when the firing, which had ceased, was renewed.   That was to them a moment of deep solicitude.   Their flesh and hearts trembled, as they looked one on the other, and on their sweet babes, and dared not ask, " Where are our protectors ?"   Then they thought of the care of the Watchman of Israel, and found support.

Crossing the river, we came to the chief, and asked, " What is all this ?"   He replied, " This is *war.*"   In a few minutes, his trusty aid, Kaiakoili, a very stout, athletic native, came from the scene of battle, and with unusual energy of manner, reported to the chief that the insurgents had fled towards Hanapepe.   We asked Kalanimoku for a guard for our house and family.   He replied, "I have but few men, and the Kauaians I cannot trust." Willing to do what he could, he issued a *tabu*, forbidding any to approach our house unbidden.   At his request, we united in prayer.   Mr. W. and myself then repaired to the fort, to dress the wounds of the bleeding, and to bury the slain.   As I ascended the walls amid these new scenes, how was I shocked and my soul filled with grief as I lifted a mat from a fallen victim, and saw young Trowbridge, whom, the evening before, I had attempted to rescue from the toils of infidelity, now lying dead on the rampart.   Covered with wounds, he lay in his blood.   He seemed to have fallen in close combat, hand to hand, and the death stroke appeared like that of a hatchet.   Another Englishman, named Smith, we found mortally wounded in the fort, as if white men had been special marks for the assailants, as needing first to be disposed of.

In a few hours, Kalanimoku, Kekauluohi, and her husband, Kanaina, Kapule and others, marched into the fort, armed.   We were struck with the martial appearance of the females, Kekauluohi, Premier, carrying a heavy pistol, and the ex-queen, Kapule, walking with a drawn sword in her hand.   Kalanimoku, on account of his strait, despatched a small schooner for Oahu, offered our families a passage, and advised us to go.   They knew not the strength and numbers of the insurgents.   They knew not whom to admit into the castle and whom to keep out, and the force was obviously small.   Even the captain of the garrison was suspected of disloyalty or great mismanagement in allowing the insurgents to scale the walls.   The approaching darkness of night might be the signal for a renewed attack.   They dared not send out to pursue the insurgents or to meet them in the field, and unless they could get help from the windward soon, Kapule and others considered their situation exceedingly perilous, and manifested unexpected concern as to the effect of our departure.   Trowbridge, and the mortally wounded young native, who expired while we were there, were buried within the walls with funeral solemnity.   We encouraged our friends to trust in the Lord, to seek his guidance, and obey his will, believing that he would not forsake those that forsake not him.

The mind of Kalanimoku seemed to be looking intently to see what Jehovah, the Christians' God, would do with him.   He does not appear to have taken any part in the contest, till he had called the missionaries to lead him in prayer, after which he left his sand bank, where he had slept, crossed the river, and took on himself the charge of the fort, and the business of restoring order.

Here the value of a trustworthy chieftain could be appreciated, and here I saw, for once, the reason which had not before been so fully obvious, why the women of rank bore arms in war, in such a country, where neither the intelligence, nor the virtue, nor the established customs of the nation would shield them from violence, if unarmed and separate from their husbands or warrior friends.

Towards night, we entered a double canoe, in the river, with our wives and little ones.   Hurrying towards the schooner in the roadstead, we were well nigh swamped in the surf, through which we had to pass.   Our children shrieked aloud as the waves dashed over us, threatening to engulf us like the raging of the rebellious multitude.   Our small stores were damaged, our water for the voyage injured ; and for a moment we felt ourselves to be in the " perils of the sea," as well as in " perils among the heathen."   We, however, reached the vessel drenched with salt water, and set sail, but our solicitude for our friends behind us, and our apprehension of an attack from the insurgents before, was scarcely diminished. For as we passed Hanapepe and Wahiawa, we had reason to suppose that if the insurgents still meant to conquer, they would deem it of material consequence to them to capture this vessel, and thus prevent Kalanimoku's appeal to the windward islands for aid. Had this been done, it is not difficult to conceive how perilous would have been the situation of our families, and that of Kalanimoku and his party.

A captive, Kamakakini, was regarded as an instigator of the revolt, was put on board this schooner, and placed in the hold, and closely bound with ropes to a stanchion, to be conveyed, as we supposed, to Oahu. On the following morning, we went to the hatchway to see and converse with him, but his place was vacated. In the silence of the night, he had been called on deck by the captain, stabbed, and thrown into the sea.

No necessity appeared for this heathen execution. It was said the captain had orders *not to land the prisoner*. But this was different from Kalanimoku's subsequent treatment of known and acknowledged leaders of the insurrection.

We had an unusually speedy passage, as if the Lord had heard us at once, and we quickly found ourselves " at the land," in Honolulu. If a strife, commenced without a preamble, manifesto, or any declaration stating the cause, and the object proposed, can properly be called a *war*, the news of the war was quickly proclaimed, not only through Oahu, but through the group.

Great sympathy for Kalanimoku and his friends was manifested when his perilous situation was made known. The startling expression, often repeated, " Mai make Kalanimoku ia Humehume ma,—Well nigh slain is Kalanimoku by George and his party,"—not only called forth the sympathy of relatives, friends, missionaries, and foreign residents, but roused the spirit of war in many a Hawaiian breast, and that of revenge, it was feared, in some, and avarice in others. Thousands were ready to rush to the field of contest. Of these, every one seemed politician enough to decide what must be done in this emergency. " He kaua, he kaua—War, war "—rung through the village and valley of Honolulu; and in a few hours a thousand men were ready to join and defend their chieftain, and bring the Kauaians under the same government with the windward islands. Gov. Boki was then in England, and his place was well supplied by Namahana. This reinforcement embarked the next day, and quickly reached Waimea, to the relief of Kalanimoku, while the insurgents were rallying at Wahiawa, the estate of George.

Through a merciful arrangement of Providence, the insurgents did not renew the attack on the fort or on Kalanimoku, but while rallying, allowed him time to obtain a reinforcement which would make such an attack useless, or destructive to their cause. Nor is it less wonderful that, after that reinforcement arrived, the leaders of the insurrection did not then hasten to propose peace on some terms rather than risk another battle. The citadel being in full possession of an experienced general, who had the resources of the nation at command, and an armed force now with him greater, probably, than ever the insurgents brought together, it was madness for the rebel chiefs to strike again for victory, or to insist on independence. But, perhaps through ignorance of the art of war, they had failed to know the strength of Kalanimoku when thus reinforced, or, through desperation, some of them preferred rather to die in battle than to submit to the government of Liholiho; and perhaps the feelings of revenge towards those chiefs of Kauai who stood by Kalanimoku impelled them to hold out for another trial of strength and military skill.

During the pause or the mustering of the forces of the two parties, Kalanimoku received from the infatuated George the following singular specimen of diplomacy, embracing a partial profession of respect to the windward government, and a strong desire to punish the chiefs of his own island who had not favored him and his party according to his wishes.

"Dear Sir,—We wish not to hurt any of the people from the windward islands, but those chiefs belonging to Kauai. Therefore I hope you will separate your men from them, and let the Atooi chiefs fight the battle, for we wish not to hurt any of you from the windward. Our lives have been threatened by Tapule, by Haupu, by Kumakeha, and by Wahine. These are the chiefs we want to go against. But your people we wish not to trouble. Send me answer as soon as you can.   Yours, &c.,

                                                        "G. P. T."

Kaahumanu being detained at Maui, after her husband's interment, Kalanimoku's express schooner hastened thither from Honolulu, to report to her. It approached Lahaina with a signal of distress, and as the captain sprung on shore, he cried out, "Ua kaua o Kauai! I kii kanaka mai au—Kauai wages war! I have come for men;" then gave the particulars to the queen. She thought the trouble had arisen because her late husband had not taken proper measures to secure the quiet submission of his son and other chiefs and people. She was ready to prosecute the war, and subdue the insurgents, and required a reinforcement of soldiers to embark at once from Maui to succor Kalanimoku, but hesitated to send any high chief. But Kaikioewa, an old chief of high rank, in a spirited address of some eloquence, said, "I am old, like Kalanimoku. We played together when children. We have fought together beside our king, Kamehameha. Our heads are now alike growing grey. Kalanimoku never deserted me; and shall I desert him now, when the rebels of Kauai rise against him? I will not deal thus with him. If one of us is ill, the others can hasten from Kauai to Hawaii to see the sick. And now, when our brother and leader is in peril, shall no chief go to succor him? I will go; and here are my men also." Asking

Mr. Richards what they should do with the rebels, he was referred to the divine rule—"love your enemies." He rejoined, "We do not go to kill Kauaians; we go to put an end to fighting. We will take the rebels and bring them to the windward, and put them to farming." Hoapili was also inquisitive as to the accordance of war with Christianity. They both asked questions difficult for a Christian missionary to answer, and some which different missionaries would, if obliged to speak at all on the subject, be likely to answer differently, respecting the lawfulness of war, and the manner of conducting it, if compelled to engage in it; but questions which showed that their consciences were awake to consider what was Christian duty in this case of insurrection. Hoopili, Kaikioewa, Kahekili (thunder), a stern warrior chief, and two companies of men, embarked immediately on board two schooners, and hastened to the scene of strife.

Soon after the sailing of this reinforcement, Kaahumanu spontaneously, like the king of Nineveh, proclaimed a fast, in order to seek God's favor. This was observed by many, with apparent propriety, on the 27th August. At Lahaina, an uninterrupted Sabbath stillness prevailed from morning till evening. Amusements and labor, and the kindling of fires for cooking, seemed to be entirely suspended; and the chiefs and a concourse of the people attended public worship, and united in presenting their confessions and supplications before the throne of mercy.

Arriving at Kauai, Hoapili united his force to that of Kahalaia, embracing the loyal warriors of Kauai, and the reinforcements from Oahu, who had joined Kalanimoku, at Waimea, and chose to lead them to battle.

On the 18th of August, a force under Hoapili marched from Waimea towards Hanapepe and Wahiawa, where the enemy held a position overlooking the valley of Hanapepe, nearly two miles from the sea-shore. Like other astrologers, Gov. Hoapili claimed some superiority over his countrymen, and doubtless supposed he could produce some impression on their minds by appearing to consult the heavenly bodies, in respect to the course to be pursued, the time and the result of the contest. He gazed much at the stars. He noticed the relative position of our principal planets, then visible, and fixed stars in the zodiac; probably more for the purpose of inspiring confidence and courage in the soldiery, as a means of victory, than for any information supposed to be derivable from the stars, as to the result of the battle, or the fitness of the time for commencing it. Heathen leaders doubtless know that the belief that success is practicable, whether that belief be encouraged by interest, experience, martial skill, astrology, or prophecy, is a powerful means of union, strength, and success in war. When Hoapili, after his repeated observations, predicted that if the loyal party should be beaten by the insurgents, the whole group of islands would be overcome by them, and there would be no place to flee to for safety, not even their own homes, he put a spur to their courage and constancy, and assumed a position not likely to be proved false.

Though the distance from the fort at Waimea to the encampment of the Kauaians was scarcely more than eight miles, the army, on the way, halted and rested on the Sabbath. The next day they proceeded, crossed the river, and ascended the heights on the east side of the valley of Hanapepe, and were drawn up in the order of battle. Silence was commanded before the onset, and prayer was offered to the great Jehovah. Then, in a curved line or semicircle, they advanced, the right and left extremes intending to pass the enemy's lines, and capture the whole force. As they drew near, the insurgents, who had taken a station behind a wall with a small field-piece, discharged it a few times with some apparent effect; for Hoapili's men, who were in its range, prostrated themselves before it at each discharge, then rose again and advanced. Some supposed at the moment that this engine of foreign war was doing the work effectually, though it was neither weakening the strength nor daunting the courage of the government troops, who returned the fire and pressed on. The insurgents, unable to stand, were beaten and routed; some forty or fifty were killed, and the rest fled chiefly to the woods, and some were pursued and taken. Kiaimakani, their boldest leader, attempted, as he fled, to conceal himself by holding up grass between himself and the passing pursuers, one of whom perceiving a motion of the grass, fired a musket ball into it " at a venture," by which the unhappy old warrior chief was killed, and his violent dealing returned upon himself.

George and Betty, and their infant daughter, fled on horseback to the mountains. The two latter were soon captured and treated with kindness. The child was, however, by Kaahumanu named Wahine-kipi, Rebel-woman. George eluded his pursuers for a considerable period. A party of men were sent by Kalanimoku to find and take him, and being led by Kalaiheana, a head man from Oahu, went into the mountains in pursuit of him. They occasionally called aloud, " O Humehume, show yourself to us. You shall not be slain, if you will make your appearance. Come, let us return to the sea-side to your father, Kalanimoku." After some weeks spent in the search, he was found and captured, and brought in a pitiable state into the presence of the dignified Kalanimoku, who, at his father's request, had been disposed to befriend him, and had commiserated him from the beginning of the contest. This noble, victorious, semi-civilized chieftain took off his own mantle and threw it over the poor, misguided young chief, thus saying, most significantly, " *Live.*" He was restored to his wife and child, and for the safety of Kauai, sent to Oahu, where he remained several years, until his death.

George, in his childhood, had been sent by his father to America, partly from apprehensions of danger to the child from jealous or aspiring relatives. He was supplied with the means of support; but Capt. R., who took the charge of him, lost both his own property and that of his ward. George labored as a carpenter's apprentice for several years, then for a time in the service of a farmer; but feeling homeless, or restless, or disposed for the scenes of war, he enlisted in the U. S. navy. He was in the engagement between the Enterprise and Boxer, and, in the act of boarding, was wounded in the side by a British pike. He afterwards went up the Mediterranean as one of the crew of the Guerrière, under Com. Decatur, and was in an engagement with an Algerine frigate. Then returning to Charlestown, he was, at the solicitation of Christian friends, released and sent to school for a season. On the sending forth of a mission to these islands, he accompanied it, not as a missionary, or as under the control of the Board, who had paid for his academical instruction and his passage home. Of course, neither the Board nor the mission was implicated in his political or seditious proceedings. He took a course contrary to their wishes and counsels, and the tendency of their instructions, though, as a son of a king, he thought he had rights to maintain by force. But how clear it is that education and civilization, without a firm belief in God's Word, will accomplish little or nothing for the heathen.

After the decisive battle, one of our promising pupils, Laanui, a chief from Oahu, who had taken part in the war, wrote back to Namahana the following brief report, which showed some advancement from the late barbarism of the country, of which Kahalaia and some others were not yet wholly cured:

"I have no captives. I regard implicitly the Word of God—of Him by whom we live, who warded off the balls from us, who is our Lord and yours; and on whose account we are without captives. In the midst of the battle, when the enemy fled, then I ceased. I went not to search for captives. I remained with your brother, Hoapili. When your brother returned to Waimea, we returned. And when we reached Waimea, there we abode, at the mouth of the river. Therefore, I have no captives at all to send up to you."

At this interesting juncture, Mr. Ellis, by the protracted and painful illness of Mrs. Ellis, was called to leave the islands. He embarked with his family on board an American ship, to return to England, by way of the United States. He had rendered most important service for about eighteen months, during which time, besides preaching and counselling the rulers, he had united with us in preparing the first hymn-book which we published for the people. He left the field reluctantly; and our missionaries and the rulers parted with him with regret. Both in America and Great Britain, he did much to bring our field to the favorable notice of the public, and to defend our cause from ungenerous aspersions.

After the fast of August 27th, Kaahumanu, about to embark from Lahaina to join Kalanimoku at Kauai, seemed interested in the preaching of the Gospel. She was seen to weep at a public lecture, and the next day sent for the missionaries, and requested them to sing and pray with her, before she left the shore. She designated as teachers three young men in her school, and wished them to be furnished with books sufficient for three large schools among her people, on the windward side of Maui. She expressed great affection for the missionaries, saying, " What we have is yours." Her sister, Hoapili Wahine, seconded her proposition for social worship. And our blind friend and coadjutor, Puaaiki, was overjoyed, and seemed ready to kiss the feet of the queen, for gratitude, because he thought she was taking a stand on the Lord's side. Grasping her hand, as her barge shoved off from the sand beach, he clung to it, wading along till he was knee deep in the water.

As she and her company, on the way from Lahaina, arrived at Honolulu, they came without delay to the sanctuary, to unite in public thanksgiving for the success which crowned the effort of the nation in restoring order at Kauai. The next day being the Sabbath, the services were well attended, both forenoon and afternoon. Namahana, Kaahumanu, her step-son, the young prince, and other chiefs, were attentive to the Word. In the morning my sermon urged the duty of following Christ and relying on him alone for pardon and eternal life, and in the afternoon, the necessity of a holy heart, or disinterested benevolence, in order to obtain the treasures of Heaven, according to the instruction of the Great Teacher to the " young ruler." Kaahumanu engaging in the work of reform, having proclaimed a fast, encouraged schools, the observance of the Sabbath, and abstinence from various evils, was, like others, supposed to be cherishing the disposition to inquire, " What lack I yet ?" Mrs. B. listening to the searching truth, watched her countenance and motions that day, and could not but feel a concern, lest (like the young ruler who did not expect a reproof after well doing), feeling too rich, high, or proud, she would turn away grieved. But agitated as she appeared when pungent truth came close home, she bore it, and no decisive marks of displeasure at the preacher, or the doctrine, could be seen in her interview with us, at the close of the service. On the contrary, she appeared unusually kind and condescending, stopped her carriage and her train at our gate, and kept us standing and talking, for a time, as if unwilling to pass on without hearing more. Thus we were encouraged.

Kealiiahonui, son of Kaumualii, whom Kaahumanu had taken as her husband, young, handsome, and naturally and usually more interesting at that period than most of the nobility, exhibited, on this occasion, a solemnity and tenderness like one under the strivings of the Spirit of God. Their connexion, in our view, was inconsistent with the rules of the Gospel, and we believed the power of the Gospel, should it result in their conversion, would dissolve it.

The next day they left Honolulu for Kauai, urging me to accompany them; but this I could not well do. The cares and labors of the station after the departure of Mr. Ellis, my esteemed colleague, seemed to forbid it. On arriving at Waimea, she repaired at once to the house of God, to offer prayer and praise. To avail herself of the advantages of the light, she spent much of her time for a few weeks, at the mission premises, where Mr. Whitney had, after the commotion, resumed his labors; and exerted herself to aid the work. The state of things at Waimea, while she was there, is thus briefly noticed by Mr. Whitney :

"I have never before seen the people give so good attention to the word of life. Last Sabbath was an interesting day. In describing the pains and consequences of a Savior's death, I perceived tears trickling down the cheeks of some, whose hearts I had supposed too hard to admit even of sympathy on the subject. Kaahumanu continues to exert her influence in the good cause."

In December, Kaahumanu having removed to the opposite side of the island for a season, caused a frail house of worship to be erected, and urged on the work of instruction by the help of several native teachers. She sent a horse and a messenger to bring Mr. Whitney to her camp, near the foot of the mountains, ten miles north of Wailua, at Kohalalele. Though he felt it very difficult to leave Waimea for a day or two, he went over to encourage them. On this occasion, he thus wrote me:

"Of the expressions of pleasure and joy I received from the chiefs at my arrival, I should say nothing, were it not to give some view of their feelings towards the great object of our labors. I have had no such meeting with chiefs. The pleasure of meeting an affectionate child could not have been expressed more unfeignedly. I have not a doubt of their sincere attachment to the mission, and of their intention to promote its interests. I preached to them, exhibiting the Savior's example. The church which Kaahumanu has built here was full, and the audience very attentive. Though at a distance from any mission establishment, the great object here is the *palapala*. Kahikona, George Sandwich, and others, are useful. I entreat you to stay where you are. I do not pretend to prophesy, but I think your presence will be more needed in a few days, at Oahu, than it ever has been before. Kalanimoku, Kaahumanu, and other chiefs are about to return."

The New York being about this time stranded and damaged at Niihau, Kalanimoku, who thought he could attend to such things better than others, proceeded thither, and had his schooner hauled up and repaired. While thus engaged he wrote me two short and pleasant notes, December 8th and 23d, subscribed *Paalua*, a name often applied to him after the death of Kamehameha and of his wife, implying that thus both eyes were closed.

" Much love to you, Bingham and Mrs. Bingham, and you all. I salute you all. Great affection for you all who remain. Exceedingly great is my love to you. Here I am, earnestly attending to the Word of God. I pray also, to our Lord Jesus Christ, and to the Holy Spirit, who will enlighten me. Let the perseverance of you all be great. Be ye strong to labor for this land of darkness. Love to the children of you all, and to yourselves also. My salutations to you all are ended.— PAALUA."

" Niihau, Dec. 23d, 1824.

" Great love to you, Bingham. This is my word to you. Speak to the professor of medicine, to doctor my mother, Ukeke, who has return-ed thither. Look you two to her sickness. I compassionate my mother because she is sick of the palsy. Do you both treat well my mother. My word is finished.— PAALUA."

His schooner being repaired, was ready at tne close of the week to be launched. The wind and tide were favorable for it on Sabbath morning, and he was urged by foreigners to avail himself of the opportunity, but though he was then in haste to return to Oahu, and he had no missionary at his elbow, he conscientiously refused to launch her till the Sabbath was past. In this, his practice accorded with his letters.

Kaikioewa, one of the conqueror's companions in former wars, a more sober and conciliatory chieftain than Kahalaia, was con-stituted governor of Kauai, and though not the most accurate in doing business, yet, with the aid of Keaweamahi, his wife, by his side, who, like some other women, was blessed with more shrewd-ness in some matters than her honored lord, he rendered important service in restoring quietude and in favoring the cause of instruc-tion and true religion—the only safe-guards of the peace of the state. "Kaikioewa and his wife," says Mr. W. at this period, " have taken a noble stand. They have begun to build a chapel, which, he says, shall be the best yet in the islands." In the course of six or eight months, that building, ninety feet by thirty, was completed, and supposed to be the best ever erected on that island.

Calling on Mr. W. one day, and learning that he was writing to our Directors, he said, with much warmth of expres-sion, " Give them my affectionate salutation. Tell them I thank them much for the good news of salvation that they have sent us. That the *palapala me ka pule*, learning and religion, shall be the business of my life." And he called on the chiefs, and head men, and people of the island, to go with him in the work of reform, though he was yet far from possessing that completeness of know-ledge, experience, and devotedness to the good of others, which are needed in a reformer. The grace of God, it is believed, ac-complished for him great things before he finished his course.

Peace being restored at Kauai, the successive return of old warriors, young soldiers, and high chiefs, from the scene of strife and victory, to Honolulu, afforded interesting occasions of thanksgiving and decisive indications of progress. Among these was Laanui, the husband of Namahana, the governess. He was an interesting young chief of the third rank, well featured, and a little above the middling stature. Having been down to take part in suppressing the insurrection, but not to get captives for self-aggrandizement, as had been formerly customary, and as some of the unchristian warriors in this case had done, he now returned, by ship, to Oahu. Before he debarked, the governess, being near the landing-place, asked me whether there or at the church we should offer prayer to God on the return of her husband. Being assured that either place, whichever she might prefer, would be very suitable for the devout expression of our gratitude, she requested me to stay by her till her husband should come on shore. She was higher than he, both as grand-daughter of the king of Maui, and relict of the Conqueror. She was taller than ordinary women, and so large as, among the chiefs, to appear rather short. She had black hair and eyes, a round, full face, large lips, a short neck—her chin almost touching her breast—and such obesity that if, as in some countries, her comeliness had been estimated by the hundred pounds of her weight, she would have been called a beauty. But she had now finer qualities to constitute her comeliness, and give her a salutary influence over her dark-hearted contemporaries.

Laanui soon landed in decent apparel of civilized fashion, and passed quietly through the crowd of natives on the quay. As he approached the governess, she kindly beckoned to him with her hand, and with affectionate voice called out, "*Mai!*—hither." Glad to be welcomed home in safety after the victory, he, with open countenance of unusual mildness for a native, came silently to her, and sat down gently by her side. They embraced and kissed each other, and wiped their tears. How wide the contrast between this and the heathen wailing on other occasions! I could not refrain from tears to see the happy meeting of this interesting pair, after their separation for so lamentable a cause. His protection and restoration they both now piously ascribed to the care of Jehovah—the Christian's God. After a few expressions of mutual joy and congratulation, and a few words as to the state of affairs at Kauai, at Namahana's suggestion, with which her husband signified his concurrence, we sang a hymn of praise, and united in thanksgiving to the King of nations for his timely and gracious aid to those who acknowledge his authority and love his Word.

One of the distinguished rebels, Kanenoho, being captured and brought from Kauai, was soon after this introduced into the presence of Namahana, amid the multitude who came around to gaze at him as a caged lion. In the verandah of Kaahumanu's framed house, the governess and Hinau, captain of the fort, conversed with the captive about the rebellion. Her closing remarks to him were touching, and highly creditable to the head and heart of one high born and so recently a proud heathen—" Compassion for you, Kanenoho. Great was the darkness of your hearts to engage in war. *Life* is the good thing. We did not wish to dispossess you of your country. Kalanimoku went down not to make war, but peacefully to take care of your islands in accordance with the charge of Kaumualii—'*E olelo pono, a hoi mai*—To have a proper talk and return.'" The prisoner wiped his eyes with his rude mantle, subdued by the kindness and fitness of her words, and the remembrance of his own folly.

I preached the same day from an injunction of our Savior, a lesson peculiarly needful for the Hawaiians at that season—" Be ye therefore *merciful*, as your Father also is merciful."

On the 16th, a small squadron returned from Kauai, having on board a company of warriors, embracing Hoapili, Kahekili, Kalaikoa, and Kapuaa, and several captives, and among them Kiaimoku (island or ship watcher), the rebel chief, of Hanapepe. Finding his cause desperate, this chief coming forth from his hiding-place to which he had fled, and surrendering to the triumphant party, threw himself on the clemency of Kalanimoku, and was treated with kindness by that noble chieftain.

These victors landed at Honolulu just before evening, and being accompanied by Laanui, and attended by a file of armed soldiers, came at once to my house with their congratulations, and made a proposition to unite the same evening in thanksgiving to God. They repaired to a house vacated by Liholiho (still absent from the country), where I met them and their friends, and was happy to lead them in the delightful service. To Gov. Hoapili, this high chief of Maui who had led the victorious little army, and marched up to the enemy's line in the face of their cannon and muskets, I put the question distinctly, " On what account would you have the company address their adorations to Jehovah?" To this he replied, and doubtless spoke the sentiments of others, " *I ke ola o kakou i ke Akua*—On account of our preservation by God."

CHAPTER X.

SIXTH YEAR OF THE MISSION, AND SECOND OF KAAHUMANU.—
1825.

Promising New Year—Association of serious females—Kalanimoku's return from
his victory—Kaahumanu's letter and return—Agency of the Spirit—Namahana
and the shipwreck—Association of men for Christian improvement—Religious
interest at Lahaina—Bartemeus Puaaiki—Progress at Hawaii—Kapiolani and
Pele—Visit to Hilo—Deficiency of means to supply schools—Result of the king's
visit to England—Return of the survivors—Visit of Lord Byron—Kaahumanu
and others candidates for baptism—National council—Outrage at Lahaina—Departure of Mr. Stewart—Decalogue and meeting of the chiefs—Non-confederacy
of church and state.

On the ushering in of the year 1825, a New Year's sermon
was preached at Honolulu, in which the dealings of God with the
nation for the last year were recounted, the speedy and universal
turning of the nation to the Lord was urged, and special displays
of divine power and grace were shown to be desirable, and were
anticipated as proofs of God's kindness and readiness to hear
the prayer of the humble and the needy. The heart of the
governess seemed to leap for joy at the prospect of good which
she felt encouraged to expect the Lord, who had restored peace,
would bestow on the land.

Under the direction of the missionary females, an association
of women to meet weekly for prayer and improvement, was
commenced on Friday of that week. It embraced, at first,
twelve or fifteen native females, among whom there appeared
some evidence of sincere love to the truth, and of understanding
the duty and privilege of prayer. Among these were Namahana
and Kaka, the wife of Naoa, the latter of whom appeared subsequently to live by prayer, and literally on her knees received at
length her summons to depart. That organization being increased
from time to time, has doubtless, in the course of twenty years,
tended not only to call into healthful action many of its regularly
entered members, and to incite others to the important duties
which it was designed to encourage, but also in some measure to
call down successive showers of spiritual blessings upon the
nation.

Kalanimoku, after his perils and the labor of some six months
at the leeward, returned to Honolulu towards the close of January. He was joyfully received by many warm friends: among
these were Namahana and Hinau, and their Christian teachers.

He was saluted by an elderly and honorable woman as the *kaula hao* (iron cable) of the country—a compliment higher than the discharge of twenty-one guns from the fort would have been. Many wept at his landing. Some of the Russian officers present wondered at the weeping of his friends who had received him safe and sound. " They would cry," said they, " if he had gone far *away ;* they would cry if he had been *killed.* Why then do they now cry since he has *returned* victorious and safe ?" But the tears of some on this occasion were more like those of a pious family at the return of a long absent son and brother, than the deafening and unmeaning or incomprehensible din of a heathen wail, formerly so frequent at these islands.

Kalanimoku and those who returned with him, and others who welcomed them, repaired spontaneously to the public altar, to offer the tribute of praise and thanksgiving which he deemed justly due to Jehovah on this occasion.

When assembled at the church, before going into the pulpit, I sat down by his side with a desire to know more definitely his views of the object for which we had assembled, and asked him to state distinctly for what he desired thanksgiving and prayer might be offered. He said, " Give thanks for God's kind care over us, and for our deliverance from death ; and pray that God would pardon our sins, and enlighten the nation and save us."

This was stated to the congregation, the reasons for it presented, and the delightful duty attempted, with a sense of the special obligations under which we all had been laid by the merciful interpositions of Providence. The following day being the Sabbath, Kalanimoku and his party attended worship. The church was well filled ; and I esteemed it a privilege to attempt to guide the meditations and prayers of the assembly, that they might consistently choose the Lord for their God, and feel their obligations to him, and consecrate their lives to him, not only for his care in delivering them from the power of earthly foes, but for his grace in providing and offering deliverance from spiritual foes, and even eternal salvation for their souls.

The words of the devout warrior of Israel furnished an appropriate and delightful theme worthy·to be adopted by those who were rejoicing in the late victory, and in the tokens of Divine favor to sinners now emerging from heathenism :—

> " I said unto Jehovah, Thou art my God :
> Hear the voice of my supplications, O Jehovah.
> O God, the Lord—the Strength of my salvation,
> Thou hast covered my head in the day of battle."
> Ps. cxl : 6, 7.

We were happy to think that this distinguished commander, who had been accustomed to heathen warfare, and who, in 1819, apparently without a thought of the God of heaven, led the forces of Liholiho against the defender of idols, now saw and felt the reasonableness of adopting the language of the inspired patriarch. It was said of him by one who was with him in his exposure when the insurgents at Kauai attacked the Waimea garrison just before the dawn, that in judging between several expedients, one of which he must adopt for himself, he would not rush into the fort, the scene of bloody strife, where it was difficult to distinguish between friends and foes ; nor would he fly to his schooner then at anchor near, and escape to Oahu, nor flee away from the arms of the insurgents, but just cast himself on Jehovah, and wait quietly just where he was, and see what the Lord would do for him.   When the assailants were repulsed with loss by the small inexperienced garrison whom they had surprised by night, he was ready to ascribe his own preservation and that of his friends, to the hand of the Lord.   Through the struggle, the right side seemed so obviously to be favored and sustained, as to produce a pretty general sentiment that it was of God ; and we found in distresses and afflictions, that he, who in wisdom and goodness makes the wrath of man to praise him, turned the calamity of war into a blessing to the nation at large, and made it contribute to the furtherance of the work of the mission and of the cause of Christianity and civilization.

Kalanimoku, re-entering his new mansion at Honolulu, appeared like a Christian nobleman, not ashamed to pray and receive daily instruction.   He soon received a cheering letter from Kaahumanu, his cousin, sister as he called her, who wrote him from Kauai the assurance of her love to the cause of Christianity and of her desire that he and the people might unite with her in furthering it, and of her purpose of visiting the different islands of the group and their principal districts, to encourage attention to schools and religion.

Order being re-established at Kauai, the Regent returned to her residence at Oahu, accompanied by Kealiihonui, Kalakua, the young prince, and others.   Their vessel, the brig Ainoa, was descried from Honolulu just before evening, Feb. 9th, and came to anchor soon after dark, when they hastened to the shore and despatched a messenger to our establishment, desiring to see the missionaries as soon as convenient.   Complying at once, we found them in a well lighted and furnished upper room of Kaahumanu's house, with Kalanimoku and Laanui and the young queens, whom Liholiho, on embarking for England, had left.   As we entered the chamber, Kaahumanu rose respectfully (a novelty to us), and received us with expressions of kindness, cordiality, and joy, which we had not before witnessed in her.   She exclaimed, " *Ua ola kakou ia Iesu Kristo,*" We have been preserved by Jesus Christ, —a just sentiment in which many heartily united with her.   We enjoyed in this friendly group a season of religious conversation and social prayer and praise, in which there was evidence that our labor, in this vineyard, had not been wholly in vain.

While many of the people retained their heathen nature, and some had the spirit of rebellion, and some were disposed to chastise and subdue rebels, and others revengefully to kill them, it was a matter of thanksgiving, and an indication of the meliorating influence of Christianity on the minds of the leaders of the nation, to find the queen, Kaahumanu, and her high chieftains so free from any charge of barbarity or cruelty in subduing those who had risen up against them. In comparison with former wars, it was wonderful that the nation passed through this war with the sacrifice of but four or five of the loyal party, and so far as we had the means of knowing, with scarcely more than half a hundred lives on the part of the insurgents—that even the most guilty who surrendered or were taken alive, were generally treated with lenity, and the praise of the victory ascribed to Jehovah. What a contrast with the terrible slaughter in former wars, when the brooks were choked with the bodies of the slain, precipices flowed with blood, whole districts were ravaged and desolated, and the murdered offered on the altars of abomination! In the first battle at Waimea, but fourteen of the insurgents were reported as killed, and in the next battle and rout, at Wahiawa, forty or fifty of the enemy, and not more than one of the loyal party, were reported as among the slain. Some probably died of their wounds, as did Smith; and a few are reported to have been wantonly killed by the victors.

The next day the queen called on us, and with a considerable number, repaired to the public altar, as others had done, to render public thanksgiving to God for his preserving care.

She shortly gave, with tears but partially suppressed, such an account of her past and present feelings on the subject of religion, as to lead us to form a very favorable estimate of her Christian character, though not yet decisive. She, with her sister, united in the female prayer-meeting, at my house, and in connexion with Mrs. Bingham, Mrs. Stewart, Mrs. Loomis, and B. Stocton, took an active part in questioning and counselling the native females. The haughty queen bowed her knees before the King of heaven, and confessed her sins, and in impressive language poured forth her earnest prayer. "Behold she prayeth!" We rejoiced in the "faithful saying, that is worthy of all acceptation, that Jesus Christ came into the world to save sinners, even the chief," and in the evidence that this once heathen ruler now acknowledged him as her Lord and Savior, and would yet serve him with the energy she had once employed against him.

How widely different the course of Kaahumanu, in celebrating the recent victory, ascribing it to the Lord, offering herself to him, and seeking the civil, moral, and intellectual improvement of the people, even of the *conquered*, from that of wasting and degrading them as her predecessors would have done, and as she herself would have freely done without the better principles inculcated by God's Word.

The missionaries had been slow to give her credit for any interest at heart in the concerns of Christ's kingdom, though she had apparently espoused the cause of reform.   But now, her changed, subdued, and amiable conduct, in contrast to that which she exhibited on our early acquaintance with her, could not but afford us comfort, and awaken the hope that she would yet shine as a gem of peculiar lustre amid the rocks and forbidding lava of these recently barbarous and heathen isles.

Her sisters, Kalakua and Namahana, exhibited also marks of change; but to most observers, not quite so striking as in Kaahumanu: nor was it the most easy for any of them to establish a reputation for piety, benevolence, and the love of equity.

Namahana, while she had charge of affairs at Oahu, acquitted herself well, and in the spring after the return of her husband from the war in Kauai, she gave repeated and happy indications of a changed character.   The following I had opportunity to witness and occasion to record.

The Royal George, an English whale ship, was run upon the reef, west of the entrance of Honolulu harbor, and wrecked at a midnight hour.   Namahana lent her schooner to aid in saving her cargo, etc., and received for the service $100, fairly earned. Without questioning her *right* to such compensation, it was suggested to her that gratuitous assistance, in such circumstances, might have been well, from one able to render it.   " What shall I do ?" she asked with some earnestness.   " Go to your house— look up to your Heavenly Father for direction; and to-morrow, you may tell me what you would *like* to do in the case."   The next day, she carried back the $100 to the captain, and laid them down at his feet, saying, 'that considering his misfortune or strait, she was willing to return the money he had paid for her assistance.' Somewhat surprised, he asked for further explanation.   She said, " I wish to do that which is best for my soul."   " We will divide it," he said: "I will take half, and you half."   "Right," she replied, " if you wish it so."   The money being then divided into two equal parts, he asked of her something in which to take away his fifty dollars.   Her purse containing small change she emptied, turned, and promptly gave to him.   The gentleman (?) noticing the care manifested in turning the purse, remarked, in my hearing, and in a foreign tongue, " See her *covetousness !*" as if the proof of liberality furnished by restoring the $100, and by giving him her purse in addition, was more than counterpoised by her care to see that it was empty.   This is illustrative of the severe manner of judging adopted by a large class of foreigners, in reference to the motives and defenceless characters of Polynesians, when, according to their knowledge and ability, they are endeavoring to be honorable, just, and even generous.   Probably few professed Christians could be found even in the most enlightened countries, who, in case of the shipwreck, would have done better than Namahana, or in the issue have deserved more the credit of liberality, docility, and self-denial.   Two years before this, she and Kapiolani had appeared much like Kamamalu and Puaaiki as to their advancement in Christian knowledge and duty ; and during that period they had considered themselves as believers of the Gospel.   Kapiolani, who had been very intemperate, and for some time after hearing the Gospel lived with two husbands, had separated herself from her junior husband some two years before this period.

At this period we had at Honolulu, besides the common schools, a class of ten chiefs attending to rudimental instruction in reading, writing, singing, and composition.

On the 18th of February, a number of serious men putting off their heathen habits, and willing to be known as seekers of the great salvation, and as, in some sense, pledged to one another to abstain from immoralities and to follow the teachings of the Word of God, united in an association for prayer and improvement similar to that formed by the females a month earlier.   Among its earliest and leading members were Kalanimoku, Laanui, Kalaikoa, Kealiiahonui, Hoaai, Kupalu, and Kaomi, whose father was a resident Tahitian, John Ii, Kaaia, Punihaole, and others. These in uniting in the association, which was in advance of the Washingtonian society, gave to each other such an account of their views and of the manner in which they had been led to attend to the things that belonged to the soul's well being, as to afford indications that the Spirit of the Lord had begun to enlighten and influence their minds.   One of them came to me, professing to be daily striving against sin, and seeking deliverance from it through the blood of Christ.   He asked if it were right for his heart to be praying to God as he was walking along the road.   Being told that it was right to pray whenever we feel inclined to it, but that it was specially suitable to offer secret prayer, he said, " I know it is right to go away to a secret place, and there kneel down in the presence of God and pray to him, but I did not know it to be proper to pray along the road ; but as I was walking along, my heart wanted to be talking with God, and I was afraid, and have come to be instructed."   He seemed relieved to be told that it was proper to talk humbly with God while walking by the way, sitting in the house, or laboring in the field, as a means of comfort, of honoring God, avoiding temptation, and securing God's favor.   He proved at length to be, in our esteem, a consistent Christian.   A like spirit appeared at the other islands, and similar associations for prayer and improvement were established at the different stations, and were obviously attended with the divine blessing.

Hoapili and some of his coadjutors returning to Maui, and others who had quietly remained there during the late struggle, now manifested increasing religious interest.   Inquirers crowded around the missionaries morning, noon, and night.   The morning and evening sacrifice was offered by many.   Some looking for the new paths, inquired, " How shall we know what things are sinful? How shall we free ourselves from sin? How shall we escape the punishment due to our sins?"

Some very freely confessed their sins, under a sense of their vileness, and made known their confidence in the new religion. One who had been distinguished for opposition to the missionary cause, being apparently subdued after a sleepless night, said to the missionaries, "I have been exceedingly wicked. I have lied and stolen, been angry and quarrelsome, adulterous and murderous. I have been hostile to you; lied about you, and scoffed at your good words. I have led the young chief into evil; have sacrificed to our old gods, and done every kind of wickedness. I am exceedingly afraid, for God is angry with me." Another said, "I have washed my vessel nearly clean outside, but still filthy within—what shall I do?"

At this period, the blind Puaaiki was brought forward as a candidate for baptism. He had been for much of the first three years of the mission, one of the more attentive hearers of the Gospel at Honolulu. Being, at first, led by the hand of another to the place of worship, he at length, by frequency, became familiar with the way, came without his guide, and was usually seen early at his place, as near to the preacher's feet as he could well get, and lending as careful an ear as any in the congregation. His long beard, his miserable eyes, his diminutive stature, and almost naked limbs, and the ravages of sin in his whole being, made him, on our first acquaintance with him, a truly pitiable object. But though a vile and miserable heathen, the Gospel met his case, and the condescending Author of salvation regarded him with divine compassion. Having become interested in the subject of religion he removed to Lahaina, where, after a heathen sacrifice by some of the opposers of religion, Puaaiki distinguished himself by his firmness and devotedness in maintaining the truth.

At a meeting of the *poe pule*, praying people, he was called on to address the throne of grace. "His petitions," says Mr. Stewart, "were made with a pathos of feeling, a fervency of spirit, a fluency and propriety of diction, and above all, a humility of soul, that plainly told he was no *stranger there*. His bending posture, his clasped hands, his elevated but sightless countenance, the peculiar emphasis with which he uttered the exclamation, ' O *Iehova !*' his tenderness, his importunity, made us feel that he was praying to a God not afar off, but to one that was nigh."

Six months later, he gave still more decisive evidence of true conversion to God, and after a careful examination, he was propounded for admission to the church. His views as to the duty of uniting with the church, and of the nature of the eucharist, were not behind those of the reformers of the sixteenth century, particularly on the doctrine of transubstantiation, as the following unpremeditated questions and answers between him and Mr. Richards will show.

"Why do you ask to be admitted to the church?" "Because I love Jesus Christ, and I love you, and desire to dwell in the fold of Christ, and join with you in eating the holy bread and drinking the holy wine." "What is the holy bread?" "It is the body of Christ, which he gave to save sinners." "Do we then eat the body of Christ?" "No, but we eat the bread which represents his body; and as we eat bread that our bodies may not die, so our souls love Jesus Christ, and receive him for their Savior that they may not die." "What is the holy wine?" "It is the blood of Christ, which he poured out on Calvary, in the land of Judea, to save us sinners?" "Do we then drink the blood of Christ?" "No, but the wine represents his blood just as the holy bread represents his body, and all those who go to Christ and trust in him will have their sins washed away in his blood, and their souls saved for ever in heaven." "Why do you think it more suitable that you should join the church than others?" "Perhaps it is not. If it is not proper, you must tell me; but I do greatly desire to dwell with you in the fold of Christ." "Who do you think are proper persons to be received to the church?" "Those who have repented of their sins, and have obtained new hearts." "What is a new heart?" "One that loves God and loves the Word of God, and does not love sin or sinful ways."

After a further season of probation and instruction, he was baptized, and received the Christian name of *Batimea*, Bartimeus. A Tahitian woman, the wife of a Tahitian teacher, Taua, was received to the church at the same time.

The island of Hawaii, during the summer and autumn of 1824, appeared to experience little of the agitation that had been felt elsewhere from the death of Kaumualii, and the war at Kauai. The missionaries and their native helpers were moving steadily forward in the work. Kapiolani and Kamakau, and their coadjutors, Kuhio and Alapai, who, side by side with Kapiolani, had been instructed in the Gospel four years, gave indications of repentance and faith, though some considered them pharisaic. They did with much apparent regularity, and for a considerable period, the very things we should expect conscientious converts to do in like circumstances. But none of them had yet been baptized.

Kapiolani expressed great interest in the public worship of God, and sought relief from the worldliness that wearied and annoyed her, by going to the sanctuary, where she could hear about God and heaven and salvation by Christ, of which she said she was never tired. She desired and enjoyed spiritual conversation too, in social intercourse with the missionaries, wherever she had an opportunity to meet them at different stations.

She put on the costume of a Christian matron, and used chairs, tables, and "hospitality" in her habitation. Having a leading mind, an ardent heart, a portly person, black hair put up in a comb, a keen black eye, and an engaging countenance, Kapiolani, the daughter of King Keawemauhili, was a vice-queen in the district assigned to her and her husband. They patronized the missionary, encouraged schools, and discountenanced iniquity, even threatening a fine for drunkenness. Their house of worship was thronged, and attentive hearers listened to the Gospel, and some were heard to inquire, "What must I do to be saved?"

At the close of September in 1824, soon after the Kauai war, Naihe and Kapiolani made an excursion to Kau to spend a few months there, both for the purpose of collecting sandal wood and promoting the cause of instruction. As they were about to launch their canoes from Kaawaloa in the midst of a concourse of their people, at their desire, Mr. Ely led them in prayer, invoking the divine guidance and protection for these friendly chiefs and their company, and those who remained at the station.

After their return to Kaawaloa, the missionary zeal of Kapiolani became still more apparent, and she sought new opportunities to favor our work. The missionaries at Hilo suffering privations, and failing to be cheered on by the co-operation of the local authorities, who had not yet aspired after the blessings of civilization or Christianity, excited the sympathy not only of fellow-laborers, but of Kapiolani. She compassionated too those of her countrymen, who in their darkness still regarded with superstitious reverence the gods of the volcano, and other false deities. To trample on the pretended authority of such deities, as well as to encourage the missionaries, she made a journey of about a hundred miles, mostly on foot, by a rough, forbidding path, from Kealakekua to Hilo. The more effectually to break the spell which held many of the people in superstitious awe, in reference to the volcano, she proposed to visit (on her inland route) the great crater of Kilauea, the pretended residence of Pele, and to set at naught her *tabus*, and disturb her fires. She was strenuously opposed in this design. Some having apprehensions that she might bring into contempt the regard which they from their ancestors cherished for the honor of Pele, and others apprehending danger to her person, attempted to dissuade her from violating the long acknowledged *tabus* of the Hawaiian Vulcan. Even Naihe, not having his mind yet wholly freed from the shackles of superstition, was unwilling to do what she proposed to do, and felt an indefinable repugnance to her exposing herself thus. Reasoning as well as she could with her husband and others, whose sincere regard for her safety she did not doubt, she perseveringly pursued her course. In approaching the region of the volcano, she was met by a prophetess claiming authority from the veritable deity. This haughty female warned her not to approach the sacred dominions of Pele, and predicted her death through the fury of the god, should she make an invasion with the feelings of hostility and contempt which she professed. " Who are you?" demanded Kapiolani. " One in whom *ke akua* dwells," she replied. " If God dwells in you, then you are wise and can teach me. Come hither and sit down." After some urging she complied. Refreshments were kindly offered her; but in the haughtiness of her assumed dignity as a supernatural being, she said, " I am a god: I will not eat." She held in her hand a piece of bark cloth. " This," said she, " is a *palapala* from the god Pele." " Read it to us," said Kapiolani. She declined, though, like the magicians of Egypt, she was unwilling to appear less authorized than others to exercise her power and authority. But Kapiolani resolutely insisted on her proving that she had a book or writing from the god by reading it. The prophetess cunningly carrying out her device, and with unexpected presence of mind holding her cloth before her eyes, poured forth a torrent of unintelligible words or sounds which she would have them believe was in the dialect of the ancient Pele.

Kapiolani producing her Christian books, said to the impostor, " You pretend to have received and to deliver a message from your god, which none of us can comprehend ; I have a *palapala* as well as you, and will read you a message from our God which you can understand." She then read several passages, and called her attention to the character, works, and will of the great Jehovah, the true God, and to Jesus Christ as the Savior of the lost. The haughty prophetess quailed; her head drooped, and her garrulity ceased. She confessed that *ke akua* had left her, and she could not therefore reply. Thus this oracle was silenced, and the deluded and deluding prophetess at length joined in the repast. The conviction of Kapiolani that she ought to proceed was strengthened ; and true to her purpose, she went forward.

The missionaries at Hilo hearing that Kapiolani had set out to visit them, were desirous to meet her at the volcano, a distance of twenty-five or thirty miles from their station. Mr. Ruggles having been for six months destitute of shoes, was unable to go. Mr. Goodrich, who sometimes travelled barefoot, undertook the journey without him, and joined Kapiolani's travelling company at the site of that great wonder of the world. She was much affected on meeting there a missionary coadjutor. She and her company of about eighty, accompanied by Mr. G., descended from the rim of the crater to the black ledge. There, in full view of the terrific panorama before them, the effects of an agency often appalling, she calmly addressed the company thus : " Jehovah is my God. He kindled these fires. I fear not Pele. If I perish by the anger of Pele, then you may fear the power of Pele; but if I trust in Jehovah, and he shall save me from the wrath of Pele when I break through her *tabus*, then you must fear and serve the Lord Jehovah. All the gods of Hawaii are vain. Great is the goodness of Jehovah in sending missionaries to turn us from these vanities to the living God and the way of righteousness." Then, with the terrific bellowing and whizzing of the volcanic gases, they mingled their voices in a solemn hymn of praise to the true God; and at the instance of the chief, Alapai led them in prayer, while all bowed in adoration before Jehovah as the Creator and Governor of all things: and the God of heaven heard.

Here was a heroism of a more sublime and immortal character than that which rushes to the battle-field. Here was a philosophy which might put to the blush the pride of Pagan Athens and Rome, whose philosophers would risk nothing in suppressing idolatry, though they admitted its pretensions were unfounded. Here was a movement which in its character, and consequences to a nation, was not wholly unlike to that of the sublime preacher on Mars Hill, whose 'spirit was stirred in him when he saw the city wholly given to idolatry.'

After this transaction, so important in its bearing upon the remaining idolatry at the islands, the company proceeded and reached Waiakea the following day. On their arrival at the missionary station, Kapiolani's feet were much swollen and lamed with travelling in the long rough way; but she would not rest till she had secured lodging for her weary party, and united with them in evening worship. She told the missionaries she had come to strengthen their hearts and help them in their work. They rejoiced in the salutary influence which she exerted in favor of education and reform, an influence felt at once and happily continued when she had returned home. " Her whole conduct here," says Mr. Ruggles, " was calculated to recommend religion to all around. Not a person came into her presence without receiving her Christian counsel or reproof. She was ten days with us, which time she faithfully spent in going about doing good."

What visitor of the great Kilauea has ever gone there with a nobler object or to better purpose, than did this noble princess, Kapiolani, on her first becoming versed and established in the Christian doctrine? She, who in her infancy had been carried by her friends through this region as Keawemauhili, her father, and his party were flying from the arms of Keoua, towards Hamakua, now, in the infancy of our mission, becomes herself a host, tramples on their ancient Pele's power, succors the missionaries in their toil and privations, and urges forward her countrymen to the victory over ignorance, superstition, sin, Satan and his legions.

Our pupils on the different islands now amounted to thousands, and the number of learners was rapidly increasing. The demand for books and stationery was far greater than could possibly be supplied by the mission. Many of both sexes, and of every age, required instruction and aid. The business of supplying and teaching all who were willing to be instructed was far greater than many of the friends of the mission supposed. To rouse the minds of the unlettered, to excite them to inquire and study, to elevate, purify, and expand them speedily, by introducing and making familiar the ideas of the existence of God and of his attributes and works, of the relation we sustain to him, of the destiny of man, a boundless heaven of eternal glory, or a fathomless abyss of endless woe, and the wondrous provision for their escaping the latter and inheriting the former, were beyond computation important, while that ignorant and degraded generation was passing away like a flood. It was a matter of grief and amazement, that when the people were so ready to be instructed, there were so few to teach them, and so great a lack of stationery and printing and binding materials, and of funds to procure them.

Multitudes sought books and teachers whom we were obliged to deny. "Many are anxious to learn," said Mr. Whitney in respect to the people of Kauai, " but for want of books and teachers must for the present be denied that privilege." One school on Oahu was taught from a single copy of elementary lessons in spelling and reading. An interesting youth begged of me a book. "Who is your teacher?" I asked. To this, without naming any person, or waiving his claim for a book, replied, " My desire to learn, my ear to hear, my eye to see, my hands to handle ; from the sole of my foot to the crown of my head I love the *palapala*." Mr. Richards wrote me, " Our books are gone. Our scholars receiving regular instruction are embraced in fourteen schools. We could establish several more had we books. There are but two where the number of books equals half the number of scholars. There are some schools where there are not more than one book to three, four, or five persons." Messrs. Thurston, Bishop, and Ely, had the supervision of a field about two hundred miles in length, coastwise, concerning the wants of which, in this respect, Mr. Bishop wrote me as follows :—

" The general cry on this island is for books and teachers. From Waipio on the north, to Puna on the south-east, the cry comes up to us. Kamakau tells us he wants four thousand books to send to Kau, where Naihe and Kapiolani are sojourning. Gov. Adams wants a *kini*, forty thousand books for his and Kaahumanu's people. *But we have not one on hand !* Twenty schools we have supplied so that they are able to make a beginning. Not half the applications from distant places have we been able to answer. There are now schools in every district on this island except Puna, and even that is soon to receive a teacher. At Hilo, things are assuming a more favorable aspect, though the missionaries are destitute of the necessaries and comforts of life, and the means of supplying the people. The chiefs and head men willingly supply them with fish, vegetables, and pigs. Bread, tea, and coffee they have none."

Such were the pressing necessities of our wilderness for years of missionary struggling, after our press was started and after the chiefs fully welcomed our labors, and many thousands of the people were ready to receive books and teachers, while millions of Christians were living very much as though there had been no heathen nations to evangelize. "Why did you not let your wants be known in the United States," it is asked, "and why were they not met at once by the Board?" Neither we nor the Board were slow to make known the wants of the field, as monthly appeals of the "Herald," and the often-repeated calls of the missionaries, will testify. The following, addressed to our beloved Secretary, is but a brief specimen of our urgency for the means of supplying books and stationery.

"Do, sir, send us *stationery* as well as *bread :* we cannot live without. Suppose that one-fifth of the population shall in a few years be furnished with books and slates, with ability to use them, what an engine our press becomes for carrying on the improvement of the nation. Had we slates and books sufficient, the number of native teachers increases so fast, that I should not be surprised if in three years from this time, there should be twenty thousand natives who shall have begun to read and write. There can be no harm in expecting great results if we take suitable measures in order to secure or produce them."

With the very inadequate amount of means allowed us, more than the anticipated twenty thousand learners were brought under instruction within three years from the date of the application from which the above paragraph is extracted. Forty thousand dollars, besides the current expenses of the mission, would have given but a scanty supply to each of the poor islanders embraced in our schools. But instead of receiving that extra $40,000, at the time, we were told that the Board was $20,000 in debt, and it was possible that we might be thrown upon our own resources for support. Besides, had there been a balance of $40,000 in the treasury, that sum might have been more needed by some other portion of the heathen world. Ashamed and grieved, we were able to give but to a *few* learners, books of proper size, and the needful amount of stationery, or to the *many* a few cheap leaves or pages to get them started and over the main difficulty while they were disposed to begin. This must exonerate the mission for the smallness of the works put into their schools, during all the early years of their progress, before the Scriptures were so far translated as to invite and warrant appropriations from the American Bible and the American Tract Societies, whose generous and well-directed grants proved, at length, so grateful to the missionaries, and to tens of thousands of the people able to avail themselves of them.

But even when more liberal things were devised and executed for the Hawaiians, even then, five thousand children in India, under the patronage and Christian instruction of the same efficient Board, were dismissed and allowed again to wander on in heathenism, because adequate funds were not contributed by the churches to provide (at a trifling expense each) for their continued instruction. The missionary who sees and feels the need of help, must be excused by the sons and daughters of affluence, if he sometimes lifts up his voice like a trumpet, to call for the means of saving the perishing.

It is now time to recur again to the king and his company, who left the islands in the autumn of 1823, for a visit to England and America.   Embarking in an English whale-ship, they passed Cape Horn, and touched and spent a little time at Rio Janeiro. Passing on thence, they reached the coast of England and landed at Portsmouth.   Their unexpected arrival there awakened some curiosity; and they were soon conducted to London.   Their presence enlisted some interest for their distant country, which Captain Cook had had the honor to bring to the notice of the civilized world.   The party was placed in charge of the Hon. F. Byng; and quarters were courteously provided for them at the expense of the British government.   Their money was placed for safe keeping in the Bank of England.   They were boarded at the Adelphi, while waiting for a royal audience.   But before the expectations of Liholiho could be realized by an interview with George IV., or with his ministers of state, sickness and death invaded the party, and beclouded and blighted their highest hopes.

On the 13th of June, 1824, Liholiho was seized with the measles, which soon became alarming.   In a few days, all this Hawaiian party were affected with this epidemic, often so severe in the case of adults.   Their age, their previous habits, their change of climate and mode of living, all probably contributed to increase the virulence of the disease, which seemed most severe in the case of the young queen.   Able physicians were employed, and their remedies were promptly applied, not without material advantage.   Boki, Kekuanaoa, and most of the company recovered. But the king and queen were unable to sustain the shock.   By the morning of the 8th of July, the hope of the queen's recovery was abandoned.   With tenderness, and many tears, the royal pair took leave of each other.   In the evening of the same day, Kamamalu, who on her departure from Oahu had so impressively and poetically pledged herself not to forsake her husband or her father's charge, finished her course among strangers, far from " the object of her father's toil," and took leave of all the earth.

The king, in his weak state, was much affected by this bereavement, which he had little expected on leaving home.   His spirits were depressed, and he rapidly declined.   The best medical skill failed.   When he saw his own case was hopeless, he said to Boki, " This is my death in the time of my youth; great love to my country."   This occurred between the time of the death of Kaumualii and the insurrection of Kauai.

To the great grief of the surviving company, he died, in the midst of his days, and before the half of his " five years," which he had required to accomplish a thorough reformation in himself, had passed away.   Thus ended his short reign of five years and two months, during which idolatry had been abolished in his country and Christianity introduced.

The bodies of both were deposited in triple coffins, one of which was of lead, with a view to their being conveyed back to their own country.

Boki and his party received sympathy and kindness from the nobility, and had opportunities of witnessing the demonstrations of the wealth and power, the civilization and Christianity of England. George IV., in an audience granted them at Windsor Castle, received them with courtesy, counselled them to respect the missionaries, and encouraged them to regulate their own affairs, and to expect his protection, should any power attempt to dispossess them, or do them injustice.*

The honorable Mr. Canning being requested by Boki to give him a code of laws for the islands, modestly replied, that the chiefs of the islands could frame their own laws better than he.

Lord Byron, the cousin and successor of the poet, and a very different man, commanding H. B. M. Frigate Blonde, was commissioned by his majesty to convey the bodies of the king and queen and the survivors of their suite back to their country. He embarked with them from Portsmouth, September 28th, 1824. On their way they touched at St. Catherine's, and (after passing Cape Horn) at Valparaiso, where another of the party, Naihekukui, the father-in-law of the present sovereign, finished his course.

The news of the king's death reached Honolulu March 9th, by the American whale-ship Almira, and great solicitude was felt as to the effect on the nation. It is not difficult to see that the death of the king and queen, in England, might have had the effect to prejudice the nation against the religion of Great Britian, and against the measures of Liholiho, in the abrogation of the public rites of their old religion. But in the wise orderings of a holy Providence, time had been afforded, and the means employed, to enlist the leaders of the nation strongly in favor of Christianity.

The missionaries labored assiduously to infix in the minds of the rulers and people, on this occasion, those controlling thoughts of the divine government which were cherished by patriarchs and prophets. " The Lord reigns. The Lord gave; the Lord hath taken away, and blessed be the name of the Lord. Jehovah is our Lawgiver, Jehovah is our King—He will save us." Such thoughts were pressed upon their attention, not in vain.

The important intelligence received at Honolulu, Kalanimoku communicated by letter to Kaahumanu, who, with other chiefs,

---

* Testimony of the present governor of Oahu—" This is what we heard of the charge of King George—' Return to Kauikeaouli and tell him that *I will protect his country.* To any evil from abroad I will attend; but the evils within the country are not *my* concern, but the evils from without.'"

[Signed] MATAIO KEKUANAOA.

was then at Manoa, a retired and picturesque valley between the mountains, in the rear of Waikiki, and about five miles north-east of Honolulu. The queen, in her answer, discreetly encouraged him to commit it all to the Lord, and to pray that his mercy might be manifested. At both places divine service was held the same day. At the close of my sermon at Honolulu, Kalanimoku made the proposition that for twelve days successively, the prayer of contrition should be offered to God, morning and evening, that he might pardon and save the nation.

The chiefs returned from Manoa, and Kaahumanu and Kalanimoku wrote and sent letters to the other islands, with kind salutations to the chiefs, missionaries, and people, apprising them of the death of the king and queen, proposing a season of humiliation and prayer on that account; exhorting them to seek consolation in the good Word of God, and to obey its commands, enjoining on the chiefs to keep the people quiet, and to remain at their posts till they should be sent for.

Namahana and Mr. Chamberlain embarked on the 11th with the despatches for Maui and Hawaii. At the close of that day, I attended evening prayers with the young prince, and also with Kalanimoku; the latter I found pleasantly and diligently teaching a number of chiefs, who sat around his table, some passages of Scripture which we had furnished him in manuscript. Notwithstanding the special efforts of the high chiefs and the general influence of the Gospel on a portion of the community, there was manifested, at some places, a disposition to give a loose to the vile passions as in the darker days of the nation. At Hilo, old enormities were attempted, and were shamelessly encouraged even by a white heathen residing in the country, who preferred the pollutions of Hawaiian customs to the pure precepts of the Gospel. The Blonde, approaching the island, passed not very far from the district of Hilo; and some fishermen went in their canoes near enough to her to see some of the native party from England, and, hastening to the shore, reported to the multitude that the chiefs were alive. The inference was made that Mr. Ruggles, who, having received the intelligence by a whale ship, had, affirmed that the king and queen were dead, had attempted to deceive them, and they therefore abused and threatened him; and for once during his residence at the island, he felt that his life was in danger from the madness of the natives. Unable to appease them, he made his way to Maalo, the head-man, and besought him, that before he should be punished or condemned, a canoe might be sent off to the frigate to ascertain the state of facts. Maalo, somewhat excited like the rest, said he would go himself, and set off, leaving Mr. R. to be looked after by the people. He soon ascertained that the report of Mr. R. was but too true. The multitude were quieted down to attend to Christian counsel on the occasion, and thenceforward the head-man

and his people put far more confidence in the word of a missionary than before.

The wisdom and sobriety of the principal chiefs was the more
noticeable, for instead of resorting to sorcery to destroy the destroyer, or multiply human sacrifices; instead of giving themselves up to the vilest abominations, or of rushing to arms to see
who among rival chiefs should have the sovereignty; the rulers
not only acknowledged the Lord's hand in prayer, but forcibly
called upon the people peacefully and submissively to bow to this
dispensation of Providence, and to offer with contrite heart their
daily prayer for his blessing, than which nothing could have been
better calculated to keep their thoughts from pollution and blood,
and their hands from violence and war. Their counsel was
generally received in a quiet and orderly manner.

During the interval between the announcement of the death of
the king and queen and the return of the survivors, Richard
Charlton, Esq., H. B. M. consul-general for the Society and
Sandwich Islands, arrived at Honolulu with his wife and her
sister. Coming as a public professor of the Christian religion,
a communicant at the Lord's table in England, and being
recommended to the authorities as "highly esteemed" by his
government, he was welcomed kindly, and for a time *expected* at
least to befriend the nation in the work of reform which had
already been successfully begun by the mission. He was certainly allowed the *opportunity* to perform important services for
his own country, for the Hawaiian nation, and for the cause of
temperance and morality.

The Blonde approached Lahaina May 4th, and being becalmed
sent in a boat with Gov. Boki, his wife, and others. Hoapili
took his seat on the beach to receive them. The report spreading rapidly, "It is *Boki*," thousands collected around, and some
began to wail. As the party landed and approached Hoapili, a
passage was opened for them through the crowd, and as they
made their way through it, he rose from his chair, threw back his
head, and with a *roar* above the ordinary compass of the human
voice, spread out his arms to embrace his daughter, Madam Boki.
The chiefs responded to the wail of Hoapili. The great multitude lifted up their thousand voices so as to drown the roar of the
surf. The young princess, however, embraced Madam Boki with
silent tears as she sat down upon the sand. Hoapili fell with his
face in the dust, and others followed his example, and chafed
their faces on the sand. This may illustrate the deepest form of
oriental prostration, with the mouth or forehead touching the
ground, as expressive of grief, or guilt, or helplessness. After a
little time, Boki said, "Where shall we pray?" A convenient
place was chosen, the loud crying subsided, and Mr. Richards
led them in prayer. After this, Boki and his wife spoke in strong
terms of the good things they had seen, and the kindness they
had received among their English friends.

The following day, Lord Byron landed, and gladdened the chiefs and the missionaries by manifesting a liberal and gentlemanly regard to the welfare of the nation, and the interests of the mission.

The company soon re-embarking for Oahu, the Blonde appeared off Diamond Point May 6th, at sunrise, and came to anchor at nine, near the entrance of the harbor of Honolulu, and fired a salute of fourteen guns, which was promptly answered by a similar number from the Honolulu fort and Punchbowl Hill battery. At half-past ten, the well-manned barges of the frigate were sent in with the Hawaiian party. To meet them, Mr. Stewart, Mr. Chamberlain, Mr. Loomis, and myself, proceeded to the wharf whence they had embarked in the autumn of 1823. Kaahumanu, her sisters, the younger queens, and others, in black dresses, assembled near the landing to receive them, and forming a line, advanced a little, and as soon as they could recognize their surviving friends, began to weep. As the passengers rose to step from the barge to the low quay on which we stood, I took the hand of Madam Boki, and the commander of the fort, in his uniform, the hand of Gov. Boki, bidding them welcome. Kekuanaoa and Manuia, and others following, formed a line, and advanced very slowly towards the chiefs. Boki lifted up his hands and eyes towards heaven, and wept aloud. Both parties approached within a few yards of each other, and gave signs of extreme grief; and as if the scenes in the death chamber of the late king and queen and of Kaumualii and the insurrection were rushing together on the attention of both parties, and overwhelming their hearts, they lifted up their voices and wept aloud. They were joined by the multitude at a little distance, while the earth around them was shaken by the heavy minute guns over their heads. Particular friends now meeting after a separation of eighteen eventful months, embraced and kissed each other in a profusion of tears. They were then seated at the house of Kaahumanu: the principal events which had affected them during the separation were briefly touched, and they repaired to the chapel to acknowledge God in his dispensations towards them and the nation. Kalanimoku, at his own house, received his brother Boki silently but cordially, and, though his health was then infirm, accompanied him to the public altar. The church was filled to overflowing. We united in a song of praise, the reading of the Scriptures, and a prayer. Then, in anticipation of what we believed the Lord, who had brought them thus far, was about to do for the nation, we sang the translation of the spirited ode, " Wake, isles of the south," adapted to Hawaiian use.

This was a happy moment for Boki to make his report on the question most immediately connected with our business, or the trustworthiness of Christianity. In a short address he expressed his conviction of the truth of the Christian religion, and recommended attention to the *palapala* and the service of God. In a more free conversation in the evening, he said the " King of Beritania," with whom he was honored to have a personal interview, after the death of the king and queen, told him to give good attention to the missionaries at the islands, for they were sent to enlighten them and do them good, and make them acquainted with the good Word of God. Direct testimony in favor of the cause of Christianity and of our mission from authority, in their esteem, so high, whatever influence it had or failed to have on the heart of Boki himself, was doubtless of importance to individuals who, for several years, had wished to know what " *Kini Georgi* " would say about it.

The early part of the ensuing day, Lord Byron and the officers and scientific gentlemen of the frigate landed under a salute, and, moving in a cheerful and brilliant procession, repaired to the Hawaiian house of Kalanimoku, where the chiefs were assembled to receive them. The procession was headed by Lord Byron in the uniform of his rank, having Mr. Charlton in his consular costume on the one hand, and Gov. Boki, in a military dress, on the other, and included Frederick Beauclerc, a young son of the Duke of St. Alban's ; the Hon. Mr. Talbot, a son of the Earl of Talbot ; the Hon. Mr. Keith, a son of Lord Keith ; Mr. Gambier, a nephew of Admiral Gambier ; the Rev. Mr. Bloxom, chaplain ; and Mr. Andrew Bloxom, mineralogist ; Mr. Davis, surgeon ; Mr. McRea, botanist ; Mr. Malden, surveyor ; Mr. Dampier, artist ; and Mr. Wilson, purser, and others.

The chiefs were seated in the place of audience—a recently built house of but one apartment, fifty feet by twenty-five, neatly thatched and carpeted with new and handsome mats spread on the ground. At the end opposite the principal entrance, on a raised platform of mats, the upper one being fine and handsomely figured, sat the young prince and princess upon a Chinese sofa, behind which stood four lofty and superb state *kahilis*—the ancient standards and insignia of rank. On their right Kaahumanu and other queens and honorable women were seated along the side of the room ; on their left, in like manner, the chiefs and honorables. A little in front, and near the centre of this line, sat Kalanimoku with his interpreters and Christian teachers. All were dressed in European fashion. Kalanimoku wore on the occasion a loose gown of black silk, well becoming his age and infirmities. The young princess had partly wrapped round her waist, above her black silk dress, a splendid yellow feather *pau*, or robe, nine yards in length and one in breadth, manufactured with skill and taste, at great expense, and designed for her anticipated reception of her brother Liholiho. In its fabrication, the small bright feathers were ingeniously fastened upon a fine netting, spun without wheels or spindles, and wrought by native hands, from the flaxen bark of their *olona*, and the whole being lined with crimson satin made a beautiful article of " costly array," for a princess of eight years.

With the exception of Kauikeaouli and his sister, all rose respectfully as Lord Byron and his suite entered. The strangers were presented severally to Kalanimoku, Kaahumanu, the prince and princess, Adams, Naihe, Hoapili, and others. Lord Byron then delivered from the King of England to Kalanimoku, a small wax figure of Liholiho, and a gold hunting watch with the royal arms on one side, and his name on the other; and to Kaahumanu, an elegant, highly finished, silver teapot, with her name and the arms of Britain engraved. In presenting this, his lordship courteously hinted that he hoped to receive a cup of tea from it through her hands. To the young prince, in like manner, he presented a rich suit of royal Windsor uniform, with splendid decorations, sword, epaulets, and military hat. At his suggestion, the young prince, not yet ten years old, put on his unaccustomed princely array, coat, sword, and hat, when his lordship playfully presented him to the queen-regent and the prime minister, expressing his desire that he might attend well to the instructions of the missionaries, and become a wise and good king.

The chiefs expressed their pleasure and gratitude, occasioned not only by these tokens of royal favor from Britain's sovereign, but the gratifying manner in which they had been presented, and more especially for the distinguished service and honor his lordship had shown them, from his country, in the noble errand for which, chiefly, he had come to the islands. Kalanimoku said to him, " I am made very happy by your coming to this country and by your kindness towards us." His lordship promptly replied, "I am very happy to have this service to perform for my king and country, and only desire to show kindness to you and your nation."

The dignified courteousness of Lord Byron, and the civility and Christian sobriety of Kaahumanu and Kalanimoku, reflected honor on the countries which they represented, and made a happy impression on the beholders. After a little conversation, the spontaneous, humble, and conscientious proposal of Kalanimoku to acknowledge God in prayer on the occasion, took us all by surprise, but commended itself at once to our consciences. One of the missionaries,being called on, led in this exercise, using in the former part the English language, and in the latter the Hawaiian, and they united in thanksgiving for Divine mercies, and in supplications and ascriptions of praise to Him who ruleth in the kingdoms of men, and doeth his pleasure in the armies of Heaven.

Respectable refreshments were then offered and received, and with general congratulations this Christian levee closed. Lord Byron commending what appeared to him to have been achieved by the missionaries in elevating the people, and learning that some members of their families were ill, generously proffered the aid and recommended the skill of his surgeon, Dr. Davis.

The chiefs of Hawaii having been sent for, came to Honolulu on the occasion of the restoration of the remains of their friends.

After their arrival, the bodies of the king and queen, being enclosed in triple coffins of lead, oak, and mahogany, which were covered with crimson velvet and richly ornamented, were removed from the Blonde, landed, and delivered to the government, amid the loud roar of minute guns.

After the barges, conveying them from the ship, reached the wharf, whence the royal pair had embarked, in 1823, the bodies were placed and borne upon two strong hearses, each drawn by a competent number of men of rank.   A procession attended them, first to the door of the church, then to the temporary mausoleum, in the following order : First, twenty men, bearing superb state *kahilis* or feathered standards, twenty to twenty-five feet in height or length, black, green, red, and yellow.   About one third of the length of the rod is set with hundreds of little stems or artificial branches radiating in every direction from the rod. These stems, branching into several divisions, have their extremities ingeniously set with tufts of short bright feathers equidistant from the rod, assuming a cylindrical form from twenty to twenty-eight inches in diameter.   Some of the rods were ornamented with bone and ivory, and multitudinous tortoise-shell rings, and the whole were very imposing.   These were followed by the marines of the Blonde, in their uniform, with arms reversed, the band playing a plaintive march ; the gentlemen of the mission, with the chaplain and surgeon of the Blonde, then the honored remains of the late king and queen, followed by the mourners, two abreast, according to rank or relationship.   Kauikeaouli, in his uniform, with crape on his arm and sword hilt, and Nahienaena, in full black, the former supported by the British consul, and the latter by Lord Byron ; then, each supported by an officer of the Blonde, Kaahumanu and Kalakua, Adams and Boki, Hoapili and Namahana.   Then followed the chiefs, male and female, of inferior rank, and many others.

The procession moved slowly on between two lines of native soldiers, and crowds of the people who thronged around.   The solemn pageant halted at the door of the sanctuary.   A few passages from the burial service were read by the chaplain in English, and a short address made in Hawaiian by a missionary.   The procession turning its course, and again moving as before, the bodies were conveyed to the thatched house of Kalanimoku.   This, but recently, had been the hall of audience, but now, arched and lined with black *kapa*, it was prepared as a temporary repository. Here the old chieftain, Kalanimoku, who called them his children, was waiting to receive them.   Halting at the door the marines rested on their arms reversed, and the bodies, being carried in, were placed upon firm platforms.   A funeral hymn closed the mournful service.   The government soon erected a more permanent but very simple mausoleum of stone, about twenty-four feet square, in which they were finally deposited with funeral solemnity.

What a lesson to the nation !   How impressively did divine wisdom show the vanity of the mirth and wine, the pomp and pride, the distinction and power, of which these departed ones, for a brief period, could once boast; and how strikingly did the hand of God stamp transitoriness on things earthly, even the most coveted and valued, in order to call the attention of the thoughtless sons and daughters of Hawaii more strongly to the things that are heavenly! How forcibly did he say to the nation, " Put not your trust in princes, but in the living God." His powerful Word, his wonderful Providence, and his almighty grace which had begun to command and control the passions and affections of these once raging heathen, laid the foundation of our hopes of peace and prosperity to the nation; and while some of them regarded Liholiho as having forfeited or thrown away his life by making his own pleasure and not the will of God his rule, there was some danger that the noise and display made over his dust, would dissipate or exclude sober thought.   But it was a matter of gratitude that the splendor and parade, the martial music and display, and the long repeated reverberations of the minute guns during much of the day, produced no apparent diminution of attention to the humble duties of the Gospel among those who had welcomed its invitations. The boldest appeals, the most searching and sin-condemning doctrines, were deemed suitable to the pulpit. The path by which such transgressors were to find the heavenly rest, was represented as narrow and straight, leading through great self-denial and many difficulties, requiring vigilance and perseverance, the renunciation or abandonment of much of what is valued by the world but is unfavorable to the interests of the soul; yet numbers of the rulers and people professed a willingness to tread that way. More than a hundred at Honolulu station offered themselves as candidates for baptism. Amongst these, Kaahumanu, Kalanimoku, Kalkua, Namahana, Laanui, Kapiolani, Kapule, Kaiu, Kealiiahonui, and Richard Kalaaiaulu, in the early part of June, while the chiefs and missionaries were generally assembled at Honolulu, being permitted, came before the congregation and the only organized church then in the island, and made a statement of their religious views, and their desire to join themselves to the Lord's people, and to walk in his covenant. They had chiefly been five years under the inspection and instruction of the missionaries, who had seen them in their heathen pollution and wretchedness; and they now represented their new feelings and views, their repentance for sin, their love to God, their reliance on Christ, their satisfaction in prayer, their desire to forsake the ways of iniquity and death, and to obey the Gospel as subsequent to the insurrection in Kauai, in Aug., 1824, and as having been established about the close of that year and the beginning of 1825.

Though all of these had, for several months at least, given much evidence of conversion, we still hesitated to baptize them, until as candidates they were set before the church and the world for the trial of a few months more, under watchful missionary care and instruction. I had been by no means willing to baptize Kaa-humanu as the wife of her late husband's son, because the Word of God appears so positively to forbid a man to have his father's wife; and Paul would not allow such a relation to exist in a church under his supervision. The queen herself and Kealiiaho-nui had come to the conclusion that their attachment to each other should not stand in the way of their consistent profession of the Christian faith, and chose to be separated. He afterwards married another, but she continued single through life.

In administering the ordinances, the missionaries have found little embarrassment from the previously existing heathen cus-toms. The chiefs and others had been chargeable with covet-ousness, extortion, oppression, idolatry, drunkenness, adultery, incest, and manslaughter. " And such were some of you," said the apostle to the Christians of his time ; " but ye are washed— ye are sanctified—old things are done away." Believing that *conversion* brings the subjects of it not only to worship God in truth, and to love his law, but makes those kind and liberal-hearted who were before naturally and habitually covetous, and enlists oppressors in the noble business of seeking the best good of their dependants, and promotes equity in judges and rulers, and true loyalty in subjects, I was slow to invite to the Lord's table those whose lives furnished no evidence of this sort that they had been born from above. At the same time I did not suppose any new tests of character, unknown to the sacred writers, ought to be set up in administering the affairs of a church gathered among the sons and daughters of Paganism. We found little difficulty from the cases of oppression, intemperance, idolatry, covetousness, polygamy, and incest, which had existed in the nation ; for when the plain " thus saith the Lord" could be shown as to what was essen-tial to Christ's welcoming a disciple to his table, if the candidate demurred or took exception, it was regarded as evidence of dis-qualification for baptism into the sacred name of the triune God. This indicates the general course of the mission in guarding the doors of the sanctuary, which may, perhaps, have assumed too much the character of the defensive, while with our voice we loudly reiterated, day after day—" Come ; for all things are ready—Enter; for yet there is room."

The numbers of the natives, both men and women, who desired admission to the church, multiplied, and some were formed into classes which met weekly, on Thursday, for prayer, inquiry, and instruction, and from which candidates were, from time to time, selected, propounded, and received to fellowship.

On the 6th of June the assembled chiefs of the nation held a council at which Lord Byron, Mr. Charlton, and the missionaries were present. Acknowledging the authority of the Christian re-ligion, this council endeavored to avoid the errors of their late king and pursue a wiser and safer course. He had, in his short reign, attempted to establish the right of dethroning Hawaiian deities, demolishing their tabus, legalizing drunkenness, polygamy, adultery, and incest, and of dispossessing the natural heirs of deceased land-holders : and, at the same time, he singularly authorized the introduction of a system of religion that inculcates equity, temperance, chastity, benevolence, and the love and service of God, to which his heart was averse. Kaahumanu, as regent, had begun to introduce a happier policy, in which she was sustained by the highest chiefs.

Hereditary claims she acknowledged, and wished them to be confirmed. As to the restraining of crime she was decided. Kapiolani stated in terms of gratulation the success of herself and husband in their efforts to prevent murder, infanticide, theft, Sabbath desecration, drunkenness, and licentiousness. The regent commended her for it, and called on the other chiefs to do the same. Kuakini adverted to the errors of Liholiho, and urged the importance of guarding the young prince, Kauikeaouli, from the distracting and contaminating influences which had been disastrous to his predecessor. He proposed that the lad, about nine years old, should be under the regular instruction of the missionaries, and be trained for active life, that he might shun the errors of his departed brother. In this there was a general concurrence. It was expected, of course, should he live to be competent, he would assume the cares of government, though now incapable of bearing rule, and though his heirship to the sovereignty was readily acknowledged.

This council, being conducted in an amicable and Christian manner, unlike the councils of heathenism and infidelity, bowed before the God of heaven and earth, acknowledging his smiles and rich gifts, and imploring his blessing on the efforts made to promote order, learning, religion, and prosperity in the realm. Here the Hawaiian people begin to assume before the kingdoms of the world the character of a Christian nation.

The chiefs being determined to encourage the missionary cause, and wishing to know whether their efforts were to be hindered or thwarted by British officials, the opinion of Lord Byron was asked in reference to the continuance of the American missionaries. He claimed no right to decide our cause, but still wished to know our object and relations. I stated, on behalf of the mission, that we were not employed by the United States' Government, and that the instructions from the American Board of Commissioners to us as Christian Missionaries, forbade our *interfering* with the civil and political affairs of the nation. He then expressed his approbation of our continuing our labors which he had already commended. Had he indulged the prejudice of some of his successors who conferred neither honor nor favor on the nation, his wishes, opinions, or objections, might have done us much harm; whereas, in this case, he forestalled the effects of the opposition of inferior men, who attempted to retard or bring into reproach the missionary cause.

Lord Byron put into the hands of the chiefs a paper in English, without date or signature, containing several hints on the principles of government, which he wished them to consider at their leisure, and which has sometimes been referred to as Lord Byron's advice, as follows ;—

" 1. That the king is the head of the people.

2. That the chiefs should swear allegiance to the king.

3. That the lands which belong to the chiefs shall not be taken from them, but descend to their legitimate children, except in cases of rebellion, in which case all their poperty shall go to the king.

4. That the chiefs shall let out their lands to the people to cultivate, that they may maintain themselves out of that cultivation, but under the chiefs' authority.

5. That a tax shall be paid to the king.

6. That a port duty shall be laid on all foreign vessels

7. That no man's life shall be forfeited but by the consent of the king in council with twelve chiefs, or the regent in time being for the king.

8. That the king or regency grant [have power to grant ?] pardon at all times.

9. That the people shall be free and not bound to one chief."

The gratuitous efforts of foreign functionaries some twenty years later, to introduce the trial of aliens, accused of crime, by a *jury of aliens*, proceeded on a principle different from that recommended by Lord Byron, or by any public officer friendly to the permanent independence of the nation. He supposed the king or regent, and twelve respectable natives of rank, were to be the proper judges in cases of the highest crimes in their dominions. Thus the integrity of the sovereignty would be unimpaired.

Great Britain, in sending out the Blonde with the bodies of the king and his consort, with their survivors, under the command of a friendly and high-minded nobleman, and, at the same time, avoiding all interference with the sovereignty or the laws of the land, conferred a high honor on the Hawaiian nation, adapted to promote their self-respect on the one hand, and their friendship and confidence towards the British government on the other.

Towards evening, the chiefs, the young prince, the missionaries, and numbers of the people, repaired to the church, and uniting in the monthly concert, offered up special prayer not only for the conversion of the world, but for the king, that he might greatly subserve the cause of Christianity in his country, and that he and the people might engage in the service, and long enjoy the favor, of the King of nations. They were appropriately addressed by Mr. Bishop, of Kailua, on the desired universal dominion of Christ, according to the prophecy, " All kings shall fall down before him, all nations shall serve him."

Lord Byron, with his scientific corps, visited Hilo, the great crater of Kilauea, and Kealakahua Bay, and caused accurate surveys to be made of Waikiki Bay, Honolulu harbor, and Hilo Bay, which has since been often called Byron's Bay. Through his kindness, Kaahumanu, Mr. and Mrs. Stewart, and Mr. Goodrich, took passage in the Blonde, from Honolulu to Hilo; Mr. G. to resume his labors there, Mr. and Mrs. S. as an experiment, under the care of Dr. Davis, of the Blonde, to resuscitate her feeble health, and Kaahumanu to encourage the missionary labors of the station. On landing, Kaahumanu sent for Mr. Ruggles to come to her. He declined. He thought her imperious and heathenish, and himself free. He would not believe that she was a disciple. She had nowhere been recognized by baptism as a Christian, and he remembered her interference with the rights of Kaumualii and Kapule, his particular friends. She sent again and entreated him. He called on her, and found he had misjudged the case. She met him in tears, threw her arms around his neck, and assured him, not only of her friendship, but of her submission to Christ, and her determination to support his cause according to her ability. She engaged heartily in promoting attention to schools and religion at that place, and acquired among the people the expressive and appropriate title, " Kaahumanu *hou*," *new* Kaahumanu. Thus unwittingly they gave a commentary on the declaration, " Old things are passed away, and behold all things are become new." The missionaries were glad to welcome her as a coadjutor, and bid her God speed.

Before leaving the islands, Lord Byron set up a memorial of Capt. Cook, almost half a century from the time of his death. On the hill of ancient lava, at the head of Kealakekua Bay, and one hundred and fifty rods from the place where that navigator fell, and near where he was dissected, he erected, on a heap of rough, volcanic stones, a small shaft, or pillar of wood, with a small plate attached, bearing the following modest and respectful inscription :—

·" IN MEMORY

OF

CAPTAIN JAMES COOK, R. N.,

WHO DISCOVERED THESE ISLANDS

IN

THE YEAR OF OUR LORD

1778,

THIS HUMBLE MONUMENT IS ERECTED BY

HIS FELLOW COUNTRYMEN, IN

THE YEAR OF OUR LORD,

1825.

Before the close of the year, the congregations at the different stations were greatly enlarged. That at Honolulu amounted to about 3000. For their accommodation Kaahumanu and Kalanimoku, availing themselves of our suggestions, conceived the design of erecting a large and permanent stone church, and began to make preparations for it : but the pecuniary embarrassment of the nation, the want of skill and efficiency then among the people, and the decline of Kalanimoku's health, prevented their accomplishing this work, and a much larger, but frail and temporary house of worship was substituted *pro tempore*.   Before this was completed, the large congregation worshipped and heard the Gospel for a time, in the open air, between the house of Kalanimoku and the tomb of the royal family.

Some 16,000 spelling books or elementary lessons, were printed, and put to use, from March to October, among as many learners, and several thousand copies of a catechism, exhibiting, in a plain and brief manner, the prominent doctrines of the Bible. These were readily received and read, and in many instances, soon committed to memory, together with a small tract of select texts of Scripture, which had been used as themes of sermons, to which hundreds and thousands of the people had listened.

All our stations greatly needed reinforcing. Mr. Whitney was left with the care of Kauai and Niihau; Mr. Ely with Kaawaloa and Kau; Messrs. Thurston and Bishop with Kailua and the northern third of Hawaii; and before the year closed, Mr. Goodrich was left with the care of Hilo and Puna; and Mr. Richards with Maui, Molokai, Lanai, and Kahoolawe. Many desired teachers who could not obtain them. From the dark island of Molokai, several men passed over the channel and came to Lahaina, saying, " What shall we blind people do ? We have heard that there is a great light in Lahaina, that will shine when the body is dead. We have hoped that it would shine on Molokai. But all is dark there yet. We have come hither to find that by which our souls may be saved ; for we hear there is a great and good Savior. But where is he ?"   Did not the same power incline these men to inquire after the true Savior, which led the sages of the East to ask," Where is he that is born King of the Jews ?"

From Hilo, Mr. Goodrich wrote to the American Board, Nov. 11th, 1825.

" The state of things at this station is very interesting. The house of public worship will not contain half that assemble to hear the Word of Life.   The chiefs have lately begun to build a new meeting-house of much larger dimensions.   Schools are rapidly increasing in all the eastern half of this island, and all that seems to be wanting is books and teachers.   I am unable to supply one twentieth part of the calls for books.   Some have already left the school, commenced by us about ten months since, and have gone out to teach others ; and many other teachers are immediately wanted.   I have taken eight or ten persons from different lands, to educate for teachers, who, finding their own food, are no expense to the mission. A wide field of usefulness is open here, on either hand.   Nearly thirty thousand souls have open ears to hear the Gospel.   Must they be left to perish because American

Christians have exhausted their charities? Cannot the churches of my dear native land afford to send out one to take part with me in this ministry of reconciliation? We do earnestly long to have some one associated with us, with whom we may take sweet counsel, and who may aid in proclaiming the good news of salvation by Jesus Christ. We find it quite trying to be left alone, so far from all our brethren; and yet we cannot think of leaving our schools and the crowded house of worship on the Sabbath. I hope that the time is not far distant when the good people of America will feel able to support another laborer in this whitening field. Honolii I find to be a valuable assistant; he continues to do well."

Every four thousand of the whole population of the Sandwich Islands specially needed at that time the labor and influence of a foreign preacher and schoolmaster and their wives, and of at least a score of native teachers as far advanced as Hopu and Honolii.

But our small number was diminished rather than increased. The entire prostration of Mrs. Stewart's health appeared, in the estimation of the mission, after consulting three medical men, to justify her removal to the United States. Dr. Blatchely, the missionary physician, was very decided, not only in the opinion that she ought to be removed, but that they ought to improve the offer of a gratuitous passage to England made by Capt. Dale, of the Fawn, availing themselves of the medical advice of Dr. Short, the surgeon of that homeward bound ship. Notwithstanding the field greatly needed all the talents and warm-hearted agency which, in circumstances of health, Mr. S. was so well able to apply to it, as a laborer just fairly initiated into the missionary work, and all the influence of his conciliatory manners and courteousness to disarm opposition; and though it is no easy thing for a laborer who has put his hand to the plough to leave the field without loss of salutary influence, or to satisfy the friends of missions, that the removal of a missionary from his peculiar sphere of action is necessary, or, on the whole, best; still, the mission consented to Mr. Stewart's return, with the hope of receiving him again in due time.

There appeared to be a prospect more fair for the recovery of Mrs. Stewart's health than of Mrs. Ellis's. Both Mr. Ellis and Mr. Stewart were desirous to devote themselves still to the missionary work, wherever their directors might deem it best to employ them: and both rendered important aid to the cause of the mission, after their return, in securing for it a friendly interest and a liberal patronage.

We were called to a reluctant parting with Mr. and Mrs. Stewart, on the 17th of October, 1825, after their residence of two years and a half at the islands. Several of the females of our mission suffered materially from debility, which was attributable in part to the climate of a perpetual summer, whose temperature in the shade by day averages 75° through the year, and in part to their solicitude for the success of our enterprise, and in part to the privations and unaccustomed modes of living and hardships to which, in straitened circumstances, they were subjected. Mrs. Stewart was so feeble that she was carried in the arms to take her last leave of Mrs. Bingham, who was equally feeble, and whose remaining course, it was then apprehended, would be sooner finished than that of Mrs. S. After the early death of our little J. Evarts, an engaging child of sixteen months, who, after a variety of suffering, was seized with croup, Mrs. B. was brought low, at a period when the demand for the strength of all the laborers was so great as to render inability to labor a peculiar trial. She was for weeks confined to her couch with alarming symtoms of a broken constitution; but the kind arm that has been so often stretched out in mercy to our mission, raised her up again, and allowed her still to have a part with her husband and others in winning the nation to Christ, and in breasting the opposition for a long time waged by unreasonable men.

Mr. Stewart, leaving his family at Honolulu, made a hasty excursion to Lahaina to take leave of his associates and his friends among the chiefs and people at the station, where he had felt himself privileged to labor. Scarcely had he embarked for this farewell visit, when the following brief account of the new demonstrations of hostility at Lahaina was received at Honolulu :

" DEAR BRO. B.,—We are yet alive, although an hour ago I had little hope of anything but immediate death. Our house was surrounded by about twenty English sailors, armed with knivès. We had but few men in the yard with us, and they unarmed. The chiefs refuse to guard us by arms, and the men, about forty in number, from the ship Daniel, appear bent on having our lives, or our consent to females going on board their ship. I need not tell you which we choose. Now there are between forty and fifty persons in our house, and as many more without; but six resolute foreigners with knives would drive them all. You can judge of our situation. Our feelings we cannot describe. For once we know the value of a Christian hope ; and a part of the time we feel a pleasure in the thought of laying down our lives in our triumphant cause. The American ships do not molest us, and some of the masters have gone so far as to tell the chiefs to guard us. The end we cannot foresee. If the sacrifice of our lives will promote our great and good cause, and there should be none but these partly enlightened people to tell the circumstances of our death, you may rest assured that we die rejoicing in the hope that we have done with trouble and with pain. Should things continue as they are, Mrs. R. must fail before many days.

" Yours in haste and confusion,
" WM. RICHARDS."

On receiving this stirring information of the outrage at Lahaina, I hastened to Kalanimoku to ask his assistance in protecting the family of Mr. Richards, noticing the apparent neglect of the chiefs of Maui. He received my appeal, and replied, " Hoapili will take care of them." " But he *does not defend* them from violence," I said. "Hoapili," he rejoined, "will sit still just like a woman till the assailants begin the attack, then he will take care of them." It was a maxim with the Christian chiefs not to resist or contend with foreigners, till the overt acts of the latter placed them clearly in the wrong, and made resistance indispensable.

In the midst of this peril, while these polluted and bloody men were threatening the lives of the missionary and his family, he reasoned with them, assured them of an unalterable determination to seek the good of the souls of the people, though at the peril, or even the cost, of life. His wife, too, though feeble and defenceless, showed herself ready to stand by her husband and share his fate, and assured those shameless invaders that in her circumstances she might reasonably have expected compassion from men who came from a Christian country ; but if it could not be shown her, except on the terms they proposed, she would sooner lay down her life than countenance such iniquity. Even this Christian heroism of a refined lady gave but a momentary check to the madness of the mob.

Mr. R. wrote to their captain, entreating him to control his men ; but he wrote back ' that he could not control his men, that they were determined not to return to the ship without women, and Mr. R. had better let them come off,' when " all would be peace and quietness." Capt. B., having on a former visit procured a native female of Wahinepio, a stout-hearted and dark-hearted chief, for the consideration, as it was understood by the chiefs, of ten doubloons, or $160, and kept her during his cruise, was doubtless in favor of this outrage of the crew, which could not have continued two or three days without his concurrence, or his appeal to the authorities for help to subdue and control his men. In this state of affairs, Mr. Stewart arrived from Oahu, and thus describes his visit :—

" We arrived at Lahaina at midnight, and as we had been delayed three days by head winds, and no time was to be lost, in despite of the great darkness of the night and the danger of the surf, I landed immediately. The mission house had been removed from the place of its original location ; but familiarity with every spot enabled me easily to grope my way through the luxuriant plantations by which it is now surrounded. But how great was my astonishment at the peculiar circumstances in which I found our inestimable and beloved friends, Mr. and Mrs. R. ! Instead of being permitted, unobserved, to come to their bed-side with the salutation of friendship and warm affection as I had anticipated, how was I surprised to meet at my first approach to the house the presented bayonet, and to hear the stern challenge of the watchful sentry, ' *Who goes there*?' and when assured that it was a friend, how inexplicable to my mind was the fact of my receiving the cordial embraces of my brother, not in the peaceful cottage of the missionary, but in the midst of the garrison, apparently in momentary expectation of the attack of a foe, and to find the very couch on which was reclining one who to us has been most emphatically a sister, surrounded by the muskets and the spears of those known to the world only by the names of savages! As soon as an explanation could be given, I learned that their peril was from false brethren, if the outcasts of a civilized and Christian country can be designated by such terms. At that very hour, three boats' crews, amounting to near forty men, were on shore, with the sworn purpose of firing their houses and taking their lives. The statement of these circumstances from them, and the unfolding of the character of my visit, made our interview most deeply affecting."

This was the beginning of a siege of violent opposition, through which the rulers and their Christian teachers were now compelled most unreasonably to pass, by men who, coming from Christian countries, better understood their obligations. But if in the commencement of a far greater and more doubtful struggle for independence in the United Colonies, when the battle of Bunker Hill was reported to a leading hero and statesman, who eagerly inquired, " Can the *militia* stand *fire ?*" and was answered decidedly in the affirmative, Washington could then exultingly exclaim, " Thank God, *American liberties are safe !*" how much more might the friends of improvement at the Sandwich Islands now affirm, " If the Ruler of the nations will enable the Christian chiefs, their missionaries, and the converts in these circumstances, to stand fire, the cause of Hawaiian morality will prevail." He did enable them to stand in repeated instances, as we shall see, as the struggle was renewed from time to time.

As it became apparent that the people were reforming, and that conscience but little enlightened by Scriptures loudly condemned what had once been exceedingly popular, the craft of a certain class of men was seen to be in danger. As the rulers, from Christian principle, knowledge, and commendable zeal, showed a determination to put a check upon the vicious practices which had long prevailed at the islands, to the disgrace even of the heathen, troubles thickened around the missionaries, arising even from sources of congratulation.

Disgusted and grieved by the shameless violation of God's laws even by men who claimed to be Christians, the missionaries were called not only to lift up the warning voice, but, in one instance, were led unitedly to address an admonition to one above middle age, who claimed to be both a gentleman and a professed Christian. Too far and too long astray to take kindly a Christian admonition, he quickly reported to his companions the rebuke, and resolved on railing and revenge rather than repentance and reform. " He sought," as he said, " opportunity to beat some of the missionaries in the street ;" he then rushed, with one of his comrades, into my house. The unbidden entrance, heavy tramp, and impious accents, as they pushed their way through to our retired bedroom where, having just returned from my labors out, I happened to be sitting with Mrs. B., who had just been raised from a three months' illness, apprised us of the object of their visit. I led them back to the room which they first entered, and asked them to be seated. The reproved offender denominated the letter which he received from us a *libel*. Being reminded that our admonition was sent him as a *private letter*, and could not at any rate be a *libel* without its being *published*, " It *is* published," he affirmed. " Who published it?" " I published it myself." " Then, sir, you are the responsible man. We have done what our duty seemed to require of us." After many words I asked him what he wished of *me*. He said " I want an apology for that letter, and if I don't get it, I'll *kill* you." Knowing that the letter had stated with sufficient clearness the incontrovertible reasons for its being written, I replied, " If the letter does not carry its own apology on its face, there is no apology to be made for it." With violence he brandished his heavy cane, and like a madman thrust it at me, while Mrs. B. sat near me, and our little first-born, five years old, at a little distance, looked anxiously through a door to see what was to become of her parents in the strange encounter. With arms calmly folded, I said, " God is my Protector." But he insinuated that I was a follower of Calvin, and calumniously accused that reformer of burning Servetus. He said, moreover, that he had the happiness to belong to a church which would not notice any complaint from us if we should make one against him, and that he would persecute us while he lived, and then leave it to his children. Having wearied himself if not us, by two full hours chiefly of impious railing, he retired with his companion.

The 5th of Dec. was a day of special interest, as the period of one of the most noticeable events in the history of the Hawaiian people. It has already been stated, that early in June, a number of the leading chiefs of the nation were set before the church and the world for further probation as candidates for admission to the church, then consisting chiefly of the pioneers of the mission and the first reinforcement from the United States. The noble phalanx thus propounded, having stood their ground well more than six months, all, at length, took on them the vows of God's everlasting covenant. Kaahumanu, Kalanimoku, Namahana, Laanui, Kapule, Kaiu, Kealiiahonui, and Richard Kalaaiaulu, were received on the first Sabbath of Dec., at Honolulu, Kapiolani a little later, at Kaawaloa, and Kalakua, later still, at Lahaina, there being, as yet, but one organized church in all the islands. Kalanimoku brought forward his little son in arms, accustomed to other offerings to other deities, and dedicated him in baptism, to the Lord. They were welcomed as fellow-citizens in Zion, and sat down with the missionaries at the Lord's table

To record the Christian vows of such a band, brought up from the depths of heathenism, with the evidence which the mission had of their penitence and faith, or true conversion, was a privilege of peculiar value. Human judgment is always fallible, but the evidence that these names, so strange to the civilized world, were written and known in heaven, with Opukahaia and Keopuolani, was, and is, a source of rejoicing, for which the thanksgivings of many have redounded to the praise of our ever gracious and wonder-working God.*

The rulers had their own peculiar responsibilities as law-givers and judges; but if the ministers of religion, few and feeble as they were, could secure their consistent and efficient co-operation in the work of reform, without compromise or confederacy, it was an object of no small importance to be perseveringly sought. But against the *union of church and state* the missionaries have, from the beginning, carefully and successfully guarded. At the same time, they have believed and taught that rulers, whether in the church or out, ought to be ' a terror to evil doers, and a praise to them that do well;' that ' he that ruleth men must be just, ruling in the fear of God, bearing not the sword in vain.'

It has been somewhat difficult for the world to decide whether the missionaries were merely independent ambassadors of Christ, or were "*state priests*" under the control and dictation of despotic or hereditary rulers, or were actually judges and rulers of the chiefs and people; or whether, in fact, there was not strictly a union of church and state, at the Sandwich Islands, after the admission of the high chiefs into the household of Christ, as brethren and sisters of the missionaries and of Christians generally. Some have conceived that the relation of the chiefs to the mission was so variable, that when their views and wishes were favorable to the Christian enterprise of the missionaries, there was, for the time, a union of Church and State; and when the rulers stood aloof, or the chief magistrate exerted a counteracting influence, or took measures unfavorable to the service of God, there was, of course, a " dissolution of the union of church and state." But this is erroneous.

The ministry of religion and the ministry of the state each has its duties; but each in its own order and place, and both for the glory of the same Master, in accordance with the Divine will.

At the Sandwich Islands, church and state have been peculiarly distinct, as the missionaries believed they ought to be, even when they have co-operated for the same end. The state, deriving all its powers from God, both rulers and subjects being bound to do God's will, and its chief magistrate being emphatically God's minister, ought to be, and in an important sense is, a *religious institution*. It is organized for self-protection, and for securing the enjoyment of certain rights which God grants to men, and the performance of certain duties mutual among men, which God enjoins. Still the state, though in fact a *religious institution*, incapable of securing its proper ends without recognizing religious

* Kaahumanu received in baptism the name of Elisabeth; Namahana, of Lydia, Kapule, of Deborah; Kealiiahonui, of Aaron; Kaiu, of Simeon; and the little lad, of Joseph Leleiohoku.

obligation, is not a *church*. Christ's church, of which he claims to be the Head, is not of this world, but has its own existence, organization, and officers entirely distinct from the state. He has constituted it not for the purpose of bearing the sword, not for the punishing of crimes, but rather that by moral means it may edify itself, teach and illustrate the Word of God, propagate the Gospel, and maintain the worship and ordinances which he has prescribed. Christ has given it, independently of the secular power, specific rules for its own discipline, and for promoting the fellowship, the spiritual growth, and high moral influence of his disciples whom he chooses out of the world, and whom he makes the salt of the earth and the light of the world.

In conformity, therefore, with these views, the Hawaiian state has had no *right* and has claimed no power to appoint the officers, or direct the action, or control the discipline of the church : and the church there has had no power and claimed no right to appoint the officers or control the action of the state. Nor have the church and state been identical or confederate.

But the ministers both of the church and of the state should, if they would be loyal to the Divine Sovereign, concur in publishing his statutes, and in inculcating the principles of truth, equity, temperance, and righteousness. The ministers of Christ are of course bound to instruct their flocks, not only in the doctrines of theology, and the proffers and promises of the Gospel, but in all the duties of a holy life, that they may know how they ought to walk and to please God. If this is faithfully done, whether the members of the flock be hereditary or constituted rulers, subjects or citizens, baptized or unbaptized, it should be expected that they would respect God's laws.

The rulers of a state ought doubtless to understand God's will, and to encourage the inculcation of just principles, and to restrain blasphemy against God and trespass against men. How happily has this been illustrated in American communities, where no union of church and state is the boast of our noble republic ! A well framed constitution of one of the most happy and prosperous states in the Union, maintains the following position :—

" It is the duty of the legislature and of the magistrates to cherish the interests of literature and the sciences, to countenance and inculcate the principles of benevolence, public and private charity, industry and frugality, honesty and punctuality in their dealings, sincerity and good humor, and all social affections and generous sentiments among the people."

Had the Hawaiian rulers, emerging from barbarism and brushing the dust of heathenism from their eyes, sought a model for their policy in the frame of society in the United States, or in the policy of the most happy states of the Union, they would have found something clearly distinguishing a Christian from a heathen or Atheistic state, something worthy to be imitated by less enlightened communities and less favored nations. They would have found there that Christianity is a part of the common law of the land; that Christian schools are encouraged by legislation; that presidents and governors appoint fast and thanksgiving days expressly for the worship of Almighty God; that Christian chaplains of legislative bodies, and of the army and navy, are approved and supported by the state for the acknowledgment and service of Jehovah, and for the inculcation of the principles of his inspired statute book, and for the special observance of the Christian sabbath.

These high and noble purposes were as worthy of the conscientious regard of the hereditary or constituted leaders of the Hawaiian nation, as of the founders of the happiest institutions in the United States; and it was a matter of admiration and congratulation to see Queen Kaahumanu and her prime minister and other counsellors, warriors, and honorable women, aiming, amid many difficulties, to secure them; aiming by their example, their office, their edicts, their counsels, their entreaties, journeyings, and personal labors among the people, to promote the very objects for which the missionaries were toiling among them.

It was ours, with the reasonable co-operation of others, to bring the Bible to the whole people: it was theirs to bring themselves, by the blessing of God, to the Bible. Whatever the rulers and people could rightfully do for themselves, or for the reformation and prosperity of the nation, it was far better for them to do than for missionaries or other foreigners. In making and executing laws adapted to the wishes, rights, and necessities of the people, building sanctuaries and school-houses, and employing their own teachers, both for the security and the training of the people, it was far better for the nation to take the responsibility and sustain the expense involved, when it was possible, than for the missionaries or their patrons. But in order to assume that responsibility, and to make the proper efforts, they needed useful hints and valuable information in respect to their duty, which they could not obtain, or would not seek or value except as coming from their tried and fast friends, and it was the more important that missionaries should be communicative, able and ready to show them what was right, and with earnestness to prompt them to do with their might what the Bible required at their hands.

But it was sometimes asked, What had the Hawaiian government to do with the Word of God? With the same propriety it might be demanded, What has ecclesiastical government to do with the Bible, or what has family government to do with the Word of God? The Bible is the inspired charter of the marriage institution which God has established, that through well regulated families he might seek a godly seed; and shall family government have nothing to do with the Bible? It is the charter, too, of the church by which the worship and ordinances of God are to be maintained, and no human device can supply its place in ecclesiastical government. Has the great Lawgiver ordained civil government, and founded the state for the execution of his will, and put his statute-book into the hands of magistrates for their guide, and yet, has civil government nothing to do with his statutes in judging of the rights and duties of rulers and subjects? Are chief magistrates to be God's ministers "for the punishment of evil doers, and for a praise of them that do well," and be denied the right to point out what is evil doing, or to publish the divine rules of duty, and the chief motives or incentives to well doing? If the safety and perpetuity of all that is valuable in a country depend on the *intelligence* and *virtue* of the inhabitants, is it not clearly the right and duty of the state or the government to take measures adapted to promote such intelligence and virtue? or may the rulers of a nation proudly say: "The intelligence and virtue and the richest blessings of our country are derived from Christianity; but let Christianity take care of itself?" Happy for Hawaii that her Christian chiefs were wiser.

Kaahumanu and Kalanimoku, and others, most fully published their views of God's Word, and regarded his statutes as binding on all, without any civil, secular, or ecclesiastical enactment to make them so. Not specifically adopting the *ten commandments* as a criminal code, or Christ's sermon on the mount as a civil code, they still sought to follow these divinely inspired teachings; but when they did this, they were seditiously resisted and ungratefully vilified. The efforts of Hawaiian rulers to restrain sabbath desecration, intemperance, gambling, and licentiousness, provoked virulent opposition from a class who either had not good sense enough to see, or ingenuousness enough to admit, that such restraint was no invasion of their rights, no obstruction to their true interests, temporal or eternal.

To enlighten and restrain from gross vices an ignorant and corrupt people, while a large portion of those who visited them from abroad, practised, countenanced or winked at these vices, and opposed such restraint, required knowledge and tact, kindness and energy, and the co-operation of all the chiefs or officers of government, with the chief magistracy. Notwithstanding it has been affirmed that the common people had no will of their own, but followed implicitly the will of the rulers, the observation of twenty years convinced me that the Hawaiians were no more ready to yield to the will of their chiefs, contrary to their own reason or inclination, than the subjects of other governments are to bow to the will of their rulers. That laws, tabus, and commands given by Hawaiian rulers should always have some influence on the multitude, was a matter of course; but then, the rulers in imposing these had a regard, not only to what their own judgment and wishes dictated, but also to what the judgment and feelings of their subjects might be supposed to approve, when the will of their rulers and the ground of it were made known to them. Kaahumanu and Kalanimoku and others needed to take heed, as every

law-making power must, not to impose laws or issue orders
which cannot be enforced.

I will close this long chapter, and the record of this eventful
year, by a brief notice of a meeting at Honolulu, near its close.
Having made a fair translation of the Decalogue, I showed it to
the chiefs as the Law of Jehovah, which we desired all might
regard as a holy rule of life. They were gratified to see
that portion of God's Word fairly rendered in their own language,
and ready for publication. Kalanimoku, in commending the excellence of the ten commandments, shrewdly remarked in reference to the tenth, that if men would observe the command which
forbids to "covet," all the rest would be easy. But that sagacious
chieftain, much as he desired to see it obeyed, did not expect that
precept to be enforced by the civil power. But he and the queen
seeing in God's law how plainly and forcibly certain crimes cogniz-
able by civil rulers, were prohibited, and concerned to see how
far the people of the realm and strangers who visited their shores
came short of obedience, and how many there were who violated
their laws, called a meeting at Honolulu with a view to urge forward the work of reform, which they had taken up in a special
manner in the spring of 1824, and in the summer of 1825; and to
secure the co-operation of other chiefs and the people in the
suppression of evils, which their orders and tabus had not
wholly restrained. It was rumored, that further regulations were
about to be made for restraining crimes forbidden in the Word of
God. Had this been strictly true, it afforded no just ground of
alarm to honest men. But scarcely had the chiefs and people
convened, when a number of foreigners intruded, and showed
their indignation that the chiefs should attempt further restraints,
or receive laws from the missionaries. To remove the impression,
if indeed it existed among influential foreigners, that the missionaries were dictating laws to the rulers, I disclaimed it in the
name of the mission, but freely admitted that I had translated for
them the Divine commands which prohibited existing evils. A
stout-hearted foreigner among the opposers, who had sometimes
threatened violence, roughly replied; "You think to stop these
things, *but you never can.*" I rejoined in one word, "I learned
long ago that 'wicked men and seducers wax worse and worse,
deceiving and being deceived;' we do not expect to stop them
wholly." Kalanimoku expressed his desire to see the laws of God
observed, and the people conforming their lives to his will; and
both he and the queen seemed determined to maintain the
Christian ground they had taken in interdicting crime, and to persevere in their efforts to bring the people to respect, not only their
own authority, but also the authority of God.

CHAPTER XI.

Arrival of the U. S. S. Dolphin—Mutiny of the Globe—Wreck of the London, Capt. Edwards—Kaahumanu's report of the course of Lieut. Percival—Outrage at Honolulu during the visit of the Dolphin—Lieut. Percival's circular—Court of Inquiry—Mr. Bishop's tour round Hawaii—Kaikioewa's tour round Kauai—Kaahumanu's tour round Oahu—Her visit to Maui—New Church at Kailua—Meeting of the mission at Kailua—Visit of the Peacock, Capt. Jones—Investigation.

In the first month of 1826, while the Christian chiefs and missionaries were pressing on, with brightening prospects, and many thousands were, from week to week, receiving instruction, while other thousands remained in their stupid and degraded state, the anti-tabu party on shore and in the whaling and merchant service, were strengthened by the arrival of a vessel of war.

The crew of the whale ship Globe, Capt. Worth, of our acquaintance, having mutinied in the Pacific, and with unprovoked madness, killed their captain, ran to the Mulgrave Islands, where they came to anchor. The dominant part of the crew went on shore, taking with them two young sailors, who, it is thought, were not accountable for the mutiny. The rest of the crew on board, designing to restore the ship to her owners, seized their opportunity, and fortunately recovered her, ran to the American coast, and reported the mutiny, the landing, and position of the crew. The United States schooner Dolphin, Lieut. John Percival, was dispatched to look after them. Meantime, the obtrusiveness and insolence of the mutineers on shore provoked the anger of one another and the vengeance of the natives; and they came to a violent and speedy death. The two young sailors, remaining entirely in the power of the Mulgrave barbarians, being comparatively quiet and discreet, appear to have been unmolested, and were happily recovered by the Dolphin, which, on her way back to the coast of America, put in for refreshments and repairs at Honolulu, Jan. 23d, and remained some weeks.

The Hawaiians had heard of the power and greatness of the United States, and though Russia, France, and Great Britain, had sent their naval vessels to these islands, yet the inhabitants knew little or nothing of American ships of war, or of the urbanity, intelligence, and elevated character of the United States naval officers. How exceedingly desirable it was that a naval commander from the U. S. arriving so soon after Lord Byron's agreeable visit, and especially at a time when hostility was showing itself among both Englishmen and Americans, against the efforts of the best rulers of the islands to restrain crime, should exert a high moral influence for good, or at least not counteract our mission, nor interfere with the municipal or civil regulations of the place.

The Dolphin came into the roads on Friday, and into Honolulu harbor on Saturday, and her commander proposed to the authorities to exchange salutes on the morrow morning. Kalanimoku and Kaahumanu declining such a secular service as unsuitable to the sanctity of the Lord's Day, the former sent this reply, " We keep sacred the Sabbath, and observe the Word of God." The Dolphin fired her salute Sabbath morning, which the natives returned from the fort on Monday morning. The little vessel was then put under repair.

Soon, the ship London, Edwards master, from New York, was wrecked on the shores of Lanai. Boki and Lieut. Percival hastened thither to render assistance ; and the latter took in charge, as a matter of honor it was said, the specie of the London, not without causing Capt. Edwards and himself some trouble about salvage in the sequel.

Returning to Honolulu, he soon made known his views of the restraints on vile women, and asked an audience with the chief rulers on that subject of grievance, which his crew, by a committee, presented to him. Kaahumanu and Kalanimoku proposed to him to write to them if he had aught to say on that matter. Kalanimoku was then too ill for such an interview. Kaahumanu prepared a condescending and conciliatory statement for the commander's information on that subject, as full as he had any right to ask or expect, to meet the strange pretence that an embargo on lewd women, at the islands, was an insult to the U. S. flag ! In this statement she maintained, 'that she had a right to control her own subjects in this matter; that in enforcing the tabu she had not sought for money; that in apprehending and punishing the offending subjects, she had done no injustice to other nations, or the foreigners who belonged to other nations ; and that while seeking specially to save the nation from vice and ruin, they had been lenient to strangers, though he very well knew, that strangers, passing from one country to another, are bound, while they remain in a country, to conform to its laws.' Boki being charged to deliver this, said the commander would be *huhu loa*, extremely angry. He delivered it, however, and in reporting to the queen, said ; " The man-of-war chief says he will not *write*, but will come and have a talk, and if Mr. Bingham comes, he will shoot him : that he was ready to fight, for though his vessel was small, she was just like fire." Seeing Boki wavering, Kaahumanu said, " Let us be firm on the side of the Lord, and follow the Word of God." Boki said, "If we meet the man-of-war chief, and then yield not to his demands, what will be the conse-quence ?'' Kaahumanu, alluding to Boki's having taken the eu-charist in England or to his standing as a magistrate, replied with dignity, firmness, and consistent principle, "You are a servant of God, and must maintain his cause." Both wept.

On the 22d of February, Lieut. P. obtained an audience at the house of Kaahumanu. She called the little royal pupil from his studies, under my instruction at Kalanimoku's, either that with her he might have the honor of an interview with a representative of the United States, or see how she would manage the matter. As Lieut. Percival had previously requested me not to be pre-sent at the interview, I insert Kaahumanu's account of it, which, in the presence of her Hawaiian friends, she gave to several mis-sionaries, and which accords well with the report of Gov. Kaha-laia and others present, and with the scenes of the drama which preceded and followed it under our own eyes. Carefully trans-lated, her narrative is as follows :—

" Percival came to the council and asked, ' Who is the king of the country ?' I pointed out Kauikeaouli. He asked again, ' Who is his guardian ?' I replied, ' I.' He asked further, ' Who has the charge of his country ?' I replied, ' I and my brother, he being under me.' He said to me, ' You are then king. I also am a chief. You and I are alike. You are the person for me to talk with. By whom are the women tabued ? Is it by you ?' I replied, ' It is by me.' He said, ' Who is your teacher that has told you that the women must be tabu by the law ?' I replied, ' It is God.' He laughed with contempt. He said, ' It was not by you ; it was by Bingham.' I said, ' It was by me. By Bingham the Word of God is made known to us.' He said to me, ' Why tabu the women ? Take heed. My people will come : if the women are not forthcoming they will not obey my word. Take care of your men, and I will take care of mine. By and by they will come to get women, and if they do not obtain them, they will fight, and my vessel is just like fire.' I said, ' Why make war upon us with-out a fault of ours as to restraining our women ? We love the Word of God, and therefore hold back our women. Why then would you fight us without cause ?' He said, ' You formerly attended properly with Kamehameha to the ships, both American and English.' I said, ' In former time, before the Word of God had arrived here, we were dark-minded, lewd, and murderous ; at the present time we are seek-ing a better way.' He denied, and said, ' It is not good—it is not good to tabu the women. It is not so in America. Why did you give women to Lord Byron's ship, and deny them to mine ? Kamehameha did not show such partiality between English and American vessels.' We all denied, and said, ' We gave no women to the ship of Lord Byron. That was a tabu ship. But why are you angry with us for laying a tabu on the women of our own country ? Had you brought American women with you, and we had tabued them, you might then justly be displeased with us.'

" Soon after this he applied to Boki to liberate the women that were fast in consequence of the tabu. Boki spoke to me about it, and I informed you. He came the evening before the outrage of the crew, and said to me, 'Send and liberate the women. If you still hold them, I myself will liberate them. Why do you do evil to the women?' I said, 'It is for *us* to give directions respecting our women—it is for *us* to establish tabus—it is for *us* to bind, to liberate, to impose fines.' He said, ' The missionaries are not good ; they are a company of liars : the women are *not* tabu in America.' He snapped his fingers in rage, and clenched his fists, and said, ' To-morrow I will give my men rum (probably the daily ration) : look out : they will come for women ; and if they do not get them, they will fight. My vessel is just like fire. Declare to me the man that told you the women must be tabu, and my people will pull down his house. If the women are not released from the tabu to-morrow, my people will come and pull down the houses of the missionaries.'

Many, including some of the Dolphin's company, could testify that in various circumstances he spoke of the tabu in a similar style. G. D. Grover, one of the Dolphin's crew, summoned by Percival, testified " that the crew had a meeting on board the Dolphin, and delegated two of their number to ' go aft ' and complain to Lieut. Percival about the *tabu*, and that the delegates brought back word that Lieut. P. would see the missionaries about it." Lieut. Paulding, of the Dolphin, being called and sworn, at the request of Percival, testified in the court of inquiry at Charlestown, " that he heard Lieut. Percival say in the cabin of the Dolphin, that the sailors would serve the missionaries right if they should pull down their houses."

There were several other crews in port, of whom many sympathized with this commander and a large part of his crew. On Sunday, the 26th of February, the commander of the Dolphin allowed double the usual number of his men to spend the day on shore at Honolulu. The violent among them, and the violent of other crews, attempted to form a coalition to " knock off the tabu."

As we were assembling for worship, in and around the house of Kalanimoku, in the afternoon, several seamen, part of whom belonged to the Dolphin, rushed into the spacious hall or saloon in the second story where were Kaahumanu, Kalanimoku, Namahana, and Boki, and a considerable number of others, and with menacing tones and gestures, made their demands and threats. " Where are the women? Take off this tabu, and let us have women on board our vessels, or we will pull down your houses. There are 150 of us—the tabu must come off: there is no other way." Thus commenced a riot which occupied the time and place of the expected divine service. These were followed by successive squads. One and another dashed in the windows of Kalanimoku's fine hall, breaking some seventy panes along the verandah. Some, I think, did not intend violence ; and one of them said to me, " I wish you to take notice who they are that are doing this; we are not *all* engaged in it."

Being apprised of the riot at the place of assemblage, and hearing the crash of the chief's windows, Mrs. B. sent to me and requested me to return home; but fearing my compliance would attract the enemy thither, I preferred to stay on the premises of the chief. Seeing soon a party of sailors directing their steps towards my house, and thinking my wife and child would instantly need my care, without a moment's further hesitation, I made speed by another direction, and reached my door a moment soonest, hoping to enter and lock it and exclude the mob; but to my disappointment I found myself, as well as the rioters, excluded. Mrs. B. not expecting me, and seeing the seamen approach, had turned the key against them, and I fell into their hands. One seized me by the shoulder, and exclaimed, " What does this tabu mean? Here he is: I have got him; come on." Another pulled me by the skirts. One said, " We are sent here by our captain." Another dashed in my windows with his club. Some crossed their clubs around me to confine me. I called out to the natives for help, but before any arrived, disengaging myself from my assailants, I returned into the chief's enclosure, whither I was followed. One who pressed me on my retreat, asked to speak with me. Putting my hand to his club, I said, " Put down your club if you wish me to talk with you." Coming around me again in the midst of the natives, they desired to know why they could not have women. One of the Dolphin's men, who appeared like an Irishman, brandishing his knife near my face, said, with malignant emphasis, " *You* are the *man*, *every* day." Namahana, standing near me, bade him be quiet. Fearing that Boki, whose duty it was to defend me, was unwilling any longer to enforce the tabu or protect the missionaries against riotous foreigners, I looked around to see if there were any on whom I could rely for immediate help, if the rioters should strike me, and seeing John Ii, Koa, Nahinu, and others whom I had instructed, standing but a few yards from me, I said to them, " *Aole anei oukou malama mia ia'u ?*" Do ye not take care of me? " *Ke malama nei no makou,*" they calmly replied, " We *do* take care." Suddenly one of the Dolphin's men struck a spiteful blow with a club at my head, which was warded off, partly by the arm of Lydia Namahana, and partly by my umbrella. It was the signal for resistance, for which the natives had waited. They sprang upon the rioters; some they seized, disarmed, and bound, and to some they dealt levelling blows. For one, knocked down senseless like an ox at the slaughter, with a two-hand club near me, I instantly felt the bowels of tenderness move, and entreated the natives not to kill the foreigners. By this time, Mr. Chamberlain and Mr. Loomis reached the scene of strife, and probably saved the life of one of the fallen sailors, over whom a stone was raised for a dreadful blow. I returned to my house, but had hardly time to correct the report there that the foreigners were killing me, and assure Mrs. B., who had heard the blows, that a kind hand had shielded me from wounds, before a company of sailors approached my premises, broke and rushed through my gate, and hastened towards my door, which I locked against them. One broke in a window; another beat with violence against the door; two applied their strength to force it, and as we looked down from the chamber window, one strangely turning his vengeance on his fellow, like the enemies of Israel, with his heavy club gave him a blow which I feared was fatal, laying him senseless on the earth. He was then lifted from the ground by order of Lieut. Percival, who with some of his officers came upon the spot about an hour after the riot commenced, and used his cane over some of the turbulent men. One of his crew attempting to force his way into the court of Kalanimoku's house after it had been cleared and closed, received on his head a severe cutlass wound from the sentinel at the gate.

In the evening of the same day, the commander waited on the chiefs and reiterated his objections to the tabu, and, while he admitted that the sailors had gone too far, expressed his unwillingness to leave the country till his vessel should enjoy the privileges that had been enjoyed by the vessels of other nations. Gov. Boki and Manuia, the commander of the fort, whose effective agency was then essential to the enforcement of the tabu, yielded to its violation in the harbor of Honolulu. An ambiguous circular, designed either to express regard for the safety and comfort of missionaries, or to palliate the outrage and confirm the prejudice of the seamen, and at the same time guard their heads from heavier blows from a wronged and offended people, was shortly addressed to the several shipmasters in port, though not agreeable to their wishes, and was shown to me by the writer. It may speak officially for itself:

" Sir,—The excitement of the seamen towards Mr. Bingham, and from the recent outrage committed by them from the belief that he has interfered with some of the civil regulations of this place, and thereby deprived them of an enjoyment they have always been in the participation of when they visit this island, I have to request you will let but a small proportion of your crew come on shore on Sunday; by complying with this request you will aid my wishes in preventing anxiety to the missionary family. I have the honor to be, Sir,
" Your obedient servant,
" J. PERCIVAL."

He moreover ordered the repair of Kalanimoku's house and mine, and put in irons two men who assailed me with knife and club; and our physician, Dr. Blatchley, applied his skill to heal the wounds of his men. After a visit of about three months, the Dolphin sailed, having obtained the proud name of " the mischief making man-of-war." With that term was associated the shout of the vile which was heard in the harbor as the first boat load of vile women was seen to pass under its flag. Never did the advocacy of licentiousness or opposition to the tabu appear

more odious.   While some exulted for a time in the partial
triumph, those citizens and subjects of other countries, and leading natives, who had been looking for something not less friendly,
wise, and honorable in a naval " chief " from the United States
than had appeared in Lord Byron, were disappointed.   But he
that makes the wrath of man to praise him, overruled this temporary triumph to the increase of the confidence of some in the
Gospel and in its propagators.   Some natives, in the heat of the
strife, witnessing the different objects and measures of the two
parties, made up their minds in favor of the religion which the
missionaries unflinchingly inculcated, amid obloquy and opposition so unreasonable : and Kaahumanu and some of the other chiefs
saw more clearly than ever the importance of attempting to free
their country from the terrible evils of licentiousness and intemperance.   .
The American Board, hearing of this outrage, and wishing to
have the escutcheon of the United States thrown over their defenceless missionaries abroad, and to see the struggling rulers of
the Sandwich Islands protected from the lawless interference of
naval officers, respectfully asked of the proper authorities an investigation of the conduct of Lieut. Percival at the islands.   This was
granted, and a careful investigation of the case by a Court of
Inquiry took place at Charlestown, by order of the United States'
government, and brought out a mass of evidence which showed
that the Board and the mission, the chiefs and the public, had
good ground to complain.   Happily for our American Republic
and for the world, a just indignation extensively prevailed
against the wrongs which were seen to have been inflicted on the
native rulers, and the enormities of the men of pride and passion,
who arrayed themselves against the cause of good morals at the
Sandwich Islands, and whose seditious and riotous proceedings did
not then cease.
But I gladly turn, as I presume the reader will, for the present,
to more quiet scenes and missionary engagements, and propose
now to sketch several excursions at a distance from the missionary
stations.
In the latter part of 1825, and the early part of '26, Mr. Bishop
made a hasty tour round Hawaii, preaching to the people, and
encouraging their efforts to avail themselves of instruction.   Sailing north by canoe, from Kailua, he touched at Kiholo, some 25
miles distant, and dined with Kapulikoliko, a reputed daughter of
Kamehameha, and spent a day at Kawaihae, giving particular attention to the wife and children, and people of old Mr. J. Young,
then resident at that place, 40 miles from Kailua.   At 2 o'clock
the second morning, he proceeded by water, and at sunrise
reached Mahukona, some fifteen or twenty miles further north,
and there the party drew up their canoe on shore, and started to
walk over to the north-east shore.   Some three or four miles, the
country appeared rocky and sterile, above which it was beautiful,

salubrious, and fertile, producing the banana, *kalo*, and sugar-cane. Passing the table land of Kohala at midday, they found a populous region sloping towards the north, cut with deep ravines and brooks, and interspersed with numerous habitations, cultivated patches, breadfruit and candle-nut trees. These trees grow on the steep sides of the ravines, along up from the sea shore to the high interior, presenting the picturesque landscape which so attracted the attention of the pioneers of the mission, as they passed round it on the day of their arrival.

In this region they found Walawala, the head woman of the district, who was just beginning to open her eyes to the light that had recently dawned on the islands. Passing several ravines which he estimated to be three hundred feet deep, he lodged at Pololu, a deep and interesting valley nearly surrounded with mountains; spent the Sabbath, and preached to large and attentive assemblies in the open air. Finding it extremely difficult to pass along the shore to the south-east, from Pololu to Waipio, on account of the abrupt cliffs overhanging the sea, and the precipitous walls of the deep ravines, he ascended from Pololu in the direction of Waimea, climbing the steep with difficulty and danger, the first hour; then ascending more gradually and comfortably three or four hours, he passed through a fertile and inhabited region, which spread its rude but verdant lawns around him. He preached in several hamlets to numbers who had not before heard the gospel. He halted at 8 P. M., and lodged that night in a cave of the mountains. The next morning, at nine o'clock, he reached Waimea, and preached to the people of that inland settlement, where a station has since been established. Thence through a forest of considerable extent, and mud and pools of water, he passed northeastwardly to the sea shore, having made a circuit or ox-bow curve of about fifty miles, and coming out at Kapulena, in sight of the point at Pololu, whence he left the shore. He preached again here, and passing over seven or eight ravines, came to Laupahoehoe, where he embarked for Waiakea, some 20 miles distant. This passage he made by night, in a tottling canoe, which required much labor to row it, balance it, and free it from the water that dashed in repeatedly. By this conveyance he worked his passage, about three miles an hour, and reached the station of Mr. Goodrich, wet, cold, and fatigued, in about seven hours, and found a cordial welcome. He attended the dedication of a house of worship just erected at that station, ninety-six feet by thirty, capable of admitting nine hundred worshippers. He spent two Sabbaths there, preached to large assemblies, celebrated the Lord's supper, and was greatly encouraged by the tokens of mercy to the inhabitants of that district. Taking leave of Mr. and Mrs. Goodrich, he proceeded to Olaa, where he preached to about one hundred persons in that little inland settlement. Thence he crossed over to Kau, by Kilauea, in the track, perhaps, of Keoua and his warriors. The volcano was in vigorous action, and the crater appeared to have been filled with fresh lava, some three or four hundred feet, during the few months since the visit there of Lord Byron and his party. The natives, Puna and others, who accompanied him, expressed the opinion that this fresh lava, thus accumulated, would find a passage for itself under ground, towards the sea.

Descending from this crater towards the habitable parts of Kau, Mr. B and his party were overtaken by darkness and rain. He thus gives their evening adventure :

" We had now to feel our way, for several miles, in an obscure foot-path, overgrown with tall grass. Darkness, intense and bewildering, succeeded. We felt our way, step by step, following close upon each other, and crawling upon our hands and feet whenever we came to a declivity. The rain poured down upon us in torrents, by which we were drenched and chilled. After wandering often from the path, and as often finding it again, we arrived at ten o'clock at Kapapala, and put up at a house belonging to Kapiolani, where, cheered by a large fire, we dried our clothes, and soon forgot in sleep the fatigues and anxiety of the evening."

Thence, after preaching to the people of the place, in the morning, he passed through a fertile region, having but a sparse population, along near the foot of the mountains of Kau, where exceedingly picturesque natural scenery was presented to them.

Abrupt cliffs and lofty peaks rose in succession on their right, to the height of two or three thousand feet. Still further in the interior, rose a lofty and beautiful mountain, covered with trees of perpetual verdure, " while over them all, like a lengthened cloud, in the distant horizon, towered the snow-capt Maunaloa, glistening splendidly" in the beams of a tropical sun.

Reaching Honuapo, they were stopped by the rain, and put up for the Sabbath, where they were received with gratifying hospitality : particularly on the Sabbath morning was he cheered with the evidence that the influence of the mission and of the Word of God was already felt there. He says ;—

" Looking out towards the western shore, I saw a company of people, about one hundred in number, winding their way around a hill, and descending to the place where we now are. When I inquired, who are these ? the answer was, ' Those who love God and are coming here to pray.' Presently another company, from another quarter ; and upon the signal being given, the most of the people of the village, about one thousand, came together. I preached in the open air, both morning and evening, with more than usual freedom, to attentive audiences. After the morning service, the school, containing one hundred pupils, taught by a son of Kamakau, assembled, and repeated every answer in the catechism, without any prompting. It is but five weeks since their teacher came."

Passing on to the extremity of the southern promontory on which he mentions a deep and fertile soil, extending back to the mountains, he embarked in the morning on board a canoe, for Kaawaloa and Kailua ; and having sailed fifty miles that day, put in at Kalahiki, preached to the people, rested till two o'clock the next morning, then, with a land breeze, reached Kealakekua at day-break, and Kailua at ten o'clock.   Thus he performed a journey of about 300 miles in a period of four weeks, preaching thirty times.   Of the state of the people of the islands, he wrote :—

" Wherever schools are established, the Sabbath is observed; all work is laid aside on that day, together with every kind of diversion The people assemble for prayer wherever there is a teacher capable of leading in that exercise, and for hearing such remarks as the teacher, or some other person present, is capable of making.   Drunkenness is suppressed by law.   In my whole tour I saw but one man intoxicated, whereas, two years since, it was a most common thing to see whole villages given up to intemperance.'

Such a readiness on the part of the 60,000 inhabitants of that island, to receive the instructions of a missionary, and such pleasing signs of their attempt to reform themselves and one another, were truly wonderful, and seemed to require, not merely the utmost efforts of four missionaries stationed on that large island, but of ten times that number, to lead the mass, at once, to acknowledge Christ, and to rise to the elevated standing of an intelligent, Christian, prosperous people.

In April, 1826, Kaikioewa made a tour around his island, Kauai, accompanied by Mr. Whitney and others.   The governor set out with zeal to instruct the ignorant people, and in every village, addressed them on the subject of avoiding a course of folly, sin, and ruin, and turning to the Lord.   Mr. Whitney preached the Gospel in almost every village of that island, at the same time, and supposed that about four-fifths of the population listened more or less to the word of salvation in the course of this tour. About six hundred were connected with the schools, a large part of whom were reading translated and published portions of Scripture.

The governor sometimes rode upon a large white mule, and might easily be imagined to resemble one of the Judges of Israel. The company sometimes travelled by land and sometimes by water, exposed occasionally to danger from the roughness of the way, or their unsafe mode of conveyance.   In some places the people seemed eager to hear and understand the doctrines of Christ, and were hardly willing to let the preacher pass on till they had individually grasped his hand, either to testify their regard to him or to receive his to themselves, after he had, with pleasure, delivered his message.   At one place, the people seemed afraid to look upon the speaker while the governor was addressing them.   But when the missionary appealed to them, saying, "Fear not, for behold we bring you glad tidings," the two or three hundred adults took courage, and ignorant and fearful as they were, like untutored children, raised their eyes and appeared interested.   Among them was a Hawaiian Albino, having a white skin, light eyes, and flaxen hair and eyebrows, whose dress, language, and manners, differed not at all from those of the common natives.   His father and mother were both believed to be natives.   At another place, he found a man, who had former- ly been employed by the chiefs to seize human victims for sacri- fice, a service for which he had qualified himself, so that, like a tiger, he would leap upon his unguarded prey and break his bones. This staunch murderer and caterer for the bloody gods of the last generation, was now willing to shake hands with a Christian missionary, and hear the commands, warnings, and invitations of the Gospel.

Keaweamahi, the wife of the governor, said she wanted to hear the chief say more about Christ and his cross, and less about Kauikeaouli, the king.   On the tour, the missionary said to her, " I am tired of your smoking."   She pleasantly inquired, " Is it forbidden in the Scriptures ?"   " No, but you make it a sin by using it to excess," was the reply.   " Here is my pipe," she said, relinquishing it and presenting it with a smile—" I will smoke no more."   Others soon followed her example, and many were reclaimed from this useless, costly, filthy habit.

The governor, in his zeal, not only exhorted the people to turn to the Lord, but from many, he obtained a promise that they would attend to God's Word, and not walk in the ways of their forefathers, but would regard Jehovah as their God.

The efforts for reform which Kaahumanu felt it necessary to make herself and to encourage others to make among the people of the land, in their ignorance, barbarism, and pollution, were not small.   The reform desired, it was obvious, could not be effected by the civil power alone, even if the rulers had been united.   The heart of the people needed to be moved by moral suasion.   They needed to be taught the reasonableness of reform, and the duty of yielding to the Divine commands, and the more so because some of the chiefs were still opposed to God's claims.

She already knew that something higher, safer, and better-than the will of a mortal ruler was required in order to the preservation of peace.   She knew enough of the enmity, turpitude, and malignity of the human heart, and its tendencies to evil, to satisfy her that it could not be materially mended by the arbitrary will alone of an earthly superior ; nor could she expect the simplest law for the check of immorality would be quietly submitted to by the mass, without the aid of moral suasion more extensively applied than it had been.   She, therefore, not disheartened by opposition, undertook journeys for the benefit of the people, and availed herself of such assistance as she could command in im- parting instruction, and bringing the Divine word to bear on the heart and conscience of the people.   Sometimes, several native teachers and Christian chiefs accompanied her; and sometimes others in the character of learners, both friends and servants. Often she had a missionary in company, not only to encourage her directly in her labor, but to do the work of an evangelist and super-intendent of schools, day by day. The labors, on these tours, therefore, were, in an important sense, a repetition, or continuation of the means among the mass, which had been blessed to the few who had been led to feel and acknowledge their importance.

In July and August, 1826, after the obstruction by the Dol-phin and other opposing forces, the queen, having matured her plan to gain more than had been lost by the infraction of the tabu, accomplished the tour of Oahu, and had opportunity in the course of a month, to see and address in person, a large part of the popu-lation of the island, giving her teachers opportunity to do the same. Her sister, Lydia Namahana, with her husband, Gideon Laanui, accompanied her. Availing myself of the facilities thus afforded for our work, I made the tour with them, employing a month to good advantage, giving my attention chiefly to preaching, and the care and establishment of schools, and reading the Scriptures. Having completed a translation of the Gospel according to Mat-thew, I took it with me, daily reading portions of it to the peo-ple, and completing the reading thus, during the tour. Several horses, two wagons, and two canoes, constituted the principal ac-commodations, as vehicles for parts of the company, much of the way. Most of the company travelled on foot, some making the whole circuit, of about one hundred and thirty miles, and some but smaller portions of it, as we passed round from Honolulu to the east, north, west, and south, then to the east again. This route affords the traveller a variety of fine scenery, grand, pic-turesque, wild, and beautiful. Small portions of the soil are cul-tivated, large tracts lie waste, and a large portion of the island consists of mountains from 1000 to 4000 feet high.

At Waikiki, the head-men and teachers, and a goodly number of people, assembled about noon, whom the regent, after she had dined, addressed on the design of the present tour, the enlightening of the people in the knowledge of the Word of God, in order that they might submit intelligently to Christian laws, and thus diminish the existing evils of the land.

Our company, consisting of 200 to 300 persons, possessed, in fact, the character of a peripatetic or travelling school. Numbers carried their books, and some fifty of them carried their slates and pencils. Those who were able, endeavored to write down the text of every sermon they heard, and to commit it to memory, and sometimes the prominent thoughts, an exercise more needful before than after the publication of the Scriptures among them. Some of the more forward, receiving daily instruction as we travelled on, put their acquisitions to use, and at different places urged on the inhabitants the importance of repentance and reform.

The Queen at Waimea, Oahu, recommending Christianity.   Page 295.

Though the medley of our company reminded me of the groups made up of scribes, pharisees, publicans, and harlots, in the beginning of the Gospel, yet, all due allowance being made for the broad phylacteries of the scribes, the formality of the pharisees, and the levity and instability of those who had hitherto sustained a character differing little from that of harlots, there was daily increasing evidence that God had already accomplished a great work among the people, and would yet do greater things.

Kaahumanu, with propriety, insisted on God's prerogative to give laws to his creatures and to punish the violators of them ; while his mercy provided for the pardon of the penitent and believing. She, therefore, called on the people in the different settlements and districts, to receive the Word of God and yield a prompt and cheerful obedience to his commands. She maintained that rulers, also, had a right to make and execute laws for their subjects, for the maintenance of order and peace, and wished them to expect that such laws would be made as would be needful. She felt and expressed concern lest the messages of the Gospel which I presented, would not be properly received by the people, because they had been so long accustomed to their darkness and hardness of heart, and still loved sin.

We spent a Sabbath at Kaneohe, and passed through Palikoolau, and on Saturday reached Waimea in Koolauloa, the residence of Hewahewa, the old high priest of Hawaiian superstition, by whom we were welcomed.

The valley of Waimea, through which a stream, from the mountainous interior, winds its way to the ocean, is almost environed by mountains rising beautifully on three sides of it, one behind another, from the sea-side to the interior, and exhibiting a fine, picturesque amphitheatre, with hamlets, trees, and plantations. At the opening of this valley where, in the days of Hawaiian barbarism, the blood of Hergest and Gooch was shed by a murderous and ungovernable horde ; the inhabitants of the place assembled with representatives of almost every district of this island, to hear of the great salvation, and to bow before Jehovah, the God of heaven. There were now seen the queen of the group and her sister, and teachers, kindly recommending to her people the duties of Christianity, attention to schools, and a quiet submission, as good subjects, to the laws of the land. To the same concourse, assembled for a purpose so different from that of those who thronged around Hergest, a generation before, I proclaimed the gospel of Jesus Christ, and urged submission and obedience to the commands of God, while the hills seemed to leap up and look askance at what the King of Zion was accomplishing for the nation.

After this service the company proceeded about five miles further, where they spent the Sabbath. A very large concourse of people assembled on the Lord's day, for public worship

in the open air. To the listening throngs I endeavored to proclaim the great salvation, and call their attention to personal duty.
In one discourse I presented the Lord Jesus Christ as the
Redeemer, who, in compassion towards our race, wandering and
lost, endured the cross, and made an atonement for the sin of
the world; and with flowing tears I urged them, therefore, gratefully to receive him, trust in him, and accept his gracious offers
of pardon and salvation. In another discourse I presented him
as the Lawgiver, Governor, and Judge of the world, and urged
them to obey his holy commands, and prepare to meet him in
heaven.

After the Sabbath we examined and encouraged, and partially
supplied with books, the incipient schools established there under
the particular patronage of Lydia Namahana and Gideon Laanui,
to whom the district belonged. There were found under Maiao
and his assistant teachers, four hundred and ninety-five male and
female pupils, and under Kaoo, one hundred and sixty-four,
amounting together to six hundred and fifty-nine pupils, chiefly
men and women.

When the chiefs had addressed and encouraged the people, we
passed on round the promontory to Waianae, the western district
of Oahu, separated from the rest of the island by a range of
mountains. Its valleys and plains, nearly level with the sea, are
interspersed with small steep mountains. The district was called
Boki's. Here we spent the third Sabbath. While there, Kaahumanu spoke with concern of the stupidity of the people. There
was a female prayer meeting, and she was invited. " This is
your time," I said, " to address them, while your heart is full of
tender concern for them, and while the opportunity is afforded
you—perhaps the last you may have to meet with the people of
this district." She went, and with kind expressions, and tender
tone and modulation of voice, well suited to their souls' eternal
concerns, gave them an impressive address, not as an imperious
magistrate, but as a maternal Christian friend, who felt for their
spiritual interests, and who relied more on truth, and faith, and
love, than on the influence of civil power for affecting their hearts
and lives, and securing their future peace. Having made her appeal to their hearts and consciences, she bowed her knees before
the King of heaven, and in an humble manner, led them in prayer.

A man in that region, pretending to know something about the
fabled god, *Kamapuaa*, assuming the form of a hog, was sent for
to tell us what he knew; but his efforts to enlighten us on that
subject, proved the ignorance, darkness, imbecility, and confusion
of the heathen mind, as did also the first efforts to lead this man
into the light of Christianity. He was once asked by a native
teacher, at a meeting for prayer and conference, to tell his
thoughts, that it might be known how he stood in respect to the
service of God. Dropping his face low towards the ground, he
stretched forth his hand, holding a small stone, and said: " What

is this? It is a stone, by which we cook food;" then holding up a little tinder, said: "What is this? It is tinder, by which we kindle a fire." Having made some advance when we arrived and conversed with him, he said: "I have been fed with the Word of God; and Jesus Christ has given me light. I know this body of dust will soon die, but my spiritual body will continue, and it is for that I want salvation." He continued with us several days, and had opportunity to learn something infinitely above the idle stories about Kamapuaa.

As we took leave of the place, the head man, Kapuiki, being personally pressed to give his heart to God without delay, said, " Such is my intention." Such personal appeals extensively and kindly made, were generally kindly received.

Kawaa, the head man of Honouliuli, in Ewa, on hearing that Kaahumanu had commenced this tour, built a large lanai, or airy and pleasant screen of green cocoanut fronds or leaves interlaced, covering about 4,000 square feet, as a sort of temporary synagogue, which afforded accommodation for the queen's company and those who assembled there on her arrival and listened to the preaching of the Gospel and the addresses of the chiefs This *Cornelius* made interesting inquiries respecting the condition of mankind, the plan of redemption, and the character, death, and resurrection of Christ.   Being told of the greatness of his sufferings on account of our sins for which he gave his life, this grey-headed man melted into tears, and exclaimed, " *Aloha ino !*" Great affection! He gave evidence subsequently of true conversion to God, united with the church, and took a leading and useful part in his neighborhood.

At Waipio, there were 383 pupils in the primary school of James Kahuhu, an active man, the yoke-fellow of John Ii, 18 of whom wrote on slates, 91 could then read, and 71 more had learned the letters.

At Waimanu, a youth, Wahapuu, being taught by Lima, was found to have learned to spell and read well, or to have mastered his spelling book, in the short space of five days.

After the toils of nearly a month on this tour, in which we had seen and more or less instructed a large portion of the population of this island, which is nearly equal to that of all the Society Islands, the party returned in safety to Honolulu, and offered unto God thanksgiving.

Soon after this tour of Oahu, Kaahumanu and her attendants visited Lahaina, where she had the happiness of seeing the young princess and a number of others propounded, and others take on them the vows of God's covenant, and stand up before the world as the professed disciples of Christ. The evidences of progress here were highly gratifying.

Many of the chiefs, and most of the missionaries, met in October at Kailua, where marked advances had been made from the time of resuming that station in 1823. As early as July, 1825, some sixty persons there declared their resolution to forsake their heathen habits and enter on the service of the Lord. Weekly meetings were established for inquirers, among whom individuals not only showed a good degree of proficiency in Christian knowledge, but also marks of hopeful piety. No little energy was exhibited by Gov. Adams and his people in promoting the new order of things, though he had not yet himself come into the ranks of total abstinence from intoxicating liquor, nor of profession of faith and repentance.

In February, 1826, Gov. Adams and the people of Kona went into the forest, cut and drew down timber for a large native church, their first one having become altogether too strait for them. In the summer, some thousands were several weeks engaged in erecting and thatching it. Its dimensions were 180 feet by 78, covering an area of 14,040 square feet, and capable of containing 4800 hearers. In September it was ready to be occupied, and the governor invited the regent and other chiefs to attend its dedication, with which they complied. The missionaries at the same time assembled there for the business of their annual convention. This new and magnificent temple had its tall, strong posts inserted firmly in the rocks of Kailua, its large roof, sides, and ends, thatched, and its corners ornamented, and. made an imposing appearance in the dingy village.

On the 27th September, it was dedicated with due formality to the service of Almighty God. The dedication sermon was preached by Mr. Ely, and the hundredth Psalm and the jubilee hymn were sung. Some 4,500 or 5,000 people, including the pupils and teachers of forty schools, joined in the solemn services. With them it was a day of jubilee and rejoicing, such as had not before been seen on that island : and the missionaries rejoiced to see such a contrast as appeared in this meeting to the crowds assembled there, six and a half years before, on the arrival of the mission.

On the succeeding day the people assembled again in the open air, to hear the voice of their rulers, and were successively addressed by Governor Adams, Naihe, the orator, Kapiolani, Hoapiliwahine, and Kaahumanu, who publicly declared their determination to follow the precepts of Christianity in the government of the people.

The same week Mr. Goodrich was there ordained as an evangelist, by the assembled missionaries, with a view to his gathering a church at Hilo, of which he then had the charge.

At this meeting of the missionaries, it was reported that schools had been established in every district of the islands, the number belonging to them estimated at twenty-five thousand, and the natives employed in teaching them, at not less than four hundred. The copies of small works printed for them subsequently to the former meeting of the mission, in June, 1825, amounted to seventy-four thousand. It was resolved to prepare from several translations of Matthew, a copy for the press, and to prosecute the work of translating the Scriptures and publishing them in small portions, as they could be made ready for the people now so ready to receive them. In this Kaahumanu, Adams, and other chiefs, took an interest.

The joint views of the mission were expressed on many points of missionary duty and labor, among which, the following appear in their Report to the Board, on the subject of the return of laborers, and missionary intercourse with the rulers :

" *Resolved,* That we consider our services as missionaries, pledged to the church for life, and that we consider it irregular for any member of the mission to take any steps towards a removal from his post, until he have the approbation of a majority of his brethren : that in order to justify the mission in approving of the return of any member to his native land, they shall be able to assign reasons for it, which, in their opinion, shall be satisfactory to the American Board, and to the candid Christian public.

" *Resolved,* That we consider ourselves required by our instructions, as well as by the nature of our office, as Christian missionaries, to abstain, like our divine Master, from interference with the political and party concerns of the nation: that we are, moreover, bound by our instructions and the nature of our office, to make known the whole Word of God, especially its prohibitions and requirements, which affect the conscience or the well-being of the soul, however opposed the prohibitions and requirements may be to the former customs and present practice of the people.

" That in perfect consistency with our instructions and the maintenance of our proper character as Christian teachers, we may give information and advice with respect to the arts and usages of civilized life and society, and may use our influence to discountenance every vice, and encourage every virtue."

Scarcely had the missionaries closed this session, when the report of another outrage at Lahaina reached them, in which the missionary might have been greatly exposed during the absence of Governor Hoapili. This event, and some notice of the largest audience probably ever assembled at the Sandwich Islands, for Christian worship, were soon after reported to the Secretary of our Board, by Mr. Bishop, who went to Kawaihaé to preach to the thousands of Kohala and Hamakua, assembled there to meet Kaahumanu, and other chiefs. Writing under date of November 3, 1826, he says :

" Mr. B. and family still remain at Kailua, where we are revising the gospel of Matthew, for the press. Mr. Richards and family have just returned to Lahaina, after a visit to this island of six weeks. His stay was protracted in consequence of information received from Lahaina, of the base conduct of the crews of several English and American whaleships, who had threatened to kill him if they could find him, because through his influence a stop had been put to prostitution. They went to his house to demolish it, but found it carefully guarded. * * * The women fled to the mountains.

" The principal spite of foreigners is levelled against our brother and fellow-laborer, Mr. B.; but you may be assured that the brethren consider it a common cause   *   *   and we feel it to be our duty publicly to give him and his measures, so far as they have come to our knowledge, our decided approbation.

" Sabbath evening, Nov. 5. I have just returned from the services of this day, where I have preached twice to a congregation of more than ten thousand listening hearers. They were assembled in a cocoa-nut grove, and I delivered my message to them in the open air. The stillness of this immense multitude, the solemn occasion upon which we had met, the thought that all this people would pass into eternity in the lapse of a few years, gave a solemnity and an interest to the scene which I have seldom felt. The Lord helped me to speak as one standing between two worlds; as an ambassador of reconciliation between God and His fallen creature, man, revealing to him a cove-nant of grace. It is a truly interesting and pleasant service to be the messenger of peace to perishing immortals; and in a special manner this service is pleasant when it is connected with the persuasion, that those for whose good we are laboring, are anxiously desirous of the light and knowledge that lead to salvation. Such, my brother, is the state of this people. There was never, perhaps, a time, when the prospect of complete success to our enterprise was greater than at present. Could you but witness, for one day, the order, the attention, the anxious, eager look, and observe the tear which starts in the eye of the tawny, sun-burnt savage, and the countenance of hope and joy, as he casts his eye upward to heaven, upon hearing the terms of pardon-ing mercy proclaimed to him, your heart would leap for joy, and you would give God thanks for having ever put it into the hearts of any to come over the wide waste of waters that divides us, to preach salvation to this people who have long been sitting in darkness and the shadow of death."

The noise in the little Hawaiian world, occasioned by the clash-ing of light and darkness, was not small. In order to guard fair-minded men from imposition by vilifiers, the mission put forth a cir-cular, signed by all the male members present at the meeting, at Kailua, making a full declaration of their object, as missionaries, and the means they were taking to secure it, asking and challeng-ing an investigation of our conduct, and protesting against the unmanly current complaints against us.

In reference to our pretended connexion or interference with the civil authority, whether to sustain or diminish oppression or abuse of power, the mission, in their circular, say:

" We have inculcated on the chiefs, not only the common duties of morality, but we have also taught them that he that ruleth men must be just, ruling in the fear of the Lord. We have endeavored to con-vince them that they were set for the punishment of evil doers, and for the praise of them that do well. We have given them general princi-ples derived from the Word of God, together with Scripture examples of their application, neither withholding instruction, nor interfering with their authority. We have also endeavored, from the same authority, to inculcate on the people their duties as subjects. We have taught them that they must needs be subject, ' not only for wrath, but also for conscience' sake, rendering to all their due.' To all we have insisted on obedience to the precepts of the Bible, which teach justice, honesty, integrity, punctuality, truth, purity, good order, union, and peace."

At such a period, the arrival of an honorable, intelligent, and high-minded gentleman from any country, would have been hailed by the missionaries, in that state of the parties.

To the mission and to the rulers, and to their opposers, the arrival of the U. S. sloop-of-war Peacock, at the Sandwich Islands, in October, 1826, was a matter of unusual interest. The two parties were earnest to learn whether they had a friend or not, in the commander, Thomas Ap Catesby Jones, Esq. The solicitude of the missionaries, though most of them were absent from Honolulu, when he arrived there, and while many efforts were made to give him an unfavorable impression respecting the mission, its members, and their pursuits, with few to correct them, was at length relieved when they came to make his acquaintance.

The residents, after an opportunity to see Captain Jones and his officers, accepted what they were pleased to call our "challenge," and proposed by letter, to the missionaries, to meet them in his presence, intimating that a fair hearing might be obtained ; though some of the officers had apparently prejudged the case, by saying, " there must be something *wrong* in what everybody *calls* wrong." Captain M. Sayre, then in port, rendered Captain Jones and our cause important service, by a prompt and friendly appeal to facts within his knowledge. The missionaries having been frank and honest, and studious to pursue a course that would bear investigation, were prompt to accede to the first proposal for a meeting, and courted a careful examination by any and all candid men. Those of us who were at Kona, Hawaii, embarked from Kailua, on board our own missionary packet, which the Board had sent us, touched at Lahaina, and took Mr. and Mrs. Richards on board, and reaching Honolulu roadstead, Saturday evening, brought the vessel into the harbor and cast anchor by night. I took Mrs. B. and our two children into the boat, and passing along by the tall ships, and the guard-boat of the Peacock, we set our feet upon the shore where my life had been threatened, and proceeded, unmolested, to the mission house, half a mile distant, with feelings not easily described.

The accustomed duties of the Sabbath being over, Capt. Jones politely called on us Monday morning. Early apprising the residents of our readiness to meet them, we proposed the appointment of a committee to arrange the matters to be adjusted. To this Mr. Charlton objected. We then proposed to meet any charge against us they would present in writing before Capt. Jones.

The parties met in Honolulu at the house of Gov. Boki. The British Consul, who had made himself conspicuous, took the lead of the meeting, called attention to our circular and challenge, and, in his usual style, made remarks respecting the chiefs, the people, the schools, and the missionaries, not very complimentary to either. One of the gentlemen appeared dissatisfied with the publication of the circular; another admitted that it would be difficult for them to find legal evidence against the missionaries, while the latter would not insist on what might be called *legal* evidence, but any evidence of wrong-doing which would convince a candid inquirer. Had the missionaries violated the laws of the land or the laws of equity, the chiefs of the country might have been supposed to be their judges; but they were generally favorable to the mission, and to each member of it in particular. There had been, indeed, some expectation that Boki, under the influence of Mr. C. and others, who seemed desirous to have him supersede Kaahumanu in the regency, would appear at this meeting against the missionaries. But in the course of the proceedings, Mr. Charlton, either as a matter of chagrin or of insinuation that the missionaries were too strongly fortified for a chief to rebuke them, or of compliment to the integrity both of the chiefs and missionaries, stated to the meeting, that " *no chief dared to testify against a missionary.*"

Capt. J., after a sufficient length of time had elapsed, and enough had been said to enable him to form some judgment of the case, rose and said, " he did not appear there as the advocate of the missionaries, to whom he had suggested some hints which he thought might be useful to them. He did not see that anything would be gained by continuing the course the gentlemen were taking, and the missionaries did not seem disposed to reply, though they had a good opportunity to do so. He thought their circular was full and fair, and if any one could show its incorrectness, the way was open for it; but as no one appeared ready to do that, or to present written charges against them, he should be in favor of adjourning:" so the assembly readily broke up. He subsequently gave to the public the following brief opinion of the case :—

" I own I trembled for the cause of Christianity and for the poor benighted islanders, when I saw, on the one hand, the British Consul, backed by the most wealthy and hitherto influential residents and shipmasters in formidable array, and prepared, as I supposed, to testify against some half a dozen meek and humble servants of the Lord, calmly seated on the other, ready and anxious to be tried by their bitterest enemies, who on this occasion occupied the *quadruple station of judge, jury, witness, and prosecutor.* Thus situated, what could the friends of the mission hope for or expect? But what, in reality, was the result of this portentous meeting which was to overthrow the mission, and uproot the seeds of civilization and Christianity so extensively and prosperously sown by them in every direction, while in their stead, heathenism and idolatry were to ride triumphantly through all coming time ? Such was the object, and such were the hopes of many of the foreign residents at the Sandwich Islands in 1826. What, I again ask, was the issue of this great trial ? The most perfect, full, complete, and triumphant victory for the missionaries that could have been asked by their most devoted friends. Not one *jot* or *tittle*—not one *iota* derogatory to their character as *men*, as ministers of the Gospel of the strictest order, or as missionaries—could be made to appear by the united efforts of all conspired against them."

Among the opinions favorable to the missionary efforts up to that period, expressed by a number of leading individuals, the following from the grey-headed Mr. J. Young, who had been intimately acquainted with the people forty years, and almost from the commencement of Kamehameha's prosperity, is very important testimony in respect to the improvement of the nation, which was the main question :—

"Kawaihae, Island of Hawaii, Nov. 27, 1826.

"Whereas it has been represented by many persons that the labors of missionaries in these islands are attended with evil and disadvantage to the people, I hereby most cheerfully give my testimony to the contrary. I am fully convinced that the good which is accomplishing and already effected, is not little. The great and radical change already made for the better, in the manners and customs of this people, has far surpassed my most sanguine expectations. During the forty years that I have resided here, I have known thousands of defenceless human beings cruelly massacred in their exterminating wars. I have seen multitudes of my fellow beings offered in sacrifice to their idol gods. I have seen this large island, once filled with inhabitants, dwindle down to its present few in numbers through wars and disease, and I am persuaded that nothing but Christianity can preserve them from total extinction. I rejoice that true religion is taking place of superstition and idolatry ; that good morals are superseding the reign of crime ; and that a code of Christian laws is about to take the place of tyranny and oppression. These things are what I have long wished for, but have never seen till now. I thank God that in my old age I see them, and humbly trust I feel them too.

"JOHN YOUNG."

Capt. Jones, as a public officer, carefully sought to promote the interests of commerce and secure the right of traders, pressed the rulers to a prompt discharge of their debts, and negotiated articles of agreement with the government for the protection of American interests, in which Kaahumanu, as regent, is conspicuous ; and secured for himself among the people the designation of " *the kind-eyed chief* "—a compliment falling on the ear of many of different classes in delightful contrast with that of " *the mischief-making man-of-war.*"

About this time, a letter ascribed to Boki, whom some men desired to see arrayed against his brother and Kaahumanu, was published in the London Quarterly as genuine. But it was full of internal

marks of having been "*manufactured*," as Lord Byron perti-
nently said, by other than Hawaiian hands. It was doubtless
intended to arm prejudice against the American missionaries. It
bears date the day after the arrival there of Lieut. Percival, and
may have been intended in part to enlist him in the crusade
against a certain tabu.   As a literary curiosity, and a specimen of the trash with which many a shipmaster and naval officer
has been saluted on his arrival at Honolulu, incorrect as
it is, it may speak for itself.   The style and idiom do not
belong to the Hawaiian nation, but are strictly low English, in
which Boki could not write or dictate a sentence.   Its orthography of Polynesian names is not such as a native would use.
When it returned to the islands, Boki disclaimed its paternity.*

* "Island of Woahoo, Jan. 24, 1826.
    "SIR,—I take this oppertunity to send you thes fu lines hopping the will find you
in good health, as ples god they leve me, at present.   Mr. Pitt (Karaimakoo) has
gon through four opperashons since you sailed from here, but thank god he is now
much better and we are in hops of his recovery, and I am verey sorry to tell you that
Mr. Bingham the head of the misheneres is trieing evere thing in his pour to have
the Law of this country in his own hands.   all of us are verry happy to have some
pepel to instruct us in whot is rite and good but he wants us to be entirely under his
laws which will not do with the natives.   I have done all in my power to prevent it
and I have done it as yet.   There is Cahomano wishes the misheneres to have the
whole atority, but I shall prevent it as long as I cane for if the have there will be
nothing done in these islands not even cultivation for ther own use.   I wish the
pepel to read and to rite and likewise to worke.   But the Misheneres have got them
night and day old and young, so that ther is verrey little don her at present.   The
pepel in general ar verrey much disctified at the Misheneres thinking they will
have the laws in their own hands.   Captain Charlton has not arrived from Öteity,
which makes me think sumthing has happened to him.   Mr. Bingham has gone so
far as to tell thes natives that neither king George nor Lord Byron has any regard
for God, or aney of the English Chiefs, that they are all bad pepel but themselves
and that there is no Redemsion for aney of the heads of the English or American
nations.   God send you good health and a long life.
    "Mrs. Boki sends her kind love to Lord Biron, and Mr. Camrone and the Honor-
able Mr. Hill.

"NA BOKE."

CHAPTER XII.

EIGHTH YEAR OF THE MISSION, AND FOURTH OF KAAHUMANU
—1827.

Position of Boki—Illness of Kalanimoku—His removal to Kailua—Visit at Lahaina—His death—Letter of Mr. Chamberlain—Return of laborers—Excursion to
Hawaii—Arrival and refusal of Romish teachers—Outrage at Lahaina by the
crew of the John Palmer—Report of Hoapili—Complaint against Mr. Richards
—Proposed trial and result.

AFTER the investigation referred to in the last chapter, the
missionaries returned to their post and pursued their work of
teaching, preaching, translating, and publishing the Word of Life,
with little reference to the good and evil report which pertained
to their chequered lot, the confidence of the Christian chiefs
in their spiritual guides being increased rather than diminished.

Boki still acknowledged Kaahumanu as regent, and his brother Kalanimoku as superior to himself in the government, published his
views at the islands in favor of Christianity, and joined with the more
stable and consistent chiefs in countenancing the evangelical labors
of the missionaries. With his fair promises he had received from
Kaahumanu the stewardship of her step-son, the juvenile king, and
engaged to act as a Christian *kahu* towards him. But he was not
steadily and decidedly one with his superiors, in reasonable endeavors to follow out the rules of Christianity, and efforts were
not wanting among the vile to lead both Boki and the child in
the sinful ways of self-indulgence. For a time, he seemed
hardly to take higher ground than Liholiho had done before he
finished his course. The declaration of Mr. Charlton, that 'no
chief *dared* to testify against a missionary,' implied that he thought
some one was disposed to oppose them, had he as much courage
as himself, and seemed disappointed that Boki did not take open
ground against the mission, when we asked for an investigation of
our course.

In the early part of 1827, the illness of Kalanimoku, who had
been some time feeble, became alarming. He had submitted three
times to the operation of tapping for the dropsy, performed once
by a Russian surgeon, once by the surgeon of the Peacock, and
once by Dr. Blatcheley of our mission.

During the two years, between the settlement of the commotions
of Kauai and his departure from Oahu for Hawaii, while he stood
like a Christian, he gratefully received many kind attentions from

his missionary friends. His having his residence near us, when, through disease, he withdrew from the concerns of public life, gave us a privilege which we appreciated, and sought to improve, of showing him the sympathies which he needed, and which our religion taught. It was worth some pains-taking to see this statesman and warrior, so lately a besotted heathen, thus receiving in his feebleness, needful comforts daily prepared for the support of the sinking frame, and to witness, from time to time, the satisfaction which precious texts of Scripture, or stanzas of hymns translated to contribute to his spiritual strength, gave him, while gratitude, meekness, and confidence marked his child-like demeanor. This course of trial appeared to his friends to be preparing that soul, once long enslaved to heathenism, to enjoy the liberty and inheritance of the sons of God. Who would not regard it as a privilege to be the humble helper of the joy and victory of such a one, reclaimed from a polluted idolatry ? He felt deeply the opposition which arrayed itself against the cause of God, and in no point more, perhaps, than when it appeared in his brother Boki. He had hoped better things of him, for he had pledged himself to be on the Lord's side, but at length gave up his profession of loyalty to Christ. Kalanimoku, in the earnestness of his solicitude for him and for the cause, though sinking himself with the dropsy, went to see his brother; and with astonishment and grief found him in his cups. Boki said, " I have sinned." Kalanimoku said, " I have heard before of your intoxication, but now my eyes see it. When I was very ill, the other chiefs came to see me, but my own brother was not among them." Boki said again, " *Ua hewa au*, I am wrong." Kalanimoku said, " It is done ; I shall leave you." He returned to his house ready to faint, and fall to the ground. He wept over the defection of his brother, and entreated his missionary friends to pray for him, because he thought God alone could set him right. He made up his mind deliberately to remove to Hawaii, if his strength would hold out till he could accomplish it.

On the 12th of January, he united with his friends in a parting prayer, near the harbor of Honolulu ; then, with trembling step, being supported by a faithful friend under each arm, he made his way to the boat, while numbers thronged around with their sympathizing *aloha*, desirous to see, once more, the venerable form of a retiring warrior and friend, to receive the parting smile and affectionate salutation of their venerated chieftain—the *iron cable* of their country. He embarked from Honolulu, January 11th, on board the brig Chinchilla, Capt. T. Meek, and touching at Lahaina on the 13th, made a visit there of four or five days among his friends, during which time Maria Hoapiliwahine, Harieta Nahienaena, and her interesting friend Henrieta Halakii and several others, were admitted to the church in the presence of a vast concourse of people ; and the Lord's Supper was administered. Of his visit there, Mr. Richards says :—

" A few days after my return from a general meeting of the mission at Honolulu, the venerable Kalanimoku arrived at Lahaina. His having proved himself the ' Iron Cable of Hawaii,' and his having been so long sick, and this being his last visit, in the apprehension of the people, all conspired to awaken deep feeling. We heard nothing, however, of that heathenish wailing which used to be practised on such occasions. Nearly all the people of Lahaina were on the beach when he landed, and it was really moving to see with what affection he met his old acquaintances. Nothing added so much to the intense interest of the occasion as the fact that he was removing from Oahu, in order that he might find a place of quiet at which to leave his remains.

" As Kalanimoku was expecting to leave Lahaina immediately after the Sabbath, and we did not expect to see him again, we thought it desirable that the sacrament of the Lord's Supper should be administered. He was much affected on the occasion, and in the evening expressed in the strongest terms the satisfaction it afforded him to see his young daughter, as he called the princess, regarding the words of her good old mother, and setting such an example to her subjects.

" The next day, the princess, at the request of the other chiefs, went to Kalanimoku with an invitation to stop at Lahaina and give up his design of proceeding to Kailua. He answered, ' that he could not deny so polite and affectionate a request, if persisted in ; but as he had given notice that he was going to Kailua, it was still his wish, if they would consent, to proceed, and if the Lord would hold him back from the grave for a little time, he would return and leave his remains beside those of Keopuolani.' To this the princess and her advisers assented. During his stay he called several times at our house, and appeared with his accustomed cheerfulness and warm affection."

He proceeded to Hawaii with comparative comfort; but shortly after his arrival at Kailua, he submitted again to the operation of tapping, and subsequently appeared so comfortable and cheerful, that the physician encouraged him and his friends to hope that he might enjoy a better state of health many years. But this hope was of very short duration. A subsequent collection of water demanded a repetition of the operation before the close of a month. Under this he fainted. He then revived a little, but sank rapidly away, and in a few hours expired—February 8, 1827. His parting advice to his people gave pleasing proof that this heathen warrior, who could once engage in drinking, gambling, and amusement beside the remains of his wife, even after he had approved of our settlement in the country, had at length learned of Jesus what his predecessors never knew.

His cheerful conformity with what he understood to be the requirements of the Word of God, his steady adherence to the Christian principles which he professed to follow since the time of his exposure, preservation, and victory at Kauai, his unvarying, warm, and operative friendship for the missionaries, his efficient endeavors to promote the cause of instruction and religious improvement among his people, his readiness to acknowledge God and to attend on his worship and ordinances, his faithfulness in reproving sin, his patience in suffering, his calm and steady hope of heaven through the atonement of Christ, whom he regarded as the only Savior, and to whom he had, as he said, given his heart, soul, and body, all combine to give him a claim to that most honorable of all titles—the title of " *Christian*."

" This world," he said, " is full of sorrow, but in heaven, there is no sorrow or pain.   There it is good; it is light; it is happy." There, we trust, through the divine teaching and discipline, the converting and sanctifying grace of God, he found his desired and expected rest.   His example still lives, and his influence will be likely to be useful to his countrymen, as long as the nation shall exist.

A competent education would have made him an accomplished statesman, who, with his piety and integrity, would have been an honor to any nation.   To the missionaries, the death of their honorable friend and patron, at that interesting crisis, was a loss which they deeply felt, and in which many sympathized.   But to none was his departure more affecting than to his superior and coadjutor, Kaahumanu, who hastened to Kailua, on hearing of his lamented departure.   She had been accustomed to look to him as kind, prompt, and sagacious, in counsel, in devising, as well as efficient and trustworthy in executing measures for the good of the nation.   She had regarded him, and often spoke of him as a brother, and mourned his loss as such.   In the settlement of his estate, she was at first thought to have done injustice to some of his heirs, but on her leaving Kailua, where she had attended to that business, she is thus kindly mentioned by Mr. Bishop, of that place, April 12, 1827 :   " Kaahumanu returns in feeble health, and we fear this may be the last time she will ever visit this island.   She is the same affectionate, consistent Christian, as formerly, and we feel the deepest interest in all her movements."

The increased responsibility and solicitude which she now felt, and her desire to urge forward the work of reform in her nation, though unaided by the arm of the true brother she had found and lost in Kalanimoku, doubtless affected her health and tended to shorten her Christian career.

Mr. Chamberlain, in a letter to the patrons of the mission, dated February, 1827, in perfect accordance with the general sentiment of the people, says: " The right of controlling the king and directing the affairs of the nation, belongs to Kaahumanu ; and even Boki has acknowledged that his power is vested in her. I had feared that the death of Kalanimoku would be the signal to resist Kaahumanu, but the present appearance of things is that peace and order are likely to prevail.   Boki has discovered a disposition to act contrary to the wishes of the higher chiefs, particularly of Kaahumanu, and his conduct has actually excited the apprehension that he is aiming to usurp the regency.   But this strange course is to be attributed more to foreign influence than to the independent actings of his own mind. Indecision is a natural trait of his character, and he is just such a tool as would suit the purpose of an artful and designing person who had an interest to promote by creating civil dissensions."

During this summer, there was a disparity between the missionary work which we had in hand and the number of laborers, which was severely felt, more especially at Maui, Kauai, and Oahu. Mr. Richards had the missionary care of the population of Maui, Molokai, and Lanai—preaching, translating, marrying those who wished to be properly married, among 30,000 inhabitants, and directing the schools, embracing more than 6000 pupils. He was at the same time superintending the building of a house for his family, the walls being of stone, forty-six feet by twenty-two, and two stories high.

Mr. and Mrs. Whitney, neither in good health, were fainting with their cares and labors at Kauai. There were fifty schools in their field, embracing 1,600 scholars. A small church, numerous inquirers, and a large and attentive congregation, demanded their attention, but reluctantly allowed them to leave for relaxation.

Mr. Loomis, our printer, and Dr. Blatcheley, yielding to the pressure, had both left Honolulu with impaired health, and returned with their families to the United States. This brought on the preacher new cares in the printing and medical departments, which, in addition to preaching to thousands, and translating, teaching, and acting as interpreter, often for the chiefs, proved, before midsummer, an overtask. Mrs. B. and Mr. Chamberlain were then my only missionary helpers at the station. A population of 25,000 belonged to the station, 8,303 of whom were then in the schools of Oahu, and needing our supervision, and not a few who wished to marry, required care and attention from the missionary. Other stations needed help. Mr. Chamberlain made a trip of thirty days to the windward stations, conveying to them supplies, and twenty-six thousand copies of our publications for the people, which would give scarcely more than one to each in their schools. At Hilo he found Messrs. Goodrich and Ruggles in the prosperous discharge of their duties, and a large worshipping assembly, not surpassed in orderly appearance by any he had seen in the islands. He returned thinner in flesh, if possible, and looking more careworn than before. He and others expressed the conviction, which I felt, that if I would prolong my life, I must seek relaxation and refreshment; for the perpetual summer of our dusty Honolulu, the cares and labors of that exciting station, and chronic hepatitis, apparently preying on my vitals, were reducing me and threatening to cut short my course. Mr. and Mrs. W. wishing to relax also, and to voyage about to recruit a little, came to Honolulu. He took part in the labors of the

station, and while he could render aid there, joined with
Mr. C. in advising me to try the effect of a visit and sojourn at some of the cooler parts of Hawaii. From the commencement of the station at Hilo, it had been desired and
expected that I should for a time join in its labors. With both
objects in view, I soon embarked with my family on board the
Missionary Packet which had been sent by the American board to
the mission. We touched at Lahaina, and attempted to pass up
the channel between Maui and Hawaii, but were met in mid-
channel by a violent wind, rushing down between the mountains.
It was night ; the waves dashed over our little vessel, knocked
off the scuttle, and damaged the schooner's boat. We looked
to the Divine Pilot for help ; our native crew struggled to pass
on ; but in the confusion, Jack, the commander, made his way
to the cabin, and exclaimed, " What shall we do? We cannot
reach Hilo." " Whither, then, can we go ?" said I. " Whither
then, indeed ?" he rejoined. " Can you run for Kailua in
Kona ?" I asked, as the waters came over us. " *Ae ; maikai ;
malaila kakou ;* yes ; good; thither go we." It was an hour of
peril. The darkness of the night, the smallness of our vessel,
the want of seamanship in our native pilot and crew, the force of
the wind and of the surges, that broke over us in a channel as
rough as any part of the Pacific, made us feel our danger and our
dependence on him who layeth the beams of his chambers in the
waters. The vessel being put on her course for Kailua, the danger diminished, and we cut our way more joyfully. Arriving
safely on the morrow, we were kindly welcomed by Gov. Adams,
and by Mr. and Mrs. Thurston, and Mr. and Mrs. Bishop, who,
with animating success and prospects, were prosecuting their
various missionary labors, translating, preaching, and teaching,
and directing several thousand learners in their schools spread
over a wide and whitening field.

After a few days, with the advice of Messrs. T. and B., we
retired to a humble cottage of Gov. Adams, at Kuahewa, about
five miles in the rear of Kailua village, and at an elevation of
about fifteen hundred feet on the western side of the volcanic
mountain, Hualalai, where they thought the temperature as favorable as that of Hilo. We found it very rurally situated, near the
native huts on one side, and the forest on the other, and in the
midst of plantations of sugar cane, bananas, potatoes, squashes,
and melons, and upland *kalo*, where vegetation was unusually
luxuriant. The temperature was agreeable : the mercury in Far-
enheit ranged from 59° to 74°, the average for two months being
68°, or ten degrees lower than at Kailua, Lahaina, and Honolulu,
at the same time. The land breeze by night, and the sea breeze
by day, were pleasant and refreshing. The latter brought to our
ears the roar of many waters, as from the sea they dashed their
surges upon the shores, from five to eight miles distant ; while
the coolness of the temperature, the release from the daily cares of

my station, and other remedies employed, contributed to arrest the progress of my disease, though the dampness of the atmosphere and of the earth floor were not favorable to the health of Mrs. B. Destitute as we were of civilized and Christian society, and of the elegancies and comforts of life, we found this season of retirement delightful and refreshing to the heart, while allowed to be moderately making preparation for the press.

After a sojourn here of two months, the duties of the mission at Honolulu requiring my return, we left our mountain retreat, and making a short visit at Kailua, and to Mr. and Mrs. Ely and the interesting chiefs at Kaawaloa, we passed over to Lahaina, and remained two or three weeks with Mr. and Mrs. Richards, to aid and cheer their solitary labors. Mr. R. had recently made an excursion through a considerable portion of his field, solemnized marriages (an almost weekly service), inspected numerous schools, and returned, rejoicing in the evidence of progress, and in view of the wide fields of usefulness spread out around him, but regretting still that the laborers were so pitiably few.

During this summer, an event occurred at the islands, of no small moment to our mission, and to the native government and people—the offer and refusal of a Papal mission.

John Rives, who went to London in the same ship with Liholiho, went over to France, representing himself as having wealth and consequence at the Sandwich Islands, contracted for goods to be carried thither, and asked for laborers to cultivate his lands and missionaries to teach his people.

Rev. John Alexius Augustine Bachelot, in July, 1826, received the title of " Apostolic Prefect (governor or commander) of the Sandwich Islands," from the pontiff and sovereign of Rome, Leo XII. Messrs. Armand and Patrick Short were united with him. An agriculturist and several artisans accompanied them. They embarked from Bordeaux on board the ship Comet, Captain Plassad (carrying cargo for Rives) and with the exception of Mr. Armand, who died on the passage, arrived at Honolulu, July 7th, 1827. Rives sailed by another vessel to the western coast of America, and never appeared at the Sandwich Islands. The government did not feel itself bound to receive Romish teachers from any country; and the people did not desire it. Whether it is right to bid God speed or not to a system of teaching which forbids free access to the Bible, and is subversive of the Gospel, or for a patriarch to appear indifferent or neutral in respect to alien teachers of his people, or otherwise, Kaahumanu, as Queen Regent, refused to receive or admit the Papal teachers, and denied them a residence. In doing this, she did no more than Vancouver had advised in respect to foreigners whom they did not want; no more than the laws of nations allow a sovereign to do, who sees reasons for it. She took the ground from which she never receded, that the papal teachers ought not to be allowed to intrude, but to depart and let the nation alone. In this, the young king and most of the chiefs concurred. She required Capt. Plassad, who brought them, to take them away. On account of her patriarchal relation to her people she had a special claim to use the prerogatives of a sovereign, in forbidding the entrance of unwelcome strangers, according to the laws of nations.

" The sovereign may forbid the entrance of his territory either in general to every stranger, or in a particular case, or to certain persons on account of certain affairs, according as he shall find it most for the advantage of the state. There is nothing in all this that does not flow from the right of the domain and of the empire. Every one is obliged to pay a respect to the prohibition, and he who dares to violate it, incurs the penalty decreed to render it effectual. But the prohibition ought to be known, as well as the penalty annexed to the disobedience. Those who are ignorant of it ought to be informed when they make their appearance in order to enter the country.*"

The appointment of a " *Prefect*," or " Apostolic Prefect," of the Sandwich Islands (commander or governor), by a sovereign pontiff with " two swords," who assumes a very general jurisdiction, and even claims all kingdoms and countries, was a measure of such a political aspect, as to have been a good reason for rejecting the stranger who bore it, and those under his direction : and if the boasted oneness and infallibility of the Romish church from the days of her departure from the standard of Christ make her responsible for all the dogmas, superstitions, and idolatries, which she has once authorized and never renounced, it is the more reasonable for a parent or patriarch not to bid God speed to its teachers in his own house, his own premises, or his own domain. If Kaahumanu had the right to forbid the *entrance* of strangers, much more their *residence*. This acknowledged principle in the laws of nations ought to have been respected by the unwelcome strangers, and the exercise of the just rights of sovereignty by Kaahumanu, for good reasons, was entitled to the respect of the sovereigns and subjects of other countries. She supposed it would be so, and appears to have had no doubt as to her duty to her people in this case.

Jealous for the honor of God's truth and affected by the delusions, follies, and sins of men, neither she nor her friends could wish the introduction of a new superstition or fatal error among the Hawaiians, or the almost certain means of civil dissensions. No earthly pontiff or potentate had a just claim to the privilege of putting any of his European militia upon the Sandwich Islands for the purpose of bringing their inhabitants to his feet. False teachers have no just right to seduce the nations or to supplant the religion of the Bible anywhere. Had Kaahumanu understood the Papal system as Luther, Zuingle, and Knox understood it, centuries ago, and as Ronge, Czerski, and numerous converted Ro-

* Vattel's Law of Nations.

manists understand it now, she would not probably have done less than to reject the offer of its teachings to her people. Boki allowed that the teaching of the Romish faith there would tend to civil strife.

But I cannot here go through the narrative of subsequent events connected with this: but such as deserve it must be given rather in the order of time in which they occurred, involving various actors in the progress of things for years. As the captain landed the Romish teachers and artisans without the permission of the government, and refused to obey the queen's orders communicated to him by Boki, to take them away, they were left in precarious circumstances at Honolulu, and received favor from Boki.

Before I left Lahaina, an outrage occurred there, on the 23d of October, 1827, the commencement of a new crusade against the tabu. Wahinepio, late governess, had died, as also her son, Kahalaia, and Geo. P. T., his rival, almost simultaneously, in 1826. Hoapili succeeded Wahinepio as governor by the appointment of Kaahumanu, and was disposed to maintain her policy.

Several women, belonging to his jurisdiction, the governor learned, were, in violation of the tabu, or government prohibition, on board an English whaler, the John Palmer, in Lahaina roadstead. Hoapili demanded of the captain, an American, to set them on shore or permit his men to fetch them : but he would do neither. The governor condescended to reason with him, and said, "When your men desert your ships and come on shore, and you apply for them, we deliver them up without hesitation. These women have broken our laws, and you would take them away. It is our right to require that you deliver up to me our people who violate our laws." Repeating this reasonable demand, day after day, unheeded, and finding the vessel about to take her anchor, and the captain being on shore, just at evening, the governor bade him send off for the offenders, while himself should stay on shore ; but this he treated with contempt. The governor, hesitating as to the next step, and fearing the vessel would sail with the women, exclaimed, "What shall we do ?" A plebeian, whose hints he valued, replied laconically, and ambiguously, "*Ka waapa.*" The boat! "Yes," said the governor, and the captain's boat was instantly taken up on dry land. The captain hastened to the house of Mr. Richards, in much perturbation. The people thronging him, thought he was intending violence to our families, and cried out, "Fasten the gate and exclude the foreigner." Mr. R., however, admitted him, when he gave us to understand the town would be destroyed in an hour from the time the taking of his boat should be known on board his ship. He was conducted to the governor's.

The mate coming on shore, obtained permission of the captain to fire on the town at discretion, if he were not released in an hour, with the caution to aim above the missionaries. Hearing of their design to fire on the town, Mr. R. hastened to the house of Hoapili, to learn his design, and found, on inquiry, it was simply to detain the captain and his boat, till the women were restored. On reflection, doubtless influenced by the kindness and peace-making suggestions of Mr. R., trusting to the honor of the captain, who promised to restore the women the next day, the governor allowed him to take his boat, and return to his ship. But before he could arrive, the ship commenced firing cannon-balls, which, by their horrifying sound, as they passed near us, and by their ploughing the ground behind us, and the relative position of the ship, the house, and the striking of the balls, appeared with little room for doubt to have been aimed at the house of Mr. R. In deciding whether to risk ourselves and families to the direct stroke of the balls, or to the falling ruins of the walls of the house, should it be struck, we took our wives and tender babes to the cellar, to be below their deadly range, and there looked up for protection to Him whose shield was still over us : and those two sisters seemed called on again to mingle their sympathies, while breasting the storm of wrath from the sons of violence, and all, to mingle thanksgiving, for the loving-kindnesses of the Lord often manifested in these troubles of the way.

Kahekili (thunder), a warrior who had command of a small battery, showed the governor his scars, and told him he was ready to repel force by force. But the governor was not disposed to in-jure the ship, or commander, or crew.

The balls passed on till the captain approached the ship and countermanded the firing. The ship sailed without discharging the women or making any reparation. The governor made a report of the transaction to his superior at Honolulu, of which the " Missionary Herald" says :—

" Let the official report be considered—its order, explicitness, free-dom from extraneous matter, and from everything like swelling and bombast, and its manly assumption of responsibility, and then let it be said whether such men are to receive abuse and insult, and their towns fired upon, not only without provocation, but when discharging a great public duty, which they owe to themselves and their persecu-tors, and whether the civilized world is to look calmly on and see the peace and the territory of the unoffending natives barbarously violated, merely because riotous sailors will not brook the restraints of civi-lization and Christianity."

The Report is as follows :

"LAHAINA, Oct. 24, 1827.

" Love to you, Elisabeth Kaahumanu.

" This is the word which I have to declare to you. We have recently been in difficulty ; of us of Maui, no one but myself is involved. What we have done was my own. This is the ground of the difficulty which you are to consider—a strict regard to God ; because you and we had said, the women must not go on board the ships for the purposes of prostitution ; I have strictly observed this edict of ours.

" There have recently gone off, secretly, several women, for purposes of lewdness. Nakoko and Mikabako, and others whose names I do not know. When I heard by the people that the ship had got possession of the women, then I requested the commander of the ship, Captain Clark, to return to me the women ; he would not consent ; he ridiculed what I said. That day passed ; next morning I urged him again ; three times I insisted on it. He said to me, ' Your efforts are vain. It is not right ; it is not thus in Great Britain ; it is not right for you to withhold women from Englishmen. Do not keep back the women that go in the bad way ; otherwise, a man-of-war will come and destroy you all.' Then I replied, ' I do not at all regard what you have said; there is but one thing that is right in my view—*that you send me back the women;* but understand, if you do not return them, I shall detain you here on shore till we get the women. Then you may go to the ship.'

" My requirement was not at all complied with. Then I sent men to take the boat. The boat was detained by me, and the foreigner was detained by me here on shore. He said to me, ' This place will be full of ships, and Maui shall be free from tabu, or entirely burnt, so that not a cluster of houses shall be left. My ship is ready to fire upon you this night.'

" I replied, ' If the guns of your ship fire, I will take care of you. You and I, and my chief, will go together to another place; if your men fire from the ship, we, the people of the island, will remain quiet ; but if the people of the ship land here on shore, to fight us, then my people will fight them. You and I will sit still and let your people and mine do the fighting. I will take care of you. If you do not give me back the women, you and I will remain here on shore, and you shall not return to your vessel. I have but one desire, and that is, *the return hither of the women.*' I ended. We continued together from the early to the latter part of the evening, when the cannon of the ship were fired. Mr. Richards had come to me, saying, ' I have come to promote reconciliation out of love to you, and out of love to them.' Mr. Richards inquired of me, ' What is your design ?' I replied, 'My only design is, that the women be returned.' We were persuaded to yield, by Mr. Richards. I therefore sent back the foreigner, but did not obtain the women.

" These are my thoughts concerning the recent doings in this place, belonging to your king. It is nearly right, perhaps ; it is nearly wrong, perhaps. He said to me, ' I shall sail to Oahu ; Boki and the Consul will come and fight you.'

" Where are you ? Look out well for Nakoko and those with her, and if you can get them, send them back here to Maui ; and if the vessel does not anchor, then give directions to Pelekaluhi (Kaikieowa). It is ended. Love to you all.

" HOAPILI—KANE."

" Capt. Clark knew perfectly well that by receiving women on board his ship and concealing them, he was violating a law of the place.

" Without reference to the immorality of such conduct, he knew that according to the usages of all countries, civilized and savage, Christian and pagan, the rulers of a place possess the right of restraining and punishing their own people. He must therefore have been aware that the demand of Hoapili was reasonable and proper, and that every attempt to evade or resist it, was dishonorable.

" The arrest and detention of the Captain, with the avowed purpose of compelling him to deliver up the criminals, was strictly defensible, on the most obvious and acknowledged principles of government. Whether it was wise in the governor to take this step, depended on his being able and prepared to proceed to extremities." *

At that time Capt. Buckle was at Honolulu, and the report of the riot by his ship, published in the United States, had just reached that place. Such outrages as were chargeable to the Daniel and John Palmer, committed by men claiming British protection, afforded the occasion, and should have had the effect, to call forth the sympathy and energy of the British Consul, to shield the chiefs and missionaries from the further infliction of such injuries. But those who knew him, or saw his interviews at that time with Captains Buckle and Clark, who met at Honolulu, did not expect his sympathy or aid in the cause of the mission, or of the government. Hoapili sent his despatch by canoe, seventy-five miles, the answer to which was awaited with solicitude. The threats of madmen who, without justice or honor, fire on a town, when told that their shots would not be returned, deserved some attention. The following note was soon received at Lahaina, from Mr. Chamberlain, who was then taking charge of the station at Honolulu, with only native helpers :

" The day the news came, the dust was literally so agitated by the wind, that frequently the ships in the harbor and the roads could not be seen. Apply this figuratively, and you may form some idea of what is passing. A very great excitement exists here, among all ranks, in consequence of the communication to the Board respecting Capt. Buckle, and nothing is talked of but the ' make o ka haole,' threatened death of the foreigner. I have heard from good authority, that Capt. B. is going up to Lahaina to obtain satisfaction. I have also been told that the captains of the English whalers have declared their intention to go to Lahaina and cause the removal of the tabu. Be prepared for the worst, and trust the event with the Lord. He has heretofore been with us, in difficulty and danger, and we know that in adhering to his word, we are in the path of duty. I feel quiet respecting the event of the brooding storm. The Lord reigneth; and he will overrule all things to the furtherance of his cause."

The chiefs and others sent letters from Honolulu informing the governor and the princess at Lahaina, of the rage and threats of the British Consul, and Captains Buckle and Clark, and of the possibility of their coming to Lahaina with a force, for bloodshed.

In the midst of such blustering, Boki, either afraid of such men or wishing their co-operation, apprised the chiefs of Maui of the threatened vengeance on Mr. Richards, with whom myself and family were sojourning, and on Lahaina, if he were not

* Missionary Herald, vol. xxiv.

given up to their rage: and he advised Hoapili not to defend him, but to let foreigner and foreigner take it out together.

The first Sabbath and the first Monday of November were days of interest and of peculiar trial, when this intelligence was communicated at Lahaina. But never, perhaps, did the missionaries feel a more calm and sweet reliance on the gracious promises and care of their Divine Protector. Nor was his aid then sought in vain. The blessed Word of God, the throne of grace, the fellowship and mutual sympathy of Christian pilgrims, men and women, in those troublous times, afforded them precious hours long to be remembered. The converts to Christianity were not slow to show their kindness; and the Maui chiefs resolved to stand their ground, having the honor and integrity to acknowledge their own responsibility in the case of Capt. Clark, and the blamelessness of the missionary in reporting to the Board the conduct of the captain of the Daniel. But Kaahumanu, then at Honolulu, took perhaps the liveliest interest in the management and termination of this struggle; and to sustain rather than surrender the cause of truth, she sent for the Lahaina chiefs and Mr. Richards to repair to Honolulu. After a week further of suspense and solicitude, being favored with a passage by Capt. Little, Mr. Richards, to meet her wishes, and myself to resume my post, embarked with our families for the stormy port of Honolulu, whither, a year before, the same two families had gone in very similar circumstances.

The next morning showed us the little forest of masts in the harbor and roadstead of Honolulu, and among them those of the John Palmer and the Daniel (or Daniel the 4th), which had engaged so warmly in the crusade against the tabu of the chiefs. The wind being off shore too strong to allow the brig to enter the harbor, she dropped her anchor in the roadstead. Capt. Little, who could not say much for our comfort in case of offered violence, lowered a boat, and another boat was sent for us by Manuia, the captain of the fort, to convey us on shore.

After some agitation in getting our wives and children down the sides of the vessel into the boats, which rocked like cradles on the agitated waves in the roadstead, we passed on safely near the tall ships in the harbor, and reaching the shore a few paces from the south gate of the fort, were met and helped out of the boat and ushered through the gate by Manuia. There stood the tall, portly, and beloved Kaahumanu, ready to welcome and shield us, having armed men on either hand, not to incarcerate but to defend, and in a dignified, motherly attitude, saluted us with cordiality and silent tears; then stepping forward, led us through the fort and out at the northern gate, and thence onward half a mile, to the mission establishment, at the eastern extremity of the village. She made us feel that the better half of the nation was pledged for our protection. With her accustomed consideration of the young king, who was then occupying the

Kalanimoku house, she wished us to stop and salute him, which, as she led the way up the long stairs into his hall, we were very happy to do. She then, though not in firm health, to do more than the highest courtesy required, proceeded with us to my residence, and there giving us her hand again, said, "I have seen you *safe* to your own house, and will now return to my own to rest, and to see the chiefs recently arrived. The *body* has been made strong by the love of the heart."

At evening we perceived our premises were guarded by armed men. Mr. Charlton seemed very solicitous to ascertain that, *aside from the testimony of natives,* "Captain Buckle could *not* be convicted of having *bought a female slave as the inmate of his cabin.*"

A highly esteemed and careful correspondent had, a little before, written me thus : " The English consul says, ' he must see Mr. Richards in person, and obtain proof of the charge against Capt. Buckle, as he is accused of a high crime, and if it cannot be substantiated by better proof than can be admitted from the natives (for the oath of a native is of no validity), there will be a *tremendous train of consequences.'* "

The chiefs and people of Lahaina, whose oath in any circumstances, had he dared to take it, would have been as good as that of their opposers, were ready to have given him the facts which would have fully confirmed the published statements of the case, what name soever he might please to attach to the crime in question. Had he been seeking to embarrass the chiefs and screen their abusers, he might have been expected to pursue the long-continued course in which he was obviously countenanced, for a time, by the American consul and others, some of whom, it is believed, at length saw their mistake.

The opinion of Mr. John Young, inclining to that of Boki and Mr. Charlton, respecting Mr. Richards, was exceedingly distressing to Kaahumanu. She had often confided in his judgment, and was accustomed to respect his opinions; but the life and reputation of a highly esteemed missionary, and the important principle of justice involved in such a decision, could not by her be so easily abandoned. In equity, her own judgment was right, but she was puzzled in her circumstances as chief magistrate, surrounded by formidable boasting, bullying enemies, to distinguish a *rightful* and a *libellous* exhibition of the misdeeds of transgressors. David Malo, a shrewd plebeian, supposing that truth might be pleaded in justification of the report of crimes, said to her, " In what country is it the practice to condemn the man who gives true information of crimes committed, and let the criminal go uncensured and unpunished ?" " None," she replied. The chiefs of Lahaina maintained that the young woman whom Capt. B. took away was *sold.* But, "in the morning," says a native writer, " came the British consul, in his official dress, with Capt. Buckle, Boki, Manuia, and several merchants, and with an air of confidence and importance, entered into the hall of council, and insisted that Mr. Richards should be punished." Kaahumanu, not seeing any cause of action, said, ' Mr. Richards had not violated the laws, but still she would send for him.' She did so; and in half an hour he was there, accompanied by those of our number who had with him been honored with the cannon balls of the John Palmer; but before they reached the hall the consul and his party hastily withdrew.

These struggles, by the blessing of God, were overruled to produce in the minds of the people a deeper conviction that there must be something good in a religion which the vilest men alone revile and oppose, and in those principles which could endure with patience and unflinching perseverance undeserved opposition and malignant contumely.

What they saw in the two conflicting parties was precisely what the religion of the Bible taught them to expect, and thus its truth was more apparent and more impressive, to show them how odious they must appear in opposing God and his holy Book.

When Mr. R. returned to Lahaina from his trial or visit at Honolulu, he was greeted by his people with unwonted interest and affection; concerning which he says:

" As soon as our doors were opened, the people began to call to express their *aloha*, good will. The number who called before breakfast we estimate at 1000. Their attachment to their teachers was never more apparent. Many of them had been made to fear that I should be sent from the islands or executed here; and when they saw that we had actually returned without injury, they were prepared to express their joy in the strongest manner. Many seemed not only to believe but to feel that the Lord was on our side. A day of fasting had been observed the week that we left, and from that time little circles continued to meet to pray for us till we returned. There never was probably any occurrence which so much endeared the missionary to the people, or them to him."

During these troubles, the native members of the church stood their ground well, and the number of candidates officially announced for admission to full communion, was greater than usual for an equal time. Some, evidently roused by the unreasonable threats and violence towards the friends of order and the propagators of the Gospel, and by the undeviating constancy of those who professed to teach its uncompromising claims, were led the more carefully to examine those claims, and their investigation resulted in their favor. Before the dispersion of the chiefs after their investigation of the alleged offence of Mr. Richards, they were invited by Mrs. Bingham and Mrs. Richards to a social evening interview at my house, of which and of a scene at my place of worship, the following sketch was shortly given to the Secretary of the American Board :—

" Towards evening all came that were invited, except Boki and his wife, and to this interesting group we should have been happy to have introduced you, and any other of our Christian friends, and I doubt not you would have been highly gratified with the interview. You would have seen the regent, once the haughty Kaahumanu, now condescending, and kind, and grateful to her Christian teachers; with her two royal sisters, Kalakua and Piia, all members of the church, bearing the Christian names of Elisabeth, Mary, and Lydia, and all endeavoring, as we believe, to copy the virtues of those Scripture characters—exerting great influence over the people in favor of reformation, and rejoicing in the mercy of God in giving them the Gospel. You would have seen the pleasing youth, the king, and his sister, rising rapidly to maturity, both possessing vivacity, and exhibiting kindness towards us; the latter a member of our church and a great comfort to the serious party; and the former as far advanced in the rudiments of learning as most of our native teachers, and, we believe, disposed to aid decidedly, the cause of the mission. You would have seen Kuakini, the Governor of Hawaii, dignified, sociable, and friendly, who has built a church at Kailua, which probably cost as many days' works as any church in America, and who has for some time been diligently assisting in translating the Gospels, and in teaching a class in the rudiments of Arithmetic. He has recently advised Kaahumanu to have laws established, written, and published. Naihe you would have met, a decided friend of similar rank, and his wife, Kapiolani, who, perhaps, is second to none in improved manners and Christian character. You would have seen the solid Hoapili, of the same rank, the Governor of Maui, recently propounded to the church, the most fearless of all in resisting foreign encroachments, foremost of all to suppress the vices which derive so much support from abroad. Another of the old phalanx of Kamehameha would have attracted your notice—Kaikioewa, now Governor of Kauai, who seems desirous to be instructed and to promote our cause; and his wife, Keaweamahi, also, who, as you know, is a respectable member of the church, admitted at Kauai. You would have seen, also, the late queen of Kauai, Deborah Kapule, and her husband, Simeon Kaiu, whom we regard as promising Christians. They recently presented their infant son to the Lord in baptism, whom they called Josiah Kaumualii, out of respect to the characters of those two men.

"You would have seen Kekauluohi, Kinau, and Kekauonohi, the three surviving women who were on our arrival wives of Liholiho. The former has for five years lived regularly with another husband, gives evidence of piety, and was last Sabbath propounded for admission to our church. Kinau, who has recently married Kekuanaoa, now appears friendly, but not pious; her husband, whom you would have seen, is like her in these respects, and is commander of a small standing force of two or three hundred men at this place. Kekauonohi has for about four years lived single, appears to be a cordial and decided friend of the mission.

"Three interesting young chiefs, Laanui, Kealiiahonui, and Kanaina, of pleasing manners and hopeful piety, would also have engaged your attention among the happy guests. Laanui, by his correct behavior for more than five years, has given us much satisfaction. He is a good assistant in the work of translation; we consult him and others of his standing, with more advantage than any of the youth who have been instructed in foreign schools. Kealiiahonui, who travelled around Hawaii a year ago, exhorting the people to obey the Word of God and the voice of the chiefs, has had an oversight of several schools, and been employed considerably with success, in teaching. He lives single, keeps a regular diary, and is foremost of his countrymen in the art of singing in our mode. Kanaina, the husband of Kekauluohi, often assists in conducting conference meetings, and is very desirous to be admitted to the church. Though we hope to admit him before a great while, yet we think a longer trial advisable. Joseph Leleiohoku, Kalanimoku's sprightly little son, and Kamanele, the young daughter of Governor Kuakini, were also present.

" We might have invited nearly as large a number of others, of the third and fourth grade of chiefs, who exhibit similar marks of improvement, and who appear to be truly friendly to the cause of the Gospel, and whose presence would have added to your pleasure, had we room and means, and strength to accommodate so many at one time. But look for a few moments at the present group—twenty-one chiefs of the Sandwich Islands, mingling in friendly, courteous, and Christian conversation, with seven of the mission family whom you have employed among them. Contemplate their former and their present habits— their former and their present hopes. They have laid aside their vices and excesses, and their love of noise and war. You see every one decently dressed in our own style. Instead of the roaring *hula*, you hear them join us in a song of Zion in their own tongue: ' Kindred in Christ, for his dear sake a hearty welcome here receive.' Listen, and you will not only hear the expressions of gratitude to us and to God, for the privileges they now enjoy, but you will hear these old warriors lamenting that their former kings, fathers, and companions in arms had been slain in battle, or carried off by the hand of time, before the blessed Gospel of Christ had been proclaimed on these benighted shores. Your heart would have glowed with devout gratitude to God for the evidence that while our simple food was passing round the social circle for their present gratification, the minds of some of these children of pagans enjoyed a feast of better things; and your thoughts, no doubt, like ours, would have glanced at a happier meeting of the friends of God, in the world of glory. When our thanks were returned, at the close of our humble repast, though you might not have been familiar with the language used, you would have lifted up your heart in thankfulness for what already appeared as the fruits of your efforts here, and for the prospect of still greater things than these.

" Again, you see the same company of chiefs joined by Boki and his wife, and the others of a lower grade, alluded to above, gathering with three thousand of the people at the humble house of prayer, when the yet novel, but cheerful sound of ' the church going bell,' breaks on the stillness of the Sabbath morning. You see a great proportion of this large congregation, decently clad in articles of foreign manufacture, and others in the best of their own, and some even richly dressed. About one-third of those present are furnished with their books of hymns, chiefly in their own binding, which many of them regard as the most valuable article they possess. They join in the worship, and you admire the order, the sobriety, the wakefulness, and the pleasing attention which pervade the assembly, while angels wait to witness the effects of the Word of God on their hearts. As I ascended the little pulpit stairs, the eyes of the congregation seemed

to greet me with a welcome.   It was the day for the communion service
and for the admission of members, and I chose for my theme the commission of our Savior—'Go ye into all the world and preach the
Gospel to every creature : he that believeth and is baptized shall be
saved, and he that believeth not shall be damned.'   I spoke of the
importance, the benevolence, and the authority of the commission,
the character of the doctrines and the precepts to be proclaimed, the
nature of evangelical faith, the design of the sacraments, and the different consequences of obeying and rejecting the Gospel.   Many
listened as though these doctrines, duties, and privileges were for them ;
and as though they were concerned in the momentous and everlasting
consequences at stake.

    " In the afternoon the congregation assembled again, a little earlier
than the usual hour, and the church took their seats in order round the
table of the Lord.   Kekauluohi first presented herself before the
church and congregation, and, at her request, her desire to consecrate
herself to God, and to obey the Gospel, was made known, and she
was propounded for admission after further trial.   Next, six others
who, about a year ago, had been examined before the church, and had
stood propounded five or six months, presented themselves for baptism.

    " Seldom has a more pleasing sight been witnessed in the Sandwich
Islands, or a more pleasing service fallen to my lot.   Here you might
have seen a man advanced in years, long versed in the abominations of
heathenism, and well acquainted with the wars of former kings, now
coming to this sacramental pool to be washed, and to pledge his allegiance to Christ, the King of kings.   His name was Kamakahiki, but
he chose to adopt the Christian name of Lazarus, the friend whom
Jesus loved.   Still more interesting was the meek, humble, and devout
appearance of his wife, Anna Waiakea, who, about two years since,
being raised from a dangerous illness, engaged to devote herself to God
as the only proper expression of her gratitude to him for his goodness to her ; and from that period, her deportment has been such as we
could wish, and such as we think, if continued, will greatly adorn her
profession.   In this little group you would have seen the interesting
youth, John Ii, one of the two whom Liholiho early, and in a very
special manner, placed under the instruction of the mission, to make
a fair trial of what our new system could do for the people.   He, and
the three other men, Kahananui, Naaoa, and Wahinealii, have, for a
long time, stood firm, even in times of considerable discouragement and
sharp trials.

    " After imploring the Divine presence and blessing, I read to them the
summary articles of faith, as they were drawn up by your revered and
lamented predecessor, when our church was organized in Boston.   On
giving their assent to these publicly, as they had done privately,
they were baptized, and thus they were admitted to a visible standing in the church of Christ in general, being baptized into his
name, and publicly professing their faith in him.   I then read
to them the covenant of our church, with which they had been
previously made acquainted.   To this they severally and publicly
signed their names with ours, ' subscribing with their hands unto the
Lord,' and thus, with our unanimous consent, they became members
of our church in particular, in full communion, and were pronounced

no longer strangers and foreigners but fellow citizens with us ; and they united joyfully with us and others in celebrating the Savior's bleeding love.

" We would adore the matchless goodness of the Lord of Heaven and earth for this display of his mercy towards us and towards the people of these isles of the sea.   May all the inhabitants of the isles soon rejoice and be glad in him.   While the friends of Zion take courage from the evidence of the Divine blessing on the preaching of the Gospel in heathen lands, let them left up their hearts in thanksgiving for the past, and in unceasing supplication for a more general effusion of the Spirit here and throughout the world."

Two days before this Sabbath scene, the chiefs proclaimed and caused to be published, written laws against murder, theft, and adultery.   The same week, the first sheet of the translation of Luke's Gospel was printed.   The Gospels by Matthew, Mark, and John, had already been sent to the United States to be printed there for the Hawaiian people, under the supervision of Mr. Loomis.

At the same time, the friends of our cause, in the United States, hailing the evidence of progress, saw it to be reasonable to reinforce our mission, though the outfit and passage of another reinforcement deemed by the Board necessary, would cost, at once, some $8,000.   Whether the Christian public would advance with the Providence of God in the work of missions was yet to be settled, as the lamented Dr. Worcester had said in 1820, after sending forth the missions to the Sandwich Islands and Palestine :

" The question is to be decided, and it may be decided soon, whether there is in this country, Christian benevolence enough—sufficiently undivided, unobstructed, and unrestrained—sufficiently resembling the charity which descended from heaven—to bear any proportionable part in the great work of evangelizing the heathen."*

---

* By the same pen it was stated in the same year, in respect to the first ten years of the operations of the American Board—" In these ten years, there has been paid from the treasury of the Board the total sum of $201,600.   For the Missions to the East, Bombay, and Ceylon, just about $100,000—for the Missions to the American Aborigines $51,000—for the Mission to the Sandwich Islands (including the outfit, passage, and settlement in 1819, 1820) $10,461 80—for the Palestine Mission $2,350 —for the Foreign Mission'school $17,340--and for various subordinate and contingent objects and purposes $20,000."

It may be added that subsequent to 1820, there were paid out from the same treasury for the mission to the Sandwich Islands, in the years ending August; in 1821, $669 70 ; in 1822, $1,071 ; in 1823, including the outfit and passage of the first reinforcement, $12,074 67; in 1824, $6,746 30; in 1825, $9,764 89; in 1826, $10,241 94; in 1827, 9,761 31—making the cost of the mission for its first eight years (besides the gifts of private friends and natives), $60,791 61.

CHAPTER XIII.

In the commencement of a new year, I will take further notice of the measures for increasing evangelical light, counteracting iniquity, and encouraging the nation to go forward in their improvement.

Soon after the difficulties in respect to the Daniel and the John Palmer, Kaahumanu wrote to her friend, the Secretary of the American Board :

" My affectionate regards to you, Mr. Evarts, and to all our kindred in that country, on account of the great blessing you have sent us—the light—the Word of God. We have given our hearts to God. We rejoice in the great salvation. Have ye good will towards us, and pray ye to God for us, that we may all stand firm together, as one in the following of Jesus Christ ; that you and we may all be saved by the Messiah, the Redeemer.

" I pity Mr. Bishop on account of his companion, the only one of yours who has fallen here. Grief for his companion and compassion for his children.

" ELISABETH KAAHUMANU."

Her honored sister wrote as follows :

" OAHU, March 12, 1828.

" Mr. EVARTS :—May you live to a good old age. I affectionately salute you and all the brethren ; this is my thought for you which l communicate to you. I am learning the holy Word of Christ and his law and his good ordinances. I have, in a small degree, acquired a very little. I have not yet acquired much. But the desire of my heart goes out to beg of him night and day, that my soul may obtain everlasting salvation in heaven. My desire and my mind, and my thoughts, I have bound up in a bundle and committed to him ; and his word and his law are what I now replace in my heart, that my house may be fully peopled by his powerful spirit, his unceasing love, and his unfeigned goodness, and his long suffering.mercy.

" O may we all be saved by him from the rising of the sun to the setting of the sun.

"Greatly does my heart fear God on account of the greatness of my sin while living in the house of mirth and feasting, until both body and soul had well nigh perished in the house of mirth and feasting. Therefore do I fear God ; and therefore does my heart repent by night and by day, every day of my life ; nor does my heart say that it is good, because I pray to God and repent of sin ; no ; it is with God to judge whether it is right or wrong. And it is mine to repent of my sins, and to cast (myself) on him, and to give him my heart, soul, and desires, that I may live for ever, through Jesus Christ.

"LYDIA NAMAHANA."

About the same time, Kaahumanu, in addressing "her friends and kindred" on the other side of the water, said, "I wish you to send hither more teachers to increase the light, in the name of Jesus Christ. That is my desire in respect to you, for great has been the kindness of God towards us, the people of dark hearts."

The American Board being encouraged by communications from the Islands, by the increased liberality of the churches, and by the readiness of missionary candidates to embark in the service, sent forth additional laborers in the autumn of 1827, to succor their little missionary band struggling there,—some ready to faint,—and to speed their work.

The following introductory communication from the Board, was addressed to the young king, still in his minority :

"To KAUIKEAOULI :

"Sincere affection for you, my young friend.

"We, the directors of missions who live here in America, have heard that you are fond of learning, and that you wish all the people of the islands to keep the Word of God. We have heard of this, and are glad.

"We send more teachers to strengthen the teachers now at the islands, and to hasten the good work of enlightening all your people. We greatly love all the teachers who have been laboring with you so many years. All our good people love them and honor them. We love also the teachers whom we now send out, and doubt not that you and all your people will receive them kindly and gladly.

"One of our friends, who is one of the society of the directors of missions, sends you a great book, full of maps, the best that was ever made in America. He writes you a letter, and wishes you to understand the maps. Mr. Bingham, your teacher, will explain them to you.

"We pray that you may be a good man ; that you may live in the fear of God, and that your soul may be saved by Jesus Christ.

"I write this in the name of all the directors of missions, and am,
"Your sincere friend,
"JER. EVARTS"
"Missionary Rooms, Boston, Nov. 2, 1827."

The reinforcement thus introduced, consisted of four preachers, —Rev. Lorrin Andrews, J. S. Green, P. J. Gulick, and E. W. Clark ; a physician, Dr. G. P. Judd ; a printer, Mr. Stephen Shephard ; and the wives of the six, together with four unmarried females, Misses Maria Ogden, Delia Stone, Maria Patten, and

Mary Ward. They embarked from Boston on board the Parthian, Capt. Blinn, and passing round Cape Horn, reached Honolulu, March 30, 1828, having during the passage suffered an unusual share of discomforts, from the discourtesy of the captain, and others. Their arrival was opportune, and was hailed by the missionaries on the ground, and by the chiefs and many of the people.

When the news that their American friends were sending helpers reached Kauai, Mr. Whitney wrote respecting Kaikioewa and Keaweamahi, " When I stated to him and his wife the news which was received yesterday that more missionaries were probably at hand, striking on their breasts, and with an emphasis too expressive for me to communicate, they exclaimed, ' Oluolu maloko,' happy within."

Kaahumanu invited them on shore, received them warmly, and gave them an official and affectionate welcome, such as might be expected from a Christian ruler in her circumstances:

" *April* 2. Kind affection for you all, ye missionaries, the company of kindred beloved. This is my sentiment ; the love and great joy of my heart towards God on account of his sending you hither to help us, that you and we may dwell together in the shade of his salvation, and that in his name we and you may labor affectionately for him. Joy is mine and great rejoicing towards you on account of his sending you hither to succor us here. My heart thanks God for our being now blessed by his causing us personally to meet together. Good will to you and us all. May our souls be saved by Jesus Christ. That is the finishing of the thought.

" ELISABETH KAAHUMANU."

The members of the reinforcement in reply, expressed their gratitude for the politeness and cordiality of their reception, and pledged themselves to seek the best interests of the rulers and people according to the Word of God, which they had come to teach and publish. Public thanksgivings were offered, and a sermon on the occasion was delivered on the theme, "How beautiful upon the mountains are the feet of him that bringeth good tidings, that publisheth peace, that bringeth good tidings of good, that publisheth salvation." The juvenile king, then at Hawaii, being apprised by letter of their arrival, soon returned to Oahu, but first kindly wrote them :

" Kaawaloa, April 12, 1828.

" I affectionately salute you, the company of new missionaries. I desire that you and we may dwell together in this country. When I arrive, then we will salute each other. Love to the company of old missionaries. " KAUIKEAOULI."

The missionaries assembled at Honolulu from the different stations, and on the 23d of the month, the older and the recently arrived held their annual convention. On the 27th, the reinforcement united with the mission church, and soon entered on the missionary work. Mr. and Mrs. Andrews and Miss Patten were assigned to the Lahaina station : Mr. and Mrs. Clark, Dr. and Mrs. Judd, Mr. and Mrs. Shephard, and Miss Ward to Honolulu; Mr. and Mrs. Gulick and Miss Ogden to Kauai. Mr. Green having an agency to perform for the American Board in exploring the North West Coast as a field of missions, accomplished it by the earliest opportunity, and returning made his report, and, with the others, entered on the work at the islands.

Never perhaps since the command was given to preach the Gospel to every creature, have missionaries entered their field of labor with a warmer welcome or under more auspicious circumstances; the heads of the nation and twenty subordinate chiefs being in favor of their work, and none to oppose their settlement; six congregations, embracing about 12,000 hearers, 26,000 pupils, and 440 native school teachers, all needing their help, and nearly 100,000 of the population waiting for the means of competent instruction, while the spirit of renovating grace appeared to be hovering over the congregations where the Gospel was regularly preached.

Having been much of the time from the commencement of the mission the only ordained missionary stationed on the island of Oahu, I was now favored to have another preacher located there, and a corps of needful helpers. Of the reception of the reinforcement and state of the field, Mr. Clark, after careful observation, says :

" Our reception by this people has been in the highest degree gratifying ; a great door and effectual is opened to us, and there are some, but I cannot say very many, adversaries. The prospects of the mission, I think, are more flattering than I anticipated. It is true we are called to witness some unpleasant sights, and from foreigners some bitter opposition ; but there is more docility and eagerness for instruction among the people generally than I expected, and among the chiefs far more politeness and intelligence. There seems to be nothing but means wanting to increase the operations of the mission to almost any extent. Meetings are thronged, books are eagerly called for, schools are established in almost every part of the islands, and we would hope in some cases the Spirit of God is giving efficacy to divine truth. I attended a church meeting a few evenings since, which strongly reminded me of similar meetings in my own land. About twenty native members of the church were present, several of them high chiefs. Four persons were examined for admission to the church, all of whom appeared to have a good acquaintance with the leading truths of the Gospel, and with their own hearts : but I was particularly interested with the simplicity and apparent sincerity of one of them—a female. After giving an interesting account of her course of life, and her present views and feelings, she was asked what she should do if the missionaries and chiefs should turn backward and speak against the Word of God. She said, with much apparent feeling, that she had not thought of that. She hardly knew what she should do : but the great desire of her heart was to follow the Word of God till she died."

At that period, Capt. Beechey, of the ship Blossom, misled, it is believed, by a distinguished resident, was, by his letters and journals, endeavoring to guard the public mind against any very favorable impressions as to the missionary work. That ship had touched at Oahu, in 1826, and having shown there, by an experiment, that a sovereign may command and compel the services of a subject, entirely against his will (as in the impressing of a resident seaman), passed on to northern seas. An American gentleman, who there fell in with him, gave us his opinion, ' that it was the design of Captains Beechey and Charlton to break up the mission cause in the islands entirely,' and though reports made by the mission were severely called in question, yet, from that period, has the evidence been gradually accumulating, that there had been solid ground for the fairest reports of progress which the mission had ever published.

The advantages of the mission to any one of the four principal islands, were enough to balance all the trouble and expense incurred on them all. Connected with the station at Lahaina, were 174 schools, embracing 6027 males and 5854 females, making 11,881 learners, more than 10,000 of whom were reckoned as reading or reciting reading lessons, and 885 as capable of writing. Mr. Richards had married 1,222 individuals in a single year, and in one instance, 59 couple in one day, in a population of about 35,000, who belonged to his missionary field. About one thousand of the people appeared to be seeking salvation, and apparently attending to the duties of religion. Among these were found persons of four generations—those advanced in years, who had grown grey in the service of idols, and who could distinctly recollect the visit of Capt. Cook and other early visitors of the islands; their children also, now past the meridian of life; their grand-children, now mature, and approaching to middle age ; and their great-grand-children among the youth, all looking at the religion of the Gospel as alike needful. The station being strengthened by another laborer, one hundred and forty teachers of the several schools were organized into a school on the Lancasterian plan, to be taught more perfectly how to teach, while monitors were in their stead, for the time, going on with their schools. The violence of the John Palmer had convinced the chiefs of the importance of greater watchfulness on their part, and of larger and better guns at their battery, sufficient, at least, to be a match for a *war-whaler*, should another ever approach. Hoapili not only prepared such means of defence, but established a guard that patrolled the beach by night, whenever danger was apprehended from shipping. That church was, at this period, deprived of several of its interesting members. One of these was Robert Haia, a useful teacher to the princess and her school. He had married Halekii, a companion of the young princess, who, from her piety and refinement of mind and manners, was regarded as the ornament of the female circle at Lahaina, and with whom he had the prospect of a happy life. A little incident in the short life of Robert is illustrative of some of the difficulties our native teachers had early to encounter.

The princess, Nahienaena, whose school he taught, and her brother, Kauikeaouli, were invited to tea at the house of a British resident, while the princess was supposed to be seriously seeking, not only to secure the salvation of her own soul, but to know how she might honor God and do good to the people in her high station. Cards being offered her, she doubted as to the course of duty, and called her native teacher Robert, and asked him if it would be right for her to play cards. He could not assure her it would be right, and she declined playing. Poor Robert, being suspected of not favoring the game, was severely beaten by the host. The princess and her brother ran away, and hastened to the house of a high chief, who reproved them for leaving their teacher in trouble.

Harry Nawaiiki, an early native convert, was remarkable for his enterprise and profitable industry, and was often employed as interpreter to foreigners, and generally to the satisfaction of the parties. Of the four who died this year out of that small church, the missionaries say : "We trust they have gone to a better state. We have heard them all plead at the throne of grace till their voice faltered. We believe they had influence in heaven while here on earth : and for ourselves we can ask no higher happiness in this life than we have sometimes felt when seeing the tears dropping from their eyes, while we talked to them of heaven and the road that leads there."

At that time, the people of Maui gave a new proof of their regard to the worship of God by their engagement in erecting their EBENEZER—a new, commodious, and durable stone church, 104 feet by 50, with good *galleries*. Its corner-stone was laid Sept. 14, 1828. " To build this house, the common people were taxed for some labor, but the real expense of the building was nearly all defrayed by the chiefs, and principally by Hoapili."

After a series of signal mercies, through God's preserving care over the lives of the laborers for eight trying years, he at length began to break in upon their number by death, but in a manner so wise and good as rather to promote than diminish the religious interest among the people which appeared at the close of 1827.

Our dear Mrs. Bishop, whom all, who knew her, esteemed and loved as an amiable and devoted missionary helper, after a short missionary pilgrimage and a season of great suffering, faded and vanished from our sight, no more to cheer on her way-worn fellow travellers. Her views of the doctrines and duties of Christianity were clear and correct, and her standard so high, that in her illness she could hardly think herself to be a Christian, and did not enjoy the full measure of the consolations of the Gospel. So comprehensive and affecting were her views of the nature of sin, and of that " holiness without which no man shall see the

Lord," that few on earth, I am persuaded, could entertain the same without deep solicitude for their own personal safety. Nor would it be strange if multitudes, who think they are floating along, pleasantly and safely, towards the haven of eternal peace, should they come to scan their motives, doings, and character, with that unsparing fidelity which determines to know the worst, should, as she did, lose their appetite for food, their relish for the engagements of earth, and even their comfort of a hope in respect to a better inheritance. February 28th, after kind messages to her pupils and the missionaries, her dying accents fell faintly on her husband's ear, "Let me depart in peace." This was followed by an increased attention to religion at Kailua.

In March, two men and four women were baptized. In June, Mr. Thurston spoke of the work of God as "advancing with power, and extending itself to the neighboring villages." Of the interest among their people, Mr. Bishop thus wrote:

"A striking trait of this revival is a deep sense of sinfulness and conviction of their lost and helpless condition, and of the necessity of divine aid to deliver them from the dominion of sin. There is nothing speculative in the nature of their convictions. Their transgressions have been too many and palpable to make it a matter of difficulty to search them out. With great ingenuousness they confess themselves to have been murderers, adulterers, sorcerers, thieves, liars, and drunkards."

In August, Gov. Adams sent the following to our Board:—

"I have received your kind letter, and also the book and portrait [of J. Q. Adams], for which I send you my grateful thanks, and also for your kind regards for myself and people. I have often heard of your kind regards for our welfare, and for the enlightening of our dark minds, and I look forward with hope when your kind wishes will be accomplished, and we shall be able to be among those who will be saved. We have a large church, and its being filled every Sabbath is, I think, a good sign that the glorious light of the Gospel is doing great good for the removing of the clouds of heathenism from our once dark minds. I shall always love the missionaries, and take care of them. With every wish for your health and happiness, and soliciting your prayers for our welfare, believe me to be your friend,

"JOHN ADAMS."

Though for years he had been as favorable to Christianity and to our mission, as this letter shows him to be, and though his wife and some twenty others were reckoned as converts, yet he was not so reckoned by the missionaries, who, though they appreciated his kindness and co-operation, could give him no encouragement to think himself converted. They required something more than a readiness to read and hear the Word of God, to aid in building churches and in supporting schools, and to treat the foreign teachers with deference and kindness. Of those who were regarded as converts at that station at that period, Messrs. Thurston

and Bishop, under date of December 10, 1828, give the following account :—

" It is not a little gratifying to witness the willingness and simplicity
with which they receive our instructions. There is no cavilling or
questioning the truth of our doctrines ; a ' thus saith the Lord,' is
a sufficient warrant for their faith ; and as far as they are able to comprehend the doctrine or duty inculcated, they are ready to put it into
practice. The prominent features of the late religious attention at
Kailua, were a deep sense of sinfulness, of danger, and of inability
on the part of the inquirer himself, to subdue the evil propensities of
the heart, or to effect any good thing. To persons of this class, our
instructions have been simple, and confined principally to an explanation of the nature and necessity of repentance and faith, together with
an entire dependence on the aids of the Holy Spirit, as the only
means of escaping from the power and dominion of sin.

" We have carefully avoided all abstruse speculations and questions
engendering strife, and as nearly as possible conveyed instruction to them
in the words of holy writ. On Sabbath, the 9th of March last, the
first fruits of our labors here were gathered into the Church. It was a
novel and interesting scene to the people of this and the neighboring
villages. Six persons, two men and four women, came forward, and
in the presence of a large concourse of people, solemnly avowed their
belief in the articles of Christian faith, took upon themselves the vows
of the covenant, and were baptized ; after which, the Lord's Supper
was administered. It was a day of deep interest to all the young converts. They afterwards came to us, and in an unaffected manner,
declared that they had in spirit partaken with us of the sacred em-
blems of our Lord's body and blood. Nor to these alone was it a day
of power. Many who had before remained undecided, became from this
time determined to seek the Lord, and have since become hopefully
new creatures.

" In August last, twenty persons, twelve men and eight women, were
propounded, but were not admitted to the church until the last Sabbath in November. This, too, was a season of solemn interest, like
the former. Many of the candidates were persons of distinction and
influence, among whom was a chief of the first rank in the islands,
Keoua, the wife of Governor Adams.

" Our worshipping congregation has been increased during the past
year, particularly on the Sabbath morning, when it is quite large, often
filling our spacious church to overflowing. People come from the
distance of seven or eight miles, and return the same day. All the
canoes belonging to the adjacent villages are put in requisition on the
Sabbath, and being drawn up on the beach together, often remind us
of the clustered vehicles near the country churches of our own land on
that day."

Mr. and Mrs. Ely, at Kaawaloa, finding their health rapidly
failing, retired from the field with the approbation of their associates, and returned to the United States.

Before the embarkation of Mr. Ely's family, Mrs. B. and myself were brought reluctantly to the conclusion that, painful as

was the pang of separation, we were called to send with them, away from our embrace, and from our field of contest, our first born daughter Sophia, at the tender age of eight years, the arms of our friends in the United States being stretched out to receive her.

The condition of the children of the missionaries in the islands of the Pacific, and the duty of parents respecting the place and the manner of their education, have often been matters of deep solicitude to the laborers, both male and female, and of no small concern to the directors and patrons of the missionary enterprise.

During twenty-one years of the mission at the Sandwich Islands, it was the general opinion of the missionaries there that their children over eight or ten years of age, notwithstanding the trial that might be involved, ought to be sent or carried to the United States, if there were friends who would assume a proper guardianship over them, in order that they might escape the dangers of a heathen country, and inherit a portion of the civil, religious, and literary privileges which their ancestors had bequeathed to them, and at the same time allow the parents more time and strength for missionary work. The desirableness of Christian missionary families among the Hawaiians was not to be questioned for a moment; they were indispensable in teaching the Christian duties of domestic life. During the period from infancy to the age of ten or twelve years, children in the almost isolated family of a missionary could be well provided for and instructed in the rudiments of education without a regular school, and without impairing, on the whole, the salutary influence of a missionary family upon the nation. But after that period, difficulties in most cases multiplied. They could not be thoroughly trained there for public life without engrossing too much of the parents' time and care. There was no employment into which the parent could with propriety thoroughly initiate them as a business for life, unless the Lord would make them true missionaries. They would be greatly exposed to be corrupted by the influence of low and vile examples around them; and the obstacles to their forming a character for usefulness were by no means small. But should these be overcome at much expense of time and labor, still the extreme difficulty in such a new field in the way of forming suitable connexions for life, was not to be overlooked in providing for the well-being of missionary offspring.

The theory that it is the duty of a missionary *mother* to guide, watch over, and educate her own children, whatever else she may do or fail to do, though plausible and agreeable, is no more true than 'that *fathers* are required to bring up their children in the nurture and admonition of the Lord.' From the relation which God has established, and the precepts he has given, they are jointly bound to provide for their children, and train them up for Christ and heaven; but not necessarily under the same roof. Otherwise, Hannah and her husband made a great mistake **in** putting their much loved Samuel in his childhood far from them, and into the family of one not distinguished as a pious disciplinarian. Should it be affirmed that they consecrated him to the Lord, it may be asked, ought not all parents to do the same with their every child? Missionary children, if their good, or the public good, required it, might with propriety, it was believed, be sent from their parents, from one town, island, or country, to another, to be trained in families, or boarding-schools, and in various ways fitted for a future useful sphere. Nor should the fondness of a parent's affection, or the pleasure of the presence and society of children, ever be allowed to interfere with the good of the child or of the public, in selecting the place of its education, or the scene or course of its active life. But there was no proper boarding-school at the islands for missionaries' children.

The missionary mother who is qualified to give her own offspring a thorough education on missionary ground, without calling in the aid of others, is, or ought to be, qualified to teach a multitude of those whose mothers cannot teach them well at all : and it is a wise arrangement of Providence, that heads of families, and the unmarried, should engage in teaching the untaught masses, and that labor-saving, boarding, and other schools, should have a place in the plan of educating and reforming the world. With this arrangement, the foreign missionary, male or female, is expected, in general, to instruct the multitude, and sometimes, as it were, in the camp or on the battle-field, while, for a time, the missionary child is committed to the hands of others, either on missionary ground or far over the sea. To aid in this, the American Board make a kind provision when necessary.*

After the departure of Mr. Ely from Kaawaloa, Mr. Ruggles was located there, and, in connexion with Messrs. Bishop and Thurston of Kailua, he labored as a lay preacher (though in slender health), attending to the details of the business of the station, and found work enough for many hands.

Prosecuting the work in that part of the field, Messrs. Bishop and Ruggles set off from Kaawaloa, on board a double canoe, Oct. 1st, and sailed round the southern extremity of Hawaii, on a missionary excursion, which was attended with great hazard. Chiefly by moonlight, they sailed pleasantly and rapidly about

---

* With similar views we subsequently sent away our second daughter, at the tender age of seven years, to our native land: and in like manner, eighteen other children of the missionaries of that field have been separated from their parents and placed in the United States in their childhood, during twenty-seven years of missionary labor there. One of Mr. Ruggles', four of Mr. Whitney's, two of Mr. Bishop's, six of Mr. Richards', two of Mr. Chamberlain's, one of Mr. Armstrong's, and one of Mr. Thurston's. Twenty-six have come from that field with their parents to remain, and three as orphans, whose parents both died in the field. Of the two eldest daughters of Mr. Thurston, grown to womanhood on the missionary field, the younger arriving in full health, died in a few days after reaching New York, and the elder has been carried through the course of instruction at Mount Holyoke Female Seminary. The eldest daughter of Mr. Whitney, educated in this country, has returned to the Sandwich Islands, to help carry out the work her parents began, and others are expected to enter the missionary field in China or elsewhere.

thirty miles with a land breeze, and by sunlight, some fifteen miles, with a sea breeze. As they doubled a point of land at Wili, the trade-winds suddenly struck them; and the swell from the south coming into collision with the current from the north, dashed the sea over their canoe, and completely swamped them. They were in imminent danger of being irrecoverably carried off to sea by the strong current there, from which a double canoe, once filled with water, has rarely been known to be brought to land. In this situation, to free the canoe of water, difficult as it was, and make it buoyant and manageable, so as to stem the current, or be driven off and lost, seemed their only alternative. In such a dilemma, the natives emptied the contents of their *poi* calabashes into the sea, baled out the water from the canoe, and resuming their places, rowed towards the nearest landing-place, about a mile distant; but there the surf was rolling on the shore so roughly, that when near the land there was danger of stranding and dashing their canoe to pieces, and breaking their bones on the rocks. The natives determining to coast along further, the missionaries not daring to proceed, leapt into the water as a sea retired, and fortunately secured a standing on terra firma, glad to prosecute their journey on foot. The natives passing on in the canoe, were shortly overwhelmed by the furious billows that swept over them. They rose to the surface, and struggled for the shore, and by their power of endurance in the water, and their skill in the surf, one after another escaped alive to the high rocky shore, against which the surges, foaming and roaring, dashed. Two of the number were taken from the water insensible. The noble canoe, the property of Gov. Adams, worth perhaps one hundred and fifty dollars, was thrown upon the rocks a complete wreck. The missionaries, who had before landed, feeling that they had not themselves the requisite skill to pilot the canoe, or to swim safely to the shore in such circumstances, sang the praise of their strong Deliverer.

They, and the captain of the canoe, apprehended that Gov. Adams would require them to indemnify him for his loss, but when he heard of the wreck, he asked if all on board escaped alive, and being answered in the affirmative, said, "I am satisfied."

Recovering a portion of their baggage, which floated ashore, they travelled on towards the habitable parts of Kau, over an almost desolate region, finding here and there a poor fisherman's hut, whose miserable tenants, when asked for food and water, replied, "We have none." The next morning, at nine o'clock, they obtained refreshments, having been twenty-four hours destitute of food and fresh water. At Honuapo a great concourse of the people of Kau assembled on the Sabbath, and heard the Gospel. On the next day, Mr. Ruggles examined twenty-five schools, embracing 1,500 scholars. Mr. Bishop married twenty couple, then revisited Hilo, where, to listening crowds of the people and the crews of nine whale-ships seeking refreshments there, he proclaimed the Gospel, free from the distractions which rum sometimes occasioned where it was sold.

CHAPTER XIV.

TENTH YEAR OF THE MISSION, AND SIXTH OF KAAHUMANU.—
1829.

Great numbers attentive to instruction—Religious interest at Kaawaloa—Progress at Hilo—State of Kauai five years after the war—Distillery at Honolulu—Insurrectionary movements of Boki—Erection and dedication of a church at Honolulu —Honolulu Fourth of July—Accession to the church—Five hundred candidates— Death of Namahana—Violent interference of officials—Memorial of Englishmen—Government orders regulating marriages and the liquor trade—Visit of the Vincennes—Capt. Finch—Despatch from U. S. Government—Reply from the Hawaiian Government—Expedition of Boki in the South Seas—Hopeful conversion of Adams.

THE events of the year 1829 exceeded in interest what I have recorded of the two preceding. The progress in the work of instruction, and the extent to which the population sought it at this period, are indicated by the fact that the number of scholars in the schools was forty-six thousand, one hundred and six, mostly above the years of childhood, and these were generally supposed to be willing to receive instruction from God's Word.

The Spirit of God was making use of the Gospel for enlightening and sanctifying those who received it. It was found that at Kaawaloa, while Mr. Ruggles had been off on a tour for examining schools, and laboring among the people at a distance from his residence, and Mrs. Ruggles was the only foreign female at the station, without any other missionary except the weekly visits of one from Kailua, fifteen miles distant, the people in the neighboring villages came to her in considerable numbers to talk about the Word of God, and to inquire the way to heaven. One of the missionaries from Kailua preaching there on the Sabbath, some two hundred of the hearers called on the preacher to make, as he said, the great inquiry, "What shall we do? We have long lived in sin: we have slighted the instructions of our teachers. Our hearts have not heretofore consented to God's Word. We are full of fears lest we be for ever lost. We come to ask, how shall we obtain salvation?" Kapiolani and others shed tears of joy when such inquirers were directed to the Savior of sinners.

When Messrs. Clark and Chamberlain visited the station in February, they were struck with the evidence of the presence of the Spirit of God. Mr. Clark says of it:

" We arrived at Kaawaloa a little after dark, and were heartily welcomed by our friends, Mr. and Mrs. Ruggles, Kapiolani, and Naihe and others. It was a time of deep interest at Kaawaloa. We felt that we were in the midst of a revival of religion. Mr. Ruggles' house was almost constantly thronged with inquirers, and a considerable number, it is hoped, have lately passed from death unto life. Mr. Bishop came down on Saturday to preach the next day and administer the sacrament. We noticed with pleasure the stillness and propriety with which the Sabbath was observed. It was a novel and interesting sight to see great numbers of the people come in canoes from villages along the shores, allowing their boats to lie crowded together till after the services of the Sabbath, then silently stretching out over the smooth bay towards evening, on their joyful way home."

The loneliness of Mr. Goodrich's family, a hundred miles from any other station, the great amount of missionary labor required in that part of the field, among 20,000 inhabitants, and other considerations, rendered it exceedingly desirable to have more laborers employed there, even if some strength should be taken from other stations, until further help could be obtained from the United States. To meet this immediate claim, Mr. and Mrs. Clark went thither for a few months with Kaio, a native teacher, who had assisted me in translations. Being on their way becalmed off Waipio, he visited the pleasant valley, some fifty miles from any missionary station, and its interesting, inquiring head-man, and has given the following brief sketch of his hasty visit :—

" We landed through a pretty high surf, though without much difficulty, and soon found ourselves in one of the most romantic spots which I ever beheld. We were surrounded on all sides, except towards the sea, by lofty and irregular precipices, over one of which poured, in perpendicular descent, a considerable stream of water. Before us was spread out a most beautiful valley, flourishing in all the luxuriance of the richest garden. I felt for a moment that we were completely shut out from all the rest of the world, though surrounded by the most sublime and beautiful of nature's works. We called on the head-man, Haa, who received us very cordially. He appeared much gratified to find that I was a missionary. He asked me repeatedly if I would not come and live there. He said they wanted some one to make clear to them the Word of God. It was very far, he said, to Kailua and to Hilo, the nearest missionary stations. Refreshments were liberally provided, after which a considerable number of people assembled in a school-house. We sang a hymn, and I addressed them in a few broken sentences ; and Kaio offered a prayer. On coming away, our boat was loaded with baked hogs, *kalo*, *poi*, &c. After leaving the shore, great numbers came swimming around our boat with *kalo* and hard *poi* in their hands, until we were obliged to reject their presents, lest our boat should be upset (or swamped). The head-man came off to the schooner with a live hog, and other articles. I presented him a set of our native books, with which he appeared pleased, and soon took his leave."

The next day they reached Hilo, and were cordially welcomed by Mr. and Mrs. Goodrich, and by Gov. Adams. The latter was sojourning in that part of the island to superintend the building of a church, on which many of the people were employed; and also to make preparation for the building of a saw-mill in the heavy forest at the base of Mauua-kea, some fifteen miles back of Waiakea, both of which objects he accomplished.

Mr. Clark engaged particularly in teaching a class of teachers, enrolling the names of eighty from different parts of that extensive missionary district, more than eighty miles in length, embracing Hilo and Puna. They were poor, and not having the means of supporting themselves steadily at Waiakea, could not attend very constantly. There was a pleasant attention to religion. " Our houses," says Mr. Clark, " were frequently thronged by persons who wished to tell their thoughts, and inquire what they should do to be saved." Such was the state of the people throughout the group at that period, wherever there were missionaries to attend to them.

Messrs. Whitney and Gulick, at Kauai, thus described the state of their field, which five years before had been in warlike commotion:

" There are seventy-four schools on this island, taught by as many native teachers. The school-houses are generally much the best and most spacious buildings in their respective villages. Several of them are at least eighty feet long, and thirty-six broad. The people seldom remain longer than two hours in schools. They usually assemble twice a day; sometimes at six o'clock in the morning, but more generally at eight, and again between three and four in the afternoon. The teachers are appointed by the missionaries after examination, and in case of improper conduct, they are rejected by the same authority. They have generally been supported, or nearly so, by the head-men in their respective neighborhoods. This has been done by the Governor's orders. He has recently directed that there be given to each teacher a piece of land, from which, with a little labor, he may obtain a supply of food. As a body, the teachers are the most moral and most intelligent young men on the island: and they appear to be usually respected and esteemed by the people. When persons from a distant village, or those with whom we are unacquainted, wish to be married, it is customary for them to bring their teacher to testify that they are not already married, or that such a connexion is not on other accounts unlawful."

In July, Mr. W. writes concerning the people:

" I have now work enough, and that of the most delightful kind. It is pointing sinners to the Lamb of God, and conducting pilgrims along the road to glory. For several weeks there has been an unusual attention to religion here. Our public meetings are usually crowded to overflowing.

" In most persons there appears to be a spirit of inquiry; in many, a deep and awful sense of the presence of God, and of their own sinfulness. Some are rejoicing in the Savior's love.

" My house, whenever I am disengaged, is surrounded with the anxious, so that I find it impossible to converse with all of them personally. I am much impressed, at times, with the simple, unaffected relation given by natives, of the operation of the Holy Spirit on their minds. A case I will relate. A young man whom I had never known as interested in religion, called upon me, as he said, to inquire. Having seated himself by my side, he said to me, with an agitated frame and a look I can never forget, ' What means this ? For weeks past I have had a load upon me which troubles me much. By day and by night it follows me, so that I cannot sleep nor rest. I have tried to get rid of it. I have prayed to God to take it away ; but it continues here.' Then pulling the Gospel of Luke out of his pocket, he pointed to the twenty-fourth verse of the sixteenth chapter, and said : ' There is my load ; oh, my soul ! to that unquenchable fire I fear I must go.' His voice and whole frame were now so agitated as to render him unable to articulate. When I told him that the Savior, whose mercy alone had long kept him from that place of torment, was now ready to take away his load, and deliver his soul from distress and perdition, he seemed a little comforted, and said, ' To him, then, I will go.'

While the missionaries were regarded as benefactors and guides, and the governor and his wife were favorable to the object of the mission, and the Spirit of God obviously present, it might be expected that the cause of the Sabbath and of temperance should receive some attention. Mr. Gulick says :

" The people are required to sanctify the Lord's day. They generally believe the Sabbath to be a divine institution, and consequently, that it ought to be sacredly observed. The natives are prohibited from all commerce in ardent spirits, and from using it, except as a medicine. This regulation has been in force a considerable time, and I believe is seldom violated ; nor am I aware that it is esteemed burdensome. The consequence is, that I have not seen an intoxicated native, nor heard of one ; neither have I known of any quarrelling among them, with one single exception, during my residence in the island."

President Humphrey gave it as his opinion, a few years since, " that if any man in the Parliament of Great Britain should move to dispense with licensing the traffic in ardent spirits, the Chancellor of the Exchequer would annihilate him." But thousands of the Hawaiians, within less than the period of a generation after they began to be instructed in morals and religion, came to the just conclusion that, encouraging the manufacture, sale, and use of distilled liquor as a drink, was wrong, both in rulers and subjects. Many a community in different parts of the United States, in France, and other civilized countries, cannot show a district school-house for the purpose of common school instruction and the occasional worship of God, where the settled or travelling preacher can assemble the people to hear the Gospel ; yet throughout the Sandwich Islands, in ten years after the mission was commenced, there was scarcely a neighborhood where such an accommodation could not be found, or where it was not, more or less, used to good purpose.

The governor's wife, Amelia, made herself very interesting, and worthy of her station, not only in her general influence in favor of the instruction of the Islanders, but by collecting and personally instructing a school of forty children, from four to eight years of age. This was a service for which she received no pecuniary compensation, but so far as she gratified the feelings of benevolence towards the needy, she doubtless found a higher satisfaction, far, than if the parents of these children had paid her in silver and gold, the ordinary wages for teaching a primary school. At one examination she gave a calico dress to each of twenty-four females in a class with herself, and the governor distributed among twenty-five teachers, clothing to the amount of $250.

Mr. Gulick, in giving a deliberate judgment on the causes of the desire for books and instruction, which was so extensive, and in some respects truly wonderful, says, " When I consider the extreme degradation and ignorance, and the proverbial indolence of the people, this eagerness to obtain books, especially portions of the Word of God, and to know something of their contents, seems as evidently the work of God, as any other circumstance connected with this mission. And I think it equally manifest that the government has had a very important agency in producing the present state of feeling."

The kindness of many chiefs in encouraging the people to learn, was wonderful, and the more so, if they still intended to oppress them.

The course of Gov. Boki was unlike that of the chiefs generally, who professed a regard to the cause of Christianity. He set up a store and tavern in Honolulu, and encouraged the manufacture, sale, and use of intoxicating liquors, and tried to introduce a measure which he might have borrowed from some city of Italy, or corrupt branch of the civilized family of nations—a measure for raising money by licensing prostitution, as well as by the traffic in intoxicating liquors, in both contrary to the best interests of the people, whatever claim the self-indulgent from other countries might make for the liberty.

He was disposed to lease land for the purpose of producing rum at the Islands, but this Kaahumanu resolutely, and for the most part, successfully prevented ; and, so far as I know, the policy of the country does not allow the product of leasehold land to be distilled.

To increase the production of intoxicating liquors, Boki, conforming rather to foreign customs than to the better policy of Kaahumanu, leased to a company of traders a building in Honolulu, which Kalanimoku, to encourage the growth and manufacture of sugar, had, before his death, built for a sugar-house. By an adroit metamorphosis, the company converted the sugar-house into a distillery, as if disposed to infix a gangrene or a consuming cancer in the heart of the nation. The principal reliance for supplying the distillery with material was the sugar-cane. But the right of soil being yet under the dictatorship of Kaahumanu, it was not the most easy to make it produce rum, without some concurrence of hers. When she saw the product of a cane-field, the soil of which belonged to the State, converted into poison, she directed the roots to be extirpated and their place supplied with potatoes. This, perhaps, more than anything else, was seized on as an occasion for accusing the missionaries of being opposed to improvements in agriculture. " I consider," said the leading distiller to me, " that you have sunk for me $7,000, in stopping my distillery : I could not get the cane of the natives to carry it on." He might have added, " How strangely these missionaries oppose manufactures and commerce! for, so scrupulous and superstitious are they, that I could not hire their cart and oxen to bring the products of the field to the distillery." It was not, indeed, deemed by us safe for the oxen of the missionaries to be seen before the face of that nation, unconsciously drawing cane to a distillery, even before the morality of the traffic in ardent spirits, as a drink, appeared to be much questioned in the United States or England. Only the preceding year, Messrs. Pomeroy and Bull, wholesale grocers in the city of New York, set the happy example there of abandoning, from principle, the traffic in distilled liquors as a drink. The same year a few united in forming the American Temperance Society.

While the distillation of the products of the cane-field was pertinaciously insisted on by those who could raise or buy the cane, and multitudes were exposed to be ruined by it, we could not safely recommend its extended culture. Riding with Kekuanaoa, at that period, near a field of cane destined to supply this distillery, partly to try his shrewdness, and partly his morality, I said to him, " Do we not judge of a tree by its fruit ?" " Yes," he readily replied. " What sort of fruit does this tree bear ?" pointing to the field. " Evil," he answered, with an arch expession, that indicated his opinion that it might well be hewn down or extirpated. Doubtless the culture of the cane, tobacco, and the poppy, is right, only where the probability is that the result will be *good*, and should not be encouraged where the probability is strong that the result will be evil. Hawaiian casuists learned to take a pretty simple view of this point.

The two filthy, noxious weeds, *stramonium* and *tobacco*, flourish in that climate and soil, but their entire extermination from the islands, and the substitution of cotton, sugar, rice, wheat, and maize, would be a good improvement, which true missionaries would desire. But Boki had more " liberality," another term there for profligacy and revelry, and though he was bound to set an example of sobriety and piety, and so far as his personal guardianship over the young king extended, he was, moreover, bound to prompt him to walk according to " the admonition of the Lord," yet he did the reverse. This course, though encouraged by foreign tempters, was the more inexcusable after his professed regard to Christianity. Efforts were made to save him from impending ruin, but with only partial success. He showed sometimes a little conscience, and sometimes a little love of character, but indulged his love of power and domination, and probably felt, with others of the faction, that an " old woman" ought not to be the superior of such a *nobleman.*

He encouraged the Papists, who claimed him as " regent," and with others, treated Kaahumanu as an " ambitious woman." With astonishing boldness, he sounded separately almost every high chief in the islands, to see if he could rely on their co-operation in his attempt to put her down and take her place; but finding no fair prospect of securing the co-operation of any high chief to crush Kaahumanu, he endeavored to encourage his sub-alterns to destroy her ; but they shrank from it. He darkly mustered forces, and tried to convince the young king that Kaahumanu was too illiberal, and that it would be well to put her down, that they might have less restraint in the pursuit of their pleasures and honors. Some of his particular dependants and friends upbraided him for his hostile movements, his aliena-tion from his relative and superior, the regent, and his readiness to involve the nation in blood and carnage. One of these, Hookea, being sick, and hearing Boki's expressions of sympathy for him, replied in the bold style of Hawaiian comparison, "I am not sick ; it is *you* who are sick." " No," said the chief, " I am not sick at all. I was ill and drank medicine, and am now quite well." Hookea replied, " *You are sick,* and so extremely sick, that no doctor of medicine can *cure* you ; you have attempted to kill your sister, and you will *die with shame.*" Another among the men whom Boki was collecting from different parts of Oahu, was an old man in the train of an elderly princess, Kalola, who was her-self among the vanquished in the conquest by Kamehameha, and not remarkable for her attachment to Kaahumanu or the present dynasty, or the Word of God. He demanded of the governor what he meant ; reproached him with his disloyalty and want of love to Kaahumanu, and of a design to destroy her, and entreated him to desist.

Boki attempted to get or to make a new division or appropria-tion of lands, without proper authority. He made purchases and distributed presents with a liberal hand. He took the sandal-wood which was collected to pay the debts of the nation, and with it purchased articles for his immediate purpose. He made contracts with traders, who, doubtless, believed the nation would be compelled to pay them if Boki, then engaged as a merchant, should fail. He tried to rouse the remaining spirit of heathenism in the land, contrary to his duty to God and the State, and to the young king and his sister, by strenuously urging their union. He accused Kaahumanu of appropriating to herself the private estate of the young king, so that he could have no land, and of reviling him by calling him a servant of David *Kamehameha* (the favorite little son of Kekauluohi) and of Ruth, the daughter of Kekuanaoa and Pauahi, who had been one of the wives of Liholiho. But these slanders recoiled on the governor, whose folly and wickedness contrasted strongly with the prudence and inoffensiveness of the queen regent.

As evidences of meditated violence were multiplied, considerable alarm was felt by the friends of God and of good order for the personal safety of the good queen. She, however, in her dignity and wisdom, appeared quite undisturbed, and quietly attended to her business, her books, her religion, and her Maker. She seemed to rely much on the affection of the people, and their knowledge of her regard for their true interests; on the rightfulness of her position and measures, and the Providence of God, in which she had been taught to trust, for the safety of her life and the triumph of her cause. She summoned no guards of warlike men around her person, nor did she, in the hour of peril, fly to the protection of the governors of the other islands, or make loud complaints of treachery or danger. While the seditious governor was surrounded with his armed men at Waikiki, she sent to tell him that she was alone at her house, and he might come and despatch her if he chose, without the carnage of war.

Kekuanaoa, a firm friend of the queen, went boldly to the governor, who would gladly have avoided the interview, and rebuked him for his ignoble and mad design to put down Kaahumanu by war. " No, no," the confused governor replied. " If you wish to kill her," continued Kekuanaoa, " there she is in such a house, unattended by armed guards, go and despatch her at once if that is what you want, but do not set the nation in arms to destroy one another in war." " *Aole*, not so," he replied. It was not easy for him to put down Kaahumanu while Christian schools were popular, and 46,000 were engaged in them.

Clear as the chiefs supposed the evidence to be that Boki (as some of his friends said about the time of the Blossom's visit in 1826) had cast off all the restraints of his superiors, and was meditating a revolt, they did not think it best to arrest him, or to take from him the subordinate charge of the juvenile king, who was still attached to his step-mother, the regent, and knew her position to be right. He, like Hushai, as a succorer of David in the council chamber of Absalom, could, if he chose, render her assistance in his position, and if not, the forcible termination of Boki's stewardship could promise little gain. He was pleased with indulgences, and of these did not complain. The high chiefs, moreover, were apprehensive that Boki had secured the support of the British and American consuls, and the Romanists from France, against Kaahumanu. The juvenile king still supported his mother, and when Boki proposed to him to take Madam Boki to a place of retreat as a signal for him to fall on Kaahumanu, a measure which could be proposed by none but a madman, the youth avoided the wily snare, and hastened to apprise Kaahumanu, and to defeat the ambitious designs of the governor. Jehovah held the shield of the Gospel over her head and over the land.

On the 8th of April, 1829, Kaahumanu and her son, passing from the windward islands to Oahu, landed at Honolulu. Mr. H., one of the respectable traders, informed us how loudly such men as Messrs. Jones, Charlton, and Butler, talked of immediate war, and of their readiness to take arms. The next day I called on the king and Boki at the Governor's "BLONDE HOTEL." The king readily engaged to resume his studies, and Boki proposed to attend again to instruction. Both came towards evening to a social cup of tea with Mrs. Bingham, and Kaahumanu being invited at the king's request, joined the circle, and all appeared quiet. The king being desirous to use his good voice in singing, we sang together at my house, not war songs, but sacred songs of praise to the God of peace. Boki had greatly impaired his reputation, and hazarded his fortune, but had not acquired a kingdom, nor could he now expect to accomplish it by force. As he appeared disposed to return to duty, the king was not now recalled, and they united in asking of me 190 books for the instruction of their immediate attendants. They also concurred with Kaahumanu and the people connected with my station in the erection of a church.

Kaahumanu and Kalanimoku, feeling unable in his life-time to build the large durable stone church at Honolulu which they had contemplated, in accordance with their desire to honor God and benefit the people, put up one of frail structure and large dimensions, but insufficient to endure the wind and weather more than a short time.

In the summer of 1829, a commodious house of worship for a congregation of 3000 or 4000 Hawaiians was erected at Honolulu, in an improved style, under the auspices of Kaahumanu and Kauikeaouli. It was 196 feet in length, and 63 in breadth, covering an area of 12,348 square feet. The posts of the building were fifteen or sixteen feet in length, ten inches in diameter, set firmly four or five feet in the earth, inclining a little inward, the better to resist the lateral pressure of the roof. The rafters were locked together at top, and firmly braced with bolted knees at the foot, like a ship's beam. Forty-four rude pillars, in three ranks, one rank under the ridge pole, and one midway between that and the side posts, supported the roof. The main framework of the ends of the building consisted of posts of unequal lengths, reaching from four feet below the surface of the ground to the rafter. The frame then being covered with small horizontal poles, about an inch and a half apart, was thatched with long strait grass, tops downwards. Two very large doors at each end, and as many smaller ones on the sides, made the ingress and egress easy for the largest congregation that a single voice could reach and teach to good purpose. To afford such advantage to the voice as was practicable in such a structure, without much expense, a floor or platform, twenty-four feet by twelve, six inches above the general area, was placed near one side, midway between the extremes of the building; and on the back part of this was erected a perpendicular casement, twenty-four feet by eleven, having the pulpit window in the centre. Before the window a small, neat pulpit of furniture wood was erected, having a little flight of stairs on each side, ascending three feet, each with a light balustrade parallel with the casement. The singular pulpit neatly panelled and cushioned, its symmetrical form and decent finish, and its obvious adaptation to the house and auditory, and the decorous, perpendicular casement with pilasters and moulding, afforded material support to the voice, and presented an object of pleasing interest, both to speaker and hearer. For an unceiled, unfinished house, rarely would a missionary ask for a pulpit more commodious or agreeable. The broad platform was found useful and pleasant in sacramental services, church meetings, and school examinations. Boki, who had earned the name of rebel, did better than had been anticipated in favoring the work.

Great interest was felt by many in the erection of this building; and when it was completed, and 'the doors of this immense tabernacle were set up,' the women spread the entire earth floor of 12,300 feet with clean mats for seats. Care was taken to have a dedicatory service favorable to the advancement of the nation, and preparation was made on the part of the king and chiefs to appear, not as mere spectators of Christian services, not as a company of rude heathen consecrating a polluted fane to the service of the abominable deities of heathenism by the sacrifice of human victims, but as a *Christian* and *civilized* " people whose God is the Lord," and " who know the joyful sound " of his salvation, offering him such service as they were able to give.

On the 3d of July this house was opened for worship, and some four thousand persons assembled in it, with the queen regent, the king, and princess, and most of the leading personages of the nation, and joined in the solemn dedicatory services. Most of the congregation sat upon the mats very closely together, three to a square yard, or one to three square feet. Hundreds were without about the doors and windows, not able to find room within.

The king, in his Windsor uniform, and his sister, in a dress becoming her high rank and improved character and taste, were seated on a sofa covered with crimson satin damask, in front of the pulpit. Kaahumanu and other chiefs sat near. A little further in front of the pulpit sat the native choir of men and women singers, aided by a bass viol. The king had been made acquainted with the part which Solomon took in the dedication of the temple, and though in his early years diffident and unobtrusive, he seemed conscientiously desirous to do what his teacher supposed would be proper for him to do on this occasion. Both he and his sister had been specially instructed to take a part in the songs suited to the occasion.

When the great congregation was ready, the king rose, and in a handsome, appropriate manner said, in few words, "Chiefs, teachers, and commons, hear : we have assembled here to dedicate to Jehovah, my God, this house of prayer, which I have built for him.   Here let us worship him, listen to the voice of his ministers, and obey his word."

The choir then, in which the king sang a good bass, and the princess a good treble, engaged in the solemn and delightful chant of the hundredth psalm, in their smooth, liquid dialect.   In this service, this young nation, just emerging from heathenism, seemed to be calling not only on one another and the whole group of islands, but on the nations of the earth generally, to acknowledge and worship the true God, in the inspired strain :—

> " Make a joyful noise unto Jehovah, all ye lands,
> Serve Jehovah with gladness ;
> Come before his presence with singing—
> Know ye that Jehovah he is God.
> It is he that hath made us, and not we ourselves :
> We are his people and the sheep of his pasture.
> Enter into his gates with thanksgiving ;
> And into his courts with praise.
> Be thankful unto him and bless his name
> For Jehovah is good,
> His mercy is everlasting,
> And his truth endureth to all generations."

The dedication sermon (a delightful service allowed me) was delivered from a part of the 132d Psalm :

> " We will go into his tabernacles ;
> We will worship at his footstool :
> For the Lord hath chosen Zion ;
> He hath desired it for a habitation—
> This is my rest for ever ;
> Here will I dwell, for I have desired it :
> I will abundantly bless her provision ;
> I will satisfy her poor with bread,
> I will also clothe her priests with salvation ;
> And her saints shall shout aloud for joy."

The great congregation, in their best attire, presenting a cloud of faces turned toward the speaker, listened with attention to the exhibition of God's condescension, kindness, and faithfulness to his church ; and the duty, happiness, and blessed results of acknowledging and worshipping him in the sanctuary.

After the sermon and dedicatory prayer, the princess, whom Kaahumanu regarded as the future partner of the throne, and who had been somewhat accustomed openly to counsel their own people, in a very dignified and impressive manner, acknowledged the supremacy of God, the King of heaven, over them all, and their duty to give him the homage of their hearts, and exhorted the people to remember and regard what her brother had said. As a young Esther she was heard with satisfaction.

The choir sang in their own language the 1st Psalm, impressively depicting the different character and end of the righteous and the wicked.

Immediately after, to the astonishment and gratification of nearly every one of the vast assembly, the king, overcoming his diffidence, though so young and unaccustomed to such an exercise, stood before the congregation and said : " *Epule kakou ;* let us pray ;" then with dignity, clearness, and appropriateness of diction, voice, and manner, addressed the throne of grace. He offered unto God thanksgiving for his merciful kindness, tendered to him not only this house of worship, but the *kingdom* also. He acknowledged his own sinfulness and that of the nation ; besought pardon, sanctification, guidance, and deliverance from evil, and implored blessings on the chiefs and people, the missionaries, foreign residents, and visitors, and ascribed to God " the kingdom, power, and glory."

Never, perhaps, did Washington exhibit more of the true dignity of the Patriarch of America, than when America's young armies were in distress and doubt, and their leader said, nearly in the language of inspiration, and with great emphasis, " Who will go forth with our armies ?—Wilt not *thou*, O God ?" Never, I am persuaded, had any Hawaiian king, in any circumstances or event, appeared more dignified than this young prince, surrounded by chieftains, the aged, middle aged, and young, missionaries and foreigners, and thousands of the people—thus leading their devotion, and in the most solemn, public, and forcible manner, acknowledging Jehovah to be his King and Savior. No candid, intelligent spectator, who could appreciate the difference between the heathen and Christian state of a nation, could have witnessed the scenes of that day without admiration at the progress which civilization and Christianity had made in nine years and three months from the landing of the pioneer missionaries, and a readiness to exclaim, " Shall a nation be born in a day ?"

This bright scene had scarcely passed away, and the first hallelujas of the new temple ceased, when a different and anxious scene occurred.

Rarely have we, for any single day, felt more deep solicitude to save the young king from the power of the world's temptations, than on the fourth of July, the day succeeding the happy dedication, when the birth of American Independence was celebrated by a festival among foreigners which, patriotic as we were, we could have wished for that time had been on the other side of the great waters, lest the excitement of the hilarity, the roar of cannon, the sparkling wine moving itself and giving its color in the cup, and the flatteries and solicitations of those who loved such things, would entirely overcome his youthful resolutions to maintain sobriety and dignity, or lead him to dishonor the cause he had so well advocated the preceding day. But through the favor of Providence we received his young majesty as our guest, during the evening, who appeared in an affable and decorous manner, as though in the house of his parents. After supper he joined us very pleasantly with his good bass voice in singing. In this art he and his sister had made as good attainments, perhaps, as any of the natives at that period ; an art of no small importance in the work of reform.

Though there was some evidence of childlike sincerity and princely honor in the king, in his transactions at the dedicatory service, yet we could not feel less solicitude lest, exposed as he was to influence exerted by ignorant, or artful, evil-minded men, who would be glad, for their own sake, to hold him back from the duties of piety, he should, after all, be drawn irrecoverably into the ruinous follies of the world, and lost to himself, his friends, and teachers, and the nation. Still we had occasion to rejoice at the important step which he took at the dedication ; for such acknowledgment of the Christians' God, though neither the faith nor the practice of any chief or subordinate subject was supposed to be constrained by it, nor any union between church and state implied in it, was rational and commendable : and it was natural for the friends of religion to avail themselves of it, as they would in the United States of an appointment and recommendation of fasting and prayer, or thanksgiving to Almighty God. Any magistrate, whether a member of the church or not, making such an appointment, is supposed to express the wish of a Christian government, and the good people of the commonwealth feel it a pleasure to comply.

It was highly gratifying to see Kaahumanu, in a public manner, the next day, take a very kind notice of the dedication service— the dedication of the house and the dedication of the kingdom, to God, and of the king's recommending obedience to his word. She confirmed it, and " wished all within the bounds of the kingdom to give good heed to the king's word, and walk circumspectly, in peace, and righteousness." In her great modesty, and in her maternal love, she rejoiced to have the youthful heir to the throne express, in his own person, the voice of the nation, or of the head of the nation. Her piety, sincerity, disinterestedness, acquaintance with the Scriptures, knowledge of human nature, and general sagacity and experience, gave her a moral power which her young son could not yet wield; and with the array of moral and religious teachers whom she cheered on in their work, she applied throughout the realm the power of moral suasion to good purpose, as the world could testify. It was God's hand moving the nation, by his own divinely appointed means. He gave the victory, and let him have the glory.

The following day, the first Sabbath after the dedication, a great concourse joyfully assembled again in the new, and to us and them, beautiful house of God, though its architecture and external decorations would hardly distinguish it from a grass thatched shed for canoes, except by its length, the number of windows and doors, and the glass over the four principal doors at the two ends. Twelve hopeful converts were baptized into the name of the Father, Son, and Holy Ghost, and fourteen other hopeful converts stood up before the congregation of worshippers, after they had been carefully examined by the church, and, at their earnest request, were publicly announced as candidates for admission, and who were subsequently received.

Among the multitude who, at that period, came to us confessing their sins, asking instruction in the way of salvation, and proposing to give themselves to God as his servants, there were at Honolulu about five hundred registered as members of a meeting of inquiry who met from week to week, and who were taught and expected to attend to Christian duties, and to take the Word of God as their guide. To these and to the Church, and to all, the ordinances of baptism and the Lord's Supper, the receiving and propounding for admission to the church, those who, in that place of temptation and danger, appeared to be taking their stand on the Lord's side, prepared to exert a Christian influence on the community, were matters of interest and moment such as had rarely been seen in those islands, and such as few expected to see so soon after the offers of the Gospel were first made there, and such as evinced the agency of the Spirit of God. With what joyfulness and courage did we, under these smiles, address ourselves anew to our work to rear the spiritual temple which there continues to rise in increasing beauty and strength!

Soon after the completion of the large church at Honolulu in the summer of 1829, the illness of Lydia Namahana, the wife of Gideon Laanui, and youngest sister of Kaahumanu, became alarming.

She had been regarded as a pillar among the *consistent* members of the church at Honolulu, and was esteemed and loved by many. As her symptoms became alarming, her compeers gathered around her according to their custom.

Kaahumanu addressed a note to her pastor, at the distance of four or five miles, to hasten to her. He came with his wife. It was evening. The bright shining of a pleasant moon, and the mournful silence that prevailed as we passed the courts of the residences of several chiefs towards the habitation of this honorable woman, were adapted to prepare our thoughts for the interview. As we entered, we heard the voice of Kekauluohi in a clear and tender manner addressing the assembled group that sat in solemn silence around the couch of their languishing friend. Among them were her two sisters, Kaahumanu, and Hoapili Wahine; her deeply afflicted husband, Laanui, Kinau, her niece, and Kakuanaoa, Gov. Boki, and Liliha, several interested members of the church, and others. She heard my voice, and slowly extending her enfeebled hand, with apparent pleasure pronounced our names. In the circumstances of a pastor on whose preaching so interesting a convert from heathenism had so constantly attended, it was to me a privilege to lead her thoughts to the sources of trust and consolation, and to find evidence that with her mind undistracted, unclouded, unagitated, her soul implicitly trusted in God, and was relying on the grace of the Lord Jesus Christ, vouchsafed to sinners who receive his Gospel. · After a precious season of prayer, bidding her farewell, we took leave. But a little after midnight, we were summoned again by a messenger, who reported her as about to depart. I hastened with others to the place. She had just expressed to Dr. Judd, in a whisper, her unabated confidence in Christ. The hand of death was upon her. The pulse in her once vigorous arm, that had warded off violence from the missionary's head, was now imperceptible. As the day faintly dawned, she said, " Hapai," which in the language of common business means *elevate, lift up,* but in that of devotion, means *praise, exalt.* It was her last audible breath, and she lifted up her eyes on the light of eternity, and her praises, we trust, before the throne. A note of wailing from the numerous company around burst forth for a moment, bringing the accents to the ear, " Alas, our friend is gone !" It soon died away, and the voice of solemn prayer succeeded, and order and solemnity prevailed.

On the Sabbath, her funeral was attended by great numbers who respected her. The procession moved from the house to the church. The remains were followed by the husband and two sisters, the king, Auhea and Kinau, Kekuanaoa and Kanaina, Boki and Lihiha, all in deep mourning. Then followed, two and two, the native members of the church to which she belonged ; then the members of the mission family, twelve in number ; then near five times that number of foreign residents ; after them, a great company of natives.

The theme of the funeral discourse was the language of Simeon, " Lord, now lettest thou thy servant depart in peace according to thy word, for mine eyes have seen thy salvation," and was supposed capable of being appropriately applied to her case. The ode entitled the Dying Christian was sung in the vernacular tongue, in which the heart-stirring language of triumph occurs :

> " Hark, they whisper, angels say,
> ' Sister spirit, come away.'
> Lend, lend your wings, I mount, I fly ;
> O grave, where is thy victory ?
> O death, where is thy sting ?"

She had seen and felt the darkness of heathenism. **She had seen** and hailed the dawn of Christianity on her country. **She** had counselled thousands of her countrywomen to follow it. Although we were sad, so soon to see her leave the work which she had begun, we had consolation not only in the divine government, but in the evidence which we had that God had displayed his grace and glory in her conversion, and that in company with those who, with ever-admiring gratitude, ascribe their salvation solely to the bleeding Lamb of God, the praise of that grace and glory would be her employment for eternity.

Honolulu, a town of dingy habitations, having a population of some five or six thousand, a harbor frequented by a hundred foreign ships a year, besides the vessels owned there, and a dusty plain on the east, and a well watered and cultivated valley on the north and north-west, and a sprinkling of exotics, restive in its warm temperature, has long been familiar with demonstrations of puerile excitement and folly, even in the full grown—and sometimes among foreign officials.

An article in the Missionary Herald at Boston, or the fall of a cow in a field of Oahu, could easily throw the foreign community into a ferment. Sometimes the ludicrous, the malicious, and the pitiable, on the part of foreigners, and the promptness and tact of the inexperienced native government to turn their noise and madness to good account, were singularly mingled. This was observable on the occasion of the shooting of a cow claimed by a resident, who, though his own cattle were accustomed to feed among the plantations of the natives, allowed his servants to kill such animals as intruded into his enclosure, especially dogs. To which of certain officials the wounded animal most particularly pertained, it was not easy to tell. They both mounted, and hastened to the place of blood, and pistol in hand, seized a native, a neighbor of ours, who they pretended had " wantonly shot a cow on the common," pinioned his arms, put a halter on his neck, mounted their horses, and in triumph made him run after them. Being nearly exhausted, he fell, and was dragged and injured by them, then cut loose by a native, S. J. Mills. Had he been a pirate or a murderer, such wanton and revengeful barbarity in arresting him unresisting, and torturing him, would not have been warranted in any country, civilized or savage. Had the chiefs put their hands upon a worshipper of images in the same manner, these very men would have trumpeted the crime the world over. He never fully recovered from the injury inflicted on him by cruel foreign hands.

Immediately Mr. Charlton, in conjunction with the other English residents, memorialized the government on the outrage against the cow, pretending that their property and their lives were in jeopardy, and inferring that if natives dared to shoot a cow of a foreigner, they might shoot the foreigners too ; they therefore begged protection for their *lives* and *property*, and Mr. C., in presenting the memorial, urged " an immediate answer, that he might send it to his Britannic Majesty's Secretary of State."

When partially civilized men are sent to barbarous countries to get their own manners mended, it is interesting to see how they are sometimes taught by semi-civilized chieftains. It was interesting to see also how the inexperienced Hawaiians managed to furnish a document, though imperfect, yet suitable for the consul to forward to his government, if he chose to do it; but still more so to see them seize on this occasion to fix rules for natives and foreigners of all grades on their shores.

They quickly issued the following edict, offering the protection of law, and showing what was forbidden and what required in respect to all, both native and foreign. They had no secretary of state, no prime minister to be intrusted with the reply. Still they drew up several articles with great explicitness, and to the point. No pistols, chains, scourges, or daggers appear, yet, considering the circumstances (embracing the time-serving policy of Boki, and the deep interest the two officials had in the result), there is a singular combination of the *suaviter in modo* and *fortiter in re*, and while with smooth words it shows the absurdity of the memorialists, it keenly rebukes the violence of two foreigners upon a native who deserved no violence at their hands for defending the plantation. The edict was signed by Kauikeaouli, and printed by the mission for the government.

OAHU, October 7th, 1829.

" I. This is my decision for you. We assent to the request of the English residents; we grant the protection of the laws; that is the sum of your petition.

" This, therefore, is my proclamation, which I make known to you, all people from foreign countries :—The laws of my country prohibit murder, theft, adultery, prostitution, retailing ardent spirits at houses for selling spirits, amusements on the Sabbath day, gambling and betting on the Sabbath day, and at all times. If any man shall transgress any of these laws he is liable to the penalty; the same for every foreigner, and for the people of these islands—whoever shall violate these laws shall be punished.

" This also I make known—The law of the great God of Heaven, that is the great thing by which we shall promote peace, let all men who remain here, obey it.

" Christian marriage is proper for men and women. But if a woman regard a man as her only husband, and the man regard the woman as his only wife, they are legally husband and wife : but if the parties are not married, nor regard themselves as husband and wife, let them be forthwith entirely separate.

" II. This is also our decision, which I now declare to you :—We have seen your wickedness heretofore. You did not warn us that your door-yards and enclosed plantations were tabu, before the time when our animals went into your inclosures; you unhesitatingly killed our animals. But we warned you of the tabu of our plantations, before the time when the animals came into them, even yours; and then it was told again to you that have cattle; but for some days past we have known your cattle to come in to eat up what we have planted; on that account some of your cattle are dead.

"This, then, is the way to obtain justice:—If you judged the man guilty, you are not forthwith to punish; wait till we have a consultation first; then, if we judged him guilty, we would have given you damages; but no, you rashly and suddenly injured the man; that is one of the crimes of two of you. And we state to you all, that the wounding of a beast is by no means equal to the wounding of a man, inasmuch as man is chief over all the beasts.

"This is our communication to you all; ye parents from the countries whence originate the winds:* have compassion on a nation of little children, very small and young, who are yet in mental darkness, and help us to do right, and follow with us that which will be for the best good of this our country.

"III. As to the recent death of the cow; she died for breaking a tabu for the protection of the plantation. The place was also defended by a fence, built by the owner of the plantation. Having secured his field by a fence, what remained to be done was the duty of the owners of the cattle, who were told by him who had charge of the plantation to bring home their cattle at evening. He did tell them so; but they did not regard it; and in the night they came in, but not by day. On that account the owner of the plantation hoped to recover damage; for many were the cattle that were taken up before, but no damage was recovered for the crops they had devoured; the owners pleaded them off without paying damage, therefore he to whom the crop belonged, determined that one of the cattle should die for destroying the crop; for it had been said that if any of the cattle should come into the enclosure, devouring the crop, such cattle should be forfeited and become the property of the owner of the crop. Many have been seized, but they were begged off and given up again; this has been done many times. Why then are you so quick to be angry? For within the enclosure was the place where the cow was wounded, after which she made her way out. What then means your declaration that the cow was wantonly shot in the common? The cow would not have been killed for simply grazing in the common pasture; her feeding upon the cultivated crop was well known by those who had the care of the plantation."

Scarcely had the chiefs issued this important edict, so necessary in reference to the general subject of Christian marriage, at the islands, as well as the quietude of the country, when they received in good time, very encouraging despatches from the United States' Government.

These were sent by the sloop of war Vincennes, under the command of W. C. Bolton Finch, Esq. It was happy for the islands, that this pleasant embassy was arranged by statesmen so

---

* This passage is ambiguous, but evidently solicits wise and mature counsels from men of countries to the north-east, *whence come the trade winds*, or figuratively, *whence come their frequent commotions*, after the adoption of the Christian religion. It was the thought of Kaahumanu, and widely different from what might once have issued from her insulted majesty. Her forbearance was very great towards foreigners, and especially those employed by high powers.

friendly to the principles of liberty, justice, learning, morality, and religion, as the Honorable J. Q. Adams and S. L. Southard. Among the respectable officers of the ship, the chiefs and missionaries were gratified to find the chaplaincy filled by their friend, the Rev. C. S. Stewart, who had, for a time, labored among them as a missionary.

The Vincennes made the islands, and put in at Hilo, October 3d, 1829. The Sabbath scene of the day following was impressive, of which Mr. S. says:—

" Such multitudes were seen gathering from various directions, that the exclamation, ' What crowds of people !' ' What crowds of people !' was heard from the quarter-deck to the forecastle.

> ' Like mountain torrents pouring to the main,
> From every glen a living stream came forth,
> From every hill in crowds they hastened down
> To worship Him who deigns in humble fane,
> On wildest shore, to meet the upright in heart.

> ' Numbers dwell remote,
> And first, must traverse many a weary mile
> To reach the altar of the God they love.' "

Attending public worship on the Sabbath at Hilo, he says :

" I can scarce describe the emotions experienced in glancing an eye over the immense number, seated so thickly on the matted floor as to seem literally one mass of heads, covering an area of more than 9000 square feet. The sight was most striking, and soon became, not only to myself, but to some of my fellow officers, deeply affecting. I have gazed on many worshipping assemblies, and of every variety of character . . . . but it was left for a worshipping assembly at Hilo, the most obscure corner of these islands, to excite the liveliest emotions ever experienced, and leave the deepest impressions of the extent and unspeakable riches of the Gospel which I have ever known ; emotions and impressions derived simply from an ocular demonstration of the power of the Word of God on untutored men, which is without a parallel in existing events, if not in the records of history.

" The depth of the impression arose from the irresistible conviction that the Spirit of God was there : it could have been nothing else. The breathless silence, the eager attention, the half suppressed sigh, the tear, the various feelings, sad, peaceful, and joyous, discoverable in the faces of many, all spoke the presence of an invisible but omnipotent power ; the power that can alone melt and renew the heart of man, even as it alone first brought it into existence. It was, in a word, a heathen congregation laying hold on the hopes of eternity : a heathen congregation fully sensible of the darkness and despair of their original state, exulting in the first beams of truth and the no uncertain dawning of the Sun of Righteousness.

" The simple appearance and orderly deportment of that obscure congregation, whom I had once known, and at no remote period, only as a set of rude, licentious, and wild pagans, did more to rivet the conviction of the Divine origin of the Bible and of the holy influences

by which it is accompanied to the hearts of men, than all the arguments, apologies, and defences of Christianity I ever read.

" Though the latest established, and long being far behind others
in success and interest, this station bids fair now to be not a whit
behind the very chiefest in its moral and religious achievements."

An accomplished scholar and gentleman, accustomed with the
eye of a limner, rapidly to trace every line of beauty visible, and
to notice the smallest as well as the greatest particulars which
could give interest to his descriptions, and having a facility in
grouping the objects of his attention, and throwing his own ardent feelings upon the canvas, Mr. S. made his delineations of
Hawaiian scenes so graphic, glowing, and beautiful, that the
reader, following him with interest and pleasure, is often led to
apprehend that a less masterly pencil would, in presenting the
same matters of fact, have given a less elegant drapery, and a
greater sombreness to the scenes and scenery of the Sandwich
Islands.   The dawning and rising light may have a mellowness
more attractive even than the beams of the vertical sun.   And
yet has the grace of God exceeded those descriptions, and carried
those anticipated " achievements " beyond the almost visionary
anticipations of this writer, on witnessing the ordinary scenes of
a Hawaiian Sabbath, and hearing of the thousands who sought
instruction in schools, and the hundreds, who every week visited
the house of the missionary, within ten years of the first sound of
salvation on those shores.

When we consider the feeble manner in which our mission had
sustained the direct labors of that station for a short period of
only five years, and the greatness of the numbers who were willing to be taught the doctrines and duties of Christianity, their
careful observance of the Sabbath, their attachment to the missionary and his wife, and their disposition to inquire what they
must do to be saved, how can we for a moment doubt, that the
Lord who chooses frail earthen vessels for his service in the Gospel,
had kindly owned and greatly blessed the missionary labors which
had been performed there?   That God was accomplishing his
wonders there, at that period, was the general opinion of our mission, as well as of Mr. S. and his fellow officers.

The Vincennes reached Oahu on the 13th of October, and
anchored in the roadstead, and at sunrise, on the 14th, fired a
signal gun for the pilot and boats of the shipping in port, by
whose aid she was towed into the harbor, in the calm of the
morning, and snugly moored in a pleasant berth.   At 12 o'clock
she fired twenty-one guns, the established national salute here,
which were returned from the forts.   The Kamehameha, in the
centre of the port, fired a salute of twenty-one guns, which was
returned by the Vincennes, making in all eighty-four guns, whose
bellowings had echoed far and wide in little more than twenty
minutes.   The captain and officers landed near the American
Consul's—were introduced to gentlemen residents and forming a

procession led by the captain, with the consuls on either side, passed through the village to the grounds of the royal residence, in the rear of the village, towards Punchbowl Hill. The house of the young king was a fine, spacious, thatched building, of peculiarly nice Hawaiian workmanship, having decent windows, and doors with side lights, decorated with crimson drapery, floored with stone and mortar, and carpeted with neat, variegated Niihau mats, and furnished with tables, chairs, mirrors, etc., an appropriate and delightful reception room of the queen regent and her son.

As the party came to the gateway of the neat palisade enclosure, the royal guards, dressed in uniform, presented arms in military style. Kekuanaoa, afterwards Governor of Oahu, in a Major General's suit, met Captain Finch, and politely conducted him into the presence of the king and chiefs, by whom he and his officers, being introduced by J. C. Jones, Esq., the American commercial agent, were very courteously received. Capt. Finch, in a neat and appropriate address, which was translated, made known the object of his visit, and presented the document from our government, which he read and handed over, and which was immediately made intelligible by a translation. The good old queen, Kaahumanu, was highly gratified with the condescension, friendship, congratulation, and encouraging counsel exhibited; and her gratitude and joy were indicated by smiles and silent tears, before the reading of the acceptable document was through; and the youthful king, just in his teens, promptly pronounced it " Maikai no, excellent indeed;" other chiefs responded in similar terms, with manifest tokens of high satisfaction.

Both they and their warmest friends had occasion to rejoice at the expressions of kindness and wisdom, in the language of a great nation, from which the Gospel of light and life, and the incipient blessings of civilization had been sent to them, by volunteers in the missionary cause, and now so distinctly approved and supported by the executive of our government.

Difficult as it might be to wield executive influence precisely right as to manner and measure, for reasons already mentioned, and others, perhaps alike obvious, the terms of the document itself and the subsequent progress and prosperity of that young and rising people will show its adaptedness to their wants at that period.

" To Kamehameha, King of the Sandwich Islands :

" *Navy Department of the United States of America.*
" *City of Washington, 20th January, A. D.,* 1829.

" By the approbation and direction of the President of the United States, I address you this letter; and send it by the hands of Captain William Compton Bolton Finch, an officer in our navy, commanding the ship-of-war Vincennes. Captain Finch also bears to you, from the President, certain small tokens of regard for yourself and the chiefs who are near to you, and is commanded to express to you in his name, the anxious desire which he feels for your prosperity and advancement in the arts of civilized life, and for the cultivation of harmony and good will between your nation and the people of the United States. He has heard with interest and admiration of the rapid progress which has been made by your people in acquiring a knowledge of letters and the true religion—the religion of the Christian's Bible. These are the best, and the only means, by which the prosperity and happiness of nations can be advanced and continued, and the President, and all men, everywhere, who wish well to yourself and your people, earnestly hope that you will continue to cultivate them, and to protect and encourage those by whom they are brought to you.

" The President also anxiously hopes that peace, and kindness, and justice, will prevail between your people and those citizens of the United States who visit your islands; and that the regulations of your government will be such as to enforce them upon all.

"Our citizens, who violate your laws, or interfere with your regulations, violate at the same time their duty to their own government and country, and merit censure and punishment. We have heard with pain that this has sometimes been the case; and we have sought to know and to punish those who are guilty. Captain Finch is commanded diligently to inquire into the conduct of our citizens whom he may find at the islands ; and as far as he has the authority, to insure proper conduct and deportment from them.

" The President hopes, however, that there are very few who so act as to deserve censure or punishment ; and for all others, he solicits the kindness and protection of your government, that their interests may be promoted, and every facility be given to them in the transaction of their business. Among others, he bespeaks your favor to those who have taken up their residence with you, to promote the cause of religion and learning in your islands. He does not doubt that their motives are pure, and their objects most friendly to the happiness of your people ; and that they will so conduct themselves, as to merit the protecting kindness of your government. One of their number, the Rev. C. S. Stewart, who resided for some time with you, has received the favor of his government in an appointment to an office of religion in our navy, and will visit you in company with Capt. Finch.

" The President salutes you with respect, and wishes you peace, happiness, and prosperity.

" SAM'L L. SOUTHARD,
. " Secretary of the Navy."

It was long a question of interest whether the rulers of the Sandwich or Society Islands had a right to make laws and enforce them in respect to foreigners, sojourning among them, or frequenting their shores. The apprehension that want of sufficient information, or impartiality, or integrity, or of a disposition sufficiently favorable to foreigners, would expose them to severity, led some of the residents and transient visitors to exert their influence against the exercise of a right, by the rulers of those countries, which is conceded to independent nations, to protect themselves by enacting and enforcing laws which shall extend to aliens, foreign visitors, or sojourners as well as naturalized subjects.

The document from our government confirmed the chiefs of the Sandwich Islands, in the opinion that they had a just right to make regulations to be enforced " on all," to secure " peace and justice," and maintained that " American citizens who violate their laws, violate, at the same time, their *duty* to their own government and country." It is obviously the duty of the citizens and subjects of any government or country to show a proper deference to the laws and the rulers of another country, while within their territory or jurisdiction. For a foreigner to show ill will, insult, or maltreatment to the rulers of the Sandwich Islands, by trampling on their laws or injuring their subjects, male or female, would be casting dishonor on the government whose protection such foreigner might claim, and, at the same time, expose himself justly to the penalty of Hawaiian law. Otherwise, any pirate or buccaneer may, at any time, set them at defiance, and any subjects or citizens of other countries on arriving there, may, with impunity, commit any depredations which they may think would be for their pleasure or advantage. This being admitted, what an awful pandemonium might be expected there! The obvious truth was simply re-affirmed that any subjects or citizens there are bound to respect the authorities and yield to their laws, and, if they violate them, " deserve censure and punishment."

Neither the Secretary of our navy, nor the rulers of the country, nor Capt. Finch and his party, nor the propagators of the Gospel, were singular in their apprehension that a lamentable degree of looseness or indecision prevailed on this subject, while men were not wanting who were ready to avail themselves of the opportunity, thus afforded them, of working mischief with greediness. The advice of Capt. F. and Mr. Stribling was useful.

The official statement of the American commercial agent to Capt. Finch, contains the following remarkable and forcible passage, which goes far to corroborate the fears of the President and Secretary, and to confirm the statements of the missionaries, in a manner which many who visited the islands in those days will know how to understand and appreciate. He says :—

" Since [during] my residence on these islands as an officer of government, I have repeatedly, in the discharge of my official duties, felt the want of protection and aid from the power of my government. I have been compelled to see the guilty escape with impunity, the innocent suffer without a cause, the interests of my countrymen abused ; vessels compelled to abandon the objects of their voyage in consequence of desertion and mutiny ; and men who might be made useful to society suffered to prowl among the different islands, a disgrace to themselves and their country, and an injury to others whom they are corrupting and encouraging to do wrong."

This tells a large part of the whole story, from which it is easy to infer the need, not only of the counteracting influences of missionary agency, but of the strong arm of wholesome law, either Hawaiian, or American, or European, to restrain men who are " *a disgrace to themselves and their country, injuring and corrupting others, and encouraging them to do wrong.*"

The President of the United States, in his sagacity, encourages the king to patronize the inculcation of the " *true religion,* the *religion of the Christian's Bible,*" and to enforce such regulations as shall prevent the mischief, here so plainly admitted and so loudly deplored by the commercial agent, and to secure " *peace, kindness,* and *justice.*"

What greater source of " injury to others " than the sale and use of intoxicating liquors, and what more indispensable regulations than such as would diminish or prevent intemperance, and licentiousness, and the profanation of the Sabbath ?

Captain Beechey's notes deserve to be compared with one of Mr. Jones's. The American whaling vessels annually cruising off the coast of Japan, and generally procuring refreshments at the Sandwich Islands, were estimated with their cargoes at $4,000,000. Capt. Beechey, doubtless, in writing for the public about the Sandwich Islands, was desirous to give useful information ; but having assured the public that fruitful fields were turned by missionary influence into barren sand, and that the king (the queen, Mr. Jones thought, would have been nearer right) had from poverty applied to Mr. Jones for a piece of bread, he must have been surprised if his eye ever fell on the official report of Mr. Jones, who so soon after said of the hundred annual American ships (to say nothing of the English), " A large majority resort to these islands, *certain here to obtain anything of which they may be in want.*" The Sandwich Islanders have often found it difficult to find a fair market for the fresh supplies which they have wished to sell from that period onward.

Before dismissing the subject of the document from the U. S. government, the joint views of the mission at the time respecting the readiness of the nation to receive it and profit by it, as expressed in a single paragraph addressed to Capt. F., may be cited, partly for the purpose of comparing them with the present general voice of political and commercial men in America, England, and France.

" Are not the people indeed prepared for such expressions of friendship and good will as the President has been pleased to make to them ? Are they not prepared to have their just rights acknowledged by so high a power as America ? Are not the rulers here prepared to be encouraged to adopt salutary regulations for the promotion of order, justice, and peace, in their own undisputed territories ? If we admit for a moment that they are not yet prepared to act with decision and discretion on all the points recommended for their consideration, what better means could have been devised than that communication from our government to raise them to the very condition to which that letter supposes them to have advanced ? But we have good reason to believe that they are prepared for just such high-toned advice ; such professions of friendship ; such acknowledgments of rights ; such congratulation for the rising prosperity of the people ; such just reprehension of every wanton abuse of their rights, or violation of law and justice by foreign residents, as that well-advised letter contains. We, therefore, heartily rejoice that the young king and his counsellors have, from so high and respectable a source, received such encouragement to take the dignified stand they ought to take, and which they are able to take among the nations ; such encouragement to go forward in promoting learning and virtue, giving protection and aid to every lawful and laudable pursuit, and of becoming, in fact, what rulers ought to be—*a terror to evil-doers, and a praise to them that do well.*"

The king's letter to the President will show how such counsel was regarded by him.

"ISLAND OF HAWAII, Nov. 23, 1829.

" Best affection to you, the Chief Magistrate of America.   This is my sentiment for you ; I have joy and gratitude towards you on account of your kind regard for me.   I now know the excellence of your communicating to me that which is right and true.   I approve with admiration the justness and faultlessness of your word.

" I now believe that your thoughts and ours are alike, both those countries and these countries, and all large countries.   We are the children—the little islands far off in this tropical climate.

" We have recently had an interview with Captain Finch, with joyfulness, and with sentiments of kindness and pleasure towards him.   I do now hope there will be a perfect agreement between you and us— as to the rights and duties of both of our governments—that the peace now subsisting between us may be perpetual, and the seat of our prosperity may be broad, and our union of heart in things that are right, such that the highways of the ocean may not diverge, because there is a oneness of sentiment in our hearts, with those distant countries, these islands, and all lands.   May our abiding by justice triumphantly prevail, that all those who come hither may be correct in deportment, and all who go thither from this country.

" This is my desire, that you and we may be of the same mind. Such, too, is my hope, that we may pursue the same course, that we may flourish, and that true prosperity may rest perpetually on all the nations of the world in which we dwell.

" Look ye on us with charity ; we have formerly been extremely dark-minded, and ignorant of the usages of enlightened countries.

" You are the source of intelligence and light.   This is the origin of our minds being a little enlightened—the arrival here of the Word of God.   This is the foundation of a little mental improvement which we have recently made, that we come to know a little of what is right, and of the customs of civilized nations.   On this account do we greatly rejoice at the present time.

" I give you thanks, too, for bestowing kindly on me the globes and the map of your country, to be a means of mental improvement for me, and also for your other presents to my friends, who rejoice with me in the reception of the favors which you have granted them.

"Long life to you in this world, and lasting blessedness to you and us in the world to come.

"KAUIKEAOULI KAMEHAMEHA III."

Several very interesting interviews occurred, in which the captain and officers of the Vincennes were brought into social intercourse with the rulers, the missionaries, and the residents, affording them opportunities of marking the advancing state of society, at Honolulu, Lahaina, and Kaawaloa. On one occasion they were received at my house, at another, at Messrs. Clark and Ruggles'; at another, at Mr. Richards'; at another, by Gov. Boki, at Nuuanu, near the Alpine pass to Koolau ; at another, at the royal palace ; which were returned by a levee on board the Vincennes.

The supper, at the palace, is perhaps worthy to be more particularly mentioned, as indicative of the national advancement at that period. The king sent out his neatly written billets to Capt. F. and his officers, to missionaries, and respectable residents, inviting them to sup with him at 7 o'clock. The company, including the chiefs, assembled about 8 o'clock, at the king's neat, newly-thatched, well-lighted palace. Its crimson damask window curtains, beautiful Niihau carpets, the long table well laid with china, glass, &c., and well supplied with substantials and luxuries, and the order and decency which appeared, made the rude structure exhibit an air of civilization. At about 9 o'clock, the large and respectable company were seated at table, with the band of the Vincennes stationed at the door ; and with the exception of the provision and offer of wine, which, in his wiser days, the king would have omitted, the whole entertainment was truly commendable, and the guests were highly gratified.

Capt. Finch courteously conveyed the chieftains of Maui and Hawaii back to their homes, on board the Vincennes, and at the same time gave the king and his suite the honor and pleasure of a delightful trip to Lahaina and Kaawaloa.

The young princess Nahienaena, and Hoapili, governor of Maui, were disembarked at the former place, and J. Adams Kuakini, governor of Hawaii, and Naihe and Kapiolani, at the latter.

At the neat and well-furnished thatched house of Naihe and Kapiolani, the distinguished nobles of the place, the gentlemen of the Vincennes, and others of the party, were received with great hospitality and civility. The refined, amiable, Christian, and matronly deportment of this Hawaiian convert, Kapiolani, for several days, filled the strangers with admiration at the advancement she had made in civilization and Christian courtesy, from the disgusting state of heathenism in which she had lived a few years before.

The Vincennes restored the young king and his sister, and the Oahu chiefs, to their homes, and departed, leaving a good impression. The intercourse of the two governments, on this occasion, was interesting, and the report of it, honorable to both. It was the means of bringing the Hawaiian islands, their rulers and people, and incipient improvement, pleasantly and conspicuously, before large classes of Christian, literary, commercial, and political men, and, like the visit of Lord Byron, tended to give consequence to that feeble and long-neglected people.

During the visit of the Vincennes, the assembled chiefs endeavored to sum up the national debts ; but Boki stated publicly that he had made no contracts for the king, but for himself, and meant to pay his own contracts. An assessment was made on the different islands, for the payment of their reasonable shares. Boki found it difficult to meet the demand for Oahu's share of the national debt, and what was due from himself. His store and hotel, however lucrative they might have been to some of his English clerks, were probably a losing concern to himself.

Being told that sandalwood was abundant at the New Hebrides, he hastily formed a project which was to repair his fortunes and restore his fame, or consummate his ruin.

An adventurer of little consideration having hinted to him that a great voyage might be made by getting the treasures of the Eremango forests, he was unwilling to give any weight to the objections which his mercantile friends could suggest, because he apprehended they wished the first chance in the speculation.

Supposing his success would depend much on his despatch and on the number of hands he could employ for cutting and carrying the wood, and for defence against the hostility of the inhabitants, he collected his dependants, hastened his preparation, and fitted out two vessels, the Kamehameha and Becket. His preparation was partly made on the Sabbath, contrary to law, and from which many augured disaster to the enterprise. The king objected to Boki's going in person, even after he had gone on board to sail. Kekuanaoa bore the message to him, and said, " The king has sent for you to quit the vessel and go on shore." Boki declined. Kekuanaoa, very ready in such cases, reasoned with him ; then with a smiling face and tall manly athletic figure, approaching the governor, threw his muscular arms around him to prove his earnestness to take him from the vessel, and said, " Come, go with me ashore." " No," said the governor, struggling from his grasp ; " I'll never go ashore till one great chief is dead." " What great chief?" said Kekuanaoa, archly ; " you, or I, or Kaahumanu, or the king?" " Never, till one great chief is dead," he repeated—indicating disappointment or revenge.

The expedition sailed Dec. 2d., 1829, a few days after the departure of the Vincennes, while the regent was at Kauai. The Kamehameha, commanded by Boki, had on board about two hundred and fifty men, four-fifths being reckoned as soldiers, Hinau and James Kahuhu accompanying Boki. The Becket, commanded by Manuia, had on board ten foreigners, one hundred soldiers, twenty native seamen, forty other men attached to Governor B., the captain's wife, and seven attendants, in all, one hundred and seventy-nine; total, four hundred and twenty-nine.

In the rapidity with which these two vessels and four hundred men were fitted off, Boki gave an unusual specimen of his energy, but it may have been the energy of desperation and not the promptness of the discharge of obvious duty. It was admitted by some who had encouraged his opposition to Kaahumanu, that his engagement in this wild enterprise was the effect of shame and disappointment. Most of those who accompanied him were opposed to the claims of the Gospel. A few men of professed and probably sincere piety were urged and induced to embark with him, on being solemnly assured by him that he would pursue a just and honorable course. The departure of such a multitude on a voyage so difficult and hazardous, was, to many weeping wives, mothers, and sisters left, an affecting and final departure.

The two vessels touched and refreshed at Rutuma, an island within eight or ten days' sail of the New Hebrides, their destination. The Kamehameha remained four days, and proceeded first. The Becket remained some ten days, and taking on board forty-seven Rutumans followed, and reached Eremango, but Boki and his company could not be found. A mast was seen, which was conjectured to have belonged to the Kamehameha. From the quantity of powder on board her, the frequent and careless use of fire in smoking tobacco, the crowded and confused state of the vessel, she may have been blown up, or foundered, and her whole company of 250 men perished together in mid ocean. The Becket remained about a month at the island of Eremango or Nanapua; but Manuia and his party did not maintain a friendly understanding with the inhabitants, but got into collision with them, fired upon them, and treated them with severity. This was disapproved by Kapalau, his friend, a member of the church at Honolulu, who was with him.

The company was speedily invaded by a mortal sickness, which carried off the captain and his kind monitor, and 180 more of their number, before they returned to Rutuma. There, twenty were left sick, and the Becket returned to Honolulu, August 3d, 1830, with only twelve natives and eight foreigners.* Thus ended this disastrous expedition, a total failure, involving the loss of more than 400 lives. But the hand of God was guarding the interests of the nation in a conspicuous and wonderful manner. The successful return of that whole company might have made strong a dangerous faction which seemed now to be greatly weakened.

Previous to the departure of Boki and his company, there were indications that Adams, Governor of Hawaii, who had been instructed nearly ten years, had come, at length, to admit the high claims of the Word of God. Up to the summer of 1829, though

* A leading one among them, Capt. Sullivan, an Irish Catholic, is supposed to have been since lost at sea in attempting to convey priests and nuns from France to the islands.

he had voluntarily aided the cause of instruction, the establishment of schools, the erection of churches, attendance on public worship, and the security of missionaries, he had never appeared to them to have his heart much interested in personal religion. It would seem difficult, if not beyond reasonable expectation, for a man of high rank, trained in heathenism, and habitually exposed to the influence of artful enemies of truth, the drinking habits and sceptical slang of foreigners, who maltreated both the English language and the Christian religion,—for a man who had some knowledge of the English, and daily took a little of the deleterious stimulus which a distinguished revivalist used to consider fatal to conviction, for a man in middle age, whose giant heart had been confirmed in the love of sin, ever to break away, and feel deeply and right on the subject of personal religion.

But, notwithstanding the adverse influence of habit, of heathenism, and of the wicked from civilized countries, which had long been felt by Adams, the missionaries at Kailua, the place of his residence, Messrs. T. and B. were, in the summer of 1829, encouraged to say of him : " Among the number of those who have given pleasing evidence of a gracious change during the past year, is Kuakini, the Governor of Hawaii, who, from being indifferent, has become our warm friend, and from a besotted sceptic has become moral and devout. He discards his infidelity, and professes his full belief in the doctrines and precepts of Christianity, as his hope of salvation. At the close of a morning sermon, on the Sabbath, he rose, and addressed his people in a pious and affectionate manner, exhorting them to turn from their sins and follies, and give themselves up to Christ. ' As for myself,' said he, ' I have resolved to serve the Lord, and to seek for the salvation of my soul through Jesus Christ. As he has given himself up a sacrifice for our sins, so do ye present your bodies, a living sacrifice, holy, acceptable to God, which is your reasonable service. Let us observe what the laws of God enjoin. If they say to us, steal, murder, commit adultery, then we will do it, but if otherwise, let us beware, for he sees us every day, and will judge us according to our deeds.' "

Whatever he did in religion appeared to be unconstrained. He read the Bible with more constancy, we think, than is common for civil rulers. But being free, he thought, like many Christians in the world, that a temperate habitual or occasional glass, and a *careful* attention to the increase of wealth, was quite allowable, and consistent with a Christian profession.

In the autumn of 1829 there was observable an increased attention to religious instruction, both public and private, and a general solemnity prevailing among the inhabitants of Kailua, and neighboring places, on the western side of Hawaii, manifested by the eagerness with which they listened to preaching, and by the increased numbers who thronged the sanctuary. On the 25th of October Gov. Adams, the only surviving brother of Kaahumanu, and sixteen others, were added to the church at Kailua. About 3000 persons were present and witnessed the solemn transaction, not as thousands do in civilized countries, as a matter of form or of curiosity, to be gazed at for the time, and then forgotten, but as a transaction implying duties and privileges which concerned them personally. It was a day of deep and solemn interest to different classes. The missionaries made this record :—

" The Lord was evidently in the midst of them by the influences of his Spirit, subduing the hearts of sinners, sanctifying, strengthening, and cheering the souls of his people, and drawing thousands to consider their ways, so that for months the houses of the missionaries were thronged with inquirers after truth and salvation, who came often in companies from five or ten to one hundred, confessing sin, such as Paul charges on the heathen, and were instructed in the plainest duties and doctrines taught in God's Word. They acknowledged great ignorance, and said, ' We have been living in darkness, and in the shadow of death. We have come to be directed in the way of light and eternal life.' "

At this period, the moral and religious societies connected with that station embraced 2500 males, and 2600 females. It is worthy of remark, that the schools and other departments of missionary work on Hawaii, had been successfully advancing for about ten years; three missionary stations had been occupied, and three churches gathered before the viceroy, Adams, united himself to the people of God, and while he had been indulging his scepticism as to the authenticity of the Bible. The same divine power which, through the Gospel, could subdue his haughty and worldly spirit, was competent, independent of civil commands or public sentiment, to subdue also the less independent and less exalted classes of the Hawaiians.

CHAPTER XV.

Associations for social worship and improvement—Infanticide once frequent—Book for children—Tour round Oahu—Waimea chosen as a new field—Romish female teacher—Tour through the windward islands—Additions to the church at Lahaina—Arrival at Waimea—Splendid Rainbow—Visit of the chiefs at Waimea —Excursion of the king to Mauna Kea—Excursion and visit to the valley of Waipio—Visit to Hilo—The great volcano of Kilauea—Inland journey from the crater to Waimea—Pulpit for a new church at W.—Journey to Kaawaloa—Temple in the wilderness—Arrival by night at Kuapehu.

THE outpouring of the Spirit of God upon the islands in 1824 and 1825, and his continued favor which followed, brought hundreds at first, and thousands at length, into praying circles or societies, the meetings of which occurred weekly at the different missionary stations, or other places. About the commencement of 1830, these associations at three of our stations, Honolulu, Lahaina, and Kailua, embraced more than ten thousand men and women ; and at three other stations, Waimea on Kauai, Kaawaloa, and Hilo, five thousand more, making the aggregate about 15,000. The men and the women met separately for several reasons : one of which was, to give the females of the mission a full opportunity to make their appeals, to read the Scriptures, and conveniently to give sisterly and maternal counsel to multitudes of their own sex, who must depend on them for much of the instruction and influence which in their peculiar circumstances they eminently needed. Another reason was, to give better scope for the awakened native talent and zeal, both of the male and female portions of the community, to employ itself in the public exercises of prayer and exhortation, and the details of religious experience, and to constitute a more perfect system of mutual watchfulness over the different members, and a more feasible mode of discipline. Multitudes were, by these associations, brought under a good influence ; and their meetings conducted in a quiet and orderly manner facilitated the access of missionaries to numbers, and afforded good opportunities to inculcate upon them, with freedom, the doctrines and precepts of the Bible. They professed to take the Word of God for their guide, to desire to be instructed in its doctrines, to abstain from known immoralities, and to pray for God's blessing on their inquiries and labors.

These pledges, the mutual watchfulness, and weekly meetings, and the reading of the Scriptures, exhortations and prayers connected with them, were doubtless of great utility to multitudes brought within their influence; withholding them from former and still existing vices, while they were not, by the terms of their engagement, exposed to the justly dreaded censures of the *church*, which must sometimes be given to disorderly members by the authority of Christ.

If, in some cases, a connexion with these associations fostered the spirit of self-righteousness, like the practice of praying in the family, or attending public worship, receiving the ordinances, or signing a pledge of abstinence from intoxicating drinks or tobacco, in more enlightened countries, this evil, I am persuaded, resulted not so much from the nature of the duties enjoined, observed, or agreed to, as from the imperfection of human nature, always inclined to commend itself for the performance of any service proper in itself, or to substitute some *form* of religion, lax or rigid, in the place of holiness of heart and life. But the missionaries being aware of this tendency, no greater, perhaps, in Hawaii than in Europe, took early pains to guard against its evils, both in respect to admissions to the associations for prayer and improvement, and to the ordinances of the house of God, and, at the same time, to secure the good that was attainable by both. Often were multitudes held back from uniting with the church on the ground that it could do them no good, unless they were truly converted, though they might think themselves to be the true disciples of Christ.   And in some cases, a union with these voluntary associations was discountenanced, because of its supposed tendency to make the members think more highly of themselves than they ought to think, though the exclusion of those who truly desired to enter, deprived them of some advantages, and exposed them with less guards to some prevailing evils.

These associations, which had different pledges or tests of membership, extending through the islands, were not all managed alike. In some places they assumed much the form of a Christian school, or a class of catechumens; and in others that of a Christian worshipping assembly, associated on terms which forbade immorality, and required of every member attention to religious instruction, prayer, temperance, and the observance of the Sabbath. Some of the meetings were conducted chiefly by missionaries, and others by natives.

At the station of Honolulu, the male association having commenced with Kalanimoku and eight or ten other serious individuals, amounted, in the early part of 1830, to 1587, of whom 1137 belonged to the district of Honolulu, conveniently situated for meeting together. The female association of the same place, which commenced with a few individuals, in January of 1825, and near the close of that year embraced about seven hundred females, including Kaahumanu and her sister, Namahana, amounted, in the beginning of 1830, to 2100; of whom 1500 belonged to Honolulu. At their weekly meeting, it was customary for one or more of the missionary females of the station to attend, and read the Scriptures, conduct the exercises, and lead in prayer, or call on native converts to do it, who humbly and unhesitatingly engaged in this appropriate and ennobling employment.

When the meeting became so very large that the house which they had erected for the purpose would not accommodate more than half their number, and a female voice could not well be heard by all in prayer, or in reading the Scriptures, or in kind expostulation and counsel, they were divided; first, into two divisions, and subsequently into many. Over each subdivision a hopefully pious female convert had a special charge, whose duty it was to have a list of the names of those belonging to it, to know their places of residence, to meet them once a week for devotion, and to look after their children, if they had any who needed such attention. Previously to these divisions, at a great meeting of these associated women, on Christmas of 1829, it was proposed by the ladies of the station that on the following weekly meeting, those who among their number had children should bring them, and they would endeavor to see what more could be done, both for the children and their mothers. Too much and too long had large portions of the children of the land been neglected by their parents and relatives, and by Christian friends who had it in their power to provide better for them. The means and opportunities for writing books for them were not wanting, but the means of publishing them, and furnishing them with suitable apparatus and encouragement, had not been adequately supplied. A first book for children, attractive and instructive, adapted to initiate them into the art of reading and to inculcate just, moral, and religious principles, and enlist their young powers in the pursuit of knowledge and virtue, was felt by all to be needed, and was now prepared and put to press. On the last Sabbath of 1829, I preached to a very large and attentive audience from Eph. vi., 1—4, explaining and enforcing, according to my ability, the duties of the parents and children who came under my charge, and whose circumstances and wants I had had almost ten years of intercourse and observation to learn.

On Friday, the first day of the new year, Kaahumanu called on us about noon with her congratulations for auspicious appearances upon the ushering in of the new year, and with her interested inquiries as to our plans and prospects for the children, and was glad to hear us report progress. As the hour for their afternoon meeting approached, mothers and children were seen coming from different directions, according to appointment, some of whom were disposed to throng the passage to the printing-house to see about the new book.

Thence they repaired together to their *hale hooikaika* [house for making strong]. At this house for religious exercises, there were about 600 within, and 400 crowded into the inclosure. The missionary females proposed to divide the company, and to lead off, to the church, the mothers and their children. About 200 women separated themselves from the majority. It was then proposed that, of the remainder, all who had been mothers, but were then childless, should rise, when a large proportion exhibited themselves,—a sad spectacle, in proof of the great mortality in the land among the children, from some cause not very apparent. The thought occurred to draw a line again, which should show what portion of these mothers had made themselves childless by the violence of their own hands, or by their voluntary concurrence in the death of their offspring. But the thought of their actually showing themselves in considerable numbers as infant murderers, on such an occasion, was too appalling and overwhelming, and it was not attempted; though many, from time to time, in a more private way, confessed that they had been guilty of infanticide.

The subject of infant murder and its causes was, of course, painful to all missionary laborers, as connected with their own neighbors, whom they were attempting to win and draw to the paths of virtue, and who, when willing to leave that work of cruelty and blood, which had been urged on by voluptuousness and by the jealousy of rude husbands and paramours, were not to be continually upbraided or interrogated as to the extent to which they had themselves carried this most unnatural species of murder. And in some instances, when we came, at length, to see here and there a mother with a little group of interesting and sprightly children, some in simple, clean attire, fitted out for school, or brought to the sanctuary, or to some special meeting of mothers, while others lamented that they had now no children to lead in the right way, it was difficult to persuade ourselves that we really understood correctly when, with their own lips, they declared they had put their own living offspring into the excavated ground, covered them with earth, and trod it down with their feet over their dying babes, and then turned away to their pleasures, as without natural affection. How could a refined and educated American wife and mother, who clings to her offspring as to her own life, readily believe what fell on her astonished ear, when a Hawaiian female, inquiring the way to Heaven, would hold up both hands with the asseveration, "These hands have destroyed one, two, three, four, or five of my own children, before or after birth?"

But mothers were not alone in this forbidding and polluting work. Husbands, and other relatives or friends, concurred, of course, or took a leading part. And thus, according to the opinion of those who had good opportunity to judge, more than half the children were destroyed during the generation preceding the introduction of Christianity, as a million are supposed to be annually, in China, to this day. From such violence attempted, there were cases of rescue, both before and after our arrival, by individuals who felt the rising of compassion or the language of conscience condemning the wrong, and were willing to assume the care and labor which a jealous and reproachful husband and father could not be prevailed on to do. Of these rescued victims, numbers have been received to the bosom of our churches, of whom Bartimeus, the distinguished blind preacher, was one, and Abba, another, a young woman, born at Hilo, and cast into a pit that she might die, rescued by a woman of Oahu, who had heard the Gospel, brought to Honolulu, adopted by her who rescued her, sent to school and church, trained in the Christian religion, taught by the grace of God, and at length allowed to sit down with her adopted mother and the missionaries, at the table of our Lord, rejoicing in the hope of heaven.

Who does not commend the compassion that snatches a Moses or a sinking child from the devouring flood? The kindness which draws a heathen infant from the pit opened by its monster mother, even though the rescued is to breathe the air of *paganism*, commends itself to consideration. How much more then the kindness of the instructed Hawaiian, who brings a heathen child from the opened grave to the Sabbath School and the House of God—to reformed society, and the light of Heavenly life! But Christianity, in the guise of Foreign Missions, hastens, not only to snatch half the children of a nation from an unnatural death, inflicted by the cruelty, or ignorance, or careless maltreatment of parents and others, and to offer them the light of life, but to rescue whole dying nations from a heathen grave, tell them of the Great Salvation, and train them for immortal glory! Happy are the communities who engage seasonably and successfully in this work.

Through the industry of Mr. Shepard and his native compositors, press-men, folders, &c., a few copies of the book for the children were ready to be presented before the prayer-meeting of the mothers and their offspring closed. They were received with great eagerness. The next day, troops of children came for more, as fast as they could be made ready for them, at the office. Within the two months after the presentation of this juvenile offering, we had, at the station, 1144 children cheerfully turning its neatly printed pages, more or less embellished with cuts, and learning its spelling, reading, and catechetical lessons, and juvenile songs. This was a specimen of the gladness with which it was received, at the different stations.

The great number of adults who had needed to be taught from the very alphabet, had taken, in some measure, the place of children, who, till their parents had learned to value instruction, were, in general, slow to attend to it. But now, it was not only more easy to enlist them, but to furnish them with teachers. These eleven hundred were, at this time, for the most part, placed under the care of thirty female teachers, who were aided, at particular times, by their foreign teachers. By the blessing of God, a new and salutary impulse was given, at the commencement of this year, to this part of Christian improvement.

The first Sabbath of this year was to us an interesting day, and the first monthly concert of the year was attended by a much larger concourse of natives than is usually seen in American congregations, on such occasions. At the weekly lecture, on Wednesday, the 6th, about 300 children were present, and many of them, doubtless, with the hope of obtaining one of the new books. More than a thousand women attended the Friday prayer-meeting on the 8th.

Never, perhaps, had it been granted me to address a more crowded and attentive assembly than on the Sabbath, Jan. 10th, when I endeavored, with great freedom, to press on their attention the inspired instruction contained in the 73d Ps. The next day, our houses were thronged, from before breakfast, till the darkness of a rainy night set in. They pressed upon us, so incessantly, their thoughts, their questions, and wants, that we could hardly find time to eat the most simple and frugal meals—a specimen of many a day, in the course of many of the laborers in that field. The number of readers and learners in the islands, at this time, was estimated at 50,000. Those who have seen the opportunity for pouring in light among a dark, heathen people, who were really waiting to be supplied, and manifesting little desire to turn away to the abominable falsehoods of heathenism or papistry, but exceedingly exposed to be led astray by the emissaries of Rome, can, in some measure, appreciate the importance of amply sustaining the press among them. It is a good school for missionaries in which to study frugality in expenditures, and economy in the application of strength ; for if each of the missionaries in the field could do ten times the labor ordinarily required of any one, and each had ten times more means of supplying the wants of the nation with books, and stationery, and school apparatus, than could then be at the disposal of each, it would all have ill sufficed to give the people a reasonable supply. Often did the missionary find it necessary to turn away from a score of the people with a simple *aloha,* or a remark, " *He hana ka'u*" [I have business], when his own desire and theirs might be to spend an evening together in conversing on the things of religion. The weary body, and often the spirit with it, was oppressed by this pressure of the people upon us, at all hours and seasons. But we rejoiced that God displayed his favor in making thousands of them willing to come to us, not only from the immediate vicinity of our dwellings, but from a distance of many miles, to visit whom, often, at their habitations, when the missionaries were so few, would have been impracticable. Nay, there was much labor to be done near at hand, as well as far off, which was out of our power. We were, therefore, obliged to employ incompetent helpers among the native population, who, though in some instances they have made us trouble, yet have, on the whole, rendered very important service to the cause ; and it has afforded us pleasure to find so many among the converts, male and female, both in the higher and ordinary ranks, who were willing, without compensation, to devote time and labor to what was, emphatically, missionary work. But they needed much training, and almost constant superintend-ance. For the 15,000 associated in different parts of the islands, for prayer and improvement, besides the numerous schools, much personal attention and careful supervision were required.

Among the leaders and teachers, Kaahumanu and her succes-sors, Kekauluohi and Kinau, were for a time numbered.

On the 7th of March, 1830, and before the troubles occasioned by the hostility and irregularities of Boki had ceased, the mis-sionaries had the happiness to see Kinau, the daughter of Kame-hameha and Kalakua, and the niece and heiress of Kaahumanu, come forward, at length, and profess her faith in Christ, her readi-ness to serve him, and her renunciation of self and sin, and enroll her name among the members of Christ's household. Her hus-band, Kekuanaoa, and others, were added to the church at the same time.

During this month, Kaahumanu, in her persevering efforts to secure the co-operation of the people in the work of reform, made another tour round Oahu. Mr. Clark, and several native teachers, who accompanied her, attended at the same time to the business of preaching to the people, and leading them in the exer-cises of public worship, and encouraging the one hundred and thirty-one schools of our circuit.

Some have supposed that Kaahumanu relied mainly on her own arbitrary will, or royal authority, to make the people religious. But those who marked her steps, heard her exhortations and prayers, and humble conversation, and the multiplied moral means employed generally, to make the people Christian, not merely in form, profession, and appearance, but in spirit and in truth, will be less likely to ascribe to her heart the intention or expectation of producing Christian virtue in others, by her will; or to the civil power, in any shape, the fact of making the people religious. Her reliance on the Word and power of God appears to me to have been as simple as that of the sons of freedom in seeking the moral improvement of the objects of their solicitude. The efforts of the queen regent, and those associated with her, were highly appreciated by the missionaries, for their moral influence, wher-ever she went throughout the islands, at a period when the popu-lation accessible, had it been divided equally among the ordained preachers of our mission, would have given each twelve thousand, and at a time, too, when Roman emissaries were watching to interrupt and thwart the evangelical efforts thus diligently made. Deference was indeed paid, as in wiser countries, to rank and office, by those who desired the good will of the most distin-guished, and by others who had sense enough to know, and honor enough to acknowledge that special deference was due to Christian rulers like Kaumualii, Kaahumanu, Kalanimoku, Kapiolani, Kinau, and others of kindred spirit and similar influence, and by all who had been led to believe that loyalty to the supreme power is as indispensable a duty as common honesty or conjugal fidelity.

At this period it was deemed advisable to occupy a new station, on the northern part of Hawaii, and to select a situation favorable to the health of those among the missionaries who appeared to be suffering from the heat of the climate, or the long-continued summer of our tropical region. In the autumn of 1829, several missionaries examined the district of Waimea, in the interior of the northern division of Hawaii, and reported in favor of its occupancy. In January the mission decided to commence the work there, with a view partly to resuscitate invalids, and partly to increase the amount of evangelical light and influence in that part of Hawaii.

Mr. Ruggles' health, and my own, were at that time nearly prostrate. To try what effect relaxation, change of scene, air, and temperature, and a sojourn in the cool, retired, lofty, and long-neglected heathen solitudes of Waimea, added to such other remedies as the medical skill in our mission prescribed, would have on our impaired constitutions, with the kind and decided advice of our fellow-laborers, we repaired to that place. Mr. R. and Dr. Judd, with their families, in the early part of the year, and myself and family in the summer—leaving Honolulu, June 14, 1830.

On the 16th of the same month, Kaahumanu and the young king, resolving to embark from Honolulu on a tour of the windward islands, called a public meeting at Honolulu, and committed to Liliha and Kinau the care of the island. Kinau being the heiress of Kaahumanu, and half sister of the late and present king, and highly esteemed for her intelligence, integrity, and firmness of character, though as yet inexperienced as a ruler, and for her attachment both to the regent and her royal son, was deemed a suitable and able coadjutor, of great importance. Kaahumanu enjoined on all, native and foreign, a heedful observance of the laws of the land, true loyalty in the support of the supreme power as the minister of God to execute wrath upon the " evil doer." The king apprised them of the intended tour by Kaahumanu and himself, leaving the charge there in the hands of Kinau and Liliha, and called on the people to acknowledge their rightful authority, and charged them to do that which was right and good according to the Word of God. Kaahumanu said to the people, " My intention is to fulfil the charge left me by my husband—to take care of his children, and to take care of the islands. I am resolved to lead this king in the right way. But aid ye me in this by walking in the right way yourselves, and helping forward the good work which is begun. These ruling mothers intrusted with the care of this island, do ye obey, according to the direction of the supreme magistrate."

Previous to the departure of Kaahumanu, she went into the precincts of her old friend Don Francisco de Paulo Marin, who had, in the days of heathenism, united with her in wickedness and idolatry, one of the rites of which was the procession of the " *Akua Makahiki*," and finding a number of people called "*palani*," who had little *kii* (images of the cross, &c.), asked them to give them up to her and not worship such things. She talked to them kindly, as if they had been her children. They gave her their trinkets, and she took a sort of pledge, that they would abandon the use of images, and the interview terminated pleasantly.

A native woman by the name of Louisa, recently returned from a cruise with a shipmaster, had undertaken to inculcate the dogmas of Romanism among the people of Honolulu. She was furnished with a manuscript manual embracing multifarious sacraments, denunciations of heresy and heretics, and exhibiting as God's laws, the mutilated or expurgated decalogue—excluding the second divine commandment, which forbids image worship, and dividing the tenth into two. When she was asked why she taught that way, she said it was because she thought Kaahumanu and all the chiefs would soon follow her. When she was asked what she understood her book to mean by the term " heretics," she said, " Those who take a part of God's Word, and reject a part." " What then do you think of those who reject the second commandment?" She could not reply. When I asked and urged her to allow me to take her book to my house and examine it thoroughly, promising that if I found it correct I might approve it, she replied, " No." " Why not?" I asked. " Because," she replied, " you don't believe it is true."

Kaahumanu took her into her family, hoping to make her comfortable in her train ; but finding her haughty and disrespectful, treated her with some severity, and after a little time, dismissed her.

This Romish woman at length assumed the office of a priestess of Rome, teaching and administering the rite of " *bapatema*," an ordinance analogous to Christian baptism. It is affirmed that she administered it to Kalola, an aged woman of rank, and thus initiated her, in her grey hairs, into the fellowship of Rome.

Kaahumanu and her company sailed on the 17th of June, 1830, for their visitation to the windward islands, to encourage education, morals, and religion, and for maintaining the peace and order of the nation. They reached Lahaina three days after my arrival there with my family, where we enjoyed a delightful season of three weeks. Thirty-three hopeful converts from heathenism were there welcomed to the fellowship of the household of Christ. Mr. R., who baptized them, and proposed the articles of faith and covenant before a great multitude, first challenged the world to object, if they had aught to object, against the character or conduct of any of the candidates, as a reason for forbidding water, or refusing their admission to the church. Such was the cautiousness with which converts, at that period, were brought to the ordinances of the Gospel.

Leaving the other travellers, and crossing over to Kawaihae with my family, we ascended at evening to the new inland station. When we had escaped from the oppressive heat on the shore, and reached the height of about 2000 feet, we were met by a slight rain and a chilly wind, which made our muscles shiver, though covered with a cloak, as we came within some twenty-five miles of the snows of the mountain. The rain and clouds passed away as we approached the place of the sojourn of Mr. Ruggles and Dr. Judd. The full-orbed moon looked serenely down from her zenith upon the hoary head of Mauna Kea, and the ample and diversified scenery around. The babbling brook, the sound of a small cataract in a glen, the rustling in the tops of the trees, at a little distance, the scattered huts of the natives in the settlement, while their occupants were hushed at midnight, and the hospitable light of a fire and lamp, beaming from a glass window of the missionary cottage pitched near the north side of the plain, over against Mauna Kea, which appeared in its grandeur, all contributed to awaken peculiar emotions, and called forth the aspiration, "May the Gospel and the Spirit of God dwell here, and the wilderness and the solitary place be glad for them."

Dr. and Mrs. Judd received us very kindly at this late midnight hour, and in a few days returned to their post at Honolulu.

Uniting with Mr. Ruggles in the labor of the station, and being assisted by John Ii, I devoted some attention to the translation of the Scriptures, and such other preparations for the press as due attention to my health and to the people would allow.

Riding out one day to call on Gov. Adams, who had done liberally for the station by the erection of the buildings, I was delighted, on my way to his temporary residence, with the grandeur and beauty of the scenery around me. The clear rippling streams that wind their way along the verdant plain, through alternate plats of shrubbery, grass, *kalo*, sugar-cane, bananas, flowering bushes, and wild vines, occasionally crossed my path. Beyond the scattered cottages, the wild cattle were grazing unrestrained on their own unenclosed territories bordering on the mountain. The green hills and mountains of Kohala, crowned with trees and shrubbery, and their sides partly cultivated and partly covered with grass of spontaneous growth, rose on the north side of the plain. The distant hoary Mauna Loa appeared in the south. Much nearer, on the south-east, the majestic Mauna Kea lifted his snowy summit in his ample form, exhibiting his peaks and precipices and piles of scoria and gravel, and his rocks and forests; and in the south-west, Hualalai, another volcanic mountain, with its terminal quiescent crater, presented no mean height and dimensions, being 9000 feet high, and forty miles long. Beyond its northern base, and very near the horizon, gleamed the mellowed rays of a brilliant setting sun, peculiarly grand in the Pacific isles, where there are few objects of great attraction. In the opposite quarter, the most majestic and splendid rainbow I had ever seen, for awhile attracted and fixed my attention, and commanded my admiration. Its southern extremity was based upon the ample side of the lofty Mauna Kea, and its rising curve bisected his frozen brow. The northern extremity rested on the abrupt termination of the mountains of Kohala to the north-eastward of the mission houses and church of Waimea. This stupendous arch, as of gold, rubies, and precious stones of other hues, was, by a hand divine, thrown quite across the broad, elevated plain of Waimea, ascending in its zenith to an unusual and lofty height, and in its perfection and beauty, appearing such as our common ancestor first saw with holy wonder and grateful adoration from the heights of Ararat.

Beneath and beyond the cloud on which this transcendent symbol of mercy was embossed, there was a wide field of azure sky, opening towards the distant Jerusalem, where my thoughts had been for a time employed in writing the history of its kings and prophets for the people of the islands. What a symbol of the gate of heaven—the open entrance to the new Jerusalem—did this grand and singular combination form ! It seemed to enhance the beauty and force of the elevated strain in the 24th Psalm, and in Handel's Messiah:

" Lift up your heads, O ye gates,
     And be ye lift up, ye everlasting doors,
     And the King of Glory shall come in."

After a pleasant interview with the governor, who was looking for his sister's arrival, and a call on a sick chief, who seemed much interested in our cause, I returned to my habitation.

Early in September, Kaahumanu and her company having accomplished their contemplated visits on Maui, Molokai, and Lanai, exhorting the people to listen to God's Word, and quietly to attend to their duties as subjects, passed over to Hawaii and landed at Kawaihae. At the special invitation of the king, I visited them there, twelve miles distant. On the Sabbath, in full sight of the once frowning and forbidding temple of abomination, built by Kamehameha, at the place where we first set foot on shore, and Kalanimoku, Kalakua, and Namahana, subsequently admitted to the Christian church, had greeted our mission, some 3000 of the people assembled in the open air and listened to the unfolding of the doctrine of God our Savior, " Who hath delivered us from the power of darkness, and translated us into the kingdom of his dear Son, in whom we have redemption through his blood, even the forgiveness of sins."

After the Sabbath, the chiefs and their attendants repaired to

Waimea, and sojourning there several weeks, made the missionaries a thorough-going *family visitation*. The king appeared affable, kind, and teachable, and the behavior of the others was equally commendable. Kapiolani, who, in her heathen state, called on board the Thaddeus on our arrival in 1820, now the Christian lady of the manor at Kaawaloa, and agreeable friend and coadjutor of the missionaries, joined the other chiefs in this visit to Waimea, and by her vivacity, intelligence, modesty, dignity, and piety, added much to the interest of the social and religious intercourse of that season.

The company of visitors to the place embraced about sixty members of churches at different stations, now constituting a sort of *Huakaihele ekalesia*, travelling church. These met on Saturday evening at my house to pray for the influences of the Spirit of God, for his blessing on the Sabbath services, and for his daily guidance of the rulers of the nation. Solemnity and tenderness of heart seemed to mark that season. God was there. The voice of the little flock was heard; and rich blessings subsequently descended there. The following morning, a great concourse assembled in a grove for divine service, and attentively heard the Gospel as summarily announced by John in the wilderness—" Behold the Lamb of God that taketh away the sin of the world." Then sixty-two communicants united there in the sacrament of the Supper, and *showed the Lord's death* in the presence of the people, in sight of the place where, eleven years before, the closing struggles, with weapons of carnage, between the opposers and defenders of idol worship, had occurred.

These Sabbath services being over, a very interesting conversation occurred, commencing while the king and Kaahumanu were at breakfast with us. The claims of religion, the recently received news of the disastrous result of Boki's expedition, the danger that had been apprehended from his ambition and restlessness, and other important matters, engaged the earnest attention of the chiefs for the forenoon. While their minds were solemn, one of their attendants, in an appropriate and touching manner, applied a passage from the first Psalm which had been recently translated for them: " He is like the chaff which the wind driveth away." . The feelings of the young king were unusually awake relative to the prospects and dangers of the state ; and for a youth of fifteen, he took an active and intelligent part in the conversation. Kapiolani coming in from the house of Mr. R., brought up the question whether the *pule palani*, papal worship, was not now the principal source of the dangers that threatened them? She and others were then making themselves acquainted with the recent translation of 2d Thessalonians. After the morning sacrifice, Kekauluohi produced her neat manuscript copy of the translation of the prominent parts of Dr. King's farewell letter to his Roman Catholic friends in Syria, which was read and listened to with intense interest, the king often interposing a question or remark. Kapiolani said to us, " These things you have long known, but they are new to us." When Naihe and I expressed to Boki our fear of the evils which would arise, if these new teachers were allowed to dwell in the land, he said, " We all worship Jehovah alike." " Not alike ! not alike !" she now exclaimed with great earnestness and emphasis : " if this is the *puli palani*, it is not the religion of Christ."

This letter, placed beside Paul's Epistle to the Thessalonians, on the *great apostasy*, could not well be misunderstood or misapplied, even by rude, unprejudiced natives.

Soon after this, the king set out with a party of more than a hundred, for an excursion further into the heart of the island, and an ascent to the summit of Mauna Kea. To watch over and instruct my young pupil, and to benefit my health, I accompanied him. The excursion occupied nearly five days, though it might have been accomplished much sooner. Crossing in a southerly direction the plain of Waimea, some on horseback and some on foot, the party ascended a small part of the elevation of the mountain, and being in the afternoon enveloped in dense fog, they halted and encamped for the night. The next day they passed over the western slope of the mountain to the southern side, thence eastward along a nearly level plain, some seven thousand feet above the level of the sea, to a point south of the summit, and encamped out again, in the mild open air. In the course of this day's journey, the youthful king on horseback, pursued, ran down, and caught a yearling wild bullock, for amusement and for a luncheon for his attendants. A foreigner lassoed and killed a wild cow.

The next day was occupied chiefly in ascending in a northerly direction, very moderately. Our horses climbed slowly, and by taking a winding and zigzag course, were able, much of the way, to carry a rider. Having gained an elevation of about ten thousand feet, we halted and encamped for the night, in the dreary solitudes of rocks and clouds. When the night spread her dark, damp mantle over us, we found ourselves in the chilly autumnal atmosphere of the temperate zone of this most stupendous Polynesian mountain. Below us, towards Mauna Loa, was spread out a sea of dense fog, above which the tops of the two mountains appeared like islands. We found it a pretty cold lodging place. Ice was formed in a small stream of water near us, during the night. As the company were laying themselves down, here and there, upon the mountain side, for sleep, I observed that the king and Keoniani, subsequently premier, and a few others, having found a cave about four feet high, ten wide, and eight deep, made by a projecting rock, which would afford a shelter from a shower, and partially from wind and cold, had stretched themselves out to sleep upon the ground in front of it. I was amused to see that their heads protruded somewhat more than six feet from the mouth of the cave, and asked, " Why do you not

sleep under the rock, which is so good a sleeping house for you?"
Keoniani, always ready, replied, " We don't know at what time
the rock will fall." Whether the apprehension that the firm rock
might possibly fall upon the head of the king that night or their
unwillingness that any ignoble foot should walk above it, or
some other fancy, were the cause of his declining the shelter,
did not appear.

In the morning we proceeded slowly upwards till about noon,
when we came to banks of snow, and a pond of water partly
covered with ice. In his first contact with a snow bank, the juvenile king seemed highly delighted. He bounded and tumbled on
it, grasped and handled and hastily examined pieces of it, then
ran and offered a fragment of it in vain to his horse. He assisted
in cutting out blocks of it, which were wrapped up and sent down
as curiosities to the regent and other chiefs, at Waimea, some
twenty-eight miles distant. These specimens of snow and ice, like
what are found in the colder regions of the earth, excited their
interest and gratified their curiosity, and pleased them much; not
only by their novelty, but by the evidence thus given of a pleasant remembrance by the youthful king.

After refreshing and amusing ourselves at this cold mountain
lake, we proceeded a little west of north, and soon reached the
lofty area which is surmounted by the " seven pillars" which wisdom had hewed out and based upon it, or the several terminal
peaks near each other, resting on what would otherwise be a
somewhat irregular table land, or plain of some twelve miles circumference. Ere we had reached the base of the highest peak,
the sun was fast declining and the atmosphere growing cold.

The king and nearly all the company declined the attempt to
scale the summit, and passing on to the north-west crossed over,
not at the highest point, and hastily descended towards Waimea.
John Phelps Kalaaulana, who had been in New England, the
only native in the company who seemed inclined to brave the
cold and undertake the labor of reaching the top, accompanied
me, and we climbed to the summit of the loftiest peak. The
side of it was composed of small fragments of lava, scoria, and
gravel lying loose and steep. The feet sank into them at every
step. Our progress was slow and difficult, by a zigzag and winding course. Respiration was labored, and the air taken into the
lungs seemed to supply less aid or strength than usual. I repeatedly laid myself down panting to take breath and rest my
exhausted muscles. On gaining the lofty apex, our position was
an awful solitude, about 14,500 feet above the level of the sea,
where no animal or vegetable life was found. No rustling leaf,
or chirping bird, or living tenant of the place attracted the eye
or ear.

Maui could be distinctly seen at the distance of one hundred
miles over the mountains of Kohala. The immense pile of lava,
once chiefly fluid, which constitutes the stupendous Mauna Loa,

rose in the south-west, at the distance of thirty miles, to a height nearly equal to that of Mauna Kea, where we stood. Very light clouds occasionally appeared above us. Down towards the sea over Hilo and Hamakua the clouds were dark and heavy, floating below our level, and towards the north, were apparently rolling on the earth to the westward towards Waimea and Kawaihae, while the wind on our summit was in the opposite direction. As the sun disappeared the cold was pinching. We occasionally cringed under the lee of the summit for a momentary relief from the chilling blast. While taking some trigonometrical observations my fingers were stiffened with the cold, and Phelps repeatedly cried out with emphasis, " *E hoi kaua, he anu.* Let us return ; 'tis *cold.*"

We descended hastily to the north-west, about twelve miles, sometimes taking leap after leap boldly down steep places of fragmentary scoria and gravel, and sometimes advancing cautiously among rocks, shrubs, trees, and wild cattle. Towards midnight we came to the place of the king's party, near the plain of Waimea, and the next day returned to the station there. As we crossed the plain, we witnessed several striking exhibitions of seizing wild cattle, chasing them on horseback, and throwing the lasso over their horns, with great certainty, capturing, prostrating, and subduing or killing these mountain-fed animals, struggling in vain for liberty and life.

Prosecuting their tour, the chiefs soon proceeded by different routes to Waipio, to meet the people of Hamakua. When they had reached that valley, at their request I joined them there. Passing through a wood of trees and shrubs of perpetual verdure, cheered by various notes of the feathered tribe, I occasionally rode under the fronds of ferns and the leaves of the wild plantain, both of which rise to the height of 12 or 15 feet. The largest species of fern on the island has a trunk some eight or ten inches in diameter, six or eight feet high, from the top of which rises a tuft of imposing, arching fronds, or neat leaves from four to nine feet in length, of a bright green, curving and tapering gracefully, and gently waving like the young leaves or fronds of the cocoa-nut. From the lofty precipice on the south-east of Waipio, I had an enchanting view of a Hawaiian landscape of singular beauty and grandeur, embracing the varied scenery around, and the deep and charming valley below; the dwelling-place of twelve or fifteen hundred inhabitants, where, generation after generation, never cheered by the voice of salvation or the sound of the church-going bell, had passed away in heathenish darkness. Numerous objects, well-defined, and at such a distance as to give them a softness, beauty, and perfection in appearance, which in a nearer view they might not have, were, in a group, presented to the eye.

The numerous garden-like plantations of bananas, sugar cane, potatoes, the cloth plant, and the *kalo*, in the different stages of advancement, from recent planting to maturity, some with narrow, and some with broad green leaves of different shade (like the Lily Ethiopica), embossed upon the silvery water, by which the surface of the beds is overflowed ; the small river flowing sometimes briskly, and sometimes slowly along its winding course, through the valley, after descending in cataracts from precipitous heights ; the unruffled fish ponds ; the quiet hamlets near the cliffs, the small scattered thatched huts of the inhabitants, with their low and diminutive doors, the tents of the travelling chiefs, pitched near the sand banks, at the sea shore ; the inhabitants moving silently about, here in a canoe, and there walking singly, and here and there in little companies, in Indian file, like the fancied Liliputians, or children of nature drawn in miniature in bright and living colors, and contrasted with the scenery by which they were surrounded ; the green, smooth, and stupendous cliffs, the lofty mountains, and the wide ocean under the unrestrained action of the N. E. trade winds, which dash its billows against the mountain walls on either side of the opening, while the canoes of the expert natives pass and repass over its fringe of surf, at the sand beach,—all afforded an interesting picture, chiefly of nature, rarely surpassed.

Scarcely a sound was heard from the valley at that soft hour, as the sun was retiring behind the western heights, except the repeated and reverberating strokes of the cloth mallet, on the bark-beater's beam.

From that position, directly down to the river, the descent of about one thousand feet was difficult, but not impracticable. With one hand clinging to little shrubs and strong grass, and with the other thrusting a sharpened staff into the earth to avoid sliding fatally down the steep, I attempted it. Friendly natives of the valley ascended part way to meet and assist me. Their ingenuity readily supplied a vehicle, by uniting bushes and branches of shrubs, and the *ki* plant for a drag. Taking a seat at their order, on the top of it, I was gradually let down this wall on this basket, by six wakeful and sure-footed natives, two before, two behind, and one on each side. With all their agility, one and another of them occasionally getting too much momentum, would suddenly slide forward a yard or two ahead of the others. We reached the bottom speedily and successfully.

The large and portly Kekauluoki had, a few days before, descended this precipice. Trying at first to creep down, her courage failed, as she saw the difficulty and felt the danger. She then had a folded mantle passed before her breast, the two ends being carried back from her sides (as if she were to draw a load) and put into the hands of several strong and trusty servants, who were to hold her from going off too fast, as she attempted to walk down before them. But as in all cases the balance or adjustment of power between the nobility and the peasantry is a matter of nicety and difficulty, the chief pressed forward too hard for their mutual safety, or they held back too hard for mutual pro-

gress, and in either case, she was in danger of falling to the
ground, at least. She at length intrusted herself to their rude
bush coach, and was easily and safely conveyed down, to their
mutual gratification.

I was very cordially received in this secluded vale. The regent,
who, with others, had been watching us in our descent, now as I
drew near courteously welcomed my arrival with her laconic compliments, " *Mai !*" hither ! " *Mama oe !*" you are light of
foot; " *Aloha*" good will. She gave me a comfortable supper,
of duck and *kalo,* or *arum* roots, baked in the ground, and tea,
which she poured and sweetened with her own hands, for me
and her son. After supper, she called for evening worship, presenting me her hymn book, from which we sang, " The Lord my
Shepherd is." The service being over, she assigned to the king
and me a small sleeping house by ourselves, for the night.

Before I finished my evening writing, I heard the king call
out in his sleep, "*Ikaika i ka heleuma,*" a sea phrase slightly
ambiguous, and might mean *spring upon the anchor.* This instance of somniloquism, I mentioned at breakfast, in the morning, with the king and queen and others. The king laughed
heartily, and said it meant "heave up the anchor quick." So
he appeared to have been commanding a ship and urging his
men to the utmost effort in weighing anchor; a very good
symbol for a chief magistrate of the Hawaiian nation, just getting under weigh. Our morning song, at family worship, such
as our hearts seemed naturally to choose, was founded on the
seventh verse of the 116th Psalm.

> " Return unto thy rest, O my soul,
>   For the Lord hath dealt bountifully with thee."

The people of the valley were called together on the 7th, and
I was happy to proclaim to them, as well as to their visitors, the
kindest invitations of the glorious Gospel, from the words of the
Savior, " Come unto me all ye that labor and are heavy laden,
and I will give you rest." Kaahumanu and the king, Kekauluohi, and Kapulikoliko addressed the people of the valley with
kindness and propriety, calling on them to attend to the commands of God, and to serve the Lord with gladness. How different this meeting from that of warlike chieftains, in the last and
former generations!

I visited Haa, the interesting head man of the valley, mentioned by the deputation in 1823. He was ill, but took a pleasant interest in our work, and to oblige me, sent a native to aid
Mrs. B. during my absence of two or three weeks. In the
course of my sojourn at Waimea, this interesting convert from
heathenism I was allowed to baptize.

Before taking leave of this region, Kaahumanu and others,
taking me out in a double canoe, showed me some of the bold
and rude features of the country along the shore, as far as the

border of Kohala to the north-west. There, the first ridge or spur of the mountains of Hamakua terminates at the shore in the most abrupt manner. It appears to have been cut down perpendicularly, or to have been broken square off, and the part that is wanting to have been buried in the ocean. The section presents the elevation of a grand pyramid, whose base I judged to be 500 yards, and height 800 or 900 feet. Honopue is a singular valley on the south of it, one eighth of a mile wide perhaps at the sea, but narrowed by the approximation of the two ridges, two miles back, where they appear to stand crowded together so closely as almost to show two hills without a valley between them. Thence a swift torrent cuts its way down between them, much obscured by the narrowness of the passage, but showing itself here and there as a white streak in the dark shrubbery. Several cascades leap from the lofty precipices along this shore, where the sloping surface is partially reeded and fluted as though furrowed down by descending streams, the solid earth at the seaside appearing to be cut abruptly down by the action of the vast Pacific for ages, finding here an impassable barrier, several hundred feet high, for many miles. The height of these cascades where they fall into the sea, as seen from our canoe, appeared from fifty to five hundred feet. Between this place and the Waiakea station at Hilo, there are more than sixty ravines and valleys, from twenty to one thousand feet deep, of which Waipio and Laupahoehoe are the more distinguished, mostly the beds or channels of mountain streams. To traverse this district of country for the purposes of missions, or of war, or of science, or of commerce, is very difficult. Gazing for a little time on this bold and romantic scenery, we landed again safely at Waipio, where the natives had caught a voracious shark, about two fathoms long ; the lobes of his liver being about a fathom ; the rim or circumference of his mouth when wide open, three and a half feet, and armed with rows of teeth :—a young leviathan, on which, in its vigor and ferocity, one would not like to lay his hand.

The king, who tells a story with spirit, said that on board their brig, Kamehameha, they hooked a shark so large and strong, that he was able to shake the brig, and that they could hear his thwacks under the bottom. His flouncing and jerking were so hard, that he made the brig rock lengthwise, till he had broken the strong shark hook, cleared himself, and made his escape. It is amusement, often, for the expert Hawaiians to capture the shark, either by hook or snare, or by diving down and putting a noose of a rope over his flukes, when this tiger of the deep appears to be sleeping with his head under a rock. But these monsters are fearful in attack, and very formidable to Hawaiians. They sometimes take off an arm or a leg, or sever the body at once. In 1826, as some hundred natives were amusing themselves in the surf unusually high at Lahaina, within sight and hearing of the missionary's door, a voracious shark came among

them, and approached an active lad of fourteen. He screamed
and struck at the monster, which instantly took off his right arm,
tore him from his surf-board, and severed his body just above the
hips; and the waves were tinged with his blood. A loud and
simultaneous cry was raised by the multitude in the water, and
on the shore—"*Pau i ka mano*—death by a shark." Several
resolute men launched a canoe, rushed to the bloody spot, and
came between the unsatiated monster and the lifeless trunk and
head of the lad, which they took up as it were out of his jaws,
brought ashore, and presented to his anguished mother, who,
though once regarding the shark as a deity, had plunged into the
sea to try to rescue her son, when she heard of his exposure.

We were at length ready to ascend from Waipio; but how
should this be accomplished? This our predecessors had found
difficult; and our successors must ever find it so. In taking leave
of this valley, let me refer to a highly esteemed visitant who had
on another occasion recently preceded us. Mrs. Dr. Judd, who,
like many a missionary lady, is not easily overawed or discouraged by difficulties in her path, having once descended into this
valley, before she had long experience on missionary ground, was
there overtaken by a storm. At the mouth or opening of the
valley, the ocean tossed its huge surges and roared. The forest-
crowned summits in the rear, and the stupendous mountain walls
on the two sides, seemed to her unscalable. The billowy clouds,
surcharged with electric fluid, shut in over head, and "poured
out water." The darkness of night coming on, enveloped the
isle. Repeated flashes of vivid lightning showed, amid the darkness, the dimensions and strength of her prison. The thunders
rolled in awful majesty over the ocean and mountains. Peal
after peal reverberated through the deep valley, and echoed from
the lofty hills. She looked anxiously around upon the fearful
scene, and thought of her own snug apartments now inaccessible.
For once her courage wavered, and her hopes of ever leaving the
famous Waipio valley failed her.

So darkness and danger have sometimes hung over our young
mission, and that infant nation whom we were attempting to
guide out of deep embarrassment and gloom, when we seemed
ready to be "swallowed up quick."

She looked upward for help and comfort. The storm passed
away. Joy cometh in the morning. The light in greater splendor beamed on the charming vale, making it more charming after
the needful rain. And in due time the egress from the valley,
as from every dark and painful strait into which that mission or
that newly instructed nation has been brought, was made practicable and pleasant, though accomplished by timely, energetic,
up-hill toil. So we, ascending the great steep near the sea, retired
from the limits of this interesting Hawaiian valley, and took our
course to Hilo, where a wonder-working God had begun especially
to record his name.

Attending to the general objects of the journey, the company reached Waiakea in a few days, where we found Mr. and Mrs. Goodrich and Mr. and Mrs. Andrews encouraged by the progress of the work, the Lord working with them.

A large church having been just completed there, was, during the visit of the regent and her company, dedicated to the worship of God on the 15th of October. A great concourse of the people, who for six years had been favored with the incipient means of knowing the Gospel and learning to read it, assembled in and about the house to join in its dedication. Many attentively listened to the dedication sermon from Isaiah lxvi.; 1, 2. "Thus saith the Lord, The heaven is my throne, and the earth is my footstool : where is the house that ye build unto me? and where is the place of my rest? for all those things hath my hand made, and all those things have been, saith the Lord : but to this man will I look, even to him that is poor and of a contrite spirit, and trembleth at my word."

The hundredth Psalm, in their language, was solemnly chanted in a very impressive manner by twenty-four singers from Oahu, aided by the missionaries. The juvenile king made an address extemporaneous, and so much founded on the sermon, or according with it, as to show that he had heard and understood it, could approve its sentiments, and recommend to his people the humble and devout service of that God who had been set forth in the sermon. He also offered a prayer in a decorous and suitable manner, much to the satisfaction of Kaahumanu and others, who longed to see him not only almost but altogether a Christian.

The next day the chiefs, in their civil capacity, called the people together, and made known to them their will. Kaahumanu, and the young king, who had some want of confidence in his own powers, being encouraged and cheered on by his friends, addressed the people in a dignified and appropriate manner. When the chiefs had communicated their thoughts, we were entertained and edified by the powers of Bartimeus, the blind orator, who has often delighted us with his fervid harangues, and who made a neat, warm, and impressive appeal, with good voice and enunciation, and manly and appropriate gesture.

At a meeting in the evening, several presented themselves as candidates for admission to the church, and were carefully examined as to their faith and experience. Several appeared to understand, believe, and love the fundamental doctrines of the Gospel, and to be built on the solid foundation ; but some failed to give the requisite evidence of true conversion to Christ.

The ensuing Sabbath I endeavored to unfold to a great assembly the instruction contained in Romans viii., 1 : "There is, therefore, now no condemnation to them which are in Christ Jesus, who walk not after the flesh, but after the Spirit;" and assisted Mr. Goodrich in administering the ordinances. We had occasion for thankfulness in receiving to fellowship five new

View of Hilo, Mauna-Kea, and Mauna-Loa   Page 385

members, and in witnessing there such demonstrations of interest in the Christian religion, where, a little before, unbroken darkness, degradation, and alienation from God had prevailed. The company of believers appeared to be refreshed, and it was remarked by one of the missionaries, that Hilo had never before had such a Sabbath.

Before leaving the place I visited the unique islet, Mokuola, the ancient place of refuge, in Hilo bay. I was struck with the grandeur, extent, and beauty of the scenery presented to the eye by Hawaii. Here appeared the smooth bay of Hilo and its ample beach sweeping round in graceful curvature, skirted with hamlets and cottages amounting to three or four hundred habitations, verdant banks, shrubbery, and a variety of trees,—the tall, valuable, and uncivilized cocoa-nut, and the shady, noble, useful bread-fruit. Among the scattered trees rose the humble yet capacious thatched church, just dedicated to Almighty God for the use of the thousands of the population of Hilo and Puna, and near it, the shapely, two story, decently finished mission-house, painted white, with its neat little portico, and raised pannel Koa door, furnishing a slight specimen of civilization, and symbol of domestic comfort, amid the richness and roughness of Hawaiian foliage. There the more frail and widely scattered dwellings of the farmer and fisherman were seen, some just raising their dingy tops above the foliage of bananas, sugar-cane, and shrubs, and some, in bold relief, standing upon a green bank or mound, and others, shaded by a single tree or copse of trees. Here extended lawns, dense groves, and extinguished, grass-covered craters presented a variety of verdure, from the lightest to the deepest green. Beyond these, along the temperate zone of the island, for many miles, stretches the belt of forests around the waists of the mountains. In the north-west, rises majestically from its ample base more than twenty-five miles in diameter, the gigantic Mauna Kea, at the distance of twenty-five or thirty miles, peering to the clouds and exhibiting its slightly broken summit, more than 14,000 feet above the ocean level. Then, further in the west and south-west the country swells gradually, from the east and south, to the lofty and ample dome of Mauna Loa, which presents its blue, extended arch, at the distance of forty-five or fifty miles, and nearly equalling the height of Mauna Kea, its only rival in the Pacific, itself a little continent of unnumbered strata of lava and other volcanic matter, heaved up in the course of ages by vast volcanic power ; the upper 5,000 feet of its height remaining unclothed with vegetation.

Such is the view of Hawaii from the bay of Hilo, a place once distinguished by its springs and rivers, falls and fairs, violence and idolatries, but subsequently more so by its showers of grace and the rising institutions of Christianity along its shores, and its unsurpassed volcanoes in the rear.

After another examination of candidates for church membership, with Messrs. Goodrich and Andrews, we had a very pleasant tea-party given by Mrs. A., where the chiefs and missionaries, as at other places, were brought together in delightful Christian intercourse. Then, after a personal conversation between the young king and myself on his spiritual concerns, I made my preparations to return to my family, by the way of the active volcano, Kilauea, on the flank of Mauna Loa, a day's journey, or about thirty miles from Hilo bay. On the 19th, I took leave of my fellow laborers and of the chiefs. So many of my native friends came to see me as to fill the room where I received them. I walked to the king's lodgings to take leave of him and those around him—led in a hymn, in which he joined freely, and in prayer. After which, many gave me their parting hand, and their *aloha*, with an additional *aloha* for *Bi-na-mu wahine* [Mrs. B.]. My faithful assistant, John Ii, and some others, set off with me for Olaa and Kilauea, the great volcano. Kaahumanu, as a token of marked civility and affection, accompanied me as far as she could conveniently, with her little two-wheeled car, when the great roughness and narrowness of the way required her to halt. I said to her, " We have travelled together this path, as far as you can go now ; our persons must now be separated." She very promptly replied, with kindness and impressiveness, " I shall go with you, and you will stay with me." Interchanging the parting *aloha*, and proposing an interchange of signals, after passing the crater, she returned in her car, and I mounted my horse, furnished kindly by the chiefs for a part of the journey which was long and fatiguing, for one debilitated as I had been. But as we advanced, the way being rough, and the animal unshod, he severely felt the inconvenience of the lava, became discouraged, and moved so slowly, that I preferred to send him back, and make my way on foot. Had I possessed the power and will ascribed to me by some who have deigned to notice me, I might surely have undertaken this journey in the palanquin or litter, or the humbler hammock of a naval officer of sufficient fortune to employ willing bearers.

The horse of my associate, John Ii, trying to avoid hurting his feet on the bare lava, would persist in stepping upon the grass and low shrubbery, beside the iron pathway, occasionally thrusting a foot into a hole or crevice in the rocks, to the no small inconvenience and danger both of the horse and his rider.

Towards evening, we reached Olaa, an inland settlement ; met a few of the inhabitants, spoke to them of the great salvation, were fed and lodged there, and the next day, before noon, we reached an elevation of some 4000 feet at the distance of twenty miles from Hilo bay.

Approaching the great crater of Kilauea, we had a fine view of the magnificent dome of Mauna Loa, stretching on some twenty miles beyond it, and rising above it to the lofty height of ten thousand feet. Evidences of existing volcanic agency multiplied around us; steam, gas, and smoke, issued from sulphur banks on the north-east and south-east sides of the crater, and here and there from deep and extended fissures connected with the fiery subterranean agency; and as we passed circumspectly along the apparently depressed plain that surrounds the crater, we observed an immense volume of smoke and vapor ascending from the midst of it. At the same time, and from the same source, various unusual sounds not easily described or explained, fell with increasing intensity on the ear. Then the angry abyss, the fabled habitation and throne of PELE, the great ex-goddess of the Hawaiians, opened before us.

Coming near the rim, I fell upon my hands and knees, awestruck, and crept cautiously to the rocky brink; for with all my natural and acquired courage, I was unwilling at once to walk up to the giddy verge and look down upon the noisy, fiery gulf beneath my feet. Shortly, however, I was able to stand very near and gaze upon this wonder of the world, which I wish 1 could set before my readers in all its mystery, magnitude, and grandeur.

It is not a lofty cone, or mountain-top, pointing to the heavens, but a vast chasm in the earth, five or six times the depth of Niagara Falls, and seven or eight miles in circumference. It is situated on the flank of a vast mountain, which has been gradually piled up by a similar agency during the course of ages. Such is the extent and depth of Kilauea, that it would take in, entire, the city of Philadelphia or New York, and make their loftiest spires, viewed from the rim, appear small and low.

But neither cities nor meadows, neither water nor vegetation, can be found in this chief of the " deep places of the earth," but a lake of lava, some black and indurated, some fiery and flowing, some cooling as a floating bridge over the fathomless molten abyss seven times hotter than Nebuchadnezzar's hottest furnace, and some bursting up through this temporary incrustation, rending it here and there, and forming mounds and cones upon it. The immense mass, laboring to escape, pressed against the great crater's sides, which consisted not of a frail Chinese wall built by human hands to resist human strength, but an irregularly elliptical wall of basaltic rocks, extending a thousand feet above the surface of the lava lake, and to unknown depths below.

Six hundred feet below the verge stretched around horizontally a vast amphitheatre gallery of black indurated lava, once fluid, on which an army of one hundred thousand men might stand to view the sublime spectacle, beneath, around, and above them.

While through the eye the impressions of grandeur, strong at first, increased till the daylight was gone, the impressions received through the ear were peculiar, and by no means inconsiderable. The fiercely whizzing sound of gas and steam, rushing with varying force, through obstructed apertures in blowing cones, or cooling crusts of lava, the laboring, wheezing, struggling, as of a living mountain, breathing fire and smoke and sulphurous gas from his lurid nostrils, tossing up molten rocks or detached portions of fluid lava, and breaking up vast indurated masses with varied detonations, all impressively bade us stand in awe.

When we reached the verge, or whenever we came from a little distance to look over, these strange sounds increased as if some intelligent power, with threatening tones and gestures, indignant at our obtrusiveness, were forbidding our approach. The effect of this on aboriginal visitors, before the true God was made known to them, may have been to induce or confirm the superstition that a deity or family of deities dwelt there, recognized the movements of men, and in various ways expressed anger against them.

If my fellow-travellers had not been cured of their superstition, or had not known me to be decidedly opposed to all idolatry, and particularly to the worship of Pele, they might naturally have mistaken my almost involuntary prostration as an act of religious homage to this discarded Hawaiian deity, which they and their fathers had been accustomed to regard as extremely unpropitious. But the missionaries had set at naught the tabus of this deity, and Kapiolani had invaded the same, and, descending into this crater, had, in a heroic and Christian manner, there acknowledged Jehovah as the only true God, and proclaimed to her countrymen that this was but one of the fires which he has kindled and controlled. This, John Ii and others with me, were ready devoutly to acknowledge.

When, seven years before our visit, Messrs. Ellis, Thurston, Bishop, and Goodrich, accompanied by Mr. Harwood, in 1823, visited this yawning gulf in opposition to the wishes of their native guide, who refused to conduct them thither, they said of it in " The Tour round Hawaii :"

" The bottom was filled with lava, and the southwest and northern parts of it were one vast flood of liquid fire in a state of terrific ebullition, rolling to and fro its fiery surge and flaming billows. Fifty-one craters of various form and size rose like so many conical islands from the surface of the burning lake. Twenty-two constantly emitted columns of grey smoke, and pyramids of brilliant flame, and many of them at the same time vomited from their ignited mouths, streams of fluid lava, which rolled in blazing torrents down their black, indented sides, into the boiling mass below."

The surface of this body of lava is subject to unceasing changes from year to year ; for " deep calleth unto deep," and the billows of this troubled ocean " cannot rest."

As night approached we took our station on the north side on the very brink, where we supposed we should be able the most securely and satisfactorily to watch the action of this awful laboratory, during the absence of the light of the sun. Though the spot where we spread our blanket for a lodgment had been con-

sidered as the safest in the neighborhood, there was room for the
feeling of insecurity, which some who had preceded me have
thus described : " The detachment of one small stone beneath, or
a slight agitation of the earth, would have precipitated us amid
the horrid crash of falling rocks, into the burning lake." Had I
believed the danger so imminent, I should have thought it prudent
to take a position somewhat further off. The mass which supported us had doubtless been shaken a thousand times, and was
very liable every hour to be shaken again ; but being in the short
curvature of the crater, like the keystone of an arch, it could not
easily be thrown from its position by any agitation that would naturally occur while this great safety valve is kept open, or the numerous fissures around it, reaching to the bowels of the mountain,
convey harmlessly from unknown depths, gases, and volumes of
steam, generated where water comes in contact with intense volcanic heat. Our position was about four thousand feet above the
level of the sea, and one thousand above the surface of the lake.

The great extent of the surface of the lava lake ; the numerous
places in it where the fiery element was displaying itself ; the
conical mouths here and there, discharging glowing lava overflowing and spreading its waves around, or belched out in
detached and molten masses that were shot forth with detonations,
perhaps by the force of gases struggling through from below the
surface, while the vast column of vapor and smoke ascended up
towards heaven, and the coruscations of the emitted, brilliant
lava, illuminated the clouds that passed over the terrific gulf, all
presented by night a splendid and sublime panorama of volcanic
action, probably nowhere else surpassed.

Had Vulcan employed ten thousand giant Cyclops, each with
a steam engine of one thousand horse-power, blowing anthracite
coal for smelting mountain minerals, or heaving up and hammering to pieces rocks and hills, their united efforts would but begin
to compare with the work of Pele here.

There was enough of mystery connected with the experiments
going on before our eyes, to give ample employment to fancy and
philosophy, and materially to enhance the sublimity of the fearful scene. For it might be asked, How can such an immense mass
of rocks and earth be kept incessantly in a state of fusion without fuel or combustion ? Or by what process could such solid
masses be fused at all, in accordance with any mode of generating
heat with which we are acquainted ? If there be combustion in the
crater adequate to the melting of such vast masses of substances,
so hard, rocky, and earthy, why is there an accumulation of the
general mass, so that millions of cubic fathoms are, from time to
time, added to the solid contents of the mountain ? But if the
bowels of the mountain are supposed to be melted by intense heat
in some way generated, could they be heaved up by the expansion
of steam or gas, while an orifice equal to three or four square miles,
like that of Kilauea, or the terminal crater on the same mountain,

is kept open ; for steam and gas might be supposed to pass through the fluid masses and escape, instead of raising them from a depth, just as steam rises from the bottom of a boiling caldron, without materially elevating the surface of its contents.

But if with one class of geologists we suppose the interior of the earth to be in a molten or fluid state, as, perhaps, originally created, and that Kilauea and other volcanoes are but openings to that subterranean, fiery, central ocean of red or white hot matter, we have no faint illustration of the bold imagery used by the sacred writers, and of their phraseology, which seems hyperbolical or even paradoxical, "the bottomless pit," "the fire that is not quenched," "the lake that burneth with fire and brimstone," "the smoke of their torment ascendeth up for ever and ever."

If such a fluid mass constitutes the main portion of the interior of the earth, it is literally "*bottomless*," and the opened surface, like that of Kilauea, may be strictly called a *lake*, a lake of fire, and as sulphur and particles of the sulphuret of iron are present, it may be called "*a lake that burns with fire and brimstone*."

After gazing at the wonderful phenomenon some twenty hours, taking but a little time for repose, I found the sense of fear subside, and curiosity prompt to a closer intercourse with Pele and a more familiar acquaintance with her doings and habits. Many who try the experiment, though at first appalled, are ready, after a few hours, to wend their way down the steep sides of the crater. Thus we descended into the immense pit from the north-east side, where it was practicable, first to the black ledge or amphitheatre gallery, and thence to the surface of the lava lake. This we found extremely irregular, presenting cones, mounds, plains, vast bridges of lava recently cooled, pits and caverns, and portions of considerable extent in a movable and agitated state. We walked over lava which, by some process, had been fractured into immensely large slabs, as though it had been contracted by cooling, or been heaved up irregularly by the semi-fluid mass below. In the fissures of this fractured lava, the slabs or blocks two feet below the surface were red hot. A walking stick thrust down would flame instantly.

Passing over many masses of such lava, we ventured towards the more central part of the lake, and came near to a recent mound, which had probably been raised on the cooling surface, after our arrival the day before. From the top of it flowed melted lava, which spread itself in waves to a considerable distance, on one side then on the other, all around. The masses thrown out in succession, moved sluggishly, and as they flowed down the inclined plane, a crust was formed over them, darkened and hardened, and became stationary, while the stream moved below it ; the front of the mass, red hot, pressed along down, widening and expending itself, and forcing itself through a net-work, as it were, of irregular filaments of iron, which the cooling process freely supplied. This motion of a flowing mass, whether larger or smaller, seen from the rim of the crater by night, gives the appearance of a fiery surf or a rolling wave of fire, or the dancing along of an extended semi-circular flame on the surface of the lake. When one wave has expended itself, or found its level, or otherwise become stationary, another succeeds and passes over it in like manner, and then another, sent out, as it were, by the pulsations of the earth's open artery, at the top of the mound. This shows how a mound, cone, pyramid, or mountain, can be gradually built of lava, and wide plains covered at its base with the same material.

We approached near the border of some of these waves and reached the melted lava with a stick two yards long, and thus did gross violence to Pele's tabu. I thus obtained several specimens red hot from the flowing mass. I have since had occasion to be surprised at the absence of fear in this close contiguity with the terrible element, where the heat under our feet was as great as our shoes would bear, and the radiating heat from the moving mass was so intense that I could face it but a few seconds at a time, at the distance of two or three yards. Yet, having carefully observed its movements awhile, I threw a stick of wood upon the thin crust of a moving wave where I believed it would bear me, even if it should bend a little, and stood upon it a few moments. In that position, thrusting my cane down through the cooling, tough crust about half an inch thick, I withdrew it, and forthwith there gushed up of the melted flowing lava under my feet enough to form a globular mass two and half or three inches in diameter, which, as it cooled, I broke off and bore away as spoils from the ancient domain and favorite seat of the Diana of the Hawaiians. Parts in violent action we dared not approach.

There is a remarkable variety in the volcanic productions of Hawaii,—a variety as to texture, form, and size, from the vast mountain and extended plain, to the fine drawn and most delicate vitreous fibre, the rough clinker, the smooth stream, the basaltic rock, and masses compact and hard as granite or flint, and the pumice or porous scoria, or cinders, which, when hot, probably formed a scum or foam on the surface of the denser molten mass.

Considerable quantities of capillary glass are produced at Kilauea, though I am not aware that the article is found elsewhere on the islands. Its production has been deemed mysterious. In its appearance it resembles human hair, and is among the natives familiarly called " *Lauoho o Pele* "—the hair of Pele. It is formed, I presume, by the tossing off of small detached portions of lava of the consistence of melted glass, from the mouths of cones, when a fine vitreous thread is drawn out between the moving portion and that from which it is detached. The fine spun product is then blown about by the wind, both within and around the crater, and is collected in little locks or tufts.

Sulphur is seen, but in small quantities, in and around the crater, and at a little distance from the rim there are yellow

banks on which beautiful crystals of sulphur may be found.   In
one place, a pool of pure distilled water, condensed from the
steam that rises from a deep fissure, affords the thirsty traveller
a beverage far better than that of the ordinary distiller.

There is, however, a gas produced by the volcano highly deleterious, if breathed often or freely.   This is one source of danger
to the visitor, which, while I was down a thousand feet below the
rim, produced a temporary coughing.

I was, perhaps, too venturesome ; but other visitors have been
far more so.

Dr. Judd having become familiar with volcanic power, in his
ardor to secure valuable and very recent specimens of Pele's
productions for the U. S. Exploring Expedition, on the visit of
Com. Wilkes and his company to this crater, descended to the
surface of the lake, and then into a *sub*-crater, in the midst of the
larger.   While busily engaged there collecting specimens, a sudden bursting up of a huge volume of fluid lava from the bottom
of the sub-crater alarmed him, and threatened speedily to over-
whelm him.   He sprang to escape, but finding the rim overhanging, he could not scale it where he was.   The flowing mass was
now too near him to allow him to return to the place where he
had descended, and its radiating heat too intense to be faced.
Escape without aid was hopeless.   The natives of the company
about the brink, alarmed for themselves, were flying for their
lives.   The doctor, giving himself up for lost, offered a prayer
to Heaven, and that moment, the last to be availing, a friendly
and resolute Hawaiian, who had been a pupil at the mission
seminary, compassionating the exposed sufferer, and facing the
approaching fiery volume, and braving its intense heat, exposed
his own life, reached down his strong hand, and firmly grasped
the doctor's, who, by their united exertions and the blessing of
Heaven, escaped with his life from "the horrible pit" and a fiery
grave.   A mighty current instantly overflowed, and they ran for
their lives before the molten flood, and ascended from the surface
of the abyss to the lofty rim with heartfelt thanksgiving to their
great Deliverer.*

This proves the real danger of meddling with Pele's palace
and trifling with her power.   Had this occurred in the days of
unbroken superstition, it would doubtless have been ascribed to
the anger of that false deity, and multiplied her worshippers.
But now such a deliverance was justly ascribed to the care and
power of Jehovah, the knowledge of whose attributes displayed
in the works of creation, providence, and grace, has introduced
the Hawaiian race into a new life.

Kilauea may be regarded as one of the safety valves of a bottomless reservoir of melted earth below the cooled and cooling
crust on which mountains rise, rivers flow, and oceans roll, and
cities are multiplied as the habitations of men.   It has been
kept open from time immemorial, always displaying active

* See U. S. Ex. Ex. vol. iv. p. 173.

power. The circumambient air which carries off the caloric, sometimes aided by the rain, is incessantly endeavoring to shut this valve, or bridge over this orifice of three or four square miles of the fiery abyss. Sometimes the imperfect bridge of cooling lava is pierced with half a hundred large, rough, conical chimneys, emitting gas, smoke, flame, and lava; and sometimes the vast bridge is broken up, and the cones submerged, and probably fused again by the intense heat of the vast fluid mass supplied fresh from the interior. This mass rises gradually higher and higher, hundreds of feet, till by its immense pressure against the sides of the crater, aided, perhaps, by the power of gas or steam, it forces a passage for miles through the massive walls, and inundates with its fiery deluge some portion of the country below, or passing through it as a river of fire, pours itself into the sea at the distance of twenty-five miles, thus disturbing with awful uproar the domain of Neptune, and enlarging the dominions of the Hawaiian sovereign.

The whole island, with its ample and towering mountains, is often shaken with awful throes, and creation here "groaneth and travaileth in pain."

In July, 1840, a river of lava flowed out from Kilauea, and passing some miles under ground, burst out in the district of Puna, and inundated a portion of the country, sweeping down forests, and as a river a mile wide, fell into the sea, heated the waters of the ocean, making war upon its inhabitants, and by the united action of this volcanic flood and the sea, formed several huge rough hills of sand and lava along the shore.

A similar flood has subsequently been poured from the summit of Mauna Loa, flowing with terrific force for weeks, and thus elevating a portion of the region between Mauna Loa and Mauna Kea. This grand exhibition could be seen from the missionary station at Hilo, a distance of about forty miles.

After spending about thirty hours at Pele's chief seat, we set off, towards evening, on the 21st, to cross the wilderness to Waimea, which required the time of a little more than two days and two nights. Walking till late, we laid ourselves down where we could find a place. The next day we continued our journey northwardly, towards Mauna Kea, lodging out in the wilderness, in the same manner, at night, the majestic mountain being half a day's walk to the north of us.

Rose at four o'clock from our mountain couch,—a day's journey from any human habitation; saw lightning at a great distance at sea—our elevation being 4000 or 5000 feet; packed our sleeping *kapa;* offered our morning sacrifice in these solitudes of the centre of Hawaii, and as the day dawned, set forward on our journey. We passed over several large tracts of lava, of different kinds, some smooth, vitreous, and shining, some twisted and coiled like huge ropes, and some consisting of sharp, irregular, loose, rugged volcanic masses, of every form and size, from an ounce in weight, to several tons, thrown, I could not conceive how, into a chaos or field of the roughest surface, presenting a forbidding area, from one to forty square miles in extent, and though not precipitous, yet so horrid as to forbid a path, and defy the approach of horses and cattle. In the crevices of the more solid lava we found the *ohelo*, somewhat resembling the whortle-berry, nourished by frequent showers and dew. At ten o'clock, we halted for breakfast; raised a smoke, as a signal for the horse keeper, at the watering-place, at the south base of Mauna Kea, to approach, and moved on, till twelve o'clock, when I was very glad to see and mount the horse sent over from Waimea to meet me. Our company having become considerably scattered, and pressing on, under a mid-day, tropical sun, were soon collected together by the loud shout, "Here's water," made by the keeper of the horse, who had very considerately brought us a calabash from Waihalulu, cold and sweet, for the refreshment of our weary and thirsty travellers. We drank round, and this gourd bottle soon sounded empty. I mounted and set forward with comfort and revived courage, leaving most of the company to proceed at their leisure. One of the keepers of the horse wishing to accompany me, girded up his loins, and like Elijah before Ahab, ran cheerfully before me, westward, along the south side of Mauna Kea, about ten miles, then northward, over its undulated, western slope, about the same distance. We halted on the ridge, half an hour, then pressed on till six o'clock, when the sun, having finished his daily race, sank with great grandeur and beauty into the western waters of the vast Pacific, sending back a pleasant fare-well to the clouds that hung over Hualalai, Mauna Loa, and Mauna Kea, the three Hawaiian mountains, and shooting upwards his diverging rays with peculiar beauty, after the last limb of his broad, golden disk had disappeared. About seven, we reached Waimea, thus completing my excursion of about 175 miles, with improved health for resuming the labors of the station.

Kaahumanu and her company passed on through Puna and Kau, and came to Kealakekua Bay, in Kona, in the course of about two months. Before they left Hilo, she addressed the following characteristic letter to the chiefs at Oahu :—

"HILO, OCT. 31ST, 1830.

"Great love to you, O Jochebed. This is my thought for you two; The words your son gave you in charge, do you remember, lest you both become quite listless. Let it be a remembrancer for you both, in the name of Christ, that it may be well with you. That thought is done.

"Here also is this thought of mine for you two—The voice of the *Palani* [Frenchman or Papist] who assented to us before; do you two look at his after course, and if he renews his work, it will be your duty to send him away, that he may be entirely separated.* That thought is finished.

* *E pono ia olua e hookuke aku ia ia a kaawale.*

" And this is my sentiment for you, Matthew Kekuanaoa. Your ship-
master fires a gun, on the Sabbath day, morning and evening. *He mea
pono anei ia, ia oe la ? Ea !* [Is this right, in your esteem ? Attend !]
Just that is my thought for you. May you and we be saved through
Jesus. Amen.

" ELISABETH KAAHUMANU."

She inserts Kinau's Christian name, Jochebed, the mother of
Moses, Lot, Alexander, and Victoria, but evidently includes Liliha, as having been jointly intrusted with the affairs of Oahu,
and reminding them of the charge given by the young king, on
leaving that place ; refers particularly to the leading French intruder, and gently reproves Kinau's husband, for what she regards
as desecrating the Sabbath, by one at Hilo bay, in his employ ;
and indicates her opinion that the violation of the Sabbath by the
commander of the vessel, may implicate the owner, if he has not
properly guarded against it. It is presumed that if she had sent
a ship to take whales, she would have ordered the captain and
crew not to take them on the Sabbath.

While the travelling chiefs were in the southern part of Hawaii,
Gov. Adams and the people of the northern part prosecuted and
completed the building of a convenient church at Waimea. To
encourage them in that work, and to increase its advantages, both
for the preacher and hearer, I managed to turn the pillars,
balusters, and newels for a pulpit, neat, decorous, commodious,
and suited to a large, rude thatched house, and to an indigent,
uncultivated people, dwelling in the poor, frail, temporary habitations of Hawaii. From two rough, green logs of the forest, two
pillars, eight or ten inches in diameter, and six feet in length, were
produced ; whether of the Tuscan or Hawaiian order, is immaterial,
provided they were sufficiently plain, neat, polished, and shapely,
and made to answer their main purpose. Placed about four feet
apart, in front, they served to support the pulpit floor three feet
high, the head of the stairs and stair-rails, and on their top a table
for the preacher's book and notes, giving to the structure put together by a carpenter, the appearance of finish, firmness, and
utility. Many a preacher waits unduly for a pulpit to be made
ready to his hands, who will not find a better place than that in
Waimea, to plead the cause of God with his fellow worms. The
house was used for public worship as soon as it was covered, and
many a true-hearted herald of the Prince of Peace would rejoice
to see what has often been seen there—a multitude of immortal
beings, withdrawn from idolatry, and sitting, with attentive eyes
and ears, to hear the messages of love from Heaven. Here an
old, grey-headed warrior, and there, a once deluded, murderous
mother ; here an agent of the bloody priests, accustomed to the
work of aiding the sacrifice of human blood, and there, groups of
those who once shuddered at his presence ; here the young man
and the young woman just entering on life's stage, and there, intermingled with the aged, middle aged, and the young, the chil-

dren but just old enough to begin the studies of the Sabbath
school,—but soon, should their lives be prolonged, to be the acting
portion of a generation engaged for good or evil ; and sometimes,
rulers and subjects waiting, as equals, in the presence of the King
of kings.   Such at that period, was this new and interesting
field, where many golden sheaves have been, and are to be
gathered for the divine Lord of the harvest.

The new station being fairly commenced, Mr. Ruggles and
family returned and resumed their labors at Kaawaloa, from which
they had been absent almost a year.   I remained with my family
another month, each week encouraged by the appearance of bud
and blossom in this wilderness ; and then, not without some conflict in our feelings, retired from this interesting spot where my
health had been benefited, the Lord's work begun, and the way
prepared for the weary to recruit, and for the strong to lay out
their strength in the care of a large population.

The dedication of the house of worship was deferred till the
chiefs, in their circuit of the island, should be again at Waimea.
They had desired me to meet them, in the meantime, at Kealakekua, where they designed to halt for a week or two.   Being
now informed of their arrival there, I undertook the journey
across, with my family.   The supposed distance is sixty or more
miles.   The region, for the most part, was uninhabited and unfre-
quented ; but we had little fear of being harmed ; on the contrary, we relied, with confidence, on such aid from the kind-
hearted people, for whose benefit we had now labored ten years,
as it was in their power to afford.   All things being arranged, we
started on our way, Dec. 29th.   Passing the principal haunts of
the numerous wild cattle, some herds of which we saw at a distance, and Mauna Kea on the left, we made our way southward,
over lava and through the desert, between that mountain and Hualalai on the west.   Just at evening, the second day, we found
ourselves wandering in a doubtful course, none of the natives with
us being able to set us right.

Night coming on, we pitched our temporary tent midway be
tween the summits of Haulalai and Mauna Loa, and rested comfortably under the protection of the Watchman of Israel.   Waked,
and rose refreshed, at day-break, in the heart of Hawaii, where
nothing of the surrounding ocean appeared.   Aiming at the supposed position of Kaawaloa, we struck across a rough field of
lava, exceedingly sharp and difficult to pass, marked with rugged
rocks, cliffs, ravines, shrubs, and trees.   About ten o'clock we
came into a track, leading over sand, towards Kaawaloa.

In these solitudes, some twenty miles from Kealakekua, we
unexpectedly fell upon an ancient temple of the Hawaiian gods,
built in a dreary wilderness, far from the habitations of men.
With what feelings must this gloomy monument of superstition
have been erected, and since regarded by dark, idolatrous natives,
who bowed to the power of Pele, or other imaginary deities even

less worthy of regard! Its form, though of little consequence compared with its abominable design, is a square, 100 feet on a side. Its walls, built of the fragments of ancient lava, were eight feet high, and four feet thick. Its entrance was by a door-way, in the middle of the wall, on the north side. The enclosed area is divided, first by an aisle, from the door to the opposite wall. On each side of this aisle was a wall about half a yard in height and thickness. The two main divisions were sub-divided by similar walls, at right angles with the aisle, into three apartments each. Around the principal structure, and at the distance of ten to twenty feet, there were eight pyramids, about twelve feet in diameter, and twelve to fifteen in height. Connected with the south-western pyramidal pile, was a small enclosure or court.

Our fellow travellers, John Ii and others, now initiated into the Christian doctrine, regarded these monuments of superstition, as relics of the work of Satan, and proofs of his triumphs over the generations that had passed away. Some of them now united here in offering to Jehovah, the God of Abraham, Isaac, and Jacob, a morning sacrifice of prayer and praise.

At almost every step for sixty miles we were reminded of Pele's power. Our road was not Macadamized, but Peleized, and by no means inviting. That day, I was thrice unhorsed, in this rough wilderness. Once my horse threw me from my saddle, upon my feet, by breaking through a shell covering of a cavity in the lava, while trotting, and in another case, by dropping both fore feet suddenly down from a rock, throwing both saddle and rider over his head, while his hind feet remained on the rock; and in another instance, still more hazardous, I was dismounted by his plunging his hind legs down into a deep chasm in the lava, which appeared to have been caused by the heaving up of this part of the island, by some subterranean force rending its iron structure, and making a long, well-defined, perpendicular fissure, fourteen or fifteen inches wide, of an unknown depth, and sufficient to swallow up a regiment. The vigorous struggles of the animal to extricate himself were unavailing; and would, unassisted, have been hopeless. A second attempt, on our part, to aid him, was successful in bringing his legs out of the fearful chasm, and he rose on solid footing, and pursued the journey as before through this rough region.

Fifty of the men of Naihe's district came out some twelve miles cheefully to meet us and help us on. Bearing off to the west, we passed through a dense wood, which affords good timber of a larse size, and came out upon the southern slope of Mount Hualalai, where, looking over upon the region between Kailua and Kealakekua, we had a fine view of the ocean.

The sun soon set, and we advanced by twilight some two miles, when the darkness of Saturday night came on, and the natives, particularly the fresh company from Naihe, who best knew the way, were reluctant to proceed in the dark, in the responsible

work of conveying Mrs. B. and three little children to their destination. But it was contrary to our wishes to lodge and spend
the Sabbath there, or to finish our journey Sabbath morning to
the place where I was expected to preach to the chiefs
and people ; and besides, the illness of our youngest urged
us forward, to seek relief for her. Dependent on their
will, in trying circumstances, it was gratifying to see they could
appreciate our reasons for venturing forward. Our Waimea
friends first moved, and were immediately joined by the others ;
and we felt our way cautiously along, for an hour and a half, Mr.
Ruggles, meantime, meeting us, and leading the way towards his
habitation. Benighted in this dark wilderness, our eyes were, at
length, all gladdened by several large candle-nut torches which
Naihe and his excellent lady had the consideration to send us,
when they perceived we did not reach their settlement by daylight.
By the light of these torches, gleaming with different degrees of
brightness, on the luxuriant vegetation around us, our company,
now amounting to a hundred, passed quietly, in Indian file, along
a narrow foot-path, amid bananas, high grasses, fern ten or
twelve feet in height, shrubs, wild vines, and trees, till just before
the closing hour of the year, when we arrived with safety and
welcome at Mr. Ruggles's cottage, at Kuapehu, two miles from
Kaawaloa landing.

CHAPTER XVI.

On the first day of the new year, I met the assembled chiefs
and people at Kaawaloa, and to our mutual joy opened to them
the Scriptures.

An attempt was made for the permanent establishment of the
Kaawaloa station at Kuapehu. Naihe and Kapiolani removed
and built there, and others gathered round them; but the people
of the district chiefly preferred the shore station as more convenient to them. But Kaawaloa, at the landing-place on the
north side of Kealakekua bay, however conveniently accessible
to the people of the district, who live much along the shores,
was cramped and rocky, being composed almost exclusively of
lava. It was hot, dry, and barren, affording neither brook nor
well, nor spring of fresh water, nor field, nor garden-spot for
plantation, though a few cocoa-nut trees, so neighborly to the
sea, find nourishment there. Kuapehu, about two miles inland,
east of the bold and volcanic cliff at the head of the bay, is, in
many respects, preferable as a place of residence. It is elevated
1500 feet above the sea; is airy and fertile, fanned agreeably by
the land breeze from the cold Mauna Loa by night, and the sea
breeze by day, making the temperature and climate about as
agreeable and salubrious as Waimea. Scattered trees around,
and the forest a little further in the rear, the banana, sugar-cane,
upland *kalo*, potatoes, squashes, goards, and melons, which its
soil produces; its high grasses, flowering shrubs, and wild vines,
all contrasted finely with the dry and sterile shore north of the
bay. Besides the ordinary productions of the country, Mr. Ruggles, Naihe, and Kapiolani had a variety of exotics—the grape,
fig, guava, pomegranate, orange, coffee, cotton, and mulberry,

growing on a *small scale*, which is the most that can be said, as
yet, of these articles at the Sandwich Islands.

An honorable woman, a hoary-headed Hawaiian convert to
Christianity, Kekupuohi, who had been one of the wives of
Kalaniopuu, the king in the days of Capt. Cook, but now a member of the church at Kailua, visiting at the thatched cottage of
Mr. Ruggles, in the midst of this scenery, and having her attention agreeably attracted by a prolific grape vine, which spread
its fruit and foliage over the door, and by the various flowers and
fruits of the garden-like court, composed an interesting ode, in
her own tongue, descriptive in part of what struck her eye, and
in part of what is seen by faith, with her own reflections; of
which the following, considering the circumstances and the
authorship, is a paragraph of peculiar beauty, which, with much
pleasure, I have translated :—

> " Once only has that which is glorious appeared.
> It is wonderful and holy altogether.
> It is a blooming glory of unwithering form.
> Rare is its stock and singular, unrivalled :
> One only *true vine*—it is the Lord.
> The branch that adheres to it becomes fruitful :
> It bringeth forth fruit ; it is good fruit,
> Whence its character is fully made known.
> Let the fruitless branch of mere show be cut off,
> Lest the stock should be injuriously encumbered,
> Lest it be by it wrongfully burdened."

In this effusion of enlightened taste, admiring gratitude, and
pious regard to the " Chief among ten thousands," as altogether
lovely, what a gratifying proof we have that Hawaiians can understand the Gospel, and that they do discriminate between the
form and spirit of religion, and that the converts appreciate the
importance of fruitfulness and fidelity, on the one hand, and the
reasonableness of church discipline on the other, " Lest the ' True
Vine ' should be dishonored and oppressed!"

Happy would it be for the church if her members in every
country entertained views as clear, as consistent and elevated, on
these important points as did this aged Hawaiian convert, once a
heathen queen, but at this period poor as to the shining things
of earth, whose habitation, wardrobe, and household furniture
together would not probably exceed in value one hundred dollars,
but as one of the " daughters of the Lord Almighty," rejoicing
in the hope of a heavenly inheritance, and an everlasting crown,
into the actual possession of which we trust she has already
entered, to the praise of divine grace.

She had been the *wahine* of some forty men, and of several
of these at the same time. On hearing the Gospel, she was one
of the first on Hawaii to give heed to it, and to befriend its
teachers. Desiring to learn to read the Word of God, she entered
as a pupil ; but from her advanced age, her dullness, and unre-

tentive memory, she found it difficult to learn even the alphabet and remember it. Before she could read at all, the missionaries, having the supervision of thousands, advised her to give up the attempt to learn. But not satisfied to remain unable to read the Scriptures, choosing one of her female attendants for her teacher, she persevered till she accomplished her object, making her book her daily companion. She put off her heathenism, and put on Christianity as a conscientious Christian. One of the most attentive hearers and one of the first fruits of Kailua, she became an ornament to the church, adorning her profession, and illustrating the transforming power of the Gospel, and the grace of God to the aged heathen who receive his offers of salvation.

During this visitation of the chiefs at Kaawaloa, numerous schools were called before them to show themselves for examination. Their coming together presented a novel scene, exhibiting something of the taste and habits of Hawaiians. Long processions of scholars and teachers, coming in from different quarters, after dark, moved in single file with flaming torches of the candle-nut, and loud-sounding conchs. Some of the schools, with their torches and conchs, came winding along around the head of Kealakekua bay, high on the steep and craggy precipices, which once echoed back the thunder of the guns of Capt. Cook's ships in hostile strife with the natives. Then near where that navigator fell in the preceding generation, the schools, embracing thousands of men, women, and children, just coming to the light, formed an immense column, still flourishing their fiery banners, and blowing their many shells of various keys, with as much spirit as if they expected the fortifications of darkness were about to fall before them.

This display was a sort of celebration of the arrival of the light and their deliverance from idols, and was to the poor people something like what the fireworks on Boston Common are to the thirty or forty thousand who go out to gaze for an hour at the shooting, soaring, arching, diverging, and exploding fire-balls and bubbles on the anniversary evening commemorative of American Independence.

The sober examination of these numerous schools the next day proved the existence of many little torch lights kindled along those dark shores, which were enlightening the path of thousands, and promising to aid them in picking out their way if they desired it, through this dark world to the heavenly city.

All appeared interested in the examination as a whole, and while we could commend improvement and attention to sober duties, we were not forward to rebuke their attempts at harmless display on the one hand, or to teach them any kind of amusement on the other, supposing this part of civilization not specifically to belong to the calling of missionaries.

It may be proper to say here that the church and mission-houses of this station, some time after Mr. Ruggles, through loss

of health, left the field, were located on the south side of Kealakekua Bay, a position which was supposed to accommodate the
people connected with the station better than the north side, or
Kuapehu in the rear.

Having completed their visit at Kaawaloa, the chiefs passed on
together to Kailua, where they were welcomed by Gov. Adams
and the missionaries.

On the 16th of January the chief rulers of the land, with the
exception of Kinau and Liliha, being there with their suites,
which added to the number and the interest of the meetings for
worship, the concourse at church on the Sabbath was immense.
It was a privilege for missionaries to lead them to the throne of
grace, and to press home the claims of the Gospel upon their
hearts. Very considerable portions of the members of all the
churches then existing in the group, at Kauai, Oahu, Maui, Hilo,
Kaawaloa, and Kailua, which this year had been declared distinct,
were present, with thousands of non-professors. Some appeared
to be feasted, comforted, and strengthened by the Word, and
others made to tremble. I was interested in the remark of my
young friend and pupil; Haalilio, that he was so *weliweli,* filled with
fear, that he could not look steadily at the preacher. After the sermon the largest number of communicants, as was supposed, that had
ever sat down together at the Lord's supper in these islands,
there, in a solemn and joyous manner, celebrated the dying love
of their Savior.

The Tuesday and Wednesday following were devoted to the
examination of the fifty schools of this missionary station, in distinction from those at Waimea, Hamakua, and Kohala, not then
entirely detached from the Kailua station, under the active and
laborious supervision of Messrs. Thurston and Bishop. The
number of scholars in the northern part of Kona were, men and
male youth, 1,520; women, 1728; of boys and girls, under ten
years, 566; total, 3,814; of whom 1,100 were able to read.

While we were at dinner, at Mr. Bishop's, on the 19th, the
sea rough and the wind driving on shore, the king's brig, Nio,
which was in sight from the door, broke from her moorings, and
was in imminent danger of being dashed on the rocks. The king
was so much interested, and so sure she would quickly be
wrecked, that he could not, he said, continue to look at her struggling in the surf, with her crew exposed; and turned his back
with exclamations of sorrow. Having been informed that the
brig had a cask of rum on board, I had a few days before invited
him to my chamber, and suggested the discharge of it into the
sea, as a precaution against harm, to which he consented. Now,
in her distress, in his trouble, and my own solicitude, I asked
him if the *Jonah* were overboard? He understood me, and said
"he had ordered its *kiola* (casting away), and supposed it had
been done." "Then," I replied, "I think she will escape;"
and we were soon made glad to see her at the command of wind

and helm, passing safely the projecting point, north of Kailua village, in spite of the sea, and steering for Oahu. When it was calm enough, the king went out with his men to try to raise the anchor she had left, and by some means, fell from his boat into the water; to him a small circumstance. Instantly recovering himself and resuming his place in the boat, his clothes saturated and all dripping, he snatched his gold hunting watch from his pocket, to save it, if possible, from being penetrated and spoiled by sea water, and handing it to a friend, with earnestness resumed his labor. His father had been disposed to labor, and most of the chiefs labor, more or less, with their own hands, on special occasions; and sometimes in hard, dirty, and hazardous work. On one occasion I saw many of the chiefs at Oahu, and three or four hundred of the people, removing a rock, about nine feet long and six feet thick, being about half embedded in the earth, and estimated to weigh ten or twelve tons. They found it difficult to dislodge it from its bed, by pulling with many ropes, by main strength. A strong pair of oxen, belonging to the mission, was added to the train, and it was dragged about twenty rods and set up as an abutment, in the Waikiki wall, at the principal gateway through it.

The people of Kona were called to meet their chiefs at Kailua on the 20th of January. The regent and her son breakfasted and attended the morning devotions with Mr. Bishop's family. The regent desired to have the young prince address the people. The steadily cherished desire in my breast, that my young pupil, towards whom thousands of eyes were turning, might well consider his position, and throw his influence on the right side, prompted me to encourage him, from the felicitous opportunity to serve his country now afforded him, and the value of the interests at stake, to employ his best powers of eloquence to make a good and deep impression on the minds of the people in favor of national improvement. He was teachable, and efforts to transfuse our views into his youthful and wakeful mind were not always in vain. The missionaries and others were gladdened by his earnest, appropriate, and impressive address to the people, who heard him with pleasure. Then the pillars of the nation stood forth, one after another, Kaahumanu, Kuakini, Naihe, and Kaikioewa, and offered able speeches, urging attention to the duties of good subjects, sincerity, faithfulness, kindness, and diligent attention to schools, and the means of salvation now within their reach, and to the service of the true God. Their object appeared to be to convince the people of the reasonableness and importance of regarding Christianity as the true source of the intelligence and prosperity of the nation, and of the future prosperity of the soul. They treated the subject as if they respected the injunction, " *Seek first the kingdom of God,*" and as if they understood the truth, that little or no valuable improvement can be permanently secured without the inculcation and adoption of Christian principles, such as were urged by the missionaries.

After the addresses, three missionaries and the king stood up in front of the pulpit, and sang the translation or imitation of the missionary hymn, " From Greenland's Icy Mountains," just then coming into use at the islands. The interesting meeting was, as usual with Christian natives, closed with prayer to the Christians' God, and the concourse dispersed with obviously pleasing impressions respecting the rulers and the value of Christianity.

The chiefs, to complete the business of their tour round this island, proceeded to Waimea on the 25th and 26th, and attended there the examination of the schools of northern Hawaii, and the dedication of their new church. Mr. Ruggles, Mr. Bishop, and myself, engaged in this service. Mr. R., as was his manner, walked over lava fields and through forests, leaving the summit of Hualalai on his right. Mr. B., according to his custom, launched his boat, and taking advantage of the land and sea breezes, proceeded along near shore, to Kawaihae. I accepted the invitation of the young king, and sailed with him to Kawaihae, in one of his brigs. The second morning we reached Waimea, we had a pleasant season of public worship on the Sabbath, with the people of Waimea and neighboring districts, and those who came from other stations; then employed the last day of January, and two or three of February succeeding, in examining, directing, and encouraging all the schools of Waimea, Hamakua, and Kohala, they having come to that place for the purpose.

In Waimea proper, there were 653 scholars, and in the rest of Kohala, 1,050, making in Kohala, including Waimea, 79 schools, and 2,703 scholars. From the interesting valley of Waipio, 498 scholars, and from the rest of Hamakua, 1,394; making in Hamakua, including Waipio, 67 schools, and 1892 scholars; total connected with the station, 145 schools, 145 native teachers, 4,595 scholars, of which 338 were children, and 4,257 adults. About 1,000 could read, and half that number write.

Before their dispersion, the closing service of this week's labor was the solemn dedication of the new church, in which the young king took a willing and active part.

Among the worshippers, a considerable number already gave indications of loving the truth, as converts to Christianity. The care of the station was soon after intrusted to the Rev. Mr. Baldwin, and subsequently to the Rev. Mr. Lyons.

During these proceedings at Hawaii, there were rumors and apprehensions of disturbances at Honolulu. Kaikeowa, of Kauai, wishing to call the attention of the government to the danger to the peace of the state, which he apprehended from the residence and labors of the papal emissaries, had made an excursion to the windward, and touching at Oahu and Maui, joined the other chiefs at Hawaii, and now returned with them to Lahaina, on their way to Honolulu.

While Kaahumanu and the king were engaged at the windward islands, the Romanists at Honolulu were erecting or enlarging their buildings, inculcating the Romish faith, and making a diversion among the people without the consent and contrary to the orders of the supreme authority, assuming that their right to do so was from a higher power than Hawaiian rulers. Those of the people whom they drew after them, and who received their images and pictures, professed to worship a God different from him whom the Christian chiefs and their missionaries worshipped. Aside from the images, pictures, crosses, &c., to which they were taught to bow with veneration, they claimed to serve *ke akua Palani*, a French or Papal deity.

A very strong desire existed among the rulers generally that the people should not be thus misled. Kaikioewa urged the removal of the papal priests from the country, if it could possibly be done by any reasonable method. He would have them once more imperatively ordered to depart; and if they still refused, for want of a vessel, he wished to procure a passage for them; he would assume the debts of Boki, and pay them, if his creditors would transport the papal priests from the islands; or he would engage a foreigner to navigate one of the king's vessels for the purpose; or if some foreigner should wish to charter one of the government vessels for the purpose of traffic, he would recommend to give him the use of the vessel a certain number of months, on condition that he remove the two papal priests to some other country.

Meantime, Liliha having heard of the loss of her husband, and apprehending she might lose her place as governess of Oahu, made warlike preparations, purchased arms and ammunition, put about a thousand men under arms, placed the men of Waianae in the fort at Honolulu, choosing for her service those least friendly to Kaahumanu's policy, for the purpose, as was supposed, of resisting the authority of the Queen Regent, as Boki her husband nad before attempted to do.

Strenuous efforts were used by certain men, English, American and French, to make it appear that the title and office of *Regent* once belonged to Boki, and afterwards to Liliha, and not to Kaahumanu, a poor apology for seditious influence. A writer in the " Annals of the Propagation of the Faith" says :

" Kaahumanu had always been ambitious to keep all the power in her own hands. But her power was counterpoised by Boki, regent of the realm, and governor of the young king. Boki was fond of foreigners, and showed himself favorable enough to the missionaries; but he thought himself obliged to use management with the old queen. He had a certain number of chiefs on his side. Several Americans and some English were also on his side, because they were with reason suspicious of Kaahumanu. The two consuls, English and American, were particularly attached to him."

The editor of the Annals says in addition :

" The old Kaahumanu never forgot her ambitious projects. Shortly after Boki's departure, she attempted to displace all his partizans, and deprive them of the dignities which Boki had conferred on them. They refused compliance, protesting that they would not resign the power entrusted to them, except to him from whom they had received it. Moreover, the wife of Boki still held the title of regent and governess of Oahu."

Neither Boki nor Liliha, with all the support they could get from natives and foreigners, could hope to supplant or supersede Kaahumanu rightfully at all, or in any way, unless the young king could be alienated from her and made to oppose her. While most of the chiefs were together in consultation at Lahaina, they heard the reports of the agitation at Oahu, and the rumor of an outbreak to be expected there. Kinau, having then a high trust there under Kaahumanu, while Madam Boki was making her preparations, as it was supposed, to detach the king from the regent and to resist her authority, or begin an attack upon her adherents, wrote the chiefs in Hawaiian as follows :—

" Love to you, Elizabeth [Kaahumanu], and Auhea, Hoapili Kane, and Hoapili Wahine. This is my word to you, which I declare that you may know. *He olelo kaua koonei. Ua paa ka pa i na kanaka o Waianae.* The language or threatening of war is here. The fortress is occupied by the men of Waianae. When you approach and anchor outside, a boat is to go out for the king, and force him away from you. That is it. Attend to that small matter. But this is what we ought chiefly to do, to rely on God. Therein let us make fully manifest our regard to him with whom is the power and the wisdom. And pray ye to God for those who do us evil. Thus also do we at this place.
                                "JOCHEBED KINAU."

On receiving such news from Oahu, the chiefs at Lahaina considered two modes of preventing a disastrous revolt; the one to land a force at different parts of that island, sufficient to secure the control of it, and the other, to send Hoapili to use his influence with his daughter, Liliha, and in conjunction with Kinau and her friends, endeavor by quiet measures to maintain the peace. The latter appearing the more wise to be tried first, Hoapili being commissioned by Kaahumanu, hastened to Honolulu, in company with Kekauonohi, and required his daughter to give up the fort to him, and herself and chief captain, Paki, to repair to Lahaina, at the order of Kaahumanu. She yielded; and Hoapili took command of the fort, established a new garrison, and quietly waited the arrival of the regent and the other chiefs. Though deep murmurs were not wholly suppressed, and though the old chief appeared far from boasting, he might have said with the triumphant Roman, " I came, I saw, I conquered."

To promote the kindest feelings among the chiefs, Mr. and Mrs. Clark seized an early opportunity to bring Hoapili and his daughter, before her departure for Maui, Kinau, Kekauonohi, and Kekuanaoa together for a friendly interview at their house, where they took a social cup of tea, and had their attention directed to the wisdom and grace of God, the Ruler of the nations, who does all things well.   The voice of praise was soon heard, not only there, but in the fort also, where warlike preparations had been so recently threatening commotion and disaster.   At this period I returned with my family to my station.   The governess and Paki soon reached Lahaina, and Kaahumanu and suite returned to Honolulu.   Kinau, in tears, received them at the Kalanimoku house, and ascribed to God her deliverance from peril; and they and their Christian teachers there, bowed together in thanksgiving for the peaceful return of the rulers, after an absence of nine months, and for the protection of those who had remained and been exposed to danger.

The utmost vigilance and activity were still required of every friend of truth and righteousness, to roll back the tide, and shut the floodgates of iniquity ; especially were missionaries and Christian rulers expected to rally round the Bible standard, and display a banner for the truth.

At a public meeting on the first of April, 1831, the young king declared the control of Oahu to be in the hands of Kaahumanu. She appointed her brother, J. Adams, to the governorship.   He declared his purpose to restrain crimes and immoralities, such as had been specified in the edict of 1829, but had not been well enforced, including Sabbath-breaking, gambling, and the traffic in ardent spirits.

In a community which had been addicted to intemperance, gambling, Sabbath desecration, and lewdness, there were those, both native and foreign, who desired full liberty to continue them as their " amusements ;" but Kaahumanu and her brother determined to check them.   It was their duty to shake their hands from the responsibility of licensing any of these evils, and of the subordinate officers to shake theirs from the pollution of taking bribes for winking at iniquity in any form.

Though no law could be comfortably and successfully carried into execution for the promotion or protection of good morals, unless the major amount of influence in the community were in favor of such a law, and though no state had been known to abolish the traffic in ardent spirits, it was deemed by the Christian chiefs a duty to put a stop to drunkenness among their people.   The friends of temperance were called on to rally, and unite to accomplish the work by sound argument, safe example, reasonable pledges of abstinence, and a vigorous support of the government.   Every communicant in the various churches was taught to discountenance and avoid the manufacture, sale, and use of ardent spirits.   No consistent friend of morality could be expected to give or take a license to traffic in distilled liquors, or engage in the traffic without a license from the authorities.

There were about two hundred and sixty foreigners at that time at Honolulu (some intelligent and respectable), most of whom claimed the privilege either of making, vending, or consuming the deleterious beverage, who, under the mal-administration of the Bokis, had enjoyed it too much to their liking ; while many a sailor boy, beset by land sharks, far from friends and home, parted with his money, clothes, reputation, and peace, at a dear rate, at the yawning, pestiferous rum holes in Honolulu. Had the proprietors been indulged to the extent of their wishes, they would have had not only successive crews from sea, but the people of the land, and foreign residents, pay them a large profit for supplying the perpetual means of excitement, drunkenness, confusion, and ruin.

Kaahumanu, Kuakini, Hoapili, Kaikioewa, Naihe, and Kinau, who took a noble stand against this terrible enemy, deserved the thanks of ship-owners, and of the world, instead of the sneers and curses of the vile, and the strenuous opposition of the proud and hardened abettors of the traffic, who, in defiance of the government, and reckless of the weal and woe of their customers, were determined to persevere in it. But unreasonable as were these dram-sellers, it is not supposed that drunkard-makers and drunkard-killers at the Islands, differed materially in heart or principle, from those of the same class in civilized towns and cities, where the general voice of the wise and good is against this dangerous traffic. In the good old Bay State, when temperance principles had taken strong hold of the community, a retailer of distilled liquor, in other respects a good, intelligent citizen, being asked by a friend who kindly reasoned against it, if he would accept a report which might throw some light on the subject, replied with scorn, " No ; I have as much light on the subject *now* as I can live under : I mean to sell rum, and I mean to get my *pay* for it on delivery, and a good profit, too ; for I will not risk my reputation and my soul without getting my pay for it."

How ought the rulers and the men of influence at the islands, to have guarded the welfare of all classes against the destructive power of such principles, struggling to countenance vice of any kind ?

The new governor looked about him for a few days, to learn who among the natives and the two or three hundred foreigners were disposed to evade and who to respect his authority ; then made such vigorous efforts to stop gambling, tippling, Sabbath breaking, &c., as to cross the path of many of the foreign population, and not a few of the native. There was some show of comtempt and resistance of his authority, which increased the rigor and roughness of the execution of his orders. A considerable number of the foreigners met repeatedly to devise means for retaining their indulgences, and drew up a remonstrance, which was signed by papists, consuls, and other leading residents, and a few shipmasters in port, and sent to the king, expressing their apprehensions and displeasure at the infringement on their practices and pleasures. In this, among many things of little moment, they were pleased, in no very complimentary terms, to say:

" The undersigned . . . . viewing with alarm the encroachments made on our *liberties, religion,* and *amusements,* beg leave to address your majesty and your chiefs in council on the subject. . . . . . To strike so sudden and so deadly a blow, to jeopardize persons and property without any means of redress, enters not into our views of moral right, nor can it be supported by any precedent from any country or from the Bible."

Oaths, curses, and threats of violence uttered by the vile and reckless, were not wanting. Nor was there room left for doubt, in the turmoil that succeeded, that the life of some of the missionaries was threatened by those who hated the measures of the governor. My peculiar circumstances and relations, at this period, may be passed chiefly in silence, and an extract of a friendly note addressed to me by Mr. R. of Lahaina, take the place of a detail.

" The present conflict, however much it has been anticipated, requires all our energies. Not that I think our enemy very powerful, or have any doubts as to the general issue ; but it requires a great deal of backaching and heartaching thought, a great deal of fervent praying, and a great deal of divine direction, to enable one to manage everything in the best way, in your present circumstances. Be assured that in my warmest prayers you are the subject of my sincerest petitions, and I take great pleasure in the firm belief that you are about to win a victory as important, in its consequences, as the struggle is painful. The Lord alone be praised for all his powerful arm is doing."

The governor not being able to see that in restraining tippling, gambling, and Sabbath breaking, he had encroached on the civil or religious rights of foreigners or natives, persevered, notwithstanding the combination against him—a combination the more unwelcome because artful men of influence, taking advantage of the youthful king's fondness for their games and caresses, endeavored to prejudice his mind against his best friends, and particularly against Kaahumanu and the governor, who were studious both of his true interests and those of the country.

The removal of Madam Boki, though allowed by the king to have been reasonable, was nevertheless felt by his young heart to involve some personal privation, and was mortifying to her admirers and supporters. Such was the love of indulgence on the part of large masses of the people, and such the combination among the foreigners against the measures of the government, that these measures could not have been sustained had not Christian principle taken root in a good portion of the different ranks of the Hawaiians, and had not the clear, decisive, and healthful tones of the pulpit throughout the islands, and the special favor of God, strengthened and cheered on the native friends of sobriety, morality, and piety.

Voluntary pledges of abstinence were encouraged by the missionaries with success. At this juncture a temperance society was formed, embracing the four noblemen, Adams, Hoapili, Kaikieowa and Naihe, and other chiefs. The resolutions which they adopted (not quite up to the standard of later times), and to which thousands in the different islands agreed, were creditable, and being translated into English, are as follows :—

1. " We will not drink ardent spirits for pleasure.
2. We will not traffic in ardent spirits for gain.
3. We will not engage in distilling ardent spirts.
4. We will not treat our relatives, acquaintances, or strangers, with ardent spirits, except with the consent of a temperate physician.
5. We will not give ardent spirits to workmen on account of their labor."

That the Temperance reform should have found so much favor among the people of the islands before it had commenced in most Christian countries, or had prospered much in America, or brought the annual expenses of alcoholic drinks in the United States, much below $100,000,000, was, to all, a matter of surprise; to many, of high congratulation; and to some, of sore vexation.

To keep open the flood-gate at Honolulu, some would sell distilled liquors under the name of beer, wine, &c., and others would give rum to the determined rum-drinkers, and sell coffee to get their pay. The British Consul tried to induce the governor to give him permission to buy up rum in quantity for his Britannic majesty's ships which might touch there. Others, admitting that the traffic was attended with great evils, argued that such ports as Honolulu and Lahaina ought to have some well regulated rum-selling houses. But *well regulated dram-shops* were seen to be out of the question in such a community, where no man of sterling virtue would keep one, and where unprincipled sailors and natives, transient, noisy bucks, and tippling residents, would give them character. There is scarcely a community in the world able to prevent the pestiferous influence of grog-shops, or to keep the habitual customers from excess, riot, and ruin. No ruler, who is responsible for the peace of the community, could, therefore, rightfully license a grog-shop in such a community as was then found at Honolulu. How utterly impracticable would it be on board a ship of war, or within the walls of a State's Prison, with the most rigid rules, to restrain rum-loving men from confusion and violence, if a rum-seller were licensed to sell or give them freely the intoxicating draught. Some dealers, admitting that there might be reasons for restraining the natives from ruining their families, their souls, and bodies, at the dram-shop, besought the governor to give them license to sell to *foreigners* only. To this he replied sarcastically, " To horses, cattle, and hogs, sell rum, but not to real men."

How difficult the task of training up the young chiefs of the nation in such circumstances, and of keeping the mind of the young king from a wrong bias, and leading him to take a noble stand independently, against the boldest and most insidious advocates of self-indulgence !

The following conversation, between him and his teacher, will show our mode of treating him in respect to it, and his affability and interest in it, immediately after the struggle.

" What is the state of feeling among the foreigners respecting the laws in favor of good morals ?"

" They say but little to me about it. Some approve and some do not."

" But were they not angry when Adams began to execute the laws respecting the Sabbath and ardent spirits?"

" Yes, some of them were angry then, and said, 'If it is to be tabu here no ships will come.' "

" Why ? *Provisions* are not tabu; why will they not come for provisions, or lawful trade, as before ?"

" Why, indeed ?"

" Do you think there is as much drunkenness among them as formerly."

" I see less of it ; but I hear that sailors continue to get drunk."

" True, and some of them pass by our doors in a state of intoxication. But how is it with Hawaiians, do they get drunk as they used to do ?"

" They have wholly left it off. But some Bolabolans here drink, and are troublesome. One of them, being drunk, threw a stick at my horse, and I ordered him to be put in irons and carried into the fort."

" Men who are instructed in the right way and turn from it, may be expected to excel in wickedness, but I have seen but one native drunk for a long time, and that was Joe Banks, who met you at the fort, on your return from the windward."

" Yes, he was drunk then, and crazy, but he has gone to the Society Islands."

" Dr. Judd told me, the other day, he had seen but one native drunk, during his residence of four years at these islands. Capt. Hussey, of the Cyrus, who says he never drank a glass of spirits at sea, in his life, has spoken with decided approbation of the shutting up of the grog-shop on the wharf, where formerly a boat's crew would get drunk in half an hour, though ordered to stay by the boat while the officer was attending to his duties; ' Now,' said he, ' it is much more difficult for them, which I think an improvement.' "

" Yes, it is better now. Mr. Reed said, the other day, ' This place is distinguished for drinking spirits; but it is a bad thing. It is not so on the Spanish coast.' Then I replied, ' It was once very bad here—formerly there was very much drinking in this place.' "

"Intemperance is a great evil, and very destructive. It is difficult to govern men who are drunken. There was a case in Wellington's army, when the soldiers got drunk and would not obey their officers. Their enemies were expected to come suddenly upon them, and several of the soldiers had to be hung, before the army could be put in order. And now, if I were really angry with the foreigners and wished to destroy them, I should wish not only to have them supplied with ardent spirits, but enticed to drink freely. Gen. M—— remarking to me on the difference between the Spanish and English and American soldiers, in their habits of drinking, said, the Spanish were, by far, the most temperate; and added, ' if I were to fight an American or British army, I would endeavor to deposit, somewhere near their quarters, a large quantity of rum. The soldiers would be sure to get it, then their defeat would be easy.' "

" I have seen that illustrated (said the king); I have seen a foreigner, angry with another foreigner stronger than himself, and fearing to attack him in his full strength, he would first entice him to drink rum till he was tipsy, and then beat him."

" Some ship-owners are afraid to have their ships come often to this port. Capt. Joy and others have been ordered by their owners not to come into this harbor to recruit, lest their men should be tempted to leave their vessel, or otherwise be led astray and induced to make trouble in consequence of the facilities for getting drunk and bringing other evils upon themselves. Capt. Beechey, of the Blossom, said to Kalanimoku, "If you do not suppress the grog-shops, I will not bring my ship into your harbor, when I return." Kalanimoku said, "I wish to suppress them, but the British consul owns one of them." " Then," said Capt. B., " put on a duty so heavy upon spirits, that nobody can afford to get drunk." Capt. Jennings said, " I wish that rum was a hundred dollars a bottle, then nobody could get drunk with it."

In this way, as well as by the persevering exhibition of divine truth, did the missionaries attempt to get his youthful majesty to guard against the pollution and ruin of drinking habits, and to save his port, the most commodious in the Pacific Ocean, from the danger and disgrace attached to it, before Governor Adams, under Kaahumanu's authority, laid his hand on this traffic and other evils, thus exposing himself to the charge of encroaching on the "liberties, religion, and amusements" of the abettors.

That those who considered themselves encroached upon by the execution of the laws, should have been inclined to favor the counteracting influence of a looser religion than that which our mission inculcated, is not surprising, though in other respects it were in their esteem valueless and even hurtful. Nor is it at all strange that men who had been accustomed to see in the cities of

Europe or America, the prevalence of such evils as the Hawaiian government were attempting to restrain, should think their prohibitions of gambling, dram-selling, prostitution, Sabbath riding for pleasure or business, &c., were too rigid and illiberal, to be enforced on foreigners within their domain. Among this class, an English trader attempted, as others had done, to induce Kaahumanu to relax, and said, "They do not prohibit these things in England or America," as though that were a good guide, had it been strictly true. Kaahumanu replied, " We do not rule *there*, but these islands are *ours*, and we wish to obey the commands of God." The trader, alluding to the restrictions on Sabbath riding for amusement and business, said, "I don't know that there is any law against riding on the Sabbath." " Indeed you do know," said the queen, " there is a law against it." "Where is it?" he demanded. She calmly, promptly, and justly replied, " Remember the Sabbath day to keep it holy."

Sincerely desirous to see the Word of God prevail, the Sabbath sacredly observed, and the cause of temperance and religion promoted, the Christian rulers rejoiced in the accession of helpers, either by the conversion of their own subjects, or the arrival of additional teachers who would attempt to carry forward the work.

Towards the close of 1830, a third reinforcement of the mission was appointed and fitted out by the American Board. The Rev. Messrs. Dwight Baldwin, Reuben Tinker, and Sheldon Dibble, and Mr. Andrew Johnstone, and their wives, embarked from New Bedford, Dec. 28th, on board the New Englander, Capt. Parker, and experiencing kind treatment from the captain and officers of the ship, reached the islands in 161 days. About 40° S. L. they had rough weather, head winds, and some dangers, and were forty-nine days beating round Cape Horn. They arrived at Honolulu, June 7th, 1831, and were gladly welcomed to the whitening field.

In reference to this reinforcement and in answer to a letter from Mr. Evarts to the queen, a letter which she highly prized, she prepared and sent the following, indicative of the calm, humble, grateful state of her mind and heart in the midst of the conflicts which tried her skill, patience, and energy; translated thus:

"OAHU, SEPT. 11TH, 1831.

" Love to you, Mr. Evarts, the director of missionaries—my first brother in Christ Jesus.

" This is for you, my thought and my joy ; I now abide by the voice of the Savior, Jesus Christ, who hath redeemed me from death. I was dwelling in the central flame of death. I was clothed and adorned in the glory and likeness of death. When I heard the voice of Jesus, as it sounded in my ear, it was refreshing to my bosom, saying thus, ' Come unto me all ye that are heavy laden, and I will give you rest.' Again, the voice of him said, ' Whosoever is athirst, let him come and drink of the water of life.' Therefore, I arose and came, and cast myself down in the shadow [protected place] of his feet, with my great trembling. Therefore, do I bear his yoke, with this thought concerning myself—that I am not able to put forth strength adequate to carry his yoke, but of him is the ability—his aid to me, by night and by day; there am I abiding continually by his righteousness and his love to me. There do I set my love and my desire, and the thoughts of my heart, and there, on Jesus, do I leave my soul. For this shall my lips and my tongue give praise continually, during the life which I now live, till entering into his everlasting glory. Such is this thought of mine for you.

"This is another thought of mine for you,—I gratefully admire the kindness of our Lord Jesus Christ in aiding us by several new teachers for us. They have arrived. We have seen their eyes and their cheeks. We have met them in the presence of God, and in our presence also, with praise to our common Lord for his preserving them on the ocean till they arrived here, at Hawaii. Now we wait while they study the native language of Hawaii. When that is clearly understood by them, then they will sow in the fields, the good seed of eternal salvation. Then, my former brethren, with these more recent, and the brethren and sisters of my own country, will all of us take up what Christ desires, on this cluster of islands, with prayer to him for his aid, that the rough places may, by him, be made plain by his power, through all these lands, from Hawaii to Kauai.

"I and he whom I have brought up [the young king], have, indeed, carried the Word of our Lord through, from Hawaii to Kauai. With the love of the heart towards God, was our journeying, to proclaim to the people, his love, and his word, and his law, and to tell the people to observe them. Thus was our proclaiming, not according to our own will, but according to the will of God, did we undertake it. Such is this thought of mine for you.

"This is one more thought to make known to you. Do you make known my love to the brethren in Christ, and to my beloved sisters in Christ Jesus. This is my salutation to you all. Pray ye to God for all the lands of dark hearts, and for the residue [unconverted], of all lands of enlightened hearts, and for us also : and thus will we, with our kindred here, all pray to God for the lands of dark hearts, and for the residue of the lands of enlightened hearts, and for you also. Thus shall we and you, unitedly, call upon our common Lord, that the nations may, in peace, follow him, and that his kingdom may be smooth and uninterrupted, that all men may turn to him without dissent, and praise his everlasting name. That is my sentiment in love to you all.

"Great love to thee. Our persons will not meet in this world, but our thoughts do meet in this world ; and hereafter will our souls meet in the glory of the kingdom of our Lord Jesus Christ—thy Savior and mine. This ends my communication to you.

" ELISABETH KAAHUMANU."

To secure the peace of the nation in the best way, could not be accomplished without much care and effort on the part of the rulers. Seeing and feeling the danger of civil divisions, of insubordination and rebellion, and believing it to be greatly increased by the introduction of a foreign superstition, or a strange religion which would admit no fellowship with theirs, the chiefs resolved on guarding against the danger, as far as they could, by removing the causes. Whatever might be the final result, fully satisfied as they were that the right of soil and the possession of the sovereignty of the islands warranted them to reject and exclude the emissaries of Rome, and that duty to themselves, to their people, and to God, required it, they set about it anew with calmness and deliberation, in a manly, open, straightforward course, and repeated the order to the priests to leave the country within three months. Warned as they had been by friendly individuals from abroad, who had spoken to them of the mischief which Romanism had done, and convinced by Dr. King's letter, and by their own observation, that it would be a great evil to the nation, they could not welcome its teachers, nor explicitly or tacitly bid them God speed.

Neither David on the throne of Israel and Judah, nor Pomare of Tahiti, nor the Patriarch of Pitcairn's island, could have safely allowed the intrusion of such aliens as teachers and leaders of their people. " He who has the right to forbid, and does not forbid, approves." If the government could not and did not welcome them, much less could our missionaries rightfully bid them God speed or encourage their continuance in that field. Nay, every friend of the nation might have reasoned as properly against the thrusting in of Romanism into the Sandwich Islands as did the wise men of the west, our revolutionary statesmen, against the introduction and establishment of that faith in Canada, who, in the address of Congress at Philadelphia, 1774, to the people of Great Britain, used the following earnest and forcible language :—

" The dominion of Canada is to be extended, that their numbers daily swelling with Catholic emigrants from Europe may become formidable to us and reduce the ancient free Protestant colony to a state of slavery. Nor can we express our astonishment that a British Parliament should ever consent to establish, in that country, a religion that has deluged your island in blood, and dispersed impiety, bigotry, persecution, murder, and rebellion throughout every part of the world."

Romanism not having changed its character materially since the American revolution, could not be expected to demean itself better at Tahiti and the Sandwich Islands than in Canada or Mexico. Nor has the experiment proved a better temper or tendency.

The priests having entered the field without asking or receiving the permission of the government, and continued there about four years in the face of the orders of the regency, claimed the right to prosecute their work independently of the native authorities.

Mr. Bachelot having been appointed " Prefect of the Sandwich Islands " by a pope who claimed jurisdiction over all the sovereigns and kingdoms of earth, denied the right of the Hawaiian rulers to prevent his residence and labors there, and refused to comply with their order to depart.

In giving an account of the rejection of his mission, he says :

" Among our *Kanacs* (Hawaiians) a *yes* is a sacred promise, but we had never obtained the formal *yes* in relation to our remaining on the islands. . . . . The yes for our remaining had never been uttered, and, moreover, it never came into my mind to ask for it till it was too late."

Mr. Hill, an Englishman, visiting the islands, and perceiving the position of the parties, endeavored to persuade the papal teachers to remove to some quarter where there would be less opposition to their remaining and more need of their labor, for it was impossible, he said, for the Romish and the Protestant religions to coalesce, and they ought not to kick against the goad. Mr. Bachelot replied :

" You say, ' we ought not to kick against the goad.' If by that goad, sir, you mean the prohibitions of men and their opposition, I will ask you, with Peter and John, consider whether it is right to obey men rather than God, and whether apostles and their successors, the evangelical laborers in China and elsewhere, have read in the Gospel that they ought to abandon the work of God because it was prohibited by the great ones of the earth, whom the low and poor have always preceded in their adhesion to the truth."*

To him, the non-permission and the magisterial prohibition of his stay by the great ones of the Sandwich Islands were of little account. He himself was *Prefect* there ; and he assumed that to disregard the order to depart was obedience to God, because God, or his avowed vicegerent, had authorized him to stay there. But neither the Pope nor any other earthly director had a right to require him to stay at the Sandwich Islands, equal to the right of that government to refuse him a residence. The authority of Kaahumanu there was paramount to that of the crowned head of Rome. Luther would have regarded obedience to the local civil ruler as obedience to God in such a case. No ruler has a right to rule in opposition to God's will. No power on earth can rightfully proscribe God's Word, or authorize blasphemy or idolatry. No government, civil, ecclesiastical, or parental, has a right to withhold God's statute-book from his subjects, because he requires them to search and obey the Scriptures. That power which proscribes the Book of God, and formally or virtually forbids its circulation and free use, has no just claim to be considered as a teacher of God's will.

While the priests denied the right of the rulers to dismiss or expel them, they supposed expediency required at least the appearance of deference ; they therefore *seemed to yield*, and pretended to seek a conveyance from the islands, while they sedulously sought to forestall and prevent the execution of the will of the rulers. When they asked for a conveyance from the

* Annals of the Propagation of the Faith, vol. x., p. 379.

islands, they asked it as a gratuity, and lest that gratuity should be granted them, they urged their unwillingness to go, and would even put up a captain to ask of the rulers an enormous sum for their passage, if they had the chance of a gratuitous passage home; then, to the chiefs, endeavor to excuse their stay, on the ground that they had no vessel to convey them away. About the expiration of three months from the removal of Liliha and the renewed order for the departure of the priests, Capt. Wendt, of the Princess Louisa, from Prussia, on a trading voyage round the world, arrived at Honolulu. He brought from the King of Prussia, presents and a friendly letter to the king, acknowledging the reception of a war-cloak from his Hawaiian majesty, recommending to his protection such of his subjects as might visit his islands, and wishing him all prosperity, peace, and happiness. The captain, who appeared obliging, learning that the king and his government were very desirous that the Romish priests should leave the country, and that they were seeking a conveyance, was ready to do a favor to both parties, and offered a free passage. But being instructed by the priests, and learning that their seeking a passage was only in pretence, and that they wished him to demand a compensation which neither they nor the government would give, at length put up the fare to more than 25,000 francs for the two.

The Apostolic Prefect of the Sandwich Islands sent to France the following account of these proceedings, which his employers published to the world :—

" That we might appear to yield in some degree to the demands of the chiefs, and to avoid irritating them, we took care when any vessel was about to depart to request, in writing, of the captain a gratuitous passage. We did this in respect to several, and as they knew our intentions, they answered us also in writing, and absolutely refused to grant our request ; for no captain was willing to engage in executing the sentence pronounced against us.

" A short time afterwards, a Prussian vessel arrived, which brought presents from the King of Prussia to the King of the Sandwich Islands. The arrival of this vessel furnished an occasion for a new attempt to compel us to leave the archipelago. The Governor of Hawaii reappeared. ' Here,' said he to me, ' is a ship from near your own country. It will conduct you to your own land.' ' What you say is reasonable,' I replied. ' But who will pay my passage ? I came here with nothing but my body and the Word of God. My heart has not been upon the things of this world. I have amassed no money.' ' Perhaps he will take you for nothing.' ' It is possible, but ask him yourself and we shall see.' Kuakini retired with this answer. The captain came to see us. I explained to him our situation. He obligingly offered to receive us on board of his vessel if we wished to depart. But if not, he told us to make the application to him in writing, and dictate the answer which we wished him to make, which was done. The Governor of Hawaii also went to see him, and urged him to take charge of us. The Prussian captain answered him that

he would do it with pleasure, but before Mr. Patrick and I could come
on board, he must be paid five thousand dollars (more than 25,000
francs). The poor governor had a great desire to rid himself of us,
but he was still more anxious to keep his money. He was, therefore,
obliged to abandon his project."

The friendly letter of Frederick William of Prussia, accompanied by a beautiful portrait of his majesty, and another of his
field marshal, the venerable Prince Blucher, together with the
interesting account which his majesty's painter gave of their
Christian character, afforded to the king and chiefs of the Sandwich Islands fresh testimony that it is not beneath the dignity
of kings and princes, and the most enlightened nobles of the
earth, to encourage learning and religion, or to promote, by their
personal example and influence, the free diffusion of the inspired
oracles at home and abroad. To that letter of the King of Prussia, Kauikeaouli returned by Capt. Wendt to Berlin, an appropriate and friendly answer, in his own hand-writing, which for
matter, style, and execution, was highly creditable to him and
his country. This correspondence took the place of a treaty of
amity and commerce, and was better than any forced agreements
dictated by men of war.

Still the trouble from the papists continued. The chiefs waited
through the summer, and till the fall ships had arrived and sailed
again, some to England, some to the United States, and some to
other coasts. Seeing no better way for accomplishing what they
believed ought to be done without further delay, they fitted their
brig Waverley for a short voyage, and engaged an English resident
to take charge of her, with the two papal teachers, or priests, as
passengers, and furnished him the following warrant:

" I, Kauikeaouli, king of the Sandwich Islands, and Kaahumanu,
and Kalua, Governor of Oahu, do hereby commission William Sumner, Commander of the brig Waverley, now lying at Oahu, to receive
on board two French gentlemen and their goods, or whatever they may
have to bring on board, and to proceed on to California and land them
safe on shore, with everything belonging to them, where they may
subsist, and then return back to the Sandwich Islands.

(Signed) } KAUIKEAOULI.
            KAAHUMANU.
            KUAKINI."

" OAHU, Nov. 5TH, 1831."

Kaahumanu asked the British Consul if he thought it right for
them to send away the papal priests. He replied that his king had
made it *tabu* for him to speak on that subject; but a few days
later he told her if she sent away a British subject she must
send him to his native country or to some of her colonies. But
by what law of nations or rule of equity she was bound to this,
he did not inform her. She called the king and counsellors together, for further consultation, on the 12th Dec., when, after a
careful review of the grounds they had taken, looking for divine

direction, they unanimously determined to persevere in their plan
for removing the priests, and resisting intemperance and idolatry.
Speaking of this interview, the following day, the queen regent
said, 'the king prayed with them, implored God's blessing on their
efforts, acknowledged their feebleness, and asked his aid and
guardianship, the out-pouring of his spirit on them, and his influence on their hearts, thanked him that he had made them
acquainted with the right way, and asked him to separate from
them those who opposed them and caused division.'   Here, her
eyes filled with tears, and her rising feelings choked her utterance.
We hoped the child was near the kingdom of God, and still hope
that his juvenile prayer, and thousands of other prayers for him,
will be answered.   With what sobriety, calmness, tenderness, and
prayerful deliberation, did the rulers endeavor to guard against the
intrusion of a system of delusion and idolatry ; a system, which
being introduced into heathen countries, always proves to be grossly
idolatrous; a system, whose Roman head, claiming jurisdiction over
all countries, aims, it is apprehended, at the subversion of every
Protestant government within its reach.

In rejecting the papal teachers, and encouraging the Protestant,
Kaahumanu endeavored to pursue that course which a dignified,
conscientious, and Christian patriarch might, in her circumstances,
have lawfully done in the fear of God, for the good of the people.
To some it was a matter of wonder to see how, like a noble
queen, patriotic as Esther, who could not bear to see the evil that
threatened her people, Kaahumanu stood up in the nation a beloved matriarch (if this term may be used for want of a better),
in the most critical state of the nation, while it was struggling
between religion and infidelity, loyalty and treachery, Christianity
and image worship, civilization and heathenism.   She well deserved from her own people the complimentary title of *Kaahumanu hou*, the new Kaahumanu, and the official designation of
Kaahumanu I., because of the intense interest she obviously felt
in the welfare of the nation, and her unwavering regard to the
authority of God in reference to her duties as a ruler.   She felt
that she could no more approve or allow the re-establishment of
image worship, in any form, than she could license dram-sellers and drunkard-makers to work at their trade, on her shores.

On the 24th of December, 1831, the Waverley being ready for
sea and for her passengers, they, having been seasonably apprised
of the time set for their departure, were waited on from their
quarters to the vessel by Kekuanaoa, subsequently governor of
Oahu.   Their baggage being carefully put on board with them,
they sailed for California, where they were debarked safely on
the 29th of January, 1832.

The reasons in brief assigned by the government, at the time,
for this measure are as follows :—

" This is our reason for sending away the *Palani* [Frenchmen or
Papists] :—In the first place, the chiefs never assented to their dwell-

ing at Oahu; and when they turned some of our people to stand opposed to us, then we said, 'Return to the country whence ye came.' At seven different times we gave them that order. And again, in speaking to them, we said, 'Go away, ye *Palani*. We allow you three months to get ready.' But they did not go during the three months, but remained eight months, saying, 'We have no vessel to return in.' Therefore we put them on board our own vessel, to carry them to a place where the service is like their own. Because their doings are different from ours, and because we cannot agree, therefore, we send away these men."

What civilized Napoleon or Alexander would have assumed the expense, hazard, and trouble, of carrying quietly away, in his own ships, unwelcome foreigners, whom he had for any cause ordered to depart? In respect to this measure, the Report of the American Board for 1832, takes this view:

"The removal of these Jesuits, in the manner in which it was performed, was the violation of none of their natural or acquired rights, and, therefore, cannot properly be regarded as persecution. No permission was ever given them to remain on the islands :—it was expressly refused, and they were repeatedly requested, and even ordered, to go away. The advice and the authority of the government being equally disregarded, the government exercised the right claimed by every civilized nation, of determining whether foreigners, at all events, shall remain within its limits; and in a manner the most considerate and humane, sent them to another country, professing the same religion with themselves. While endeavoring to estimate the merits of this case, we should endeavor to place ourselves in the circumstances of the chiefs of the Sandwich Islands."

The papal priests, whose clerical friends had invited them to California, gave the captain a certificate "that they had been treated on board by him with as much consideration and interest as they could expect, and had been debarked safely with all their baggage at San Pedro." By this he was able to satisfy his employers that he had executed his trust according to contract. Mr. Bachelot says, moreover, that "before they were landed, the captain sent information to a farmer who knew who they were, and who visited them on board, and then sent a man to take charge of their baggage, who supplied them with provisions and slept with them." They were shortly welcomed by their clerical friends, who had assured them that they were needed there, and might be useful. These facts should have shielded that government from the defamatory charges of brutality and wanton cruelty in the removal and disembarkation of the papists, by which their enemies attempted to provoke the indignation of French naval officers.

It should be observed, that these men were not alone denied a residence. Mr. Hill, who had shown himself very friendly, said to Kaahumanu, "When I return to this country, I want you to let me have a little spot of ground, and build a small house and live here." "I shall not assent to it," was her prompt reply; for she did not think it safe to pledge him a residence without knowing the capacity in which he should come. Capt. Cole applied for permission to open a shop at Lahaina. Gov. Hoapili, fearing he would sell rum, refused. The trader appealed to Kaahumanu, and said he wished to have the same privileges of trading at Lahaina that were enjoyed at Honolulu. She replied, " You sell rum at Honolulu contrary to our orders, and we do not wish it." He therefore failed. An Englishman at Waimea, Hawaii, being directed to leave, urged the king to allow him a residence there. The king referred him to Gov. Adams, who, having been encroached on by the foreigner, confirmed and repeated the order for him to depart. He treated the governor contemptuously to his face, calling him " *no gentleman.*" The governor condescended to reply with a spice of native irony, and in common English phrase, " *You* are a gentleman, and because *I* am not, do you clear out." Several Russians, who attempted to establish themselves in Kauai before the introduction of Christianity, had been sent away. An American resident having attacked with pistols another American, accusing him of having taken away his wife, the government required both the assailant and the wounded man to leave the country.

About the time, but before the papal priests were sent away, I called at a little cluster of huts, where I found several of their followers sojourned, being employed daily in building a stone fence between the dry plain and the plantations in the rear, along between Punchbowl Hill and Waikiki. Many hundreds of the people were, from time to time, called out to work on this wall, on which the chiefs labored with their own hands. But this was the ordinary mode of executing public works : the other was special, and though I saw and heard neither chains, whips, nor instruments of torture, it was regarded as *punishment.* This was the only instance of punishment which I ever saw inflicted on Hawaiian subjects who claimed to be papists. I asked Kaahumanu by what authority they were made to labor there. She said, " By the law against idolatry ; for they have violated that law in renewing the worship of images."

The prohibition of image worship had been deemed right from the commencement of the reign of Liholiho. *Christianity* did not come to reinstate images of any kind as objects or instruments of worship, in the confidence and affection of these recently heathen idolators. Nor could we, from the beginning, pronounce the tabu inhibiting the *malama kii* or *hoomana kii* [image worship or idolatry] to be wrong, nor could we make such a distinction between the worship paid by a Jew under Hezekiah to the brazen type of Christ, and that rendered by a native to the host, the cross, and the image of the Virgin, as to show that the one was opposed and the other conformed to the sacred oracles.

Both before and after the arrival of Romish priests, Kaahumanu and the king, and other chiefs and native teachers, were accustomed to say, " *Mai malama kii. Mai hoomana kii. Mai hoomana i ke akua e.*" " Serve not images. Worship not idols. Worship no strange God." All the missionaries, instead of objecting to that style, held uniformly the same language. Our method of treating this subject publicly may be illustrated by the following brief sketch of a sermon at Honolulu, towards the close of 1831. To my church and congregation, where I freely maintained that as a church or church members we had no weapons to oppose error but the sword of the Spirit, the Word of God, I preached, about a month subsequent to the date of Capt. Sumner's commission, from Mark xii., 29, 30 : " Hear, O Israel, the Lord our God is one Lord, and thou shalt love the Lord thy God with all thy heart, with all thy soul, and with all thy mind, and with all thy strength :" Showing first that Jehovah alone is the object to which religious worship can properly be addressed ; and, secondly, that the duty required was a sincere, spiritual service—a supreme devotedness of the heart to God, implying, in particular, obedience to the *first, second, third,* and *fourth* commandments of the decalogue ; and, thirdly, that such worship and service should be rendered to Jehovah alone—because of his glorious perfections which he alone possesses,—because of the various exhibitions of his goodness in what he has done for us,—and because his favor and our salvation through Christ, would thus be secured ; then presenting and illustrating in the simplest manner, the inferential truth, that to worship any other object than the one Lord—the living and true God—is obviously wrong, as the ancient gods of Hawaii, whose worship had been suppressed and abandoned ; Baal of Canaan, whose worship Elijah resisted ; the calf of Aaron, which he pretended was a god who had brought them out of Egypt, and which Moses destroyed with just indignation ; and the calves at Bethel and Dan, set up by Jeroboam to turn away Israel from the true faith and worship, for which the nation was punished ; the brazen serpent which God had given them to be looked at when they were bitten by fiery flying serpents, but which Hezekiah, in a rational zeal for God, destroyed when the people bowed down to it and worshipped it ;—in all which cases the reasonableness of rejecting and opposing idolatry was apparent, whether the worshippers professed or not to " hold a feast to the Lord " around a calf, or to honor their Deliverer by bowing to a serpent.

The people could not be blamed for concluding from observation that Romish worship is idolatrous ; for the teachings of Rome would bring them to the same conclusion.* Protestants of

* The council of Trent, by which Romanism was stereotyped, declares that " it is lawful to represent God and the Holy Trinity by images, and that the images of Christ and the saints are to be duly honored, venerated, and worshipped, and that in this veneration or worship, those are venerated who are represented by them." In the creed of Pope Pius the Fourth, it is written by his infallibility, " I also believe that the saints who reign with Christ are to be worshipped and prayed to, and that

every class, and every friend of the principles of freedom, might be justified in using every argument to forestall the establishment by foreign agents of an idolatrous and sanguinary *politico-religious* system among the recently rescued Hawaiians.

To carry forward the work with energy, while the field was fairly open, and so inviting, the American Board and the patrons of the mission wisely increased the number and the facilities of the laborers, and enabled them to put in operation new and systematic measures for raising the qualifications of native teachers, and for training up a future native ministry, by means of boarding-schools and a missionary seminary, on a broader scale than in the first years of the mission was practicable, while a nation of unlettered heathen were on the hands of a few, to be instructed in almost everything needful for them to know. During the last year of the laborious and prosperous course of Kaahumanu, soon after Gov. Adams succeeded Liliha, the mission put into operation a missionary seminary, at Lahainaluna, under the care of the Rev. L. Andrews. This was opened in Sept., 1831, with twenty-five young men, as pupils. The number, in the course of the year, was increased to sixty-seven. The scholars, many of them, were married, and had to provide lodgings for themselves and their families, to build their own school-house, with the direction and aid of the teacher, and raise or procure their own food. But such was their laudable desire to obtain the advantages thus offered, that while pursuing their studies, they labored patiently, month after month, the first year, to erect, under every disadvantage, the walls and roof of their school-house. The stones they collected without team, and brought their timber from a distance by human muscle. It was all up-hill work—analogous to that which, for years, had been performed, before an enterprise like this, requiring so much of native energy and hearty co-operation, could be successfully undertaken.

The object of this seminary was to extend and perpetuate the religion of our Lord Jesus Christ, which the mission had labored,

their relics are to be venerated; and I most firmly assert that the images of Christ and the Mother of God, who was always a virgin, are to be had and retained, and that due honor and worship is to be given them." A bull of a learned pope of the present century promises to excuse the poor Irish, for so many days or years, from the pains of purgatory, if they will, at certain times, offer this ejaculation:—"Jesus, Mary, Joseph, I give my ardent soul to you." The Bishop of Treves, a representative of Rome, maintains that he has the coat worn by Christ, which fell to one of his murderers, and exhibits it as a relic for hundreds of thousands of the deluded people to visit and worship, some of whom invoke it as though intelligent and divine— "Holy Tunic, I come to thee. Holy Tunic, I pray to thee. Holy Tunic, pray for me."

The Romish system sanctions the killing of men for repudiating her dogmas. The defenders and apologists of Rome say, "When Rome puts heretics to death, their blood is no more than the blood of thieves, man-killers, and other malefactors." The Romish notes to the Rheimish Testament still defend the killing of heretics, and maintain that children ought not to spare their own parents, if they are heretics. Laws, built on this system, condemn to death such Christians as maintain that the wafer consecrated by a priest is still *bread*, and that the Scriptures forbid image worship. For this Maria Joaquina was, at Madeira, lately imprisoned a year, and condemned to be hung; but she is said to have found, with other persecuted victims, an asylum in Trinidad (1847).

eleven years, to introduce, and to aid in accomplishing its design to secure for the nation the blessings of Christianity and civilization, to disseminate sound knowledge throughout the islands, to train and qualify school-teachers for their respective duties, not only by acquainting them with literature and the knowledge of the arts and sciences most needful for them, but with the proper usages and habits of civilized and Christian life, and eventually to educate young men of piety and promising talents to become preachers of the Gospel, and ministers of Christ, for the maintenance and dissemination of pure religion among their dying fellow men. The intention of the mission was to allow fifty to enter annually, who could pass a respectable examination in reading, writing, mental arithmetic, and topographical geography, and whose age did not exceed twenty-five years. The proportion of pupils from the different islands was 18 from Hawaii ; 14 from Maui, Molokai, and Lanai ; 10 from Oahu, and 8 from Kauai and Niihau. The period for the course in general was four years. The course of studies, introduced gradually, were, for the first year, Arithmetic, Geometry, Trigonometry, Sacred Geography, Hawaiian Grammar, Languages to a select class.

2d year. Mathematics, embracing Algebra, Navigation, and Surveying, History, Languages for a select class.

3d year. Mathematics continued, Natural Philosophy, Church History, Languages for a select class.

4th year. Astronomy, Chemisty, Moral Philosophy, Church History, Languages for a select class.

During the whole course, more or less attention, every week, is given to biblical instruction, embracing the interpretation of Scripture, evidences of Christianity, Archæology, and Sacred Geography, Composition and Elocution. Systematic Theology was contemplated, as soon as sufficient advancement and preparation for it should be made. Music, vocal and instrumental, Penmanship, Drawing Maps, Engraving, Printing, Binding, Carpentery, Turnery, and Mason work, all received some attention, at least, from individuals—connected with needful exercise and profitable labor.

The juvenile king was offered the privilege of attending the school, with five of his favorite young men. They went to the spot, in 1832, before it was possible for the mission to afford the accommodations, apparatus, and books necessary for the comfortable and rapid progress desirable, and much to be regretted as it was, he declined the offer.

From a very early period of the mission, at the request of Kalanimoku and Kaahumanu, he, with Haalilio, his bosom friend, and private secretary, and, at length, trustworthy commissioner to foreign courts, received instruction from me, as my other cares and labors, and his engagements and amusements would admit. He, as well as his gay young friend, having naturally, good powers of mind, and an aptitude to learn, whenever he gave himself the time and trouble for it, made very good attainments ; though since the weighty cares of government have come upon him, convincing him that it is no trifling amusement to be king of a nation,(which, though very small, must provide for its own wants at home, and have a part to act with other nations, and, therefore, requires wisdom,)if he should now feel regret that so much of his youthful years had been allowed to run to waste, in respect to application to study, he would by no means be alone in it.   That he highly prizes the advantages of early education, his active and steady patronage of it, throughout his realm in general, and among the young chiefs in particular, affords a happy proof.

The students were selected by missionaries and chiefs at the different islands and stations, whither they were expected to re-turn, to aid the cause of improvement, when qualified for it.   The walls and roof of the school-house being erected by their own hands, the pupils, in the summer of 1832, went to the mountains for plank and timber for writing-tables.   There was no saw-mill in the island, and the pupils had no team to aid them in their work, nor capital to procure its accomplishment.   They must cut down trees, and hew them away to the thickness of the plank needed; then bring them on their shoulders, or drag them on the ground, by hand, for miles.   This was the common method of procuring plank and boards, by natives, throughout the islands, before the pit-saw and the saw-mill, moved by water power, were introduced.   The pupils collected stone for a floor, hewed them a little, laid them down and pointed them with lime-mortar.   Then they collected coral for lime, and went to the mountains for fuel to burn it, and brought it on their shoulders, made a kiln and burned it, then plastered the walls of the house, outside and in, and made their writing-tables, seats, window-shutters, door, &c.   A new class entered this year, greatly enlarg-ed the school, and engaged with courage in the erection of a new building.

What class of pupils in America, without funds or patrons, would have shown more zeal, or have undertaken to build their own school-house, with all these disadvantages, and board and lodge themselves, while pursuing their studies ?

What severer trial of the voluntary principle could have been made or desired ?

The students were often hungry, but studied as patiently as when full fed.   The chiefs partially granted a valuable piece of land (though they refused a title) for the aid of the seminary, on which the students could raise their own vegetables, &c.   The Ameri-can Board, from time to time, increased the means of erecting suita-ble buildings and of furnishing a library and apparatus, and have sus-tained there three teachers and their families, well adapted to the design of the institution.

Had the affluent friends of missions then seen the importance of furnishing the means of a speedy and thorough education for a competent number of teachers for the nation, as the missionaries saw and felt it, when they looked upon the pupils, half naked and half starved, sitting on the ground to study, and hoped that from among them might arise the teachers, doctors, lawyers, statesmen, and preachers of the kingdom, can it be supposed they would have been slow in granting them the needful aid? But then we had this excuse for them—many and greater heathen nations needed their aid still more, and, therefore, we could not willingly defraud the greater by unduly pressing the claims of the lesser.

A species of superstition once existed at the islands analogous to the *grave-worship* of the Chinese, and the worship of relics in other countries. This was supposed to have nearly ceased before the attempt to introduce Romanism. It was, however, obvious that the tendency still existed in the nation to revive that superstition. The zeal of Kaahumanu led her as early as 1829 to visit the *Hale o Keawe* at Honaunau, a cemetery associated with dark superstitions, and surrounded with horrid wooden images of former generations. The regent visited the place not to mingle her adorations with her early contemporaries and predecessors to the relics of departed mortals, but for the purpose of removing the bones of twenty-four deified kings and princes of the Hawaiian race, and consigning them to oblivion. But at that time she thought Naihe was wavering in respect to their removal, and Kekauluohi, whose father's bones were there, she thought still cherished an undue veneration for them; and Boki she feared would treat her with abuse and violence if she should disturb the house or remove its mass of relics. But when she saw it *ought* to be done, she determined it *should* be done : and in company with Mr. Ruggles and Kapiolani, she went to the sacred deposit, and caused the bones to be placed in large coffins and entombed in a cave in the precipice at the head of Kealakekua Bay. In doing this she found an expensive article of foreign manufacture, comparatively new, placed near the bones of the father of Kekauluohi, and which appeared to have been presented as an offering since the date of the prohibition of the worship of idols.

In September, 1831, the regent made her last tour round Oahu. This she accomplished in about eight days, in company with Kauikeaouli and others. They both charged the people not to revive image worship, warning them not to return to vain idols, and commending to them the worship of the Lord Almighty. They said, " There is one only living and true God : it is Jehovah. Let us, O ye people, listen to his word, and obey his law." In one instance I heard from the mouth of the king, " If ye worship images, ye shall be punished." In this journey of eight days, or 150 miles, I preached twenty-one times to large companies of the people, ' as though God did beseech them by us, praying them in Christ's stead to be reconciled to God.'

A part of our company crossed over the mountains between Waialua and Waianae. On a ridge where our horses were led, the fine horse of Haalilio unfortunately got off the track; and finding his situation perilous, he reared to leap with vigor up to the path, lost his balance, went over backwards, and falling, slid helpless and rapidly down the steep, and was killed.

Just at the close of the year, the nation was called to mourn the loss of another of its reformed and useful chieftains. Naihe, the friendly chief of Kaawaloa, and acting governor of Hawaii during Adams's residence at Oahu, died December 29th, having received a stroke of paralysis forty-four hours before his departure. He was perhaps more conservative than his compeers. He had been slow to give up the old superstitions of his ancestors; and when Kekuaokalani, in 1819, refused to renounce his idols and the governmental tabus, Naihe was slow to oppose him, and by some was thought to be inclined to join him, but finally separated himself from the defenders of the idols. When the zeal of Kapiolani led her in 1824 boldly to invade the domain of Pele, he felt utterly unwilling to advise it, but allowed her to follow her own conscience and discretion in the case. When the general abandonment of the use of tobacco was recommended by the missionaries, Naihe, like thousands more enlightened and more civilized, felt that it would be a great privation, but still in the main submitted to it. When Kaahumanu wished to incase the bones of the deified kings in coffins for interment, Naihe thought he had no boards for the purpose, while his wife stood firmly by Kaahumanu in the measure. But when the *vices* and *crimes* of men which, if unrestrained, he believed implicated civil rulers, required his attention, he stood forth beside Kapiolani as a champion; and when the Gospel at length appeared to gain the control of his heart, he became a firm and steady supporter of good morals and the Christian religion. As a Christian, he was an able coadjutor of the mission. As a magistrate, he was vigilant and decided, and bore " not the sword in vain." He was a very constant attendant at the house of God, and exerted habitually a good influence over the people, and was by them much respected and loved. Mr. Ruggles said of his departure:

" Hawaii feels the loss of Naihe, but we have good reason to think that though the loss to us is great, it is infinite gain to him. His widow, Kapiolani, is still with us. She is a precious sister; a burning and a shining light in the midst of her benighted conntrymen. The chief desire of her soul seems to be the conversion of sinners, and she is always ready for every good word and work."

During this year, the mission printed for the people in their own language about 7,000,000 pages, embracing considerable portions of translations of the Scriptures, both of the Old and New Testaments.

CHAPTER, XVII.

IN the close of the last chapter, the close of Naihe's course, which occurred a year from the visit of the chiefs to his place on their tour round Hawaii, was recorded.

Kaahumanu felt deeply the loss of faithful coadjutors on whom she had leaned for counsel and aid in the maintenance of good order, and in improving the condition of the people. She visited Kapiolani in her affliction, and being refreshed by her society and wisdom, proposed to come, after a little time, and take up her abode with her. But Kapiolani said, " You will never perhaps come back to Hawaii." This proved to be a true conjecture.

The queen closed her visit there and at Kailua, and proceeded to Lahaina, earnestly endeavoring to improve the condition of the people and secure the best interests of the nation. One object which she had particularly in view, was to regulate the system of governmental support so as to secure that equity and economy in the different branches which she herself had conscientiously practised.

Her solicitude was greatly increased at this period by the determination of Kauikeaouli in his youth to unite himself, contrary to the wishes of the queen and the leading chiefs, to one much below his rank, which it was apprehended might disturb the succession; for, according to custom, the children of his sisters, Kinau and Nahienaena, would in that case claim or hold higher rank than those of the king.

Kamanele, the daughter of Gov. Adams, had been proposed as the most suitable, as to age, rank, and education; but he preferred Kalama, the daughter of Naihekukui. Princes, doubtless, have a right to choose their own companions, though if they expect their offspring to enjoy a peaceful possession of the throne, the constitution, established usage, or will of the nation, should be respected. No small agitation existed for a time. His wishes in this matter, however, eventually prevailed.

Hearing that a reinforcement of our mission was expected to

arrive soon, the queen hastened her return to Honolulu, in order to meet and welcome them as coadjutors in promoting the work of God and the good of the nation. She came early to my house and took tea. She was unusually feeble, and unusually affectionate. The interests of the nation pressed upon her ; and she looked with unwonted confidence to the aid supplied by our mission. She kindly called on the other mission families in our quarter of the village the same evening, before she returned to her house. This is remembered as her last visit to the missionaries.

Kinau having been called to Kauai by the illness of Kaikioewa, but wishing to welcome the new missionaries, and fearing she might not be present on their arrival, wrote me a note expressive of her confidence in our helpers, saying :

" Should the kindred, yours and ours, arrive, do you salute them, and say to them, ' Your sister in Jesus, our redeeming Lord, sends you salutations.' "

On the 17th of May, 1832, as the members of the mission were assembling at Honolulu to transact the business of their annual convention, a large reinforcement, opportunely sent forth by the Board, arrived by ship Averick, and were gladly welcomed to the field. This reinforcement consisted of the Rev. Messrs. Wm. Alexander, R. Armstrong, D. B. Lyman, J. S. Emerson, E. Spaulding, C. Forbes, H. R. Hitchcock, L. Lyons, Dr. A. Chapin, and their wives, and E. Rogers, printer. The united bands assembled at the house of Mr. Chamberlain, and lifted up their hearts in songs and thanksgiving and prayer, rejoicing that Providence had so seasonably sent so large an accession to the phalanx of missionary laborers to join in reaping the harvest of Hawaii, and in sowing the good seed in other islands of the Pacific.

The next day they were presented to the king and chiefs. The royal residence was carpeted anew for the occasion with the figured mats of Niihau. About forty painted chairs were arranged for seats on three sides of a parallelogram, the king's seat being in the middle of the shortest side. As the company entered he rose respectfully, and as they were introduced to him successively, he gave each his hand and his *aloha*. We were then seated on the long rows of chairs, a formidable array of missionaries, thirty-two in number, such a corps as probably never before sat together in the court and under the smile of an earthly prince.

The commissions by the American Board, and the protections from the U. S. government which had been given to the missionaries, were presented and explained to the king, and inspected and approved by him. Mr. Armstrong said in behalf of the reinforcement, " The object for which we left our homes and came to these islands is to teach the Word of God, to show the way of life, and to promote to the extent of our ability the true interests of the nation, and the salvation of all who shall come within the reach of our influence." To this the king courteously replied, " I give you our affectionate salutation. You are freely permitted to enter on your work. We were in darkness, unable to help ourselves. You have brought us the means of light and salvation. We rejoice in the blessings thus bestowed on our country."

Kaahumanu, though suffering from weakness and pain, sat in her armed-chair, and received them cordially at her dwelling. She saluted them kindly, expressed her high satisfaction on ac-count of their arrival, then covered her face with her handker-chief and wept tenderly. Doctor Chapin, the physician of the reinforcement, tendered to her the sympathy which he and his associates felt for her in her illness, and expressed the hope that God would restore her as he had those who had been danger-ously ill on board the ship that brought them. He said, " We come to you as your children to seek your good, and to promote the temporal, spiritual, and everlasting good of your people." She replied, " That *one* object is yours and ours. You and we shall be united in the same pursuit."

On the Sabbath following, the new missionaries were delight-ed with the opportunity of meeting with the great congregation for Christian worship, and thought that what they saw and heard that day exceeded the accounts, which, before they embarked, they had read in the journals of the mission. After the invoca-tion and reading of the second Psalm, the native choir, then em-bracing the young king, joined with the missionaries in singing the Christian welcome, a Hawaiian hymn, often used to intro-duce public worship and sometimes the communion service at the Lord's table, and may be thus translated :

" Birthmates, welcome, well beloved,
　　Whom the Lord hath sanctified—
　To him, be our best affections ;
　　For him be this hour employed :
　　　Come and worship
　　Your and our exalted Guide.

" Glorious is His guardian kindness,
　　Who provides a peaceful home ;
　Glorious only is his power,
　　By whose aid thus far we're come :
　　　O adore him,
　　Blessed Leader of our way.

" Jointly let us seek his counsels,
　　And his law together hear ;
　Yield our hearts to his commandments,
　　Steadfast thus, we'll persevere,
　　　Still rejoicing
　　In our Prophet just and true.

" What the Lord hath done to bless us,
　　We'll admire and praise with joy ;

What he suffered for our trespass,
Shall our grateful songs employ :
Thanks we render
For the saving Sacrifice.

" Thus with hope and faith augmented,
We'll draw near to Christ in love ;
And when this sojourn is ended,
We shall meet again above ;
There united,
We shall separate no more."

It was a day of mutual rejoicing. Thousands of the people and nearly all the missionaries in the group were present. Kaahumanu, unable that day to attend, sent in her Christian salutations to the missionaries, assuring them that her heart was there. When this was mentioned, and the state of the field, embracing more than 100,000 souls waiting for and needing the aid of new laborers, was exhibited, many a heart was tenderly touched, and the aspiration called forth that God would shower down the blessings of his grace on the nation, and enable the laborers to thrust in the sickle and reap, and gather fruit unto eternal life.

We exulted not only in the actual success, but also in the anticipated triumphs of the Gospel. The translation of the New Testament had been completed, and most of the books of it had been printed and circulated, and the final portion was nearly through the press.

There was, ere long, however, one source of deep solicitude, which cast a sombre shade over the prospects of the nation and of the mission. It was the illness of Kaahumanu, which continued, and soon became alarming. Dr. Judd, with the co-operation of Dr. Chapin, prescribed such remedies as medical science seemed to require, but without staying the progress of her disease. Her expectation of recovery seemed to leave her without perturbation. She had labored with such assiduity from the time she embraced the Gospel, that the nation, or nearly all, had heard her counsels, and become acquainted with her views, from her own lips, and had been permitted to see something of her Christian example. She had not, subsequently to her conversion, appeared ambitious to seek the distinctions coveted by the world, or to make personal display, or idle demonstrations of superior wealth, rank, or power. Martial honors she counted as of little value. She loved retirement, notwithstanding her care of the nation, and her persevering efforts to promote the good of all classes.

Withdrawing now from Honolulu, she was conveyed to her humble cottage which had some time before been built for her accommodation, in the retired, quiet, and perhaps more salubrious valley of Manoa. She was so feeble as to need to be carried on her bed. Her servants, who loved her, and were attentive to her wishes, raised over her couch an ingenious covering to shield her from the sun, and give her free air, and bore her gently along upon their shoulders, with comfort to her. Halting, and taking a little refreshment at Punahou, a favorite spring two miles from the harbor, and near the entrance to the valley of Manoa, she passed calmly on three miles further, among the mountains, as one retiring from the cares of office, the guardianship of the State, the agitations of Honolulu, the bustle of the world, and the sorrows of a life of almost three score years, five-sixths of which had been spent in heathenism.

As we repeated our visits and attentions to her in this retreat, she expressed her love to Christ, and represented herself as having an unshaken reliance on him as her Friend and Savior. She bore her pains with unmurmuring patience, took with due promptness the medicines prescribed for her by our physicians, and resigning herself to her heavenly Father's guidance, received the cup at his hand, and bore the rod with dignity, and, like Melancthon, manifested no anxiety about recovering or remaining longer on the earth. The chiefs gathered around her with tender concern, and most of the missionaries visited her in these trying hours. Dr. and Mrs. Judd and Dr. and Mrs. Chapin spent some days with her, and felt it to be a privilege to be near her, and to do what it was possible for skill and kindness to do to save her life and comfort her heart. She was tenderly affectionate to friends around her, especially to the missionaries and their wives, and seemed grateful for what was done for her in kindness. She had, especially from the close of the war at Kauai, cherished a high regard for the missionaries, their directors, and patrons. In the warm friendship and steady confidence which she so uniformly manifested towards those with whom she had most acquaintance, and the reasonable gratitude she so often showed to those whose Christian instructions and respectful attentions she had most frequently received, there was a reward of no small value. For several years she had devoted a portion of her time to studying the successive portions of the Scriptures as they were translated, printed, and put into her hands, and in reading the hymns and hearing them sung, which seemed to help her religious affections, her tenderness of heart, her faith, hope, and joy.

During this illness, the printing of the translation of the New Testament was completed for the benefit of thousands of the people. We quickly had a copy of it put into neat red morocco binding, and presented to the queen in her feeble state. She took the sacred prize in her hands, as she lay upon her lowly couch, glanced through it to assure herself of what books it was composed, and looking at it attentively again and again, both inside and out, emphatically pronounced it " maikai," excellent, wrapped it in her handkerchief, laid it on her grateful bosom, gently clasped her hands unusually delicate for a Hawaiian, over it, and placidly looked upward towards its source, as though she had seasonably received the precious boon, the last will and testament of her Savior, as a passport to glory.

Even in the paroxysms of distress, she would attend to the reading of the Scriptures and the exercises of devotion. The consoling words of Christ to his sorrowing disciples were read to her: "In my Father's house are many mansions. I go to prepare a place for you, that where I am there ye may be also." Subsequently, when able to say but little, in allusion probably to this provision, and perhaps to the former custom of Hawaiian rulers setting out to visit some portion of their domain when it was announced to them that a house had been erected for their reception and sojourn there, she said, as we were sitting around her couch, "The way that I am going—the habitation is prepared—send the thoughts thither with joyfulness."

Though the hand of death was on her, she expressed solicitude for me, lest I should be too much fatigued in my impaired state of health; still, as she was engaging in the struggle with the last enemy, she wished me to be near her; and the kind feelings of a Christian mother towards a son, in such circumstances, could hardly have been more obvious and disinterested. After a severe paroxysm, as if the golden bowl were broken, I stooped near her, and said, "Elisabeta, this perhaps is your departure. Stay yourself on Jesus: he is your Physician, your Savior. We wish you to stay with us; that would be our joy; but we think the Lord will soon take you from us." She replied, "I will go to him, and shall be comforted."

Retaining her reason apparently to the last, as she descended into the dark valley, she sent back to us intelligible signals, to show us where her soul was resting and looking for aid. A little before the power of utterance failed, she ejaculated meekly the language of the penitent, confiding soul, giving itself to Christ, as found in two lines of a Hawaiian hymn, which she valued, and which, with their context, indicated the humble, penitent, and believing posture of her soul, as she was about to present herself before him at the threshold of his heavenly temple. The fifth and sixth lines of what I here translate were audible:

> "Now will I go to Jesus,
>   My Lord who pitied me,
>   And at his feet lie prostrate,
>   For there I cannot die;—
> *Lo, here am I, O Jesus,*
>   *Grant me thy gracious smile:—*
> But if, for sin, I perish,
>   Thy law is righteous still."

Perceiving herself to be dying, she called me; and as I took her cold hand in mine, she inquired, "Is this Bingham?" I replied, "It is I." She turned her languid and friendly eyes upon me for the last time, and said, "I am going now." Her brother and sister, Adams and Hoapili-wahine, her husband's children, Kinau, Kauikeaouli, and Nahienaena; her niece, Kekauluohi, several members of the mission families, and others, looked and listened with intense interest as the dignified sufferer manifestly felt the cold waters of Jordan. Giving her our *Aloha*, I bade her " Farewell—go in peace—lean on Jesus, and dwell with him for ever." Breathing more and more faintly for ten or fifteen minutes, this ruling mother of the reformed nation fell asleep, no more to be affected by the applause or reproach of human breath. She died just before the dawn, June 5th, 1832.

As she rested from her labors, her relatives and attached attendants wept tenderly over their much loved friend, whose going in and out among them had now for ever ceased, and united in prayer to the Christian's God ; and when the morning rose, conveyed her body to her house at Honolulu. Many attended, weeping. The nation felt the shock. None, perhaps, felt it more deeply than the missionaries, whose firmest helper had left them in the midst of their struggle, and who were overwhelmed at the thought that there was not a mortal on earth, who could then fill her place as a leader of her people.

At their convention, they immediately adopted the following minute :—

" Whereas God in his mysterious and holy providence has seen fit to visit this nation by a deeply afflictive stroke, which has removed by death the Queen Regent, Elisabeth Kaahumanu, a distinguished reformer of her nation, a kind friend, and benefactress of the missionaries, a firm supporter of their cause, and faithful comforter of the brethren, and of the infant churches in these isles, in whom much confidence has been deservedly placed by the commercial, political, and Christian world, but especially by the people and missionaries of the Sandwich Islands: *Resolved*, That the business of the general meeting be suspended till after her interment, that we may unitedly pay to her the last sad honors due to her remains, and that a funeral sermon be preached at each of the stations, as a tribute to her worth, and as a means of consolation to the afflicted people, and of furthering the cause of piety and national improvement, which was so dear to her heart from her conversion to her dying hour."

Preparations being made, while the lamentations of the people were continued, a great concourse assembled in the afternoon of the 8th of June to attend her funeral. Her remains, carefully enclosed in an appropriate coffin, covered with crimson velvet, and attended by a long procession of the relatives of the deceased, and other chiefs, residents, strangers, missionaries, members of churches, and others of the people, were conveyed from her house to the church that had been built under her auspices, and where she had dropped the tear of gratitude, penitence, and joy, in the presence of the great congregation, when the Gospel of the dying and exalted Savior, whom she loved, had been proclaimed to her and her beloved people. Some desired to hear the strains of martial music, but the king said his mother did not desire such things, and the missionaries preferred to move in silence.

The slow and solemn tolling of the bell struck on the pained ear as it had never done before in the Sandwich Islands. In other bereavements, after the Gospel took effect, we had not only had the care and promise of our heavenly Father, but a queen-mother remaining, whose force, integrity, and kindness, could be relied on still. But words can but feebly express the emotions that struggled in the bosoms of some who counted themselves mourners in these solemn hours; while memory glanced back through her most singular history, and faith followed her course onward, far into the future.

Thousands now thronged around, not to exult in the vanquishment of an oppressor; not to rend the air with deafening heathen wailing to frighten away evil demons; not for the libidinous and revolting customs of their pagan state, on the departure of a sovereign; nor yet with the rage of war to decide who next should hold the reins of government; but to mourn over a great one who, in the midst of her course of usefulness, had fallen in Israel, and to bow in worship before the God of Abraham, while a Christian church disposed of the remains of a mother and sister, in the consoling hope of her putting on the robes of immortality. Assembled in and about the great sanctuary, their attention was directed to the appropriate words of the Apostle to the Gentiles, who had also been born out of due time:

"I have fought a good fight. I have finished my course. I have kept the faith. Henceforth there is laid up for me a crown of righteousness, which the Lord, the righteous Judge, shall give me in that day; and not to me only, but unto all them also that love his appearing."

Though, like Paul, she entered the service at a late period in life, yet few have encountered more opposition, or fought more successful battles with the workers of iniquity, during a lifetime, than she had done in the short space of eight years. She was bold and energetic when the cause of Christ was assailed or needed her support; but humble and retiring when her own honor or emolument merely, was in question. She suffered with meekness a measure of reproach and abuse, which few would have risked for the sake of religion: and when she was required no more to struggle on in this warfare, she laid down her armor; and few have left brighter evidence of exchanging earth for heaven, and worldly rank and distinctions for glory everlasting.

Having lived half a century in heathenism, she at length is led by grace to bend her unaccustomed knees in prayer, and having her stout heathen heart subdued, she enters on a new life, earnestly inquiring, "What shall I render unto the Lord for all his benefits towards me?" Instructed and transformed by the Gospel, she gives the noble answer herself, "I will make his Word the man of my counsel, and will endeavor to induce all under my influence to honor and obey it." Adopting this in spirit, and carrying it out in practice, what an example of the power of the Gospel and grace of God has she given, not only for the permanent benefit of her own nation in the passing and succeeding generations, but worthy of the regard of the rulers and subjects of other countries !

While those who, for twelve years, had labored for her good, were, with other friends, called mournfully to see her remains deposited in the tomb prepared for the royal family, so early after her Christian character had become established, they could rejoice in the evidence that in meekly resigning her high place here on earth, she passed away to paradise, to the possession of an unfading crown, and an everlasting inheritance.

How could the place of such a ruler be supplied ? The eyes of some were turned to heaven for help. The presence and powerful arm of the Lord were made manifest, and were still thankfully acknowledged. The quietude of the nation, notwithstanding the shock, the harmony among the chiefs, the undisturbed state of our young churches, and the spirit of tenderness and inquiry among the worshippers of Jehovah, afforded proof that the Gospel had extensively taken root in the land, and 'the days of KAAHUMANU' will long be referred to as days of progress and prosperity to the nation in respect to schools, morals, government, and religion.

The king was yet too young to sway the sceptre alone, and by the arrangement of his father and queen-mother, and surviving chiefs and himself, his sister, Kinau, the heiress both of Kamahameha and Kaahumanu, was to act as premier or queen-mother, her concurrence being essential to the constitutionality and validity of every regal enactment. She was publicly recognised by the king, who gave her the official title of KAAHUMANU II. But she had not, like Kaahumanu I., the dictatorship or sovereignty which their honored queen-mother had exercised by the will of her husband, the Conqueror, and by her heirship to the domain of Kekaulike, and the concurrence of the young heir to the throne. Kinau became the chief agent, or premier of the realm, and exercised an office similar in responsibility to that of the king, and one which, in some sense, has been permanently established, though its prerogatives were liable to be modified by change of circumstances.

Kinau was a woman of excellence, after her conversion to Christianity. She had been a wife of Liholiho; then, after his death, the wife of Kahalaia, who died shortly after their marriage. She afterwards married Kekuanaoa. In her Christian character, modesty and firmness were remarkably combined. She was dignified and comely, but not handsome. She had a good figure, though she was smaller in stature than most of the chiefs. High in rank and office, she was condescending and courteous. She was affable, but not loquacious. In her dress, manners, habits of temperance and sobriety, and in her dignified attention to courteous and intelligent strangers, she was exemplary. Though above her husband by birth and station, by education and piety, yet in the love and deference which she uniformly manifested towards him, the complacency which she seemed to feel in him, and the satisfaction which his honorable and gentlemanly conduct gave her, she appeared interesting and amiable. Although she was young for so important a station, she possessed an uncommon share of the confidence of the king and the other chiefs, and she entered on the duties of her office at a period when experience, wisdom, and tact, were demanded, and with the feeling, we believe, that her utmost skill and energy would be required to fill her place, and that her success depended on the blessing of the Lord, and the prevalence of the principles of his Gospel. In a public address to the people she declared her intention to pursue the policy and carry out the measures of Kaahumanu; and the king called on the nation to acknowledge her authority.

It was feared that the lovers of iniquity to be found among aliens and many thousands of the native population, not yet subdued by the Word and Spirit of God, would take occasion to indulge themselves the more freely under the new government. It was, therefore, the more needful that the example of every friend of truth and righteousness in those dominions should lend the support of a healthful influence to the cause of improvement.

At that period, the missionaries declared it to be their main business to inculcate that Divine Word which could not be softened down to meet the wishes of any class of men or women, high or low, and at the same time, unitedly resolved ' to encourage improvements in agriculture and manufactures; habits of industry in the nation; neatness in the habitations and dress of the inhabitants; punctuality in all engagements, especially in the payment of debts; justice and temperance in rulers in the execution of law; and loyalty, order, and peace, among their subjects, in all the relations and duties of life; and also to recommend to the people daily to commit to memory each a verse of Holy Scripture, as the means of enlightening and purifying their souls.'

About the close of Kaahumanu's public labors, and the entrance of Kinau upon the duties of her office, the attention of the American Board and of the American Christian public was much attracted to the Washington Islands—a division of the cluster usually denominated the Marquesas. Missionaries were sent to the Sandwich Islands with the expectation that if the mission there approved of it, they would be established on the Washington Islands. The mission took up the subject with earnestness, made diligent inquiry as to the field, and resolved to consult freely with their fellow-laborers in the South Seas, and to survey the Washington Islands to see what we could do for them.

For this service a deputation was sent forth in the summer of

1832, consisting of Messrs. Whitney, Tinker, and Alexander, assisted by Kaiu, a native convert, and Kuke, a convert and teacher from Huahine. They proceeded to the Society and Georgian Islands, held several interesting consultations with the missionaries of that group, then visited the Washington group, and, for a few days, looked at the field with care and prayerfulness. They returned in safety, and notwithstanding the revolting manners, gross idolatries, and forbidding aspect of the Washington Islands, reported in favor of attempting to supply them with the Gospel, provided the missionaries at the Society Islands should not, in the course of a few months, find occasion to object, or the London Missionary Society find the means of supplying that field with the Word of life.

During the absence of Mr. Whitney from Kauai, there were striking indications of the revival spirit among his flock. A little before his departure, he preached to them a sermon on the life and death of Kaahumanu, and then a parting sermon, and in company with Kaiu, one of the principal members of his church, left them in an interesting state in the care of Mr. Gulick, his associate, who shortly after speaks of the outpouring of God's Spirit there.

Who can doubt that the consistent manifestation of Christian solicitude for distant tribes is adapted to awaken attention to the value of the Gospel and the salvation of the soul among those who have been already evangelized? or that any church which endeavors duly to water, shall itself also be watered?

I hastened to assist Mr. G. in the important duty of pointing sinners to the Lamb of God, and sailed from Honolulu with two native assistants, Paulo Kanoa and Daniel Oleloa, in a vessel of twenty tons, which we imagined to be about the size of the ships used by the fishermen of Galilee, on the sea of Tiberias. We came into Waimea roads by moonlight. Three men from the village conveyed me in a canoe from the vessel to the shore. One swell after another lifted and urged us shoreward. Being near the beach the stern was turned towards it, to give me a better chance to land with dry clothing. "There comes a large sea," cried one; "look out." I sprang and stood up on the top of the canoe, as it was borne forward. The wave curled nobly, and its white crest swept foamingly over the whole length of the canoe, drenching the men and wetting me to the knees as it tossed us on the shore. The wave retiring, left the canoe heavy with water on the sand beach.

Saluted by the repeated *aloha* of the friendly natives, I was conducted to the missionary's residence, about a quarter of a mile from the beach, in a line parallel with which stood the neat, new houses of Mr. Gulick, Mr. Whitney, and Gov. Kaikioewa.

The governor's little palace, or cottage, stood on elevated ground, overlooking the narrow, level, cultivated valley of Waimea, in which the cocoa-nut trees growing near lifted their evergreen and palmy tops to its sills or threshold. It was somewhat showy, being of one story, finished and painted white, having good windows, a neat and spacious verandah in front, supported by shapely pillars, and dormer windows in the attic. In front of the line of these three dwellings, which ornament the village and evince an advance towards civilization, stood their spacious church, frequented by throngs of worshippers.

Early in the morning the people began to come to the house of Mr. Gulick. The first I met was an old man, who was an adult in the days of Cook's first visit, half a century before, and till recently regardless of his salvation. He said, giving me his hand and his *aloha*, "God has brought us together." "Yes, through his goodness we meet; let us give our hearts to him." A silent tear stole down his aged cheek, and not his alone. An elderly woman, almost blind, who had professed her faith in Christ, grasping my hand in both of hers, expressed her gratitude that she had before seen me, and was again allowed to meet me, and as she spoke of God's loving kindness, her obscured eyes filled with tears. Gentle tears rolled down the faces of others who stood by, while some sat on the ground in silence, with drooping heads, the reverse of the levity so common among the people. The forwardness and apparent readiness of these two aged persons to devote the evening of life to the Savior, led to the reflection that eleventh hour laborers are more likely to be found among the recently idolatrous Hawaiians than where Christian light has long shined, been more intense, and more habitually resisted. Had the eleventh hour laborers been called upon every hour of the day, and every hour had resisted till the eleventh, they might then have been passed by as hopeless; or they might as easily have resisted the last as any former call. But as the light burst in upon the Hawaiian race, the call was simultaneously given to all classes, of every age; and a very large proportion of the hopeful converts there have been among the aged and the middle aged.

Mr. G. and myself spent much of our time in personal conversation with those who came to us for that purpose, instructing them, putting to them unexpected questions, and hearing their answers, or attending to their spontaneous statements and inquiries. We endeavored to form a distinct judgment of the case of each, giving to each direct advice, a passage of Scripture, or a tract, to show them their own character and condition, and the adaptedness of Christ to meet their necessities, and his readiness to save the penitent and believing.

Among many who came on the first day of my visit, was an old warrior, formerly of Oahu, an officer of the government in 1792, mentioned by Capt. Vancouver in the narrative of his transactions with the people there. I had met him before on the back part of Kauai, while in his unawakened heathen state, and was glad to hear him now tremblingly inquire.in an humble and teachable posture, " What must I do ?" He took a humble seat at my feet and said, " I am a great sinner." As I addressed him, he looked at me with earnestness, his heart being awake and his hearing impaired. On being asked why he condemned himself as a great sinner, he said, " I have worshipped images, and served false gods. I am an idolator. I am a man-slayer, too. Some of the people of Oahu, when Kehehili was king, killed some men of Britain [Hergest and Gooch], at Waimea. Vancouver came to Waikiki and demanded the murderers. The king sent me to take them and deliver them up. I searched for them ; but they were gone ; I could not find them. I seized three other men and gave them up to Vancouver in return for the Englishmen that had been killed. He gave me a loaded pistol to shoot them ; and I shot them. I am a murderer—a great sinner. When Brown came to Waikiki, I showed him the harbor of Honolulu, not before known to foreigners. He showed me dollars, and said, ' These are the best *waiwai* (treasures or goods) of my country.' I wanted them, and stole three forties. I was seized, put in irons, and the dollars were taken back. I am a thief."

How clearly did conscience point out the crimes of his heathen state, idolatry, shedding blood, deception, coveting, and taking what belonged to others ! The violent sacrifice of human beings to the Hawaiian deities, had been the prominent feature of their religion, which had stifled conscience and encouraged manslaughter and murder. Extremely base, barbarous, and criminal as was the conduct of this high office-bearer of a heathen monarch, it was no more than what was customary among priests and chiefs in those days of darkness and cruelty. Dreadful and pitiable as was that execution of pretended murderers to satisfy justice, how much more dreadful would have been the bombardment and destruction of the villages and inhabitants of Waikiki and Honolulu, for the offences of the Waimea murderers ! And if this execution, sanctioned by Vancouver and the government, now stung the heart of the old warrior on getting a glimpse of Gospel light, what will the concentrated light of eternity do to the despisers of inspired truth who have slaughtered villages or shed the blood of nations, with no greater regard to justice or the authority of God than governed this savage and his degraded countrymen ?

And what now could be said to this awakened heathen different from what should be said to every violator of divine law as written by the finger of God on the heart, or on tables of stone, " Fly to Christ, who died for sinners, even the chief ; repent, and trust in him for pardon and eternal life."

Towards evening, the people gathered, by hundreds, to the church, to pray and hear the Gospel, and I presented that portion of it which records the death of Christ and the two malefactors, showing the design of his death, the penitence and wisdom of the one, and the hardness and folly of the other, who died with him, and urging them to believe on the crucified Savior. A general solemnity, stillness, and attention prevailed. The next day, many came to converse. I admitted ten to the study to begin with, called their attention to the invitation of Christ, "Come unto me all ye that labor and are heavy laden, and I will give you rest," bowed with them before the mercy seat, and conversed carefully with each. Several wept. From the eyes of one woman large tear-drops fell freely and silently, upon her native robe, and a large man, wiping tears from his face, sobbed like a little child in its sorrows. In some, there appeared an indistinctness, and in others a good degree of clearness of vision in respect to their sins, the mediation of Christ, the method of justification by faith, and the insufficiency of their own works to save them. More than half appeared to be under the influence of the Spirit of God, and some to be trusting in Christ.

As the sun declined it was delightful again to meet a concourse of the people, who seemed, so spontaneously, to go up to their temple to pray and hear, at the hour of the evening sacrifice;—a most rational and happy method of spending the hour before sunset, which myriads devote to frivolous amusement.

The next day, walking out to see some of the people, at their homes, I called at the neat white cottage of Deborah, which had about it a few shrubs and doves; but found her at the house of Haupu, whom she called her father. In, and about his habitation, which was above the ordinary size, and, according to the new fashion, consisted of three apartments, were twenty or more persons, unusually still for such a number of natives. An elderly woman saluted me, and in answer to inquiries about her spiritual state, said she had given her heart, soul, and body, to Jesus, sat down by the feet of Deborah, and engaged quietly in conversation with her. People from neighboring houses, and some from a distance, dropped in, one after another, till sixty, then eighty, and even a hundred were assembled, among whom were four old warriors, including the man who had confessed himself an idolator, thief, and murderer, and one, who, since the establishment of the mission, had been guilty of drunkenness and manslaughter, in which his own wife was the victim of his heathen violence. As they seemed ready to hear, I addressed them from the words of the Prophet,—"It is time to seek the Lord, till he come and rain righteousness upon you," urging them to seek him at once, to seek earnestly, and seek *continually*, till he should pour on them his spirit and his free salvation. Several were in tears. One of the natives gave a short, kind, and pertinent exhortation. After a hymn, Paul Kanoa offered a prayer. Native Christians engage in prayer with great propriety, both as to matter and manner, but rarely, or never, by a committed form. They often use Scripture phraseology, not in a stereotype order, but adapt their thanksgivings, confessions, and petitions to the circumstances in which they are placed, uttering them in a natural, slow, distinct, and reverential manner. A part of Kanoa's prayer, here, translated, may serve as a specimen. " O Jehovah, the God of Abraham, Isaac, and Jacob, thou art the God of the living and not of the dead. The living live by thee. We have assembled in thy presence to praise thee, and to pray unto thee, because we are burdened with sin and are distressed. O, rain upon us now ; and let the power of the Highest overshadow us. The hearts of the chiefs and the people are in thy hand, and thou canst turn them. Bless the missionaries, who have sowed the good seed here, which has produced, some an hundred fold, some sixty, and some ten. Bless those who have gone to carry the Word of God to Nuuhiva [Marquesas], and to other parts of the world."

On coming to Mr. W.'s house, we found assembled and assembling there, about 150, who had come to converse. One woman seemed agitated, and was trembling. I spoke to the company the Word of God, led them to the throne of grace, and conversed with several who had come seven or eight miles, and who appeared serious and earnest.

On the Sabbath, the church, 155 feet in length, and 48 in breadth, was filled at half-past nine o'clock, A.M. About 2,000, or one-fifth of the inhabitants of the island, were present. After the sermon, on the words quoted by Christ, from Isa., and applied to himself,—" The Spirit of the Lord is upon me, because he hath anointed me to preach the Gospel to the poor," &c., about three hundred stood up to signify that they had resolved to give themselves up to Christ, to follow him, renouncing their sins. They had had line upon line, from the missionaries—They had had the Gospel preached to them from time to time—Mr. Whitney had labored there twelve years, and Messrs. Ruggles and Gulick several. They had been favored with evangelical tracts, and portions of the Old Testament Scriptures, and the entire New Testament. Great pains had been taken to guard them from mistake and self-deception, and the Spirit of God was obviously among them. Still, the doubt that hung over their case was a great check to the joy which would naturally arise from such an exhibition of readiness to serve the Lord.

The governor and his wife were absent. Kaahumanu was dead. The king was not over-strenuous in regard to Christianity ; but here were the same demonstrations of the power of truth and of the Spirit of God, as had been exhibited at Honolulu, Lahaina, Kailua, Kaawaloa, and Hilo, in the days of Kaahumanu. Among 300 who showed themselves, on this occasion, one man appeared to be seized with convulsions, which I regarded as proving nothing for or against the genuineness of the work. Mr. Gulick noticed, at other times, cases of bodily agitation, among the people, such as trembling, falling down, and loud weeping, which he supposed to be produced by the Spirit of God. Of this work, he says :—

" Our public assemblies, however, have been still and solemn, and remarkably attentive to the messages which were delivered. Persons from almost every part of the island, have been brought to a sense of their lost condition, and are now rejoicing in hope. From the pagan priest, down to the humble devotee of superstition, all classes, and every age, except the very young, have felt, as we are fully persuaded, the sacred influences of the Holy Spirit. There was a depth and pungency in their convictions which I had never before witnessed at the islands, except in a few cases. A vast majority of the cases of conviction are found at this station and one other place, where nearly all the missionary labor has been bestowed."

I returned to Oahu, in the king's brig, commanded and manned by natives, who made an unusual passage from Koloa to Honolulu roads, in forty hours, without tacking ship, or altering any principal sail. A Hawaiian mother and her little daughter were passengers. Having heard that one of the four sons of that mother, at Honolulu, a lad of fourteen or fifteen years of age, had, during her absence, been involved in guilt or calamity, through the influence of rum on a sailor, I asked her if she had heard the tidings from Honolulu. "No," she said, "what tidings?" "That your son, Henry, has killed a foreigner with a club." "Oh! I am in heaviness!" she exclaimed. "How could he do such an evil deed? I charged my sons to do right, and left them, to visit a sick relative; and that child has done this evil deed and brought us into straits. I am distressed: must he not die?" "That is the law of the king, concerning murder; but if the foreigner was chiefly in fault, or if your son did not intend to kill, perhaps he will escape." "That is the law of the king," she repeated with a deep sigh. As we came into the roads, the elder brothers came on board, kissed their mother, and said, "A foreign sailor, having drunk rum, came into the house and abused Henry. Henry expostulated with him and led him out. He was struck by him with a cane, and returned blow for blow, with a hard wood stick. They separated. Henry returned to the house. The sailor went to the tavern, and died there, the same night, from a blow on the temple." The youth, the son of a foreigner, was sentenced for manslaughter, for a limited time, to Kaahoolawe—a sort of state's prison.

Trying as this case was to the mother and the brothers, the signs of distress and interest in the case were not more unequivocal than I supposed I had seen in many others, during my visit at Kauai, in reference to their own guilt, and the means of rescue from final ruin.

In the course of the same year—the first after the death of Kaahumanu, there were also very encouraging appearances among the people of Maui. The missionaries at Lahaina said, "We do, even here, see the footsteps of our Lord, and witness indubitable evidence that the Holy Spirit is at work on the hearts and consciences of men." Their monthly concert was attended by about 800 persons. They had a Bible class of 250 members— and thirty-four classes of men of forty each, and nearly the same numoer of women, studying a verse a day of the Scriptures. Many called to see the missionaries, and spoke of their attach- ment to the truth, their love to the Savior, their desire to associate with his people, and with them to sit down at his table, to com- memorate his death. Some were examined and admitted to church ordinances. " Were we to admit all the applicants," said Messrs. Richards, Spaulding, and Chapin, " nearly all the adult population would soon be in the church."

A new station was this year taken at Wailuku, East Maui, of which Mr. J. S. Green, removing from Hilo, where he had labored about a year, took charge, with the fairest prospects of success among a large population.

At this interesting period, the U. S. frigate Potomac, Com. Downs, arrived from (Qualla Battoo)—a ship that ploughed the ocean at an expense equal to that of all the operations of the American Board, among all the nations to whom they were offer- ing the Gospel. The several classes at the islands looked with interest to see what advantage could be gained to their cause by this visit, and especially to see whether the intelligent and liberal commander would favor the puritanism of the missionaries, and the measures of the government to restrain iniquity, or the looser maxims of those who thought the mission required too strict a regard to temperance, chastity, and the Sabbath, and maintained that the measures of the government, in respect to gambling, Sabbath-desecration, Romanism, and the traffic in intoxicating liquors, were too rigorous.

The state of the nation, the efficiency of Kinau and Gov. Adams, their earnest desire to know how to secure the best inte- rests of the nation, their teachableness and the inexperience of the king, rendered it important that prudent counsels, such as should tend to consolidate the government on a basis firm and safe, and provide for the interests of the current and succeeding genera- tions, should prevail.

The divine will being the foundation of all human authority, it was not difficult to infer, nor unsafe to teach, that no lawgiver, legislator, or magistrate, had a right to contravene the will of Heaven by requiring or licensing that which God forbids in his Word. Some, both residents and visitors, supposed the strict- ness of the missionaries and the Christian chiefs might be made a plea or occasion for withdrawing the young king from their influence, and for encouraging him to take a looser view of duty or public responsibility than the Bible authorizes, and more con- genial with their own. The maxims of men, the policy of human governments, and the examples of civilized statesmen, were, by some, deemed a guide more suitable for Hawaiian rulers than the principles of the Bible.

The commander of the Potomac, in his intercourse with the missionaries, was courteous, and, in some important points, coin- cided with their views as to the duty of the rulers. He urged the importance of securing the rights of property, encouraging agriculture, industry, justice, and punctuality in the fulfilment of all business contracts. He did not, however, think it well for the rulers to shut out rum and Romanism from their country. Learning that efforts had been made to stop the traffic in distilled liquors, and that Romish priests had been excluded, and some of their followers put to hard labor, and treated with severity, he advised a more liberal course. He said the king could expel or exclude the priests of Rome, if he chose to do so, but that Roman Catholic countries might object to it, and stated to him "that all civilized nations were in favor of free toleration." He was asked if he meant to be understood to include Italy, Spain, and Portugal, as countries in favor of full toleration. This inquiry was construed, by some, as an apology for Hawaiian intolerance. The Commodore then asked the king why he punished his subjects for their opinions. He replied, "that his subjects were not punished for their *opinions*, but for image-worship, and other offences distinct from mere opinions."

While the Potomac was at that port, a grog-shop keeper, who went from the same country and in the same vessel with the pioneers of the mission, and set up his shop in the same village where they established presses, schools, and churches, hoisted over it the American flag and pennant, which he thus dishonored. He entertained many of the frigate's crew while on liberty, furnishing them the means of intoxication. Finding himself supported in it by high influence on ship and shore, he boasted that during the ship's visit he had cleared $900. It was dangerous to pass his door at the time, and Gov. Adams had occasion to accommodate some of his customers, from time to time, with iron handcuffs, but was requested not to punish the landlord, who had "entertained the frigate's men so kindly."

To men who deemed grog-shops "a necessary evil," notwithstanding the wish of the rulers to prevent the dreaded consequences, it was of small account how much cost and trouble they made the government, how annoying and corrupting the example of their customers must be to the villagers, or how shameful a demonstration they gave the people of what civilization, without Christian principle, could produce.

Rev. Mr. Grier, the chaplain, Lieut. Ingersol, Mr. Warriner, the teacher of mathematics, Mr. De Selden, and others, were very friendly to the missionaries. The liberal sum of $200 was, with the concurrence of the commander, contributed on board the frigate to aid the church and congregation at Honolulu in procuring a church bell. To this the congregation added about as much more to complete the purchase money for a bell of 550lbs, and erect a small tower, frame, and wheel, for its suspension. The bell, then in that market, soon reported itself to the satisfaction of many, and has since summoned many thousands to go up to the house of God with joyfulness and thanksgiving.

About that time, the king and chiefs became acquainted with a proposed plan for taking·possession of their country, by some who loved the *soil* more than its owners. A pamphlet reached them, published in London, addressed to a NOBLE LORD, by a Mr. James, a disappointed adventurer, who had seen Botany Bay, and visited the Sandwich Islands, and who considered it "*mortifying to an Englishman to walk upon the soil, enriched by the blood of Cook, and not feel that it was his own.*" He boldly recommended to the British government "the occupancy of the Sandwich Islands on 'THE PLAN OF A PROPRIETARY GOVERNMENT,' either colonizing them, or granting them to a joint-stock company, to be sold for the benefit of the company, and for the support of a foreign governor." Awkwardly attempting a defence of what the natives called his "covetous design," he shamelessly averred "that the chiefs were semi-barbarian, and very oppressive; that neither the government, laws, letters, nor religion there ought to be regarded as an objection to the measure; that the people earnestly desired to be taken out from under the oppression of the chiefs and missionaries; that all the foreign residents, American and English, desired to have a British governor, who would promote the settlement of the country, and wished him to make their wishes known as soon as he should arrive in London—*all to a man*, except the missionaries, who desired no change, but to have the islands all to themselves; and that under the proposed arrangement, the islands might be made another West Indies for the extensive and lucrative production of sugar, cotton, coffee, tobacco, rum, &c."

To him who supposed the British government, the residents, and the expected colonists, to be as corrupt as himself, these reasons, specious and puerile as they were, seemed to warrant a great nation to abolish the native government, and dispossess, enslave, or drive into the sea, the aborigines. It is well for all parties that the influence of American missionaries, ever friendly to the continued independence of that nation, stood in the way of such aggression, though they had neither sword, nor spear, nor cannon, to resist it.

"Horton James" was not appointed Prefect or Governor of the Hawaiian Islands. The British government was rich enough without making those islands another Naboth's vineyard, and too honorable to carry out this Haman-like plan, for seizing the possessions of a feeble, friendly, confiding people.

Whatever some other power might be disposed to do, and whatever different influence a different class of missionaries might exert, in reference to the subjugation of the country, none can justly blame the rulers for being on their guard against alienating their soil, or allowing it to pass into the hands of those who hated their sovereignty, or countenancing a class of religious teachers who, it was feared, would unite with those who desired that in their place some other power might rule.

CHAPTER XVIII.

THIRTEENTH YEAR OF THE MISSION AND FIRST OF KAUIKEAOULI,
OR KAMEHAMEHA III.—1833.

Kaomi's Faction—Kauikeaouli asserts his majority and supremacy—Premiership of Kinau—Missionary efforts for sea-faring men—School at Oahu for the children of Foreigners—Seamen's Chaplaincy at Honolulu—Fifth Reinforcement of the Mission—Visit of the ship of war Challenger, Captain Seymour.

THE elements of confusion were still obviously at work, and heart-burnings but too manifest. There were numbers possessing influence, who yet loved the indulgences and follies of heathenism, and regarded the restraints of Christianity as irksome. Several young men, belonging to a class attached to the king, and distinguished from the rest of their countrymen by the term *Hulumanu* (Feather or Bird-feather), were among the advocates of a system of loose morals and vile sports. Among these, Paki, Namauu, and Kaomi, were, for a time, conspicuous. The latter was a native born son of a naturalized Tahitian, by a Hawaiian mother, and possessed considerable shrewdness. He early manifested a desire to be instructed, and for a time made good progress—became a teacher and exhorter of his countrymen, and, after four or five years, desired baptism. But this was not granted. Then, getting entangled in love affairs, he denied the authority of God's Word, attached himself to the irreligious, and declared that he had tried religion, and found there was nothing in it, and would now try anew the pleasures of the world. He acquired such an influence over the *Hulumanu*, and with the king, as to become his counsellor, and obtained the somewhat ambiguous title of *Keliikui* (engrafted king).

The king wished Kinau to purchase for him a ship. Having consulted her ablest counsellors, and believing it to be unwise just then to augment the public debt, she respectfully declined, but without fully satisfying the king.

Kaomi and his party coinciding with the libertinism of influential foreigners, entered boldly on a course, which gave some occasion for alarm lest the peace of the nation should be broken, and the interests if not the lives of Kinau and her friends put at hazard. Revelry and the old games were encouraged, under the auspices of Kaomi.

Gov. Adams, then at Hawaii, and Hoapili, the king's stepfather, the substantial governor of Maui, at Lahaina, being apprised of the state of things, both repaired to Honolulu, to do what they could to maintain the *pono*—the right policy—and secure the

nation from confusion and disaster.   Hoapili arriving first, and
studying to manage so as not to give offence, said to the young
king, "Let us return together to Maui, and those who have misled you, stay here."   He declined.

About the middle of March, 1833, the king proposed to the
chiefs his "wish to take into his possession the lands for which
his father toiled, the power of life and death, and the undivided
sovereignty."   This would have required a degree of wisdom and
weight of character which rarely fall to the lot of a youth of seventeen or eighteen.   The high chiefs, supposing (perhaps without sufficient reason) that it was his design to set aside Kinau,
to abrogate the existing laws, and to promote the plebeian Kaomi, or Liliha, to the second rank in the kingdom, demurred.
There was no small agitation.   Rum-drinking and licentiousness
increased.   But Providence still watched over the nation and over
the cause of moral improvement.   The king summoned the chiefs
and people to assemble to hear his pleasure.   A slight rumor was
heard, that war was at hand.   At the time for the meeting, many
of the praying women assembled in their usual place, and had a
solemn and tender season ; asking God's providential care over
the interests of the nation.   At that hour, some expected and
others feared that Kinau would not only be degraded by the king,
but exposed to abuse and violence from Kaomi's party.   In the
gathering of the great assembly, in the open air, Kinau, with dignified step, walked through the crowd, and came up to her
brother, and saluting him, uttered her noble motto, " *We cannot
war with the Word of God between us !*"

He announced his majority, asserted his claim to the sovereignty,
and lifted his hand to designate the next highest officer, while the
three candidates for it were around him—a moment of deep interest to many : and happy was it for him, and for the nation, that,
as he brought it down, he could not, as he said afterwards, but
prefer the daughter of Kamehameha, his father ; and confirmed
Kinau as *Premier*.

She made a conciliatory address, modest, firm, and kind, assuring the people that she understood her position, and was ready
for the duties of her office.   No governmental measure, she supposed, could be strictly constitutional, without her concurrence or
assent.   This was, at length, conceded, though an attempt was
made to evade it for a time.   On the following day, I sought and
obtained an interview with his young majesty, and assured him
that my love for him was not exhausted, and that while it was
possible, it was my intention to persevere in seeking his best good,
and urged him to seek the divine guidance and favor.   The next
day, he attended church, and on the morrow, applied for two hundred copies of the last number of the New Testament, in their
language, for his *Hulumanu* to read.   Believing that exercise to
be good employment for his " bird feathers," we readily furnished
the required copies, and encouraged their daily use.

The agitation was unfriendly to the progress of schools and attention to the one thing needful. Restraints were withdrawn from the manufacture, sale, and use of intoxicating liquors. Kinau, Adams, Kaikioewa, and Hoapili, however, conscientiously refused to grant licenses. Kaomi recommended the opposite policy, and a large class of foreigners favored it. Two among them, self-esteemed wise, whose position gave them undue influence, maintained that rum-selling houses, which they allowed to be a nuisance, were a *necessary evil*, because eating-houses were necessary in such a place, and nobody could get a living by selling victuals alone. The king, too, supposed, like more enlightened princes, that his revenues might be augmented by encouraging the traffic, and by granting licenses.

To take a share in the spoils and honors, American shippers sent by the Rasselas and otherwise, quantities of intoxicating liquors, to the islands, to exchange for money and the products of the country, with natives and foreigners who were reckless enough to buy ; among whom were some of the king's agents. Thus a traffic that supplied the means of intoxication to natives, residents, and transient seamen, was claimed to be *necessary*, not for the well-being of the Hawaiian public, but for the *support* of drunkard-makers and drunkard-killers, though it might hinder the success of expensive voyages and the prosperity of the country, ruin families, shipwreck the fortunes, and sacrifice the reputation and lives of the customers, a " support " like that of a bag of specie grasped by a drowning man.

Certain places, for a time, appeared to be consecrated to Hawaiian saturnalia and exempt from the action of the laws of order which were still applicable to the largest portion of the islands, and giving the appearance of a petty state within a state. Sabbath riding, for amusement, was attempted at Honolulu, but could not be made popular, and never has been, since Adams seriously threatened to confiscate the horses of those who would persevere in thus desecrating the Sabbath.

The missionaries had occasion for solicitude, but not for despondency. The means that had a thousand times been tested successfully, in the work of reform, were still available. They applied themselves afresh to the work of preaching and teaching, translating and publishing the Scriptures, preparing and putting to use such works as were needful for the discipline of the native mind, and for the better understanding of the doctrines of the Bible; and about a hundred of the best native teachers were called from their schools and put under instruction. Our work continued much as before, though for a time, somewhat more difficult than it might have appeared to be, had not the sober chiefs felt constrained to say, as they did with impressive emphasis, " *Kaahumanu is dead.*"

But as there had been no *union of Church and State*, there was no disruption or change of relation when the king attempted the exercise of supreme power, in his own person alone, and to pursue a policy at variance with that of Kaahumanu. Kinau proclaimed a fast, as Esther once did, and as Kaahumanu had also done.

In all ages, the name of the Lord has been a strong tower to his people. To him they are accustomed to look for the continued existence and prosperity of his church. And to him his people there then looked for the success of the struggle of light and love against the powers of darkness and malevolence, though the contest appeared to lie long in even balance.

The six hundred members of the church, in different parts of the islands, for the most part, stood their ground firmly. Samuel J. Mills, and the young princess, and a few others, were drawn into the snare of the devil, and occasioned disappointment and grief. But during the year after Kaomi's commotion, there were one hundred and twenty-four additions to the churches—a number greater than the average annual additions, during the seven years of Kaahumanu's membership. With regard to the supposed influence of her authority, wish, or example, it has been extravagantly said, "that the will of the chiefs was the will of the populace," and "that thousands joined the ranks of Christians from unworthy motives, carried along with the current." Scarcely more than half a thousand were admitted to the churches at the Sandwich Islands during the Christian life of the queen regent, though tens of thousands availed themselves of schools and other means of improvement. During this commotion 20,000 were reported as readers in the schools. At Honolulu, where, in the excitement, it was said by a boastful foreigner, that not forty would be found at church, there were still 2,000 in the congregation, about half of whom were studying the daily verse of Scripture.

The island of Oahu suffered much, for a time ; the other islands less.

Never, perhaps, has the king had a better demonstration that the new religion had struck deep root in Hawaiian soil, than at the time when the influence of the infidel Kaomi, and his coadjutors, was applied to check or destroy it ; and his young majesty was constrained to say openly, " The kingdom of God is strong."

Most obviously was the arm of the Lord revealed for the maintenance of his cause, as it had often been from the beginning. Whatever " current " may be supposed to have been created in favor of Christianity by the united influence of the Gospel and Kaahumanu and her coadjutors, during her administration, there were every year strong counter influences acting against Kaahumanu and the Gospel, and in conformity with the corruption of human nature ; influences such as were manifest in 1826 in the sympathy with Lieut. Percival, and in 1827, with Captains Buckle and Clark, and were more fully demonstated in 1828 and 1829, by Boki and his faction, and in 1830 and 1831 by the same faction in the name of Liliha. The same kind of counter influ-

ence was employed in 1832 and 1833 by Kaomi and the Hulumanu, and the whole host of the friends of the traffic in intoxicating drinks.

Under Kaomi, who was encouraged by high authority, his party
were emboldened to take a course which they acknowledged to
be wrong. Hawaiian infidels set a singular example to the whole
fraternity, when, as we expostulated with them, they admitted
that they chose the *wrong* rather than the *right*. But the church
was still shielded. In the progress of religion at the islands for
twenty-six years, though much personal influence has been exerted favorably by high chiefs and the Queen Regent, it has so
happened that no earthly king has been the head or even a member of the Hawaiian church. But the King of kings has been its
constant Helper : He alone was worthy of our trust in respect to
the safety of the church and the prosperity of his cause.*

In all the struggles of the mission, a regard to the purity,
security, prosperity, and best interests of foreign residents and
seafaring men was habitually cherished by the missionaries. The
claims of our own countrymen are sometimes urged from considerations of patriotism and in opposition to the claims of foreign
missions, without a due regard, perhaps, to the migratory habits of
the seamen and foreign traders (connected with the commerce and
navy of the United States), equal in numbers to the whole population of the Sandwich Islands. At almost every foreign missionary station there is opportunity afforded for doing good to the
citizens of the country from which the mission emanated, indirectly, by showing the benevolent nature and beneficial influence
of the Christian religion, and by direct efforts to bring them to a
saving acquaintance with its life-giving truths. The argument
from patriotism in favor of Home Missions might, in various
ways, be applied to Foreign.

The moral and religious interests of the foreign residents at
the Sandwich Islands, and of the masters, officers, and sailors,
chiefly American, who, from year to year, have visited those
distant shores since 1819, have received a share of the sympathy,
labor, and care of the foreign missionaries there, from the very
commencement of their work. This indeed seemed reasonable
and necessary in order to the completeness of the effect contemplated. If the natives are expected to dwell in peace and
purity, under the Gospel's precious vine, those who mingle with
them should be so instructed and impressed by its members and
professors, and their Divine Director, as not wantonly to " waste
it like the wild boar out of the desert." All classes who mingle

---

* The sentiment of Luther, the reformer on this point, though expressed in his
bold, rough phraseology, was suited to strengthen the feeble: " We tell our Lord
God plainly, if he will have his church, then he must look how to maintain and
defend it, for we can neither uphold nor protect it. And well for us that it is so.
For if we could or were able to defend it, we should be the proudest asses under
heaven. Who is the church's Protector that hath promised to be with her to the end.
and the gates of hell shall not prevail against her ? Kings ? Deists ? Parliaments
Lawyers ? Marry no such cattle."

in the business of life, or whose influence is mutual, should be simultaneously instructed in the same religion that is necessary for all. Thus the teaching and converting of the heathen nations may have a powerful influence in purifying, converting, and perfecting our own countrymen. So the adults and children of heathen countries must both be instructed in the Gospel, or neither will be likely to be extensively and savingly reclaimed.

During a period when the whole Hawaiian nation seemed especially to claim the utmost efforts of every member of our mission and many more, Mr. Clark, by the special direction of the American Board and the wish of the mission, and of some of the foreign residents, devoted a portion of his time, studies, and public labors, to the department which might properly belong to the Seaman's Friend Society, until they were, agreeably with our wishes, induced to send forth a chaplain to those islands. Messrs. Spaulding, Chamberlain, Johnstone, and others, also aided in that cause.

As a specimen of the efforts of our mission in that department, it may be stated that during two years of Mr. Clark's labors, he usually preached once a week in English, and by the aid of the American Bible Society, and the American Tract Society, distributed eighty-five Bibles, and thirty-six Testaments, and thirty or forty thousand pages of tracts. Mr. Chamberlain, during the same period, and from the same sources, distributed to 420 foreigners, chiefly sailors, 310 Bibles, and 112 Testaments, and 10,000 pages of tracts.

Among those who availed themselves of the labors and influence of foreign missionaries, there were happy instances of reformation and hopeful conversion. Several have united with the churches there. Masters and officers of vessels, in several instances, suppose themselves to have derived important benefits from the labors and influence of the missionaries, through the grace of God, to whom all the praise is due.

Previous to the appointment of a seaman's chaplain at Honolulu, we were glad to see some, even of those who disliked the puritanism of our mission, come forward and boldly advocate the cause of education in favor of the children of Hawaiian mothers. The American commercial agent urged his associates to effort in this cause, from what he affirmed the American missionaries had accomplished " *by human power alone*," as proof of what they themselves could do, by the same power, if they would undertake it with earnestness. The residents of Honolulu proposed to establish a school, exclusively for the children of foreigners, if one of our lay laborers would devote himself to them. This appearing rational, Mr. and Mrs. Johnstone were ready to take charge of such a school, provided the proprietors would build a suitable house for it, and defray the reasonable expenses of maintaining it. Gratuitous aid being expected from foreign visitors, the erection of a suitable and permanent building was undertaken with spirit, and promptly accomplished. Mr. John-stone tendering his resignation as an assistant missionary of the American Board, was eventually discharged, and with Mrs. John-stone, a woman of energy in the cause of education, continued the instruction of the school for years with vigor and success.

Some of the active patrons of the school, though they would call it a "*charity* school," wished to exclude *religion* from it. Others would allow the reading of the Bible, but a majority voted to exclude from the school every religious book except the Bible. The conscientious teachers, however, who had left their home and country chiefly to aid the cause of human salvation, regarded the immortal interests of their pupils, who had little religious advantages at home, as too dear to be neglected at school. They therefore endeavored, and especially on the Sabbath, to train their pupils for heaven hereafter, as well as for usefulness in time.

The increase of the foreign community at Honolulu, and of the number of ships and seamen visiting the islands, and of the healthful concern in the United States, both for the good of sea-men and for their salutary influence on the heathen whom they visit, at length induced the American Seaman's Friend Society to send forth a faithful chaplain for that port. The Rev. John Diell was heartily welcomed there on the 1st of May, 1833. The Oahu Charity School-house, where we had for a time preached in English, was readily granted for his temporary use on the Sab-bath. On the following day he entered on the duties of his office, taking for his motto, " Hinder me not, seeing the Lord hath pros-pered my way." Having brought many of the materials from America for the purpose, he soon had a commodious seaman's chapel erected and dedicated, with reading-rooms and library in the first story, and an audience room in the second, sufficiently large to admit 200 hearers. The frame sent out by the Society was, by the liberality of the Hon. Thos. W. Williams, of New London, Conn., conveyed to the islands, freight free, in one of his whaleships frequenting the Pacific.

Kinau, the premier, showed her public spirit, and the king his liberality, and both their approval of the object, by granting the Society a site for the chapel in a favorable location in that part of the town of Honolulu most frequented by seamen, and most convenient for the business community, in which he was expected to exert an evangelical influence; and also a pleasant place for the chaplain's residence, more retired, in the northern part of the village. The establishment of this chaplaincy was a great acqui-sition. The Seamen's Friend Society devised a good thing when they resolved to accomplish it. They have been happy in their selection of agents to fill it, and in the prospects of its usefulness both to residents and seamen, and the native community.

Some, for whom it was kindly designed, have treated it with contempt; some have been disposed to countenance it, and not a few in their long and toilsome voyages have hailed the Honolulu Bethel flag, floating over the tower of the chapel, as the symbol of peace and hope, and have visited its sanctuary with pleasure and advantage.

The successful establishment and maintenance of that chaplaincy was a matter of rejoicing to the friends of the nation. It was a great relief to the missionaries of the Board to have a faithful preacher, distinct from our community, enter on the work of pleading the cause of temperance, peace, and righteousness, among the seamen and residents, on the same principles which we had inculcated, and by which we were still endeavoring to enlist and save the native population ;—one detached from the nation, somewhat more than it was proper for us to be, who might stand up with a shield over its peace against the shafts of evil, too often felt from the regions of the ocean.

At the same time that Mr. Diell was sent to assume that part of the labor at Honolulu, for which the Seamen's Friend Society wished to provide, the American Board sent another reinforcement to this mission—the Rev. Lowell Smith, and the Rev. Benjamin W. Parker, and their wives, and Mr. Lemuel Fuller, a printer. But the latter arriving in a state of health too much impaired to warrant his entering on the work, soon returned to his friends. The others were hailed as needed fellow-laborers in a field that required all our energies, though one of them was expected to proceed to the Marquesas.

During the unsettled state of the government, when the danger of winking at crime needed to be impressed on the mind of the young king and others who were pleased with Kaomi's policy, the ship of war, the Challenger, Capt. Seymour, arrived from Great Britain, and the commander demanded the execution of two Hawaiian sailors, accused of having thrown overboard and drowned their captain, a British subject, run the little vessel to Fanning's Island, and scuttled her. To secure the object of the Challenger, application was made to Kinau at the fort. She said, " The king claims the power of life and death, and has not committed to me the disposal of those men.". . . . Mr. Charlton intimated that "the king had pardoned them, and given them land." But they applied to the king, and one of them, we were told, gave him to understand that if he alone were responsible for the administration of government, they would have either the murderers of their countrymen, or him in their place.

The mutineers were confined on board a brig commanded by Nahinu, one of the Hulumanu, and owned by the government. I visited the unhappy prisoners there, offered them the Gospel, and labored to lead them to make their peace with God, but had reason to fear that all was unavailing. Mr. Charlton, alleging that " a rescue was to be attempted," asked and obtained a guard from the Challenger to watch the vessel in the harbor. The next day the accused were hung at the yard-arm of the brig. Capt. S. thanked Kinau for the assistance she had rendered him in bringing those men to justice. Strange as the proceedings, from beginning to end, appeared, the result tended to convince the king and chiefs, that if they had not the energy and the will to restrain or punish such crimes, there were other powers that could and would do it for them, even if some were determined to spare the life of the murderer.

Gov. Adams remained at Honolulu till the 1st of August, then returned to his permanent residence at Kailua. Kaomi fell into neglect, and ere long, faded away and died, none seeming materially to feel his loss, or to envy the fleeting honors and pleasures of such an infidel despiser of revealed religion.

The following beautiful and striking allusions to the change of policy attempted, which she had occasion to deplore as deeply as any missionary friend of the cause of righteousness, I pencilled in Hawaiian from the mouth of Kapiolani. The transition is bold and delicate, and the air of romance or fable abates nothing from the force of the rebuke to the wrong-doer, whoever he might be.

> " Love to thee, my sister Waahila,
>   My sister Waahila, rain of Kona,
>   In the days of Kanaloa, descending, gentle, and fine,
>   Enlarging the opening blossoms of the *ohia*.
>   " Thou didst crown thyself with a rainbow coronet,
>   Richly adorned was the interior of Naniuapo,
>   Then flourished the shrubbery of Waiakekua.
>   " Thou playest a god to trample down without cause ;
>   Recklessly to confound the right policy :
>   The bud, the tender shoot, the stem is broken by thee—
>   The shoot of that which is excellent and holy."

Kapiolani was again called to give up some of her missionary friends and helpers. Mr. Ruggles, who, as a pioneer, entered the field in 1820, and labored at different places about fourteen years, much to the satisfaction of the people, finding his health greatly impaired, and having taken the advice of several physicians and of his associates, left his station at Kaawaloa, about the close of this year, in the care of Mr. Forbes, and early in January, embarked with Mrs. Ruggles and two of their children, and returned to the United States, leaving to their native and missionary friends the hope of their re-entering the field with renewed vigor. But this hope was not realized. Two missionaries' children of 7 years, Lucy W. Bingham and Emilie Whitney, were by the same ship sent over the wide waters to their friends.

CHAPTER XIX.

FIFTEENTH YEAR OF THE MISSION AND SECOND OF KAMEHAME-
HA III.—1834.

Steady progress of the Churches—The schools during the apparent reverse—Books
and printing for the nation—Almanac and Newspaper—Religious interest at Hilo
and Kailua—Mission to the Washington Islands—Kaahumanu's opinion of prayer
and effort—London Missionary Society's efforts—Voyage to the Marquesas—Reception of the Mission—Character and condition of Marquesans—Objections to
the continuance of the Mission—Return to the Sandwich Islands.

It is a happy proof of the power of the Gospel and the presence of the Spirit of God at the Sandwich Islands, that whatever
adverse forces have been brought to bear down against the missionary cause, there has been an onward progress in the churches
from their first establishment, so that they have generally been
enlarged year by year, notwithstanding the mortality that has
prevailed and the causes of defection by which some fell away,
and all the efforts made to promote worldliness and a contempt of
religion among the mass.

During the most trying period of their history, from the time
when Kaomi, the "*engrafted king*," was attempting to grow and
flourish where he did not belong, the year ending June, 1834, the
additions to the churches were 124, and the excisions for apostasy
but five during the same time, and the whole number from the beginning reckoned as entirely excommunicated, was less than one to
each church. In July, 1834, there were in the ten churches, twenty-
seven members under discipline, and debarred the communion, as
is customary there with those who walk disorderly; two at Honolulu, eleven at Lahaina, three at Kaawaloa, two at Waimea on
Hawaii, and nine at Kailua. But most of these expressed a desire to return to their duty. The number of marriages solemnized
by the missionaries, the same year, was more than 1100, or equal
to 112 to each station.

In the meantime, preaching was maintained by twenty-three
preachers, so as to supply, in a measure, 67,000, or about one half
of the whole population. The missionaries and their female
helpers, had under their *personal* instruction twenty-nine schools
embracing 1,847 scholars, fourteen of these schools being instructed by female members of the mission. Besides these, there were
in the instruction of the members of the mission, 185 in singing
schools, 980 in Bible classes, and 2190 in Sabbath schools, not
including the multitudes taught by natives.

The indispensableness of the schools under native teachers, imperfect as they were, not being fully understood by all, they were, in some instances, suspended by the missionaries, on the supposition that they had done their work. Still the efforts of the mission in the cause of education were undiminished, especially in raising the qualifications of teachers and furnishing books. The works, chiefly small, prepared by the mission for the people, up to this period, and printed in the native language, amounted to more than forty ; the number of copies being 859,000, and the aggregate of pages 36,640,920. Of these, 25,000 copies were printed at the expense of the American Bible Society ; 55,000 at the expense of the American Tract Society ; 40,000 at the expense of Mr. William Williams of Utica; and 739,800 at the expense of the American Board. These were widely diffused, and gladly received and read by thousands. This year the mission prepared and published a *Hawaiian Almanac*, for 1835, and in conformity with the suggestion of the Board, resolved on the publication of a semi-monthly newspaper of eight quarto pages, called " *Ke Kumu Hawaii*," *The Hawaiian Teacher*. The editorship was assigned to Rev. R. Tinker, who, before the close of the year, removed from Wailuku to Honolulu, and took charge of it. Two thousand copies were issued. Its columns, to which missionaries, natives, and others contributed, were read with pleasure by many.

Of the need and design of such a work the mission, at their convention in June, expressed their views in the following resolution :—

" That the periodical press may be advantageously employed in the Sandwich Islands, to exhibit truth in an attractive form before the eyes of several thousand readers; to open the sources and supply the means of useful knowledge in the arts and sciences, history, morals, and religion ; to point out existing evils, their character, seat, extent and consequences, their causes, and the remedy; to make a newly and partially instructed people acquainted with the results of the experience and discoveries of past generations and with the success or defeat of the enterprises of the passing age; to supply deficiencies in the books printed, and to elucidate by various methods of simple and figurative language, diagrams, engravings, etc., every subject brought before the people, from the simplest elements of knowledge to the highest points of instruction aimed at by the mission."

A smaller paper was commenced in February of this year, for the Mission Seminary, by Mr. Andrews, called the " *Lama Hawaii*"—*The Hawaiian Luminary*. The issuing of the Kumu Hawaii was commenced Nov. 12th, 1834.

About the close of 1833, and the early part of 1834, a protracted meeting at Hilo, and other labors of Messrs. Goodrich, Lyman, and Dibble, appeared to be attended by the influences of the Spirit of God, and a few souls appeared to be gathered from among their best instructed pupils, though they could hardly hope " that a deep and saving impression could be made on the mass of the population of their wide field, unless a mission family should be stationed at each of the more important places along the whole extent of its sea coast."

At Kailua the Sabbath school increased; Gov. Adams took part in it, and heard a class of his people recite their weekly seven verses of Scripture which they committed to memory: thirteen hopeful converts were added to the church in August, and a wakeful attention to the means of grace was manifested by numbers.

At this sifting period, Messrs. Thurston and Bishop said of their charge what many a minister would be glad to say, but what few are able ordinarily to say, at least in some particulars, though the Hawaiians were regarded as naturally dilatory and indolent:

" The church as a body appear well, and live in harmony with each other, and many individuals of them are valuable helpers to us in all our social meetings, as well as in carrying into operation any measure we put on foot.

" Our Sabbath congregations, as also our weekly and morning prayer meetings, are more frequented than formerly, and more fixed attention to the preached Word prevails. We attribute this favorable state of things, under the divine blessing, principally to the happy influence of our morning prayer meetings. The impulse to religious feeling there received at the beginning of each day, accompanies them through all the succeeding hours. We meet at five o'clock, which, at this season, is an hour and a quarter before sunrise, and continue together an hour, which is so much time gained from the empire of darkness. The number that attend is from two to three hundred."

Where, in England or America, could a daily morning prayer meeting of two to three hundred, more than an hour before sunrise, be kept up by about equal numbers of professors and non-professors of religion, for many months, like that at the so recently heathen village of Kailua? Could this be accomplished with spirit, who can doubt that the interests of religion would be greatly promoted by it?

During the struggles of 1833 and 1834, at the Sandwich Islands, and especially at Honolulu, the mission renewed its efforts to convey the Gospel to the Marquesas or Washington Islands, which, as a part of the history of the mission, deserve a record here.

When Kaahumanu's attention had been called to that dark portion of the human family, as needing the Gospel, and prayers were offered and plans proposed to help them, she expressed a willingness to co-operate, if possible, and her opinion was incidentally elicited on a point which was to her new. I said to her, " Suppose we offer our prayers that God would convert the Marquesan people to Christ, and we still withhold the Word of God from them, what would you think of such prayers?" After a very few moments' reflection on the importance of using efforts, if possible, corresponding with the object of the prayers we offer, she replied with decision, " *Ua hala ia pule. Such prayers miss their mark.*"

The sentiment in its bearing on the conversion of the heathen world is of great value. Whatever prayers are offered for the heathen by those who are unwilling to do what belongs to them to do to secure the answer, or to turn the answers to good account, should they be granted, may well be considered as *missing their mark*. If the supplicant can do nothing for the object but pray, then he is doubtless accepted according to what he hath, and not according to what he hath not.

Does not this, in part at least, explain the fact that the ten thousand thousand prayers offered for the conversion of heathen nations, unaccompanied with corresponding efforts, or while the light of God's Word is not given them, fall to the ground? Can such petitions be the " fervent and effectual," prevailing " prayer of the " obedient " righteous man," which the Scriptures assure us " *availeth much?*"

The London Missionary Society having made efforts, at different periods, to evangelize the Marquesans, and not having, as was supposed, the adequate number of laborers to man the field so as to make a strong impression, the American Board believing that a detachment of the laborers sent to the Sandwich Islands could operate advantageously at the Washington Islands, and no conclusive objection having been made from any quarter, the annual convention of our mission in 1833 resolved on the occupancy of that field. In accordance with the wishes of the American Board and of their own, Messrs. Alexander, Armstrong, and Parker, with their wives, were intrusted with the important service of attempting to preach the Gospel, and translate and publish the Bible for the Marquesans. It was an arduous, a self-denying, and hazardous service; but there was a spirit given them to undertake it which was well expressed in the motto of a sermon which one of them preached on the occasion—" The God of heaven he will prosper us, therefore we his servants will arise and build." The faith and courage with which the ladies, two of them with their tender babes in their arms, set off in this new enterprise, were highly commendable, and their unshrinking heroism too admirable to be soon forgotten.

This detachment from our mission embarked on board the brigantine Dhaulle, Capt. Bancroft, and sailed from Honolulu on the 2d of July, 1833, with fair trade winds, touched at Tahiti on the 24th of the same month, and reached Nuuhiva, the place of their destination, on the 10th of August. They were welcomed on shore on the 15th by the aged Hape, the head chief of Massachusetts Bay : and having removed their baggage and such means of support, for a time, as they carried with them, and which required to be guarded with much care, they were, on the 21st, left by their captain in their novel and untried situation to prosecute their work.

So far as they could then judge, all the chiefs were favorable to their settlement there. Still, the sense of *insecurity*, except in the special providence of God, was not an entire stranger or unfrequent guest. The curiosity of the natives was much excited by the white women and their children. They tried to get them in their arms, and the native females to clasp the gentlemen in theirs. Their rudeness, lasciviousness, shouts, and uncouth movements, were shocking in the extreme; and the insubordination, destitution, barbarism, cannibalism, love of war, and the awful moral darkness that covered the land, were truly appalling. There they found heathenism in its native deformity and loathsomeness—with very little of the *law* of God legible on the heart.

It would, perhaps, be well for those who are inclined to think men more virtuous and happy without the revealed will of God than with it, to take time and opportunity to look in upon the soul of the cannibal, or the equally monstrous sacrificer of human blood; of the self-immolating widow, and of the orphan child trained by heathen priests to light the death-fire that is to seize upon their mother, and of the fiendish father who throws back his daughter, bound, upon the flames, if she emerges and attempts to flee from the fiery trial, the intolerable torture, and awful death which she could not voluntarily endure. And those who think missionaries who take up their abode among the barbarous or degraded heathen, while they refuse to mingle in their vices and their sinful pleasures, choose such a situation because of its felicities, might be benefited, perhaps, by accompanying Brainard among our Indians, Martin in Persia, Mrs. Judson in Burmah, Hall in India, Williams in Polynesia, or any of the missionaries, English or American, on the Marquesas, or among any strictly heathen people on earth.

If, after years of toil, privation, and danger, with many prayers and efforts for the temporal, spiritual, and eternal good of the degraded and doubly ruined heathen, God should so fulfil his promise that those who "trust in the Lord and do good, shall dwell in the land and be fed"—that their habitations, clothing, and table, and the state of society around them assume the air of comparative comfort, and both they who sow and they who reap rejoice together; shall it be set down to the disparagement of the spirit of missions—as proving it sordid, selfish, or wholly undistinguishable from the spirit of the world?

The missionaries entering the Marquesas found no suitable habitations for their reception or accommodation. Hape, the chief, offered them the temporary use of his, which they accepted; and introducing several slight partitions, the three families had each about twelve feet square, and a common store-room of similar size, where their goods and chattels were placed. Here they took lodgings. Here, surrounded with cruel, warlike, cannibal barbarians, they began their missionary work in the midst of the chaotic ruins of the fall, now overspread with the deep and dreadful gloom of paganism. Here, for a season, they toiled, feeling themselves safe no further than they had the divine protection; but cherishing the buoyant hope that the rays of the Sun of Righteousness would in due time dissipate that gloom, and cheer and purify the dark heathen heart of the polluted Marquesans, one of whose sons had been taught Christianity in the United States, and had given evidence of true conversion to Christ.

Thomas Patu, here referred to, was an interesting youth who had been carried to the United States. The gentleman with whom he lived for a time in one of the cities of the Union, used to allow him to visit the theatre; but he, at length, professed himself disgusted, and declined, saying, with his national pride, " Too much negro there." He afterwards embraced the truth, was partially educated in our country, gave good evidence of love to the Savior, and died in the faith, as one of the first fruits of Marquesan soil, where a harvest, it was hoped, would follow in connexion with a persevering cultivation.

The form and stature of the Marquesans were thought to be more noble, on the whole, than those of the Hawaiians; and the women, vile as they were, more comely; though some of the people were horridly tattooed. But the men were distinguished more for pride and independence of feeling, than any other natives whom the missionaries had seen in the Pacific Isles. They were struck with the lofty air with which these swarthy, half naked sons of ignorance would pace the deck of a foreign vessel, as if the ship and the ocean were at their command, though they were as poor as Robinson Crusoe's goats, and knew about as little of navigation, law and government, morals, and the duties and decencies of human society. Their religion was much like other Polynesian tribes. Though English missionaries had visited them, at different times, and though a deputation from our mission had expostulated with them on the folly, sinfulness, and abomination of idolatry; human sacrifices were still offered by the people. They were believed, or pretended to be, availing to avert sickness or death, in some of the higher classes. A *king of the gods* being sick, in Massachusetts' Bay, the people went to the valley of the Taipis, and killed two or three of the people for sacrifices.

Petty wars appeared to be the delight of the inhabitants; not, apparently, for establishing a supremacy or acquiring wealth, any more than boxers or wrestlers aim at it. The people were all sovereigns, almost as much as the citizens of the United States, and having no formal laws, each did what seemed good in his own eyes. In every respect, so far as appeared, there was as much of the independency of nature as could be desired; and the inhabitants were left, in the utmost freedom, to choose or reject the Christian doctrine, without the fear or favor of any man. But this absence of subordination to parental, patriarchal, or magisterial authority was found, as it always will be, unfavorable to a rational and cordial subjection to divine authority, and less favorable to the reception of the Gospel message, than habitual subjection to law or to despotic power, even when oppressive. In Christian communities, those children who are most restrained by vigilant and inflexible family government, make the best citizens and subjects of the King of kings. Thus the distrained sons and daughters of Africa, in the West Indies, when fairly made acquainted with the Christian doctrine, were found to be more ready to embrace it, than the free negroes of the United States, or the uncontrolled, Marquesans, or the indomitable Indians of America, and the unrestrained Arabian or African. It is not for the *loss* but for the *abuse* of freedom that God gives over his creatures to "a reprobate mind," to incurable blindness and ruinous hardness of heart. It is not for the possession or rightful *exercise* of power, but for the *abuse* of it, that many of those who hold places of power on earth, are left to take their portion in what earth can give, without a better inheritance, while, to the poor and oppressed, the Gospel offers an enduring inheritance and an unfading crown, which are by them more readily and gratefully accepted.

The rule which was exercised over the subjects, at the Sandwich Islands, was favorable to the reception of Christianity, while the want of the same, at the Marquesas, was unfavorable, both to the propagator of the Gospel and to those to whom it was offered. The want of vigorous civil government, in the days of Noah, left men the more fitted to despise the preacher of righteousness. Take away, entirely, all the restraints of law, in London, Paris, New York, and Philadelphia, and what would become of those cities, in ten years, or in the course of a generation? Society could hardly exist there. The healthy portions of the community would retire to communities where the protection of government could be enjoyed. Anarchy and confusion are always unfavorable to schools, to virtue, and religion. It is true the Gospel might be preached, but the Gospel as really requires obedience to parental and civil authority as to any other rule which God has given. True obedience to a righteous law is virtue, but without obedience to law there is no virtue.

The true philosophy of alienation from God, or of the blindness and degradation of the heathen mind, or the obduracy of the human heart, will not support the hypothesis that " the heathenism of oppression is a greater hindrance to the reception of the Gospel than the heathenism of idolatry," if it is practicable to make such a distinction. But since oppression is almost always the concomitant of idolatry and ignorance, the question of their obstructive force can have little or no bearing on the duty of the churches of Christendom to proclaim the Gospel, and publish the Bible, the world over, without further delay. Well may we rejoice that the benevolent and general command comes with paramount authority, to the whole church of Christ—" Teach all nations—Preach the

Gospel to every creature." The specific command to " break every yoke " applies to those who make or bind it.

The missionaries found, notwithstanding the apparent independence of the Marquesans, a strange mixture of lordliness and meanness in the men, and wantonness and abjectness among the women, which, had they not been idolators, would have made the Gospel, once understood, specially welcome to them.

Sometimes, the first or lawful husband, being too proud, too mean, or too lazy to do what was reasonable for a husband to do, to provide for a family, a subordinate husband was taken in to perform the little labor deemed necessary, as a compensation for sharing in a woman's love. But if the wife showed him much favor or affection, she was pretty sure to be beaten by her lordly husband, who could not reconcile the feelings of pride and independence with the abject condition of equality with the menial paramour of his wife.

Some, with all their haughtiness and stout-heartedness, never dared to leave the little valley that gave them birth, lest they should be roasted and devoured, or at least murdered, by the men of blood in their neighborhood.

The fountains of moral life were all corrupted, and the whole aspect of society was uncouth, wretched, vile, and repulsive.

Contemplating the deep degradation and wickedness of these tribes, the sickening and appalling aspect of the whole nation, one of the missionaries said, " I bless God that I am not to live always." Still, the missionaries there, glancing the eye of faith upward, could sing :—

> " Give to the winds thy fears;
> Hope and be undismayed :
> God hears thy sighs, and counts thy tears ;
> He shall lift up thy head."

They procured materials, and erected houses, made themselves acquainted with the rude barbarians, visited the neighboring districts, and found the inhabitants few in number, scattered, and divided into small hostile tribes, far less accessible than much larger numbers who were still unprovided for, at the Sandwich Islands, and who remained comparatively indifferent to the claims, the warnings, and the proffers of the Gospel.

After months of toil, and a further consultation with one or more of the English missionaries, whose patrons still hoped to man both parts of the Marquesas, their thoughts turned back towards the Sandwich Islands, where the government had efficiency, wisdom, and integrity enough to make it a blessing rather than a curse to the governed, and where places enough unoccupied were waiting for them.

The facilities and prospects here they contrasted with the darkness, difficulties, and smallness of the field there. The fickleness, doubtful character, or cupidity of some on whom they had placed confidence, distressed them.

The old chief, Hape, apparently friendly, on the visit of the deputation, and the landing of the missionaries, appeared for a time disposed to favor them; probably with the expectation of immediately gaining health and wealth from their hands. Perhaps a thoroughly instructed and experienced medical adviser might have been the means of his restoration, and of securing the whole weight of his augmented influence in favor of Christian teachers. Medicines, given him by Mr. Armstrong, temporarily relieved his sufferings, but did not arrest his fatal decline. He was here disappointed, and demanded why Jehovah did not cure him if he could?

It is supposed, too, that the natural *cupidity* of this chieftain was excited by seeing, in one collection, the whole of the stores, clothing, household furniture, apparatus for schools, etc., belonging to three families, all placed in his own house and within his power. He asked for one thing and another; and the brethren endeavored reasonably to meet his wishes, till they found that giving him only increased his covetousness. It were well for the world, if in the wise administration of the Great Benefactor of all, this result were confined to heathen Marquesas.

Numbers came by night, to steal; some thrust in a pole, with a hook, to pull out clothing, and others reached through windows or through the thatching, taking what was at hand.

Drunkenness and licentiousness were encouraged by the shipping. The young chief, Kemoana, told the missionaries, that once he drank no rum, and when a ship-master first induced him to taste it, he, on tasting, told the captain it was not good, and he did not like it. The ensnarer replied, " Drink a *little*, and by and by you will *love* it." Many a reformed man can tell us what that *love* of *rum* is, which this friend of civilization was trying to cultivate in this youthful heathen chieftain.

When the chiefs learned that prostitution was wrong and ruinous, several of them proposed to prevent the women from boarding the vessels. But one of the guards of the beach being bribed for a trifle, by the ship-men, no further effort was made by the chiefs to suppress that evil. It is a wonder that they should have proposed or attempted it at all, with so little instruction and so little force. Little was done, on this subject, by the efficient Hawaiian chiefs, till thousands of the people had been taught to read the commands, threatenings, and promises of God; and four years of missionary toil had passed away. And even then, they needed to be prepared to resist, by irresistible force, the force that was meanly and wickedly brought to bear against them in support of so base and ruinous a practice.

The appearance of a small congregation of half a hundred Marquesans, during public worship, which, for several months, the publishers of salvation maintained, on the Sabbath, was a severe trial of the faith and patience of men and women who were endeavoring to do for them whatever could be reasonably required at their hands. Says Mr. A., "Some lie and sleep; some laugh and talk; and others mock and mimic the preacher, and endeavor to excite laughter in others. Here one sits smoking a pipe. There another, twisting a rope, and often, there is such confusion that the preacher can scarcely hear himself speak. When we request them to sit still, and hearken to our words, they reply, ' Yes, let us all sit still and listen.' One says to another, ' Sit you still there,' and makes a motion as though he would strike him or throw a stone at him ; the other must retaliate, and this excites laughter. Not unfrequently, numbers will rise and go off, laughing and mocking." They refused the offer of salvation.

The tribe, in Massachusetts Bay, were threatened with invasion from the warlike and superstitious Taipis, who wanted human sacrifices, and *for them, the missionaries formed a part of the people, and were equally eligible for sacrifices and for the cannibal feast; and they intended to make them suffer, in full measure, the consequences of a war which themselves were laboring to bring upon the people.*

The first day of April, the missionaries observed as a day of fasting, prayer, and consultation as to duty, and concluded to retrace their path to the Sandwich Islands, for various reasons; but the one conclusive, in their minds, said Mr. Alexander, is this ; " The population, in this field, capable of being brought under the influence of missionaries, is too small to justify the Board in sustaining a mission here, when such vast fields, in other places, are calling for their efforts."

The English missionaries, as well as the American, have found peculiar difficulties to encounter, at the Marquesas ; though their hopes of ultimate success have not been relinquished. Mr. Rogerson, who, for some time, labored at one of those islands, under the patronage of the London Missionary Society, being convinced that the place was unfit to be the residence of civilized females, removed to Tahiti, with his wife and three children. Those of the people who had grown to years of maturity, seemed as much as ever attached to their own superstitions, and the youth could not be prevailed on to assemble regularly to receive instruction. There had been a war at Tahuata, and two persons had been killed, baked, and eaten. In writing from Tahiti to the Sandwich Islands, he says,

" A short time previous to this war, a native of Dominica, who was over on a visit to Vaitahu, set fire to our dwelling, chiefly, with a view, as we supposed, of plundering. He was seen climbing over the fences, by a Spaniard, who came and told us, though not aware of his real intention. We perceived the fire in time, however, and had it speedily extinguished. The wretch we also apprehended, who would speedily have been cut to pieces for the diabolical act, had we given consent. All that we requested was that he might be sent home, which was done

early the next morning. Mr. Stallworthy was at the windward side of
the island, at the time.   One of our children was within three yards of
the part of the house that was set on fire.   The Lord our God was gracious unto us ; and may a sense of his goodness be impressed upon
our hearts, and may we be enabled to show forth his praise and promote his glory."*

After a residence of eight months at those islands, with some
difficulty, our mission families effected an embarkation from their
perilous condition, on the 16th of April, and arrived at Honolulu
safely, on the 12th of May, 1834.

There was need of large and repeated reinforcements to maintain the older ports and to man new ones, while adverse agencies
were so much on the alert to circumvent the Gospel.

Mr. Armstrong was located on the northern part of Maui, Mr.
Parker at Kaneohe, on the northern part of Oahu, and Mr. Alexander at Waioli, on the northern part of Kauai, all new stations,
where they entered into the work of bringing the Hawaiian nation
to Christ.

At Kaneohe, twelve miles north of Honolulu, the people of
Palikoolau, and at their head, Amasa Kaiakoili, once the trusty
warrior friend of the late Kalaanimoku, but now a Christian brother in declining health, with great readiness erected a small
thatched church, which was dedicated Nov. 30th, in connexion
with a protracted meeting held at that place.

In the progress of this year, two of our number, Mrs. Rogers,
on the 23d of May, and Mr. Shepard, on the 6th of July, peacefully finished their Christian and missionary course. On the 12th
of July, Mr. David Douglass, a scientific traveller from Scotland,
in the service of the London Horticultural Society, lost his life in
the mountains of Hawaii, in a pitfall, being gored and trampled
to death by a wild bullock captured there.

---

* I have not altered my views of heathenism or Christianity since the uncivilized
" *Tipee*" has sought, through the presses of civilization in England and America, to
apologize for cannibalism, and to commend savage life to the sons and daughters of
Christendom, instead of teaching the principles of science and virtue, or the worship
of our Maker, among idolaters, man-eaters, and infidels.

CHAPTER XX.

New station at Molokai—Progress in a year—New station at Waialua—New
station at Ewa—Idolatrous efforts—Influence of the schools—Severe test of the
pupils—Zeal of. Hoapili—Marriage forbidden to those who could not read—Co-
operation of Kawailepolepo at Wailuku—Manufacture of Cotton introduced—
Religious interest at Kauai—Shipmasters against license—Temperance petition.

As the Board supplied the means, the mission endeavored to
multiply its posts, and enlarge its sphere of labor and influence.
Soon after the active course of Kaahumanu was terminated, the
mission proceeded to occupy a new post on the island of Molokai,
whose population had as yet been greatly neglected, and concerning whom the demand was felt to be forcible—"Why is Molokai still utterly destitute of a foreign missionary ?"

A station was chosen at Kaluaaha, near the eastern end of the
island, of which Mr. Hitchcock took charge, Nov. 1832.
He found it salubrious and agreeable as a field of missionary toil.
His *parish*, to use a familiar term, embraced about 5000 souls,
living sparsely around the shores of the whole island, most of
them being poor, destitute, and ignorant. Many of their habitations were not more than two or three times as large as a common
bedstead, being from seven to nine feet square on the ground, and
no taller than to allow a man of ordinary stature to stand erect
under the ridge-pole. The neglected human occupants of these
diminutive tents or frail huts will hardly bear a description ;
women with arms, neck, chest, feet, and ankles naked ; men
with " the *wretched malo*," a narrow girdle round the middle,
" covering," as Mr. H. said, " scarcely more of the whole surface
of the body than a pair of shoes ;" children often with no clothing but their swarthy skin ; then, to complete the catalogue,
various tribes—cats, dogs, pigs, fowls, goats, mice, cockroaches,
flies, musquitoes, fleas, and lice—the two latter, as well as most
of the others, being then deemed edible by the islanders.

Within a year many habitations, more comfortable, were built,
having separate sleeping apartments, and other accommodations
which gave them an air of neatness and comfort before unknown
there. Then a spacious school-house was erected to ornament
the village at the station, and soon, as in commencing other stations, a rude and roomy temple to Jehovah. Hoapili Wahine,
who had a special charge of Molokai, encouraged the labors of
the station.

Before the close of 1835, the natives, with a very little aid, erected, with their own hands, and at their own expense, a commodious church, highly creditable to a people who had been so ignorant and indolent. It was ninety feet by forty-two, and would admit 1200 hearers; the walls being of stone, laid up with mortar made of earth mixed with grass, plastered on both sides with lime mortar, and whitewashed. Its well constructed roof was thatched with the long, strong, sear leaf of the pandanus or screw pine, the corners and ridge of the building being ornamented and secured by a raised, thick, dark border of the *ki* leaf. Light or straw colored mats nailed to the nether side of the beams, concealing the timbers of the roof from the audience, and similar mats spread on the ground for flooring, gave the spacious audience room the appearance of neatness and finish suited to the climate and the taste of the people. A block of mason-work, three feet high, formed the base of the pulpit. On the 6th of December, the house was filled to its utmost capacity, hundreds standing around without, and was joyfully dedicated to the worship of the true God, when Mr. Richards preached the dedication sermon from the spirited words of the Psalmist, " Enter into thy resting-place, thou and the ark of thy strength."

About the same time, or July, 1832, the second station on Oahu was taken at Waialua by Mr. Emerson, assisted for a time by Mr. Clark, and under the patronage of Laanui. The districts of Waianae, Waialua, and Koolauloa, extending coastwise about fifty miles, and embracing a population of 7300, were connected with the station, among whom about 1600 could read. In 1834 a station was taken, and a congregation collected, at Ewa, fourteen miles west from Honolulu, where Mr. and Mrs. L. Smith were located, after they had resided a short time at Molokai.

A protracted meeting was held at Ewa in April, 1835, which continued five days, several of the missionaries of Honolulu and Waialua assisted Mr. Smith in the services, and nearly a hundred of the natives from other stations were present, some of whom returned impressed with divine truth. " The special influence of the Spirit of God," says Mr. S., " most evidently rested upon the congregation, not only during the meeting, but for several weeks subsequently. The amount of good accomplished on the occasion will be best known at the great day. One year ago the prospects around us were dark and discouraging, but a brighter day has dawned upon us; and we hope and pray that it may be a long and blessed day to these benighted Hawaiians."

After rioting and drunkenness, and the ancient dance and revelry had by the haters of truth been attempted to be revived, and a partial return to idols, house burning, and violence, appeared in the district by the no-government ultraists, the king and chiefs saw the necessity of laws for the lawless and vile for the protection of all, and they encouraged the enforcement of reasonable restraints. But in carrying this measure, three *idolators* were arrested for idolatry, and taken before the chiefs at Honolulu. This was another instance in which the civil arm was stretched out against idols. And though it is exceedingly difficult for any Christian government to define idolatry so as to oppose it by civil enactments, still the Christian rulers and the king himself supposed that any attempt to re-establish idolatry ought to be repressed by the secular power.

Could any man think of blaming Mr. Smith for not interfering with the police in the case of their arresting idolators in his district who were attempting to seduce the people back into heathenism? The law was thought to be reasonable, and the execution of it could not of course be complained of. But the law did not propose to change men's *opinions*, but to prevent practising and teaching image worship or idolatry.

At Puna, the south-eastern district of Hawaii, an idolatrous party wishing to honor Hapu, a woman who had died among them, canonized her, as well as they knew how, and associated her name with Jehovah and Jesus, of whom they had heard through the Gospel, as one towards whom their prayers and veneration were to be directed. They built a shrine for this new worship, this fatal " corruption of the truth," this " totally perverted Christianity." They valued the remains of this prophetess, not indeed the Romanist's " Queen of heaven "—the " all powerful Virgin "—but her sister, born of Hawaiian parents, and being as worthy of the religious homage of pagans as the Jewish Mary is of that of Christians. These honored relics two young men placed in a prominent position, and called on the people to make pilgrimages thither to avoid speedy destruction. Maintaining at the same time that they believed in and worshipped the true God and Jesus Christ whom the missionaries had proclaimed, they enticed a number to hear and follow them. A considerable crowd assembled and engaged in this monstrous service, so analogous to that which Rome in a course of generations devised, and for centuries has practised.

Hearing of this insufferable abomination, Mr. Dibble and a young chief hastened thither to remonstrate and expostulate with the leaders and their dupes. These rude natives had not the learning and tact to defend their half-Christian and half-pagan worship.

On the arrival there of a watchful and earnest missionary and the young Christian chief, a large part of the worshippers disappeared. The rest, on hearing the remonstrances of a missionary and his coadjutor, professed a willingness to forsake the idolatrous part of their worship. The temple, therefore, which had been erected to the worship of Jehovah, Jesus, and their deified prophetess, was immediately devoted to the flames, as a useless and polluted thing.

It was wisely ordered that the means should be at hand for

saving the nation from this monstrous imposture, and that no foreign power was present to give it currency by force, by precept, or by example, or to prevent its speedy abandonment or suppression. There was too much scriptural knowledge in the land for the prevalence of such an anti-scriptural system without some foreign influence to sustain it.

The schools at the Sandwich Islands, springing suddenly into existence, among a barbarous and unlettered people, extending rapidly over the whole territory, everywhere gaining favor, and in less than fifteen years embracing a third of the entire population, notwithstanding the fewness of the missionaries, and the necessity for their furnishing every lesson in every department of instruction, and the greatness and variety of the pulpit, pastoral, and miscellaneous labors they had to perform, might, to some, be an object of ridicule and scorn, and to others, a matter of astonishment and admiration. The mere announcement of more than half a thousand Christian schools and fifty thousand learners, in the heathen wastes of the Sandwich Islands, in less than half the period of a generation from the time when they had not a book or an alphabet, may lead some to inquire, What kind of schools could they be? Who were their founders? supporters? teachers? What their design, use, accommodations, and prospects of permanence, and their connexion with the missionary work?

It may be difficult to give a just idea of their structure or their value, but whatever they were, they were put in operation and sustained, from the beginning till now, to a very great extent, by native energy, the missionaries encouraging them, preparing books, and furnishing, by means of funds from home, the largest part of the supply to the schools. We had not, for the first fifteen years, the means of building school-houses, nor paying native teachers, nor has much aid ever been furnished for that purpose, except in a very few instances. Their school-houses were much like their dwellings, temporary thatched buildings, and as destitute of furniture as could well be conceived; but still they formed a rallying point and a shelter from the rain, sun, and wind. Of the common schools, the missionaries, in attempting to give a brief but exact account of their design, character, and influence, say to their directors in 1835 —

" The missionaries and their wives and helpers have, up to the present time, endeavored to cherish the schools as a primary means of reforming the nation. They have had classes under their own immediate instruction, amounting sometimes to not less than 1000 individuals of different ages. But the mass of those who have attempted to learn, embracing those numerous collections of people called schools, in the different parts of the islands, have been under the instruction of incompetent native teachers. The aggregate of learners has, at some periods, amounted to 50,000. Probably more than four-fifths of these

were advanced to years of maturity, and not a few beyond middle age.   Most of them had their ordinary occupations of life to
attend to, as though no school existed.

"While it has been our business to teach a few hundreds
personally, and superintend their efforts to teach others, our
steady aim has been to extend a moral and religious influence
over the whole community by means of the widely extended
and, in some respects, loose school system.   Whatever may have
been the defects of that system, it should be understood that the
design of it has not been merely or mainly literary ; that mental
culture has not been in the common schools, especially of adults,
our most prominent object ; for in those points of view, hundreds
of schools, under native teachers, embracing thousands of readers,
would hardly deserve the name of schools, as that term is ordinarily understood in the most enlightened countries as the nurse-
ries of science and literature.   But the general object has been
to supply, in some measure, the want of family government and
education ; the want of a well regulated civil government ; to
restrain from vice and crime, and to supply amply, by a mild and
salutary influence, the want of the power once derived from a
horrid superstition.   It has afforded, to a great extent, by the
pen, slate, pencil, and book, a substitute for the pleasure which
the people once derived from games of chance, and of skill, and
strength, connected with staking property ; and in many cases
instruction imparted by dictation and the exercise of joint recitation or cantillation of moral lessons by classes, has been a happy
substitute for the heathen song and dance, where ignorance of
the value of mental culture, or a want of interest in the subject
of education, or the incompetency of the teacher, rendered a
severer method of application impracticable.   When this easier
method of communicating and receiving some knowledge of what
we desired to teach has served to enlist the stupid pupils at all,
they have been ready to try to learn the art of reading and
writing where the means have been supplied.   And as these have
been acquired by numbers, the desire for books and other studies
has been increased beyond our ability to meet it.

"While then we have labored to afford the people the means
of learning the arts of reading and writing, geography and arithmetic, for the discipline of mind and the purposes of life, and to
facilitate their access to the sacred Scripture, it has been our
steady aim to bring to bear constantly on the dark hearts of pagans
and their children those moral and evangelical truths, without the
presence and possession of which the design of their rational
existence cannot be secured.   While our school system does indeed
contemplate the disciplining of the mind, and affords important
means and facilities for it, it has always contemplated chiefly a
moral influence over the heart and life which the want of family
and civil government, and the want of an adequate number of
the preachers of the Gospel, has made indispensable.   We have,

therefore, in our first books, inserted such plain precepts in the
science of duty as every reader can understand ; and have added
evangelical tracts and portions of Scripture as reading lessons
for all our schools ; and have endeavored to give them an influence similar to that of Sabbath schools, as far as circumstances
would allow.   And we believe their agency has been, and still is,
in that respect, far more indispensable than that of Sabbath
schools in the United States or Great Britain."

What better means could have been adopted to secure the
attention of such a rude nation, and to get their eyes and ears turned
so generally towards the foreign teachers ?   Nay, had the expansion and elevation of the intellectual powers of such a people been
the main object of any class of men, who should, in the place of
the foreign missionaries, have undertaken to raise the nation, it is
hardly conceivable that a few dozen foreign teachers, by any
other process, could have gained more general attention, acquired
more general confidence, or introduced more elevating and expanding ideas into the minds of the mass of the nation in so
short a period than was done by means of our schools, of which
some of us have been almost ashamed to speak, because they fell
so much below what we desired to see in successful and triumphant operation, or so far short of the best schools which have,
for generations and centuries, been coming to their present maturity and perfection in the most enlightened Christian states.

The simplest ideas of the true God and of the soul, and of our
relation and duties to God and his creatures, are the most elevating,
expanding, and purifying that can be first introduced into the
minds of the heathen, whether aged or middle aged, in youth or
childhood.   The Egyptians, in the days of Moses, the Athenians,
in their glory, and the proud Romans, in the days of the Cæsars,
before the Gospel was preached among them, did not possess so
much elevating and purifying knowledge as was taught in our 900
schools, among 50,000 learners, the first half generation after the
missionaries set foot on those dark shores, when eclipsed in night
and excluded from all true philosophy and true religion ; for,

" The law of the Lord is perfect, converting the soul ;
  The testimony of the Lord is sure, making wise the simple."

During that short period, to some 30,000 of the people, the
New Testament, or the Gospels and other portions of Scripture
and useful books, had been made available.

But how could Hawaiians, naturally unaccustomed to mental
effort and so little able to appreciate education, be induced to
engage in the work of instruction, so extensively as they did,
when no compensation was offered them from abroad further than
the few books they were required to teach ?   The readiness with
which the brethren and sisters of the mission engaged in teaching
school, gave to the employment a consequence and respectability
in the eyes of the people, and doubtless had some influence in

inducing numbers to engage in imparting to others what they had acquired, and with no compensation from the chiefs or people above their daily food and shelter. Some were doubtless influenced by loyalty to their chiefs, some by loyalty to Christ, some by the pleasure of communicating, and some by the pride of distinction.

It was at some hazard, that from year to year, their constancy should have been put to so severe a test, with so little mental and moral training as they had received, and so little apparent advantage to themselves or their families derivable from their employment as teachers.

So in the first years of the Mission Seminary, it was no small hazard to require the pupils to build their own school-house, under every disadvantage, and raise their own food while prosecuting their studies. With the aborigines of the American continent, and doubtless with other tribes, it would have produced disgust and occasioned defeat. But when the teacher took up the first stone and carried it to the spot, the scholars followed him, and they labored on together till the building was up, and accommodations for study supplied. Rarely has a school appeared more truly interesting than that high school, at Lahainaluna, withdrawn a mile and a half from the town which they overlooked, laboring at their new building, and pursuing their studies, often hungry, with almost no shelter from the sun and rain, no furniture, and very little school apparatus; when they held their slates in a perpendicular position to prevent the descending showers from washing out their questions, and refused to be dismissed till their lesson was completed. Numbers of these were hopefully pious, and a large portion wished to be qualified for teaching.

Severe as was this test in the early years of the school, it was a species of training which was needed to bring out the voluntary principle, to give scope to the feelings of responsible men as members of the community, and an example of laboring directly for the benefit of successors, to which few or none in the nation had, without the Gospel, been accustomed. Though there was danger of producing discouragement or disgust, as in every attempt to induce a severer application to industrial pursuits, among a people of their habits, who had so many temptations to indolence, yet, what better could have been done for a public school, collected from all the stations and islands of the group, when no funds from any quarter had been provided for the express establishment of such a school, and when hundreds of millions of heathens, in other lands, more destitute, were demanding tenfold more than all the missionary funds that were contributed by all Christendom ? Though sometimes ready to blame ourselves for not laying out more for the education of the people, yet when we received increased funds and facilities for the support of boarding-schools, we could hardly avoid the feeling, that by those grants to us, other portions of the heathen world, destitute of preachers, had been defrauded.

The countenance given by friendly chiefs to the pupils in this school, to the common school teachers, and to all who wished to learn, though it was less than the missionaries desired, was still valuable, and sometimes remarkable.

Hoapili, the viceroy of Maui, in his zeal for general education, and the good of the people, in 1835, exempted the native teachers from all public labor except teaching, required all the children above four years of age, to attend school, and ordered that no man or woman, in his jurisdiction, unable to read, should have license to be married. He had probably heard of some such edict, by some sovereign of Europe, and wished to try the experiment. Submission to such a rule, among a population of 30,000, who, fifteen years before, could not read at all, was a grand proof of the progress of elementary education. The governor, doubtless, relied much on the general prevalence of ability to read among the marriageable, and on the ability of the public teachers quickly to supply the deficiency, in case any persons unable to read were in haste to enjoy the privileges of wedlock.

This was intended, not as an obstacle to marriage, but as a spur to education, so far, at least, as to enable the people to read God's Word. He assumed that where schools were so generally patronized, and the means of acquiring the art of reading so universally available, none who were unwilling to learn could be suitable persons for training up families. His intention was not to dishonor the divine institution of marriage, but to honor it by raising the qualifications of the candidates for it. Furthermore, the refusal of the governor to give license to be married to such as could not read, was not, like a law of the Medes and Persians, unalterable; but an experiment to stimulate the dilatory to a little healthful mental effort, a measure which, if it should prove oppressive or unwelcome to the people, could, at any time, be recalled by himself, or vetoed by the supreme authority.

In a land of such corruption, as commerce found, and would have perpetuated, at the Sandwich Islands, a due regard to God's design, in respect to this relation, and to the specific rule given by the apostle to the Gentiles, should have facilitated, rather than obstructed the pathway to wedlock, and guarded, with sleepless earnestness, the avenues to impurity and licentiousness. " Nevertheless, to avoid fornication, let every man have his own wife and every woman her own husband." Disregard to this injunction and the long continued interdicting of marriage to great numbers to whom God had made it lawful and " honorable," might, in pagan countries, or partially Christianized countries, be expected to tend to licentiousness, blasphemy, and hypocrisy, and to a misanthropy which would, with unflinching hand, consign to the dungeon or the stake, the defenders of God's truth and institutions. Nay, a systematic and authoritative forbidding to marry might be used for training a disencumbered militia that could easily spread themselves far and wide, obsequiously to extend a gigantic human institution, acknowledging a virgin as its chief, and adorable patroness in heaven, and a voluptuous worm as its head on earth. But against such abuses, the rulers were on their guard. In no country, perhaps, is marriage made more easy than at the Sandwich Islands. No man thinks it is necessary to wait till he has a house or a farm, or a shop, or even a whole suit of clothes, in order to take a wife, nor do the women make these qualifications a *sine qua non*, when they seek or accept the hand of a husband.

Children and youth from twelve to sixteen years of age sometimes claim the privilege.

The rulers not only encourage marriage, but guard the institution with much care, among all ranks. There was no doubt of the kindness of Hoapili's intentions in requiring a knowledge of the art of reading in the candidates for marriage, or in requiring the children, above four years old, to attend school, and their parents or guardians to send them, or to allow them to attend, more or less ; yet his measures seemed somewhat arbitrary, I will not say, oppressive, for oppression is the abuse of power, to the injury of the weaker party, or the laying on of unreasonable burdens. But if the rulers, who, in seeking the best good of the subjects, sent their children to school, provided for their instruction, and considered it the right and duty of every one to have access to the written Word of God, and ability to read it under such provisions, essential to rightful marriage, were, therefore, to be considered oppressors, what must be said of them, had they officially denied their subjects the privilege of learning to read, or the free use of God's statute book, or the privilege of lawful Christian marriage, such as God intended for the human race ?

At this period, it was easy to see that a lax discipline, a weak, careless, ill supported government, which should allow the riotous to annoy the peaceful, and the malevolent to prey with impunity upon the well disposed subjects, must be more intolerable than rigid laws vigorously executed, by the firm hand of well supported hereditary chieftains.

The efforts of those who professed to love the Gospel were prized by the missionaries, and by the well disposed among the people. They were invariably favorable to schools among the common people. Among those of rank who had derived advantages from the Mission Seminary, was Kawailepolepo, from the church at Honolulu, who, before he had completed the course, was put in charge of Wailuku, a district on the northern part of Maui. He conscientiously and humbly endeavored to aid the cause of improvement, and the interests of the nation, rather than his personal gratification or aggrandizement, to the high satisfaction of the missionaries there, Messrs. Green and Armstrong. Of him, they were, at this period, pleased to say, " In all our school operations, and indeed in everything else that is good, we have the hearty co-operation of our worthy young chief, who was three years at the high school, and can, in some measure, appreciate the value of learning. In this we are highly favored." He very kindly assisted in the erection of a house for Mr. Armstrong, in various ways aided the station, and appeared to persevere unto the end as a consistent Christian and true soldier of Christ.

Under the auspices of friendly chiefs, and assisted by their wives, Messrs. G. and A. addressed themselves to their work, preaching, translating, and teaching. They had a school of adult men, more than thirty of whom they hoped to see qualified for teachers, a school for adult females, attending to reading, writing, singing, and arithmetic, a school of 200 native children taught by native monitors, two select classes of fine promising girls, and, fitting for the Missionary Seminary, a school of eighteen promising lads, as capable of learning as any class of boys in America. These different schools, after their daily exercises, were often brought together, at one place, and kindly addressed on the momentous concerns of the soul. A Sabbath school, of four or five hundred children, engaged their attention, of which they said, " This is a noble field of effort, a field in which, no doubt, angels would delight to labor." They had still a vastly wider field to superintend, in the numerous schools of east Maui. This year, Miss L. Brown commenced there, teaching the women to card, spin, knit, and weave, thus introducing the domestic wheel and loom, for the manufacture of cotton of Hawaiian growth. Her first class, of six or eight young women, learned readily, and in about five months, produced ninety yards of cloth, woven chiefly by Miss B. The girls learned, in this period, to be good spinners, and began to use the loom. Successive classes have been taught, in the same way there, and in other parts of the islands.

Governor Adams took so much interest in the domestic manufacture of cotton, that he introduced it into his own family, and had his young wife and others taught to use the wheel and loom successfully.

Mr. and Mrs. Whitney, maintaining the station at Waimea, Kauai, alone, after Mr. Gulick removed to Koloa, were, from the middle of July to the middle of October, afflicted with her severe illness, far from medical aid; during six or eight days of which she was considered in imminent danger, before they could obtain a physician from Oahu. The people, wakeful and inquiring, demanded an increase rather than a diminution of missionary labor. Much of this time, Mr. W. was enabled to teach forty scholars, two hours a day, preach twice on the Sabbath, attend two Sabbath schools, and have a prayer meeting every morning, at daylight, in the church, where a passage of Scripture was read and expounded. "God has been with us," he says, " in these meetings, and I can look at them with the sweetest reflection that there I have spent some of the most precious moments of my life."

Such attention to the spiritual advancement of the people, and such a readiness on their part to avail themselves of it, so as daily to bring a large congregation together, at break of day, to pray and sing, and hear God's Word, were preparing the way, under the influences of God's spirit, for greater things than these.

But further toils and further trials were needed, before the great harvest could be gathered in.

One of his useful helpers, Simeon Kaiu, being almost ready to supply the place of a foreign teacher, in a destitute village, in order to meet the wishes of the people on the eastern part of Kauai, and that he and Deborah Kapule, his wife, might be nearer their estates, removed with her and their retinue, embracing sixteen members of the church at Waimea, to Wailua; where he was to employ his useful talents in the work of instruction.   " Scarcely had they got settled," says Mr. W., " before their beloved teacher, Simeon, was suddenly cut off, by death. It was a severe stroke to the little colony, to this church, and to the island and nation. He was a man of sound judgment, excellent temper, and active piety. For ten years, he had adorned a profession of the Gospel ; and was taken from us, just at a time when we were hoping he would, in a good measure, supply the place of a foreign teacher.   His wife, Deborah, and the other members of the church will remain in that district, with the hope of obtaining a missionary to live with them, after our next general meeting."

No missionary is stationed there.   Deborah remained there ; but at length gave up her profession, and has, by her worldliness, greatly disappointed and grieved her Christian friends, who had regarded her both as pious and useful.   How many, in other lands, who remove and dwell far from the ordinances of God's house, like Deborah, give up their religion, and take the world for their portion !   Worldly as she is, she seems to favor neither the ancient nor modern superstition.   May she yet return to her duty, and find mercy.

In June of this year, the sixth reinforcement of our mission was welcomed to these shores.   It consisted of the Rev. T. Coan, who had explored the dark regions of Patagonia as a field of missions, but found his work at Hilo ; Mr. H. Dimond, the first regular bookbinder sent to the Sandwich Islands; Mr. E. O. Hall, the fifth printer; their wives; Miss Hitchcock, and Miss Brown, teacher of the domestic manufacture of cotton.   In their instructions, signed by the Rev. Secretaries B. B. Wisner, R. Anderson, and D. Greene, the earnest hope of the Board and the views of the Prudential Committee, in respect to their object, are thus summarily expressed :—

" The service you are to perform among the heathen is commanded by the God of heaven, and is therefore a practicable service.   Missions are nowhere impracticable.   There is no great Saharian desert which cannot be cultivated in the mind of this world.   Revolted as the human mind is from God, and corrupted and debased, it is, through God's grace, recoverable.   By the voice of the Son of God, as heard

in the Gospel, it can be and will be renovated.   That voice you are to
be on the Sandwich Islands.   There you may find multitudes of souls,
for whom Christ died, who never heard of his redeeming love.   You
carry to them tidings of that amazing fact of exhaustless interest, of
inconceivable importance.   Who that hath reflected upon the subject
can think lightly of your enterprise ?   You go, leaving

> ' Home, and ease, and all the cultured joys,
> Conveniences, and delicate delights
> Of ripe society, in the great cause
> Of man's salvation.—
> High on the pagan hills, where Satan sits
> Encamped, and o'er the subject kingdoms throws
> Perpetual night, to plant Immanuel's cross,
> The ensign of the Gospel, blazing round
> Immortal truth; and in the wilderness
> Of human waste to sow eternal life ;
> And from the rock, where sin, with horrid yell,
> Devours its victims unredeemed, to raise
> The melody of grateful hearts to heaven.'

"It is with joy, therefore, the Committee bid you go in the name
of Christ, in the full belief that He will be with you, and crown your
efforts with his blessing, and at length receive you into those mansions
which he has prepared for the rest of his missionaries."

In 1834, a Total Abstinence Society was formed at Lahaina,
sixteen masters and eighteen officers of whaleships at once
uniting in it.   A considerable number of foreign visitors at Honolulu, by a respectful memorial, urged the king and chiefs to
suppress the traffic in distilled liquors.   No missionary ever more
frankly and decidedly admonished the king to check the destructive vices of intemperance and licentiousness than did Capt.
Joseph Allen, of Nantucket, in his farewell letter to the king on
taking his final leave of the islands.   On an emergency the following appeal was made to the governor of Maui, by respectable
shipmasters lying at anchor in the roads of Lahaina :—

"LAHAINA, Nov. 17, 1835.

" Gov. HOAPILI,—We, the undersigned, have come to this good
country to refresh our ships with fruit and vegetables.   These we find
in great abundance, for which we leave you our dollars and cloth.   We
do not any of us like to go to Oahu, because bad men sell rum to
our seamen.   We like your island, because you have a good law preventing the sale of this poison.   But now, after lying here in peace
for some weeks, a vessel has come among us from Oahu with rum for
sale.   Our seamen are drinking it, and trouble is commencing.   We now
look to you for protection.   We think that as these men have violated
your wholesome regulations, and given your visitors so much trouble,
they should be punished by fine or otherwise, and sent immediately
from the island, after having all the rum thrown into the ocean.

FRANKLIN RIDDELL,	JAMES PIERSON,	EDWARD HARDING,
CHRYSTOPHER ALLYN,	GEO. HAGGERTY,	TIMOTHY W. RIDDELL,
PHILETUS PIERSON,	RICHARD WEEDEN,	RODOLPHUS N. SWIFT,
HENRY LEWIS,	DAVID BAKER,	ELIJAH DAVIS,
CHARLES G. BARNARD,	ISAAC BRAYTON,	JAMES B. WOOD,
GEORGE ALLEY,	JOHN HENDERSON,	GEORGE ALLEN."

The Fliberty-Gibbet was ordered away, and the natives forbidden to trade with her till the captain should have given indemnity to the injured.

Among the various efforts for the promotion of the cause of temperance, the following memorial, *sui generis*, by the chiefs and people of the Islands to the king, is probably the first formal, written petition ever presented to a Hawaiian monarch, and the first by any people to their sovereign on this important question. It was moved at a great popular temperance meeting at Honolulu, and drawn up by a native committee of that meeting, in their own language and style.

" HONOLULU, Nov. 26, 1835.

" Know thou, O King Kaukeaouli, this is our mature and undisguised sentiment. We make our earnest petition to you. Let the purchase of spirits and the retailing of spirits at the rumselling houses, and the distilling of spirits come to a total end—just these three things.

" We believe the kingdom would not be impoverished should these several things cease, for the people and foreigners too are ensnared by these evil things.

" Thou thyself hast seen the drunkenness, contentions, the wounds, and death of the people and foreigners, by means of ardent spirits, during thy reign.

" Not ourselves alone thine own people understand this evil, but certain shipmasters know the evil of this thing: and on account of it many are bound in irons through the prevalence of this traffic, both of natives and foreigners.

" Wherefore, we greatly desire these evils may be utterly abolished; not for our individual benefit only is this petition set forth that this course may be abandoned, but for your own good, O king, and that of your chiefs and people.

" We who abominate the practices here complained of, therefore set our names under this writing to oppose the wholesale traffic, the manufacture, and the retail of spirits at these islands. Let your true consent be also subjoined to forbid these things, for thou knowest it would not be adverse, but a great safeguard to the people of this country and of other countries here in thy kingdom, O king. And if thou understandest this matter, make known thy will, that we may see and hear."

This was at once signed by three female chiefs of the highest rank, Kinau, Kekauluohi, and Kekauonohi, and three highest male chiefs on Oahu, Kekuanaoa, Aikanaka, and Paki. Then the names of 1958 of the people of Honolulu district, and 846 of other parts of the island, were given in, concurring in the design. Thousands of the people on the other islands united their influence to secure this important object, which was at length consummated, so far, at least, as to free the government almost entirely from the responsibility of the deleterious traffic. Who knows what such a petition sent up by the nobles and people of Great Britain to the throne, would accomplish in the temperance reformation of the world?

CHAPTER XXI.

In commencing the record of a new year, it is with pleasure I
give a brief sketch of an interesting enterprise in that quarter of
the world by two philanthropists from England—Daniel Wheeler,
a preacher of the Society of Friends, and his son Charles, both
having spent some time in Russia endeavoring to improve the
condition of the lower orders. Voyaging in their own strongly
built sloop, the Henry Freeling, they touched at many points, and
visited many missionary stations in the Pacific between Van Die-
man's Land and Hilo, teaching temperance, righteousness, and a
serious regard to the Word and Spirit of God. They arrived at
Honolulu, December 25, 1835, and remained at the islands about
six months, or till near the close of June, 1836, and visited most
of our missionary stations. In their intercourse with the rulers,
they endeavored to impress them with the importance of equity
to the common people, recommended the prohibition of the influx
of intoxicating drinks, and of the traffic that makes and kills
drunkards, and the restraining of the flood of licentiousness that
drowns men and women in perdition.

To make speedy and thorough work of stopping drunkenness,
Friend Wheeler not only advised the king to prevent the importation of spirits, but to buy up at once and pour into the sea what
could be found on his shores. How widely different from the
counsels which France, Rome, the world, and Satan, have urged
with vehemence and perseverance, at the Sandwich and Society
Islands!

In Friend Daniel Wheeler's public discourses to the people,
which our missionaries readily interpreted, though there was a haze
more or less dense about them, some of the grand doctrines of
the cross were seen to shine out through it. He spoke of the
depraved state of men, by nature "dead in sin," the necessity
of the regeneration of sinners, who must be "raised from death
unto life" by the Spirit of God; justification by faith, of "the

true and living worshippers, redeemed from sin and reconciled to God by the righteousness of Christ;" sanctification or the duty of obedience to the commands of Christ; the union of all his true disciples in one " society of friends to God, to one another and to the whole race," and the obligations of every man to use the light which he has in the service of his Maker, whether that light be *conscience, reason, written revelation,* or the *internal influence of God's Spirit.**

His disregard to visible sacraments, audible prayer, and singing, were, perhaps, hardly noticed by the people ; and as to the peculiarities of his colloquial and denominational style, they could not be distinguished in the Hawaiian language, and are probably known only to the English.

While these friends were with us, to give a specimen of the running to and fro before our eyes for the increase of knowledge, which it is desirable should be multiplied a hundred fold, I may mention that Mrs. B., in that corner of the world, had the pleasure one evening of receiving at her table the Rev. Samuel Parker, from his exploring tour on the Rocky Mountains and the Columbia River; the Rev. Daniel Lee, of the Methodist mission in Lower Oregon; the Rev. Mr. Beaver, from England, chaplain of the Hudson's Bay Company's station at Fort Vancouver, on the Columbia River, and his wife from Wales; the Seamen's Chaplain for Honolulu, the Rev. Mr. Diell, and his lady; Mr. P. A. Brinsmade, a friendly and liberally educated temperance merchant of the place, from New England; and the philanthropic Friends Daniel and Charles Wheeler, from England and St. Petersburg.

A sketch of one of our native helpers, who in February of this year was transferred from Hilo to Wailuku, may here be appropriately given.

Soon after we began to preach the Gospel at Honolulu a poor blind heathen, with untrimmed beard and almost destitute of covering, was repeatedly led by a little heathen lad to our place of worship, and early became a constant and interested attendant. He learned, ere long, to find the way to our little thatched church without his guide. He was generally found to be in his place in good season, and as near the preacher's feet as he could well be, and holding as attentive an ear as any one in the assembly

While many of his countrymen were enjoying the pleasure and prospect of learning to read and write, and of acquiring, by means of books, a variety of useful knowledge, he, from the loss of sight, was denied this privilege, but was doubtless led by that means the more to cultivate the power of memory, for which he became distinguished. His best mode of acquiring ideas for a

---

* A Bostonian Restorationer, who heard him address a large concourse at Honolulu, and who had flattered himself that a loose morality would find more lenity at his hands than at those of our missionaries, said, in his disappointment, " He is as much of a blue-stocking as any of them."

long period, was by hearing sermons which he early learned to love.

With his retentive memory, listening for years to evangelical preachers, who, with great plainness, let the Scriptures speak freely in their obvious import, he was able to gather up and retain many ideas, a fund of Scripture and other valuable matter, somewhat methodically arranged so as to be available in teaching others. He began early to recommend instruction, and to exhort others even of high rank to attend to the concerns of their souls, among whom was Kamamalu, who died in England after a short period of Christian instruction at the islands.

His poverty and helplessness, and sense of dependence, as in other ages and countries, were, it may be presumed, favorable to his reception of the gracious proffers of the Gospel. The offer of spiritual sight to the literally blind, and of the riches of heaven to the miserably poor, and of the glorious freedom of the sons of God to those who suffer unwelcome subjugation in any land, it might be expected would be peculiarly welcome. And this has been proved in many instances at these islands.

The meekness, docility, and apparent gratitude with which he listened to the same heavenly message which Christ, amid the opposition and scorn of the great and proud, had preached with acceptance to the poor, led us early to hope this poor, sightless immortal would enjoy a celestial light, and inherit a crown incomparably more valuable than that of his earthly sovereign, who looked down upon him as on a worm.

After giving some evidence of loving the truth as it is in Jesus, he, at the request of Queen Keopuolani, removed from Honolulu to Lahaina, where he continued his attentions to the means of grace. In the summer of 1825, he was there admitted to the fellowship of the church as the first native received to the Lord's table in the Sandwich Islands. There were, at the same time, several of high rank, and others, at the different stations, coming out before the world with their professions of being on the Lord's side, who took the vows of the covenant a little later.

As the mental powers and Christian character of Bartimeus became more fully developed, he took an active part occasionally at prayer and conference meetings, became a good speaker, was employed as an assistant at different stations, and at length received a license to preach. He was a distinguished master of his mother tongue. His elocution was flowing and forcible; his enunciation distinct, though sometimes rapid. His memory was good, and after he began to love the truth, he gathered up useful knowledge with rapidity, and seemed to make Christian attainments apace.

Such was his acquaintance with the character and habits of his countrymen, with the Sacred Scriptures, and the modes of reasoning exhibited by the missionaries, that he could readily make a happy and forcible appeal to an assembly of the people.

I have sat with pleasure, as my brethren have done, and heard him pour forth a torrent of fervent words and useful thoughts, which caused me to admire the grace of God to such a degraded heathen, and to feel it to be a privilege to sit at his feet, while the love of Christ and of souls was in his heart and the language of Christian eloquence was on his tongue. His gestures were appropriate, graceful, and forcible. His voice was winning. Standing erect, in a manly posture, or bowing himself a little forward, stretching forth the hand, like Paul on the stairs, though he could give neither flashes of fire, nor the softer expressions of deep-toned kindness, by the glance of his eyes, he often labored with tears to persuade the people to forsake their sins, and poured forth his fervid appeals to rouse them to immediate compliance with the divine injunctions.

A few years after his admission to the church, he removed to Hilo, where, for several years, he rendered important assistance. He returned to Maui, about the middle of February, 1836, and subsequently labored at Honuaula and Wailuku. Of his entrance there, a missionary, who was then slow to see the evidence of piety and intelligence among the native professors of religion, says :—

" I called upon Bartimeus, the blind man, from Hilo, to address the congregation, as he had just arrived. He did so, and afforded us great satisfaction by his excellent and timely remarks. I am uniformly pleased with this man, he is so humble and well instructed in things pertaining to the Kingdom of God. He is going to make the tour of East Maui. I trust he will be instrumental of great good."

He, not long after, gave to the people of Wailuku an impressive address, in favor of an increased attention to the education of children, and of a more prompt and generous support of the native teachers; for notwithstanding what had been done by Hoapili, Auwae, Kawailepolepo, and others, in favor of schools, he was not satisfied that the chiefs or the parents had yet come up to the proper mark. He referred to numbers of the children who, he thought, were corrupted and led astray by careless, indiscreet, ignorant, or wicked parents, and to many little ones left to themselves, and allowed to run wild like the goats. He boldly reflected on the chiefs for their indifference in regard to the prosperity of the schools, and urged the importance of the voluntary efforts of the people. He demanded of the great assembly, if they had looked upon the happy effects of the Gospel, at the islands, for fifteen years, and were yet unbelieving as to the value of education. He thought civilized nations domineered over the chiefs and people, and treated them as though they were little children, because they were deficient in knowledge, and therefore education should be encouraged as the means of protection and independence. With vehemence, and skill, and kindness, he urged his countrymen to support the teachers well. He alluded to the cost of a heathen education in those things which were worse than useless. He said :—

" In the time of dark hearts, I learned the *hula* (singing, drumming, and dancing, or heathen revelry). I learned also the bloody *lua*, the business of a bandit. I learned the *ka-ke*, a dialect known to few. In that period of night, I was taught *mischief*. But did it *cost* nothing ? Was there nothing paid to those teachers of evil-doing ? Ah, I remember the hogs, the *kapas*, the fish, the *awa*, and other things which we paid them, and paid them freely. We thought it right to pay such teachers. But how is it now ? Here are men of our own blood and nation, whose business it is to teach us and our children good things, the things of God, and salvation, our Bibles, geographies, arithmetics ; and ought we not promptly to support them ? How can they continue to teach if they have nothing to eat and nothing to wear ? Will they not, ere long, be disheartened ? Who can work long when he is hungry ? Let us take hold with our own hands and help the teachers freely, seasonably, and efficiently."

Others concurred, and a new impulse was given, and increased efforts were made to support the cause of education.

About the middle of the year 1836, the assembled missionaries made to their patrons the gratifying report, " that in the progress of a year, 1850 pages of new matter had been added to the publications for the Hawaiians ; that 151,929 copies of various works, amounting to 11,606,429 pages, had been printed, at a cost of $5,336 48;—10,546 volumes bound, and 36,050 pamphlets folded, stitched, covered and cut, and made accessible to such as wanted them ; and another edition of the New Testament was expected to be called for as soon as it could possibly be printed, as well as other reprints and new works." The preaching of the Gospel and other ordinary means of grace, and several protracted meetings in different places, were accompanied by the blessing of God. The special presence of the Lord was felt and acknowledged in many of the congregations a part of the year; 212 hopeful converts were received to the fellowship of the churches, 1358 marriages were solemnized by the missionaries, two churches organized, 249 children baptized, and 14,500 hearers, attending on the stated preaching of the missionaries, heard from Sabbath to Sabbath the words of eternal life The chiefs and people having looked another year at the claims of Christianity and its effects on those who received it as from God, were settling down in the conviction that the *temperance, righteousness,* and peace which it promoted and enjoined, rendered it worthy of consideration. Several chiefs who had opposed, now became favorable to the missionary work ; several high chiefs, joined by 3000 of the most respectable natives of Honolulu and neighboring stations, petitioned the king to suppress entirely the manufacture, sale, and intemperate use of ardent spirits on the islands. Twenty-five shipmasters petitioned the government to suppress all the grog-shops at Honolulu.

This is a brief sketch of one of the three years subsequent to the anti-missionary movement of the " engrafted chief," Kaomi, and his irreligious coadjutors of 1833, when, with the king's " signet," as it were, he licensed rum and ruin, to take their course, except where conscience, the Gospel, missionary influence, Christian governors, and the kingdom of God, were strong enough to oppose Satan and his legion. But during this period of misrule, the population diminished at a fearful and lamentable rate.

Nothing was more reasonable, therefore, than that the missionary laborers, who believed that God was just as ready and just as likely to crown with his blessing the labors and prayers of the spiritual cultivator and seedsower as of the physical or natural, should put forth their united and their best efforts for a spiritual harvest of immeasurable value.

The annual convention of the mission was a meeting of great interest. An unusual glow of brotherly love was manifest. Great harmony, not associated with indifference as to what should prevail, but with earnestness and watchfulness as to matters of moment, marked the deliberations which were continued for days together. Many and important subjects they discussed with patience and candor, and kind feeling, and in most cases their decisions were remarkably unanimous. Devotional exercises were happily intermingled.

During the convention, we sat down twice at the table of our Lord, once with the native church at Honolulu, when thirty-nine native converts made a public profession of their faith, and were baptized and received to the communion of God's people, and once as a mission church, distinct from the native converts, the services being in English; but in the former case, as usual, in the Hawaiian language.

The attendance on the ordinance, by the missionaries and their wives and children, and a few select natives, was a deeply interesting, melting, heavenly season. Messrs. Thurston and Richards, with their wives, presented their infants to God in baptism; Persis G. and Lucy G., the two eldest daughters of Mr. and Mrs. Thurston, gave themselves to the Lord and his people, and took on them the vows of his everlasting covenant, and sat down with the missionaries at their Master's table. This was a matter of tender and joyful interest, to welcome to the full communion of the church the first fruits among our own offspring there, while some of their contemporaries returned to the United States, were welcomed there in like manner to the bosom of the American church. Many an eye was suffused, and many a heart swelled with gratitude and overflowed with praise in witnessing and taking part in this scene. Some among the other children being cared for, prayed for, and labored with for their immediate conversion, manifested tenderness, while some parents were almost ready to say, "They made me keeper of the vineyards, but mine own vineyard have I not kept."

The mission felt encouraged to go forward with new zeal and faith in their work, to call upon one another and upon the native Christians, and upon the patrons and friends of the mission, to offer their most earnest prayers that the year of labor on which they were to enter, as they separated from the convention, might be among the dying Hawaiians "a year of the right hand of the Most High."

The prayers of faith and the labors of faith were employed that year, if they have ever been at the Sandwich Islands. And God in his providence called the multitude at home in the eager pursuit of wealth to pause and consider whether an inheritance above were not worth an unusual share of attention; and many, seeing their earthly gains and fancied wealth vanishing, stood amazed in a posture of waiting to see what the Lord would do.

At the Sandwich Islands, the missionaries saw that unless Christianity could arrest the causes of desolation, the ruin of the nation was certain. They were constrained to say:

"The angel of death stands over the land with a drawn sword. The anger of the Lord has kindled a fire upon the nation which will burn to its entire destruction, unless it be speedily extinguished. With us the present is truly a time of hope and fear. It is also emphatically a time of effort. If the work of destruction is ever arrested here, it must be done soon. According to the present ratio of decrease, it will be but a few years before the pall of death will be spread over the whole land, and these valleys, once full of people, will be solitary. These shores, once teeming with myriads, will either become silent as the house of death, or be peopled with a new race of men. But we hope better things are in reserve for this people; that these fearful clouds will, ere long, pass away, and the work of destruction cease. But should the consumption determined go through the land in indignation, a remnant will be saved; and we feel more and more that we are to labor for this people as 'pulling them out of the fire.' We greatly need help to apply at once, and in every part of the islands, the only sovereign antidote to this dreadful contagion, and we are happy to learn that our Macedonian cry has not been unheeded."

With such views, the laborers went forth again to sow and reap, and were everywhere cheered on by divine encouragements.

Mr. Thurston, at Kailua, says of the converts at that station, in October of 1836:—

"The church, as a body, I think appears well, and many of the members are truly engaged in religion, and are men and women of prayer, anxious for the salvation of souls. There is more deep feeling, repentance, and humility in the church at the present time, than I have witnessed before for a number of years. There is among the people generally more seriousness, and a better attention has been given to preaching for a number of months than has been usual. There are many instances of deep conviction, and some, it is hoped, of real conversion to God. The Spirit of God is evidently operating upon the hearts of sinners, and some, it is believed, have submitted themselves to the Lord Jesus to be his for ever. The Lord be praised for any evidence that souls are born of God! 'It is not by might nor by power, but by my spirit, saith the Lord.' 'For Zion's sake will we not rest, till her righteousness go forth as brightness, and her salvation as a lamp that burneth.' "

The same month, Mr. Clark (who in 1834 removed from the station at Honolulu, to take part in the instruction of the Mission Seminary), as though from the hills of Lahainaluna he saw the cloud as that of a divine hand, stretched forth to indicate the rain, says :—

" We have reason to think that God has been visiting us with the influences of his Holy Spirit. We hope that a few of our best scholars have recently become the followers of Christ. Others are more or less serious. We deeply feel our responsibility and our need of the prayers of God's people. Unless our pupils become pious, the labor and money laid out on them will be in a great measure lost, and in some instances worse than lost."

The last month in the year, Mr. Coan made the tour of Hawaii, passing to Hamakua, Waimea, Kailua, and Kaawaloa, then round through Kau, Puna, and Hilo.

Of the latter part of this tour he gives such an account as to lead us to think the Spirit of God attended his preaching while passing, as it were, through a wilderness of about 100 miles of those neglected coasts. In Puna he examined more than twenty schools and more than twelve hundred scholars. He says ;—

" From the time when I landed in Kau till I reached home, a period of eight days, I preached forty-three times, and often to congregations that listened with much interest and many tears. In a thickly populated district of Puna where I spent the Sabbath, I found a most interesting state of feeling. Multitudes flocked to hear, and many of them seemed pricked to the heart under the influence of the truth. Here I spent two days and preached ten times, the interest seeming to increase to the last. All the intervals between the hours of preaching, were filled up in conversing with natives, who pressed upon me to receive instruction. So great was the throng that I was not able to speak with one half of those who labored to get access to me. I had literally no leisure so much as to eat ; and one morning I found myself constrained to preach three times before breakfast, which I took at ten o'clock. I could not move out of doors, in any direction, without being thronged by people from all quarters, and multitudes who could find no other opportunity to converse, stationed themselves by the wayside, sometimes singly, and sometimes in companies of three, five, ten, etc., in order to speak with me, as I passed. Some followed me from village to village, for several days, to hear the Gospel. Among these was the old high priest of the volcano, brother of the old Priestess, of whom Mr. Stewart speaks in his journal. This ancient priest of heathenism was noticed as giving fixed attention to preaching at the time when Mr. Lyman and myself passed through that district, a year ago. He has since been several times to our station, a distance of forty or fifty miles, and spent a number of weeks, to hear the Word of God; and within a few days past, we have examined him, with reference to his admission to the church. During this examination he gave something of the history of his life, and among other things he confessed that he had been a highway robber and a murderer. He said that he had killed two men with his own hands, for no other reason than to obtain their kapas (native clothing), and food not amounting probably to more than fifty cents in value. He seems penitent, and we think he is truly converted to God. His sister, the priestess, still lives in Puna, but she evinces no relish for the Gospel. I found her, in one of my meetings, in a small village through which I passed, and I had a close personal conversation with her on the interests of her soul. But she seems utterly opposed to the claims of God upon her heart. In receiving such men as this old priest into the church, I am often reminded of Paul's language to the Corinthian Church—1 Cor. VI: 9, 10, 11. All the sins there mentioned have been common to most of our church members in the days of their heathenism; and even this catalogue does not express half the former character of many. If you wish to see the full drawn portrait just add the list of crimes that are recorded in Rom. Chapter 1st.

"I reached home from this tour of the island, in just thirty days from the time I left.

"One week after my return, I went out, through the district of Hilo, to preach and examine schools, etc. This tour occupied about a week, during which time I examined 1200 scholars, and preached more than twenty times.

"Hilo is one of the most picturesque and verdant districts in the Sandwich Islands. Puna is low and level, several miles from the shore, and is little else than a vast field of lava, covered in some places with a thin soil, and in other places of five to fifteen miles in extent, entirely naked, and glowing and glittering under a tropical sun. There are no streams, and very little fresh water in that district. Hilo, on the other hand, is an inclined plane, with bold and precipitous shores. The land rises rapidly from the sea, to the centre of the island, where it is crowned by the lofty Mauna Kea, which is usually mantled in snow. Travelling in Hilo is very difficult and dangerous, on account of the numerous ravines and precipices, by which the land is everywhere broken. All these ravines form channels for so many rivers or torrents, which come leaping and foaming along their rocky beds, dashing down innumerable precipices, and urging their noisy way to the ocean. In times of great rains, these streams run rapidly, and rush along with such maddening energy, as to prevent swimming or fording them. When there is less rain, they are shallow, and can be forded, at certain places, or passed by leaping from rock to rock, with which their beds are filled. While passing through the district, for thirty or thirty-five miles, I took occasion to number the principal ravines over which I passed; and without measuring, or pretending to accuracy, I reduced them, according to the best of my judgment, to the following classifications; 14 were from 200 to 1000 feet deep; 16 were from 50 to 100; and 22 were from 20 to 50. All these 63 ravines are the channels of streams of water. In many places, the banks of the ravines are perpendicular, and can only be ascended by climbing with the utmost care, and descended only by letting one's self down, from crag to crag, by the hands. In times of rain, these precipices are very slippery and dangerous, and in many places the traveller is obliged to wind his way along the sides of a giddy steep, where one step, of four inches from the track, would precipitate him to a fearful depth below."

What a field for a missionary do these two districts of Hilo and Puna constitute! A district, seventy or eighty miles in extent coast-wise, embracing some thirteen or fourteen thousand inhabitants, most of them poor and destitute, and utterly precluded from rising to affluence, with their embarrassments arising from the nature of their location, their want of skill, or their want of capital, of facilities for transportation, and of a market for their productions. And such, to a great extent, was the condition of the mass of the Hawaiian nation, proving that a home market for their products was indispensable to the adequate supply of the wants of the nation, and that agriculture and manufactures must both be greatly promoted among them, before they can rise above penury.

When Christianity was fully recognised by the nation, the need of cultivating the arts was not the less apparent to the mission and to the intelligent visitors and friends of the nation, than before; and by some, the missionaries were pressed to go into it, somewhat beyond their original design; because it was seen to be indispensable. On the subject of Hawaiian agriculture, the mission have said, " that a land, enjoying one of the finest climates in the world, with a soil as good for cultivation as any on which the sun ever shone, should remain, to a great extent, untilled, is a subject on which we feel intense interest, as connected with the future destinies of the nation." Some portions of the soil are indeed excellent, and might, doubtless, be made much better, but there have been found difficulties not yet overcome, in securing that productiveness, in exportable products, which is found in many other countries. Very much of the surface of the country must ever be unproductive. Its basaltic rocks and lava plains, its precipices, and ravines, its contiguity to the sea, its exposedness to winds, excess of rain in some places, and to drought in others, and to numerous enemies to products of various growth found there, may baffle the skill and keep in check the ardor of the husbandman for a long period.

The introduction of the plough, the domestic wheel and loom, the scissors and needle, the different processes of house-building, the manufacture of sugar, the culture of the cane and the mulberry, engraving and printing on copper, etc., have all received our attention and encouragement; and still more the training of men to the business of printing and book-binding, to supply the nation with reading and elementary works, as one part of the process of raising up the nation to take its rank among the civilized families of earth.

The printers and binders who entered the service, for that purpose, under the direction of the American Board, have had an important field of usefulness, and the satisfaction of seeing their skill, patience, and toil, turning to good account, in a double sense. Laborers, in these departments, sufficient to produce 50,000 volumes a year are employed, in connexion with the mission helpers. The native printers and book-binders at our office, uniformly exhibit commendable industry and sobriety; and their wages being paid them at fair prices, by the piece, are not interfered with by the chiefs or lordlings of any class; and few of the dealers in intoxicating drinks ever get a shilling of them for their deleterious drugs. On this subject, the testimony of Mr. Dimond, who left New York and joined our mission, to direct our book-binding, is highly creditable and important. In 1836, he wrote as follows:—

" I have fifteen men in the bindery—folders, sewers, forwarders, and finishers; and a shop of more orderly men, of the same number, can hardly be found in America. I am quite certain that the same number of men, taken promiscuously from among the book-binders of New York, would suffer in the comparison. Although they are paid in money, and generally have some about them, I have never known one of them to get intoxicated; and only one, on one occasion, to drink rum, although it can be obtained, at any time, in the village."

The native printers and binders do not work as rapidly nor as skilfully as American and English workmen; still they labor diligently, patiently, and honestly, and can perform every part of the process well, from the laying and setting the type to the gilding and lettering of a neat volume. A considerable portion of the product of their labor is sold at cost, though most of the people find it difficult to pay money for the books which they wish to possess.

The missionaries, intent on providing a needy nation of 125,000 souls, with ample means of instruction in every useful department, and unwilling to have the ordinary useful arts of life neglected, applied to their Directors specifically for forty-six additional missionary laborers, to be sent at once, pointing out the location and the work for each; and before the close of this year they, moreover, sent to the A. B. C. F. M. and other philanthropists, a memorial on the importance of increased efforts to cultivate the useful arts among the Hawaiian people. These appeals, approved by the majority of the chiefs of the islands, though they did not meet the full response desired, were sent forth with pleasing hope and were received with kindness. The memorial is as follows:—

" The introduction and cultivation of the arts of civilization must, it is believed, have an important bearing on the success of the preaching of the Gospel, and the permanence of evangelical institutions in the Sandwich Islands.   But if there were no immediate connexion, and the influence of the latter could be permanent without the former, still the arts and institutions of civilized life are of vast importance to the happiness, improvement, and usefulness of any nation where they are, or may be, properly fostered.   Of the importance of both, our Directors were aware, when they instructed us to aim at raising up the entire population of these islands to an elevated state of Christian civilization, and to get into extended operation and influence the arts, institutions, and usages of civilized life and society.

"As our great aim has been to win the nation to Christ, we believe we have begun right in preaching the Gospel, translating the Scriptures, making books, establishing schools, and by their means giving the people access to the Bible and other means of knowledge.   God has granted his blessing on these efforts.   A great change has been effected in the religious views of the nation, and a radical change in their religious institutions.   But the improvements in the civil policy of the government, and in the science of political economy, have by no means kept pace with the progress of Christianity.   How could this be otherwise, on the supposition that our influence was felt chiefly where we wished it to be ?   Our business was to rouse a stupid nation to the immediate concerns of their souls, and if any have been made wise unto salvation, it is not to be expected that they should of course be made equally wise in the things of this life.   The reception of the Gospel by the majority of the royal family did not abrogate their hereditary title to the soil ; and though the Bible inculcates justice in rulers, it does not show the *modus operandi ;*—it does not prescribe the form of government, nor direct the specific methods of administration.

" We were not sent to this people in the character of *civilians* or *politicians ;* nor should we be likely to be acknowledged as such by the rulers, or by the churches at home, should we be disposed to assume that character.   We were, moreover, cautioned against interfering with the party politics and commercial interests of the people ; and our engagements have been sufficiently numerous and important without giving much attention to law, agriculture, manufactures, commerce, &c.   Little could be expected from other sources of information to which the people have had access.   The few items of salutary advice which they have received from intelligent foreigners, have generally been deemed interested advice, as coming from a class of men, the majority of whom, intent on their own gains, are willing to elevate themselves by the depression of the people.   So far as we know, the foreign mechanics who are employed in the islands uniformly refuse to teach the natives the trades which they exercise ; and the course pursued by the public agents stationed here, seems to us to embarrass and depress, rather than to enlighten and elevate the nation, unless we admit that they can rise by opposition.

" Great as the change has been in the religious aspects of this nation, it is not to be supposed that the great mass of the people are controlled by the principles of Christian benevolence, or that they are prepared for freedom, or capable of being as yet governed on the principles of civil liberty.   Nor would we propose a *radical* (or revolutionary) change in the constitution or form of government, but would wish to see *the rights of the people better defined, better understood, better respected by those in power and better maintained by themselves,* so that the condition, both of the rulers and the ruled, may be vastly improved, and the general happiness and prosperity of all classes may be greatly promoted and rendered permanent. To accomplish this, great wisdom, and enterprise, and benevolence are requisite.

"The people need competent instruction in *agriculture, manufactures,* and the various methods of *production,* in order to develope the resources of the county (which are considerable), for though there is a great proportion of waste and barren territory in the group, yet either of the principal islands is doubtless capable of sustaining quadruple the whole population, were its resources properly and fully called forth. They need competent instruction immediately in the science of government, in order to promote industry, to secure ample means of support, and to protect the just rights of all. They need much instruction and aid in getting into operation and extended influence those arts and usages which are adapted to the country, calculated to meet the wants, call forth and direct the energies of the people in general, and to raise up among them intelligent and enterprising agents, qualified to carry on the great work of reform here and elsewhere.

"There are various obstacles to be met at the outset. The people are *poor* as well as ignorant. They have not the capital nor the encouragement to enter on any great plan of improvement in bringing forward the resources of the country. Though the people, as a body, perform considerable labor for themselves and drudgery for superiors, yet there is a great deficiency in the amount of profitable industry. Hitherto the right of soil has been considered as belonging to the sovereign or royal family, and the common people have not been able to acquire an indisputable title to any portion of it, or a trustworthy lease, by which the occupant might consider himself as permanently settled, and secured in the occupancy of a piece of land, the products of which, beyond a certain rent or tax, should be his *own.* The same rule applies to the fisheries, the salt beds, and other means of support. The evil will not probably be eradicated till the common people are themselves better qualified to manage their own affairs ;—till they have more knowledge, forecast, integrity, stability, patriotism, and loyalty, so that while they should employ their powers economically, and exercise an intelligent regard to their own private rights, they could reasonably be expected to defend with greater firmness the interests of their country, and the just rights of their rulers.

"The sentiment seems to be of ancient date, that ' the sovereign cannot govern chieftains whose lands are not at his control, and that hereditary chiefs cannot easily govern *independent* landholders under them.' This principle is not eradicated by the introduction of the Gospel, and will probably yield only to the progress of moral and intellectual improvement. Owing, therefore, to the natural condition of the people, their ignorance, poverty, and subjugation, their labors are not the most cheerful or well-directed; their strength is applied at a great disadvantage : there is a great waste of human muscle in the cultivation of the soil, in the transportation of its products, and other heavy burdens, and the unaided performance of much that might be done or facilitated by the power of domestic animals, water, steam, machinery, &c.

" What would the common people of the United States think if they had to supply themselves, their state and town officers, their lawyers, doctors, and school teachers, with the simple article of fuel by carrying it five miles on their shoulders in bad roads, without hat or shoes, and cultivate the ground for their sustenance, without plough or team ? Yet such is the disadvantage at which the muscular strength of a great portion of the men at the Sandwich Islands is applied, though it is easier to cultivate water *kalo* by hand, than maize or wheat. What man in New England would be ambitious to build a house for his son, if he must go to the Green Mountains, and bring the materials on his own shoulder a distance of twenty miles ? And who, it may be asked, could be expected to perform more of this kind of labor than obvious personal necessity requires, or superior authority compels ?

" There must be, therefore, a great deficiency in the productive industry of the country, until an increase of knowledge shall enable the people to apply their strength or capital to better advantage, and the motives to enterprise and exertion shall be more extensively and powerfully felt.

" If we suppose one or two thousand of the people are under the influence of Christian motives, one to a hundred, or one to fifty ; the great body need more powerful promptings and encouragements to effort and enterprise than they now have, and unless something more can be done for the people, they will not provide well either for the rising or future generations : they will not sustain good schools for the education of their children : they will not raise up and maintain a competent number of well trained ministers, physicians, lawyers, legislators, etc., nor will they have manufacturers and merchants of their own to conduct the business of the country. But foreign speculators may be expected to seize on the advantages which the country affords for agriculture, manufactures, and commerce : and an inevitable influx of foreign population, induced only by the love of pleasure and gain, would doubtless hasten the waste of the aborigines ; and at no distant period, the mere mouldering remnants of the nation could be pointed out to the voyager.

" The inquiry then becomes highly interesting to the Christian philanthropist, By what means can a wise and generous policy be introduced into the administration of the civil power without abrogating the form of a hereditary monarchy ; the equitable rights of the subjects be secured ; the resources of the country developed ; national economy and wealth advanced ; schools and evangelical institutions made prosperous and permanent ; and the temporal and spiritual good of the present, the rising, and the future generations of the people be most effectually promoted ?

" It is obvious that more vigorous efforts ought to be made in the department in which we, as propagators of Christianity, are appropriately engaged, and that corresponding efforts should also be made in the other departments, for the purpose of making improvements in legislation, in the execution of law, in medicine, agriculture, manufactures, and commerce. There is no reasonable doubt that teachers and laborers of the right stamp, who are ready to devote themselves to Christ and the people in these departments, would be received and made useful.

"If, in the opinion of the Board, these could not be employed under their immediate direction, as the teachers of printing and binding now are, let another Society be formed on similar principles, as a coadjutor, and send forth teachers and laborers for the specific object, not only to the Sandwich Islands, but to any other countries where a similar necessity exists for that kind of aid.

"Or if that should appear less practicable, let a company be formed on Christian and benevolent principles, for the express purpose of promoting the interests of this country by encouraging the cultivation of sugar-cane, cotton, silk, indigo, and various useful productions adapted to the soil and climate; and the manufacture of sugar, cotton, silk, clothing, hats, shoes, implements of husbandry, etc.

"Let this company, or the agents to be employed by the society above named, consist of men of approved piety and established character.

"1. A general superintendent, possessing weight of character, liberal endowments, thoroughly acquainted with the science of law, and capable of giving advice in the affairs of government.

"2. Four agriculturists acquainted with the growing of cotton, cane, &c., and the manufacture of sugar, to superintend plantations, that is, one for each of the principal islands.

"3. A merchant to transact the mercantile business of the Society or company, both in the islands and abroad, supplying the people at a reasonable rate with such articles as they need, receiving raw cotton, cane, cash, &c., in payment more to their advantage than selfish men will do.

"4. A cotton manufacturer, with competent machinery or the means of making it, who should work all the cotton raised by the company or received in barter for goods, and this product should be offered by the merchant for sale to the people, and if not demanded by them, exported to the coast.

"The company, or the principal agents employed by the Society, might consist of seven persons, as above named, who might have pious artisans to assist in the business, and in giving the needful instruction to the natives in the various arts; or if they prefer it, the following artisans may be associated in the company, viz: a blacksmith and carpenter, to assist each of the agriculturists, a wheelwright, a mill-wright, paper-maker, type-founder, house-joiner, cabinet-maker, cooper, tanner and currier, harness and shoe-maker, plough-maker, mason, tailor, and hatter, all ardently devoted to Christ, and ready to give their services to the Sandwich Islands' nation, much on the same principle as evangelical missionaries are expected to do. Each of these might undertake the instruction of a number of natives in their respective arts, as a printer and bookbinder has done.

"The agriculturists and cotton manufacturer, besides endeavoring to enlist the chiefs and head men in the business, would give employment to a considerable number of natives of regular habits, who living on the plantations, or in houses of their own in the neighborhood, might obtain a comfortable support, both adults and children, and become possessors of property of their own earning, besides paying their own annual taxes to the government.

" Should the agriculturists have the control and profits of land, they would pay a rent to the government which would be better than is now received, as they would probably occupy chiefly ground that is not now tilled at all.   Thus the government would be an immediate gainer, besides the ultimate and immediate advantage to the people. A *school*, either under the direction of the mission or of the company, should be maintained in connexion with every establishment.

" The Society, or company, on entering on this plan, would need a ship freighted with materials, implements of husbandry, and other articles, and to be always at their service.   A considerable amount of funds would be requisite to get under weigh ; but it is believed the enterprise would pay for itself, in a pecuniary point of view, in a few years, and the persons engaged in it obtain an economical support for themselves and families.

" The profits of the whole establishment at these islands, above the original and current cost, must be devoted to the support of schools, or churches, charitable institutions, or internal improvements in the nation, according to the judgment of the company, for the benefit and elevation of the people, conformably with regulations to be approved by the A. B. C. F. M., or the S. I. Mission.

" The warmest and most invariable friendship should be cherished between the mission and the company, and they should invariably co-operate, though in reality they be distinct.

" Such is the outline of a plan to hasten the elevation of this people, and to secure permanently the blessings of civilization and Christianity—a plan which we propose to our patrons and the friends of the nation, with the earnest desire that the experiment may be tried.

" Could this, or something like it, be carried into immediate operation, we should hope that it would greatly facilitate the Christianizing of the present generation, and help to lay the foundation for the morality, intelligence, and piety of the next.

" Should such a class of men come upon the ground, and there should be any hesitation on the part of the government as to granting the use of land, and such facilities as might be desired at first, all the artisans could doubtless find employment in a more individual capacity, and support themselves at wages ; the merchant, the civilian, and the agriculturists, could act as teachers, undoubtedly, to good advantage to the people.

" There is room for *benevolent* exertion, and *much* benevolent effort must be made from some quarter, more than the present class of missionaries ever expect to perform, or the islands will not be filled with schools and churches, and fruitful fields and pleasant dwellings, and the full blessings of Christianity ultimately secured to the Hawaiian race."

This memorial was drawn up in July, 1836, and its purport and design made known to the government.   In August, of the same year, the king and chiefs of the nation united in a brief memorial, to their American friends, not only concurring in the general application, but specifying the kind of teachers whom they needed, and offering their patronage.

The document is singular in the history of nations, and

shows an acquaintance with the wants of a young people, and their gratitude and confidence towards the good people of the United States, and a degree of readiness to co-operate in measures for the good of all classes. It is addressed to those who had already sent them teachers of learning and religion.

"LAHAINA, AUG. 23, 1836.

" Love to you, our obliging friends in America. This is our sentiment as to promoting the order and prosperity of these Hawaiian Islands. Do give us additional teachers, like the teachers who dwell in your own country. These are the teachers whom we would specify, a carpenter, tailor, mason, shoemaker, wheelwright, paper maker, type founder, agriculturists skilled in raising sugar-cane, cotton, and silk, and in making sugar, cloth manufacturers, and makers of machinery to work on a large scale, and a teacher of the chiefs in what pertains to the land, acording to the practice of enlightened countries; and if there be any other teacher that could be serviceable in these matters, such teachers also.

" Should you assent to our request, and send hither these specified teachers, then will we protect them, and grant facilities for their occupations, and we will back up these works, that they may succeed well.

(Signed) KAUIKEAOULI,   KAAHUMANU 2D,   LELEIOHOKU,
          NAHIENAENA,   KEKAULUOHI,   KEKUANAOA,
          HOAPILI KANE,   PAKI,   KANAINA,
          MARIA HOAPILI,   LILIHA,   KEKAUONOHI,
          ADAMS KUAKINI,   AIKANAKA,   KEALIIAHONUI.

This appeal, sixteen years and four months after the settlement of our mission among them, shows not only a becoming readiness in the rulers to receive instruction in what pertains to the affairs of this life, as well as in what refers to the life to come, but as in all that our mission proffered, a willingness to consult the good of their subjects generally, by encouraging general instruction in whatever branches of knowledge, industry, or improvement, the mission and its friends were able or willing to give it. Kaikioewa, Keaweamahi, Konia, and Kapiolani, had they been present, would have concurred.

From the first efforts of Kaahumanu to procure for herself a well finished dwelling-house, one and another from among them erected for themselves permanent and pleasant habitations, furnished them as they were able, and by degrees, accommodated themselves to a residence in them, and occasionally invited their missionary and other friends to join them in a social evening party, of which, as proof of their readiness to imitate the example set them, and their success in it, one or two instances may be noticed. At the time of the convention of our mission, in 1834, Miriam Kekauluohi having, with her husband, Kanaina, built an elegant two story house of rock coral, near the mission houses, at Honolulu, received and entertained, one evening, at a well furnished table, thirty-three missionaries, including men and women, presiding herself with the dignity of a Christian matron. The year following, Kinau and her gentlemanly husband, on entering a house newly built, partly in Hawaiian and partly in foreign style, finished and furnished with considerable elegance, gave to numerous invited guests, a gratifying proof of their advancement in civilized life. Kekauluohi, having tried the routine of civilized domestic life, about two years, in her well finished and furnished habitation, received, at a Christian tea-party, the king, and some twelve or fourteen chiefs—all who were then at Honolulu, except the feeble and unhappy princess—and several missionaries and well-informed natives. The table furniture was respectable—the lamps, candles, and glass-shades were elegant—their bread, biscuit, cake, and tea, chiefly of their own preparing, all good ; and the order of the table was managed with kindness and regularity. Two or three tunes were played on a barrel organ, which had been recently and obligingly presented to Kinau, by Capt. Valiant, of the French Corvette, Bonite. After tea, the company being conducted to the large upper drawing-room, united, as was customary, in a hymn and prayer.

To the missionaries, who were deeply solicitous to devise and put in operation the means of similar advancement among the common people, it did not seem too much to hope, when these memorials were prepared, that enterprising men of skill, and virtue, and force of character, might be found, who, under such a pledge from the authorities of the country, and with such a soil and climate as the Sandwich Islands possess, would enter on these employments. It was clearly obvious that the chiefs, in this state of their progress, eminently needed a teacher, well versed in the principles of political economy, of law and government, and thoroughly acquainted with the language, habits, dispositions, and wants of the people, and the capabilities of their soil. But such a teacher it was difficult for the world then to furnish.

The memorial of the chiefs, and the memorial of the mission on the cultivation of the useful arts, and a printed circular of the mission, expressive of their views of the duty of the friends of Christ to engage in greatly increased numbers in spreading the Gospel speedily through the world, were conveyed to the United States by the Rev. William Richards, on his visit with his family, to his native shores. Mr. Spaulding, with constitution greatly impaired, retired, with his family, from the field the same month. Leaving the Lahaina station in charge of Mr. Baldwin, who became established there, and whose constitution did not find Waimea congenial. Messrs. R. and S. embarked in December, and reached the United States in about five months. Mr. S., with feeble voice and the use of one lobe of his lungs, for a time pleaded the cause of the mission not in vain, and soon faded away. Mr. R. remained about six months, attending to the objects of his visit, and having disposed of six children, returned with Mrs. R., a lonely mother, to the islands and to their two youngest in 1838.

CHAPTER XXII.

THE close of 1836 was marked by the last illness and afflictive death, at Honolulu, of the young princess, Nahienaena. This beautiful flower, once the pride of the nation, and once the joy of the infant church at Lahaina, having been blighted, through the power of the great enemy, was now cut down, and passed away. During the days of her wasting sickness (as for weeks before) efforts were made to lead her to repentance; but with what success is not yet fully known. She was induced to confess her sin and folly, and once more, in her distress, to call on the name of the Lord. She left a faint hope that she may be found to have been heard in an accepted time. Many tears and loud lamentations, among her friends, testified to the interest they felt in her case. Her remains were enclosed in an elegant coffin (having one of lead closely sealed within), and kept some weeks, in the house of her brother. The lofty kahilis of state there stood motionless over her. Her superb, princely robe of feathers, was displayed, and other tokens of respect, intended to correspond with her rank, were exhibited. The gay and bustling little world of Honolulu was partially hushed by this event, and by the influence of the Spirit of God on the people, while the body of the princess reposed in silence. A series of protracted meetings having been arranged, for the different stations, on Oahu, were anticipated with interest. The marriage of his majesty with his favorite Kalama, was solemnized on the 4th of Feb., 1837. Soon after this the remains of his sister, with considerable pomp and display, a large military guard being called out to attend, were borne, in procession, to the church, where a concourse assembled. A sermon was delivered on the occasion, and a great degree of order and solemnity prevailed. A ship was purchased and fitted up, on board which, the king removed the remains of his sister, to Lahaina, where they were deposited beside her mother.

On Oahu, protracted meetings, of six days each, were successively held at Honolulu, Ewa, Waialua, and Kaneohe, and attended with interest, by great numbers. The preaching, exhortations, prayer and inquiry meetings were accompanied with the blessing of God. The missionaries passed from station to station, with some of their people, and felt themselves refreshed. The presence of the Spirit of God was manifest, at all these meetings. " The Holy Spirit," says Mr. Parker, of Kaneohe, " was evidently with us. The church was awake to pray. Those who had hardened themselves in sin, trembled under the exhibition of divine truth."

That the Gospel should strip away the pride of self-righteousness among the degraded heathen, as it does in thousands of instances, is one of the wonderful phenomena which the missionary is allowed to witness. Self-justification, before the Spirit sets home the Gospel, and self-condemnation after, for the violation of God's law, and for the death of Christ, are illustrated in the experience of many a Hawaiian. The following is a specimen. A hopeful convert at Wailua, attempting to persuade his fellow sinners to come to Christ, said, in an address to the children, " You have heard of the wickenness of the Jews who crucified Christ. It was *I* who drove the nails into his hands and feet. It was *I* who pierced his side with a spear. By my sins, I have consented to all that the Jews did to the Messiah. Formerly I thought that I was as good as others: but now I see that I am guilty of violating every command of the decalogue. I am ruined by my sins. I hope for mercy only in Christ."

Difficult as it is, in a Christian country, to convince the sinner that he is responsible for the sufferings of Christ, it may be supposed to be far more difficult to do it in the Sandwich Islands, or any heathen country. Enlarged views of the need of an atonement, and a clear conviction that Christ's sufferings were for us, that he bore our sins in his body, on the tree, and that sin in us, as really as the wrong-doing of the Jews of his time, caused his unparalleled sufferings and death, are necessary to the feeling of high personal responsibility for the indignity and wrong inflicted on our Substitute, the agony he freely bore, and the blood he freely poured out for our salvation.

The aborigines of the Oregon, when they were told that their sins were the occasion of the sufferings and death of Christ, rejected the doctrine, not only as incompatible with their *honor*, but as impossible, from the distance of time and place. Another Indian of North America, whose tribes have not been remarkable for integrity, a sense of justice, or a regard to character, age, or sex, but who, like all the race, are given to self-justification, when he was told by a missionary, that the Messiah, Jesus of Nazareth, who had done no wrong, was put to death by wicked men, replied with earnestness, " It must have been *white* men then, for Indians never kill a good man." So when History mourns over the bloody persecutions which myriads of martyrs have suffered at the hands of Rome, one of her prelates declares, with about as much truth as the Indian apologist, " Holy mother Church never persecutes." Thus the generation which killed the Son of God, absolved themselves from the charge of persecution, and most men feel free from all responsibility for the sufferings which he endured on Calvary, and for the reproach that is now cast upon his name and upon his cause.

The congregation at Honolulu, the seat of the government, amounting to three or four thousand, and the population of the district, embracing about 12,000 souls, besides the numerous visitors there, were deemed large enough for two, and as a dangerous heresy was watching to thrust itself in there, we established a second church in the same village with the first, but half a mile distant. The charge of this was assigned to Rev. L. Smith, who found abundant room and opportunity for missionary labor. For many months, he devoted much of his time to the instruction of children, and in February, March, and April, had a season of spiritual interest and a number of hopeful conversions among them. Mr. Bishop took charge of Ewa.

The prayers and hopes of the American churches were greatly encouraged in respect to the Sandwich Islands; and at the close of 1836, the American Board, desirous to ensure the victory, sent forth, December 14th, a large and timely reinforcement, consisting of four preachers, one physician, a secular agent, and eight male school teachers, the wives of these fourteen, and two unmarried female teachers. Their passage from Boston was delightful. Their accommodations were good, their captain kind and courteous, and his officers obliging, and the crew respectful. Their arrival, April 9, 1837, was opportune, and their reception cordial. The spirit of harmony prevailed on board ship. Morning and evening prayers, preaching on the Sabbath, and other means of grace suited to promote a revival, persevered in (though for a time despised by some of the ship's company), were attended with the reviving influences of God's Spirit, much like what was, at the same time, experienced at the islands. Capt. Sumner, one of the officers, and several others of the ship's company, appeared to renounce the world, and to choose the service of God, and desired to unite with his people.

The examination of these before the native church, at Honolulu, and their taking on them there, in the presence of that nation, and of the world, and of angels, the vows of God's covenant, was one of the most interesting scenes that ever occurred in those islands, where the transaction was between sea-faring men and the natives. To the latter, it was a wonderful demonstration of the power of religion, and of the sameness of the spirit produced in the foreigner and the native, when both bowed to the authority of God's Word, and they were led to rejoice, not only that a number of white men had on the ocean been hopefully born of God, but that an acquaintance between seamen and missionaries was favorable to the piety of the former, and the good name of the latter. Both the government and the mission gladly hailed the arrival of the reinforcement, and welcomed them to the whitened field.

In June, by the general convention of the mission, the new laborers were distributed over the field as they were needed, and located as follows:—Mr. Johnson at Waioli, Dr. Lafon at Koloa, Mr. Locke at Waialua, Messrs. Cook and Castle at Honolulu, Mr. Munn at Molokai, Mr. McDonald at Lahaina, Messrs. Conde and Ives at Hana and on Hawaii, Messrs. Bliss and Bailey at Kohala, Mr. Knapp at Waimea, Dr. Andrews at Kailua, Mr. Vanduzee at Kaawaloa, and Mr. Wilcox at Hilo ; Miss Marcia Smith resided for a time at Kaneohe, then at Honolulu; and Miss L. G. Smith first at Lahainaluna, and afterwards at Waimea.

By this arrangement the largest force of lay laborers ever sent forth at once by the American Board, with the four new preachers, were soon allowed advantageously and cheerfully to enter on their work.

About this period, the mission was tenderly and impressively admonished by the Divine Master's dismissing from their labors, and taking home to himself, two young and loved sisters of the consecrated band—Mrs. Dibble at Lahainaluna, a few months earlier, and Mrs. Lyons, while at the general meeting at Honolulu, in June. Their assembled associates, tenderly touched, gathered around the remains of the latter at her funeral, and sang the following parting dialogue hymn, composed on the occasion :

" Farewell, beloved companions,
My precious friends in Christ ;
He sends his welcome summons,
To call me home to rest :
I tread the dark lone valley
My Shepherd trod before ;
Through Jordan's flood he leads me,
To heaven's sweet, holy shore.

" Go, pilgrim, to thy Savior—
Thy toilsome course is run ;
Now rest from all thy labors
And cares beneath the sun :
No more shall sin molest thee,
The world no more control ;
Go, praise the Lamb who blest thee,
Whose love shall fill thy soul.

" Go, pilgrim, to thy Savior ;
On joyful wings ascend ;
On his almighty favor
Let all thy hopes depend :
His all-sufficient merit—
His rich atoning blood,
Brings sinners to inherit
The kingdom of our God.

" Farewell, dear fellow laborers ;
O live for Christ and heaven ;
Toil on for that blest Savior,
Whose life for you was given :
Bring back blind rebel mortals
From sin's dark dangerous way ;
And guide them to the portals
Of heaven's eternal day.

" Farewell,—I trust my Jesus
To take my sins away ;
Now on that head most precious,
My soul her hand would lay :
To that sole hope for sinners,
My SAVIOR, KING, and FRIEND,
Kind angels, lend your pinions,
And help my soul ascend.

" Go, pilgrim, to thy Savior ;
A short, a kind adieu ;
Far holier friends will hail thee,
Where joys eternal flow :
By angel bands attended,
Go, take thy crown there given ;
And when our toils are ended,
O may we meet in heaven."

At the close of a very interesting meeting of the assembled and united bands of missionaries, they went forth to their work with courage and hope. But the addition of so large a band of lay laborers and ministers as in the reinforcement had been sent

by the American Christian public into the field where so many
of their missionaries were already toiling successfully, brought
up anew and with much force, the question whether the Hawaiian
public ought not to support them with more efficiency than the
young churches, the rulers, or the common people had felt themselves able or bound to do.

The Christianity which we were endeavoring to establish in
the islands clearly teaches that the worshippers of God should
sustain the expenses of that worship, and that those who enjoy
the preaching and ordinances of the Gospel should take part,
when able, in supporting its ministers. The question as to the
ability and duty of the Hawaiian churches to support the missionaries devoted to them, had been occasionally discussed and
viewed differently by different missionaries, together with the
practicability of self-supporting schools. The islands belonged
to the people, and in one sense, the nation, if unmolested from
abroad, was able to support its preachers and teachers. But the
right of property not being well defined, it was not easy to say
that the chiefs ought, from the funds raised by taxation, to give
much for the support of missionaries, nor was it safe to decide
that the cultivators of the soil, when taxed, as it was supposed,
quite enough by land proprietors and the government, ought to
tax themselves so much as to support both the native teachers
and the missionaries needed for the community. The poverty
of the common people being general, it was deemed the duty of
the more favored parts of Christendom to meet this emergency
by supplying to the missionaries the natives' lack of service.
Still it was even then urged by some that the same arguments
which proved the duty of Christ's people in enlightened countries to diffuse the Gospel through the world, proved the duty of
Hawaiian Christians to bear a part in it, either by aiding the support of the press and the missionaries among themselves, thus
diminishing the drafts on missionary funds, or by contributing to
those funds to send the Gospel to heathen nations.

From time to time I laid this subject before the hearers of the
Gospel at Honolulu, the more intelligent and generous of whom
admitted that there were claims upon them; and for the year
ending June, 1837, I was happy to report, aside from the avails
of books purchased and various comforts supplied to the mission
families by the people, the following contributions, chiefly in
specie, for various public objects:

For a pulpit and bell for the church at Ewa, - -	$90 25
For Rev. S. Parker, exploring agent of the American Board in the Oregon, - - - - -	78 00
For the mission in Upper Oregon, - - - -	92 50
For the Methodist Mission in Lower Oregon, - -	20 00
For the railway over the rock at Nuuanu-pali, - -	50 00
For building a new stone church, - - - -	2,350 00
Total,	$2,680 75

On another occasion, while engaged in building their church, the same church and congregation contributed in money and various articles, to the amount of $444 in aid of the mission among the Indians of the Oregon, furnishing a small printing-press, the first employed on the western side of the Rocky Mountains. A large portion of these contributions, as did others from year to year, came from the poor, though it is believed they were not in the end the poorer for having made them ; for the needful stimulus to exertion thus supplied, in favor of public objects, resulted in the increase of industry and economy in respect to private.

A good degree of native energy displayed at other places was at the same time reported to the convention of the mission. From January 1, 1836, to January 31, 1837, under the patronage and direction of Gov. Adams, a stone church, 120 feet long, 48 wide, and 27 high, was erected at Kailua, having a high gallery and pulpit, good windows, a shingled roof, a steeple, and bell, thus giving to the place where the mission first landed, a pleasing and important feature of a Christian village in New England.

About the same time, a *dobie* meeting-house, 90 feet long, 42 wide, and 15 high, was completed at Ewa. It was plastered, lighted with glass windows, still rare in the Pacific, furnished with a low, neat pulpit, and being situated on ground elevated a little above the plain, became a grateful ornament to that portion of the country ; but it was soon found too strait for the multitude of worshippers who had put their hand to the work, and were disposed to throng their new temple for worship or instruction. Other houses of public worship were at the same time built at Lanai, Olualu, and Kaanapali, distant from the residence of any missionary. In the islands in general, more than fifty school-houses, in native style, were erected in the course of the year.

With these indications of ability, of the growing energy and willingness of the people to help themselves, the mission at this meeting harmoniously adopted the following minute on the duty of the Hawaiian churches and their pastors as to the domestic support of the Gospel :—

" As it is obvious that the churches who need to be taught almost everything which it is important that they should know, in order to be active, united, pure, happy, and useful, in the highest degree, and who need all the power of persuasion which the ministry can employ to secure the same object, could better forego every luxury, and part with every cent of their increase than to be destitute of preaching and pastoral labors ; therefore, *Resolved*,

" 1st, That it be considered the duty of the churches in the Sandwich Islands to take efficient measures, and make vigorous efforts for the support of their own preachers, either wholly or in part, as God shall give them ability, availing themselves of such aid as may be freely given by the congregations which share with them in the advantages of the preaching and pastoral labors which they enjoy.

"2dly, That it be considered the duty of the missionaries to teach their people what they may reasonably be expected to do for the support of the Gospel both at home and abroad, and how they may most advantageously aid this object, with a faithful exhibition of the motives to enlist them in this work, but then leave the churches and individuals to judge voluntarily for themselves what and how much they will do in this cause.

"3dly, That no civil enactments should be requested to secure a support for the missionary, except for the purposes of protection, but that the king, chiefs, and landlords, be encouraged to aid in constructing public buildings, and sustaining charitable or evangelical institutions and schools among the people, both by grants and donations from their own property, by direct labors or appropriations from what they would have a right to demand for private or public use, were no such objects before them, and by affording facilities and encouragements to the people to build school-houses, pay their teachers, and contribute something annually, at least, for the support of their pastors.

"4th, That owners of vessels among our church members be, in a particular manner, requested to favor the objects of the mission generously by transporting lumber, supplies, and mission families without charge, when convenient; and whenever a large amount of freight is taken for us, or considerable inconvenience is required of them, that they be requested to favor our common cause by moderate, reasonable, favorable terms of freight ; and that favors thus done *apparently* for the mission, but in reality for the nation, should be regarded as gratuitous on the part of the individual rendering the favor, and as such be duly acknowledged."

Here was a manifest advance in the minds of the missionaries towards a systematic method of securing domestic aid to the cause of the Gospel, and it was followed by spirited efforts on the part of some of the churches, and some of the rulers ; and there has subsequently been a general advance in the nation towards assuming the expenses of preaching and all kinds of teaching which they choose. But the wishes of the American churches in respect to this have, through different causes, been deferred.

The papists, in Europe, unwilling to allow their plans in the Sandwich Islands to be defeated by the expulsion of the apostolic prefect and his associate, sent thither, Mr. Robert Walsh, and Mr. Murphy. At the same time, Messrs. Bachelot and Short were directed to leave California, either to re-occupy the Sandwich islands, or if they could not secure a residence there, to take some other post in Oceanica.

Mr. Walsh, the Irish priest, educated in France, arrived at Oahu, about the close of Sept., 1836. As soon as it was known that he had come as one of the Pope's clergy, to renew the work left by Messrs. Bachelot and Short, he was denied a residence by Kaahumanu 2d, and ordered to leave the country. The British Consul claimed for him a right to remain as a British subject, regardless of his character, office, or design ; still he was not only required to depart, but forbidden to propagate the dogmas of Rome. But both orders he disregarded, and treated the will of the goverment with contempt while he enjoyed the assurance of British protection.

Mr. Murphy being supposed to be a Romish priest in disguise, was required to leave, and he departed, but to return again. Messrs. B. and S. left California where schools were few and the people ignorant, and destitute of the Bible, and came to the Sandwich Islands, whence they had been expelled, and where they were not needed, and could not expect to be admitted.

Mr. Bachelot thus wrote to France, from California :—" Nov. 3d, 1836. A ship is at last found which is willing to run the risk of carrying us to the Sandwich Islands. Our affairs are far from being in a good condition, and I know not how we shall be re- ceived. According to all probability, we shall be treated as enemies."*

They placed little reliance on a forced construction of the ar- ticles of agreement between the king and Lord E. Russell, which was a commercial arrangement, engaging that Englishmen might come and build houses, provided the king's consent be specifically obtained. The qualifying phrase—" Ke ae ke Lii—if the king shall consent," was understood, both of entering the country and building houses, etc. To suppose the king stipulated for the un- conditional admission of Jesuitical teachers, deserters, or hostile invaders, or persons for ever banished from his territories, is not only preposterous, but firmly denied by the king and his court, and other trustworthy witnesses, who were present when the agreement was made with Lord Russell, an agreement which the king finally allowed might be interpreted " according to the law of nations."

Messrs. B. and S. arrived in the Clementine, April 17th, 1837. Mr. Short attempted to land in disguise, and to reach his former habitation by a circuitous route, unobserved by any in authority. But their arrival was soon known, and the governor of Oahu ordered them to depart in the same vessel that brought them. He reported them to the king, then at Maui, who immediately issued an edict, declaring the act of expulsion by Kaahumanu to be still in force, sustaining the governor, and requiring the priests to leave his shores without delay, as follows :

" Ye strangers all from foreign lands who are in my dominions, both residents, and those recently arrived, I make known my word to you all, that you may understand my orders.

" The men of France whom Kaahumanu banished, are under the same unaltered order up to this period. The rejection of these men is perpetual, confirmed by me at the present time. I will not assent to their remaining in my dominions.

* Probably the consul and every ship-master who understood their case at all, knew they would not be welcomed by the rulers ; but it was said the captain who brought them averred,—" I would carry the devil there, if I could get my pay for it."

" These are my orders to them, that they go back immediately on board the vessel on which they have come, that they stay on board her till that vessel on board which they came, sails; that is to me clearly right, but their abiding here I do not wish.

" I have no desire that the service of the missionaries who follow the Pope should be performed in my kingdom, not at all.

" Wherefore, all who shall be encouraging the Papal missionaries, I shall regard as enemies to me, to my counsellors, to my chiefs, to my people, and to my kingdom.

" (Signed), KAMEHAMEHA III."

Kinau, the prime minister, called the two priests before her, and insisted on their leaving the country, urging them to go on board the Clementine. But they refused. Haalilio said to the prefect, Mr. Bachelot, " If you can force a residence here against the will of the king, then *you* are the sovereign."

The king availed himself of the teachings of Vattel, and so far as appeared endeavored to conform to the law of nations.*

Having thus begun, in accordance with their own views of sovereignty, and with the advice of a British naval officer, the young king was happy to find their policy supported by the doctrines of Vattel.

When he was interrogated by Captain Valiant, a French naval officer, with respect to the reception or rejection of Romish priests, the king affirms that he supposed the captain to acknowledge his sovereignty and to acquiesce in his right to exercise it as he had done.

After hearing the king's account of what had been done, Capt. V. said, " Why do you not desire the Catholic religion ?" " I replied," said the king, " I do not desire that religion here, lest my kingdom should be divided." Captain V. continued, " Perhaps it would be well to have some foreigners here of that religion." " I said to him," added the king, " it would not be well. If the people of my kingdom were enlightened, perhaps it might be well." To this Captain V. assented, saying, " You know the nature of your kingdom."

In pursuance of the settled policy, the Gov. of Oahu, having

---

* A respectable French writer on international law, establishes this doctrine ; " Since the lord of the territory may, whenever he thinks proper, forbid its being entered, he has, no doubt, a power to annex what conditions he pleases to the permission to ᵉⁿᵗᵉʳ. This is a consequence of the right of domain. The sovereignty is the right to command in the whole country, and the laws are not simply confined to regulating the conduct of citizens towards each other, but also determine what is to be observed by all orders of people throughout the whole extent of the state. In virtue of this submission, foreigners who commit faults are to be punished according to the laws of the country. For the same reason, disputes that may arise between foreigners, or between a foreigner and a citizen, are to be determined by a judge of the place. The foreigner cannot pretend to enjoy the liberty of living in the country without respecting the laws. If he violates them he is punishable as a disturber of the public peace, and guilty of a crime against the society in which he lives; but he is not obliged to submit, like the subjects, to all the commands of the sovereign ; and if such things are required of him as he is unwilling to perform he may quit the country."— *Vattel.*

the positive orders of the king for the purpose, required the expelled priests to go on board the Clementine which brought them
from California.   On their reaching the deck, the commander and
owner, Mr. J. Dudoit, then with the crew, left the vessel, carrying
the flag, which was British.   The British Consul, in accordance
with his inflammatory policy, dishonoring it, burnt it in the streets
of Honolulu.

The king still considering the rights of sovereignty invaded by
the vessel and by the priests, and not at all redressed by a whole
crew deserting a vessel and throwing themselves upon his shores,
supposed it proper still to order the vessel to depart instead of
seizing and confiscating it.   Sustained by a standing law of the
land requiring the authorities to prevent desertion from vessels,
and to do what they could to return them, he directed the commander to return with his crew on board the Clementine ; but
they refused.

Messrs. Jones and Charlton pretended that the act of the government in obliging the priests to leave the shore and go on board,
was " piratical," though it was done in their own harbor and in
self-defence.   Mr. Charlton considered the Irish priest from
France as a British subject, and in reference to a supposed en-
croachment on his right to come and live and labor there as a
Romish teacher, at his own option, he, in his correspondence with
the king, made a declaration which, to his majesty and some
others who had become acquainted with him, appeared extraordinary :—

" It has always been my most ardent wish to promote harmony and
good feeling between my countrymen and your majesty's subjects, but
I cannot allow British subjects to be ill treated or molested in their
lawful pursuits, and depend upon it, that His Britannic Majesty's government will not allow a British subject to be injured in person or
property, without severely punishing the aggressors.   I have the honor
to be your majesty's most obedient and humble servant."

At this juncture, H. B. M. ship of war, the Sulphur, arrived,
and the commander, Capt. Belcher, very readily joined with Mr.
Charlton in defeating the purposes of the government, and resolved to set the priests on shore, and take charge of the Clementine.

He and the consul waited on the queen premier, and proposed
to set the priests on shore.   She forbade him.   He said, " I shall
do it."   " Then you wish," said she, " to take the sovereignty
and deprive us both of it."

She desired him to be more reasonable, and not rashly to act on
mere *ex parte* representations.   He said, " I must go according to
the consul."

Does the law of nations require a commander of an exploring
ship of war to follow the will or orders of a consul, in defiance
of the laws or of the sovereign of a country ?

During this interview, the French ship La Venus, Captain

Thouars, arrived at the port of Honolulu, and the captain repaired to the prime minister, and united in the wish that the priests might be admitted on shore.

An attempt was made to explain to him the ground on which the priests were not allowed on shore, and Mr. C. said to Capt. Thouars, " Mr. Bingham is the cause of all this trouble." When I expressed my dissent by saying, " That is not correct," the consul rejoined—" Mr. Bingham, if you insult me again, I will horse-whip you." Whether he intended to prevent any explanation, or to alarm my native friends as to my personal danger in order to carry his point, or to convince the Frenchman that American missionaries could be maltreated with impunity, or to bring the vengeance of France on our band, subsequent events help us to conjecture. When I asked him if he thought my correcting him was intended as an insult, he replied, " No, it was something else I was thinking of."

Capt. Belcher retired from this audience, to remove, as he said, under the cover of his guns, the priests to the shore, and take the Clementine, and he threatened to arrest me if his men should be hurt in doing it.*

In defiance of the authorities, he set the priests on shore, took possession of the Clementine, and sent her to Maui.

A week later, the king and his chieftains granted these despisers of his authority an audience on the same question of the residence of those priests on shore.

The king chose Mr. Bingham for interpreter, but Messrs. Charlton and Belcher refused him, and sent for Mr. Bachelot, whom they had put on shore contrary to the positive edicts of the king and chiefs, and brought him in without proper consent, to act as interpreter. When he had with difficulty interpreted a sentence for them, into imperfect Hawaiian, which the king, in a quiet time and from a welcome speaker, could have understood, he followed him with the forcible interrogation, " What ?" The obtruded interpreter labored through the sentence again, which was followed by the " What ?" from the king. The interpreter, increasing the energy of his voice if not the lucidness of his style, repeated his task ; and the king, with increased self-possession, renewed his significant interrogatory, " What is it ?" Thus mildly rebuking the discourteousness of those who had attempted to obtrude on him one who trampled on his authority, and who was here in his dominions without his consent, he, in his turn, refused to do business for them through the interpreter of their choice.

The obtruded priest, unsuccessful as interpreter, assumed the censor, and with some shrewdness, and not a little rudeness, said to the king, " You don't understand me because you don't wish to." Thus ended his official services for the day.

By this time a foreign officer, whom, had it not been for the extreme boorishness of his manners, I should have taken for a lieutenant of the French Navy, came and stared me malignantly in

* Mr. Short says, " Capt. B. threatened to hang Mr. Bingham at the yard-arm."

the face, placed his back against me, and crowded me back hard upon a sideboard against which I was quietly standing with folded arms. As I attempted to escape sideways from this incipient Lynching, he, suddenly wrenching his body either to prevent my escape or to consummate the outrage, gave me a blow with his elbow, which was chiefly warded from my breast by my still folded arms. His strange movements being perceived, one of the counsellors, John Ii, came and kindly placed himself between us and defeated his repeated attempts to approach me, for a time, as we stood behind the captains.

Another interpreter was called in, through whom the two captains and the British consul in vain attempted to gain the consent of the king to the residence or sojourn on shore of the two expelled priests. Mr. Andrews, of our mission, was, at length, employed as the fourth interpreter, as agreeable to both parties.

Here the necessity of having an interpreter, not connected with the mission, became obvious, and my being rejected became a matter of relief to me, and the successive labors of Mr. Andrews, Mr. Richards, and Dr. Judd, as authorized interpreters, who resigned, successively, their connexion with the mission, succeeded.

Before the discussions of the day were through, the company got into some confusion, as some papers which Captain Thouars wished to put into the king's unwilling hand, were allowed to fall to the floor. Then the officer before mentioned as insolent, again approached me, and clapping his sword, said, with a malign stare, " Do you see this ? Do you see this ?" intending, doubtless, to make the impression, that should all arguments fail to introduce Romish teachers into the island, the sword could accomplish it. The late premier said to the insolent officer, "What does this mean ?" She also called the purser of the king's man-of-war, in his side arms, to sit beside me. Monsieur Dudoit also used his efforts to restrain the officer from further violence.

The rulers, by this specimen, saw what Romanism was disposed to do, and probably never felt a stronger determination not to bid it God speed in the country. The king subsequently asked me, " Would the United States make war with me if that Frenchman had killed you ?" I replied, " They would surely inquire into it first, to see who was the blame-worthy aggressor." To this commotion the king alluded forcibly in his letter to William IV.,(sent by the Imogene,)as " the near approach of battle."

Captain Belcher, proposing to guarantee the departure of Mr. Short, asked the king to allow the priests to sojourn temporarily with Mr. Charlton. To this the king decidedly objected. The captain considered it insulting. The king offered to state his reasons if the captain wished to hear of the wrong-doing of the consul, who, he supposed, conspired with others against his sovereignty, and could not properly be trusted with men, who, under papal authority, opposed his government. In his complaint to William IV., the king said, "I utterly refused to let those missionaries stay, because they were under the authority of the pope." Assuring his Britannic Majesty that his consul had wrongfully aided the introduction of Papal priests, he says, "Those things which I have seen are much like the covetous designs of Mr. Horton James. I have seen a sentence of his letter like this—' Introduce a foreign government among the natives, and remove the chiefs and Christian missionaries.'" In withholding confidence from such a man, he thought himself authorized by well known facts.

Mr. Dudoit, through Mr. Charlton and Capt. Belcher, presented a claim upon the Hawaiian government of $50,000, for damages for sending the priests on board the Clementine while under English colors. If the vessel had not been seized or confiscated by the government, why were damages tenfold above reasonable demanded? If she had been seized by the government, what right had Capt. Belcher to take her and send her to sea as far as Maui? And if he did not think she had been taken by the government, why did he apply formally to the king, as he subsequently did, to get her released? To this application, the king replied, "Neither I nor Kinau have seized the vessel."

The captain and owner had deserted her. The English consul had burnt her flag. Capt. Belcher had cut her out, and taken possession, and concurred in demanding enormous damages to the owner. No wonder he was solicitous to get the king's permission to allow the vessel to proceed on her voyage, and to allow the priests whom he had put on shore, a temporary stay. To accomplish the latter he made the following engagement:—

"His Britannic Maj. Ship Sulphur, Honolulu, July 21, 1837.

"I, Edward Belcher, commanding his Britannic Majesty's ship Sulphur, engage for Mr. Short that he will quit this island by the first favorable opportunity which offers for Manilla, Lima, Valparaiso, or any civilized part of the world ; and that in the event of no opportunity offering before the arrival of a British vessel of war, he will be received on board of her. I further engage that he will not act contrary to the laws of the country.

"EDWARD BELCHER,

"Com. of H. B. M Ship Sulphur, and Senior Officer of the British Navy present."

The following day, the king gave this cautious consent to the temporary stay of Mr. Short, the Irish priest :—

" We consent that Mr. Short shall reside unmolested at Honolulu, until a favorable opportunity offers to quit this country, either for Manilla, Valparaiso, Lima, or other civilized portions of the world. We farther guarantee that no obstruction will be offered to the Clementine pursuing her voyage.

"KAUIKEAOULI."

The commander of La Venus gave the following :—

"Honolulu, July 21, 1837.

" The undersigned, captain of the ship, commander of the French frigate La Venus, promises, in the name of Mr. Bachelot, that he will seize the first favorable opportunity which offers to quit these islands, to go either to Manilla, Lima, Valparaiso, or any civilized part of the world ; and in case such an one is not presented, on the arrival of the first French man-of-war which visits these islands, he shall be received on board. In the meantime, Mr. Bachelot shall not preach.

" A. DU PETIT THOUARS.

"Post Captain commanding the French frigate La Venus."

Thus these two commanders, having insisted on the temporary stay of the two priests, concurred officially in their final expulsion, and in restraining their preaching while they remained. The following agreement also was made between the king and Capt. Thouars :—

"Honolulu, Sandwich Islands, July 24, 1837.

" There shall be perpetual peace and amity between the French and the inhabitants of the Sandwich Islands. The French shall go and come freely in all the states which compose the government of the Sandwich Islands.

" They shall be received and protected there, and shall enjoy the same advantages which the subjects of the most favored nations enjoy.

" Subjects of the king of the Sandwich Islands shall equally come into France, shall be received and protected there as the most favored foreigners.

"KAMEHAMEHA III.

" A. DU PETIT THOUARS,

" Capt. Commander of the French frigate La Venus."

Whether this be a treaty or not, it ought not to be interpreted so as to involve an absurdity. And if the engagement is binding at all, it binds France to the offices of peace and friendship, and surely furnished her no excuse for violating her permanent obligations by declaring an unjust war upon the islands, demanding and extorting unreasonable concessions as to their soil, money, and sovereignty. It was doubtless mutually understood that fugitives from justice, deserters from ships, Romish teachers, and armed invaders, though not specifically excepted, were not included in the pledge of free entry and passage, in either country.

The rulers did not waive the right which most of the governments of Europe have at different periods exercised to exclude a certain class of teachers. After hearing the opinions of a British officer, which in principle accorded with those of Vancouver, Vattel, and their own, they issued at Maui an edict inhibiting the teaching of the dogmas and exhibiting the ceremonies of the papal religion, and forbidding its priests to enter the country without a special permission and bonds for a seasonable departure.

The premier having learned from Capt. B., of the British ship of war Imogene, that the Europa was expected to bring Romish priests from Valparaiso, notwithstanding the opposition of the government to their intrusion, took measures to prevent their landing without bonds for their departure in a reasonable time, so great were the apprehensions of trouble from that quarter. Knowing the objections of the government, Mr. Skinner, the supercargo of the Europa, on receiving Mr Maigret, a Romish priest from France, on board as passenger, required him to give bonds that he would not land at the Sandwich Islands without permission from the government.

On the arrival of the Europa in Honolulu roadstead, with five passengers from Valparaiso, the premier, on the 2d of November, 1837, apprised them and the captain that propagators of the papal religion must not land without first giving, for the protection of the kingdom, bonds that they would speedily depart, and receiving her written permission to come on shore. Three Chilian passengers promptly replied that they were citizens of the republic of Chili, whom political difficulties had obliged to flee from their country, and that they were not merchants or of any other profession, and wished permission to remain only till they could get a passage to Manilla or some other country. They were, without further hesitation, permitted to land.

But the Romish teachers, not willing to give bonds, or to declare to the Premier their office, lest it should obstruct their landing without, wrote her as follows :—

"The undersigned, passengers on board the Europa, promise not to interfere with the laws and regulations of the Sandwich Islands during their sojourn, and to leave the islands the first favorable opportunity.
"L. MAIGRET.
"J. C. MURPHY."

Not satisfied with this reserve on the main point, Kinau promptly wrote them the same day as follows :—

"Salutations to you, L. Maigret and J. C. Murphy, on board the ship Europa.

"I have received your writing to-day, and have seen what you have made known ; but you have not stated to me definitely in writing what countrymen you are, and what your employments, and how long you wish to stay. You have not informed me in writing to what country you wish to go by the first favorable opportunity. On this account, I request you to make a clear statement of these points in writing, and if you, or either of you, are priests of the religion of the pope or of any other office, make it known to me ; do not hide it from me, for this only is the reason why I hesitate to allow you to land. I do not desire propagators of that religion to dwell here ; that is taboo (forbidden).

By me,   "KAAHUMANU II.

Honolulu, Nov. 2, 1837."

The next morning, Mr. Dudoit brought the following from Mr. Maigret, claiming to be a Frenchman simply :—

"Oahu, Nov. 3, 1837.

"This certifies that I, Louis Maigret, a Frenchman, came on board the ship Europa as passenger at Valparaiso, and my object was to remain here until I could get a passage to the Marquesas or the dangerous Archipelago Islands, and that I will conform to the laws and regulations of government at all times.

(Signed)   " L. MAIGRET."

In her view, he evades the main point of her earnest inquiry, lest he should not be permitted to land as a Papal priest without giving bonds. The queen then inquired of Mr. Dudoit if Mr. Maigret were not a priest, and he frankly replied in the affirmative, as he intimated Mr. M. ought to have done. She said, " He has concealed that fact."

Mr. Murphy, who, if he were not a priest, had a good opportunity and good reason to tell her so, did not reply; but being declared by the British Consul not to be a priest, he was allowed to land. By an English Quarterly, this man is represented as a Jesuit priest, who, in disguise, had aided in the introduction of Romish priests at Tahiti.

Mr. Dudoit, finding the government would not, without bonds, allow Mr. Maigret to land, as a Papal priest, sought for permission to transfer him from the Europa to a small schooner to pursue his voyage. To this the government readily acceded, on Mr. D. giving the following pledge or bond to Kaahumanu II. :—

" MADAM,—I bind myself to fulfil the same obligation as the captain of the Europa, that is, should Mr. Maigret land after his embarkation on board the schooner Honolulu, without the permission as your letter expresses, I will pay the fine.

" I have the honor to be, &c.,
" JULES DUDOIT."

Whether the party, on the arrival of the Europa, accomplished or not the " *circumventing* " of the governor who endeavored to conform to law, Mr. Maigret's answers, " some time afterwards," he himself represents as characterized by " a *frankness* which displeased some persons." How far they differed from his notes is not clear.*

Mr. Short embarked from Honolulu, Nov. 2d, on board an Eng. schooner, and reached Valparaiso the following January.

Mr. Maigret, having purchased a schooner for the prosecution of their missions in the Pacific, was permitted to pass on board

---

* The following is his account of this matter:—" When we were seen, a pilot was sent to forbid us to enter. However, the captain was permitted to go and make his representations. Some time afterwards we received a visit from the governor, by circumventing whom permission had been obtained to enter the port. But as everybody on board knew very well who I was, and as I had kept nothing secret from anybody, Kuanaoa soon found that he had been deceived. He then asked me to what nation I belonged, and whether I was a priest. I answered at once, and with a frankness which displeased some persons, but I could not betray my conscience to please them. Nevertheless, the governor pretended to believe that I was acting in concert with those who had deceived him, and that was one of the reasons why I was not permitted to set foot on shore. I earnestly protested that I had never denied my country, nor endeavored to conceal from the government of the Sandwich Islands my quality as a priest and a missionary. All was in vain. He would not even permit me to pass on board another vessel."—[*M. Maigret's letter to the Archbishop of Calcedony, dated January* 26, 1839.]

of it in the harbor from the Europa.   Mr. Bachelot thinking himself recovering from his disease (probably rheumatism), and Mr.
Maigret hoping that the sea air would re-establish his health, they
embarked together for the Gambiers, via Ascension, or with the
intention of spending a few months together at Ascension, before
proceeding to Gambiers or Valparaiso.   They embarked from Honolulu Nov. 23d, and Mr. Bachelot, instead of gaining, soon lost
strength, according to the report of Mr. Maigret, who says :—

"After the first day of our voyage, he grew worse.   He suffered
much in the joints of his arms and legs, and could scarcely stand
erect.   Soon his mind became confused.   He saw things that no one
else could see, and heard what no other person could hear.   He prayed
often, and his rosary never left him.   On the 4th of Dec., about five
o'clock, he ceased to speak, and I applied to him the indulgence of a
good death."

Mr. Short says; "Mr. B. came from California to the islands
with the intention of passing on to the islands of the south, or at
least to retire to Valparaiso, if not allowed to remain in his mission."

Instead of taking a *favorable* opportunity to go to some *civilized* port, according to stipulation, by Capt. Thouars, if he and Mr.
Maigret chose an *un*favorable time, and an *un*suitable vessel to
go to a *barbarous* island, neither Capt. Thouars, nor the Hawaiian
government, nor the American missionaries, are responsible for
it, whatever may be said of those who sent him back to Oahu.

In these facts, or in the conduct of the government towards Mr.
Bachelot and Maigret, we have the head and front of the offending
of the Hawaiian government against the French nation.

If the agreement with Capt. Du Petit Thouars is to be construed
so as to guarantee free entry and passage to all Frenchmen, without regard to circumstances or character, then it was violated in
refusing free entry and passage to Mr. Maigret, and in expelling
Mr. Bachelot, in which the contracting parties concurred at the
same time.   But an interpretation of such latitude would seem to
allow either the French or the Hawaiian sovereign to send an army
of soldiers, or Jesuits, or a colony of convicts into the other's country, which would be an absurdity not contemplated by the contracting parties.   "Every interpretation that leads to an absurdity,"
says a distinguished writer on international law, "ought to be
rejected."   To claim, under this agreement, that subjects of
France who would not conform to the laws of the country, or
fugitives from justice, or mutinous seamen from French ships,
might come and go freely at the Sandwich Islands, would be
manifestly absurd, and the restraining of such subjects of France
would be no infraction of this engagement.

But to this subject I must again refer after a further change of
agents and circumstances two years later, or in the record of 1839,
and in the meantime glance at the progress of the great revival.

From the first efforts to plant the Gospel in the wide districts of Hilo and Puna, the field there has ever presented the prospect of a great harvest; and it has been always difficult to make the world understand how much of darkness and of light, how much of wheat and of chaff were to be found there, at any one time. All, indeed, may be said to abound there from the time when the printed Gospel was given to the people, in 1828, with ability to read it, though it may still be difficult to tell which predominates.

But the labors and the apparent harvest can be briefly stated, without the detail of the toils of fourteen years previous to the great revival. I will here speak of one effort of Messrs. Coan and Lyman, in a protracted meeting of two weeks' continuance, commencing the 5th of Feb., 1837. During the first week, the following order of exercises was pursued, daily. A prayer-meeting, at the break of day; preaching to children, at eight o'clock in the morning, a church prayer-meeting being held at the same time. Preaching to the whole congregation, at ten o'olock A. M., and at two P. M. A meeting for the anxious and inquiring, at four P. M., and a church prayer-meeting at the same hour. From eight to nine in the evening, social prayer of the two mission families. The spare time, not occupied by the above engagements, was devoted to conversation with those who, in great numbers, filled the houses, and beset the paths of the missionaries. Mr. Coan says:—

" The meetings were full and solemn. Many came from the most distant parts of our field, 50 or 60 miles, to attend this meeting. The Holy Ghost came, at the commencement of the meeting, and many were awakened under the first sermon, which was preached from these words : ' Verily, verily, I say unto you, the hour is coming and now is, when the dead shall hear the voice of the Son of God, and they that hear shall live.' These words of Christ seemed to be clothed with his almighty power, and to receive a literal fulfilment at the time ; for some that were ' dead in trespasses and sins' give pleasing evidence that they heard the voice of the Son of God, and that they passed from death unto life.

" About three hundred attended the inquiry meeting, many with tears and evident conviction of sin, and many, as is always the case here, not knowing why they came. The church seemed much aroused, and to have an unusual spirit of prayer poured upon them. The attention of multitudes of all classes was called up to subjects of ' weal or woe.' Some cases of conviction and hopeful conversion were as distinctly marked as most cases in the United States. How many souls were born again, we know not. Some we believe are—we hope many.

" As the attention of some children seemed to be arrested, we resolved to continue the meeting one week longer, with special reference to their conversion. During that week, they were assembled to hear the Gospel three times a day. The church also met to pray for them and our evening meeting was also continued in their behalf. Impressions were made on many of them, and some give evidence of con version. * * Mr. Lyman and myself preached alternately, and divided all the labors of the meeting equally between us. Our hearts were one in the work, as they are in all our mutual labors, and we find that two are better than one.

"On the second day, after the close of our meeting, we sent out the church members in all directions to bring in the aged and decrepit, that we might tell them that God's house is not full—that there was room for them. About 200 were collected; some maimed, some halt, some blind, some withered to a skeleton, some bowed nearly to the earth, some trembling with decrepitude, some covered with sores, and all of them tottering on the last verge of time. Many who were unable to walk without support were led by friends, or were brought in canoes. It was an affecting spectacle, and Mr. L. and myself labored to pull them out of the fire, feeling that it was the last opportunity that we might have with many of them, as a large number of them do not attend preaching on the Sabbath, either from infirmity of body, or indisposition of heart. They listened with attention, and some seemed affected. What the fruit will be the Judgment will reveal."

What a picture of wretched and perishing creatures laid by the side of the Gospel pool! West's painting of the sick at the Temple, receiving healing mercy from the Savior's hands, might help one's conceptions of the need of help in such a case. The power of the same Savior was equally needed for the recovery of the health of the souls of this motley and miserable group.

Messrs. Coan and Lyman, in May of the same year, say:—

"Our church has been united and happy through the year. Many of its members seem to grow in knowledge and grace, and we feel more and more comfort in them as we gain more and more evidence that they are really 'members of Christ's body, of his flesh and of his bones.' No instance of church discipline has occurred at Hilo the past year."

What a charming, peaceful, healthy church, of seventy-one members, scattered over two wide, rough districts, waiting for the windows of heaven to be opened, and a shower of blessings to fall upon them! Can such a church and such spiritual guides wait long in vain?

On the 1st Sabbath of Nov. thirty-one hopeful converts were received to the church at Hilo, and the following week was devoted to the labors of a second protracted meeting. Concerning this, Mr. Lyman says:—

"The arm of the Lord was visible in every stage of the meeting. Some of our church members are very much aroused to the duty of prayer, and are now able to understand, as they never did before, the Scripture, 'The Spirit helpeth our infirmities—the Spirit itself maketh intercession for us with groanings that cannot be uttered.' There is, in fact, every evidence that this is a genuine work of the Holy Spirit."

Of the same work and meeting, Mr. Coan says:—

"Many came from the distance of fifty or sixty miles to hear the

Gospel. It was a season of deep and solemn interest. God's Word was with power, and his work was glorious. Multitudes wept and trembled; and hundreds evidently think they are converted. How many will bring forth fruits meet for repentance remains to be seen. Of one thing we are sure, that God is in this place, and that he has spoken to many hearts. We expect to return with many sheaves for Christ."

In September, 1837, Mr. Lyons, at Waimea, reported for the northern district of Hawaii, 155 schools, 5,010 scholars, 5,000 Sabbath school scholars, a singing school of 80 scholars ; the number of books disposed of in a year, 10,000, including all kinds, from the " Child's First Lessons," up to the New Testament. The blessing from heaven was hailed with solemn gladness and thanksgiving, and increased courage and hope. Mr. L. says :—

" Soon after the church was purified of some of its unworthy members, the Lord seemed to smile upon us. The Spirit came down in the midst of the people. Meetings became solemn. Truth made a deep impression upon the mind. The torpid conscience was aroused. Sinners trembled in view of impending ruin. The Savior was presented as able, willing, and waiting to save. Hundreds flocked to the inquiry meeting, where prayer was offered for their perishing souls. The Lord was nigh. Angels looked on, and rejoiced over the repentance of some of the sable sons of Hawaii. To me, this was a season of thrilling interest. I had labored long and arduously, I had wept over the desolations of Zion and the wilful stupidity of sinners. Clouds and darkness had overhung my way. The Gospel, though often preached, had fallen powerless on the heart. How cheering, then, to be visited with a ray of light from heaven! How soul-ravishing to see those, once so stupid and immovable in sin, rising, and turning, and fleeing from the wrath to come, and laying hold on eternal life."

For a short time after this, there were fewer of the manifestations of the divine presence there and self-examination and humiliation were required and resorted to. And Mr. L. says :—

" We resolved to repent and give ourselves more to prayer, and be more in earnest in our efforts to save souls. The Lord looked on. His ear hearkened to the voice of our supplications. The Holy Spirit came down, and sinners were awakened. The old man of grey hairs, and the child of ten years, also, became alarmed. They saw the wrath of God hanging over them ; and seemed to feel that they were sinking to hell. Jesus was pointed out as the only refuge."

A protracted meeting was held for a week. The exercises were well attended. Sometimes crowded audiences listened to the truth. The Spirit of God was believed to be present, working silently yet effectually on the hearts of many who had grown old in sin. The Sabbath came. Multitudes thronged the house of God. Sixty-one individuals, embracing two blind men of grey hairs, and several children, stood up before God and angels and men, and made a public profession of their attachment to Christ and their determination to devote the remainder of their lives to his service. These, with the others who had entered into solemn covenant, sat down at the Lord's table, and seventy-five more candidates were propounded.

At Kailua, Kaawaloa, and Kohala, the presence of the Spirit of God was acknowledged, and at nearly all the mission stations in the islands. Agitation from Romish influence, the demonstrations of the power of God's Spirit, and the unusual disturbance of the waters of the ocean around us, were simultaneously felt.

On the 7th of Nov., 1837, occurred a very singular phenomenon at the different islands of the group. It was the irregular rising and falling of the waters of the ocean, not easily accounted for. On the northern parts of Hawaii and Maui, particularly at Hilo Bay and Wailuku, it was disastrous to the inhabitants who were exposed, and unexpectedly visited by it. The waters suddenly receded from the shore, then returned with great strength, rising ten or fifteen feet above high water mark, and stretching upon the land far beyond its ordinary bounds, overwhelming and demolishing more than 100 habitations of the natives, destroying some and endangering many lives. It occurred at seven P. M., at the time of low tide, and when there was little wind. On the south side of Maui the waters rose about eight feet; and further west still less.

At Wailuku, the waters, after the first recession of fifteen or twenty rods from their ordinary limit, " stood up as an heap " or a precipice, and rushed back upon the beach, overflowed the banks, and carried away an entire hamlet of twenty-six native grass houses, with their effects and occupants, some forty or fifty rods inland, throwing most of the wrecks of houses, broken canoes, fowls, beasts, men, women, and children, into a pond, two miles in circumference, in the rear of the village.

Some of the people who saw the unlooked for recession of the waters, though they were Hawaiians, had the quickness of wit and the self-possession to conclude there would quickly be a corresponding procession, or overwhelming influx, and, making seasonable speed, fled to a place of safety. But the mass were taken entirely unawares by the overwhelming and irresistible surge ; their houses were instantaneously demolished over their heads, and all submerged or floating at once, and the outcries of the astonished sufferers mingled with the roar of the sea.

Such a calamity, falling suddenly on an American or European village, at evening, might be expected to destroy many of the lives exposed. But the natives, with commendable address, applied their almost universal power of swimming, to relieve themselves, while the stronger were assiduous and successful in aiding the children and the infirm. By the blessing of God, all escaped but two at this place. One of these was a mother who was carried out of the flood by her son, safely, as he supposed, rejoicing that he could aid her in such peril. But how was he disappointed when he laid her on dry ground, to find that she had been overpowered by the shock and was dead !

The same phenomenon, as it occurred at the missionary station in Hilo, is thus described by Mr. Coan, Nov., 1837, in connexion with a work of grace :—

" But God has recently visited this people in judgment as well as mercy. On the 7th inst., during the time of our protracted meeting, at 7 o'clock P. M., as we were calling our domestics together for evening prayers, we heard a heavy sound as of a falling mountain upon the beach. This noise was succeeded by loud wailing and cries of distress, extending for miles around the shores of the bay. l immediately ran down to the sea, where a scene of wild ruin was spread out to our view. The sea, by an unseen hand, had all on a sudden risen in a gigantic wave, and this wave, rushing in with the rapidity of a racehorse, had fallen upon the shore, sweeping everything (not more than fifteen or twenty feet above high-water mark) into indiscriminate ruin. Houses, furniture, calabashes, fuel, timber, canoes, food, clothing, everything floated wild upon the flood. The water rushed up valleys, carried away fish-ponds, and swept over many low plantations of food. So sudden and unexpected was the catastrophe, that the people along the shore were literally ' eating and drinking,' and they ' knew not, until the flood came and swept them all away.' The wave fell upon them like the bolt of heaven, and no man had time to flee or to save his gar-ment. In a moment, hundreds of the people were struggling with the raging billows, and amidst the wreck of their earthly all. Some were dashed upon the shore ; some were drawn out by friends who came to their relief. Some were carried out to sea by the receding current. Some sank to rise no more till the noise of the judgment wakes them. Through the great mercy of God only eleven were drowned. Twelve individuals were picked up while drifting out of the bay, by the boats of the Admiral Cockburn, an English whaler then in this port. The master, Capt. Jones Lawrence, kindly ordered his boats to go in search of those who were floating off upon the current, and by the prompt and timely aid of his men twelve were saved from impending death. The whole scene was one of deep and painful interest. Multitudes came out of the waters without so much as a garment left them to cover their nakedness. Half frantic parents were searching for their chil-dren. Children were weeping for their parents. Husbands were run-ning to and fro in the crowds inquiring for their wives. Wives were wailing for their departed husbands. The loud roar of the ocean, the cries of distress, the rush of hundreds to the shore, and the scene of desolation there presented, all combined to render the scene one of wakeful and thrilling interest. Had this providence occurred at mid-night, when all were asleep, hundreds of lives would undoubtedly have been lost. But in the midst of wrath God remembered mercy.

" The water remained but a few minutes upon the shore, and then re-turned with a rapid rush far below low water mark. Again it returned upon the land ; but with less violence than at the first, and thus, after several influxes and refluxes, it retired to its ancient bounds. It was said by those on board the ship, that the water rushed by the ship at the rate of eight or ten miles an hour."

About a hundred houses, filled with their customary occupants and with many strangers, were demolished. Eleven were drown-ed, and one sufferer died soon after.

CHAPTER XXIII.

Progress of the great revival—Religious interest among children and youth—Means
employed to save souls—Mode of preaching at the islands—Great additions to
the churches—Chaplain, teacher, and interpreter for the king and chiefs.

THE year 1838 was at the Sandwich Islands emphatically
a year of the right hand of the Most High. The Sabbath that
closed 1837 was at Honolulu a day of peculiar interest. The
preaching of the gospel to a great multitude was evidently set
home with power in the case of many individuals. The following
morning, with the new year, commenced a series of protracted
meetings for the worship of God, and the increase of religious
interest throughout the island of Oahu. As the first rising sun
showed his bright disc in the east, the church and congregation
at Honolulu, filling one of the largest houses of worship on the
islands, united in solemn prayer for the outpouring of the Spirit
of God, not without the hope that the prayer accompanied by
the well directed efforts of the professors and ministers of religion
would be speedily answered.

There had been for a time a waking up among the hearers of
the Gospel on this island, and indeed throughout the whole group.
And during the progress of this meeting for a week, there were
many who appeared to give heed to the things that belonged to
their peace, and who afterwards declared that at that time their
hearts chose the Lord for their King, their Savior, and their
Portion. At the other stations, a similar degree of interest was
felt in the course of their protracted meetings at Ewa, Waialua,
and Kaneohe. Indeed there was a shaking among the dry bones
through the nation. The preachers of the Gospel prophesied
according to their ability, and with deep impressions of the
responsibility of their office, called on the people to *hear the
Word of the Lord.* The Spirit of God most manifestly hovered
over the islands. The Gospel proved to be the power of God
and the wisdom of God for the recovery of the lost. Our ears
were allowed to hear and our eyes to see glorious things in our
Hawaiian Zion. The year of Jubilee had come, and thousands
of the liberated appeared to be coming to Zion, and celebrating
the praises of their Deliverer.

Many appeared oppressed with a sense of sin, or filled with
apprehensions of the wrath of God which should fall upon the

ungodly, the impenitent, and unbelieving.   Lukewarm and cold
professors of religion were revived, or apparently converted
anew.   Those who had witnessed a good confession, labored with
ardor to save souls, and earnestly interceded with God to pluck
their fellow sinners as brands from the midst of the burning.

The missionaries at all the stations, standing, as it were, between
the living and the dead, with the scenes of eternity before them,
and seeing many thousands of the people ready to hear and
inquire, insisted largely on the cardinal points, the ruined condition of the sinner and his exposure to everlasting death; the
utter inexcusableness of his continuing his rebellion against God;
his need of justification through the righteousness of Christ; the
freeness and fullness of redemption through his blood; the duty
of immediate repentance and faith as the condition of pardon;
the necessity of the aid of the Spirit of God in the work of
regeneration and sanctification; and the importance of immediate
submission to his guidance, teaching, and commands.

The gracious visitations of the Spirit of God from on high,
which at this period were joyfully hailed at all the stations, as
wonderful and glorious, as the expected answer to united prayer,
the expected blessing on the means which the Lord of the harvest had most specifically and peremptorily enjoined, led, we
believe, unusual thousands to crowd the doors of the sanctuaries,
where they were addressed with unusual earnestness, and where
the united cry of many ascended to heaven.   With thousands
the missionaries held personal conversation, endeavoring to know
their thoughts and their state, and to lead them to Christ or to
confirm them in faith and hope.   Examining great numbers, and
selecting such as appeared to be born of God, they propounded
them for admission to the church, and after some probation,
usually two or three months, baptized those who in the judgment
of charity were the true disciples of Christ.   In midsummer, it
was found that the aggregate additions to the churches were equal
to the three thousand added at Jerusalem on the day of Pentecost,
and the two thousand immediately after, and that 2400 more had
also been propounded for admission.   There was always need of
care and caution in bringing forward candidates.   Certainly not
less in a season of excitement, or unusually extensive attention
to religion, when thousands of native members were urging their
relatives and acquaintances to come into the ranks of the Lord's
people, and many thousands were soliciting baptism and admission to the Lord's table.

There was some diversity of opinion among the missionaries
as to the extent of personal acquaintance with candidates necessary to warrant their admission, and as to the length of probation
which ought to be given; yet all required what they deemed
good evidence of true repentance, or of a radical change of heart
by the Spirit of God.   Strong fears were indulged by some that
hundreds of candidates with whom the missionary could have

but a limited or short acquaintance, had been admitted to church fellowship too hastily, and partly on the opinions of their countrymen. Whether a minister and church are any more liable to misjudge of the qualifications of candidates under a shower of divine grace than in ordinary times, admits of a question. In many cases the acquaintance of the missionary with the candidates was familiar and long.

The blessing of heaven appeared to attend the efforts of the mission and others for the rising generation. Six hundred children and youth were reckoned at this period among the converts. At the Mission Seminary there were twenty men and sixty-four boys under the care and instruction of Messrs. Andrews and Clark,* eight of whom, having evidently shared in the general revival, were this year admitted to the church. In the female boarding-school at Wailuku, there were thirty-three girls under the care and instruction of Mr. and Mrs. Green and Miss Ogden. They applied themselves with becoming diligence to their studies and appropriate labors. They made their own clothes, braided bonnets for themselves, and assisted in making clothes for the indigent students in the Mission Seminary. They were respectful, obedient, and attached to their teachers, easily managed, and being under strictly Christian influence, gave promise of aid in the work of elevating the nation. Here too the gracious influences of the Spirit were experienced, and ten of these precious souls appeared to be born of God, and were this year admitted to the church.

At Hilo, the interesting school of boys under the care and instruction of Mr. and Mrs. Lyman, and whom they were preparing to be the future teachers of the nation when maturity and the advantages of the Missionary Seminary should be conferred on them in due course, shared in the revival influence. There were thirty-one pupils in the school. Many of them were bright and apt students, of sober habits, and good morals. Seventeen of them giving evidence of conversion, were this year baptized and welcomed to the fellowship of the church.

The character of the native school teachers through the country was gradually rising. Some, trained in the station schools, and others at the Mission Seminary, with special reference to school teaching, conducted their schools with diligence, energy, and success. Pupils were taught to read and value the Scriptures. Children were instructed to love one another, to respect their parents, to obey their Creator, and to love and trust the Savior. In many schools the voice of prayer and praise was heard. In the schools generally a religious influence was felt; the number of hopeful conversions among quite young pupils was highly encouraging: and the mission felt and acknowledged the importance of the machinery of schools in the work of enlightening,

* Mr. Dibble, who had left Hilo and joined the Seminary, was this year absent on a visit to the U. S.

civilizing, and elevating the heathen world, and especially the Hawaiian race.

While such an influence was exerted by the missionaries, by the Word and Spirit of God, and by the schools, there seemed less amount than usual of restraint by civil laws or magisterial power. Yet thieving was scarcely known among the people; the missionaries rarely locked a door; the Sabbath was very generally observed as the *Lord's* day; and it was exceedingly rare for a native in any part of the islands to be known to be intoxicated.

In whatever village a missionary would appoint a religious meeting, any day or hour of the week, he could rely on having an attentive audience and encouragement to hold forth the Word of Life. In some places, the rude people in numbers called on the name of the Lord with *loud voices simultaneously ;* and in others, they attended to the duties of religious meetings with quiet and silent demonstrations of interest in their object.

Under the guidance of the missionaries generally, notwithstanding the greatness of the crowds that assembled and the interest felt, the meetings were orderly, and were conducted with ease and pleasure.

Among the institutions ordained by heaven for raising up a godly race, the prominent are the *family*, the *magistracy*, the *church*, and the *Christian ministry*. But in a ruined heathen nation, how little aid in the work of reform can be derived from the family arrangement till that is purified, regulated, and elevated! By this time, however, not only had Christian marriage come to be generally respected, the fidelity of husbands and wives greatly promoted, and the happy bond of parental and filial affection cemented ; but family *religion* had been introduced, and family prayer, morning and evening, now prevailed in the country to a much greater extent than the public profession of religion. Very many throughout the islands, who were not members of the church, had family worship, whereas in some Christian countries there are many professors of religion who do not usually have family devotions. The extensive attention to family religion at the Sandwich Islands has doubtless been highly beneficial, and been attended with rich blessings from heaven.

The influence of the *magistracy* has been variable.

The existence and light of nineteen *churches* at this period in different parts of the country, their prayers and songs and solemn ordinances, the rite of baptism, and the sacramental showing of the Lord's death before the world, were mighty in the hand of God. The general diffusion of the New Testament, and portions of the old, published at the expense of the American Bible Society, and of numerous evangelical tracts by the aid of the A. Tract Society, two or three hundred hymns and other works by the American Board, were among the means of promoting extensive revivals of religion. Nor should *the committing to memory daily of a verse of Scripture* by thousands, be overlooked.

But, as in other countries, the labors of the *ministry* in connexion with the prayers, faith, and obedience of believers, the preaching of the Gospel was the grand instrumentality by which God has caused his name to be honored there.   And whether that Gospel has been set forth through earthen vessels, foreign or native, it is 'by the foolishness of *preaching*'that God is pleased to save those that believe.

I have been often asked what *kind* of preaching do the Hawaiian people require, and what *method* of presenting truth do the missionaries find the best adapted to their minds?

They need to have the same doctrines and duties presented, and much the same arguments and considerations urged, and in much the same form and style, as other sinners in any part of the world.   A diversity of talent has been employed among them. A great diversity in the modes of preaching, conducting meetings, communicating divine truth, and maintaining a healthful Christian intercourse with the people, has been exhibited by different missionaries, and by the same missionaries at different times.   I know of no *one* method of dealing with Hawaiian sinners or Christians successful at all times to lead them to do their duty to God and man, or to lead the impenitent, the lukewarm, or worldly formalist, to Christ and heaven, or to lead on the faithful disciples to the highest achievements in the Christian warfare, or in the extension of Christ's kingdom.

At first, as in the case of children, or of those whose minds had been unaccustomed to reason correctly, great plainness and simplicity in presenting divine truth were required, and care, time, and patience to gain attention and to train the conscience. But in 1838, when the New Testament had become a common book among the people, and when the Gospel had been preached to some thousands stately, and others occasionally, from five to eighteen years, there was a considerable diversity in the attainments of those who composed the congregation wherever a missionary preached.

At this period, the same style of sermons, prayers, songs, interrogations, and exhortations, which proves effectual in promoting revivals of religion, conversion, or growth in grace among a plain people in the United States, was undoubtedly adapted to be useful at the Sandwich Islands.   The *directness* of Peter on the day of Pentecost, and of those who are distinguished for winning souls in the United States, would be equally suitable to the Hawaiians.   The beginning with a text of Scripture is of course not essential to the success of a sermon, though it should be a fair and forcible exhibition of God's will on some point or points of immediate concern.   It may be the exposition of an inspired clause, verse, paragraph, parable, or chapter.   A sermon to the Hawaiians may be short or long, with little or no formality.   It may consist of a few appropriate sentences like that in the Philippian jail, "Do thyself no harm," we are here not to expose, mislead, or injure, but to aid you—" Believe on the Lord Jesus Christ, and thou shalt be saved;" or it may embrace the amount of matter usually delivered in a sermon from half an hour to an hour long, especially if a question, as is not uncommon, is occasionally asked by the preacher, and responded to either right or wrong by some one of the congregation; and if there are *tracks* made in the discourse which can be followed or retraced, or such distinct heads, divisions, inferences, &c., as can be distinguished, or could be noted down by such as wish to preserve the outline or substance of the discourse.

A rule of our travelling Methodist brethren to prefer the plainest texts as the most important and the most effective, is, doubtless, of some importance among a people so recently instructed as the Hawaiian race.

While there is great agreement among the missionaries as to the doctrines and duties to be inculcated, there is some difference of opinion as to the mode of preaching best adapted to benefit the people.   One preacher, who deems the native mind too stupid to take in ideas of religion or to act by ordinary impulses, thinks it best to single out detached ideas and present them with simplicity itself, or such singleness and force," as to come," as he would say, " right down. upon the mind of a native, as a well directed hammer comes down upon the head of a nail."   Another, who knows that even iron can be " *hammer hardened*," prefers a more insinuating and winning mode of opening the heart and introducing purifying truths, naturally unwelcome, and of pouring in knowledge, demanding and expecting a little more voluntary labor of the hearer to receive and retain instruction.   Another, supposing that one prominent truth in a sermon is better than two, " chooses one single truth, presents it in various attitudes—turns it over, as it were, on this and on that side, that it may be clearly seen." Another presents several great truths in the same discourse, and repeats his prominent thoughts with clearness, as matters of testimony, like Peter and Stephen.   Another, believing that religion is the work of a rational soul, and that the process of reasoning is essential to the establishment of a solid faith, and pure and permanent principles, endeavors to call the mind of his hearers into action, and to lead them, step by step, as they can see the way, to form just conclusions from comprehended and admitted premises, to notice the connexion of one truth with another, and feel the obligations of duty arising from acknowledged relations.   Some, if not all of the preachers in the mission, have tasked their powers in trying the various modes—the hammering, insinuating, winning, pouring, reiterating, leading, or inductive methods, and have found them all to be useful when their own hearts, impressed with the amazing importance of the divine themes they are called to handle, are warm with love, and strong in faith, resting on the promise of the Savior, " Lo I am with you alway, even unto the end of the world."

The question may be further answered by referring to the teachings of the Bible, not designed for one class or tribe alone, but adapted to all nations, and as well to the Hawaiian as to the proud Jew or the learned Greek. Comparing Scripture with Scripture, our preachers at the islands have, from the beginning, allowed the very words of the sacred writers to abound in their discourses, partly because the words which the Holy Ghost teacheth are the best, and partly because it was necessary that all, for a time, and very many still, should learn by the *ear*, the testimony which God has given to guide and save the soul.

As the arts and sciences are to be taught at the Sandwich Islands by the same process as elsewhere, so is the Gospel of salvation. The human mind, the human heart, the human soul, may safely be regarded as essentially the same in all ages and countries. Much the same process is required to teach it to comprehend and compare quantities and numbers in London and Honolulu, or to lead it to understand and appreciate the Gospel, at Jerusalem, Mars Hill, Lahainaluna, and Hilo, where a few years ago the people had never seen a plough or a book. The Hawaiian and the German may alike begin by adding the thumb to the four fingers on one hand to find the sum of five, then subtract it to find the difference between one and five; and in a few months, extract the cube root of a given number, or on the black-board, promptly, as we have seen native boys, demonstrate the square of the hypotenuse of a right angled triangle to be equal to the sum of the squares of the two sides, and by the same process, too, by which all, in other lands, are trained to do this.

Besides the labors of the pulpit, or preaching to assemblies of the people, much was to be done by personal conversation, by simple testimony, by argument, by exhortation, and appeal, either privately or openly, to individuals, or small companies, at the house or study of the missionary, by the way-side, at the habitations of the natives, and in common and Sabbath schools, the occasional inquiry meeting, and the weekly meeting for reviewing the Sabbath sermons.

It is worthy of remark that missionaries, even with a limited acquaintance with the language and ancient religion of the country, were able to be useful.

Too much account, I am persuaded, is sometimes made of the knowledge of the ancient mythology or customs of the people, and of the rites and maxims of heathenism, the form of words and the graces of elocution, the trickery and trade of the tragedian. The voluble Hawaiian convert, versed in the language and superstitions of his country, was allowed to have greatly the advantage of the foreign missionary in those particulars; yet the latter, having a more extensive acquaintance with the Bible, the great subject of redemption, and the nature of the human mind, has much the advantage on the whole, and though he should never name their former heathen rites or superstitions, is better able to rouse, elevate, and guide the minds of the people.

An acquaintance with what is true and useful, and with the mode of introducing it into the minds of others, is of vastly more importance to a preacher, teacher, or lecturer, than a knowledge of all the errors, prejudices, superstitions, and abominations, with which the minds of his hearers may have been filled.

Though an acquaintance with the vernacular language of the heathen is a great acquisition to the missionary, it is not *essential* to his success. No foreign missionary, perhaps, ever preached with more power or success to the heathen, since the days of miracles passed away, than did David Brainerd to the Indians by an interpreter, before he had much acquaintance with their language, style, customs, and superstitions. While a comparative stranger and foreigner, before he could speak their language, treating them as lost sinners for whose salvation Christ had made provision, he had a wonderful out-pouring of the Spirit connected with his preaching and prayers, and the felicity to think *three-tenths* of his hearers were converted, within a few months from the commencement of his labors among them.

What encouragement is thus given to the ardent disciple of Christ, the Sabbath school teacher, the student in college, and the candidate for the ministry, to seize on the opportunities offered for walking in Brainerd's steps, to make known Jesus and the resurrection to the wise and unwise, the semi-civilized and the barbarian! And how wise and benevolent the injunction of the Savior appears—" Go teach all nations to observe all things whatsoever I have commanded you,"—a system of religion equally adapted and equally indispensable to all, and so successful, at this period, at the Sandwich Islands.

This Gospel was laboriously inculcated on many thousands of the people who were spread over wide fields for individual preachers, parishes, or districts, each from twenty to eighty miles in length. Some of the missionaries preached four or five times a week, some ten, and some, occasionally, twenty or twenty-five times.

The natives who took part in the work employed a variety of talent, each in his own way. Many of their services were doubtless owned by the great Head of the Church as the means of promoting his cause.

For a time, a question occupied some attention, whether the process through which the people appeared to come over from the world to Christ or from heathenism to Christianity, were not *too long*, and whether the method of dealing with them adopted by the missionaries, especially in the long probation given to candidates, or the slowness with which the missionaries came to an opinion favorable to the piety of those who offered themselves, were not calculated to mislead the people in regard to the nature of conversion, and consequently in respect to their personal duty.

Some of the people doubtless thought that a considerable time was requisite for the sinner to pass through the successive stages of seeking and praying for a new heart, inquiry, conviction, distress, repenting, submitting, choosing God, and trusting in Christ, and setting the affections on heavenly things.

At a protracted meeting at Honolulu during the great revival, I heard Bartimeus, in an able plea, urge on his countrymen the duty of immediate repentance, and the practicability of instantaneous conversion. With earnestness, fluency, and force, he cited for his purpose the cases of Zaccheus on the Sycamore tree hastening down at once to obey the Savior's call; the dying thief on the cross, at once confessing and forsaking sin and trusting in Christ; the trembling jailor of Philippi, who, on first hearing the Gospel, believed, and the three thousand, who, on the day of Pentecost, were added to the church before the close of the day. These, with other considerations, he urged impressively, to prove that every impenitent sinner ought instantaneously to repent and obey the Gospel.

The same duty was diligently inculcated from every pulpit connected with our mission. This native pleader, growing in knowledge and experience, and the power of persuasion, was, as has before been mentioned, licensed to preach, and after some years, finished his useful course as a soldier of the cross and a faithful ally of the missionary band. As they laid this beloved brother and coadjutor in the grave, they felt that " a great man had fallen in Israel," and believed that he had gone to receive a crown—an immortal crown, to be bestowed by grace, rich and wonderful grace, on one who had been the most abject, debased, neglected, and miserable among the sons of paganism.

How glorious does the Savior appear in gathering such trophies into his kingdom!

During the year ending June, 1838, there were received into sixteen churches, 4,973 hopeful converts.* During the whole year, the work of the Divine Spirit appeared to be going on gloriously at nearly all the stations, and also wherever the Gospel was diligently proclaimed and the general means of grace carefully employed. " Persons of all ages," say the mission, " have been subjects of the gracious visitations of the Spirit, from opening childhood to decrepit old age. The boarding school and Sabbath school scholar, together with many who had been neglected, have sought, and it is hoped, have found the Savior."

It was to the missionaries a matter of wonder, and it is a matter of lasting gratitude, that God appeared in mercy for the Hawaiian race at the very period when the churches in the United States were, in part, withholding their contributions, and the Board were

---

* The additions at the different stations were as follows; Waimea (Kauai), 18; Waioli, 38; at Waialua (Oahu), 127; Ewa, 329; Kaneohe, 43; Honolulu 1st, 134; Honolulu 2d, 49; Kaluaaha, Molokai, 14; Lahaina (Maui), 2; Wailuku, 208; Kailua (Hawaii), 62; Kealakekua, 81; Hilo, 639; Kohala, 629; Waimea, 2,600.

cutting down the expenditures of their missions, and restricting their laborers beyond former precedent, and without the knowledge of the missionaries at the Sandwich Islands, till these heavenly showers came upon them. This gracious visitation, therefore, was not only for the immediate subjects of it, but designed by a wonder-working God to prevent his faint-hearted people from giving over the heathen world to perish, and at the same time to humble them for that want of faith in him, which had held them back from the reasonable, voluntary sacrifices, which he required for his work abroad. For their omissions, doubtless, in part, at least, he was then scattering to the winds of heaven their mountains of fictitious wealth, and their hills of grasped and solid treasures, which they were fondly hoping would soon rise to mountains, and afford them the privilege of aiding the missionary cause in a more princely manner, than they had felt able to do. We, therefore, looked upon this divine interposition as of great importance in reference to the general evangelization of the world.

The mission, and the rulers, had now waited two years, after sending their memorials to the United States, for a civilian, and teachers of the arts, independent of the mission; but received no response. The American Board, though deeming the subject of great importance, did not think it properly belonged to them to send a civilian. But divine Providence, always exercising a peculiar care over the nation, from the moment of the renunciation of idolatry, did not leave them destitute, in this emergency. To avail themselves of what was within their reach was a duty to which they were prompted by their own sagacity, and by the suggestion of intelligent residents.

The increasing intercourse of the rulers with the representatives of foreign nations, and with others, resident and transient, rendered it obviously important that some trustworthy and competent interpreter should be more devoted to that business, than it was convenient for pastors and translators, on whom they had, in part, relied, ordinarily to be. The necessity for having an interpreter and teacher for the chiefs, had become so apparent to them, and so urgent, in 1837, that they applied to Mr. Andrews, a teacher of the Mission Seminary, to engage in that work, and offered him a moderate salary, for a year. Though he did not fully accept the offer, he asked his patrons for a " conditional dismission," that he might be the teacher of the king and chiefs, in politics, law, and political economy, and their interpreter in the transaction of business. In the summer of 1838, the king and chiefs applied to Mr. Richards, to enter into their service as chaplain and interpreter, and teacher of political economy, law, and the science of government.

Accepting the responsible office, he, on the 3d of Aug., 1838, completed his arrangements with the chiefs, and entered partially on its duties at once. From that period, the government engaged to give him a salary of $600, and paid it quarterly. But until a dissolution of his connexion with the American Board could be effected, though he could preach anything which Christ and his apostles taught, he could teach nothing unsuitable for a minister of Christ, or a foreign missionary to teach : much less could he bear the standard of a civil office, or become a minister of state.

The teaching of the principles of moral philosophy, of equity and justice—the foundation of law, and the introduction of any of the useful arts, was, with the consent of the government, lawful for any missionary, without giving any nation ground, justly, to complain. Interference with the party interests of chiefs, or with their civil power, would have been improper ; or to advise or assist them in their business, any further than they desired it, would have been objectionable. And some missionaries, wishing to keep far within the line, were very slow to give an *opinion*, even where the magistrate requested it, or sought it with diligence, lest they should sacrifice their appropriate influence as ambassadors of Christ, and the mission should be censured for interfering in civil matters.

It was a satisfaction to the rulers now, to have a teacher in their affairs on whom they could call as their *own*, and it was a relief to the other members of the mission to have the chiefs' teacher stand in the breach, to supply, and far better than any man who could then be obtained for it out of the mission, their need, as far as he was able. Nothing was more reasonable than that the government should support the teacher, so exclusively devoted to it for the public good, and it was an important step in advance in civilization, which that government took, when they assumed the expense of such an agency.

Mr. R. tendered his resignation as a missionary ; and his connexion with the Board was dissolved as soon as possible.

He immediately commenced translating a work on political economy, and lecturing to the king and chiefs. Kinau, the premier, took a deep interest in this method of acquiring the needed knowledge that was thus attainable; and the king and others listened with attention and advantage.

Meantime, the power of the Spirit of God accompanying the diligent use of the various means of grace, continued to be manifest throughout the islands, and the year 1839 commenced with the prospect of an increasingly rich and glorious harvest.

CHAPTER XXIV.

TWENTIETH YEAR OF THE MISSION, AND SEVENTH OF KAMEHA-MEHA III.—1839.

Translation of the Bible—Death of Kinau—Appointment of a Premier—Suspension of the punishment of native papists—Visit of L'Artemise to Oahu—Warlike manifesto of Capt. Laplace—Correspondence of the missionaries and their consul —Measures of residents at Honolulu—Agreement between Capt. Laplace and Kauokaeouli—Visit of the United States' ships Columbia and John Adams—Testimony of the officers of the squadron—Voice abroad—Death of Mr. McDonald and G. P. Judd, jr.—Native elegy.

Two important points in the progress of the mission and of the nation were at this period regarded as of special interest and importance, and, in some sense, particularly related to each other—the *entire translation of the Bible,* printed, published, and open to the whole people, and a code of laws based on the principles of civil liberty, and suited to a limited monarchy, and the moral and intellectual advance of the people. The former point was reached in 1839, and the latter in 1840.

God's Word, the finishing sheet of which was struck May 10, 1839, has from the commencement of our mission been prominent in our teaching—prominent in all the schools, taught or superintended by our missionaries. The entrance of God's Word giveth light. He has honored the nation that has nobly welcomed his Word to their families and to their schools. God has honored the rulers who have encouraged its general circulation and free perusal among the whole population. In this the Hawaiian chiefs made more progress during the first nineteen years of the labors of the missionaries than the rulers of Italy, Portugal, and Spain, have made in half as many centuries, with all the aid of bishops, cardinals, and popes. Nor do I believe any anti-Christian power can ever make the free circulation and reading of the Bible unpopular in the Sandwich Islands, unless through the influence of Satan the people can be seduced into gross idolatry and the abominations of heathenism, which the Bible so uncompromisingly rebukes.

We are happy to think the Hawaiian translation of the Bible, the labor of a number of hands during a period of fifteen years, is a good translation, giving in general a forcible and lucid exhibition of the revealed will of God; a translation highly acceptable to the best native scholars, and one which all evangelical Christians can patronize and use with confidence. A few foreign words are introduced, and a few original words retained; for " Sabbath," *Sabati;* for "baptizo," *bapetizo;* and its verbal noun

bapetizo ana. For the Supreme Deity we use three terms with
discrimination; for the Hebrew " Jehovah," we use *Iehova*, and
ascribe to him all the divine attributes, and deny to him all im-
perfections. For " Alohim " and " Theos," we use *Akua*, and
give it the same definition; for " Adonai " and " Kurios," we use
Hɩku, which corresponds to the word Lord. But I must not
enlarge.

While churches were rising, the blessed work of revival was
going forward, and thousands of the natives were flocking like
doves to their windows, Kinau, the Premier, the kind, modest,
firm, and sagacious patroness of the cause of reform at the islands,
was laid suddenly on her last sick bed. Many interested friends
gathered around her, and made such efforts as were in their
power for her relief. But the summons had come in the very
morning of her days, and the time of her departure was at hand.
At the commencement almost of a public career of great usefulness, she suddenly reached the goal. She had come into office
in troublous times, but she had acquired the full confidence of
the king, and was generally and highly respected. In connexion with the king and her husband, the governor of Oahu, she
had greatly encouraged the erection of the two churches at Honolulu. The missionaries thought she could not well be released
from her post, in which she had endeavored to supply the place
of Kaahumanu.

She had begun, with readiness of mind, to attend to the principles on which the government was to be improved and administered, and much reliance was placed on her Christian spirit to
make her follow just where truth and duty could be shown to
lead. From the time of her conversion there had been a very
marked improvement in her habits and manners. Not an approach to immodesty in dress, in words or actions, appeared in
her, or blamable gaiety, levity, or austerity of manners. Intemperance and Sabbath breaking were no more expected of her
than of the missionaries who were assiduously laboring to oppose
these evils. She once invited two naval officers to breakfast with
her. The higher eventually, when the time came, instead of
accepting her civility, sent his apology, that he had the evening
before drunk too much wine, and was too unwell. The captain,
who accepted the invitation, and was kindly entertained at a
well furnished and well spread breakfast table, and was served
with as fine fish and coffee as could often be found, said, " No
lady in Washington could have given a better breakfast, or received a guest more genteelly."

In her spacious and well furnished apartments, which had the
air of civilization, she, on one occasion, very courteously received
and entertained on a pleasant evening, at a well supplied table,
forty-four missionaries, male and female, the king and eight or
ten chiefs, and about twenty missionary children. At her request,
a blessing was implored at the commencement, and thanks re-

turned at the close of the supper. Serious and cheerful conversation marked the interview, and singing and prayer followed the repast. In the piety and sobriety of the Christian chiefs on such occasions, there appear more particularity and scrupulousness than in many who have had far greater opportunities of learning and feeling obligation to the Author of every good and perfect gift which they enjoy.

Having been seized with mumps and afterwards by paralysis, she sank rapidly, and, April 4th, left her husband, an interesting group of children, her mother, Hoapili-wahine, her half sister, Kekauluohi, her half brother, the king, who in his youth sometimes called her " mother," and a numerous circle of Christian friends, to mourn their loss in her early departure from earth.

The disposition of Kinau and her predecessor, Kaahumanu, after their hearts had been made to welcome Christianity, and to cherish a lively hope of an inheritance in heaven, would, I think, have led them to greater retirement and quietude than the cares and honors of their elevated and responsible office would admit. The more readily would they have sought retirement if they could have assured themselves that the government would without them have been wisely and efficiently administered. They had begun to study the mysteries of redemption, and to find sources of higher pleasure than the distinctions of wealth and rank could give ; and though they had not, perhaps, the full measure of internal resources and satisfaction in the enjoyment of God in retirement which led Lady Jane Grey at first to decline in favor of her cousin the offer of a crown—a crown which to her she believed would be a crown of thorns to torment her if it should not cause her death—still they showed as decided a desire to benefit the nation by retaining and executing their office, as almost any uninspired rulers of ancient or modern times.

Where intrinsic moral worth is associated with rank and power, we cannot fail to admire the union of the modesty which draws back from the allurements, the honors, and responsibilities of office, with the disinterested heroism which fearlessly assumes and executes high trusts when the possessor is providentially called to it, as were Moses, Esther, Kaahumanu, and Kinau. The latter had expressed a willingness to resign and retire ; but the interests of the nation appeared to forbid it. So to those who offered promotion, Lady Jane, when duty appeared doubtful, said, " My liberty is better than the chain you offer me, with what precious stones soever it be adorned, or with what gold soever it be framed." The need of her wisdom and influence to guide the nation in the way of life did not prevail with her to accept the crown, nor the commands of the Duke of Northumberland, nor the entreaties and promises of the Duke of Suffolk, till her loved husband, Lord Guilford, employed all his influence to accomplish her coronation.

No friend of the Hawaiian nation could have desired Kaahumanu or Kinau to retire from office, and to have their system of government suddenly changed by a revolution in their time, to a popular form.

The missionaries collectively said of Kinau, " She sustained the highest rank in the nation next to the king; for stability of character she has left no equal; she was ever awake to the interests of the nation, and showed no ordinary skill in managing its concerns, even in the most troublous times; she set her face against the prevailing immoralities, and gave satisfactory evidence of a readiness to make any personal sacrifice for the purpose of promoting Christian morals and the best interests of the nation."

The next day after her funeral services, Kekauluohi was proclaimed her successor and initiated into her office, and the people were called on to yield her due obedience, but Kinau's infant daughter, Victoria, was considered as her superior in rank.

The following edict was issued by the king:

" HONOLULU, JUNE 8TH, 1839.

" The explanation of Kamehameha III. respecting the descent of the authority of Kaahumanu II. to her heir and successor, Victoria Kamehamalu II., in whose place, however, Miriam Kekauluohi is to act for the present.   This is his proclamation:

" Hear, ye chiefs, patricians, plebeians, and people from other lands, for I make this explanation that you may understand.

" The authority hitherto possessed by my mother Kaahumanu II. until her decease, is now transferred to my other mother (*Miriam Kekauluohi*) though Victoria Kamehamalu II. is her superior, but still under my direction.

" Furthermore : no documents nor notes, referable to government, after this date, which have not my own signature, and also that of Miriam Kekauluohi, at the bottom of said writing, will be acknowledged as government papers."

Whether the office be that of Queen, Premier, Prime Minister, or Secretary of State, it was an office of high responsibility, and its occupant was expected to understand the wishes of the sovereign, and of the chiefs and people; to advise for the public good, and to act as a check to prevent injustice and oppression. Difficult as were the duties of the office, and trying as were the circumstances of the nation at that period, Kekauluohi entered on her public duties with much propriety, though to the exposure of her spiritual prosperity.

Scarcely ten days had elapsed before it was reported that a number of subjects at Waianae, called *Palani*, accused of *malamakii*, image worship, had been called before the chiefs, and that some of them were treated with severity.   Addressing a note to the Premier, I inquired of her as to the fact, and she returned me the following answer :

" JUNE 18TH, 1839.*

" Salutations to you, Bingham.

" I have seen your letter. We have exercised that oppression. But it is brought to an end. Henceforth it will, doubtless, be the rule to admonish. Love to you and Mrs. Bingham.

" KEKAULUOHI."

Whether it were from the increase of the knowledge and power of religion, or the extreme difficulty found in distinguishing between the *belief* and practice of those who called themselves *Palani*, and *idolatry*, against which a law had been in force twenty years; or the direct advice of the missionaries not to punish their subjects for being *papists ;* or the remonstrances of others, or all together, the king and his government, from that period, are considered as having receded from the execution of that law upon them.

The king allowed and encouraged his chiefs to guard against sedition and idolatry, and if they found any of his subjects practising or teaching image worship under the name of *palani* [papist] to admonish and teach them better. Two women were shortly sent to the governor's residence in the fort, where he, lodging elsewhere that night, proposed to examine them in the morning. Returning from Punahou in the morning, I was requested by a resident to go with him to the fort, and see and assist to liberate two women who, he said, were there, bound in a most painful posture, for being Catholics. Expressing doubts as to their being punished for being Catholics, I stated that I had learned from the Premier herself that punishment was not to be inflicted on that account; but I would go with him to the governor. We took the same road to the gate of the Premier, at whose house the governor was. The resident passed on towards the fort, and his place of business. I apprised the governor of what I had heard, and asked his attention to it. He quickly despatched a messenger, and started himself, and met the two women coming from the fort, under the escort of several foreigners, who, unbidden, had gone, into the fort to release them, concerning whom the author of the Supplement to the Sandwich Islands Mirror says: " The gentlemen succeeded in liberating the prisoners." The governor, surprised at this bold interference, said to the gentlemen : " *Your* business is to take care of your stores—that is the road to them. The government of the island and fort is *mine*—this is *my* path." He remanded the women to the fort, examined them as to what they had done, gave them his advice, and dismissed them. On the subaltern he imposed a fine for binding the women (in handcuffs) and keeping them in a painful posture through the night, in the open air, and required him to offer them remuneration ; but

*" Aloha oe, e Binamu. Ua ike iho nei au i kau wahi palapala. Ua hana iho nei makou i ua hookaumaha la. A ua hoopauia ae nei. Eia paha, ma ke ao aku ka pono o keia hope. Aloha oe, a me Binamu wahine."

this they declined. The reason this man assigned for what he had done was, that he had undertaken to examine them himself, in the absence of the governor, and as they showed an unwillingness both to answer and to renounce their adherence to papacy, it had been proposed to him to confine them as he had done.

The king has most distinctly declared in his letter to the American Consul, " that their confinement was not by the order of the chiefs."

In the midst of scenes of surpassing favor to these poor gentiles, in which God was so abundantly smiling, both on their civil and religious institutions, we are brought in our narrative to recur to the further interference of France and Rome.

Now the success of the Gospel is allowed to have been the greatest throughout the Sandwich Islands when the stern resistance of the government, against every species of idolatry, was such as to allow no teacher of it to disturb the people. But though the persevering opposition of the government to Romanism, for twelve years of the progress of the Gospel among them, may not have originated the unexampled success, it may have materially modified it, inasmuch as it secured the undisputed circulation of the Scriptures, in the language of the country, and their free use in all the schools, and by the people generally.

So far as the authority of the rulers was exerted in the fear of God, and in love to the people, against what they justly regarded as idolatrous in their old religion, and in the papal, as against Sabbath desecration, intemperance, and licentiousness, there can be no reasonable doubt that it was noticed with favor by the Sovereign, who will not divide his glory with another, however specious the claim, or gorgeous or imposing the appearance of a rival. Why should it not always be so, under the government of the Infinite, who has said, " Him that honoreth me, I will honor ?"

After two years of the unexampled success of the Gospel, from the last rejection of the papal priests, the French Frigate, l' Artemise, of sixty guns, C. Laplace, commander, came into Honolulu roadstead, July 9th, 1839, and the captain, after an interview with Mr. J. Dudoit, sent to the chiefs the following most singular Manifesto.

" His Majesty, the king of the French, having commanded me to come to Honolulu in order to put an end, either by force or persuasion, to the ill-treatment to which the French have been victims at the Sandwich Islands, I hasten, first, to employ this last means as the most conformable to the political, noble, and liberal system pursued by France against the powerless, hoping, thereby, that I shall make the principal chiefs of these islands understand how fatal the conduct which they pursue towards her will be to their interests, and perhaps cause disasters to them and to their country, should they be obstinate in their perseverance. Misled by perfidious counsellors ; deceived by the excessive indulgence which the French government has extended towards them for several years, they are, undoubtedly, ignorant how potent it is, and that in the world there is not a power which is capable of preventing it from punishing its enemies; otherwise they would have endeavored to merit its favor, or not to incur its displeasure, as they have done in ill-treating the French. They would have faithfully put into execution the treaties, in place of violating them as soon as the fear disappeared, as well as the ships of war which had caused it, whereby bad intentions had been constrained. In fine they will comprehend that to persecute the Catholic religion, to tarnish it with the name of idolatry, and to expel, under this absurd pretext, the French from this archipelago, was to offer an insult to France and to its sovereign.

" It is, without doubt, the formal intention of France that the king of the Sandwich Islands be powerful, independent of every foreign power which he considers his ally; but she also demands that he conform to the usages of civilized nations. Now, amongst the latter there is not even one which does not permit in its territory the free toleration of all religions; and yet, at the Sandwich Islands, the French are not allowed publicly the exercise of theirs, while Protestants enjoy therein the most extensive privileges; for these all favors, for those the most cruel persecutions. Such a state of affairs being contrary to the laws of nations, insulting to those of Catholics, can no longer continue, and I am sent to put an end to it. Consequently I demand in the name of my government,

" 1st. That the Catholic worship be declared free throughout all the dominions subject to the king of the Sandwich Islands; that the members of this religious faith shall enjoy in them all the privileges granted to Protestants.

" 2d. That a site for a Catholic church be given by the government at Honolulu, a port frequented by the French, and that this church be ministered by priests of their nation.

" 3d. That all Catholics imprisoned on account of religion since the last persecutions extended to the French missionaries, be immediately set at liberty.

" 4th. That the king of the Sandwich Islands deposit in the hands of the Captain of l'Artemise the sum of twenty thousand dollars as a guarantee of his future conduct towards France, which sum the government will restore to him when they consider that the accompanying treaty will be faithfully complied with.

" 5th. That the treaty signed by the king of the Sandwich Islands, as well as the sum above mentioned, be conveyed on board the Frigate l'Artemise, by one of the principal chiefs of the country; and, also, that the batteries of Honolulu do salute the French flag with twenty-one guns, which will be returned by the frigate.

" These are the equitable conditions, at the price of which the king of the Sandwich Islands shall conserve friendship with France. I am induced to hope, that, understanding better how necessary it is for the prosperity of his people and the preservation of his power, he will remain at peace with the whole world, and hasten to subscribe to them, and thus imitate the laudable example which the queen of Tahiti has given in permitting the free toleration of the Catholic religion in her dominions; but if, contrary to my expectation, it should be otherwise, and the king and principal chiefs of the Sandwich Islands, led on by bad counsellors, refuse to sign the treaty which I present, war will immediately commence, and all the devastations, all the calamities which may be the unhappy but necessary results, will be imputed to themselves alone, and they must also pay the losses which the aggrieved foreigners, in these circumstances, shall have a right to reclaim.

"The 10th July (9th according to date here), 1839.

"(Signed),   C. LAPLACE.

"Captain of the French Frigate l'Artemise."

Is this new method of "*persuasion,* the most conformable to the system pursued by France against the powerless," under false representations, to make unjust demands, and threaten *immediate war* if they are not at once complied with? Is this the boasted, noble liberality of the policy of France? and was her abstaining from this, for a time, "excessive indulgence" to the chiefs of the Sandwich Islands, by which they had been deceived? The rulers of the islands needed only *equity,* and if Laplace means, simply, that France had not before invaded the country for excluding a priest who had no right to remain, let him put it to the score of her honor or justice, instead of lenity or indulgence where she had a right to punish. But if France had been wronged by the exclusion of Mr. Bachelot, this had been already adjusted by the captain of the Venus and the king, who, in 1837, engaged that, "Peace and amity between France and the Sandwich Islands shall be perpetual." Yet, to make out an insult to France, Laplace pretends that the expulsion of the French was under the *absurd pretext* that Romanism is idolatrous. If to treat Romanism as idolatrous is an insult to France, or other Catholic nations, then the accomplished and noble queen, who has been received by the citizen king with high demonstrations of respect and friendship, must have set the example at her inaugural; and many a Protestant creed must be very offensive to France. But to oppose *alien* teachers of idolatry or of blasphemy, or to expel them in accordance with international law, is not 'absurd,' though it might be impolitic to punish idolatry in subjects.

The assertion that the French were subjected to the most cruel persecutions, and the imputation by Laplace to the king, of a continued punishment of his subjects for being Catholics, and of the continued imprisonment of Frenchmen, an allegation and imputation the more unmanly and inexcusable because the king was too far away to repel them before the stroke of vengeance was to fall upon his people, must be regarded as a gross abuse.

Intimating that the French could have no religion but the *papal,* and misled by others as to persecutions against the French, he makes the bold allegation; "In the Sandwich Islands the French are not allowed publicly the exercise of their religion, while Protestants are allowed the most extensive privileges; for these all favors, for those the most cruel persecutions."

Such a state of affairs as he pretends to describe did not exist at the islands. Subjects of France, as such, had been treated with the same consideration as men from other countries, as really before as after the visit of Laplace. Two French priests had, indeed, been sent away, as has been fully stated in the narrative of 1827, 1831, and 1837.* The prohibition of the entrance and residence of papal teachers was not restricted to France. Indeed French Papal Catechists had long been at Honolulu in the guise of artisans.

The king had moreover endeavored to assure the French government of his desire of friendship, and his willingness to admit the French as freely as others in the prosecution of any lawful business. But to welcome one religion and refuse another, or to admit one class of teachers and reject another, was not *contrary to the law of nations*, whatever wisdom, charity, or policy in the case might require. Pretending to reason with the king against intolerance, and in support of a demand at the mouth of the cannon, that the king shall conform to the usage of civilized nations, the author of the Manifesto affirms with singular effrontery, that among them "there is not even *one* which does not permit in its territory the *free toleration* of all religions." *All* religions, spiritual and formal, evangelical and heretical, Protestant and Papal, Mahomedan and pagan—*all freely tolerated by all civilized nations!*

He throws out the unmanly reproach that the noble and energetic chiefs had violated treaties, as soon as the ships of war that had put them in fear had departed. They had violated no treaties, even if their agreement with naval officers had been regarded as treaties. If he means that after the Venus left they refused to admit papal priests, without a guarantee for their seasonable departure, he doubtless knew, or might have known, that they refused to admit them without such guarantee when two ships of war were present, and their two commanders were trying a whole week to induce them to do so. Refusing to admit them afterwards was but the continuation of their policy, which they assured the commanders they meant to pursue, the whole responsibility of which they assumed themselves. There was in this, therefore, neither ground for the charge of perfidy nor cause for war or punishment.

"As a mere question of international law, upon which ground it was placed by Captain Laplace in his Manifesto, it would not be difficult to satisfy any one who has the least knowledge of that subject, that he was clearly in the wrong. The pretence that to refuse to tolerate the propagation of any and every religious creed is contrary to the established usages of all civilized countries; in other words, that it is inconsistent with the law of nations and the acknowledged

---

* "The few remaining Frenchmen who lived at those islands, of which there were not above four, and the three whale-ships which had for two years before alone represented their commerce, had been treated with all the respect and hospitality enjoyed by the most favored nation."—*Jarves' History of the Sandwich Islands*, page 323.

rights of sovereignty, was as new in theory as it was unfounded in fact. And there would be still less difficulty in showing that to refuse to receive the teachers of any particular religion as such, merely because they happened to be the subjects of the king of the French, was no violation of the agreement of July, 1837, between the Sandwich Islands and the commander of the French frigate la Venus, even if that agreement had been sanctioned by the French government so as to give it the binding force of a treaty. It appears to be nothing more than a mere commercial treaty to place the subjects of the contracting parties in the territories of each government upon an equal footing with those of the citizens and subjects of the most favored nations. And your committee are not aware that it was ever before claimed by any nation, that such a stipulation secured the right to the subjects of the contracting parties mutually to introduce their own religious tenets against the wishes of the government, merely upon the ground that the citizens of another country were permitted to inculcate the principles of a religion adopted by such government, and which was generally professed by the inhabitants of its territories who had emerged from the darkness of heathenism."—[*Report of the A. B. C. F. M.*]

To induce a speedy compliance with his demands, he commends " the example of the Queen of Tahiti, in permitting the free toleration of the Catholic religion in her dominions." Though it was afterwards found that she and her people had been disgusted with his ungrateful and overbearing treatment of them after they had helped to save from wreck his frigate, which had struck a rock. If she had been compelled by him to admit Romish priests, she had not assented to the yielding of her subjects to their authority or dictation; and by late accounts, not one of them had adhered to Rome.

The conduct of Capt. Laplace, therefore, to say nothing of his ill treatment of Americans, was obviously contrary to the law of nations, and probably influenced by misrepresentations on which he too hastily resolved on hostilities. If the French have had no better pretext for a war with the Tahitians, the civilized world will not be censurable for sympathy with the natives manfully struggling to maintain their independence against powerful and haughty invaders.

Capt. Laplace then threatened the people with the evils of an unjust war, and though he would impute those evils to the king and chiefs alone, and would make the nation indemnify the foreigners for the loss they might suffer, the principles of international law would impute them to him and his accomplices.*

---

* " He who wages an unjust war is chargeable with all the evils, all the horrors, of war: all the effusion of blood, the desolation of families, the rapine, the acts of violence, the ravages, the conflagrations, are his works and crimes. He is guilty of a crime against the enemy whom he attacks, opposes, and massacres without cause; he is guilty of a crime against his people whom he forces into acts of injustice, and exposes to danger without reason or necessity; against those of his subjects who are ruined or distressed by the war, who lose their lives, their property, or their health in consequence of it; finally, he is guilty of a crime against mankind in general, whose peace he disturbs, and to whom he sets a pernicious example."—*Vattel.*

The manifesto, as a whole, is a clear index to a most palpable interference per force in the religious affairs of the nation in opposition to its will. And "it is certain," says Vattel, "that no one can interfere, in opposition to the will of a nation, in its religious affairs, without violating its right, and doing it an injury."

The British Consul, Mr. Pritchard, affirms that Com. A. Du Petit Thouars, in stipulating that *Frenchmen* should be received at Tahiti, allowed that if the rulers did not wish the Roman Catholic religion to be taught in Queen Pomare's dominions, they might make a law to that effect; and that they did make a law prohibiting all except the Protestant religion being taught there; and that subsequently the Frenchmen of the Artemise put themselves in a most hostile position, and demanded with a threat of burning the town, that that law should be abrogated; and he adds, "We are now daily expecting Roman Catholic priests to enter in among us, and sow the seeds of discord in this missionary field, which probably may terminate in a civil war."*

The most unreasonable hostility of Capt. Laplace to the American missionaries, is a matter deserving a historial notice in distinction from his hostility to the Hawaiian government.

In a letter to the American Consul, he condemns and proscribes American Protestant clergymen, and dooms them to the horrors of the war, which, he apprises their consul, he is about to commence upon the country, if the terms which he dictates are not

---

* The Flag Ship, p. 330–32. The views of the natives of Tahiti of the ungrateful and oppressive course of this man-of-war may be gathered from a letter from Tahitian Christians of Taimo to the church at Honolulu :—

" Peace be to you, through our Lord Jesus Christ, the Messiah. This is our word to you. We sympathize with you in your trembling at the evil at Honolulu—your being troubled by the man-of-war ship that has been at your islands.

"This is the communication of the church at Taimo. Let us be strong in our religion—let us stand by the Bible and hold it fast, and not the religion of the pope. Let us by no means listen to those words which are not according to the Gospel of the Messiah.

"We will make known to you our troubles occasioned by the man-of-war ship which has gone to your islands, but came to ours first. The ship struck on the rocks, and came to our harbor at Papaete, and took her cargo out and put it in a house belonging to the queen. We treated them well. We gave them timber to repair their vessel. We gave them food. When the vessel was finished, they commended Pomare because none of their things were stolen, and none of their people were ill-treated, under the government of Pomare in Tahiti.

" After this was a meeting of the governors and the people in authority with the captain of the ship of war. He asked for land to build a church for the Catholics, and we did not agree to it. They said they must fire upon us, that the island might be theirs, and that they might establish the Catholic religion in Tahiti. We were greatly oppressed. We were hushed at the mouth of the cannon, and agreed that they should have a house of worship. But we did not desire their form of religion. We value the religion of Jesus Christ taught by the missionaries from England— the Gospel of Jesus Christ which Paul and the apostles taught.

" This is what we have to say to you, brethren :—Be in earnest and hold fast the religion of Jesus, and not the papal religion, or any other that is not like the religion of Jesus the Messiah, which is the true. Let us stand firmly by the Gospel, though our bodies perish through our obedience to Jesus the Messiah."

complied with. Stating the day and the hour when he intends to commence hostilities, with the strong force at his command, unless the king yields to all his demands, he adds :—

" I consider it my duty to inform you, Monsieur le Consul, that I offer asylum and protection on board the frigate Artemise to those of your compatriots who may apprehend danger, under these circumstances, on the part of the natives, either for their persons or property. I do not, however, include in this class, the individuals who, although born, it is said, in the United States, make a part of the Protestant clergy of the chief of this Archipelago, direct his counsels, influence his conduct, and are the true authors of the insults given by him to France. For me they compose a part of the native population, and must undergo the unhappy consequences of a war which they shall have brought on this country.

" (Signed)   C. LAPLACE. "

As the king had offered no insults to France, that part of the Protestant clergy who were from the United States could not, of course, be authors of his alleged insults. Whatever construction shall be put upon the acts of the government towards France, the American clergy in general, and in particular, ought to have been exempt from these gross, unmanly charges, and much more from the vengeance which Capt. Laplace threatened.

He could name amongst them no offender against France. But without naming an individual, or offering, or possessing any proof of wrong doing, by any one of them, he brands a class as enemies of France. " For me," a foreign despot declares, " for *me*, they compose a part of the native population, and must undergo the unhappy consequences of a war which they shall have brought on this country."*

For several days and nights the war-threatening Artemise, with her guns loaded and shotted, lay abreast of the village of 6,000 souls, and of our mission houses, families, and presses, and the

---

* " In a verbal conversation with the American consul," says Mr. Jarves, " Laplace informed him, that the American flag would prove no protection to the proscribed individuals ; that if a man of his vessel was to be injured, it was to be a war of extermination—neither man, woman, nor child, were to be saved."—[*Jarves' History of the Sandwich Islands.*]

" An armed French ship," says the Rev. Mr. Taylor, an Episcopal clergyman, who soon after visited that port, " anchoring within cannon shot distance of the town of Honolulu, with every means of communicating with a helpless and harmless government, but without asking for any explanation, presenting ex-parte accusations, and making peremptory demands of the surrender of the sovereign's prerogatives, the cession of lands, and a deposit of $20,000 as a security for the future obsequious obedience of his Hawaiian Majesty, Kamehameha III., to the King of the French. Nor is this all, or one half. Along those streets of Honolulu, and in full view and reach of the shotted guns of a French ship of war, is a number of interesting families, who, for their intelligence, urbanity, and generous self-devotement to the cause of philanthropy and the Christian religion, would do honor to any nation, as they have abundantly honored, as American citizens, the people of the United States, now denounced, expatriated, proscribed, and pointed out by a French Post Captain as the special mark, in case of hostilities, for devastations, calamities, insults, and horrors threatened by cannonading, and by landing a lawless crew from a French man-of-war."—[*The Flag Ship*, p. 315.]

walls of our large church rising by the patient and cheerful labors
of converts from heathenism, and which did not stop till the
French despoiled them of $20,000. The king, whose signature
to certain unreasonable and arbitrarily dictated terms was demanded, was then at a distance on another island, unable to
arrive in season, if, on his arrival, he should be ready to comply
with them. So little honor or justice was now to be expected of
so rash a commander, who offered proscription and hostilities to
clerical citizens of a friendly power, with whose character he
was almost wholly unacquainted, that they did not think it worth
while to write him. To complete the picture, there were on
shore and near us, some united with France and Rome against
our mission, and others seeking an alliance with them for very
questionable purposes.

But in the midst of these commotions and threatening dangers,
through divine goodness, the missionaries and their wives, confiding in God, could, together, sing :—

> " Howl, winds of night, your force combine,
>   Without his high behest ;
> Ye shall not, in the mountain pine,
>   Disturb the sparrow's nest."

The honored youth who was providentially elevated from a
stocking-loom, did not, when he flung that apposite strain from
his pious harp, expect it would ever be re-echoed by a band of
defenceless, pioneer propagators of the Gospel, men and women,
on the shores of the Sandwich Islands, actually exposed to bombardment, conflagration, and massacre, by a French force, in order
to introduce there the priests of Rome. Though buoyant and
hopeful, they did not fail to feel for the nation, for themselves, and
for their cause, which, for twenty years, had been so dear to
their hearts. They had not been trained to stoicism, nor to recklessness, when danger from false principles or barbarian force
threatened disaster to themselves or others; nor yet, to act on
the principle that—

> ———" Whatever pangs surround,
> 'Tis magnanimity to hide the wound."

Every reasonable effort which could be made without compromise of principle they were ready to make to avoid the blow which
pride of power and wounded bigotry had aimed at the cause of
Protestantism and its supporters ; though they knew Captain Laplace had no more right to fire on the town, or on the missionaries,
than they had to blow up his ship with a torpedo for what he had
done at Tahiti, or for his note to the American consul, threatening
an unjust war on American Protestant clergymen. They believed,
as did the consul and other friends, as well as the bold public
accusers of the missionaries, that Capt. Laplace identified the
American Protestant clergy generally with the native chiefs,

preachers, and people, condemned them for their influence, threatened them, and treated them all as enemies, and in the name of France, put himself in the position of a warlike foe to them all.* It can hardly be supposed that Captain Laplace would have threatened the nation or the American missionaries with the horrors of war, and thus exposed his country to the rebuke of the whole world, if he had not been deceived and misled by interested counsellors. From his violence and injustice the members of the mission at Honolulu, and Messrs. Richards and Tinker who had resigned, appealed to their country, and taking the official notice of the consul, rather than the threat of the post-captain, as the occasion of their appeal, thus addressed their consul :—

"To P. A. BRINSMADE, ESQ., UNITED STATES CONSUL.

" Sir :—We learn from your official communication to the American citizens, at this place, that the commander of the French frigate, now in the roads, having demanded of the authorities of this nation satisfaction for *alleged offences* against the French nation, threatens speedy hostilities in case his terms are not complied with ; and that in that case he offers asylum and protection on board his ship, to all American citizens except *Protestant clergymen*.

" We regard ourselves as proscribed by this exception, our persons, our lives, our families, and a considerable amount of property of three chartered societies in the United States, the A. B. C. F. M., American Bible Society, and the American Tract Society—exposed to violence without our having in any way violated our duty or forfeited our protection as American citizens, or in any way, either secretly or openly, having offered any insult or injury to the great, enlightened, powerful, and deservedly respected nation of the French.

" We, therefore, respectfully solicit the protection of the United States for ourselves and our associates throughout our mission, forty unoffending citizens of the United States and their families, and request you to take such measures and use such means as may seem to you proper, and within your reach, for the security of our just rights as citizens of our common country, to which we are bound by a thousand ties though separated by thousands of miles, and which, we are happy to say, is now on terms of amity with France."

The next day, they received the following reply :—

" UNITED STATES CONSULATE, SANDWICH ISLADNS, JULY 12TH, 1839.

" Gentlemen :—Your communication of yesterday, soliciting the protection of the United States for yourselves and associates throughout the mission, against the intended aggression upon your American rights, on the part of the French naval force, now lying off this harbor, has been received at this consulate.

* The Sandwich Islands Gazette of the same month, July 27, 1839, contained the following :   " We cannot believe it possible that Capt. Laplace would have identified the *Protestant clergy*, at the Sandwich Islands, with the native population, as the enemies of France, without the most positive proof of that fact." . . . . " We hesitate not to accuse the *missionaries* of being the great first cause of all these persecutions; all these acts of inhumanity ; all these unjustifiable deeds which have been perpetrated by the natives of these islands."

"In reply, I can only say that my consulate, established by the authority of the United States, and acknowledged by this government, is under the protection of the American flag. Within its office and enclosure I offer you such asylum and protection as it may afford by its neutral position in relation to the nations whose differences are in progress of adjustment. I am offered from the authorities of this country all the means of defence which I may deem necessary.

"I am, gentlemen, with entire respect,

"Your most Obt. Servant,

"(Signed),   P. A. BRINSMADE, U. S. Consul."

When the hostile intentions of Captain Laplace against the government and the missionaries were known, a committee of the foreigners voted, on the 10th, "that a letter be addressed to the captain of the French frigate, for the purpose of ascertaining what *arms* or *assistance* he could afford, or what *co-operation* might be expected from him in the event of hostilities," and on the 11th they apprised him, " that in case of actual hostilities, their persons and property would be in imminent danger, and the more calamitous from the unhappy circumstances of the foreigners not being in possession of arms and ammunition sufficient to make their most energetic efforts for defence, against the evil disposed, effective," and " to supply this deficiency they made their appeal to him, in that ' perilous moment,'" as they said, assuring him " that the arms required would not, probably, exceed 50 muskets, 100 pistols, and 50 cutlasses, as many of the foreign residents were already possessed of the necessary arms and accoutrements." They were to have two brass guns, and appointed a chief Director, and four assistants, with power to organize the foreign residents into a force for mutual protection, and to make such other arrangements as might be necessary." Captain Laplace tells us how far he regarded these residents as his allies, when, commending their loyalty, he replies—

" I am sensible, gentlemen, how much the aid of so many brave English and Americans would secure still more the success of my arms ; but unhappily, to my regret, I am unable to furnish them with the means of defence which they want ; for all my men are to be employed in the attack on the town and the defence of the frigate. I have prepared forces sufficiently strong, that in giving a dreadful blow, the French shall be the masters and the protectors of the town at the same time. "

Doubtless it was the intention of the Post Captain and the expectation of some of the armed enemies in the camp, that the constituted authorities of the place should be *French*.

While this alliance was forming, the committee of vigilance deemed it wise " to inquire of the native authorities in what light they would consider the foreign residents, in case of hostilities, whether as *enemies* or *friends*, whether they would be left to their own resources, or whether they could depend on the rulers for assistance in any measures which might seem advisable in order to protect their lives and property from any attacks on the part of the native population, who might break through the restrictions which they believed the chiefs would impose." In their communication they said :—

" The committee have every confidence that the government will pursue such a course as will render it unnecessary for the force, now off the harbor, to proceed to extremities; but if such a calamity should threaten us, we wish, in harmony with the constituted authorities of the place, to be prepared to defend ourselves against the aggressions of a lawless multitude."

The premier, with some perturbation, thus replied :—

" Gentlemen :—I have received your communication, and hasten to express to you the sentiments entertained by the chiefs, at this place, in regard to foreign residents. It is proper that we should protect the subjects of other lands ; and be to them instead of their own rulers, inasmuch as this is enjoined upon us, to contribute according to our ability to the safety of their subjects resident at these islands. And were there no stipulations to this effect, I would have you understand that it is my mind and pleasure to do it. I have, therefore, sent a herald through the streets, to command the people to keep quiet, to avoid all disorder ; especially within the enclosures of the foreigners.

 " I am happy to comply with any reasonable plan which you may meditate for the safety of the persons and property of all the foreigners residing here. While I live, you shall lack nothing which will promote your peace ; but should I be taken away, it will devolve on my friends to protect you. Should evil approach you from the sea, I have no power over that, nor strength to assist you. If any mischievous natives should plunder you, I give them into your hands, during these days, to determine their demerit, and when our perplexity is passed I will see to it that they are justly punished.

" (Signed),   KEKAULUOHI."

What then was the part of wisdom for the local authorities in respect to the demands and threats of Laplace? If the law of self-defence, if the usages of nations, if international law, give the right to repel unlawful violence, it will hardly be questioned that the natives had a right to muster all their force for resistance. According to the established laws of nations they might have charged and manned the guns of their forts, entered their stern protest against the misrepresentations and unreasonable demands of the manifesto, and proposed better terms for adjusting their differences; and if they failed thus to satisfy their *foe*, they might have repelled force by force, and not allowed a boat's crew to land alive. But if France was now determined to fall upon the nation or despoil it of its independence wrongfully, what would she not do if they had sunk her frigate at anchor, or killed or captured her crew in battle in repelling an attack? France had many more ships of war and many men. The premier judged that

" wisdom is better than strength," and that negotiation with the
king of the French, after a partial surrender, would be safer than
warlike resistance against a naval officer who was unwilling to
hear any explanation, and who claimed to be acting in the name
of the sovereign of France.

Having collected $20,000, partly from their own funds on hand,
and partly from a loan, which he obtained at high interest, among
the foreign merchants, the governor carried it off to the frigate
with the dictated articles, signed by the premier and himself, but
not by the king, and ordered a salute from the fort. The king
arrived from Maui, the next day. The sacred hours of the Sabbath were disturbed by martial bands from the Artemise, passing
through the streets with martial music and fixed bayonets, and
by a military mass, celebrated on shore, under the direction of
Mr. Walsh. The king saw and felt the degradation and mortification ; and though he did not reverse the proceedings of the
premier and governor, and though he regarded the loss of $20,000
as a matter hardly to be thought of in comparison of the infringement of his sovereignty, he is reported to have said, " They ought
to have waited till the war-club touched the forehead."

The French Post Captain and Consular Agent then presented
the terms of another treaty, some of which were unwelcome and
unworthy of a great nation—terms which would further despoil
the king of his sovereignty as to resisting the influx of intoxicating drinks and the offences of aliens—and which were urged
upon him, amid the excitements which the invasion of his rights
and the threat of war had occasioned. And his hasty compliance, contrary to his convictions, his interest, and the prosperity of his people, can hardly be accounted for, except on the
supposition of his being panic-struck by the proceedings of
Laplace, in the name of the king of the French.

" Article 1st. There shall be perpetual peace and friendship between the king of the French and the king of the Sandwich Islands.

" Article 2d. The French shall be protected in an effectual manner in their persons and property by the king of the Sandwich Islands,
who shall also grant them an authorization sufficient so as to enable
them juridically to prosecute his subjects against whom they will have
just reclamations to make.

" Article 3d. This protection shall be extended to French ships
and to their crews and officers. In case of shipwreck, the chiefs and
inhabitants of the various ports of the Archipelago shall assist them
and protect them from pillage. The indemnities for salvage shall
be regulated, in case of difficulty, by arbiters selected by both
parties.

" Article 4th. No Frenchman, accused of any crime whatever, shall
be tried except by a jury composed of foreign residents, proposed by
the French Consul and approved by the government of the Sandwich
Islands.

" Article 5th. The desertion of sailors belonging to French ships shall be strictly prevented by the local authorities, who shall employ every disposable means to arrest deserters, and the expenses of the capture shall be paid by the captain or owners of the aforesaid ships, according to the tariff adopted by the other nations.

"Article 6th.   French merchandises or those known to be French produce, and particularly wines and *eaux de vie* (brandy), cannot be prohibited, and shall not pay an import duty higher than five per cent. *ad valorem.*

" Article 7th.   No tonnage or importation duties shall be exacted from French merchants, unless they are paid by the subjects of the nation the most favored in its commerce with the Sandwich Islands.

" Article 8th.   The subjects of King Kamehameha III. shall have a right in the French possessions to all the advantages which the French enjoy at the Sandwich Islands, and they shall moreover be considered as belonging to the most favored nation in their commercial relations with France.

" Made and signed by the contracting parties the 17th of July, 1839.

" (Signed),   ⎰ KAMEHAMEHA III.
                   ⎱ C. LAPLACE,
                   " Post Capt. Commanding the French Frigate l' Artemise."

The fourth article, if duly ratified by the two governments, gives to any French consul the power to prevent the punishment of Frenchmen, for no court of his Hawaiian majesty could try a Frenchman, accused of crime, if his consul could not or would not propose a jury to suit himself, or should persist in proposing one of aliens, which the government could not approve.   Any number of Frenchmen, then, might, with the connivance of the consul, set Hawaiian law at defiance to any extent, by depredations on the other foreigners or on the native community.   Even the regicide and the killer of heretics might hope to escape.   The king, who was but a youth, though he objected to this article, did not see the extent to which it would curtail his power or throw it into the hands of aliens.

To the sixth article there were most obvious objections.   The rulers had seen the mischief arising from intoxicating liquors, and had laid a heavy duty on wine, prevented the distillation of spirits in their own country, and inhibited their importation. To prostrate those regulations, and open the flood-gate now to intemperance, might be disastrous both to the health and morals of the nation, and equally so, perhaps, to the rum-loving portion of the community from abroad, and would defraud the government of a portion of revenue justly due, if such products were to be imported by foreigners.   If France, or rather the French consul, the Romish priests, and a part of the residents, and others, must be permitted to bring brandy and wine, why should the French government object to allowing a reasonable duty of fifty or five hundred per cent. ?

A staunch apologist for this new policy said, " Capt. Laplace was perfectly justifiable in *insisting* that the wines and brandies

of France should not be prohibited; those constitute the principal articles of French produce, (exports?) and the interest of
that country required that every country should be open to receive
them." Was it then necessary that his Hawaiian majesty and all
other governments should be governed by the *interest of the French*
in opposition to their own? On that false principle only were
the severe measures of Laplace justifiable. But France is too
magnanimous to maintain or admit such an absurdity; and Laplace himself affirmed that " the French government had respect
only to the advantage of all civilized nations." And the French
consul admitted that " it was very little to the interest of France
that brandy should be free, but intimated that further punishment
on the Hawaiians was admissible for their former treatment of
the French." But it could hardly be believed that the French
government, knowing the injustice of these two articles, and
the king's earnest objections to them, would ratify and make dis-
graceful, a treaty, honorable, in other respects, to both countries.

The suggestion that if he refused to sign the treaty as it was,
he would surely have trouble, had undue influence with the king
and his inexperienced and alarmed friends around him. That
kings should have *trouble*, while the world is so wicked, whether
they yield to unjust claims or not, is a matter to be expected of
course : and if it was the will of the French to bring brandy and
wines to the islands on their own terms, Laplace had taught his
young majesty that he could not enforce the existing laws against
it, and " conserve friendship with France."* He, therefore,
yielded, though with a sense of injury, not easily relieved.

The silence of his missionary friends at this important juncture
has been seriously called in question by moral men, so strong is
their repugnance to that disastrous anti-temperance measure.
Even the courteous commander of the U. S. Exploring Expedition maintains that the missionaries, as true friends of the nation,
and teachers of Christian morals, having stood aloof while Capt.
L. was forcibly urging the claims of the Catholic priests, ought
now to have interposed their objections and influence to prevent
him from securing the free admission of brandy also. But if
they had a right to interpose at all, it is questionable whether any
of them, except his interpreter, knew the danger of his being
thus ensnared till he had given his name. His own customary
counsellors among the high chiefs, or intelligent people, would
doubtless, had they been allowed the opportunity, have remon-

---

* "There can be little doubt, that the original suspension of this traffic in relation to which the American missionaries were known to have exerted an active influence, had much greater influence in placing these faithful ministers of the cross out
of the pale of that protection which the laws of civilized warfare always give to non-
combatants, than all other causes combined; and that the commander of the Artemise,
if not the French Government itself, was actually deceived by the false representations of those who were or wished to be engaged in the demoralizing business equally
destructive to the temporal and eternal welfare of the human race."—[*Report by Chancellor Walworth.*]

strated against these provisions of the treaty, and against which the king should have stood firm, " till the war-club had struck the forehead."*

It is the boast of civilization and Christianity that they recognise the sisterhood of nations, so that the powerful and the weak, the great and the small, may dwell side by side in the enjoyment of equal rights of sovereignty and independence, so long as they respect the authority of international law. But French naval officers in the Pacific have violated the great compact of nations, repudiated the claims of international law, in respect to the Sandwich and Society Islands, and struck down the shield that had saved them, even before they were evangelized.

Laplace did indeed say in his manifesto, with the appearance of honor, " It is without doubt the formal intention of France that the king of the Sandwich Islands be powerful, independent of every foreign power, and that he consider her his ally." Why then should he proceed to despoil him of the power which properly belonged to him? Was it a mere *formal* intention, announced with a show of honor to secure confidence and respect for the moment, while no sincere intention existed, or was supposed to be proper or politic in the case. Subsequent events must show whether " France intends the king shall be powerful and independent."

The Clementine, belonging to Mr. J. Dudoit, soon brought from Valparaiso Romish ecclesiastics—the Bishop of Nilopolis and three priests, including Mr. L. Maigret, with the paraphernalia of Romish delusion, or imposture, and intoxicating liquors, before sternly resisted by the rulers.

Among the " brave English and Americans " on whose co-operation the Post Captain had relied for the success of his arms, while trampling on the principles both of civil and religious liberty, one of the former and five of the latter sent him a letter of thanks and adulation, and commended for imitation " the *manly, noble, disinterested,* example " which he had set for " the *simple, confiding children of nature,* so long deluded by designing and interested counsellors !"

But the friends of law and order, the friends of the independence of the Hawaiian nation, and of the protection of American citizenship in the persons of missionaries, were justly shocked with what they regarded as the outrageous, oppressive, and calumniating proceedings of that naval commander.

* A gentleman then on the ground thus notices this measure:—" This was brought to him at five o'clock P. M., on the 16th, and he was required to sign it by breakfast the next morning. No amendment of the objectionable features was allowed; it must be signed as received, or not at all. The king desired time to consult with his counsel; this was refused. Neither the consul nor Laplace dared openly to commit themselves by saying to him, that if he refused, war would ensue; but it was bandied about among his attendants, so as to reach his ears, that in such an event, there would be no end to the trouble; that this frigate would be succeeded by a larger force, and ultimately his island would be taken possession of. It was a successful design to entrap the king through his fears."—[*Jarves' History.*]

Soon after the departure of the Artemise, with 20,000 dollars of the people's money, and other spoils, there came into the same port two vessels of war from the United States—the frigate Columbia, Com. Read, and the John Adams, Capt. Wyman—too late indeed to check the rashness of their predecessor, but not too late to turn his mistakes to good account. These ships came from a land of freedom, and a land of Bibles; and the authority of Scripture, the sanctity of the Sabbath, and the duty of obeying God, were acknowledged by those who held commissions on board: and the power of the same Gospel, which was subduing the nation to Christ, had been specially felt by some on board while passing through the Atlantic, Indian, and Pacific Oceans.

The missionaries were as desirous as others were afraid to have these men investigate and report their case onward from 1826, when Captain Jones had opened his eyes and ears to whatever opposers might wish to present against them. They earnestly and repeatedly requested Com. Read to make a careful investigation of the ground on which they had been proscribed by a French officer, and either in person or by a board of officers under his appointment, to consider the questions whether they had by any act or acts, instruction, influence, or course of life, lost their American citizenship, or forfeited the protection of the United States, and whether, as a body or as individuals, they were in any way the authors, or blamable cause, of any persecutions at the islands. This they urged not only on their own account, but for the benefit of their countrymen of whatever calling, for if the principle on which they had been proscribed and threatened with hostilities were to be established and allowed, the interests of all Americans there were in jeopardy. But several important reasons led Com. Read respectfully to decline, while he assured the missionaries he considered them entitled to his protection, and that he could not believe they had acted or meant to act as the *enemies of France*. The officers necessary to compose the court of inquiry were employed in a court-martial, after which the season was found to have advanced too far to allow sufficient time for the required service.

But after a visit of about five weeks, high-minded and intelligent officers of the squadron voluntarily authorized the publication of an account of the proceedings connected with the visit of the Artemise, drawn up with fairness and ability by Mr. S. N. Castle, and also gave to the world their own opinions and testimony in opposition to Laplace and his coadjutors and admirers:

" We, the undersigned, officers of the United States East India Squadron, having, upon our arrival at this place, heard various rumors in relation and derogatory to the American mission at these islands, feel it be due, not only to the missionaries themselves, but to the cause of truth and justice, that the most unqualified testimony should be given in the case ; and do, therefore, order one thousand copies of the annexed article and correspondence to be printed for gratuitous distribution, as being the most effectual mode of settling this agitated question in the minds of an intelligent and liberal public.

" Being most decidedly of opinion that the persons composing the Protestant mission of these islands are American citizens, and, as such, entitled to the protection which our government has never withheld, and with unwavering confidence in the justice which has ever characterized it, we rest assured that any insult offered to this unoffending class will be promptly redressed.

" It is readily admitted that there may be in the operation of this, as in all other systems in which feeble man has any agency, some objectionable peculiarities ; still, as a system, it is deemed comparatively unexceptionable, and believed to have been pursued in strict accordance with the professed principles of the society which it represents ; and it would seem that the salutary influence exerted by the mission on the native population ought to commend it to the confidence and kind feelings of all interested in the dissemination of good principles.

GEORGE A. MAGRUDER, Lieut.	JOHN HASLETT, Surg. of the Fleet.
ANDREW H. FOOT, Lieut.	JOHN A. LOCKWOOD, Surgeon.
JOHN W. TURK,* Lieut.	DANGERFIELD FAUNTLEROY, Pursr.
THOMAS TURNER, Lieut.	FITCH W. TAYLOR, Chaplain.
JAMES S. PALMER, Lieut.	ROBERT P. PEGRAM, Master.
EDWD. R. THOMPSON, Lieut.	JOSEPH BEALE, Ass't. Surgeon.
AUGUSTUS H. KELTY, Lieut.	J. HENSHAW BELCHER, Prof. Math.
GEORGE B. MINOR, Lieut.	ALEX. G. PENDLETON, Prof. Math.

" *Honolulu, Oahu, November* 1, 1839."†

The American consul, who had just succeeded Mr. J. C. Jones, appealed to his majesty on the main question, as follows :—

" United States Consulate,
" Sandwich Islands, Oct. 26th, 1839.

" Sir :—As the opinion seems to be to some extent entertained that American citizens residing in the Sandwich Islands as missionaries, under the patronage of an Incorporated Institution of the United States, have exerted a controlling influence upon the framers of the laws of this country, I have very respectfully to inquire, if they have ever

---

* Now LIVINGSTON.

† " The commissioned ward-room officers of the squadron, with but few exceptions, subscribed the letter which effectually nullifies the malicious reports sent abroad with anonymous signatures in a scurrilous paper, formerly called the Sandwich Islands Gazette, but now appearing as the Sandwich Islands Mirror. Several copies of the letter being struck off, that the objections might be met by the officers themselves, produced a temporary excitement. The French consul addressed a communication to Commodore Read, purporting that he had been informed of the publication of a letter by the officers reflecting on the character of Capt Laplace and the French government, and as the representative of that government deemed its notice incumbent on him. On reading it, and hearing an explanation of the motives giving rise to the letter in question, the commodore, deeming it unexceptionable, stated that he could take no measures to suppress it. The French and English consuls, with the residents, were distinctly given to understand, that the letter originated solely with the officers of the squadron, not an individual on shore suspecting their intention until it was subscribed, and that it contained a full and free expression of their opinions for which they were responsible, and from which they should not recede."
—[*Letter of A. H. Foot, Nov.* 2, 1839—*New York Observer.*]

had any voice in the passage of laws affecting the interests of other foreigners, and particularly whether they ever had anything to do in the measures adopted by your government for the prevention of the intro- duction of the Catholic religion into the country. And whether in the treatment which has been shown to any subject of the government of France, they have directly or indirectly recommended the course pursued by your government, and also, whether in the attempts made under your authority to suppress the public exercises of the Roman Catholic religion on the part of your own subjects, they have countenanced those attempts. If they have in any of these respects controlled the action of your government, will you be pleased to inform me very explicitly in what manner and to what extent. An early reply will be a favor.

"With the highest considerations, I have the honor to be,
"Your Majesty's most obt. servt.,
"P. A. BRINSMADE,
"United States Consul."

"To His Majesty, KAMEHAMEHA III.,
"King of the Sandwich Islands."

Severely censured and chastised as the king had been on the allegation of intolerance, he had now the opportunity to throw responsibility on the Christian teachers of the nation. But in the manly assumption of responsibility in respect to the acts of his government, he exonerates them, and gives them credit for using their influence not to aid oppression, but the acquisition of useful knowledge, and the prevention of intemperance, and persecution for religious opinions, and also proposes an investigation. His reply, an index to the natives' advancement, is thus translated :

"Kauwila House, present residence of the
"King of Hawaii, Oct. 28th, 1839.

"My respects to you, the American Consul.

"I have received your letter asking questions respecting the American missionaries, supposed, by some, to regulate the acts of my government under me ; I, together with the chiefs under me, now clearly declare to you, that we do not see anything in which your questions are applicable to the American missionaries. From the time the missionaries first arrived, they have asked liberty to dwell in these islands; communicating instruction in letters and delivering the Word of God has been their business.

"They were hesitatingly permitted to remain by the chiefs of that time, because they were said to be about to take away the country. We exercised forbearance, however, and protected all the missionaries, and as they frequently arrived in this country, we permitted them to remain in this kingdom because they asked it, and when we saw the excellence of their labors, then some of the chiefs and people turned to them in order to be instructed in letters, for those things were, in our opinion, really true.

"When the priests of the Romish religion landed at these islands, they did not first make known to us their desire to dwell on the islands, and also their business. There was not a clear understanding with this company of priests as there was with that ; because they landed in the country secretly without Kaahumanu's hearing anything about their remaining here.

" When the number of the followers of the Romish religion became considerable, certain captains of whale-ships told Kaahumanu of the evil of this way, and thus Capt. D . . . informed me of a great destruction in Britain in ancient time, and that his ancestors died in that slaughter, and he thought a like work would soon be done here. That was the company who informed us of the evil of the Romish religion, and also a certain French man-of-war, and a certain British man-of-war approved of what we did.

" In as much as I do not know of the American missionaries having had anything to do in my business with the chiefs, I have, therefore, inquired of them the chiefs, and they say, no, in the same manner as I now say no, to you.

" Some of them, however, have told me of having known certain things done by certain missionaries, viz., what Mr. Bingham said to Kaahumanu, " I have seen some people made to serve at hard labor on account of their having worshipped according to the Romish religion. Whose thought is that ?' Kaahumanu said to him, ' Mine.' Then he that spake to her objected quickly, saying, ' It is not proper for you to do thus, for you have no law that will apply.' When he said, that, then Kaahumanu immediately replied to him with great strength, ' The law respecting idolatry ; for their worship is like that which we have forsaken.' Mr. Clark also, and Mr. Chamberlain spoke to Kinau while Kaahumanu was yet alive, and objected to said conduct, and afterwards Dr. Judd. And at a certain time Mr. Bingham and Mr. Bishop disputed strongly with Kinau on account of the wrong of punishing those of the Romish religion.

" And now, in Kekauluohi's time, Mr. Richards disputed strongly with Kekuanaoa, urging the entire abolition of that thing, and that kindness should be bestowed on them, that they might be pleased, giving them also an instructor to teach them the right way ; and thus, also, he said to Kekauluohi and to me.

And afterwards, when Mr. Bingham heard by Mr. Hooper that certain women were confined in irons at the fort, he went immediately and made known to Kekuanaoa the wickedness of their confinement for that thing, and when Kekuanaoa heard it, he immediately sent a man, and afterwards went himself to the fort to set the prisoners free, for their confinement was not by order of the chiefs.

" Should it be said by accusers that the American missionaries are the authors of one law of the kingdom, the law respecting the sale of rum, or if not, that they have urged it strongly, I would say, a number of captains of whale-ships commenced that thing, thousands of my own people supported them, and when my chiefs saw that it was a good thing, they requested me to do according to the petition of that company, and when I saw that it was really an excellent thing, then I chose that as a rule of my kingdom.

" But that thing which you speak to me of, that they act with us, or over-rule our acts, we deny it, it is not so.

" We think that perhaps these are their real crimes : Their teaching us knowledge. Their living with us, and sometimes translating between us and foreigners.   Their not taking the sword into their hand and saying to us with power, stop, punish not the worshippers in the Romish religion.

"But, to stand at variance with, and to confine that company, they have never spoken like that since the time of Kaahumanu I., down to the time that the Romish priest was detained on board the Europa.

"I think perhaps these things are not clear to you; it would, perhaps, be proper, therefore, that the American missionaries should be examined before you and Commodore Read, and us also.

"Thus I have written you with respect.

"(Signed)   KAMEHAMEHA III."

The ironical reproof to missionaries is a keen rebuke to their calumniators, while the right to punish the disloyal is not renounced.[*]

The North American Review and the American Board expressed the sense of the enlightened American public on the main points in question.   The former says :—

"Was it ever heard before that the legitimate government of an independent state has not a right to declare that an alien religion shall not be taught by aliens within its borders ? . . . France had no right to force missionaries on the Sandwich Islands to reclaim them from the bloodiest and most impure idolatry.   . . .   We think the moral judgment as well as the international law of the world will recognise the sacred right of a people, in so interesting and critical an era in the history of its efforts and opinions, to be let alone."

The language of our Prudential Committee on the treatment of their missionaries, is as follows :—

"And what had these missionaries of the Board done to call forth the proclamation of outlawry which was issued against them ?   The reason assigned by the French officer is that they directed the counsels of the king of the Sandwich Islands, influenced his conduct, and were the true authors of the insult given to France.   He holds them to be the real authors of whatever the government of the islands had done adversely to the papal interest.   This is not the place for the Committee to go into a formal defence of the missionaries on this point.   But they certainly will interpose for the defence of their brethren, whatever force there is in their own positive declaration that Capt. Laplace had no proper evidence of what he asserts, and that his assertions are untrue."

On the same point, a committee of the Board, Chancellor Walworth being chairman, say :—

"Your committee, upon examination of the subject are gratified to

---

[*] "Whatever appeared to them as *idol-worship* was considered the sign of disloyalty, hence the authorities insist upon it that they have punished only for idolatry according to a law which existed a number of years before the Catholics came to the islands.   It was in their estimation merely a political offence, having nothing to do with the merits or demerits of religion, any further than it affected their political institutions, and therefore not entitled to the name of *religious persecution.*—S. N. C."

[*Polynesian, Vol.* 2, *p.* 74.]

find these devoted missionaries of the Cross cannot, with justness, be charged with having done anything inconsistent with the spirit of our free institutions and their strict duty in this respect.   As faithful Protestant missionaries and teachers, it was as much their duty to warn the people of their charge against what we believe to be the great and leading errors of the Romish church, as it was to inculcate the doctrine of the Holy Trinity, and that there is no hope of salvation to fallen man, except through the redeeming blood of a Divine Mediator.

   " The utmost that can be charged upon your missionaries there, is, that all of them did not actually interpose their influence to prevent the Catholic religion from being proscribed by the government, as tending to restore idol-worship which had been prohibited, and to which, it was supposed, by the Sandwich Islanders, to be in some measure assimilated."

   The Board united in adopting the following:—

   " Resolved, that in the opinion of this Board, no just grounds of complaint existed against any of its missionaries in relation to the professed cause of the visit of the French frigate, l'Artemise, to the Sandwich Islands, in July, 1839."

   Will civilized nations accept the interference of Laplace as a favor to them ?   Will the civilized world look with indifference upon this interesting struggle,—the rulers of the islands, on the one side, enduring with unusual patience and forbearance, unlawful encroachments, yet with manly energy, refusing to receive the last and stereotyped edition of Romanism and foreign spirits; and on the other, the sleepless cunning of Jesuitism, the proud assumptions of the Potentate of the Seven Hills, and the naval power of the citizen king, all attempting to force the admission of the teachers of eschewed error upon those carefully guarded, but still defenceless shores, and to open the flood-gates of inundation and ruin ?   Such meekness, and wisdom, and reasonable opposition to immeasurable wrong-doing, on the part of the weak, with right on their side, and such contempt of just rights and claims, and such abuse of power rarely paralleled in the history of the world, on the part of the strong, will, where true virtue and honor dwell, naturally call forth deserved sympathy for the Hawaiian race, and awaken zeal in the wise and good 'to put an end'to such tyranny, and to pour evangelical light into the dark places of the earth, till neither this " fatal error," nor pagan delusion, nor vile intemperance, nor grievous oppression, shall find favor among the great, or victims among the weak.

   Many in Great Britain and France, looked with deserved indignation on the outrages committed by the French against the Protestants in the Pacific.   Among those who take a noble stand against them, is Count Agenor de Gasparin, a young French nobleman, Master of Petitions, and member of the Chamber of Deputies.   Speaking of the attack on the Sandwich Islands, in a work which he published, he earnestly says:—

" Ah! we are cowards; in that immediately after such a crime, French [Protestant] missionaries did not depart for Honolulu, and that we have not since lifted up our voice daily to denounce that savage act, that incredible abuse of our flag. The true love of the Gospel, as well as the true love of France, would have suggested another course. Strong and unceasing protests should have rendered for ever impossible the repetition of such barbarous deeds; deeds to which the public conscience would then have put an end, by judging them as severely as we ourselves. But, at least, the consequences of that inauspicious day serve as a most serious warning to our church—that for three years we have seen the Christian government, the independent government of the Sandwich Islands, obliged to bow its head under the outrages of a people ordinarily noble and generous !

" That government believed it to be its duty to use against the Catholic missionaries a right, which it would have been more liberal, doubtless, not to have exercised, but which has never been denied to the Catholic States of the South of Europe, when they have armed themselves against Protestant missionaries. It did not forbid *the French* to enter its territory, but only French *ecclesiastics* coming to exercise their ministry, and to contend against the established religion ; just as it is not to the French that the Roman or Neapolitan States deny admission to their territory, when they interdict French pastors coming to exercise their ministry, and to oppose the established religion.

" But it was not *principle* which led to this conduct. It was prejudice. It was hatred. There has been a monstrous alliance between the policy of the State and a religion which is no longer that of the State. The violence which installed the Romish worship in all its pomp, in the midst of a nation but recently won over to a true, spiritual worship, at the same time opened its ports to spirituous liquors from France. The same day two prohibitions were removed under the menace of our guns, that relating to Catholicism, and that relating to *brandy !*

" This last act serves to characterize the expedition. No one, in fact, can be ignorant of the moral and physical ruin which brandy has always produced among a savage people, and the scenes of debauchery which immediately followed the ratification of our infamous treaty, are a commentary too eloquent to need any other.

" But, though its first effects have been deplorable, the eternal Word of our God is sufficiently powerful to put a stop to them. It will not shrink before Rome, nor before the accursed traffic which the French Consul and others have not feared to undertake. It will fortify consciences but little disciplined, before which a subtle heresy attempts to cast new difficulties. It will recover, it will raise, it will regenerate those who are hurried away by their baser passions. Is not what it has already done for the Sandwich Islands an earnest of what it will yet accomplish there ? Where can we find in the annals of government a social transformation which can compare with that which sixty poor American missionaries have effected among 130,000 savages ? The sailors who calumniate them, forget to compare the security which they enjoy there now, with those fierce and sanguinary traits which formerly rendered so terrible those copper-colored and tattooed tribes, among whom the illustrious Cook lost his life. It is only necessary to mention it to vindicate the work accomplished at the Sandwich Islands. It is enough to point to men who formerly treated women as creatures of an inferior order, who neither suffered them to sit at the same table, nor to eat from the same dishes with themselves; who sustained towards them no other relations than those of libertinism ; but who now, through the influence of married missionaries, understand the sanctity of the marriage tie, respect their wives, and taste, for the first time, the sacred joys of the family.   *   *   *   It is enough to point to those who formerly destroyed more than one half of their offspring, but who now encourage them with tender solicitude and love. It is only necessary to enumerate the schools, the presses, the journals which are established in a country where so lately the language was neither written nor formed, and where now Bibles and tracts are printed, and everywhere distributed among more than 10,000 readers. It is enough to enter the churches, or to walk the street on the Sabbath. Everywhere, in spite of the disorder which the French have produced, we discover both outward respect for religion, and true conversion of the heart.

" Such are the fruits of those Protestant missions, so much decried, and against which it is still so popular, in France, to bring the most odious accusations. Let those who accuse them, examine before they attack. Let them compare before they proclaim, as they are wont, the immense superiority of *Roman Catholic* missions.' '*

The illness and death of Mr. McDonald were among the afflictions of the mission at this period. But having trusted in Christ, and consecrated himself to his service on the missionary field, yet being called to leave it ere three years had completed their course, he honored the Lord in the trying hour by the simplicity and strength of his faith, and the Lord was with him when heart and flesh failed. As he descended to the Jordan he exhorted his fellow laborers to be faithful to their own souls, to the people, and to God. In parting with his little children, on their behalf—

" He sought, with look that seemed to penetrate
The heavens, unutterable blessings, such

* The following may illustrate the nobleman's remark, and afford some apology for the mistakes of Frenchmen respecting the Sandwich Islands—" The holy and consoling exercises of the Catholic priests were contrasted with the cold preaching of the Protestant ministers and the disinterested labors of the first with the covetousness of the second. The Methodists have always been the same in this last respect; but in some things they have seen fit to change their sentiments. Hitherto they had taught that baptism is not necessary in order to salvation; but May 7th, 1838, they declared that it was necessary for all the world to be baptized. They also established a certain kind of public confession, but wholly for their own advantage. Each of the natives was to come into their assemblies and tell some of his faults before all the world. He was then to give some money, vegetables, poultry, or something else, and so receive *absolution* . . . . . None of our dear neophites have been sentenced to capital punishment, nor to any of those tortures so common in the history of the first martyrs; for that is not the disposition of the *kanaakas.* And, besides, the Protestant ministers, according to whose mind everything continues to go on in these islands, take good care not to permit it; they are afraid the shedding of blood would render them odious; and their chief care, after that of persecuting, is to prevent compassion from declaring itself in favor of their victims." [*Annals of the Tr. de Prop. de la Foi, at Lyons.*]

> As God to dying parents only grants
> For infants left behind them in the world."

The brethren and sisters around his couch, at his request, sang the sweet hymn :—

> " Rock of Ages, cleft for me,
> Let me hide myself in thee."

He responded with the emphasis of faith—

> " Thou must save and thou alone,
> Simply to thy cross I cling."

He closed his earthly mission September 7th, 1839.

Soon a young missionary child, Gerrit P. Judd, Jr., was called to leave his parents, sisters, and brothers, being seized with a singular disorder, which no remedies could arrest, and in about a week closed his young career of promise, Nov. 13th, 1839, at the age of ten years and eight months.   When the dear child, distinguished for intelligence and activity, saw that he must die, his parting counsels to his little companions, urging them to be prepared to meet him in heaven, were both melting and consoling, and helped his afflicted parents to say, when they had prepared their first born for the grave, " The Lord gave, and the Lord hath taken away, and blessed be the name of the Lord."

The following beautiful elegy was written on the occasion in the Hawaiian language by Hoohano, a native student of medicine, then in delicate health, who had been instructed at the Mission Seminary, and who soon followed his little friend along his "lonely pathway," both leaving some evidence of having been reconciled to God through the death of his Son.

Hawaiian poetry is not accurately measured, either in respect to the succession of feet, or the length of the lines ; nor did it exhibit, prior to the introduction of sacred hymns by the missionaries, any chiming at the end of the lines.   As the Hawaiian songs were unwritten, and adapted to chanting rather than metrical music, a line was measured by the breath ; their *hopuna*, answering to our line, was as many words as could be easily cantilated at one breath.

Though this piece has no more measure or chime than the compositions of the ancients or of Ossian, yet every line of it is *poetry*, and of no inferior order compared with the ancient Greek and Latin odes.   It is one of many respectable specimens of poetic composition, among the instructed Hawaiians, of a Christian character and salutary tendency :—

> " Farewell to the beautiful flower of the Doctor's garden !
> It has fallen and vanished away.
> The flower that budded first did blossom fair;
> Its splendor was seen ; its fragrance exhaled :
> But the burning sun came, and it withered,
> And that beautiful blossom has fallen !

The occupant of the garden then wondered
That a single flower should have fallen.
He sought it, but found it not again; it was gone;
It had perished; it had mingled with the dust.
Alas! what a pity for the flower plants,
Which grow up well, and lo! they are withered!
All the flowers bowed their head, smelling the fragrance,
They stood around in great sorrow.
Alas! alas! O my blossom that has fallen!

The chief tenant inquired of his landlord,
' What thinkest thou concerning this flower
Which thou did'st plant in my border?
The Lord replied,
' I have taken away the image of all its glory;
Its bud has fallen and is mingled with the dust.'

How beautifully did the plants flourish!
Compassion great for the tenant resident,
Mourning and searching with great lamentation!
' Whither, O Gérrita, hast thou gone?
When wilt thou return to thy birth-mates?
Alone hast thou gone in the way that is lonely;
Thou hast gone a stranger by an unknown path.'

O Gérrita, Gérrita! Behold we all
Are falling flowers, and soon shall fall.
Where art thou? Go thou, and be a kind welcomer for us all.
O, Gérrita, Gérrita! thou goest at the pleasure of thy Lord,
And none can forbid thy design. Go thou,
Travel on, till thou art wholly gone, along the lonesome pathway:
Then ascend the ladder of God,
And pass within the glorious walls of Jerusalem;
And enter into the peace of God's kingdom.

Thou art singing hymns with good angels;
A never-ceasing employment is thy employment there.
O Gérrita, Gérrita!
Deeply we mourn that we cannot behold thee:
For ever hast thou gone from our sight,
And wilt return hither no more."

CHAPTER XXV.

The translation of the Bible—The Hawaiian constitution—Progress of the great
revival—State of the churches—Departure of a pioneer missionary.

THE spring of 1840 was a new era in the progress of the nation.
A written constitution, or declaration of rights, and a new code
of written laws were framed by the instructed natives, carefully
discussed, and in the course of the year adopted. The mission
rejoicing in every effort of the rulers to secure the just rights of
the people, to encourage industry and thrift, to restrain vice and
punish crime, took encouragement from this evidence of progress
probably more than the mass of the people themselves.

The supposition that the limiting of the rulers by *written* and
equitable laws would at once annihilate the burdens of the people,
would be unreasonable. Educated native judges and attorneys,
enlightened jurors and government officers are requisite, in order
to honor and execute a well devised system of *statute law* in
connexion with the existing *common law* that ought not to be
annihilated.

In putting on the untried armor of their new system even
gradually, there were, of course, difficulties not instantaneously
to be overcome. Few men, even in enlightened countries where
published laws are voluminous, thoroughly understand the principles of law so as to be trusted with its application, in cases
even of frequent occurrence, without a learned jurist to instruct
them in the particular cases. At the islands, some of the elder,
more experienced, valuable chiefs, but not educated as civilians,
were employed to fill important offices. But, though they possessed considerable tact and sagacity in following the established
system, they were slow to comprehend, and slower still to execute a new system of law, and sometimes made so incorrect an
application, as to throw discredit on the law itself, or on the
whole remodelled system.

Advance in legislation was made from year to year, before a
constitution was written out. Care was taken to instruct the rulers
of the islands as to the basis of personal rights, *i. e.*, the *gift by
God*, and the *earnings of personal labor*, physical and mental.
Every man derives his right to life and liberty directly from God;
but the right to anything else of which he can justly claim possession must be the result of human effort. But how far does per-

sonal *labor* give a personal *right* to its products? The general maxim urged by some, that *what a man makes is his own*, admits of exceptions, and the chiefs thought they could see such exceptions, because in communities, private interests must not be pursued to the destruction or detriment of public. A man's right, therefore, to the products of his own labor may, in some instances, be disputed. If he makes noxious articles which the interests of the community require should be prohibited, if in opposition to the will or weal of the State he makes a destructive liquor, a distillery, or anything that proves a nuisance; if he builds a house or a fence of another's materials, or on another's premises; or if he needlessly makes something for himself during the time belonging to the government, to parents, to guardians, to masters, to landlords, or to God, his right to such things might be questioned by the community.

In the Hawaiian bill of rights, the chiefs endeavored to incorporate in few words the general basis of personal rights, both of the chiefs and common people, and to guard against perversion; and this they have accomplished with, perhaps, as much *precision and consistency* as the Americans, who affirm " that all men are born free and equal, possessing certain inalienable rights, life, liberty, and the pursuit of happiness."

With distinguished and commendable care do the Hawaiians of 1840 acknowledge the paramount authority of God, in which Kaahumanu had set them a noble example, and the importance of an unwavering purpose in legislation not to contravene his Word.

The following translation I have made with care from the original, published at the islands as the Constitution of 1840:—

" God has made of one blood all the nations of men, that they might alike dwell upon the earth in peace and prosperity. And he has given certain equal rights to all people and chiefs of all countries. These are the rights or gifts which he has granted to every man and chief of correct deportment,—life, the members of the body, freedom in dwelling and acting, and the rightful products of his hands and mind: but not those things which are inhibited by the laws.

" From God also are the office of rulers and the reign of chief magistrates for protection; but in enacting the laws of the land, it is not right to make a law protecting the magistrate only and not subjects; neither is it proper to establish laws for enriching chiefs only, without benefiting the people, and hereafter, no law shall be established in opposition to the above declarations; neither shall taxes, servitude, nor labor, be exacted without law of any man in a manner at variance with those principles.

" PROTECTION FOR ALL.

" Therefore let this declaration be published in order to the equal protection of all the people and all the chiefs of these islands while maintaining a correct deportment, that no chief may oppress any subject, and that chiefs and people may enjoy equal security under the same system of law; the persons, the lands, the dwelling enclosures, and all the property of all the people are protected while they conform to the laws of the kingdom, neither shall any of these be taken except by the provisions of law.   Any chief who shall perseveringly act in opposition to this constitution, shall cease to hold his office as a chief of these Hawaiian islands ; and the same shall apply to governors, officers of government, and land agents.   But if one condemned shall turn again and conform himself to the laws, it shall be in the power of the chiefs to reinstate him in the standing he occupied before his trespass.

" FOUNDATION OF LAWS.

" According to the principles above declared, we purpose to regulate this kingdom, and to seek the good of all the chiefs and all the people of these Hawaiian islands.   We are aware that we cannot succeed by ourselves alone, but through God we can ; for he is King over all kingdoms, by whom protection and prosperity may be secured ; therefore do we first beseech him to point out to us the right course, and aid our work.

" *Wherefore resolved :*

" I. No law shall be enacted at variance with the Word of the Lord Jehovah, or opposed to the grand design of that Word.   All the laws of this country shall accord with the general design of God's law.

" II. All men of every form of worship shall be protected in their worshipping Jehovah, and in their serving him ; nor shall any one be punished for merely neglecting to serve God, provided he injures no man, and brings no evil on the kingdom.

" III. The law shall support every unblamable man who is injured by another, all shall be protected in every good work, and every man shall be punishable who brings evil on the kingdom or individuals. Nor shall any unequal law be established to give favor to one through evil to another.

" IV. No man shall be punished unless his crime be first made to appear, nor shall he be punished without being examined in the presence of his accuser ; when the accused and accuser have met face to face, and the trial proceeds according to law, and guilt is established before them both, then punishment shall follow.

" V. It shall not be proper for any man or chief to sit as judge or juror to try his own benefactor, or one directly connected with him. Therefore if one is condemned or acquitted, and it shall soon be known that some of the triers acted with partiality to favor whom he loved, or perhaps to enrich himself, then there may be a new trial before the impartial.

" EXPLANATION OF THE POSITION OF THE RULERS.

" The nature of the position of the chief magistrates and of the policy of the country is this :—Kamehameha I. was the head of this kingdom or dynasty.   To him pertained all the lands from Hawaii to Niihau.   But they were not his own personal property ; they belonged to the people and the chiefs, and Kamehameha was their head and the dictator of the country. Therefore no one had before, and no one has now, the right to convey away the smallest portion of these islands without the consent of the dictator of the kingdom.

" These are the dictators, or the persons who have had the direction of it from that time down, Kamehameha II. and Kaahumanu I., and at the present time Kamehameha III. To these persons only has belonged the direction or dictatorship of the realm down to the present time ; and the documents written by them only are the documents of the kingdom.

" The kingdom is to be perpetuated to Kamehameha III. and to his heirs   And his heir shall be one whom he and the chiefs shall appoint during his lifetime ; but if he shall not nominate, then the appointment shall devolve solely on the nobles and representatives.

" PREROGATIVES OF THE KING.

" This is the king's position :—He is the sovereign of all the people and all the chiefs. At his direction are the soldiers, the guns, the forts, and all the implements of war of the kingdom. At his direction is the public property, the revenue from the poll tax, the land tax, and the three days monthly labor tax, to accord, however, with the provisions of law. He shall possess his own private lands, and such as shall be forfeited for the annual tax.

" He is the chief judge of the supreme court, and to him belongs the execution of the laws of the land, the decrees, and the treaties with other countries, in accordance with the provisions of the laws of this country.

" It is for him to make treaties with the rulers of all other kingdoms, and to hold intercourse with ministers sent hither from other countries, and to consummate agreements.

" It is for him to declare war should a period of distress arrive, and the chiefs could not well be assembled ; and he shall be commander-in-chief of the army. All important business of the kingdom not committed by law to others, belongs to him to transact.

" OF THE PREMIER OF THE KINGDOM.

" It shall be the duty of the king to appoint a chief of ability and high rank, to be his prime minister, who shall be entitled *Premier* of the kingdom, whose office and business shall be like that of Kaahumanu I. and Kaahumanu II. For in the life-time of Kamehameha, the questions of life and death, right and wrong, were for Kaahumanu to decide, and at the time of his death he gave charge, ' Let the kingdom be Liholiho's, and Kaahumanu the prime minister.' That policy of Kamehameha, wherein he sought to secure a premier, is to be perpetuated in this Hawaiian country, but in accordance with the provisions of law.

" ' This is the business of the premier. Whatever appropriate business of the kingdom the king intends to do, the premier may do in the name of the king. The words and acts of the kingdom by the premier, are the words and acts of the king   The premier shall receive and acknowledge the revenue of the kingdom, and deliver it to the king. The premier shall be the king's special counsellor in all the important business of the kingdom. The king shall not transact public business without the concurrence of the premier ; nor shall the premier transact public business without the concurrence of the king. If the king shall veto what the premier counsels or attempts, *that is a negative.* Whatever important public business the king chooses to transact in person, he may do, but only with the approbation or consent of the premier.

" OF GOVERNORS.

" There shall be four governors in this Hawaiian country ; one of Hawaii, one of Maui and the adjacent isles, one of Oahu, and one of Kauai and the adjacent isles. All the governors from Hawaii to Kauai shall hold their office under the king.

" This is the character and duty of the office of governor. He is the director of all the tax officers in his island, and shall sustain their orders which he shall deem right, confirming according to the provisions of law, and not his own arbitrary will. He shall preside over all the judges of his island, and execute their decisions as above stated. He shall choose the judges of his district, and give them their commissions.

" The governor is the high chief (viceroy) over his island or islands, and shall have the direction of the forts, the soldiers, guns, and all the implements of war. Under the king and premier shall be all the governors from Hawaii to Kauai. Each shall have charge of the revenue of his island, and shall deliver it to the premier.

" In case of distress he may act as dictator, if neither king nor premier can be consulted. He shall have charge of all the king's business on the island, the taxation, improvements, and means of increasing wealth ; and all officers there shall be under him. To him belong all questions and business pertaining to the government of the island, not assigned by law to others.

" On the decease of a governor, the chiefs shall assemble at such a place as the king shall appoint, and together seek out a successor of the departed governor, and the person whom they shall choose and the king approve by writing, shall be the new governor.

" OF CHIEFS OR NOBLES UNDER THE KING.

" In the public councils of the chiefs, these are the counsellors for the current period. Kamehameha III, Kekauluohi, Hoapili wahine, Kuakini, Kekauonohi, Kahekili, Paki, Konia, Keohokalole, Leleiohoku, Kekuanaoa, Keliiahonui, Kanaina, Ii, Keoniana, a me Haalilio, and if a new member is to enter, the law shall specify it. These persons shall take part in the councils of the kingdom. But if the council choose to admit others merely for consultation it shall be allowable, the specified counsellors only being allowed to vote. No law shall be enacted for the country without their consent.

" In this manner shall they proceed : They shall meet annually to devise means for benefiting the country and enact laws for the kingdom. In the month of April shall they assemble at such time and place as the king shall appoint. It shall be proper for the king to take counsel with them on all the important concerns of the kingdom in order to secure harmony and prosperity, or the general good, and they shall attend to all the business which the king shall commit to them.   They shall retain their own personal estates, larger or smaller divisions of the country, and may conduct their affairs on their own lands according to their pleasure, but not in opposition to the laws of the kingdom.

" OF REPRESENTATIVES ELECTED.

" Several men shall be annually chosen to act in council with the king and chiefs, and to devise with them laws for the country.   Some from Hawaii, some from Maui, some from Oahu, and some from Kaui, shall the plebeians choose according to their own pleasure.   The law will determine the method of choosing and the number to be chosen. These chosen representatives shall have a voice in the government ; and no law can be established without the consent of the majority of them.

" OF THE MEETINGS OF THE LEGISLATURE OR PARLIAMENT.

" There shall be an annual meeting as aforesaid, but if the chiefs choose another meeting at another time, they may meet at their discretion.

" In the assembling of parliament, let the hereditary nobles meet by themselves and the elected rulers meet by themselves.   But if they choose to take counsel together occasionally at their discretion, so be it.

" In this manner shall they proceed : The hereditary chiefs shall choose a secretary for their body, and on the day of their assembling he shall record all their transactions ; and that book shall be preserved, that what they devise for the kingdom may not be lost.

" In the same manner shall the elected representatives proceed ; they shall choose a secretary for themselves, and on the day they assemble, to seek the good of the kingdom, and agree on any measure, he shall record it in a book, which shall be carefully preserved, in order that the good devised for the country may not be lost.   And no new law shall be established without the consent of a majority of the nobles, and of the elected representatives.

" When any act or measure shall have been agreed on by them it shall be carried on paper to the king, and if he approves and signs his name and also the Premier, then it shall become a law of the kingdom, and it shall not be repealed except by the body which enacted it.

" OF THE TAX-OFFICERS.

" The king and premier shall choose tax-officers and give them a commission in writing.   They shall be distinct for the separate islands.   There shall be three, or more or less for each island at the discretion of the king and premier.

" A tax-officer having received a commission, shall not be removed without a trial.   If convicted of crime he may be removed : but the number of years the office shall continue may be previously limited by law.

" This is clearly the business of the tax-officers : They shall apprise the people of the amount of assessment that they may hear beforehand at the proper time.   They shall proceed according to the orders of the governors and the provisions of law.   And when the time for paying taxes shall arrive, they shall collect the amount and deliver it to the governor, and the governor to the premier, and the premier to the king. The tax-officers shall also direct the public labor for the king, but may commit its details to the land-agents, presiding themselves over them in this work. They shall also have charge of any new business which the king may design to extend through the kingdom; but in their doings they shall be subordinate to the governors. They shall be arbiters of the tax laws, and in all cases where land-agents or landlords oppress the peasantry, and in every difficulty between land-agents and tenants, and everything specified in the tax law established June 7th, 1839.

" In this manner shall they proceed : each shall exercise his office in his own district. If a difficulty arise between a land-agent and a tenant, the tax-officer shall investigate it, and if the tenant is in fault, the tax-officer and land-agent shall execute the law upon him. But if the land-agent is in fault in the judgment of the tax-officer, the latter shall call the other tax-officers of the island, and if they agree with him, judgment against the land-agent is confirmed, and the governor shall execute the law on him. But if any believe the tax-officer to have erred, the governor may be apprised and try the case over again, and if he is believed to have erred, the case may be made known to the supreme judges, and they shall try the case anew.

" OF THE JUDGES.

" The governor of each island shall choose judges for the island according to his own mind, two or more, at his own discretion, and give them a written commission. When they receive this they shall not be removed without trial, but the law may limit their term of office.

" In this manner shall they proceed : The court days shall be declared beforehand, and when the appointed day arrives, they shall proceed with trials according to law. To them shall be given jurisdiction in respect to all the laws except those connected with taxation, and to the difficulties between land-agents, landlords, and tenants. The governor shall sustain them and execute their judgment. But if their judgment is thought to be unjust, he who thinks so may complain or appeal to the supreme judges.

" OF THE SUPREME JUDGES.

" The elected representatives shall choose four judges to assist the king and premier ; and these six shall be the supreme judges of the kingdom. This shall be their business ; cases of difficulty not well adjusted by the tax-officers or island judges, they shall try again according to law. The court days shall be declared beforehand, that those who are in difficulty may apply. And the decision of this court shall stand. There is thereafter no appeal. Life and death, to bind and release, to fine and not to fine, are at their disposal, and with them the end of controversy.

" OF CHANGES IN THE CONSTITUTION.

" This constitution shall not be considered as fully established until the people generally shall have heard it, and certain persons as herein

mentioned, shall be chosen, and shall assent to it, then firmly established is this constitution.

"And thereafter, if it be designed to alter it, the people shall be
first apprised of the nature of the amendment intended to be introduced, and the next year, at the meeting of the nobles and representatives,
if they agree to insert a passage or to annul a passage, they may do it
lawfully.

" This constitution above stated, has been agreed to by the nobles,
and our names are set to it this eighth day of October, in the year of
our Lord, 1840, at Honolulu, Oahu.

(Signed), "KAMEHAMEHA III.
KEKAULUOHI."

The house of nobles, or hereditary lords and ladies, consisted
of the king himself, a female premier, four governors of islands,
four women of rank, and five chiefs of the third rank. The people were allowed to choose by districts annually seven men to be
members of the national legislature for a year : two from Hawaii,
two from Maui and adjacent islands, two from Oahu, and one
from Kauai, the government bearing their expenses. The proposition was also distinctly made to increase the number after a time.
The right of suffrage, so far as to vote for one or two men to act
in making laws and appointing supreme assistant judges, was extended to all, but guarded with peculiar care. Whoever wished
to avail himself of it, is permitted to send up his vote or petition
to the throne, in company with others, in this form :—

" To his M., K. III.
' Love to you. We write to inform you of men of Hawaii whom we
know, men of wisdom, men of probity ; ——— is the name of one,
and ——— is the name of the second. We desire them to act in council with the chiefs this year."

The men who receive the majority of votes in their district are
chosen, and are by the premier apprised of their election, and thus
entitled to a seat in the parliament or national council. This not
only gives a spur to mental improvement, but tends to ensure the
blessings of civil liberty.

Not by the noisy and turbulent demand of the people, but by
the respectful solicitation as it were of the highest hereditary
rulers, these elected members are invited to come up and take part
in the weighty concerns of making laws for the nation, without a
disastrous revolution, and without prostrating the feelings of loyalty, or evincing the slightest tendency to anarchy.

Where has the world ever seen a monarch so freely limiting his
own power, inviting the common people to send representatives
to aid him and his high-born counsellors in making laws, or a
hereditary aristocracy, of their own accord, extending the right
of suffrage to the lower orders, to elect legislators who should
have an equal voice with themselves in the legislature ? In this
particular the king and chiefs of the Sandwich Islands stand unrivalled. Washington and his compeers performed a noble ser-

vice in securing the rights of the common people of their country, but none of them, from a hereditary throne, stooped to invite every man in the nation to have a voice in legislation, and a share with the sovereign and his nobles in the administration of the civil power.

In respect to education, the Legislature, when providing for schools in every district, is pleased to say :—

" The basis on which the kingdom rests is wisdom and knowledge. . . In the estimation of the nobles and the representative body, schools for the instruction of children in letters are of great importance. We are firmly determined to give protection to schools and to teachers of good character, and also to deal rigidly with all those who oppose the schools or embarrass their operations."

On the same subject they urge the duty of giving the children the advantages of schools, because no person unable to read can hold office under the government or have license to marry a wife or husband. Their code of written laws, enacted before and after the constitution, and published among the people with the constitution, is too voluminous to be inserted in this volume, and it is almost superseded by the insertion of the entire constitution.

How they meet the difficult question of providing a revenue for the support of the general and local government the reader may wish to see. A *poll* tax is laid on the people of one dollar each man, and half a dollar each woman, except school teachers, the aged and infirm, and foreigners ; a quarter of a dollar each boy, and an eighth of a dollar each girl, between fourteen and twenty years of age. The annual *land* tax is from five to twenty dollars on a farm or plantation according to its size and value. Where money cannot be obtained, five pounds of coffee, or fifteen of cotton, or thirty-three of arrow root or of swine on the foot, may be substituted for a dollar. The *labor* tax on men, except schoolmasters, and the infirm and those that give support to their own children or orphan relatives to the number of three, or to invalids to the number of four, three days per month, or $4. 50 per year, for their landlord : and three days per month,or $4. 50 per year for the king. If some extraordinary public work of the kingdom, for the benefit both of the chiefs and people, require it, six days extra per month, may, for the time, be exacted of each. Parents who support five or more children are exempt from taxation, but their children, when able to labor, from fourteen to twenty years of age, are taxable. This revenue is about $65.000.

The nation of Hawaiians hitherto had been to a remarkable degree a common stock community, the soil, fisheries, and products being considered as in some sense belonging to the state and at the king's disposal. No portion of the soil was so separated from the common stock as to belong to a private citizen or subject, though most of the chiefs were considered as subjects. This organization of the State of course modified the action of the rulers, so that when they were disposed to do the best that was possible in their circumstances for the public good, they were liable to be censured by some, who, as citizens of a free republic, had been accustomed to the title of *sovereigns*.

From various causes, the common people were accustomed to spend less time and effort on the soil and fisheries from which they gained their subsistence, and therefore made them far less productive to themselves and their superiors, than a reasonable amount of well directed industry would make them. A portion of the *time* of the tenants was required on public plantations, or public buildings, or houses, or fences for landlords, governors, kings, &c. This labor was often of little value, even when rightfully exacted, compared with the free intelligent labor of enlightened communities. Public spirit needed to be increased and well directed.

To aid the cause of Christianity, the erection of school-houses, the support of school teachers, and the erection of churches, claimed their attention. Wherever the people much desired a school, they were willing to do something towards erecting a building that might be called a school-house. And whenever the people came to desire the preaching of the Gospel, and could obtain a missionary, the erection of churches became a matter of desire among them. For the expense and labor of erecting such buildings it was reasonable that the nation or the people should feel themselves responsible, instead of taxing for that purpose, the charity of the Christian community that sustained the mission.

Kings, queens, and governors, taking a rational view of this subject, have directed or favored these enterprises in a commendable manner, appropriating a portion of the time of the people which was at their disposal for the public good, and allowing the people to take for this purpose timber and other materials, the property of the state, and encouraging them to give a portion of their own time, strength, skill, and earnings to the work. Commencing with frail and perishable materials, and making improvements from time to time, as Christianity extended its influence, and the energy and ability of the people increased, and large portions of the rulers and people came to cherish the desire to have the advantage of large, commodious, and durable churches, they at length built them of solid materials, at a cost of two or three thousand, up to twenty or thirty thousand dollars. Some of their churches have been built by the worshippers without any special direction of the rulers, further than to grant the site and the materials belonging to the state for the purpose; and others have been built partly by public labor, or that which was at the disposal of the ruler, and partly by the spontaneous and voluntary labors of the people; and others still almost solely by the labor which was supposed to be due to the king, or governor, or both.

Towards the close of 1835, the young king, advancing to manhood, signified to the premier, Kinau, that three things of special importance he desired to see as soon as possible—a ship of war for his service, a palace for his residence, and a new church for the worship of God. Kinau thought it wise to secure the church first, at least to mature the plan and make a beginning. The erection of a large stone, or coral rock, church at Honolulu had for several years been in contemplation, while the people of the island, 27,000, constituted one missionary district, the head men and chiefs residing much at Honolulu. To Kalanimoku and Kaahumanu, and others, such an object had appeared highly desirable, but not till now attainable. Nor was it now attainable without the aid of temperance and Christianity.

In the early part of 1836, a public meeting of a popular form was appointed on the subject at Honolulu. The king and high chiefs resident there, the head men, and a great concourse of the people, assembled to transact business. Gov. Kekuanaoa, by nomination and lifting the hands, a novel measure, was chosen chairman. The projections of a church 144 feet by 78, with basement, audience-room and gallery, vestibule and tower, were presented and explained; the question of their ability and willingness to erect such a church discussed and settled in the affirmative. For the people and the rulers said, " Let us build." It was understood that besides the materials which they could furnish, and the labor which they could devote to this object, some thousands of dollars would be needed for procuring materials and labor, boards, nails, glass, sashes, trimmings, lamps, &c. The king, and Kinau, and the governor, entered into it with spirit. His majesty encouraged the people to engage in the enterprise heartily, and a good degree of enthusiasm was manifested by all classes present.

To raise money for the object, a subscription was opened on the spot before the great assembly. The question was asked, Who among you will subscribe and give thousands for this new house of God? The king took the pen, and, in the presence of the chiefs and people, subscribed, as we expected, the princely sum of $3000. None else chose to subscribe a thousand. The question then followed, " Who will give by the *lau*, four hundred?" Kinau subscribed $400. " Who will give hundreds or forties?" Kekauluohi, Liliha, and Paki, subscribed each $50, and Kekuanaoa $40, and said he meant to do much more. " Who will give by twenties?" The wife of the king, Kalama, Kanaina, Haalilio, Konia, and others, subscribed $20 each. " Who will give tens?" A good number subscribed ten each; smaller sums were asked for and subscribed down to one dollar, the number of subscribers increasing as the sums diminished, till the names of those who announced themselves to the scribes for a dollar each, amounted to about 1000, and those for higher sums, to near 500. The whole amount subscribed within a short period amounted to little less than $6000. Another thousand would probably have subscribed from an eighth to half a dollar each, if that had been asked. Of the whole subscription, very little failed to be paid in due time, and without any dunning, though most of the subscribers were poor, and probably destitute of money when they put down their names.

Besides the subscriptions in money, the rulers gave a considerable portion of the stone, lime, and timber, for the building. The stone was cut from the reef or flats washed by the sea at high tide. The lime in great quantity was produced from the coral. The timber was brought partly from their own forests, and partly from California and the Columbia; the shingles from the N. W. Coast; boards, nails, glass, sashes, and lamps, from Boston; and a timepiece for it, presented by J. H., Esq., from Charlestown.

In prosecuting this work, the need of trucks, carts, and teams, became very obvious, and we took pains to get them brought into use, to relieve the people from carrying such heavy materials on their shoulders, or dragging them half a mile on the bare ground without wheels.

The people were benefited not only by the introduction of wheels, drawn by hand, and by oxen and horses, but also by bringing into use a variety of useful tools, and the mechanical powers, the lever, the wheel and axle, the screw, the crane, and the pulley.

Knowledge, dexterity, invention, and energy, among the people, for the subsequent construction of bridges, private and public buildings, of a durable and respectable character, were greatly promoted by this work. To call forth the ingenuity and energies of thousands of the people on a great enterprise of public value, in which they and their children were to have an equal interest with their rulers, one especially connected as this was allowed by all to be with the honor of God and the promotion of his kingdom, was an object of no small importance in the education of the nation.

For the accomplishment of this part of the result, it was desirable that the hands of the natives should do as much of every part of the work as, without neglecting other duties, they could advantageously do in procuring and fitting materials, and putting them in their proper place in the building. By this means their knowledge of masonry and carpentry was materially augmented, and their judgment improved, in respect to the business of life.

Judging that the surface of the ground allotted for the building, though competent to sustain ordinary dwellings, could not safely be relied on to sustain the pressure of the massive walls and tower and internal work of the church, and the immense audience which was expected to crowd it, they excavated the earth to the depth of six feet, entirely removing the soil and substratum of volcanic ashes or cinders which had doubtless come from the Punchbowl crater in its vicinity, and laid the foundation firmly on a broad, level rock of submarine formation of considerable extent, which had by some means been here elevated a little above the level of the ocean. On this rock they reared the walls of the basement, 44 inches thick, and about 12 feet high. Then the builders, proprietors, and missionaries assembled and laid the corner stone of the new temple. The stone, weighing about half a ton, had been procured by Paki at Waianae, and transported under his direction, to Honolulu. Beneath it, was placed a Hawaiian Bible, just completed, a volume of Mathematics, in native, and another on Anatomy, indicating the basis of Christian and missionary institutions at the islands, and a brass plate with the reign, the date, and the object for which the church was erected, neatly engraved by Kapeau, a native pupil at the Mission Seminary. Though in the ceremony, the formality of pronouncing the corner-stone " square, level, plumb, and durable " was omitted, yet the fitness and durableness of the Corner-Stone in Zion, and the glory of the spiritual temple which God was rearing on it, were commended to the people ; and the divine blessing was invoked on the enterprise, on the founders, laborers, and worshippers, who there seeking the gate of heaven, should consecrate their service to the Father, Son, and Holy Ghost.

Above the basement, the walls being narrowed by five inches on the outside and six within, were then carried up 33 inches thick to the sills of the gallery windows, and thence being narrowed six inches more within, were carried up 27 inches thick to the plates. The immense roof having an extended span, and the ceiling, supported by king and queen posts, rest on the walls without the support of pillars. The building is well lighted, though not in the most tasteful style, having twenty windows on each side above the basement, which, with the ends, has a proportional number. The gallery windows and the doors are arched. The floor of the building is six feet above the surface of the ground. The front is ornamented with four pillars of the Hawaiian order, nearly four feet diameter and twenty-six in height, about two-thirds of their shaft projecting from the wall, with which they are firmly united. The blocks of coral-rock, somewhat porous, but strong enough to make good walls, being cut out with axes, pried up, trimmed by pattern to their proper form and size, and weighing from two hundred to twelve hundred pounds, were laid up in good lime mortar, most of the work being done by native hands. The building appears shapely and firm, an ornament to the town of 8000 inhabitants, and may stand centuries as a monument of the favor of God to the nation, and of the rapid advancement of the people in Christianity and civilization during the first quarter of a century of their acquaintance with the Gospel. In the erection of this stately edifice, the active men among about 1000 communicants of that church, being divided into five companies, labored by rotation many days and weeks with patience and zeal.*

* After the taking of $20,000 from the people by the French, which was not restored till the interest on it at 12½ per cent. per annum would have been equal to

It argued courage for the people to undertake a work of that kind which could hardly be accomplished at an expense less than $20,000, and it proved their perseverance to carry it on for six years, till they were permitted to open it, July 21, 1842, for the worship of God and the use of generations. That was an honored people who reared that house of prayer, so large, costly, firm, and commodious, and, to their eyes, so rich, grand, and beautiful :—a happy and honored people were they after their toil, when they received from the hands of Kamehameha III. a title-deed of it, as a rich possession for Protestant worship :— honored and happy people, who assembled by thousands, with the king, chiefs, and missionaries, to set it apart, and having the question put to them, " To whom do you dedicate this house?" replied with joyful acclamation, " To Jehovah our God, for ever and ever."

The people or the professors of the Gospel connected with the station at Kealakekua, under the care of Messrs. Forbes and Ives, erected for themselves a commodious and substantial church, 120 feet by 57, the particulars of which I gather from Mr. Forbes. The stones were carried on the shoulders of men forty or fifty rods. The coral for making the lime, they procured by diving in two or three fathom water, and detaching blocks or fragments. If these were too heavy for the diver to bring up to his canoe with his hands, he ascended to the surface to take breath, then descending with a rope, attached it to his prize, and mounting to his canoe, heaved up the mass from the bottom, and when the canoe was thus laden, rowed it ashore and discharged his freight. By this process they procured about thirty cubic fathoms, or 7,776 cubic feet. To burn this mass, the church members brought from the mountain side, upon their shoulders, forty cords of wood. The lime being burned, the women took it in calabashes, or large gourd shells, and bore it on their shoulders to the place of building, also sand and water for making the mortar. Thus about 700 barrels each, of lime, sand, and water, making about 2,000 barrels, equal to 350 wagon loads, were carried by women a quarter of a mile, to assist the men in building the temple of the Lord, which they desired to see erected for themselves and their children ; a heavy service, which they, their husbands, fathers, sons, had not the means of hiring, nor teams to accomplish. The latter had other work far more laborious to perform for the house. The sills, posts, beams, rafters, &c., which they cut in the mountain, six to ten miles distant, they drew down by hand. The posts and beams required the strength of forty to sixty men each. Such a company, starting at break of day, with ropes in hand, and walking two or three hours through the fern and underbrush loaded with the cold dew, made fast to their timber, and addressing them-

the principal, the builders of this church were encouraged by the acceptable donation of $1.479, a sum made up chiefly by a few friends of that nation in New York, Brooklyn, and New London, and of a pulpit and communion table from New Haven.

selves to their sober toil for the rest of the day, dragged it over beds of lava, rocks, ravines, and rubbish, reaching the place of building about sunset. To pay the carpenters, and workmen who laid up the walls, the church members subscribed according to their ability, from one to ten dollars each, and paid in such things as the workmen would take, produce or money. Thus with a little foreign aid, amounting to two or three hundred dollars, besides the labor and care of the missionary, the people erected a comfortable house of worship, valued at about $6,000.

Efforts very similar have been made by the people of Kohala, Hana, Wailuku, Koloa, Waioli, Kaneohe, Waialua, Waimea, Kailua, Ewa, Honolulu 2d, Kaluaaha, and Lahaina, and some other places, but I will here detail but one more which illustrates the spirit of those who welcome the Gospel, a particular trait of Hawaiian character, and the action of missionary example upon it. The Hawaiians are not only inclined to live in hamlets and villages, but to labor in companies, even where the work could be accomplished by single hands. And in such cases they must have and obey a leader, chosen, hereditary, or self-appointed, who plans for them and cheers them on. The people of the district under the care of Mr. Coan, in building a large new church at Waiakea, Hilo, devoted voluntarily much toil, and exhibited ingenuity, energy, and good will, dragging down for the purpose heavy timber, six miles from the forest. Mr. Coan says:—

" In order to stimulate and encourage the people in this great work (for it is truly a great and heavy work for them), I have often gone with them to the forest, laid hold of the rope, and dragged timber with them from morning to night. On such occasions, we usually, on our arrival at the timber to be drawn, unite in prayer, and then fastening to the stick proceed to our work. Dragging timber in this way is exceedingly wearisome, especially if there be not, as is often the case, a full complement of hands. But what is wanting in numbers is often supplied in the tact and management of the natives, some of whom are expert in rallying, stimulating, and cheering their comrades by sallies of wit, irony, and if the expression is allowable, of good-natured sarcasm. The manner of drawing is quite orderly and systematic. They choose one of their number for a leader. This done, the leader proceeds to use his vocal powers, by commanding all others to put theirs at rest. He then arranges the men on each side of the rope like artillerists at the drag-rope. Every man is commanded to grasp the rope firmly with both hands, straighten it, and squat down inclined a little forward. The leader then passes from rear to front, and from front to rear, reviewing the line to see that every man grasps the rope. All is now still as the grave for a moment, when the commander, or marshal of the day, roars out in a stentorian voice, ' Kauo, draw !' Every one then rises, bending forward ; every muscle is tense, and away dashes the timber, through thicket and mud, over lava and streamlet, under a burning sun or amidst drenching rain. No conversation is allowed except by the marshal, who seems to feel it his privilege during his incumbency, to make noise enough for all.

About once in half a mile, all stop to rest, and then proceed again. If the company flag after an hour or two, choosing to walk erect, holding the rope loosely, then the brilliant marshal has a thousand smart things to say to arouse their zeal and provoke their muscular energies. I will give one sententious phrase, " Bow the head—blister the hands—sweat." If the marshal finds his voice exhausted, he resigns voluntarily or through the modest hint of a friend ; and another is chosen to fill his place. All is done in good-nature."

The same people who were thus laboring to honor the Lord by building a house of worship, were ready to attend on his ordinances, whether they had a house sufficiently large to accommodate them or were obliged to sit in the open air. Their pastor says :—

" Once in three months the whole church meet at the station to eat the Lord's Supper. Our last communion was on the last Sabbath in April. Perhaps there were five thousand present. For want of a convenient house for the occasion we met in a grove of cocoa-nut trees on the sea-shore. The assembly was immense, and the scene overwhelming. Before us was the wide Pacific heaving its broad breast to the breath of heaven. Behind us were the everlasting mountains rearing their summits above the clouds, and forming an eternal rampart against the western sky. Beneath us was a little spot of earth once ignited by volcanic fires, rocked by earthquakes, and more than once submerged with a flood. Above us was the vaulted sky, that glorious mirror, that molten looking-glass spread out and made strong by the hand of Omnipotence. Around us was a landscape of inimitable beauty, clothed with verdure, teeming with life, and smiling in loveliness. The softer and sweeter features in nature blended with the grand, the bold, the sublime, combined to render the scene enchanting."

Here a great multitude just recovered from the darkest heathenism, a multitude, such as Christ once fed by his miraculous power, having heard his glorious Gospel, often unite in commemorating the dying love of Him who made and who has redeemed the world.

In coming to the close of twenty-one years from the abrogation of the ancient tabus, and the 21st year of the mission, we are called to notice what the Lord had done for the nation in respect to government, education, morals, and religion. The constitution and laws, the production of a people so recently barbarous, whose first lessons in their own language had been printed but eighteen years, may be referred to as a monumental record of advancement. The Bible entire, printed in two editions of 10,000 copies each, and welcomed by the nation, as another : six boarding-schools, 12 station schools and 357 common-schools, embracing 18,000 scholars, as another ; and as another still, the establishment and enlargement of eighteen churches to be the light and glory of the land. How wonderfully does the grace of God rear his spiritual temple in the Sandwich Islands, by the influences of his Spirit copiously shed down on the nation, and thus through the divine Word bring into his visible kingdom and to his ordinances so large a proportion of the population during the last four years of the history of the nation and of the mission.* Not less than 20,000 were, in this period, added to our churches, all of whom, at the time of their admission, were regarded by the missionaries and their native Christian friends, as hopeful converts and disciples of Christ. Should we suppose that through haste or error one-fifth of the whole had entered the church unworthily, it may be added that three or four thousand more not then baptized, considered themselves as converts, and were subsequently admitted.

Though the American missionaries entered on their work at the islands more than forty years subsequently to the discovery by Capt. Cook and the death of that navigator, numbers of the Hawaiian people who were contemporary with him, lived on amid the ravages of war and pestilence, to hear of the great salvation from the lips of the missionaries, and some even to see the great revival of 1837—1840. Bending with age, with locks silvered or whitened for the grave, those who saw the wars of Kalaniopuu, Kahekili, and Kamehameha, and the slaughter of human victims on the altars of superstition, and were surrounded by those by whom multitudes of helpless infants suffered a violent death, now came to the altar and temple of the living God, and though their eyes were growing dim with the dust of years, and the days of their probation about to close for ever, they now, with wonder, saw a glorious light, as they were taught to look up to the Lamb of God. As they looked around on the state of society to mark the contrast with that of their early days, they beheld thousands of children now connected with Sabbath and other schools, provided by missionary, parental, and governmental care, and groups of them here and there singing " Hosana " in the temple. The

* The following table will show the additions to the churches during the four years ending June, 1837--1840.

Islands.	Stations.	1837.	1838.	1839.	1840.
KAUAI.	Waimea	5	18	69	20
	Koloa	10		37	15
	Waioli	10	38	9	
OAHU,	Waialua	8	127	202	174
	Ewa	10	329	742	174
	Kaneohe	8	43	85	59
	Honolulu 1st	14	134	390	275
	Honolulu 2d		49	672	438
MOLOKAI.	Kaluaaha		14	59	59
MAUI.	Lahaina	6	2	131	131
	Lahainaluna			20	3
	Wailuku	11	208	200	192
	Hana			62	58
HAWAII.	Kailua	29	62	92	372
	Kealakekua	4	81	262	385
	Kohala		629	149	80
	Waimea	21	2,600	2,300	419
	Hilo	23	639	5,244	1,499
Total		159	4,973	10,725	4,179

age of darkness, of wars, of infanticide, and of human sacrifices, had passed away, and the age of schools, of wholesome laws, of Bibles, of spiritual sacrifices, and revivals, had come.

Though as much had, by the favor of God, been gained as the pioneers expected in their lifetime, when they sought their home in that region of darkness, yet, in some sense, the work of the mission was but begun.

To lose health at such a time, or to be called to leave such a field in such a state, was a trial greater than that of leaving one's home and country to convey the Gospel to the heathen.

In the course of this year, Divine Providence seemed to indicate that one or both of the ordained pioneers of the mission should leave the ground temporarily, at least, though both could not well be spared at once. Mr. and Mrs. Thurston, who thought it their duty to convey their children to the United States, myself, and Mrs. B., with health much impaired had permission to visit our native land. Mrs. B. was too much worn out to go without her husband. Mr. T. chose to stand at his post at Kailua, and send his family with mine, and trusted the arrangement for their children with Mrs. T., the Board, and private friends. Mr. Armstrong took my post at Honolulu. With the full approbation of the mission, our two families embarked from Honolulu Aug. 3d, 1840, while numbers of my people, with anxious looks and tender tears, came around, and the parting *aloha* was exchanged with the mutual desire and hope of meeting there again. We touched at Tahiti and Pernambuco, and reached New York in safety, Feb. 4th, 1841, six months and two days from Oahu, and twenty-one years, six months and eleven days from Boston.

STONE CHURCH AT HONOLULU.

CHAPTER XXVI.

FIVE YEARS FROM THE ADOPTION OF THE CONSTITUTION TO THE
INTERNATIONAL ACKNOWLEDGMENT OF HAWAIIAN INDEPEND-
ENCE. 1841—1845.

Visit of the United States Exploring Expedition—The last generation of chiefs—
Institution for the young chiefs—State of the Mission Seminary—Female Semi-
naries—Boarding-Schools for boys—School for the children of Missionaries—
Church discipline—New efforts to secure Independence—Recognition at Wash-
ington—Visit of the French ship Embuscade—Visit of the English ship Carysfort,
Lord Paulet—Provisional cession of the islands—Restoration by Admiral Tho-
mas—Acknowledgment and guarantee of the Independence of the Islands by
England and France—Naturalization—Rëinforcements 8, 9, 10—Public Morals—
Haalilio—Representatives—Treaties—Speech from the Throne—Conclusion.

WITHOUT the advantage of further observation at my post, which
had become to myself and family a home of interest, from which
we have been providentially detained, but having been favored
with the correspondence of the missionaries, well written letters
from natives, received by ship, intercourse with the Hawaiian
commissioners while in the United States, and free access to voluminous communications from the Hawaiian Islands, found in
the archives of the American Board and elsewhere, I shall, without the formality of an Appendix, endeavor to bring down the
narrative of events there since 1840, but with less minuteness
and more dependence on the accounts of others.

Shall a nation be born in a day? However that question may
be solved, the Hawaiian nation, after twenty-one years of acquaintance with Christianity, is but a youth taken from the filth and rags
of heathenism, washed and trimmed, supplied with clothes and
books, and endowed with a healthy and manly constitution, but inexperienced, and unable to form a mature, symmetrical, and efficient
character, without the influence of good society, as well as that of
the school and the church; and now needs the impress which the
correct example and counsels of the older and more mature nations
of the earth ought, in their wisdom, to be willing to give it, while
its true foster parent, with unabated solicitude, still watches over
its progress.

The United States Exploring Squadron, which for some months
had been looked for at Oahu, arrived there in Sept., 1840,
and made a survey of the islands. Commodore Wilkes and
Captain Hudson took a happy and decided stand against intemperance, and the rash doings of Captain Laplace and his coadjutors, and in favor of the independence and progress of the nation
and of the prosperity of the schools and the mission. The visit

was made useful not only to the cause of science and commerce, but beneficial to the cause of the American Board, who, in the report of 1841, say of it :—" The mission was much pleased and encouraged by the visit of the United States Exploring Squadron, which spent seventy days at the islands, in the autumn of the last year. The deportment of Commodore Wilkes and Captain Hudson and other officers, and of the scientific corps, towards the mission and towards the government of the islands, was such as became the representatives of a great Christian nation."

In the progress of twenty-one years, from 1819, many of that class of the chiefs who were above middle age or prominent in the nation, when our mission first visited them, passed away, and the rest, with the exception of Kapule, within five or six years, and their places will know them no more for ever. The funeral of Liliha, ex-governess of Oahu, occurred before I left the field. Near the same period, in Jan., 1840, Hoapili, the aged and venerable governor of Maui, finished his course of life, of humble faith, of attachment to the Word and house of God, and of patriotic devotion to the interests of his country, both as a magistrate and as a citizen of Zion. His widow, Hoapili Wahine, of similar excellence and influence, followed him in Jan., 1842. The missionaries and the people of Maui, who had rejoiced over them, deeply felt their loss. In May, 1841, the nation lost one of its brightest ornaments, and the mission one of its fairest fruits, by the death of Kapiolani, whose precious life, in the midst of her prayers, exhortations, and useful influence, was brought to a close by a cancer. For nearly twenty years, she had befriended the mission, and for fifteen, had greatly adorned the Gospel, and endeared herself to the friends of improvement among the people of her nation. In her opposition to superstition, whether Hawaiian or Roman, and her support of the truth, she was kind, decided, dignified, and triumphant, while she exalted Christ and abased herself and made her adorning that of good works.

As that class of chiefs whom we found on the stage in 1820 were leaving it, one after another, and younger ones were taking their places, it was deemed highly important to win and educate their juvenile heirs, who were expected eventually to be the acting chiefs of the country. It had been difficult to detach them from their numerous attendants, and difficult otherwise to teach them in our families, and equally difficult to train them properly in any of the schools for the common people. The object was, however, made to appear so important, that the mission and both the parents and the children came at length to concur in the design of a boarding-school exclusively for this interesting class. Such an institution was therefore established at Honolulu in 1839. A house was erected in the form of a hollow square, suited to accommodate a mission family and some twenty boarding and lodging pupils with school-room, parlor,

Mission Seminary at Lahainaluna.   Page 581.

dining-room, bed-rooms, etc. The charge of it was committed to Mr. and Mrs. Cook. The expenses of the institution, including the buildings, the scholars, and the teachers (after the first year or two), are sustained by the parents or the government, the king being the special patron of the school.

John Ii and his estimable wife, Sarai, are attached to the institution, and exercise an important and useful guardianship over these royal and noble pupils. The parents of the pupils are highly satisfied with the management and success of the school. The pupils have signed the temperance pledge, which they observe with constancy. They take exercise with the teachers on horseback and otherwise. The boys ride well. All sing, and usually join in the morning and evening song of praise. They are among the most constant attendants at church on the Sabbath. They have school exercises five and a half days in the week, and spend much of their evenings in reading, and writing journals. The boys sometimes read while the girls sew. They are taught both in English and Hawaiian. Misses Jane and Bernice play prettily on the piano-forte. The school presents a happy, promising group of 14 children and youth of rank, who in their attainments and manners are engaging and respectable. The commander of the Exploring Expedition says: " I have seldom seen better behaved children than those of this school. They were hardly to be distinguished from well bred children of our own country, were equally well dressed, and nearly as light in color."

Some four years later, a reply, in English, made by one of the female pupils in the name of the school, to a naval officer, who had wasted his eloquence in favor of balls, will illustrate their docility, advancement, and amiableness: " Our teachers seek our good, sir. They have experience, and know what is best for us. We have confidence in their judgment, and have no inclination to do what they disapprove."

The Mission Seminary at Lahainaluna, established in 1831 for self-supporting students, assumed, from the 23d of July, 1837, the form of a boarding-seminary for children from seven to twelve, and youth from twelve to twenty years of age.

The principal building has been enlarged and greatly improved, and furnished with apparatus by the Board. A printing office, and comfortable habitations for the families of three ordained teachers and an assistant, have been added from the same source. The establishment, including the dormitories of more than a hundred students, form a village of some interest.

Mr. Andrews having been principal of the seminary about ten years, resigned in 1841, and subsequently entered the service of the government, as a judge, in cases connected with foreigners. In 1842 it contained 107 pupils, and up to that period, it had sent forth a number of valuable classes, of which 144 members were then living, and of whom the mission say :—

" Of these, 105 are usefully employed as teachers ; thirty-five are officers of government, of whom eight devote a part of their time to teaching; seven are engaged in other useful employments; eleven are doing nothing or worse; seventy-three are church members in regular standing ; nine are officers of churches; ten are openly immoral ; a few are occasionally employed as preachers, though without a regular license. The graduates of the seminary are generally reported as efficient helpers in the missionary work."

A theological class of six members in this seminary was placed under the tuition of Rev. S. Dibble, in 1843, but his early death occasioned a vacancy in that department of instruction which has not been constantly supplied. In 1844 the number of students was 131. Twenty-eight were graduated, each giving a pledge to refund to the institution twenty dollars for each year's board and tuition, unless their useful labors as teachers of their countrymen should be deemed by the faculty an equivalent in the cause of the mission.

The hopes of the mission, and of the friends of the nation in respect to its future teachers and officers, are in a measure suspended on this institution.

The boarding-school for girls, or the Female Seminary at Wailuku, under the care of Mr. and Mrs. Baily and Miss Ogden, having buildings completed suited to accommodate a family and seventy pupils, affords to some sixty promising girls and young women, instruction not only in Christianity, but in geography, mental and written arithmetic, moral philosophy, natural theology, reading, writing, drawing, composition, and various arts adapted to the station of Hawaiian females. In 1843 the mission give this gratifying report of it.

" The moral, mental, and physical training at this school seems to be of a high character. At daylight the pupils repair to their gardens, where they exercise till they are called to prayers at half-past six. They breakfast at seven. After breakfast, they are employed for an hour in sweeping their rooms and putting all things in order. The time from nine to eleven is spent in study and recitation. The next half hour they spend as they please. From half-past eleven to twelve, they bathe and prepare their dinners, which they take at twelve. From dinner until two is at their own disposal, and much of it is spent in study. From two till four they give their attention to spinning, weaving, sewing, knitting, making mats, etc., under the instruction of Miss Ogden. The time from four to five they devote to exercise with the hoe. They sup at five, and the remainder of the day is at their own disposal. At the evening devotions, they recite the daily food (or the verse of Scripture for the day), and receive such religious instruction as may seem appropriate."

A considerable number of those who have been educated here have been married to graduates from the Mission Seminary, and have entered on the duties of life with a better prospect of usefulness among their contemporaries, than if these advantages had not, through Christian kindness, been conferred on them.

This school has shared, at different times, in the influences of the Spirit. In 1843, the principal, describing their seriousness and inquiring state of mind, says :—

" So far as we know, all met to pray in little circles, every morning or evening, or both. They often arose long before the light of day, to engage in this blessed work. The taste for play seemed to vanish ; and all appeared, in a greater or less degree, to feel that the salvation of their souls was the great thing to be attended to."

Efforts properly to seclude the girls from that portion of the native community whose influence is hurtful, have been so successful as not to obstruct but greatly to promote the happiness of the cheerful, industrious group.

In 1839, Mrs. Coan of Hilo undertook to sustain and teach a boarding-school for girls, with such aid as she could obtain from the pupils and their parents, and other natives. Twenty girls were taken under her instruction and superintendence, the annual expenses of the school, aside from the support of Mrs. C., being about $400. The pupils are clothed in a cheap cotton fabric— sit at a table spread with kalo, potatoes, fish, and arrow-root. They work in a beautiful garden, for exercise and pleasure, are taught in school the common branches. They form a group of happy hearts and bright faces, are easily governed, are attentive and affectionate, and repeatedly blessed with the influence of the Spirit. Within six years from the commencement of this enterprise, the girls of the oldest class were nearly all married and appeared well, and a new class had taken their place under their persevering teacher.

The boarding-school of equal promise under the charge of Mr. and Mrs. Lyman from 1837, has continued to flourish, having from thirty to sixty boys as pupils. In 1845 thirty-five were church members, seventeen had entered the Mission Seminary at Lahainaluna, and twenty-three others were prepared to enter it who could not then be received.

At Waialua, Oahu, a manual labor boarding-school for boys was established, of which Mr. Locke laid the foundation and took the charge. The pupils numbered from fifteen to twenty-two, and were taught the common branches. The boys labored in the field a part of the time to train them to business and to procure their living. The experiment advanced with promise for a few years; but afflictions early clustered on the school. The first born of Mr. and Mrs. Locke, returning from the field, was drowned in the river. Next Mrs. L. was removed by death, and shortly after, Mr. Locke finished his race, which he had, as a missionary, but recently begun. Their three little orphan daughters have been brought by Mr. A. B. Smith to the United States to find an asylum in the bosom of Christian kindness.

At Waioli, Kauai, in the neighborhood of grand and picturesque scenery, a select school has been established, for training teachers and fitting scholars for the Mission Seminary, and for the business of life. It is partly a boarding-school, as many of the pupils are boarded by church members, and partly a manual labor school, systematic instruction being given in that department. It has been chiefly under the care of Mr. and Mrs. Johnson, and affords instruction to from thirty-five to seventy-five boys.

Station or select schools are maintained at nearly all the stations, as model schools, and as the means of bringing forward the rising generation to take their part in teaching, and in other duties of life. One of these was taught at Honolulu by Mr. and Mrs. Knapp in a first rate school-house built by the natives.

Numerous common schools are provided for by the state, and are under governmental direction, affording scope for a minister of instruction, and a number of native school inspectors, but somewhat embárrassed by papists. A school for the education of the children of the missionaries, the Board has established at Punahou, about two miles north of east from the harbor of Honolulu. Mr. and Mrs. Dole took charge of it in 1841. Miss M. Smith, and since the death of Mrs. Dole, Mr. and Mrs. Rice have taken part in the institution. In 1845 seventeen boarding-scholars and seven day-scholars were favored with its valued advantages.

The native churches, for the first twenty years of the mission, were independent of each other, and were generally in the care of a missionary or *Episcopos* Apostolic. Other officers have been introduced during the great revival.

In the government of those churches, whether Congregational, or Presbyterian, or under the direction of an *Episcopos*, discipline has been generally prompt and rigid. The tests of membership, and the by-laws of some of them, are, perhaps, more severe in some respects than most evangelical churches adopt.

The missionaries, who, like evangelical ministers generally, require *perfection* in professors of the Gospel, but not as indispensable to communion, for various reasons wished the Hawaiian churches and habitations to be as free from tobacco smoke as a lady's parlor.

Before the Gospel was extensively acknowledged, the people, though able to command few luxuries, were fond of smoking tobacco, and all classes, men, women, and children, indulged extensively in the practice, which would be injurious in any community. They usually cultivated and cured the article for themselves, and made their own pipes, commonly of wood. In the practice of smoking they often exercised a pleasant, sociable disposition, amid their destitution, and the pipe was, doubtless, a more common treat among them than tea, coffee, or wine in any country. A circle meeting on any occasion, generally lighted a pipe and passed it round, each taking two or three whiffs, throwing the last into the chest. The design was sometimes mischievous, and the effect generally evil. A long match of the shreds of kapa

was often seen slowly burning for lighting the smoker's pipe, by
which means their frail habitations were sometimes ignited and
burnt down, occasionally with the loss of life.

When the evils of the habit, as filthy, expensive, unnecessarily stimulating, and deleterious to health and life, were pointed
out by the missionaries, and abstinence recommended, many natives relinquished the practice, became tetotalers, and urged their
countrymen to abstain, and in a few years, thousands pledged
themselves not only to abstain from intoxicating liquors, but
from tobacco, and some of the native churches adopted the rule
not to receive smokers.   In 1843, the mission briefly notice
this subject thus :—

" Many of us believing the cultivation and use of tobacco to be an
immorality, tending to diffuse evil and not good in the world, have
conscientiously taken of our candidates for church fellowship, the
pledge of total abstinence in this matter, consequently when they violate their pledge they become subjects of censure.   Many of our number do not agree with those in the ground taken on this subject ; but
this difference of opinion does not alienate our feelings nor disturb the
spirit of brotherly love.   We agree to differ, still loving each other as
brethren, and still holding ourselves open to argument and conviction,
and still praying that the Spirit of truth may lead us to see eye to eye
in this and all other things."

As the influence of drinks and drugs on the human constitution
and on human society is much the same in all countries, it might
be safe perhaps to make no test in regard to their use for the converts of one country, which should not be applicable to those of
another.   Nor should converts from heathenism whom Christ
accepts, and who are bound to honor him in his ordinances, be
required, in order to enter the church, to pledge themselves to
any course of virtue or abstinence to which the will of God or the
general good, do not bind both them and others, whether they are
pledged or not.   Still, if any native church which has its rights,
thinks it has authority from Christ to make by-laws for itself, to
receive none to its fellowship who use any particular drug or drink,
it must be allowed to try it, if such church is not equally bound to
guard against schism, and to facilitate rather than embarrass the rightful use of the ordinances according to their design as the means of
approaching and honoring Christ. In my apprehension, preaching,
and Christian counsel, instead of *ecclesiastical authority*, are appointed for the management of these and many like matters ; while
scandalous offences which, if persisted in, prove *apostasy*, are to be
rebuked and restrained by the authority of the church, and while
the conscience of the true disciple is allowed to gain light and
strength under the edifying power of Christian ordinances, too
often undervalued.

Let us now turn again to the government.

To secure the recognition, explicit acknowledgment, and guarantee of Hawaiian independence among the great powers of the earth, was an object of deep interest to Kamehameha III., and his more intelligent chiefs and the friends of order and justice, who were acquainted with the circumstances of the people. The nation, therefore, came forward, not to demand by their numbers, wealth, or power, but to present their claims, though few and poor and weak, to be received into the family of Christianized and civilized nations.

To bring the condition of his country under the consideration of the government of the United States, and of the sovereigns of France and the British empire, the king, in 1840, endeavored to engage the services of a legal gentleman of the United States, but after spending a thousand dollars found that unforeseen difficulties prevented his accomplishing the embassy.

Feeling his difficulties and dangers, the king, in the autumn of 1841, addressed letters on the subject to the King of the French, the Queen of Great Britain, and the President of the United States, and sent them by a confidential hand, to ensure their safe delivery.

The same year I was permitted to visit Washington, when I presented to Congress a copy of the Bible in the Hawaiian language, and in the capitol, detailed briefly the progress of events at the islands from 1819 to 1841.

In 1842, the king resolved on employing an embassy, with power to negotiate; and to meet the case, appointed Sir George Simpson, a high-minded and philanthropic Englishman, Governor of the Hon. Hudson's Bay Company's territory, and Mr. William Richards, well acquainted with Hawaiian affairs, and full in the confidence of the government, and Haalilio, the king's friend and secretary, a Hawaiian of distinguished worth.

A visit of Sir George at this time at the Sandwich Islands, gave him a good opportunity of judging for himself of the state of things there. He returned to England; and in July, 1842, Messrs. Richards and Hoalilio embarked to go by the shortest route to Washington, and thence to London and Paris.

Being kindly received at Washington by the President, they, by correspondence with the department of state, presented to the consideration of the government, the condition of the Hawaiian Islands, and the wishes of their sovereign. The correspondence between them and Mr. Calhoun was, by Pres. Tyler, laid before Congress, with the following favorable message :—

To the House of Representatives of the United States.

" I communicate herewith to Congress copies of a correspondence, which has recently taken place between certain agents of the Government of the Hawaiian or Sandwich Islands, and the Secretary of State.

" The condition of those Islands has excited a good deal of interest, which is increasing by every successive proof that their inhabitants are making progress in civilization, and becoming more and more competent to maintain regular and orderly civil government. They lie in the Pacific ocean, much nearer to this continent than the other, and have become an important place for the refitment and provisioning of American and European vessels.

" Owing to their locality, and to the course of the winds which prevail in this quarter of the world, the Sandwich Islands are the stopping place for almost all vessels passing from continent to continent across the Pacific ocean. They are especially resorted to by the great numbers of vessels of the United States which are engaged in the whale fishery in those seas. The number of vessels of all sorts and the amount of property owned by citizens of the United States which are found in those Islands in the course of a year, are stated, probably with sufficient accuracy, in the letter of the agents.

" Just emerging from a state of barbarism, the Government of the Islands is as yet feeble ; but its dispositions appear to be just and pacific, and it seems anxious to improve the condition of its people by the introduction of knowledge, of religious and moral institutions, means of education, and the arts of civilized life.

" It cannot but be in conformity with the interest and the wishes of the government and the people of the United States that this community, thus existing in the midst of a vast expanse of ocean, should be respected, and all its rights strictly and conscientiously regarded. And this must also be the true interest of all other commercial States. Far remote from the dominions of European Powers, its growth and prosperity as an independent State may yet be in a high degree useful to all, whose trade is extended to those regions ; while its nearer approach to this continent, and the intercourse which American vessels have with it —such vessels constituting five-sixths of all which annually visit it—could not but create dissatisfaction on the part of the United States at any attempt, by another Power, should such attempt be threatened or feared, to take possession of the islands, colonize them, and subvert the native Government. Considering, therefore, that the United States possesses so very large a share of the intercourse with those Islands, it is deemed not unfit to make the declaration, that their Government seeks, nevertheless, no peculiar advantages, no exclusive control over the Hawaiian Government, but is content with its independent existence, and anxiously wishes for its security and prosperity. Its forbearance in this respect, under the circumstances of the very large intercourse of their citizens with the Islands, would justify this Government, should events hereafter arise to require it, in making a decided remonstrance against the adoption of an opposite policy by any other Power. Under the circumstances, I recommend to Congress to provide for a moderate allowance to be made out of the Treasury to the Consul residing there, that, in a Government so new and a country so remote, American citizens may have respectable authority to which to apply for redress in case of injury to their persons and property ; and to whom the Government of the country may also make known any acts committed by American citizens of which it may think it has a right to complain."

The subject was referred to the Committee on Foreign Affairs, the Hon. **J. Q.** Adams being chairman, who concurring with the President, and happily grouping the claims of the little Sandwich Islands with populous China, made a report highly honorable to its author, and to the body which adopted it, as follows :—

" The Committee on Foreign Affairs, to whom was referred the message of the President of the United States of December 30, 1842, concerning the present condition of the relations, commercial and political, of the United States with the Sandwich Islands and with the Chinese Empire, and recommending to the consideration of Congress the expediency of adopting measures for cultivating and improving those relations, respectfully report :

" That, concurring in the views of the President, as expressed in the message, with regard to the intercourse with those remote regions, suited to the best interests of the United States, and adapted to the promotion of benevolence and good will between brethren of the human family, separated heretofore not only by geographical distances to the utmost ends of the earth, but by institutions, in both extremes, of barbarism and of civilization, alienating from one another the various tribes of man, children of one common parent, and born for mutual assistance in the purpose of promoting the happiness of all— they report for the consideration of the House, two bills, to enable the President to carry into effect the purposes set forth in the message.

" Peace—friendly, social, and commercial intercourse—and the reciprocation of good offices with *all* nations, was proclaimed as the fundamental policy of this Union, from the day and in the instrument with which the North American people, till then English colonists, ' assumed among the powers of the earth that separate and equal station to which the laws of Nature and of Nature's God entitle them.' At that time more than one half the surface of the habitable globe was hermetically sealed up against them, and inaccessible to them. A series of events, all emanating from one beneficent Providence, but wonderfully various, and seemingly antagonistical in their original character, have unlocked or burst open the gates of countries ranging from the equator to the pole, in both continents of America, in the central darkness of Africa, and in the continental islands of Australasia.

" At that time the Sandwich Islands were yet undiscovered by the race of civilized man ; and China, from ocean to ocean, had surrounded herself, from ages immemorial, by a wall, within which her population, counting by hundreds of millions, were pent up in sullen separation and seclusion from all the rest of mankind. Within one year from the day when the United States were first acknowledged as a nation, the discoverer of the Sandwich Islands (the most illustrious navigator of the eighteenth century) perished on their shore by the hands of their savage barbarian inhabitants.

" It is a subject of cheering contemplation to the friends of human improvement and virtue, that, by the mild and gentle influence of Christian charity, dispensed by humble missionaries of the Gospel, unarmed with secular power, within the last quarter of a century, the people of this group of islands have been converted from the lowest debasement of idolatry to the blessings of the Christian Gospel ;

united under one balanced government ; rallied to the fold of civilization by a written language and constitution, providing security for the rights of persons, property, and mind, and invested with all the elements of right and power which can entitle them to be acknowledged by their brethren of the human race as a separate and independent community.   To the consummation of their acknowledgment, the people of the North American Union are urged by an interest of their own, deeper than that of any other portion of the inhabitants of the earth—by a virtual right of conquest, not over the freedom of their brother man by the brutal arm of physical power, but over the mind and heart by the celestial panoply of the gospel of peace and love."

Acknowledging the independence of the islands as formally as was their custom, the government appointed Mr. George Brown as a commissioner to reside at the Sandwich Islands as the representative of the government of the United States. He repaired to his post, where he was kindly received by the king and chiefs, and for a time was highly respected, and apparently friendly to the native government.

Mr. Charlton, the British Consul, finding the king had sent Commissioners on this embassy, suddenly left the islands on board a vessel where Mr. Alexander Simpson had engaged a passage for himself, sending back from that vessel in Honolulu roads, Mr. Simpson, deputed to exercise the consular functions *pro tempore*, and hastened to England, not to aid the commissioners in so noble and desirable a plan, but apparently to circumvent them by creating a prejudice at the foreign office against the government of the Sandwich Islands.

But Sir George Simpson, Capt. Jones of the R. N., and Messrs. Richards and Haalilio, by a timely and fair statement of facts, were able at length to counteract the intended mischief.   Those English gentlemen had both visited the islands of Hawaii, and becoming acquainted with the clashing interests there, and the shameful conduct of some of their fellow subjects and others, had been favorably impressed with the honesty, honor, integrity, and efficiency of the Hawaiian government, and its readiness to administer justice, if unmolested by foreign powers.

The Earl of Aberdeen, glancing through the consul, could not perceive any good reason for his deserting his post uncalled, disapproved of the insolent bearing of his official communications, and easily disposed of most of his complaints, leaving one question for him to settle at Oahu, whether his deed of a large part of Honolulu were genuine, forged, or otherwise fraudulent ; removed him from his office, and appointed Gen. Wm. Miller as consul general for the Sandwich and Society Islands.

Before the commissioners could reach Paris, the French Sloop of War Embuscade arrived at the islands, and the following correspondence occurred between Captain Mallet and the king, touching national claims, national rights, and national dignity.

SIRE,

I have the honor to inform your majesty, that since the treaties of July 12th and 17th, 1839, French citizens and ministers of the Catholic religion have been insulted and subjected to divers unjust measures, concerning which your majesty has not, probably, been informed. Subordinate agents, ignorant or ill disposed, and without any special order from the government, have thrown down churches, threatened the priests, and compelled their disciples to attend Protestant places of worship, and Protestant schools. To effect this, they have employed a course of treatment repulsive to humanity, notwithstanding the treaty of July 12th, signed by your majesty and the commandant of the French frigate Artemise, grants free exercise to the Catholic religion, and an equal protection to its ministers.

" Persuaded that your majesty has no intention that treaties, entered into in good faith, should be annulled, and also that it is incumbent upon you to treat all religions with favor, therefore I shall demand that you will adopt such measures as shall defend the adherents of the Catholic faith from all future vexations.

" I demand, therefore, of your majesty,

" 1st. That a Catholic High School, with the same privileges as the High School at Lahainaluna, be immediately acknowledged, and that a lot of land be granted to it by Government, according to promise.

" 2d. That the Catholic schools be under the exclusive supervision of Catholic Kahukulas (Inspectors) nominated by Kahunas of the same faith, and approved by your majesty ; and that these Kahukulas enjoy without infraction all the privileges granted by the law.

" 3d. That the Kahunas have power to fill, temporarily, all vacancies that may occur in consequence of the death, absence, or loss of office of any of the Kahukulas.

" 4th. That for the future, permission to marry be given by Catholics, nominated by the Kahunas, and approved always by the government of your majesty : and that in case of death, absence, or loss of office, the Kahunas have power, provisionally, to grant permission themselves.

" 5th. That hereafter Catholics be not forced to labor upon schools, or churches of a different faith, and that the relations of children, who may embrace the Catholic religion, be not ill-treated on this account.

" 6th. That severe punishment be inflicted upon any individual, whatever may be his rank or condition, who shall destroy a Catholic church, or school, or insult the ministers of this religion.

" Furthermore, I demand of your majesty that you will confirm to the French mission the land which was given it by Boki, when regent of the kingdom, which land has always been considered as belonging to said mission ; and also, that you legalize the purchase of the land made by his lordship, the Bishop of Nicopolis, by a sanction which will confirm it to his lordship, and to his heirs for ever.

" I will not conclude what relates to the Catholic clergy without praying your majesty to give me proof that the Abbé Maigret has signed a writing, by which he acknowledges himself a British subject Should this prove to be a mere calumny, invented for the purpose of ruining a French priest in the estimation of the inhabitants of these isles, and that of your majesty, I demand that the author of this calumny, John Ii, the inspector general, retract in writing, declaring either that he lied about it, or that he had been deceived. As a Frenchman, I deem it important to be fully satisfied on this point.

" There is still another subject, concerning which I must demand some explanation of your majesty. According to article 6th of the treaty of July 17th, French wines and spirits were to be admitted into the islands of your government, on paying a duty of five per cent. Was it not for the purpose of eluding this article (not to say violating it) that the sale of brandy has been limited to a certain number of gallons ?

" I cannot prevent your majesty from enacting such laws as the prosperity and well-being of your subjects seem to you to demand, but I consider it my duty to inquire how you can reconcile the 6th article of the treaty of July 17th, with the last law concerning the sale of spirits in the islands of your kingdom. It would give me great pleasure to be informed on this subject, in order to make my report to the Admiral, Commander in Chief of the French Forces in the Pacific Ocean, that he may decide upon such a course as he shall judge expedient for the maintenance of treaties and of our national dignity.

" I have the honor to be, with the most profound respect, Sire, your majesty's very humble servant.

(Signed), " S. MALLET.
" Captain of the Sloop of War Embuscade."

" HONOLULU, SEPTEMBER 4TH, 1842.

" To S. Mallet, Captain of the French Ship of War, the Embuscade, Greeting :—

" We have received your letter, dated the 1st inst., and with our council assembled, have deliberated thereon, and we are happy to receive your testimony that if there are instances of difficulty or abuse in these islands, they are not authorized by this government, and we assure you that we hold in high estimation the government of France, and all its estimable subjects. It is the firm determination of our government to observe the treaties with all nations, but the written laws are a new thing, the people are ignorant, and good order can only be preserved on the part of the government by affording the protection of the laws to all who will appeal to them at the proper tribunals.

" On the introduction of the Roman Catholic religion it was understood that toleration was to be fully allowed to all its priests and all its disciples, and this has been done as far as lay in our power, and no one can prove to the contrary ; but it is impossible to put a stop to disputes and contentions between rival religions, and the evils and complaints which result therefrom.

" The laws favor literature, and as soon as the French priests are ready to found a High School for the purpose of imparting it to their pupils, and teachers are ready, it shall find a location.

" The School Laws were formed to promote education in these islands, and not sectarianism, and no one should ask the government

that they be altered to favor any particular sect.   Any man qualified
for teaching, being of good moral character, is entitled to a teacher's
diploma, this by reason of his acquirements, not his sect.   No priest
of either sect can give diplomas.   Likewise marriage is regulated by
law, and no priest, of either sect, can perform the ceremony except the
parties obtain a certificate from the governor or his officer, and why
should the laws be altered ?   Difficulties often arise on this subject, and
we should regulate our own people.

" The laws require the people to labor on certain days ; some for
the government, and some for the landlords to whom the labor is due
according to law, and the kind of labor is regulated by those to whom
the labor is due.

" The laws are not fully established in all parts of the islands, and
probably an ancient custom has been practised, by which the owner of
land would pull down the house of one who built thereon without his
cheerful assent, but if the owner of the house complains to the judges,
they should grant a trial, and if no satisfaction is obtained, then the
governor will grant a trial, and if that decision is unjust, an appeal
must be made to the supreme judges, who will sit twice a year.

" The ground occupied by the French priests in Honolulu, is held
by the same tenure as that of the priests of the Protestant religion, and
some other foreigners; and negotiations have been commenced which
it is to be hoped will give equal justice to all.

" When John Ii arrives from Kauai, that case will be adjusted,
and if he denies the charge which you have presented, a trial will be
granted.

" Please do us the favor to assure the admiral that the present laws
do not contravene the 6th article of the treaty of the 17th July.   Brandy and wines are freely admitted here, and if any one wishes a license
to retail spirits, he may procure one by applying to the proper officers.
Those who retail spirits without license are liable to punishment.
Please inform him also that we have sent ministers to the King of
France, to beg of him a new treaty between us and him.

" Accept for yourself the assurance of our respect and our salutations.

(Signed),   " KAMEHAMEHA III.
(Signed),   " KEKAULUOHI.
" Translation certified to be correct by G. P. JUDD."

This dignified answer, and the fact that his majesty had sent commissioners to France for the purpose of negotiating with the government of Louis Philippe, may have deterred the captain from
further encroachments.

The king, having received a protest from two British subjects
against acknowledging Mr. Simpson as acting consul, on the
ground of his declared hostility to the government, refused to
receive him.

Her Majesty's Ship Carysfort arrived at Honolulu early in
Feb., 1843, and her captain, Lord George Paulet, after an interview
with Mr. Simpson, the deputy consul, commenced a course of
proceedings which equity could not detail but with grief, as the
following correspondence, published by authority of the Ha-

waiian government, will, with little or no comment, demonstrate :—

"*Her Britannic Majesty's Ship Carysfort, Oahu, 11th of Feb.*, 1843.

Sir,—Having arrived at this port in Her Britannic Majesty's Ship
Carysfort, under my command, for the purpose of affording protection
to British subjects, as likewise to support the position of her Britannic
Majesty's representative here, who has received repeated insults from
the government authorities of these islands, respecting which it is
my intention to communicate only with the king in person :

" I require to have immediate information by return of the officer
conveying this despatch whether or not the king (in consequence of my
arrival) has been notified that his presence will be required here and
the earliest day on which he may be expected, as otherwise I shall be
compelled to proceed to his residence in the ship under my command,
for the purpose of communicating with him.

" I have the honor to be, sir, your most obedient, humble servant,
" GEORGE PAULET,   Captain.
" To Kekuanaoa, Governor of Oahu, &c., &c."

" *Honolulu, February* 11*th*, 1843.

" Salutations to you, Lord George Paulet, Captain of H. B. M.
Ship Carysfort :—I have received your letter by the hand of the officer,
and with respect, inform you that we have not sent for the king, as we
were not informed of the business, but having learned from your communication that you wish him sent for, I will search for a vessel and
send. He is at Wailuku on the east side of Maui. In case the wind
is favorable he may be expected in six days.

" Yours with respect,
" M. KEKUANAOA."

On the king's arrival at Honolulu, he received the following :—

" *H. B. M. Ship Carysfort, Honolulu harbor, Feb.* 16*th*, 1843.

" Sir ;—I have the honor to acquaint your Majesty of (with) the
arrival in this port of H. B. M. ship, under my command, and according to my instructions I am desired to demand a private interview with
you, to which I shall proceed with a proper and competent interpreter.

" I, therefore, request to be informed at what hour to-morrow it
will be convenient for your majesty to grant me an interview.

" I have the honor to remain your majesty's most obedient, humble
servant,
" GEORGE PAULET, Captain."

The fact and the day of the private interview and the accompanying interpreter, he fixes himself, and wished to be informed
of the hour, when the king, without attendant, officer, or interpreter, will meet his lordship, who received the following appropriate reply :

" *Honolulu, February* 17*th*, 1843.

" Salutations to you, Lord George Paulet, Captain of Her Britannic
Majesty's Ship Carysfort.

" Sir :—We have received your communication of yesterday's date, and must decline having any private interview, especially under the circumstances you propose. We shall be ready to receive any written communication from you to-morrow, and will give it due consideration. In case you have business of a private nature we will appoint Dr. Judd our confidential agent to confer with you, who, being a person of integrity and fidelity to our government, and perfectly acquainted with all our affairs, will receive your communications, give all the information you require (in confidence), and report the same to us.

" With respect,

" KAMEHAMEHA III.

" KEKAULUOHI."

Her Britannic Majesty's Ship Carysfort, Oahu, 17th Feb., 1843.

" Sir :—In answer to your letter of this day's date (which I have too good an opinion of your majesty to allow me to believe it ever emanated from yourself, but from your ill advisers), I have to state that I shall hold no communication whatever with Doct. G. P. Judd, who, it has been satisfactorily proved to me, has been the prime mover in the unlawful proceedings of your government against British subjects.

" As you have refused me a personal interview, I enclose to you the demands which I consider it my duty to make upon your government ; with which I demand a compliance at or before four o'clock P. M., to-morrow (Saturday), otherwise I shall be obliged to take immediate coercive steps to obtain these measures for my countrymen.

" I have the honor to be your majesty's most obedient, humble servant,

" GEORGE PAULET, Captain."

" Demands made by the Right Honorable Lord George Paulet, Captain R. N., commanding her Britannic Majesty's Ship Carysfort, upon the king of the Sandwich Islands.

" First. The immediate removal by public advertisement, written in the native and English languages and signed by the governor of this island and F. W. Thompson, of the attachment placed upon Mr. Charlton's property ; the restoration of the land taken by the government for its own use and really appertaining to Mr. Charlton, and reparation for the heavy loss to which Mr. Charlton's representative has been exposed by the oppressive and unjust proceedings of the Sandwich Islands government.

" Second. The immediate acknowledgment of the right of Mr. Simpson to perform the functions delegated to him by Mr. Charlton ; namely, those of Her Britannic Majesty's acting consul ; until Her Majesty's pleasure be known upon the reasonableness of your objections to him. The acknowledgment of that right and the reparation for the insult offered to Her Majesty through her acting representative, to be made by a public reception of his commission and the saluting the British flag with twenty-one guns—which number will be returned by her Britannic Majesty's ship under my command.

" Third. A guarantee that no British subject shall be subjected to imprisonment in fetters, unless he is accused of a crime which by the laws of England would be considered a felony.

"Fourth. The compliance with a written promise given by King Kamehameha to Captain Jones of the Curacoa, that a new and fair trial would be granted in a case brought by Henry Skinner, which promise has been evaded.

"Fifth. The immediate adoption of firm steps to arrange the matters in dispute between British subjects and natives of the country or others residing here by referring these cases to juries, one half of whom shall be British subjects approved by the consul, and all of whom shall declare on oath, their freedom from prejudgment upon, or interest in, the cases brought before them.

"Sixth. A direct communication between His Majesty Kamehameha and Her Majesty's acting consul for the immediate settlement of all cases of grievances and complaints on the part of British subjects against the Sandwich Islands government.

"Dated on board H. B. M. Ship Carysfort, at Oahu, this 17th day of February, 1843.

"GEORGE PAULET, Captain."

He, at the same time, apprised Captain Long, of the U. S. Ship Boston, then in port, that the Carysfort would be prepared to make an attack on the town, at four o'clock, P. M., the next day, unless his demands were complied with.

The government of a people, once savage and delighting in war, and ready to attack and destroy even unoffending naval officers, and capture ships, were now disposed to peace and equity, and resolved to yield rather than break friendship with Great Britain, and made the following reply, which was construed to concede more than was even temporarily intended :—

"Honolulu, Feb. 18th, 1843.

"Salutations to Rt. Hon. Lord George Paulet, Captain of H. B. M. Ship Carysfort ;

"We have received your letter and the demands which accompanied it, and in reply, would inform your lordship that we have commissioned Sir George Simpson and William Richards as our Ministers Plenipotentiary and Envoys Extraordinary to the Court of Great Britain, with full powers to settle the difficulties which you have presented before us, to assure Her Majesty, the queen, of our uninterrupted affection, and to confer with her ministers as to the best means of cementing the harmony between us.   Some of the demands which you have laid before us are of a nature calculated seriously to embarrass our feeble government, by contravening the laws established for the benefit of all.

"But we shall comply with your demands, as it has never been our intention to insult Her Majesty, the queen, or injure any of her estimable subjects ; but we must do so under protest, and shall embrace the earliest opportunity of representing our case more fully to Her Britannic Majesty's government through our minister, trusting in the magnanimity of the sovereign of a great nation which we have been taught to respect and love,—that we shall then be justified.

"Waiting your further orders,
"With sentiments of respect,
"KAMEHAMEHA III
"KEKAULUOHI."

After an interview, and acknowledgment of the acting consul, such exorbitant demands were made and peremptorily urged, that the king deemed it impossible to comply and preserve his independence, and being urged by various parties to cede his country to one of the Great Powers (though his " constitutional *right*" to do so without the consent of the people is questionable), he considered that subject with much pain.   He found that the United States would not accept it.   He felt that France had injured him, so that his people would never forgive him should he cede his country to France, and having great confidence in Queen Victoria, whom he could not suspect of having authorized either Mr. Charlton, or Mr. Simpson, or Lord George Paulet to oppress him, yielded to the pressure, and in concurrence with the premier, made with anguish the cession of his country as follows :—

" In consequence of the difficulties in which we find ourselves involved, and our opinion of the impossibility of complying with the demands in the manner in which they are made by her Britannic Majesty's representative upon us, in reference to the claims of British subjects ; We do hereby cede the group of islands known as the Hawaiian (or Sandwich) Islands, unto the Right Honorable Lord George Paulet, Capt. of her Britannic Majesty's ship of war Carysfort, representing her Majesty Victoria Queen of Great Britain and Ireland from this date and for the time being ; the said cession being made with the reservation that it is subject to any arrangement that may have been entered into by the Representatives appointed by us to treat with the Government of her Britannic Majesty, and in the event that no agreement has been executed previous to the date hereof, subject to the decision of her Britannic Majesty's Government on conference with the said Representatives appointed by us ; or in the event of our Representatives not being accessible, or not having been acknowledged, subject to the decision which her Britannic Majesty may pronounce on the receipt of full information from us, and from the Right Honorable Lord George Paulet.

" In confirmation of the above, we hereby affix our names and seals, this twenty-fifth day of February, in the year of our Lord one thousand eight hundred and forty-three, at Honolulu, Oahu, Sandwich Islands.

" KAMEHAMEHA III.
" KEKAULUOHI."

The same day Lord Paulet made the following proclamation :—

" A Provisional Cession of the Hawaiian or Sandwich Islands having been made this day by KAMEHAMEHA III., King, and KEKAULUOHI, Premier thereof, unto me, The Right Hon. Lord George Paulet, commanding Her Britannic Majesty's Ship Carysfort on the part of Her Britannic Majesty, Victoria, Queen of Great Britain and Ireland ; subject to arrangements which may have been or shall be made in Great Britain, with the Government of H. B. Majesty.

" I do hereby proclaim,

" FIRST, That the British Flag shall he hoisted on all the Islands of the Group : and the natives thereof shall enjoy the protection and privileges of British subjects.

" SECOND, That the Government thereof shall be executed, until the receipt of communications from Great Britain, in the following manner :—namely, by the native king and chiefs and the officers employed by them, so far as regards the native population ; and by a Commission, consisting of King Kamehameha III., or a deputy appointed by him, The Right Honorable Lord George Paulet, Duncan Forbes Mackay, Esquire, and Lieutenant Frere, R. N., in all that concerns relations with other powers (save and except the negotiations with the British Government), and the arrangements among Foreigners (others than natives of the Archipelago) resident on these Islands.

" THIRD, That the laws at present existing, or which may be made at the ensuing Council of the King and Chiefs (after being communicated to the Commission), shall be in full force so far as natives are concerned ; and shall form the basis of the administration of justice by the Commission, in matters between foreigners resident on these Islands.

" FOURTH, In all that relates to the collection of the revenue, the present officers shall be continued at the pleasure of the native King and chiefs, their salaries for the current year being also determined by them, and the archives of Government remaining in their hands ; the accounts are, however, subject to inspection by the Commission herebefore named. The Government vessels shall be in like manner : subject, however, to their employment if required for Her Britannic Majesty's service.

" FIFTH, That no sales, leases, or transfers of land shall take place by the action of the Commission appointed as aforesaid, nor from natives to Foreigners, during the period intervening between the 24th of this month, and the receipt of notification from Great Britain of the arrangements made there : they shall not be valid, nor shall they receive the signatures of the King and Premier.

" SIXTH, All the existing *bona fide* engagements of the native King and Premier shall be executed and performed as if this Cession had never been made.

" Given under my hand this twenty-fifth day of February, in the year of our Lord one thousand eight hundred and forty three, at Honolulu, Oahu, Sandwich Islands.

" GEORGE PAULET,
"Captain of H. B. M. S. Carysfort.

" Signed in the presence of
" G. P. JUDD, *Rec. and Int. to the Govt.*
" ALEX. SIMPSON, *H. B. M. acting Consul.*"

This document was publicly read, and the national flag lowered and the British hoisted in its stead. The king addressed the people in a few words well adapted, by their tenderness, wisdom, and force, to keep them from resenting the injury which the nation had received, and to inspire them with confidence that their cause would be more favorably judged in Great Britain, as follows :—

" Where are you, chiefs, people, and commons from my ancestor, and people from foreign lands? Hear ye, I make known to you that I am in perplexity by reason of difficulties into which I have been brought without cause; therefore I have given away the life of our land, hear ye! But my rule over you, my people, and your privileges will continue, for I have hope that the life of the land will be restored when my conduct shall be justified."

He sent despatches to Great Britain by B. F. Marshall, Esq. He deputed Dr. Judd, who had resigned his commission as assistant missionary, to take part in the commission which entered on the labors of the provisional government, no easy or enviable task.

Not only was the Hawaiian banner brought down temporarily, but the standard of loyalty was lowered among the people, and the useful principle of deference to kings, constitutions, and laws partially undermined, for the people had lost, in a measure, their hereditary and constitutional king and protector, the *breath* of the nation, the power to speak for itself, being surrendered to other hands, the barriers against intemperance, licentiousness, and Sabbath desecration were weakened or broken down, and a species of anarchy manifested itself; but thousands of the believers of the Gospel, the salt of the land, stood firm in their integrity, mourned over the follies and wickedness of the lovers of pleasure and sin, and strove to avert the mischief which this partial revolution threatened, and with their friends desired a speedy restoration. Finding it impracticable to act with the British commission without participating in a policy which he deemed enormous, the king protested and withdrew in the following manner :—

" Know all men, That according to private instructions given to our Deputy, he on the 10th of May issued a Protest on our behalf in the following words :

" Whereas, the undersigned was by Commission dated Feb. 27, 1843, appointed Deputy for his Majesty Kamehameha III., to the British Commission for the Government of the Sandwich Islands, under the Provisional Cession thereof unto Her Most Gracious Majesty Victoria, Queen of the United Kingdoms of Great Britain and Ireland :

" And whereas, in the prosecution of business by the Commissioners, many acts have been passed and consummated affecting the interests of foreigners, resident on these Islands, and acts which virtually abrogate the *bona fide* obligations of the Government existing at the period of the Provisional Cession ; to which acts the said Kamehameha III. did refuse assent through me his Deputy :

" And whereas, by an order issued April 27, 1843, to the Acting Governor of Oahu, and by subsequent orders, dated May 8th, 1843, issued to all the Governors of these Sandwich Islands, the Commissioners, to wit, the Rt. Hon. Lord George Paulet, Captain of H. B. M. Ship Carysfort, and Lieut. John Frere, R. N., did virtually abrogate one of the existing laws of these Islands, by forbidding the imprisonment of persons found guilty of fornication, except in certain cases, not specified in the laws, as will appear more fully upon reference to said orders, violating thereby the solemn compact entered into under the Provisional Cession.

" Now, therefore, Be it known to all men, that I, the said deputy for the said King, KAMEHAMEHA III., do by these Presents, enter this my most solemn Protest against the acts, especially those above recited, of the said Commissioners, which have not the signature and approbation of me, the said Deputy, as will appear more fully upon reference to the Records of said Commission.

" And I do hereby most solemnly protest against the said Right Hon. Lord George Paulet, and Lieut. Frere, Commissioners aforesaid, and all others whom it may concern, holding them responsible for their violation of the solemn Compact or Treaty entered into on the 25th day of February, 1843.

G. P. JUDD, Deputy for the King."
Honolulu, Oahu, Sandwich Islands, May 10, 1843.

" On the next day our Deputy withdrew from the British Commission by the following document, acting in our place and stead.

" Whereas, the undersigned Deputy for the King KAMEHAMEHA III., did, on the 10th day of May inst., enter his protest against certain Acts of the British Commissioners for the Government of the Sandwich Islands :

" And whereas, the undersigned has been verbally informed this day, by the Rt. Hon. Lord George Paulet and Lieut. Frere, that one of the laws as made at the recent Council of the King and Chiefs, viz., ' A law for the Licensing of Public Auctioneers,' shall not go into operation.

" And whereas, it now appearing evident to the undersigned that the terms of the Compact or Treaty entered into on the 25th of February, 1843, will not in future be respected by the British Commission :

" Therefore, Be it known to all men, that I, the said Deputy, Do by these Presents, resign my seat in the said Commission, thereby withdrawing the said King KAMEHAMEHA III., from all future responsibilities in the acts of the said Commission.

G. P. JUDD, Deputy for the King.
Done at Honolulu, Oahu, Sandwich Islands, at the Office of the British Commission for the Government of the Sandwich Islands, this 11th day of May, A. D., 1843."

" We, therefore, publicly make known that we, KAMEHAMEHA III., the King, fully approve and acknowledge the Protest and withdrawal of our Deputy as our own, and declare that we will no more sit with the British Commissioners, or be responsible for any acts of theirs which may encroach on the rights of foreigners.

" The Rt. Hon. Lord George Paulet and his Lieut. John Frere, having enlisted soldiers under the title of ' the Queen's Regiment,' maintaining them as a standing army out of funds appropriated by us for the payment of our just debts, which expense we consider quite uncalled for and useless ; they having enforced their demand for the payment of the money by a threat of deposing from his trust an officer of the Treasury, although contrary to the orders of the King and Premier to him, made known to the British Commissioners :

" By these oppressions, by the trial of natives for alleged offences against the native government, cases which come not properly under their cognizance, and by their violating the laws, which, by the Treaty, were to have been held sacred until we hear from England; we are oppressed and injured, and feel confident that all good men will sympathize with us in our present state of distress; and now we Protest in the face of all men, against all such proceedings both towards ourselves, and foreigners, subjects of other Governments, on the part of the Rt. Hon. Lord George Paulet, Captain of H. B. M. ship Carysfort, and his Lieut. John Frere, R. N., and take the world to witness that they have broken faith with us.

By me, (Signed,) KAMEHAMEHA III.
(Signed,) KEKAULUOHI, *Premier.*
"Lahaina, Maui, Sandwich Islands, June 24, 1843."

The king's bold stroke in appealing to the honor of the British queen, the hasty measure of giving away the life of the land in the hope of its resuscitation, and the decided recession from the Paulet commission may have prevented a bloody collision, and the final loss of his sceptre, and been among the means of placing the independence of the islands on a firmer basis than before.

Apprised of the proceedings of Lord Paulet, which seemed inconsistent with the known wishes of the British Government, Rear-Admiral Thomas, commander of the British naval forces in the Pacific, hastened to check the growing evil, and turn back the turbid flood.

He arrived at Honolulu, July 26th, and declining the cession, promptly and honorably applied himself to the work of restoration, and was hailed as a deliverer. To secure an interview with the king, he addressed the following note to the Governor :—

"Her Britannic Majesty's Ship Dublin, } off Honolulu, 26th July, 1843. }

"Sir,—It being my desire to obtain the honor of a personal interview with His Majesty, King Kamehameha III., for the purpose of conferring with His Majesty on the subject of the Provisional Cession of his dominions, I have to request that you will be pleased to intimate my wishes to His Majesty, in order that he may appoint the time and place where such interview may be held.

"I have the honor to be, Sir, your most obedient humble servant,
"RICHARD THOMAS,
"Rear-Admiral and Commander-in-Chief of H. B. M. Ships and Vessels in the Pacific.

"To Kekuanaoa, Governor of Oahu."

The king having returned from Maui to greet Commodore Kearney, of the U. S. Navy, gladly welcomed Admiral Thomas also. After five months of embarrassment and suffering under the misrule of the new powers, the 31st of July opened a brighter scene, as the following will show :—

"DECLARATION

Of Rear-Admiral Thomas, Commander-in-Chief of Her Britannic Majesty's Ships and Vessels in the Pacific, in relation to the events which transpired at the Sandwich Islands, and consequent upon the visit of Her Britannic Majesty's Ship Carysfort, in February, 1843.

" To King KAMEHAMEHA III., and the Principal Chiefs of
THE SANDWICH ISLANDS.

"Immediately that the Commander-in-Chief was made acquainted
at Valparaiso in June, 1843, of the Provisional Cession of the Hawaiian Islands unto the Right Honorable Lord George Paulet, as the
then and there Representative of Her Majesty Queen Victoria, he
hastened to the spot to make himself fully acquainted with all the circumstances, and, if possible, the motives which led to such an unlooked
for event.

" His first duty on arrival was to seek a personal interview with His
Majesty Kamehameha III., and to ascertain whether these difficulties
in which he found himself involved, and the opinion which His Majesty appeared to entertain of the impossibility of complying with certain
requisitions which had been made, were so utterly insurmountable as
to call upon him to renounce the sovereignty of those Islands for the
time being, likewise whether the Cession was a free, unbiassed, and
unsolicited act of Sovereign Power.

"The Rear-Admiral having ascertained that the difficulties to which
allusion is made in the deed of Cession might be surmounted ; having
convinced His Majesty that he had not properly understood the principles of justice and good faith which invariably guide the councils of
Her Majesty, the Queen of Great Britain, in all their deliberations, particularly respecting their relations with foreign powers ; and that whenever it becomes necessary to vindicate the rights of British subjects or
redress their wrongs, the Government scrupulously respects those rights
which are vested in all nations in an equal degree, whether they be powerful or weak, making it therefore a rule not to resort to force until every
expedient for an amicable adjustment has failed ; having moreover
learnt that His Majesty entertained the hope that his conduct was
capable of justification, and that such justification he thought would
restore to him the authority he had ceded under supposed difficulties ;
and having moreover assured His Majesty that whilst it is the earnest
desire of the Government of Great Britain to cultivate by every means
a good understanding with every Independent Nation, and to prevent
any of its subjects from injuring those of other sovereigns, either in
person or property, wherever they may be located : and that, when it
can be avoided, rather than urge compliance with demands which are
likely to embarrass a feeble government, its object is to foster, and
even *assist* by kind advice or good offices such as may be disposed to
seek its friendly interposition, requiring only in return equal privileges
for such British residents as may have been granted to the subjects of
the most favored nation. Lastly, His Majesty having given his assent
to new proposals submitted to him for the amicable adjustment of the
pending differences which led to the temporary cession of his authority,
THE COMMANDER-IN-CHIEF of Her Britannic Majesty's Ships and
Vessels in the Pacific, for the reasons herein stated, and as the highest
local representative of her Majesty Queen VICTORIA, Queen of the
United Kingdom of Great Britain and Ireland, HEREBY DECLARES
AND MAKES MANIFEST that he does not accept of the Provisional Cession
of the Hawaiian Islands, made on the 25th day of February, 1843,
but that he considers His Majesty KAMEHAMEHA III., the legitimate
King of those Islands : and he assures His Majesty that the senti-

ments of his sovereign towards him are those of unvarying friendship and esteem, that Her Majesty sincerely desires King Kamehameha to be treated as an INDEPENDENT SOVEREIGN, leaving the administration of justice in his own hands, the faithful discharge of which will promote his happiness and the prosperity of his dominions.

" Although it is the duty of every sovereign and his ministers and counsellors to do all in their power to prevent any of their subjects from injuring those of any other nation residing among them ; nay more, that he ought not to permit foreigners to settle in his territory unless he engages to protect them as his own subjects, and to afford them perfect security as far as regards himself ; yet Great Britain will not consider the public character of the legitimate sovereign of a state but recently emerged from barbarism, under the fostering care of civilized nations, if at all implicated by the aggression of some of his subjects, provided the government does not directly or indirectly sanction any acts of partiality or injustice, either by conniving at whilst they are planning or being executed, or by allowing the perpetrators to remain unpunished.

" If, unfortunately, a case should occur in which there is an evasion or denial of justice on the part of the government towards British subjects, the course to be pursued is clear, and it would then be the duty of the Commander-in-Chief in such cases of real grievance which shall remain unredressed, to obtain that which BAD FAITH and INJUSTICE have denied.

" The Commander-in-Chief confidently hopes that this act of *restoration* to the free exercise of his sovereign authority, will be received by the King of the Sandwich Islands as a most powerful and convincing proof not only of the responsibility he is under to render immediate reparation for real wrongs committed upon British subjects or their property, but also of the importance which attaches to the maintenance of those friendly and reciprocally advantageous relations which have for so many years subsisted between the two nations ; and he further hopes that neither His Majesty nor his successors will ever forget that to the illustrious circumnavigator Captain Cook, as the first discoverer, the inhabitants of the Sandwich Islands owe their admission into the great family of civilized man, and from the lips of Vancouver (another Englishman) Kamehameha I. heard mention for the first time of the true God, which ultimately led to the abrogation of a false worship, idolatry, and human sacrifices, and by the well directed energies, the ceaseless perseverance of the American Missionaries to the establishment of a religion pure and undefiled, accompanied by the advantages of instruction and civilization, the which combined and duly cultivated, bring in their train, security of life and property, social order, mental and moral improvement, internal prosperity, and the respect as well as good will of other nations more advanced in the knowledge of the true faith, and the science of good government.

" Blessings and advantages of this nature the government of Great Britain is desirous of increasing and promoting among the inhabitants of the Sandwich Islands by every honorable and praiseworthy means in its power ; and thus to enlist the sympathies of the sovereign and his ministers on the side of justice, which is the basis of all society, and the surest bond of all *commerce.*

" Given on board Her Britannic Majesty's Ship Dublin, at Honolulu, Island of Oahu, this thirty-first day of July, in the year of our Lord one thousand eight hundred and forty-three.
(Signed) " RICHARD THOMAS."

A parade of several hundred English marines appeared on the plain of Honolulu with their officers, their banners waving proudly, and their arms glittering in the sunbeams. Admiral Thomas and the suspended king proceeded thither in a carriage, attended by the chiefs and a vast multitude of the people, who formed a line parallel with the troops. The English standard bearers advanced towards his majesty, their flags bowed gracefully, and a broad, beautiful Hawaiian banner, exhibiting a crown and olive branch, was unfurled over the head of the king and his attending chieftains, which was saluted by the English troops with field pieces, then by the guns of the Carysfort, whose yards were manned in homage to the restored sovereign. Then succeeded the roar of the guns of the fort, Punch-bowl Battery, the admiral's ship, Dublin, the United States' ship, Boston, and others. The day was a day of rejoicing and congratulations, enhanced by the issuing of the following edict :—

" AN ACT OF GRACE

" Accorded by His Majesty King KAMEHAMEHA III., by and with the advice of his Chiefs in Council, to all his Subjects upon the occasion of his resuming the reins of Government.

" WHEREAS certain difficulties and apparent misunderstandings have recently arisen between Us and the Government of Great Britain, in the course of which some of our subjects, subsequent to our Provisional Cession of the Sovereignty of the Islands to Great Britain, and up to the period when we resumed the exercise of our Kingly Power, have accepted office, and otherwise performed acts not so required to do by Us, or our duly constituted Authorities. And, whereas, certain persons have been imprisoned within the time abovementioned not by our Authority,

" WE, anxious to express our Gratitude to God, and to give the fullest proof of our attachment to the English Nation, and to manifest our joy at the Restoration of our National Flag, hereby Proclaim,

" FIRST, That none of our subjects shall be punished by our Authority for any act committed by them or any of them to the injury of our Government between the 25th of February, 1843, and the date hereof.

" SECOND, That all prisoners of every description, from Hawaii to Niihau, be immediately discharged.

" THIRD, All Government business will be suspended for ten days after this date, that all persons may be free to enjoy themselves in the festivities and rejoicings appropriate to the occasion.

" Given at Honolulu, Island of Oahu, this thirty-first day of July, 1843.
(Signed) "KAMEHAMEHA III.
(Signed) " KEKAULUOHI."

The native soldiers, whom Lord Paulet had enlisted under Victoria, came bending to their hereditary sovereign and kissed his hand.   The king and chiefs repaired to the stone meeting-house to offer public thanks for the singular interposition of Providence in favor of the nation.   The king made a short address, stating that according to the hope expressed by him when he ceded the islands, ' *the life of the land* ' had been restored to him ; that now, they, the people of his islands, should look to him, and his rule over them should be exercised according to the constitution and laws.   This address was followed by the interpretation of the declaration of Admiral Thomas ; after which, John Ii (a counsellor and orator) delivered an animated address suited to the joyful occasion.   He referred to the gloom which had shrouded the nation, and the despondency which had brooded over many minds, but which were now dispelled, and succeeded by hope, and joy, and brightening prospects.   He referred to the auspicious event of the restoration as of the LORD, who had been mindful of the nation in its low estate, and as demanding from all, gratitude and praise.   The sentiments of the 126th Psalm apparently inspired his heart : " When the Lord turned again the captivity of Zion, we were like them that dream.   Then was our mouth filled with laughter, and our tongue with singing.   Then said they among the heathen, ' The Lord hath done great things for them.' "

What a contrast between this scene and that of a human sacrifice in a heathen temple, which the orator of the day once saw offered by his prince, Liholiho, and his father !   It affords pleasure to add here, the testimony of the American Board, 'that the whole deportment of Admiral Thomas, while at the islands, towards the king and his people, and the mission, was of the most courteous and honorable character; and his example, counsels, and influence will long be gratefully remembered.'

The king being restored to the free use of his sovereignty under the constitution, and once more regarding himself as the head of the people, took the lead again by example and influence, and by such means as were in his power, to favor the cause of temperance and order.   Ashamed, as he said, to persist in rum-drinking when, as the " father of the people," and the guide of the chiefs, he ought to lead none astray, he had signed the temperance pledge with his chiefs, in April, 1842, and since that period, emptied from his storehouse into the sea, about 120 gallons of ardent spirits, instead of allowing this portion of his stores to be used or sold.   'He has carefully refrained from intoxicating drinks, both in times of the deepest adversity and on the most festive occasions.'   His chiefs uniting with him, and more than 20,000 church members, and the mass of the people, would, if allowed by foreign powers, stand up together for the abolition of the deleterious traffic in such drinks; and now, while Ireland is starving, and millions of bushels of bread-stuffs are in the British isles annually converted into alcoholic drinks, the Hawaiian legislature will not allow the products of the soil to be converted into intoxicating liquors, because it tends to famine and ruin. Surely they have a right to demand liberty to free their country from the evils of rum, and none has a right to restrain them. "In this respect as well as in others," says the report of the American Board for 1844, "the example and influence of Admiral Thomas of the British, and of Commodore Jones of the U. S. Navy, strengthened and encouraged both the native population and the missionaries. Following the misrule and licentiousness consequent upon wresting the government out of the hands of the legitimate rulers, their counsels and aid were most opportune for the restoration of things to order, and a healthful moral state."

In the meantime the Earl of Aberdeen had, as early as the 1st of April, 1843, apprised the Hawaiian Commissioners that Her Majesty's government had determined to acknowledge the independence of the Sandwich Islands, under Kamehameha III. We gladly hail the judicious and friendly influence of public officers, and I record with pleasure the following testimony of Dr. Anderson, Sec. of the A. Board, respecting Sir Geo. Simpson:—

" For his judicious counsels in their civil affairs, and the lively interest he manifested in the progress of education and Christianity at the Islands, while on a visit there ; as well as for his great and well-directed influence in their behalf in London, the Hawaiian government and all who seek the welfare of that people are under lasting obligations to Sir George Simpson, the chief factor of the Hudson Bay Company."

The disavowal of Lord Paulet's proceedings by the British government, and the course of policy intended by it, were communicated by the Hon. Mr. Fox to the Sec. of State at Washington, and welcomed by the friends of Hawaiian independence.

" *Washington, June 25th*, 1843.

" Sir : Her Majesty's government, previous to the departure from England of the last steam-packet, had already received information, though not officially, of the provisional occupation of the Sandwich Islands, in the name of Great Britain, by the officer commanding Her Majesty's ship ' Carysfort.'

" I am directed by the Earl of Aberdeen to state to you, for the information of the government of the United States, that the occupation of the Sandwich Islands was an act entirely unauthorized by Her Majesty's government ; and that, with the least practicable delay, due inquiry will be made into the proceedings which led to it.

" The British government had already announced to certain commissioners, who arrived in Great Britain in March last, on the part of the king of the Sandwich Islands, that Her Majesty had determined to recognise the independence of those islands under their present chief.

" To that determination Her Majesty's government intends to adhere. At the same time, however, it is right that it should be understood that the British government equally intend to engage, and, if necessary, to compel the Chief of the Sandwich Islands, to redress whatever acts of injustice may have been committed against British subjects by that Chief, or by his minister or agents, either arbitrarily, or under the false color of lawful proceedings.

"Instructions which, during the past year, were addressed by Her Majesty's government to the British consul residing in the Sandwich Islands, and to the naval officers employed on the Pacific station, enjoined those officers to treat upon all occasions, the native rulers of the Sandwich Islands with forbearance and courtesy; and, while affording due and efficient protection to aggrieved British subjects, to avoid interfering harshly or unnecessarily with the laws and customs of the native government.

"It has been the desire of the British government, regulating the intercourse of its public servants with the native authorities of the Sandwich Islands, rather to strengthen those authorities and give them a sense of their own independence by leaving the administration of justice in their own hands, than to make them feel their dependence upon foreign powers by the exercise of unnecessary interference. It has not been the purpose of Her Majesty's government to seek to establish a paramount influence in those islands for Great Britain, at the expense of that enjoyed by other powers, All that has appeared requisite to Her Majesty's government has been that other powers should not exercise there a greater influence than that possessed by Great Britain.

"I avail myself of this occasion to renew to you the assurances of my distinguished consideration.   H. S. Fox.

"Hon. Abel P. Upshur, &c., &c."

The Commissioners having obtained in England the desired pledge, proceeded to France, where they encountered many obstacles from the currency there of misrepresentations and unreasonable complaints against the Hawaiian government, such as the Captain of the Embuscade put together and endorsed in his letter of Sept. 1, 1842, to Kamehameha III. The Commissioners happily met them at once, and made an able defence of the conduct of the Hawaiian Government towards the subjects of France, and Catholics generally. The French and English Governments united in the recognition and guarantee of Hawaiian independence in this

"DECLARATION.

"Her Majesty, the Queen of the United Kingdom of Great Britain and Ireland, and His Majesty the King of the French, taking into consideration the existence in the Sandwich Islands of a Government capable of providing for the regularity of its relations with Foreign Nations, have thought it right to engage, reciprocally, to consider the Sandwich Islands as an Independent State, and never to take possession, neither directly or under the title of Protectorate, or under any other form, of any part of the Territory of which they are composed.

" The undersigned, Her Britannic Majesty's principal Secretary of State for Foreign Affairs, and the Ambassador Extraordinary of His Majesty, the King of the French, at the Court of London, being furnished with the necessary powers, hereby declare, in consequence, that their said Majesties take reciprocally that engagement.

" In witness whereof, the undersigned have signed the present declaration, and have affixed thereto the seals of their arms.

" Done in duplicate at London, the twenty-eighth day of November, in the year of our Lord one thousand eight hundred and forty-three.

(Signed) ABERDEEN. L. S.
(Signed) ST. AULAIRE." L. S.

By Belgium also, the Hawaiian Islands, already on terms of amity with Russia and Prussia, and other countries, were acknowledged as a sister nation. At this time, P. A. Brinsmade, Esq., was endeavoring to effect on a large scale the introduction of Belgian capital, labor, and machinery, into the Sandwich Islands, under certain limitations by the king.

During these struggles of the Hawaiian government to settle their relations with foreign powers on a proper basis without subjugation, the American Board, with the co-operation of the American Bible and Tract Societies, and the agency of their missionaries, used their endeavors to urge the nation forward to a state of *independence* in respect to foreign missionary aid. Messrs. Richards, Andrews, Green, and Judd, of our mission, having resigned as missionaries and been discharged, with the expectation of contributing to the stability of Hawaiian institutions, took, with other foreigners, the oath of allegiance to His Hawaiian Majesty, and became his adopted naturalized subjects.

Dr. Judd was appointed Secretary of State, and subsequently (March 9, 1844) John Ricord, Esq., a citizen of the U. S., took the oath of allegiance, and was " commissioned to be the Attorney-General of the Hawaiian Islands." Mr. Green gathered a church at Makawao, Maui, over which he watches, and through which to him the promise is fulfilled, " Thou shalt be fed." Mr. Tinker and Dr. Lafon having resigned, Mr. Munn, having buried his wife, Mr. Vanduzee (both with impaired health), and Mr. Bliss, retired from the field and returned to the U. S.

During the period in question, the Board, considering the unanswerable reasons for strengthening their mission there, to complete their work in the proper time, sent forth, in quick succession, their eighth, ninth, and tenth reinforcements, who entered into the labors of their predecessors—the eighth, Messrs. Dole, Bond, and Paris, and their wives, who arrived May 21, 1841; the ninth, Mr. Rowell and Dr. Smith, and their wives, who arrived Sept., 1842; the tenth, Messrs. Whittlesey and Hunt, and their wives, Messrs. Andrews and Pogue, and Miss M. K. Whitney, daughter of one of the pioneer missionaries, who, providentially escaping shipwreck in a violent storm, reached the islands, July 15, 1844.

The Propaganda, who might well relinquish the field, have employed a number of laborers, and lost others intended for their work.   And " What will they do?" it is asked.   Much what the same class would do in New York city and in the Valley of the Mississippi.   They may be expected, besides inculcating some truths of importance, to inculcate much error, and to *do what they can to shut out the Bible from schools, lead the unguarded to bow to Mary and the Host, and make magistrates do penance and homage to Rome.*   The Lord enables the watchful and praying disciples to guard against their wiles, though greatly exposed, and in some instances to show a degree of shrewdness and wisdom in judging of their pretensions, which some would hardly expect in their circumstances.   To give a specimen or two : one of the priests attempted to convince Keikenui, a convert under my care, that a special blessing was promised them by Christ, in consequence of their having been *reviled* and *opposed.* The convert (subsequently a preacher at Waialai, Oahu) replied, " Probably you are not reviled and opposed for your adherence to *Christ,* but for your adherence to *Mary.*"   When Mr. Walsh demanded of Kapiolani her authority for thinking the papal worship *idolatrous,* she referred him to the second commandment of the decalogue in the Hawaiian Bible, as forbidding their use of images, pictures, and the host.   To palliate their practice, or insinuate that Protestants do the same, or to puzzle the noble princess, he demanded, " Why do your missionaries put pictures into your books?"   She promptly replied, " To illustrate the subjects taught ; and when we understand the subject, we can tear the pictures or throw them away : but *you bow down* to *yours,* and *pray* to them."

But whatever influence they have employed to subvert the converts, to prevent subjects from sustaining government regulations in respect to schools and marriages, and to turn away the nation from the Bible and from our mission, thus far, though they claim thousands of baptismal converts, they appear not to have broken the peace, or greatly disturbed the order, or checked the growth of the Protestant churches.   Neither rum nor Romanism has yet triumphed there where the Word of God has been so free and powerful.   The great revival which, after repeated and wonderful outpourings of the Spirit on that heathen tribe, commenced about the close of 1836, was not checked by the disastrous events of 1839 and 1842 ; nor for ten successive years, did that shower of divine grace cease to descend on that waiting people who honored the Bible, and were laying up its life-giving truths in their hearts.   In its progress with different degrees of power at different times and places, this work brought into our churches many thousands of those who, from the days of Kaahumanu, belonged to the associations formed in 1825 for prayer and improvement, and thousands who were accustomed to commit to memory weekly, seven verses of the Scriptures, and other thousands who with these classes, attended the means of grace. Ten thousand, three hundred and twenty-one at the different stations made a profession of their faith during the four years subsequent to June, 1840; i. e. 1,473 in '41; 2,442 in '42; 5296 in '43; and 1,110 in '44. These, together with the 20,036 of those added to the churches in the four previous years, make the total for eight successive years, 30,357. One of the churches, the largest perhaps in the world, embraced 6,000 members in good standing, and under one bishop.

The mortality of the members was at the same time great. In some of the churches the cases of discipline were numerous, and in one or two the excisions were many, while in most, the great majority of the members, even in trying circumstances, appeared to stand their ground well.

Mr. Paris, in 1842, gathered a new church of 200 members at Waiohinu, in Kau, the dominion of the ill-fated Keoua, near the close of the last century. In that district, where his arrival was hailed, hopeful converts were multiplied, and in one year, 848 were added to the church. Of more than a thousand members, he says, in 1844, " A large majority hold fast their profession, grow in grace, and give the most decided evidence of piety." So of 800 members of the church at Lahaina, where many good habitations are erected by the people, and where hundreds of ships are supplied, Mr. Baldwin says, " There have been few cases of discipline; and a goodly number of our communicants appear to have always been engaged in religion."

Several churches have for years contributed freely in aid of their preachers; and that at Wailuku, Maui, have spontaneously assumed the expenses of their pastor Mr. Clark. Several natives have been formally licensed to preach at out stations, and hundreds of others employed as church officers or lay preachers. The religious contributions of the people for seven years from 1837, amounted to $19,987, and during the same period they multiplied houses of worship and school-houses, many of a substantial character, in their valleys and settlements. The large churches and congregations dwelling in wide districts hold their meetings for worship in many places, and the exercises, when they have no missionary, are soberly conducted by themselves.

" The moral condition of the islands," says the Hon. G. P. Judd, " may compare favorably with that of any other country. During the year last expired (May, 1845) 497 whalers, manned by 14,905 sailors, refreshed in our ports, and yet the disorders complained of were very few."*

---

* According to a list of vessels kept by Mr. S. Reynolds, a merchant at Honolulu, that port, in twenty years from 1824, received fifty-two visits from ships of war, and 2008 from other vessels, 1712 being whale ships—about three-fourths American.

The average times in which vessels direct from other parts of the world, reach these islands, are nearly as follows:—from California, 20 days; Tahiti, Columbia River, and N. W. Coast, 25; China, 60; Sidney, 84; New York, 146; Boston, 153; London, 159.

The same mercy which watched over the nation seemed to follow their interesting commissioner, Haalilio, in all his journeyings and engagements abroad.

The primary object of the embassy being happily accomplished, he revisited the United States with Mr. Richards on his way home. After an interview with the Hon. Mr. Calhoun, Secretary of State, and the renewed assurance that the independence of the islands would be respected by the U. S. Government, rejoicing in the brightened prospects for the Sandwich Islands, they embarked from Boston for Hawaii, Nov. 18, 1844. But Haalilio was then low in health. Disease had marked him for a prey during his last visit in Brooklyn, waiting a passage home. While he was receiving kind and skilful attentions at the hospital in Boston, where judicious friends advised him to go, his powers were rapidly prostrated by consumption. He, however, embarked with some hope of reaching his native country, and of personally reporting to his king and friends what he had seen, and heard, and experienced from the hand of the Lord, and there publicly devoting himself to his service.

Haalilio was a man of intelligence, of good judgment, of pleasing manners, and respectable business habits. Few men are more attentive to neatness and order, at home, on shipboard, or in foreign climes, than he was; and few public officers possess integrity more trustworthy.

He had, during his embassy, read his Hawaiian Bible twice through, besides his various useful reading in Hawaiian and English. Though, like many other instructed and reformed Hawaiians, he had made no public profession of religion, yet to Mr. Richards and myself, who enjoyed happy intercourse with him, he gave good evidence of piety, and we consented to give him baptism. He appeared to love the Bible, secret and social prayer, and the duties of the Sabbath and the sanctuary, and often called on the Lord for his mother, his king, and his country. He was gratified by the sacred regard paid to the Lord's day in England and the United States, and shocked at its obvious desecration in France and Belgium. He received Christian kindness with gratitude, and injuries without retaliation; and appeared to bow with resignation to adverse dispensations of providence. He would, with Mr. R. and myself, take part in social prayer; and by the humility of his confessions, the fervor of his petitions, and the earnestness of his thanksgivings, he showed that prayer, with him, was not a mere form, nor an unusual or unwelcome exercise.

On the evening of the Sabbath, just before his death, speaking of his sufferings and the prospect of his immediate departure, he said, " This is the happiest day of my life. My work is done—I am ready to go "—then lifted up the prayer, " O my Father, thou hast not granted my desire once more to see the land of my birth, and my friends that dwell there, but I entreat thee, refuse not my petition to see thy kingdom, and my friends who are dwelling with thee."

Though denied the felicity of seeing his native land again, he sought and found, we believe, that "*better country.*" On the bosom of the Atlantic, taking leave of the world, he embraced the neck of his ardent friend, kissed him, and asked, "What more have I to do here?" After a little conversation on the heavenly state on which he expected soon to enter, receiving the assurance that his dying charge to his king and countrymen should be faithfully delivered, he once more stretched out his withering, cold, hand and as his final *aloha*, with a smile, grasped the hand of his companion. Then apparently resigning himself to Christ, he engaged in prayer—his supplicating voice died away—and in a few minutes, his spirit took its flight, to prove, we trust, by actual fruition, the unspeakable value of the blessings bestowed through the Gospel on Hawaii. There, often, many a convert sings as he did—

"From wandering, O my soul, return,
Unto thy resting-place,
Surpassing is the bounteousness
Of thy Redeemer's grace.

"O Lord, my soul hast thou redeemed,
And made my feet stand sure ;
By thee, my tears are dried away,
And death has lost its power.

"Up to God's temple I will go
With his acknowledged friends ;

I'll sing the holiness of Him
On whom my peace depends.

"My pledge to follow Him I give—
I'll ne'er forsake his way :
His, truly, is my fleeting life,
My life through endless day.

"Him will I worship here below,
Through all my earthly days ;—
Through endless ages in yon world,
Will I rehearse his praise."*

His remains were, by the waiting chiefs and people, received in a shroud; the return of his coadjutor was welcomed with mingled emotions of grief and joy; and the report of the embassy received both with congratulation and mourning.

A large number of the respectable foreign residents united in a testimonial of their esteem for the departed, and in a letter of condolence and of respect to the king.

About the same time, April 2, the people, in the exercise of the *right of suffrage*, chose and sent to the legislature the following representatives, viz. : Iosua Kaeo, Iona Kapena, Paulo Kanoa, Namauu, Iona Piikoi, Beniti Namakeha, Kaisara Kapakea, and J. Y. Kanihoa.

Notwithstanding the happy results in general of the foreign embassy, the difficulties in which the government had been involved in 1839, by Captain Laplace, were not yet removed, and strenuous efforts were not wanting among foreign officials to perpetuate them, and to make Great Britain and the United States participate largely in the responsibility and the spoils, particularly in reference to the introduction of intoxicating liquors, and of an alien or consular jury for the trial of foreign criminals.

The United States Government, in 1845, appointed the Hon. ANTHONY TEN EYCK as Commissioner, and the Hon. JOEL TURRILL, as Consul, to the Sandwich Islands, who have been con-

* "*Himeni Hawaii,*" p. 210.

veyed thither by a government vessel, under command of Commodore Stockton, and cordially welcomed there by Kamehameha III.

Treaties with England and France, nearly parallel, (with the exception of the words "or *delit*," misdemeanor, interposed by the French after "*crime*" in the third article), were in March, 1846, substituted in the place of all former Hawaiian agreements with those powers.

"It being desirable that a general convention should be substituted for the various Instruments of Mutual Agreement at present existing between Great Britain and the Sandwich Islands, the following Articles have, for that purpose and that intent, been mutually agreed upon and signed between the governments of Great Britain and the Sandwich Islands, and it has been determined that any other treaty or conventional agreement, now existing between the respective parties, shall be henceforward abrogated and considered null and of no effect.

"I. There shall be perpetual peace and amity between the United Kingdom of Great Britain and Ireland and the King of the Sandwich Islands, their heirs and successors.

"II. The subjects of her Britannic Majesty residing within the Dominions of the King of the Sandwich Islands, shall enjoy the same protection in regard to their civil rights, as well as their persons and properties, as native subjects ; and the King of the Sandwich Islands engages to grant to British subjects the same rights and privileges which now are, or hereafter may be, granted to or enjoyed by any other foreigners, subjects of the most favored nation.

"III. No British subject, accused of any crime whatever, shall be judged otherwise than by a jury composed of native or foreign residents, proposed by the British Consul, and accepted by the government of the Sandwich Islands.

"IV. The protection of the King of the Sandwich Islands shall be extended to all British vessels, their officers and crews. In case of shipwreck, the chiefs and inhabitants of the different parts of the Sandwich Islands shall succor them and secure them from plunder. The salvage dues shall be regulated, in case of dispute, by arbitrators chosen by both parties.

"V. The desertion of seamen embarked on board of British vessels, shall be severally repressed by the local authorities, who shall employ all means at their disposal to arrest deserters ; and all reasonable expenses shall be defrayed by the captain or owners of the said vessels.

"VI. British merchandise, or goods recognised as coming from the British dominions, shall not be prohibited, nor shall they be subject to an import duty higher than five per cent. ad valorem. Wines, brandies, and other spirituous liquors are, however, excepted from this stipulation, and shall be liable to such reasonable duty as the Hawaiian government may think fit to lay upon them, provided always that the amount of duty shall not be so high as absolutely to prohibit the importation of the said articles.

"VII. No tonnage, import, or other duties, shall be levied on British vessels, beyond what are levied on vessels or goods of the most favored nation.

"VIII. The subjects of the King of the Sandwich Islands shall, in their commercial relations with Great Britain, be treated on the footing of the most favored nation.

" Done at Honolulu, the 26th of March, 1846.
"ROBERT CRICHTON WYLLIE,
" WILLIAM MILLER."

It is to be hoped that, with all the intelligence of the king and his nobles and representatives, and their readiness to give equity to their people and other nations, with all the foreign talent which, under the oath of allegiance, he employs at his court, and the assured friendship of Britain, France, and the United States, he will yet be able to effect a treaty with these powers on the terms of *reciprocity*. His subjects are to " be treated on the footing of the most favored nation." But they are yet by no means placed by treaty on the footing of the subjects of the other contracting powers.

The government immediately laid a duty on foreign spirits and wine, as high as Christian nations will now endure. It has also established a press, and placed it under the direction of J. J. Jarves, Esq., a naturalized subject, a gentleman of acknowledged talents, who publishes, weekly, " The Polynesian."

The regular assembling of the Legislative Council, according to the constitution, for the transaction of the business of the nation, is now a matter of no little interest. On the 20th of May, 1845, soon after the return of Mr. Richards from his foreign embassy, who has been made Minister of Instruction, they assembled at Honolulu in a respectable hall prepared for the purpose. The entrance of his majesty into the hall of legislation was announced by a salute. As Christian law-makers and guardians of the realm, they bowed in prayer before the God of nations. The king, in a full, new, and rich military suit, surrounded by governors, nobles, representatives, ministers of state, foreign consuls, naval commanders, clergy, etc., presented a speech from the throne worthy of the Christian princes and judges of the earth, and indicating their regard to the Word of God, as the foundation of their prosperity, and affording evidence that to do right was the object and business of their united constitutional body. From his manuscript he thus addressed the Council :—

" NOBLES AND REPRESENTATIVES OF THE PEOPLE:

" We have called you together to deliberate on matters connected with the good of our kingdom. In the exercise of our prerogatives we have appointed Gerrit P. Judd, Esq., to be our minister for the Interior affairs of our kingdom, Robert C. Wyllie, Esq., to be our minister for Foreign Relations, and John Ricord, Esq., to be our Law adviser in all matters relating to the administration of Justice. We have ordered our ministers to lay before you reports of their several departments.

" The independence of our kingdom has been most explicitly recognised by the United States, Great Britain, France, and Belgium. From each of these powers we have received the most friendly assurances. It is our wish to cultivate the relations of peace and friendship with all nations, and to treat the subjects of all with equal justice.

"With this view, we recommend to your consideration the better organization of our Courts of Justice, the division of powers, and a careful revisal of the laws.

"The laws regulating licenses, the tenure of lands, the registration of vessels, the harbor regulations, the duties, the fines for punishment and correction of offences, the laws for the collection of debts and taxes generally, deserve your attention.

"Our minister for the Interior will lay before you the estimate of expenses required for the ensuing year, for which it is incumbent on you to provide with a due regard to economy and the means of the people.

"It is our desire that you take measures to ascertain whether the numbers of our people are diminishing or increasing, and that you devise means for augmenting the comforts and the happiness of the people of our islands.

"We consider it the first of our duties to protect religion, and promote good morals and general education; it will therefore be your duty to consider by what means those blessings can be best promoted and extended among the people of these islands, and also among the foreigners resident in our dominions. We are well aware that the Word of God is the corner-stone of our kingdom. Through its influence we have been introduced into the family of the independent nations of the earth. It shall therefore be our constant endeavor to govern our subjects in the fear of the Lord; to temper justice with mercy in the punishment of crime; and to reward industry and virtue.

"The Almighty Ruler of nations has dealt kindly with us in our troubles, in restoring our kingdom, together with special guarantees for its existence as an independent nation. May He also aid you in your deliberations, and may He grant his special protection to us, to you and our people."

The Legislative Council then unanimously passed resolutions of thanks to the Governments of Great Britain, France, Belgium, and the United States, for recognising the independence of the Sandwich Islands. The sacred volume is honored in this royal speech. To the estimation of the sacred writings by the Protestant portion of the nation, the following extract from an ode of 100 lines by their own young poets in 1834, is a further index:

> "O Holy Bible, glorious prize, extended through these isles;
> No other treasure can compare with this most sacred pearl:
> An everlasting treasure this, for all the men of God,
> Who furnished with it, travel on with staff and spear and sword."*

On that true *corner-stone* let that kingdom stand. Happy may that people be whose God is Jehovah!

If the magnanimity of sister nations will allow the Hawaiians true independence, though thus far their numbers have diminished since their discovery, they will stand, rise, and flourish, and be a blessing to the world.

Solomon built the temple by the aid of thousands of hands, and at the expense of millions of talents, but the LORD built the

* *Kumu Hawaii*, vol. iv., p. 60.

house with his own laborers and his own gold, and there, favored his people with his presence, and there revealed his salvation.

The American Board, under the same Divine Builder, have sent forth (and well sustained) sixty-five men and seventy women, to build the Lord's house at the Sandwich Islands, whose operations have cost, of gold and silver, $650,000; and of time, an amount equal to that of an individual, 1100 years.

During the progress of their work, the American Bible Society have, in addition, liberally granted to the mission in money, $40,500; and in Bibles and Testaments, $1,920 37=$42,420 37; from which $838 33 have been returned to them.

The American Tract Society have also generously aided the mission in the circulation of evangelical tracts approved by their different denominations, to the amount of $19,774.

Twenty thousand Bibles, thirty thousand New Testaments, and more than seventy other works, prepared, written, translated, or compiled by the missionaries, have issued from our mission presses. The printing from January, 1822, to June, 1845, amounted to 149,911,383 pages.*

A considerable part of the outlay is still available for the purposes of the mission—forty permanent dwelling-houses, at eighteen stations, two printing offices, four presses, and a

* CATALOGUE OF HAWAIIAN BOOKS AND TRACTS.

	Pages		Pages
Elementary lessons, 4, 8, and 16 pp., 100,000 copies.		Little Philosopher [Abbott's]	40
		English and Hawaiian Grammar	40
Decalogue and Lord's Prayer	4	First Teacher for Children	32
Scripture doctrines, a Catechism	8	Tract on Astronomy	12
Thoughts of the chiefs	16	Maps of Sacred Geography	6
Sermon on the Mount	16	Sixteen Sermons	144
Hawaiian Hymns	60	Tract on Lying	8
First Book for children	36	Attributes of God	12
Universal Geography	216	First Book for teaching English	36
New Testament	520	Moral Science	12
Fowle's Child's Arithmetic	66	Key to Colburn	76
Animals of the earth, with a chart	12	Heavenly Manna	72
Catechism on Genesis	56	Hymns for Children	122
Geometry for Children [Holbrook's]	64	Hawaiian History	116
Tract on Marriage	12	Algebra [Colburn's]	44
Sacred Geography [Worcester's]	100	Anatomy	60
Geographical Questions	44	Scripture Lessons	152
Bible Class Book, Abbot & Fisk's, vol. i	62	Mathematics, Geometry, Trigonometry,	
Colburn's Intellectual Arithmetic	132	Mensuration, Surveying, and Navigation	168
History of Beasts	192	Tract on Intemperance	28
Lama Hawaii [Newspaper]	100	Bible Class Book, Vol. II	36
Hawaiian Almanac	16	" " " Vol. III	40
Vocabulary	132	Child's Book on the Soul, [Gallaudet's]	66
Compend of Ancient History	76	Natural Theology [Gallaudet's]	178
Sacred Geography	84	Nonanona [Newspaper]	00
Union Questions, vol. I	156	Articles of Faith and Covenant	00
Colburn's Sequel	116	Church History	340
History of Beasts for Children	84	Moral Philosophy [Wayland's]	215
Hawaiian Teacher, 4 vols., 4to	720	Pilgrim's Progress	324
Child's teacher	96	Tract on Popery	23
Daily Food, for 1835, with Notes	36	Keith's Study of the Globes	80
Hawaiian Grammar	32	Volume of Sermons	296
First Reading Book for Children	48	Sandwich Islands' Laws [by Government]	92
Tract on the Sabbath	12	English and Hawaiian Lessons	40
Universal Geography [Woodbridge's]	203	Keith on the Prophecies	12
Daily Food, for 1836, with Notes	123	Dying Testimony of Christians and Infidels	40
Maps of U. Geography	9	Algebra [Bailey's]	160
Scripture Chronology and History	216	Reading Book for schools	340
Hymns revised and enlarged	184	Messenger, semi-monthly	8
Hymns with tunes	360	History of the Sandwich Islands in English	464
Linear Drawing	36	Hawaiian Bible	200

bindery, and commodious seminary and school buildings for boarding schools. A large portion of their laborers are still toiling on in the dust and sweat of that incessant summer, to build according to the divine rule. Of the fourteen pioneers, I gratefully record it, after twenty-seven years, four men and the seven women are still living to praise God for his faithfulness to them, and for his surpassing favor to that mission and that nation. Wm. Kanui, after wandering twenty years, has returned to his duty as a teacher. But one of the *fourteen* has died in that field. Mr. Whitney drawn, like Moses, from the flood in March, 1820, licensed at Honolulu and ordained at Kailua, used and laid down his silver trumpet at Waimea, and, March 20th, 1846, ascended from the mount of Lahaina-luna, rejoicing in that blessed Savior, whom, for nearly a generation, he had proclaimed to the islanders, and who, as he said, 'held him by the hand, and was leading him along' to the missionary pilgrim's home. There, we trust, he will greet many from the shores of HAWAII REDEEMED.

A nation has been raised from blank heathenism to a rank among enlightened nations, to the enjoyment of letters and laws, of Christianity and the hope of heavenly glory. Whatever troubles may yet assail them, there is ground to rejoice that the foundation of the spiritual temple of Jehovah has there been firmly laid, and its superstructure commenced which is to rise in future generations. The builders there and elsewhere have many adversaries, but the benignant Lamb shall overcome them. His servants must be multiplied, and many a heart, constrained by the love of Christ, will be found to say—

" The voice of my departed Lord, ' Go TEACH ALL NATIONS,'
Comes on the night air, and awakes my ear."

If the American Board and its friends and laborers have not done too much for that nation in a generation past, and who will say they have toiled or expended too much? those who are on the Lord's side, grateful for what *God has wrought* there, will be encouraged to attempt and expect the same, or "greater things than these," for other nations, till, in every tongue, they shall harmoniously hymn the Messiah's praise, and earth's ransomed millions shall swell the strain which these converted islanders have recently learned and gratefully adopted :—

"E ke Ola, Lua ole !
E ukuia kou make e :
Lanakila kou aloha ;
Nau 'na mamo, e maha'i:
Make oe i mau ohua—
Nou ko makou mau naau ;
Nou ka ikaika ;—Nou na uhane ;—
Nou ka nani oia mau."

"O Redeemer, matchless, glorious !
Let thy anguish be repaid :
Reigning, make thy love victorious ;
In thy seed, be satisfied :
Thou wast slain, blessed Lamb, to win us—
Let us live and die for thee ;
Worthy thou of all within us ;—
Thine shall endless glory be."

MISSIONARIES OF THE AMERICAN BOARD, TO THE SANDWICH ISLANDS.

ABBREVIATIONS.—Colleges and Universities,—A. C., Amherst; B. C., Bowdoin; D. C., Dartmouth; Dick., Dickinson; H. C., Hamilton; M. C., Middlebury; N. J. C., New Jersey; U. C., Union; W. C., Williams; Y. C., Yale.—Theological Seminaries,—Andover, Auburn, Bangor, E. Windsor, Princeton, Union, Lane, N. Haven.

NAMES.	BORN.	GRADUATED.	EMBARKED.	EN. THE ISLES	CHIEF LOCATION.	LEFT.	DECEASED.
Rev. Asa Thurston.	Fitchburg, Ms., Oct. 12, 1787.	Y. C., 1816, Andover, 1819.	Boston, Oct. 23, 1819.	Apr. 1820.	Kailua, Apr. 12, 1820.	Visited U. S. '41.	
Mrs. Thurston, (Lucy Goodale.)	Marlboro', Ms., Oct. 29, 1795.		" 1819.	"	"		
Rev. Hiram Bingham.	Bennington, Vt. Oct. 30, 1789.	M. C. 1816, Andover, 1819.	Boston, Oct. 23, 1819.	Apr. 1820.	Honolulu, Apr. 19, 1820.	Aug. 3, 1840.	Feb. 27, 1848.
Mrs. Bingham, (Sybil Moseley,) [daigna. Canan-	Westfield, Ms., Sept. 14, 1792.		" 1819.	"	"	"	Mar. 20, 1846.
Mr. Samuel Whitney, N. Haven.	Branford, Ct., Apr. 28, 1793.	Ord. Kailua, Nov. 30, 1825.	Boston, Oct. 23, 1819.	Apr. 1820.	Waimea, July 25, 1820.		
Mrs. Whitney (Mercy Partridge).	Pittsfield, Ms., Aug. 14, 1795.		" 1819.	"	"		
Mr. Daniel Chamberlain.	Of Brookfield, Ms.		Boston, Oct. 23, 1819.	Apr. 1820.	Honolulu, Apr. 19, 1820.	March 21, 1822.	
Mrs. Jerusha Chamberlain.			" 1819.	"	"	"	
Thomas Holman, M. D.	Cooperstown, N. Y.		Boston, Oct. 23, 1819.	Apr. 1820.	Kailua, Apr. 12, 1820.	1821.	
Mrs. Holman, (Lucia Ruggles.)	Brookfield, Ct.		" 1819.	"	"	"	*
Mr. Samuel Ruggles.	Brookfield, Ct., Mar. 9, 1795.		Boston, Oct. 23, 1819.	Apr. 1820.	Waimea, Hilo, Kuapehu,	Jan. 6, 1834.	
Mrs. Ruggles, (Nancy Wells.)	E. Windsor, Ct., Ap. 18, 1791.		" 1819.	"	"	"	*
Mr. Elisha Loomis.	Middlesex, N. Y., Dec., 1799.		Boston, Oct. 23, 1819.	Apr. 1820.	Honolulu. Apr. 19, 1820.	Jan. 6, 1827.	*
Mrs. Loomis, (Maria T. Sartwell, Utica.)	N. Hartford, N. Y. Au. 25, '96.		" 1819.	"	"	"	
Rev. William Richards.	Plainfield, Ms., Aug. 22, 1793.	W. C. 1819, Andover, 1822.	N. Haven, Nov. 19, '22	Apr. 1823.	Lahaina, May 31, 1823.	Res'd, 1838.	Nov. 7, 1847.
Mrs. Richards, (Clarissa Lyman.)	Northampton, Ms. Jan. 10, '94.		" 1822.	"	"		
Rev. Charles Samuel Stewart.	Flemington, N. J. Oct. 16, '98.	N. J. C. 1815, Princeton, '21.	N. Haven, Nov. 19, '22	Apr. 1823.	Lahaina, May 31, 1823.	Oct. 17, 1825,	*
Mrs. Stewart, (Harriet B. Tiffany,)	Stamford, Ct. June 24, 1798.		" 1822.	"	"	"	
Rev. Artemas Bishop.	Pompey, N. Y., Dec. 30, 1795.	U. C. 1819, Princeton, 1822.	N. Haven, Nov. 19, '22	Apr. 1823.	{ Kailua, Mar. 11, 1824, Ewa, 1836,		
Mrs. Bishop, (Elizabeth Edwards, Bost.)			"	"			Feb. 28, 1828.
Mrs. Bishop, (Delia Stone, Roch't, N. Y.)	Bloomfield, N.Y. May 26, 1800		Boston, Nov. 3, 1827.	Mar. 31, 1828.	(Married, Dec. 1, 1828.)		
Mr. Levi Chamberlain, Boston.	Dover, Vt., Aug. 28, 1792.		N. Haven, Nov. 19,'22	Apr. 27, 1823.	Honolulu, Ap.27,1823-'47.	Visited U. S. '46.	
Mrs. Chamberlain, (Maria Patten.)	Salisbury, Pa., Mar. 3, 1803.		Boston, Nov. 3, 1827.	Mar. 31, 1828.	(Married, Sept. 1, 1828.)		
Mr. Joseph Goodrich, Ord. Kailua, 1826.	Wethersfield, Ct.	Y. C. 1821.	N. Haven, Nov. 19,'22	Apr. 27, 1823.	Hilo, Jan. 24, 1824.	Jan. 23, 1836,	
Mrs. Goodrich, (Martha Barnes.)			"	"	"	"	
Mr. James Ely.	Lime, Ct., Oct. 22, 1798.	{ Ordained Honolulu, June 4, 1825.	N. Haven, Nov. 19,'22	Apr. 27, 1823.	Kaawaloa, Apr. 9, 1824.	Oct. 15, 1828.	*
Mrs. Ely, (Louisa Everest.)	Cornwall, Ct., Sept. 8, 1792.		"	"	"	"	
Abraham Blatcheley, M. D.	East Guilford, Ct.		N. Haven, Nov. 19,'22	Apr. 27, 1823.	Honolulu, Apr. 27, 1823.	Nov. 6, 1826.	
Mrs Blatcheley.	N. J.,		"	"	"	"	
Miss Betsey Stockton.	——, Ct., 1796.		"	"	Lahaina, May 31, 1823,	Oct. 17, 1825,	
Rev. Lorrin Andrews, Maysville, Ky.	• • • • •	Jeff. C. — Princeton, 1825.	Boston, Nov. 3, 1827.	Mar. 31, 1828.	Lahaina, 1828, Lahainaluna, 1831.	Res'd, 1842,	
Mrs. Andrews, (Mary Ann)			"	"			
Rev. Ephraim W. Clark, Peacham, Vt.	Haverhill, N.H., Ap. 25, 1799.	D. C. 1824, Andover, 1827.	Boston, Nov. 3, 1827.	Mar. 31, 1828.	{ Honolulu, Mar. 31, '28. Lahainaluna, 1834. Wailuku, 1843.		
Mrs. Clark, (Mary Kittredge.)	Mt. Vernon, N. H. Dec. 9, 1803		"	"			
Jonathan Smith Green, Pawlet, Vt.	Lebanon, Ct., Dec. 20, 1796.	Andover, 1827.	Boston, Nov. 3, 1827.	Mar. 31, 1828.	[Vis. N. W. C., 1829.] Lahaina, 1830, Hilo, 1831, Wailuku, 1832, Mount Pleasant, 1842.	Rea'd, 1842.	
Mrs. Green, (Theodocia Arnold.)	E. Haddam, Ct., Apr. 3, 1792.		"	"			

MISSIONARIES OF THE AMERICAN BOARD, TO THE SANDWICH ISLANDS.

NAMES.	BORN.	GRADUATED.	EMBARKED.	EN. THE ISLES	CHIEF LOCATION.	LEFT.	DECEASED.
Rev. Peter J. Gulick.	Freehold, N.J. Mar. 12, 1797.	N. J. C. 1825, Princeton, '27.	Boston, Nov. 3, 1827.	Mar. 31, 1828.	Waimea, July 15, 1828. Koloa, '34, Molokai, '42	Res'd 1842.	
Mrs. Gulick, (Fanny H. Thomas.)	Lebanon, Ct. April 16, 1798.			"	"		
Gerrit P. Judd, M.D.	Paris, N.Y., April 23, 1803.		Boston, Nov. 3, 1827.	Mar. 31, 1828.	Honolulu, Mar, 1828.		
Mrs. Judd, (Laura Fish.)	Kingsboro', N.Y., Apr. 26, 1800		"	"	"		
Mr. Stephen Shepard.	Of Champion, N.Y., b. Pa. 1801		Boston, Nov. 3, 1827.	Mar. 31, 1828.	Honolulu, March, 1828.	Jan. 6, 1835.	July 6, 1834.
Mrs. Shepard, (Margaret C. Slow.)	Durham, Ct., Sept. 29, 1798.						
Rev. D. Baldwin, M. D., Durham, N. Y.	Northford, Ct., 1805.	Y. C. 1821, Auburn, 1829.	N.Bed, Dec, 28, 1830.	June 7, 1831.	Waimea H., 1831, Lahaina, 1835.	Vis. U. S. 1837.	
Mrs. Baldwin, (Charlotte Fowler.)	Skenateles, N. Y., 1805.		N.Bed, Dec. 28, 1830.	June 7, 1831.			
Rev. Sheldon Dibble.	Troy, N. Y., April, 1808.	H. C. 1827, Auburn, 1830.	N. York, Oct. 9, 1839.	Apr. 10, 1840.	Hilo, Aug., 1831, Lahainaluna, Nov. 1831.		Jan. 21, 1845.
Mrs. Dibble, (Maria M. Tomlinson.)	Manlius, N. Y., 1809.		N.Bed. Dec. 28, 1830.	June 7, 1831.	"		Feb. 20 1837.
Mrs. Dibble, (Antoinette Tomlinson.)	Chester, Ms., Aug. 6, 1799.	A. C. 1827, Auburn, 1830.	N.Bed. Dec. 28, 1830.	June 7, 1831.	Lahainaluna.	Oct. 23, 1847.	
Rev. Reuben Tinker.	Chester, Ms. Aug. 24, 1809.			June 7, 1831.	Wailuku, Honolulu.	Res'd 1838.	
Mrs. Tinker, (Mary T. Wood, Madison,O.				June 7, 1831.	"	1841.	
Mr. Andrew Johnstone, N. Bedford, Ms.	Scotland.				Honolulu, June, 1831.	Res'd 1834.	
Mrs. Johnstone, N. Bedford, Ms.					"	"	
Miss Maria C. Ogden.	Philadelphia, Feb. 17, 1792.		Boston, Nov. 3, 1827.	Mar. 31, 1828.	Honolulu, June, 1831.		
Rev. Wm. P. Alexander.	Paris, Ky., July 25, 1805.	Princeton, 1831.	N.Bed. Nov. 26, 1831.	May 17, 1832.	Washington Isles, 1833. Waioli, 1834, Lahainaluna, 1842.		
Mrs. Alexander, (Mary Ann McKinney.)	Wilmington, Del. Jan. 5, 1810		N.Bed. Nov. 26, 1831.	May 17, 1832.	"		
Rev. Richard Armstrong.	Turbotville, Pa., Ap. 13, 1805.	Dick. C.1827, Princeton, '31.	N.Bed. Nov. 26, 1831.	May 17, 1832.	Wash. Isles, 1833, Wailuku, '35, Honolulu '40.		
Mrs. Armstrong, (Clarissa Chapman.)	Russell, Ms., May 15, 1805.		N.Bed. Nov. 26, 1831.	May 17, 1832.	"		
Rev. John S. Emerson.	Chester, N. H., Dec. 28, 1800.	D. C. 1826, Andover, 1830.	N.Bed. Nov. 26, 1831.	May 17, 1832.	Waialua, July, 1832.		
Mrs. Emerson, (Ursula S. Newell.)	Nelson, N. H., Sept. 27, 1806.		N.Bed. Nov. 26, 1831.	May 17, 1832.	Lahainaluna & Waialua		
Rev. Cochran Forbes.	Goshen, Pa., July 21, 1805.	Princeton, 1831.	N.Bed. Nov. 26, 1831.	May 17, 1832.	Kaawaloa, Kealakekua.	Oct. 23, 1847.	
Mrs. Forbes, (Rebecca D. Smith, New'k)	Springfield, N.J. June 21, 1805		N.Bed. Nov. 26, 1831.	May 17, 1832.		"	
Rev. Hervey R. Hitchcock.	Gt. Barrington, Ms., Mar. 13, 1800.	W. C. 1828, Auburn, 1831.	N.Bed. Nov. 26, 1831.	May 17, 1832.	Kaluaaha, Nov. 1832.		
Mrs. Hitchcock, (Rebecca Howard.)	Owasco, N. Y., Dec. 2, 1806.		N.Bed. Nov. 26, 1831.	May 17, 1832.	"		
Rev. David B. Lyman.	N. Hartford, Ct. July 29, 1803.	W. C. 1828, Andover, 1831.	N.Bed. Nov. 26, 1831.	May 17, 1832.	Hilo, 1832.		
Mrs. Lyman, (Sarah Joiner.)	Royalton, Vt., Nov. 29, 1806.		N.Bed. Nov. 26, 1831.	May 17, 1832.	"		
Rev. Lorenzo Lyons.	Colrain, Me., Apr. 18, 1807.	U. C. 1827, Auburn, 1831.	N.Bed. Nov. 26, 1831.	May 17, 1832.	Waimea H., 1832.		
Mrs. Lyons, (Betsey Curtis.)	Elbridge, N. Y., Jan. 10, 1813.		N.Bed. Nov. 26, 1831.	May 17, 1832.	"		May 14, 1837.
Mrs. Lyons, (Lucia G. Smith, Truxton.)	Burlington, N. Y., 1810.		Boston, Dec. 14, 1836.	Apr. 9, 1837.	(Married July 14, 1838.)		
Rev. Ephraim Spaulding.	Ludlow, Vt., Dec. 10, 1802.	M. C. 1829, Andover, 1831.	N.Bed. Nov. 26, 1831.	May 17, 1832.	Lahaina, 1832.	Dec. 26, 1836.	
Mrs. Spaulding, (Julia Brooks.)	Buckland, Ms., Ap, 7, 1810.		N.Bed. Nov. 26, 1831.	May 17, 1832.	Lahaina, 1832.		June 28, 1840
Alonzo Chapin, M. D.	W. Spring'ld, Ms. Feb. 24, '05.	A. C. 1826.	N.Bed. Nov. 26, 1831.	May 17, 1832.	Lahaina, 1832.	Nov. 1835.	
Mrs. Chapin, (Mary Ann Tenney, Bost.)	Newburyport, Ms. May 9,1804		N.Bed. Nov. 26, 1831.	May 17, 1832.	"	"	
Mr. Edmund H. Rogers.	Newton, Mass, 1805.		N.Bed. Nov. 26, 1831.	May 17, 1832.	Honolulu, Lahainaluna.		
Mrs. Rogers, (Mary Ward.)	Middlebury, N. Y., 1799.		Boston, Nov. 3, 1827.	Mar. 31, 1828.	Married 1833.		May 23, 1834.
Mrs. Rogers, (Elizabeth M. Hitchcock.)	G.Barrington,Ms. Oct. 4, 1802		Boston, Dec. 5, 1834.	June, 1835.	Married July 12, 1836.		
Rev. Lowell Smith.	Heath, Ms., Nov. 27, 1802.	W. C. 1829, Auburn, 1832.	N. Lord., Nov., 1832.	May 1, 1833.	Kalunaha, Ewa, 1834, Honolulu, 1836.		
Mrs. Smith, (A.W. Tenney, Brandon,Vt)	Barre, Ms., Dec. 4, 1809.		"	"	"		

MISSIONARIES OF THE AMERICAN BOARD, TO THE SANDWICH ISLANDS.

NAMES.	BORN.	GRADUATED.	EMBARKED.	EN. THE ISLES.	CHIEF LOCATION.	LEFT.	DECEASED.
Rev. Benjamin W. Parker.	Reading, Ms., Oct. 13, 1803.	A. C. 1829, Andover, 1832.	N. Lond. Nov. 21, '32	May 1, 1833.	{ Wash. Isles, 1833, Kaneohe, Dec. 1834.		
Mrs. Parker, (Mary E. Barker.)	Branford, Ct., Dec. 9, 1805.		N.Lond.Nov.21,1832.	May 1, 1833.	"		
Mr. Lemuel Fuller, Providence.	Attleboro', Ms., Apr. 2, 1810.		N.Lond.Nov.21,1832.	May 1, 1833.		Dec. 1 1833.	
Rev. Titus Coan.	Killingworth, Ct. Feb. 1, 1801.	Auburn, 1833.	Boston, Dec. 5, 1834.	June 6, 1835.	{ Patagonia, 1833, Hilo, Aug. 1835.		
Mr. Henry Dimond, N. Y. city.	Riga, N. Y., Feb. 17, 1810.		Boston, Dec. 5, 1834.	June 6, 1835.	Honolulu, 1835.		
Mrs. Coan, (Fidelia Church.)	Ct.		Boston, Dec. 5, 1834.	June 6, 1835.	"		
Mrs. Dimond, (Ann Maria Anner.)	New York city.		Boston, Dec. 5, 1834.	June 6, 1835.	"		
Mr. Edwin O. Hall, Rochester, N. Y.	Walpole, N. H., Oct. 21, 1810.	A. C., 1828, Auburn, 1831.	Boston, Dec. 14, 1836.	Apr. 9, 1837.	Wailuku, Kaluaaha.		
Mrs. Hall, (Sarah L. Williams, Brooklyn)	Elizabethtown, N. J., Oct. 27, 1812.		Boston, Dec. 14, 1836.	Apr. 9, 1837.			
Miss Lydia Brown.	Warren, Ms., Aug. 28, 1804.		Boston, Dec. 14, 1836.	Apr. 9, 1837.	Kohala, 1837.	1841.	
Rev. Isaac Bliss.	Elbridge, N. Y., July 25, 1811.		Boston, Dec. 14, 1836.	Apr. 9, 1837.	Hana, 1837.	"	
Mrs. Bliss, (Emily Curtis.)	Charlton, N. Y., Feb. 3, 1807.		Boston, Dec. 14, 1836.	Apr. 9, 1837.	"		
Rev. Daniel T. Conde.	Jericho, Vt., June 17, 1810.	U. C. 1831, Auburn, 1834.	Boston, Dec. 14, 1836.	Apr. 9, 1837.	Hana, Kealia.		
Mrs. Conde, (Andelucia Lee.)	Goshen, Ct., Feb. 10, 1809.		Boston, Dec. 14, 1836.	Apr. 9, 1837.	"		
Rev. Mark Ives.	Haddam, Ct., Nov. 18, 1810.	U. C. 1833, E. Windsor, '36.	Boston, Dec. 14, 1836.	Apr. 9, 1837.	Koloa, 1837.		
Mrs. Ives, (Mary A. Brainard.)	Chesterfield Co., Va., Dec. 17, 1801.		Boston, Dec. 14, 1836.	Apr. 9, 1837.			Sep. 29, 1846.
Rev. Thomas Lafon, M. D. (Mo.)	N. Bedford, Ms., June 30, 1812	(Dr. Nelson's School.)	Boston, Dec. 14, 1836.	Apr. 9, 1837.	Kailua, 1837.	Rev'd. 1841.	1840.
Mrs. Lafon, (Sophia L. Parker.)	Putney, Vt., June 24, 1809.		Boston, Dec. 14, 1836.	Apr. 9, 1837.		"	*
Seth L. Andrews, M. D. Pittsford.	Woodbury, Ct., Jan. 12, 1807.	D. C. 1831.	Boston, Dec. 14, 1836.	Apr. 9, 1837.	Honolulu, 1837.	Vis. U. S., 1842.	
Mrs. Andrews, (Parnelly Pierce.)	Cazenovia, N. Y., Au. 12, 1808		Boston, Dec. 14, 1836.	Apr. 9, 1837.			
Mr. Samuel N. Castle, Medina, O.	Sudbury, Vt., Oct. 25, 1810.		Boston, Dec. 14, 1836.	Apr. 9, 1837.	Kohala, Wailuku.		
Mrs. Castle, (Angeline L. Tenney.)	Exeter, N. Y.		Boston, Dec. 14, 1836.	Apr. 9, 1837.	Honolulu, 1837.		
Mrs. Castle, (Mary Tenney.)			Boston, Nov. 2, 1842.	1843.			
Mr. Edward Bailey.	Holden, Ms., Feb. 24, 1814.		Boston, Dec. 14, 1836.	Apr. 9, 1837.	Waioli, 1837.		
Mrs. Bailey, (Caroline Hubbard.)	Holden, Ms., Aug. 13, 1814.		Boston, Dec. 14, 1836.	Apr. 9, 1837.			
Mr. Amos S. Cooke.	Danbury, Ct., Dec. 1, 1810.		Boston, Dec. 14, 1836.	Apr. 9, 1837.	Honolulu, 1837.		
Mrs. Cooke, (Juliette Montague.)	Sunderland, Ms., March 10, 1812.		Boston, Dec. 14, 1836.	Apr. 9, 1837.	"		
Mr. Edward Johnson.	Hollis, N. H., 1813.		Boston, Dec. 14, 1836.	Apr. 9, 1837.	Waimea H., Honolulu.		Mar. 28, 1845.
Mrs. Johnson, (Lois S. Hoyt, Warner.)	Salisbury, N. H., 1809.		Boston, Dec. 14, 1836.	Apr. 9, 1837.	"		
Mr. Horton O. Knapp.	Greenwich, Ct., Mar. 21, 1813.		Boston, Dec. 14, 1836.	Apr. 9, 1837.	Waialua, 1837.		
Mrs. Knapp, (Charlotte Close.)	Greenwich, Ct., May 26, 1813.		Boston, Dec. 14, 1836.	Apr. 9, 1837.	"		
Mr. Edwin Locke.	Fitzwilliam, N. H., June 18, 1813.		Boston, Dec. 14, 1836.	Apr. 9, 1837.	Lahaina, 1837.		Oct. 28, 1843.
Mrs. Locke, (Martha L. Rowell.)	Cornish, N. H., Nov. 9, 1812.		Boston, Dec. 14, 1836.	Apr. 9, 1837.			
Mr. Charles McDonald.	Easton, Pa., Dec. '24, 1812.		Boston, Dec. 14, 1836.	Apr. 9, 1837.	Kaluaaha, 1837.	1844.	Oct. 8, 1842.
Mrs. McDonald, (Harriet T. Halsted.)	New York city, Dec. 6, 1810.		Boston, Dec. 14, 1836.	Apr. 9, 1837.		1841.	Sept. 7, 1839.
Mr. Bethuel Munn, Benton, N. Y.	Orange, N. J., Aug. 28, 1803.		Boston, Dec. 14, 1836.	Apr. 9, 1837.	Kaawaloa, 1837.		
Mrs. Munn, (Louisa Clark.)	Skeneateles, N. Y., Mar. 3, 1810.		Boston, Dec. 14, 1836.	Apr. 9, 1837.	"		Aug. 25, 1841.
Mr. William S. Van Duzee.	Hartford, N. Y., Jan. 12, 1811.		Boston, Dec. 14, 1836.	Apr. 9, 1837.		1839.	
Mrs. Van Duzee, (Oral Hobart.)	Homer, N. Y., Feb. 3, 1814.		Boston, Dec. 14, 1836.	Apr. 9, 1837.		"	

MISSIONARIES OF THE AMERICAN BOARD, TO THE SANDWICH ISLANDS.

NAMES.	BORN.	GRADUATED.	EMBARKED.	EN. THE ISLES	CHIEF LOCATION.	LEFT.	DECEASED.
Mr. Abner Wilcox.	Harwinton, Ct., Apr. 19, 1808.	. . . . .	Boston, Dec. 14, 1836.	Apr. 9, 1837.	Hilo, 1837, Waialua.		
Mrs. Wilcox, (Lucy E. Hart, Norfolk.)	Cairo, N. Y., Nov. 17, 1814.			"	"		
Miss Marcia M. Smith, Truxton.	Burlington, N. Y.		Boston, Dec. 14, 1836.	Apr. 9, 1837.	Honolulu, Punahou.		
Rev. Daniel Dole.	Bloomfield, Me., Sept. 9, 1808	B. C., 1835, Bangor, 1839.	Boston, Nov.14, 1840.	May 21, 1841.	Punahou.		
Mrs. Dole, (Emily H. Ballard.)	Hallowell, Me. June 11, 1808.		"	"	"		Ap. 27, 1844.
Mrs. Dole, (Mrs. Charlotte C. Knapp.)	(Of Honolulu.)		Boston, Dec. 14, 1836.	Apr. 9, 1837.	(Married 1845.)		
Rev. Elias Bond.	Hallowell, Me., Aug. 19, 1813	B. C., 1837, Bangor, 1840.	Boston, Nov.14, 1840.	May 21, 1841.	Kohala,		
Mrs. Bond, (Ellen M. Howell.)	Portland, Me. Dec. 29, 1817.			"	"		
Rev. John D. Paris.	Stanton, Va., Sept. 2, 1809.	Bangor, 1839.	Boston, Nov.14, 1840.	May 21, 1841.	Waiohinu.		
Mrs. Paris, (Mary Grant.)	Albany, N. Y., Apr. 27, 1807.			"	"		Feb. 18, 1847.
Mr. William H. Rice.	Oswego, N. Y., Oct. 12, 1813.		Boston, Nov.14, 1840.	May 21, 1841.	Hana, Punahou,		
Mrs. Rice, (Mary Sophia Hyde.)	Seneca Village, N. Y., Oct. [11, '1813.			"	"		
Rev. George B. Rowell.	Cornish, N. H.	Andover, 1841.	Boston, May 2, 1842.	Sept. 21, 1842.	Waioli, Waimea,		
Mrs. Rowell, (M. J. Chapin.)	Newport, N. H.			"	"		
James W. Smith, M. D.	New York City.		Boston, May 2, 1842.	"	Koloa.		
Mrs. Smith, (M. Knapp.)	Greenwich, Ct.			"	"		
Rev. Asa B. Smith.	E. Williamst'n, Vt. July 10 '09	M. C., 1834, N. Haven, 1838	Mar. 2, 1838.	1843.	Oregon, Waialua.	1845.	
Mrs. Smith, (Sarah G. White.)	W. Brookfield, Ms. Sep.14,'13	Union, 1843.		"	"	"	
Rev. Eliphalet Whitlesey.	Salisbury, Ct. July 13, 1816.		Boston, Dec. 4, 1843.	July 15, 1844.	Hana.		
Mrs. Whittlesey, (Elizabeth Baldwin.)	Frankfort, N. J., Aug. 29,1821	Auburn, 1843.		"	"		
Rev. Timothy Dwight Hunt.	Rochester, N. Y.	Lane, 1843.	Boston, Dec. 4, 1843.	July 15, 1844.	Kau, Lahainaluna.		
Mrs. Hunt, (Miss Hedges.)	Newark, N. J.			"	"		
Rev. Claudius B. Andrews.	Kinsman, O.	Marietta, 1840, Lane, 1843.	Boston, Dec. 4, 1843.	July 15, 1844.	Kaluaaha.		
Rev. John F. Pogue.	Wilmington, Del.Dec.29,1814	Lane, 1843.	Boston, Dec. 4, 1843.	July 15, 1844.	Koloa.		
Miss Maria K. Whitney.	Waimea, S. Islands.		Boston, Dec. 4, 1843.	July 15, 1844.	Honolulu.		
Rev. Henry Kinney.	Amenia, N. Y., Oct. 1, 1814.	Union, 1847.	Boston, Oct. 23, 1847.				
Mrs. Kinney, (Maria L. Wadsworth.)	Cleveland, O. May 30, 1822.		"				
Rev. S. G. Dwight.	Northampton, Ms. Jan. 18,'15	Union, 1847.	Boston, Oct. 23, 1847.				

MISSIONARIES OF THE LONDON MISSIONARY SOCIETY, TO SANDWICH ISLANDS.

NAMES.	BORN.	GRADUATED.	EMBARKED.	EN. THE ISLES	CHIEF LOCATION.	LEFT.	DECEASED.
Rev. William Ellis, (Society Islands.)	England.		Feb. 4, 1823.		Honolulu.	Aug. 1834.	
Mrs. Mary Ellis,	"				"	"	

MISSIONARIES OF THE SEAMEN'S FRIEND SOCIETY TO S. ISLANDS.

NAMES.	BORN.	GRADUATED.	EMBARKED.	EN. THE ISLES	CHIEF LOCATION.	LEFT.	DECEASED.
Rev. John Diell.	Cherry Valley, N. Y.	H. C., 1829, Andover, 1832.	N.Lond. Nov. 21, '32.	May 1, 1833.	Honolulu.	1840.	* At Sea.
Mrs. Diell, (Caroline Platt.)	Plattsburg, N. Y.			"	"	"	
Rev. Samuel C. Damon.	Holden, Ms.	A. C. 1838, Andover, 1841.	1841.	1842.	Honolulu.		
Mrs. Damon, (Miss Mills.)	Natic, Ms.		"	"	"		
Rev. Townsend G. Taylor.		M.C., 1844, Union, 1847.	Oct. 1847.		Lahaina.		
Mrs. Taylor, (Persis G. Thurston.)	Sandwich Islands.			"	"		